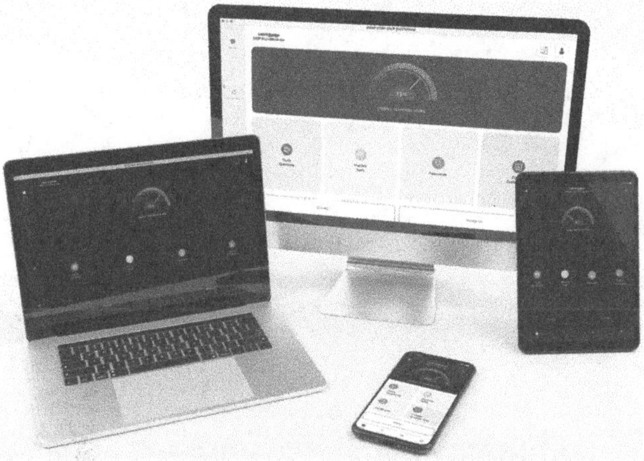

Big Book of HR Exam Practice Questions

Big Book of HR Exam Practice Questions

Sandra M. Reed,
SPHR, SHRM-SCP

SYBEX
A Wiley Brand

Published by John Wiley & Sons, Inc., Hoboken, New Jersey.

Published simultaneously in Canada and the United Kingdom.

ISBNs: 9781394255368 (paperback), 9781394255382 (ePDF), 9781394255375 (ePub)

For general information on our other products and services, please contact our Customer Care Department within the United States at (800) 762-2974, outside the United States at (317) 572- 3993. For product technical support, you can find answers to frequently asked questions or reach us via live chat at `https://sybexsupport.wiley.com`.

Wiley also publishes its books in a variety of electronic formats. Some content that appears in print may not be available in electronic formats. For more information about Wiley products, visit our web site at `www.wiley.com`.

Library of Congress Control Number: 2024939919

Cover image: © Jeremy Woodhouse/Getty Images

Cover design: Wiley

SKY10138302_012126

To my daughter, Clara Paigey, the light of my life, to show you that anything is possible when you do it with your heart. Always, always fall forward. Love, Mama.

Acknowledgments

Every time I have the privilege of working on a writing project, the idea of "standing on the shoulders of giants" comes to mind. As an introvert, I am highly dependent upon the extroverts who adopt me during these times, and this book was no exception.

I want first to share my gratitude and appreciation to my editors. To Kenyon Brown for his belief in me and willingness to hear my ideas, to Brad Jones for his ah-mazing organizational skills (seriously, I would have been underwater multiple times without his upbeat nudges), and to James Galluzzo, a bright star in his own right, whose technical editing skills absolutely made the final result better.

I also want to take a moment to acknowledge the drive behind a lot of my professional efforts: young adults. My son and daughter-in-law, nieces, nephews, interns, and the early professionals I coach are starting their careers, and I know from firsthand experience how the world can seem overwhelming at times for our youth, especially with the economy and social unrest and the lack of effective and accessible mental health treatment. Writing certification preparation books is my small way to support individuals who perhaps couldn't afford to go to college or follow a traditional career path yet still have that drive to succeed in alternative ways; I think of you all when I am writing. You can and will do big things despite barriers that, at times, may feel insurmountable.

Finally, being married to me ain't easy, yet my husband does it with tons of grace, patience, humor, and love. I am eternally grateful to have him as my partner in life.

About the Author

Sandra M. Reed, SPHR, SHRM-SCP, is a leading expert in the certification of HR professionals. She is the author of *HRCI's Official Guide to the Human Resource Body of Knowledge*, the *SHRM CP and SCP Exam Preparation Guide*, and numerous other exam preparation books, SHRM case studies, learning modules, and training for adult students. Reed has an undergraduate degree in industrial-organizational psychology and a graduate degree in organizational leadership. She is a master practitioner of the Myers-Briggs Type Indicator (MBTI) personality assessment and the owner of a business consulting group that specializes in strategy, organizational effectiveness and design, and leadership development for small businesses. Find her at `www.sandrareed.co`.

About the Technical Editor

James J. Galluzzo III, SPHR, PMP, is an HR strategic professional with nearly 30 years of experience. During his service in the United States Army, he found his professional calling in the HR branch of the Adjutant General's Corps and retired as the chief of leadership development for the 40,000 Army HR professionals around the world. He has served as a director of HR in government and private-sector organizations and is an HR subject-matter expert and program manager helping to transform the Army's HR training and development as it fields the most comprehensive HR information system (HRIS) in its history. Additionally, James has been an adjunct instructor, author, and content creator for training HR professionals.

Contents at a Glance

Contents

About This Book

One of the most common questions that I get about professional HR certification is, "Which exam should I take?" My answer is always the same: "It doesn't matter, just start somewhere." There have always been multiple options when it comes to getting certified, and the HRCI and SHRM exams are both excellent places to start. This is because both exam suites establish the foundational knowledge and competency awareness that can help you grow professionally. From there, you can choose to specialize in any of the domains of HR, whether it's becoming a Certified Compensation Specialist, Safety Specialist, or Workplace Inclusion Specialist, the list is long, and options abound. Starting with the generalist exams, such as those offered through HRCI and SHRM, sets the baseline from which you can grow.

While Chapter 1, "Introduction," goes into more detail about how to use this book, I encourage you to complete each chapter in its entirety. The questions are designed to prepare you for exam day in both function and form.

Reader Support for This Book

I have partnered with MindEdge to offer stand-alone, online preparation courses that serve to take a deeper dive into key exam and human resource concepts as a companion to this book and my other study guides. These courses are also pre-approved for *after* you successfully certify for re-certification credits. You can find the catalog online at `https://catalog.mindedge.com/sandrareed`. Additionally, the officially licensed mobile app for this material can be found at `www.learnzapp.com/apps/hr`.

How to Contact the Publisher

If you believe you've found a mistake in this book, please bring it to our attention. At John Wiley & Sons, we understand how important it is to provide our customers with accurate content, but even with our best efforts, an error may occur.

To submit your possible errata, please email it to our Customer Service Team at `wileysupport@wiley.com` with the subject line "Possible Book Errata Submission."

Chapter 1

Introduction

"You are what you do, not what you say you'll do."

Carl Jung

Welcome to *The Big Book of HR Practice Questions*! Your decision to invest in your professional development speaks volumes about your commitment to excellence and your dedication to advancing in the field of human resources (HR).

As the opening quote suggests, the process of preparing to sit for a certification exam requires taking action. It is not enough to simply think about or say that you want to accomplish something. True mastery of any topic requires work, patience, consistency, and access to resources that support a successful outcome. This book is designed to be a functional practice question guide for exams offered by the Human Resource Certification Institute and the Society for Human Resource Management.

- **The Human Resource Certification Institute (HRCI):** The Human Resource Certification Institute (HRCI) is an organization that offers certifications for HR professionals, validating their expertise and competency in various HR domains. Through rigorous examination and ongoing professional development, HRCI aims to elevate standards in the HR industry and empower professionals to advance their careers. This book is mapped to HRCI's exam content outlines for four exams:
  - **Professional in Human Resources (PHR):** The PHR certification caters to HR professionals who possess one to four years of experience in executing programs with a tactical/logistical focus, highlighting their operational duties within the organization's HR department.
  - **Professional in Human Resources, international (PHRi):** The PHRi certification is tailored for HR practitioners situated in a single international setting (non U.S.-based company), affirming their professional-level proficiency, knowledge, and skills to advance their careers in HR. Through the PHRi, individuals showcase their expertise in universally recognized technical and operational HR principles within an international context.
  - **Senior Professional in Human Resources (SPHR):** The SPHR credential targets senior HR leaders in the United States with four years or more experience in strategizing rather than executing HR policies. SPHR professionals typically oversee HR department objectives and strategize and implement business plans and technology, all while comprehending the broader HR requirements of the organization.
  - **Senior Professional in Human Resources, international (SPHRi):** The SPHRi certification is tailored for HR leaders located outside of the United States,

acknowledging their senior-level competency in generally accepted HR principles encompassing strategy, policy development, and service delivery within a single international setting.

- **The Society for Human Resource Management (SHRM):** The Society for Human Resource Management (SHRM) is a professional association dedicated to advancing the HR profession by providing resources, training, and networking opportunities to its members. Through advocacy, research, and education, SHRM strives to empower HR professionals worldwide to become strategic partners in their organizations' success. They have developed an exam Body of Applied Skills and Knowledge (BASK) for two exams that this practice guide is mapped to:
  - **SHRM Certified Professional (SHRM-CP):** An individual pursuing an SHRM-CP certification typically engages in HR or HR-related tasks or is aspiring toward a career in HR, with a focus on operational responsibilities. It's advisable for candidates to possess a basic understanding of HR concepts as they prepare for the certification.
  - **SHRM Senior Certified Professional (SHRM-SCP):** The SHRM-SCP certification is designed for individuals who have a minimum of three years of experience in executing strategic-level HR or HR-related responsibilities. Alternatively, it's also suitable for SHRM-CP holders who have maintained their certification for at least three years and are either currently working in or transitioning into strategic-level roles within the HR domain.

What sets this book apart is its practical approach. Each question is carefully crafted to mirror real-world scenarios and challenges encountered in a typical day in HR. Each question is also designed to get you familiar with how the questions are presented on the HRCI and SHRM exams. By engaging with the questions in this book, you'll not only test your understanding of key concepts but also hone your ability to critically think through situations, make informed decisions, and apply your work experience to find the correct answers.

Many athletes are familiar with the age-old adage, "Practice makes perfect." Yet, imagine a professional golfer heading to the driving range, swinging away for hours with the wrong form and the wrong club, and lacking the proper mindset. That practice might end up engraining the wrong techniques rather than properly refining the skills necessary for success.

This same principle applies to exam preparation! It's not just about practice; it's about perfect practice. To stack the odds in your favor, you need the right tools and resources for effective performance, and that's where this book comes in. It's designed to be an important resource in your preparation cache.

Success when facing a difficult exam requires planning and effort, not unlike when preparing for a marathon, embarking on a job search, or taking on new responsibilities at work. It will take perseverance and a commitment to yourself. The journey begins by understanding your own motivation.

Know Your Why

Mae Jemison was the first African American woman to travel in space, a physician, an engineer, and a passionate advocate for STEM education and exploration. From an early age, Dr. Jemison was captivated by the mysteries of the universe. This curiosity fueled her passion for science and drove her to pursue studies in chemical engineering and medicine. This led her to apply to NASA's astronaut program, despite facing barriers as a woman and African American. Jemison's personal "why" was rooted in a deep-seated desire to understand and explore the cosmos, propelling her to space aboard the Space Shuttle Endeavour in 1992. A true space pioneer and role model, Jemison's story reminds us that overcoming internal and external barriers to success requires a whole lot of guts, planning, and perseverance.

Why are you taking a professional certification exam? The answer to the question "why" serves decision-making, drives behaviors, and satisfies in a way experts call *intrinsic motivation*. Intrinsic motivation refers to the internal desire or drive to engage in an activity or pursue a goal solely for the enjoyment, satisfaction, or inherent interest it brings. This type of motivation often leads to higher levels of engagement, persistence, and creativity in tasks or goals pursued. Of course, there is nothing wrong with being motivated by external factors either; in fact, for some, the idea of recognition or monetary rewards is a key driver. When pursuing successful HR certification, it is useful to understand your own intrinsic and extrinsic motivators, such as the following:

- **Self-investment:** People often take professional certification exams to invest in themselves, aiming to boost their skills and knowledge for personal and professional development.
- **Pay increase:** Getting certified can help bump up your earnings by more than 25%. This is accomplished by showing employers and clients that you've got the expertise and competencies they're looking for, which can lead to better job opportunities and higher salaries.
- **Role-modeling:** When you become certified, you're not just doing it for yourself; you're also setting an example for others around you, inspiring them and encouraging them to keep pushing forward in their own careers.
- **Excellence:** Sitting down for a professional certification exam isn't just about passing a test; it's about showing your commitment to being the best in your field, demonstrating your dedication and staying on top of industry trends and standards.

This process is tough, and at times it might even be stressful. Knowing your why is your benchmark, the place that tethers you to the reasons you get up early to study, stay up late making flashcards, and watch MBA-level videos while on the treadmill. A quick mindset shift can help when those study days seem long. As Simon Sinek said, "Working hard for something we don't care about is called stress. Working hard for something we love is called passion."

The Exam Content

The profession of human resources has a framework from which university courses are taught, research is conducted, and best practices are formed. This framework is built around the human resource body of knowledge (HRBoK), and exam content often reflects these guidelines. While each exam has its own functional area categories, there are core knowledge and competency themes that are covered across all of the HRCI and SHRM exams. This book includes exam questions in the following HR domains:

- **U.S. Labor Laws (covered in Chapter 2):** Regulations governing employment practices and worker rights in the United States
- **Business Management and Strategy (covered in Chapter 3):** Developing and implementing plans to achieve organizational goals and maintain competitiveness
- **Talent Planning and Acquisition (covered in Chapter 4):** Strategically identifying, recruiting, and retaining skilled individuals to meet organizational needs
- **Learning and Development (covered in Chapter 5):** Cultivating employee skills and knowledge through training and educational programs
- **Total Rewards (covered in Chapter 6):** Comprehensive compensation and benefits packages designed to attract, motivate, and retain employees
- **Risk Management (covered in Chapter 7):** Identifying and mitigating potential threats to the organization's success, including legal, financial, and operational risks
- **Employee Engagement and Retention (covered in Chapter 8):** Fostering a positive work environment and implementing strategies to enhance employee satisfaction and loyalty
- **Employee and Labor Relations (covered in Chapter 9):** Managing interactions between employees and their employers, including negotiations, conflict resolution, and union relations
- **Ethical Practice and Corporate Social Responsibility (covered in Chapter 10):** Adhering to moral principles and implementing socially responsible practices to benefit society and stakeholders
- **Managing a Global Workforce (covered in Chapter 11):** Overseeing HR activities across international borders and diverse cultures
- **Diversity, Equity, and Inclusion (covered in Chapter 12):** Promoting fairness, respect, and opportunities for all individuals regardless of differences in background or identity
- **Workforce Analytics and Technology (covered in Chapter 13):** Leveraging data and technology to inform decision-making and optimize human resource processes
- **Human Resource Competencies (covered in Chapter 14):** Demonstrating proficiency in various HR functions, including communication, problem-solving, and strategic thinking
- **Leadership (covered in Chapter 15):** Guiding and inspiring individuals or teams toward shared goals and objectives
- **Organizational Design and Development (covered in Chapter 16):** Structuring and evolving the organization to enhance efficiency, effectiveness, and adaptability

Regardless of which exam you plan to sit for, it is recommended that you download the detailed exam content descriptions. You can find the PHR and PHRi (PHR/i) exam content outline here:

`www.hrci.org/certifications/exam-preparation-resources/exam-content-outlines`

The SPHR and SPHRi (SPHR/i) exam content outline can be found here:

`www.hrci.org/certifications/exam-preparation-resources/exam-content-outlines`

Finally, the SHRM Body of Applied Skills and Knowledge (BASK) can be found here:

`www.shrm.org/credentials/certification/exam-preparation/bask`

Types of Questions

To maintain their accredited status, exam administrators must maintain a controlled firewall between themselves and the item writers. This means the authors who write the exams do not have access to special content. They are building the items, options, and correct answers from their position as a subject-matter expert (SME) who has worked as an HR practitioner. Each question is submitted for review and refined until it reaches the beta phase. At this point, the question is placed on the exam as a "pre-test" item for validation before it becomes part of a candidate's official score. For example, on the PHR exam, there are 25 items on each exam that are not part of the scaled score. You will not know which exam items these are.

All six exams share similarities in the types of questions you will encounter. There are questions designed to measure knowledge and questions designed for you to apply your situational judgment.

Knowledge Items Knowledge items are typically questions that assess your understanding of fundamental concepts, principles, and theories in human resources management. You are required to recall and apply your knowledge of HR practices, laws, regulations, and organizational policies. Knowledge items serve to evaluate your depth of understanding and proficiency in various HR domains, ensuring you possess the necessary foundational knowledge to excel in HR roles.

Situational Judgment Items Situational judgment items on exams present you with realistic scenarios or workplace dilemmas relevant to the subject matter being tested, such as management or professional ethics. You will be asked to evaluate the situations and then select the most appropriate course of action from a list of options provided. These items assess not only your knowledge of theoretical concepts but also your ability to apply that knowledge to real-world situations, providing a more holistic measure of your competence and decision-making skills.

The correct answer on the situational judgment items on the SHRM exam are crafted by vote. This means a question goes out to field practitioners who "vote" on the correct answer. In many HR situations, the answer is not necessarily rooted in facts or evidence but rather best practices that require discernment and critical thinking skills. This is also why on all of the exams it can feel like there are many possible correct answers, and thus, it's important that you take the exam that is best supported by your practical experience. For candidates with less than five years of generalist experience, that would be HRCI's operational PHR/i or the SHRM-CP. For senior HR professionals, consider the more strategic SPHR/i or SHRM-SCP.

The tests will measure your knowledge and your ability to apply that knowledge in real-life situations. The following are the types of questions you will encounter:

- Multiple choice/multiple option
- Drag and drop
- Fill in the blank

Multiple Choice/Multiple Option

A multiple-choice or multiple-option exam item starts with a clear stem or statement that presents a problem or scenario. This is followed by several possible answer options. In a multiple-choice question, one of the answer options presented will be correct. In a multiple-option question, one or more of the answers options will be correct. The other options will likely sound plausible or will closely resemble the correct answer, but they are incorrect. The intent of the questions is to assess your understanding and ability to differentiate between the correct and incorrect options. The following is an example of a situational judgment multiple-choice question:

> A manufacturing company recently relocated its corporate headquarters, resulting in changes to HR operations, including implementing a new quarterly performance management system. The department manager expresses concerns to the HR director about the increased workload and system efficiency. How should the HR director respond to the supervisor?
>
> **A.** Offer additional training sessions to help supervisors and employees adapt to the new performance management system.
>
> **B.** Ignore the concerns raised by the department manager and proceed with the implementation of the new system.
>
> **C.** Provide the department manager with additional resources or support to help alleviate the increased workload.
>
> **D.** Revert to the previous performance management system to address the concerns raised by the department manager.

Drag and Drop

A drag-and-drop question assesses your knowledge as well as your ability to organize information or concepts effectively, offering a more interactive and engaging assessment experience. It requires that you match a set of terms to their corresponding description. The following is an example of a drag-and-drop question:

Match the HR principle with its corresponding definition:

Principles	Definitions
1. Equal Employment Opportunity (EEO)	A. Ensuring fair treatment of all employees regardless of their race, gender, age, or other protected characteristics.
2. Diversity and Inclusion	B. Fostering a work environment that embraces and respects individual differences, perspectives, and backgrounds.
3. Performance Management	C. Establishing processes and systems to assess and improve employee performance, productivity, and development.

Fill in the Blank

A fill-in-the-blank question is a statement or sentence with one or more blanks strategically placed to test your understanding of specific concepts or terms. The blanks are placed in a manner that requires you to recall and accurately provide missing information or complete the statement correctly. This type of question evaluates your knowledge in a more targeted manner. Here is an example of a fill-in-the-blank exam item:

> Title VII of the Civil Rights Act of 1964 was originally passed specifically to prohibit employment discrimination on five protected class characteristics including __________, __________, __________, __________, or __________.

A. Age, disability, sexual orientation, marital status, or veteran status

B. Race, color, religion, sex, or national origin

C. Age, gender identity, compensation discrimination, educational background, or socioeconomic status

D. Physical appearance, accent, genetic information, immigration status, or pregnancy status

Exam Preparation

There is no one-size-fits-all approach to studying. Some individuals learn best under pressure, so a shorter preparation window makes perfect sense. Others require a more planned out and predictable schedule, so 10–12 weeks makes more sense. The key is to understand how you learn and play to your strengths.

Regardless of your pace, it is recommended that you take as many practice assessments as possible. This not only helps you become familiar with question structure but also allows you to see where your greatest strengths and opportunities for improvement are. From this, you can plan to spend extra time in the more difficult areas and brush up in the areas where you are scoring the highest.

Exam Scoring

Speaking of scoring, the exams are not graded in the traditional academic way of A, B, C, D, or the dreaded F. Instead, they are scaled scores based on the degree of difficulty in the random question mix that you draw on exam day. Think of it this way: out of the thousands of exam items available in the master database, you will receive between 115–134 questions, depending on your exam. This means a few things:

- **Over-preparation is essential to success.** While we know what percentage of questions you will get in each of the content areas, we cannot know which domain topics you will be tested on. For example, the SHRM-CP exam will have 134 questions, and the HR expertise domain of the Workplace will account for 14% of the total. This means you will have only approximately 19 questions related to this functional area. Take a look at Table 1.1 for an example of this concept in action.
- **Foundational knowledge is also essential for success.** While the purpose of the exams is to measure competencies, the tests (and the real world) will require that you are able to draw from a bank of knowledge to make evidenced-based decisions, critically think through multifaceted problems, and align HR programs with business results. This will require memorization of facts, models, and theories.
- **The test is just a snapshot of time.** The exams have varying pass rates, ranging from 50% to 70%. Many people don't pass the first time, and that is OK! The process of getting ready is just as important to your career because the knowledge you gain during the preparation process is invaluable. It is possible that the questions you get on exam day just won't align with your experience or knowledge, but it does not mean that you aren't a great HR professional. Review your results, refresh your memory in the areas your under-performed, and retest as soon as possible.

TABLE 1.1 SHRM-CP Exam Weights

SHRM-CP Exam: 134 Questions	Percentage of the Exam	Total Number of Questions
Leadership	17%	23
Interpersonal	16.5%	22
Business	16.5%	22
People	18%	24
Organization	18%	24
Workplace	14%	19

Studying Best Practices

There are several other study best practices that can help prepare you for the big day:

- **Know your learning style:** Do you prefer to learn by seeing, hearing, or touching? Visual, auditory, and tactile learners all have a preferred way of taking in information, and aligning your preparation activities with your style will help to maximize retention. For visual learners, use colors and categorization methods to create presentations that sort and organize the information. For auditory learners, record yourself reading the material out loud, and subscribe to the various podcasts and YouTube channels that are listed at the end of each chapter in this book. Tactile learners, look for opportunities at your place of work to see the HR process in action and consider typing up your notes. Typing offers a tactile learning experience through physical engagement and muscle memory development. For all types, use a variety of study resources to enhance your understanding such as textbooks, online courses, academic journals, case studies, and reputable websites.
- **Finish this book:** Getting familiar with the question formatting is essential to establishing comfort with the exam style. Even if you are confident with your knowledge of a subject, use the practice questions to time yourself or simply to brush up.
- **Create study aids:** Create your own study aids, such as flashcards, summary notes, or mind maps, to condense and organize key information. These aids can be especially helpful for memorizing definitions, laws, or key concepts. The best way to learn something is to teach it, so consider teaching the material to someone else or discussing it with peers to deepen your understanding and retention of the material.
- **Stay organized and manage your time effectively:** Develop a study schedule that allocates sufficient time to cover all the necessary material before the exam. Break down your study sessions into manageable chunks and set specific goals for each session. Prioritize topics based on their exam weights and your understanding of them. Also, make sure to take regular breaks to avoid burnout.
- **Consider joining a study group:** Surround yourself with a group of likeminded individuals, and you are likely to feel supported as you get ready for the test. Joining a study group can provide valuable insights and perspectives from peers, facilitating a collaborative learning environment, and discussing concepts and practicing problem-solving together can enhance comprehension and retention of key materials.
- **Self-study:** Even if you are part of a network of like-minded individuals, it may be helpful for you to access micro-learning sessions for topics you are less familiar with. I have partnered with MindEdge to offer professional-level online content that is 100% self-paced and in alignment with the HR exams. Take a look at `https://catalog.mindedge.com/sandrareed`.

What You Think About Matters

In the 1960s, Aaron Beck and Albert Ellis introduced cognitive behavioral therapy (CBT), now one of the most prevalent therapeutic approaches. It is primarily utilized in treating disorders such as anxiety and depression. For many people, test anxiety is an incredibly real presence in their life, and the CBT technique can be helpful to practice long before the day of the exam arrives. At the core of CBT is the idea that "what you think about, you bring about." This is illustrated in the "Cognitive Triangle" presented in Figure 1.1.

FIGURE 1.1 The Cognitive Triangle

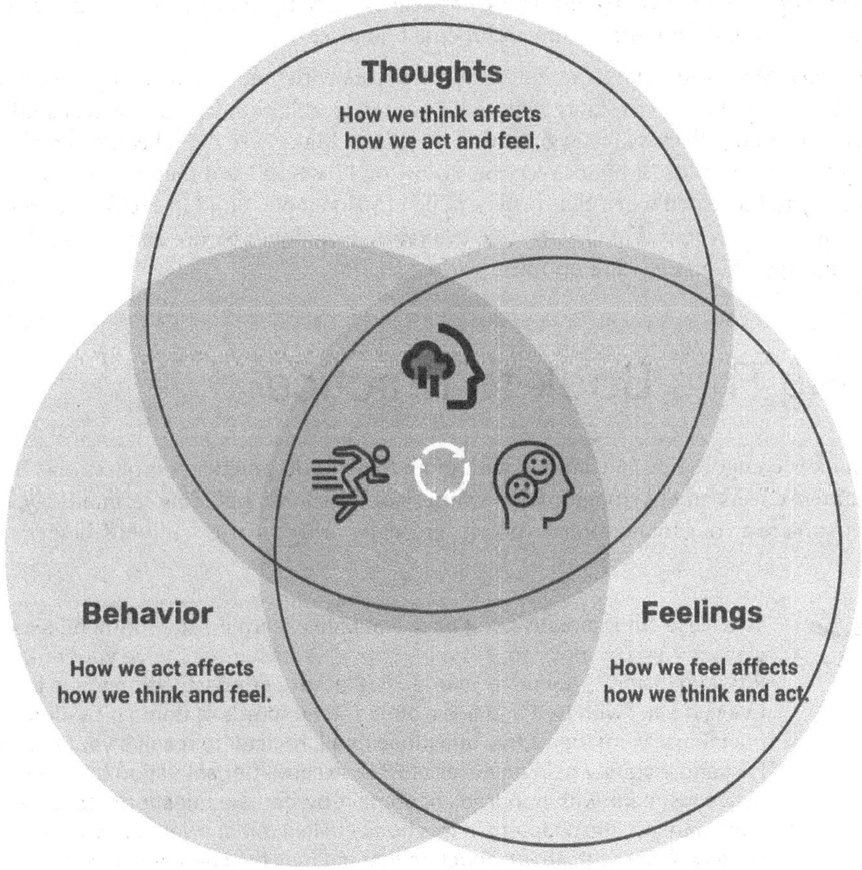

When studying for the exams, understanding and utilizing the Cognitive Triangle of thoughts, feelings, and actions can be instrumental in optimizing preparation and performance:

- **Thoughts:** Monitor and manage your thoughts about the exam. Instead of dwelling on fears of failure or inadequacy, cultivate positive and empowering beliefs about your abilities and preparation. Practice cognitive restructuring techniques to challenge and replace negative thoughts with more realistic and constructive ones. For example, instead of thinking "I'll never be able to remember all this," reframe it to "I've studied diligently and am well-prepared to tackle this exam."
- **Feelings:** Recognize and regulate your emotions related to studying and taking exams. Anxiety and stress are common emotions during exam preparation, but they can be detrimental if left unchecked. Engage in stress-reducing activities, such as deep breathing exercises, mindfulness meditation, or physical exercise the morning of test day to manage anxiety and promote a calm and focused mindset.
- **Actions:** Align your study strategies and behaviors with your cognitive and emotional states. Break down your study material into manageable chunks and create a study schedule that reflects realistic goals and deadlines. Make sure the schedule is realistic! So many students allot "8 hours every Saturday for 12 weeks" and then are surprised, frustrated, and defeated when that proves to be unsustainable. Build in breaks and time off for special occasions. Finally, practice relaxation techniques before and during the exam to manage test anxiety and optimize performance.

Using This Book to Practice

This book is composed of 16 chapters with more than 1,000 practice test questions. Each of the chapters covers an HR domain with a variety of questions, including terminology, that can help you test your foundational knowledge, real-world scenarios, and HR best practices.

NOTE

To access our interactive test bank and online learning environment, simply visit `www.wiley.com/go/sybextestprep`, register to receive your unique PIN, and instantly gain one year of FREE access after activation to the interactive test bank with two practice exams and hundreds of domain-by-domain questions. More than 1,000 questions total!, register to receive your unique PIN, and instantly gain one year of FREE access after activation to the interactive test bank with hundreds of domain-by-domain questions. To optimize your learning, the chapters in this book are laid out in a very specific way. Each chapter starts with an introduction that outlines the chapter's objectives and scope. A case study follows to illustrate real-world applications or short scenarios related to the topic. After the case study comes the bulk of the chapter, the practice questions.

After the practice questions, you will find a section titled "Key Research" that is designed to enrich your knowledge on important topics and connect you with online, expert sources to deepen your understanding. This section is followed by simple "Terminology" questions to test your knowledge on important terms and concepts to aid comprehension. The "Conclusion" section summarizes key points and identifies the weighting of the chapter topic on the HRCI and SHRM exams. Pay special attention to the last section titled "Additional Resources." These resources are designed for multiple learning styles by suggesting podcasts, YouTube channels, and more websites to invite further exploration and reflection, ensuring a cohesive and informative chapter experience.

Appendix A has the answers to the practice questions, along with an explanation for the correct and incorrect options. The exams count any unanswered question as "incorrect," so you don't want to leave any question blank. Appendix B contains the correct answers for key terminology, and Appendix C provides insights into the key research questions.

Conclusion

Building a career is a commitment requiring passion, focus, and intention to gain experience and education one step at a time. Setting yourself up for success requires that you have access to the right resources and that you "perfectly practice" for optimal performance on exam day and throughout your career.

Thinking about your "why" offers you a benchmark from which to return when the exam process feels overwhelming. Reminding yourself that many others have gone before you and have been successful can help sustain you when a concept feels particularly complex or you are questioning your own capabilities.

Understanding the exam dynamics around the content areas and question format serves as a reminder that you are not being tested on all things. There is a framework of expertise that defines the practice of human resources, and it is likely you are not starting from scratch—you are starting from experience. Trust your talent. This commitment to excellence in your career will pay off, even if it takes you a little longer than others. "Comparison is the thief of joy," so meet yourself where you are and remember that a career is a journey, not a sprint. Best of luck as you get started on this next step!

Chapter 2

U.S. Labor Law

Labor law in the United States is a complex and multifaceted field that governs the relationship between employers and employees. It has evolved to protect workers in areas such as fair wages in the 1930s, employee rights to work in an environment free from discrimination in the 1960s, and whistleblower and other protections in areas such as healthcare in the 1970s. In 1970, when the Occupational Safety and Health Act was passed, the worker fatality rate was 18 out of 100,000 workers. Twenty years later, that number was cut in half (`BLS.gov`).

Understanding these laws is crucial for both employers and employees, and HR is the conduit for this learning and application. Risk management activities protect the employer from costly fines and protect workers' rights.

In this chapter, we will focus on some of the key principles, statutes, and regulations that are covered on the HRCI and SHRM exams, as well as look at relevant global practices where appropriate. This wide range of topics includes the following:

- **Employee relations laws:** We will discuss the National Labor Relations Act, Labor Management Act, and Labor-Management Reporting & Disclosure Act, which protects the rights of employees to organize and bargain collectively.
- **Wage and hour laws:** We will discuss the Fair Labor Standards Act and its amendments, which set standards for minimum wage, overtime, and child labor and compensable time, along with paycheck management and record-keeping.
- **Discrimination protections:** We will examine Title VII of the Civil Rights Act, the Age Discrimination in Employment Act, and other key anti-discrimination laws in terms of the protected class characteristics and enforcement agencies such as the Equal Employment Opportunity Commission.
- **Employee benefits:** We will discuss the Employee Retirement Income Security Act and Patient Protection and Affordable Care Act, shedding light on the regulation of voluntary pension plans and mandated health insurance protections.
- **Health and safety:** We will explore the Occupational Safety and Health Act, a vital law ensuring safe workplaces for all.
- **Family and medical leave:** We will discuss the Family and Medical Leave Act, including the rights it provides to employees for family and medical-related leave.
- **Additional protections:** We will discuss the Americans with Disabilities Act, Genetic Information Nondiscrimination Act, Equal Pay Act, and Fair Credit Reporting Act with an emphasis on their significance in promoting equal opportunities and fair treatment in the workplace.

This chapter serves as a valuable starting point and resource for both education and reference, enabling individuals to assess their understanding of these critical labor laws and regulations.

Real World Scenario

Navigating U.S. Labor Law Compliance Through HR Audits

In the complex landscape of labor law compliance in the United States, employers face numerous challenges to ensure that they adhere to the myriad regulations and statutes governing their workforce. This case study examines the experience of Compliance Corp, a midsize company, in managing labor law compliance and using HR audits as a strategic tool to mitigate risks.

Background and Problem

Compliance Corp operated in the highly regulated healthcare industry. With numerous federal and state labor laws, including the Fair Labor Standards Act (FLSA) and the Family and Medical Leave Act (FMLA), compliance was a paramount concern. However, the company encountered instances of noncompliance that raised concerns about potential legal and financial liabilities. While no formal complaints came to the attention of the board of directors, they looked to their HR teams for a proactive solution.

Diagnosis

Recognizing the critical importance of labor law compliance, Compliance Corp embarked on a journey to assess its adherence to these laws. The company identified the following key issues:

- **Wage and hour compliance:** Instances of overtime violations and misclassification of employees
- **FMLA compliance:** Concerns regarding consistent application of FMLA leave and documentation
- **Record-keeping practices:** Incomplete or inaccurate employee records, including timecards and payroll records
- **Employment discrimination:** Concerns about the prevention of workplace discrimination and harassment

Strategies

To address these issues, Compliance Corp implemented a comprehensive HR audit strategy that included the following:

- **Internal HR audit team:** The company established an internal HR audit team comprising seasoned HR professionals and legal experts to conduct regular audits.

- **Wage and hour audits:** Compliance Corp conducted regular audits of employee time and attendance records, ensuring compliance with FLSA regulations and addressing any wage and hour issues promptly.
- **FMLA audits:** Compliance Corp reviewed FMLA policies and practices to ensure consistent application, accurate record-keeping, and timely response to leave requests.
- **Record-keeping enhancement:** Compliance Corp invested in modern HR information system (HRIS) software to improve record-keeping accuracy and completeness.
- **Training and awareness:** Mandatory training programs were initiated to educate employees and managers about discrimination and harassment prevention.

Results

As a result of its HR audit initiatives, Compliance Corp experienced several benefits.

- **Reduced legal and financial risks:** Identifying and rectifying noncompliance issues minimized the risk of costly lawsuits and fines.
- **Improved employee morale:** Clearer policies and consistent enforcement fostered a positive work environment, boosting employee morale and reducing turnover.
- **Enhanced reputation:** Demonstrated commitment to compliance and ethical practices improved the company's reputation among both employees and clients.

Conclusion

Compliance Corp's actions illustrate how U.S. labor law compliance necessitates proactive measures, particularly in highly regulated industries such as healthcare, transportation, and financial services. By leveraging HR audits as a strategic tool, the company not only mitigated risks but also enhanced overall workplace practices. Compliance Corp's experience serves as a valuable lesson for businesses operating in the United States, emphasizing the importance of diligent labor law compliance and the benefits of regular HR audits in minimizing legal, financial, and reputational risks.

Labor Law Employment Law Cheat Sheet

HR has many acronyms in its lexicon, particularly when it comes to employment law. Additionally, most acts are triggered once an employer reaches a certain size, and you will need to know this to critically think through many of the exam questions. Use this cheat sheet to get started:

- **Age Discrimination in Employment Act (ADEA):** Applies to employers with 20 or more employees.

- **Americans with Disabilities Act (ADA):** Applies to employers with 15 or more employees.
- **Americans with Disabilities Act Amendments Act (ADAAA):** Applies to employers with 15 or more employees.
- **Consolidated Omnibus Budget Reconciliation Act (COBRA):** Applies to employers with 20 or more employees.
- **Deferred Action for Childhood Arrivals (DACA):** A federal program that provides work authorization to undocumented immigrants who were brought to the United States as children regardless of the size of their employer.
- **Employee Polygraph Protection Act (EPPA):** Applies to most employers, but there may be certain exemptions based on industry and size.
- **Employee Retirement Income Security Act (ERISA):** Generally applies to private-sector employers that offer employee benefit plans.
- **Equal Employment Opportunity Commission (EEOC):** Enforces various anti-discrimination laws, and the size requirement varies depending on the specific law being enforced.
- **Fair Labor Standards Act (FLSA):** Applies to most employers engaged in interstate commerce or the production of goods for interstate commerce.
- **Family and Medical Leave Act (FMLA):** Applies to employers with 50 or more employees within a 75-mile radius.
- **Health Insurance Portability and Accountability Act (HIPAA):** Applies to healthcare providers, health plans, and healthcare clearinghouses that handle protected health information (PHI).
- **Immigration Reform and Control Act (IRCA):** Requires businesses to verify the employment eligibility of their workers by completing Form I-9 and maintaining records to prevent the hiring of unauthorized immigrants.
- **Labor Management Relations Act (LMRA), Taft-Hartley:** Governs labor relations for covered employers, including those in industries such as manufacturing and transportation.
- **Labor Management Reporting & Disclosure Act (LMRDA), Landrum-Griffin:** Applies to labor organizations and their officers.
- **National Labor Relations Act (NLRA), Wagner Act:** Generally applies to most private-sector employers.
- **National Labor Relations Board (NLRB):** Administers the NLRA, which covers most private-sector employers.
- **Occupational Safety and Health Act (OSHA):** Applies to most private-sector employers.
- **Older Worker Benefit Protection Act (OWBPA):** Applies to employers who offer early retirement incentive programs.

- **Patient Protection and Affordable Care Act (PPACA):** Applies to different employer sizes, with specific requirements for large employers (generally 50 or more full-time equivalent employees).
- **Pregnancy Discrimination Act (PDA):** Applies to employers with 15 or more employees.
- **Pregnant Workers Fairness Act (PFWA):** Applies to employers with at least 15 employees.
- **Title VII of the Civil Rights Act of 1964 (Title VII):** Applies to employers with 15 or more employees.
- **Uniformed Services Employment and Reemployment Rights Act (USERRA):** Applies to all employers, regardless of size.
- **Worker Adjustment and Retraining Notification Act (WARN):** Applies to employers with 100 or more full-time employees, or 100 or more employees who work a combined total of 4,000 hours or more per week. WARN also applies to single-site employers where more than 50 employees are being laid off.

TIP

The trifecta of labor laws related to labor unions has two names: the name of the act itself and the names of the authors of the act. SHRM's Body of Applied Skill and Knowledge (BASK) refers to these laws by *both* of their names, so it is recommended that you are familiar with each.

- National Labor Relations Act (NLRA) also known as the Wagner Act
- Labor Management Relations Act (LMRA) authored by Taft-Hartley
- Labor Management Reporting and Disclosure Act (LMRDA) referred to as the Landrum-Griffin Act

Labor Law Practice Questions

1. Anna is an HR professional responsible for ensuring that her company complies with federal labor laws. She wants to stay current on these laws to avoid any legal issues and provide the best guidance to her organization. Which of the following methods would be the BEST way for Anna to stay current on federal labor laws?

   A. Rely on the company's legal department to provide updates on labor laws.

   B. Attend an annual HR conference that covers a wide range of HR topics.

   C. Subscribe to a reputable HR industry newsletter that provides regular updates on federal labor laws.

   D. Review federal labor laws on an ad hoc basis when specific issues arise.

2. Emily is an HR professional responsible for coaching employees on their rights and responsibilities within the company. She wants to ensure that employees are well-informed and understand their roles in compliance with company policies and regulations. Which of the following methods would be the BEST way for Emily to effectively coach employees on their rights and responsibilities?

   A. Conduct one-on-one coaching sessions with each employee to discuss their rights and responsibilities individually.

   B. Organize group workshops or training sessions to educate employees collectively on their rights and responsibilities.

   C. Provide employees with a written handbook outlining their rights and responsibilities and encourage them to review it independently.

   D. Send periodic email updates to employees with information about their rights and responsibilities.

3. Nemo's Shellfish is a small organization with limited resources and is considering hiring external resources to help it comply with labor laws. Nemo's wants to make the most effective and efficient use of its resources. What are the key considerations the company should consider when hiring external resources for labor law compliance?

   A. Hire a large consulting firm with a broad range of services to ensure comprehensive compliance.

   B. Conduct a detailed assessment of the organization's specific compliance needs and budget constraints before selecting external resources.

   C. Rely on free online resources and government websites to navigate labor laws.

   D. Hire individual consultants with expertise in specific areas of labor law to address immediate concerns.

4. Eleanor, a pregnant employee, recently informed her supervisor about her pregnancy and her intention to take maternity leave in a few months. Since then, she has noticed a change in her work assignments and responsibilities, with some of her tasks being reassigned to colleagues. She suspects she might be facing pregnancy-related discrimination. Which of the following actions would be a violation of the Pregnancy Discrimination Act?

   A. At Eleanor's request, her supervisor reassigns some of her tasks to other colleagues to accommodate her pregnancy-related limitations.

   B. Eleanor's supervisor denies her request for a temporary modification of her work schedule to attend prenatal appointments.

   C. Eleanor's supervisor provides her with reasonable accommodations, such as allowing her to take more frequent breaks, to help her cope with pregnancy-related discomfort.

   D. Eleanor's supervisor offers her a promotion to a higher position in the company, but Eleanor declines because of her pregnancy.

5. In 2011, the EEOC filed a lawsuit against Verizon Communications Inc., alleging employment law violations. The case involved claims of disability discrimination and failure to provide reasonable accommodations to employees with disabilities. The court eventually ruled in favor of one of the parties. Which of the following statements is true regarding the EEOC versus Verizon employment law case?

   A. The EEOC's lawsuit against Verizon was dismissed, and the court found in favor of Verizon, ruling that there was no evidence of discrimination or failure to provide reasonable accommodations.

   B. Verizon was found liable for disability discrimination and failure to provide reasonable accommodations, and the court awarded substantial damages to the affected employees.

   C. The case resulted in a settlement between the EEOC and Verizon, with both parties agreeing to resolve the matter through mediation.

   D. The EEOC withdrew its lawsuit against Verizon after reaching an out-of-court settlement that included a commitment from Verizon to improve its disability accommodation policies.

6. Chidi works as a guard for a private security company. His employer is concerned about recent thefts in the workplace and asks Chidi to take a polygraph (lie detector) test to determine whether he has any knowledge of the thefts. Chidi is uncomfortable with the idea of taking the polygraph test and is unsure about his rights. Which of the following statements about the EPPA is correct in this situation?

   A. Chidi's employer can require him to take a polygraph test since it is related to workplace security.

   B. Chidi's employer can request a polygraph test only if they have a reasonable suspicion of his involvement in the thefts.

   C. Chidi's employer is prohibited from requesting or requiring him to take a polygraph test in this situation.

   D. Chidi's employer can require him to take a polygraph test as long as they provide him with a copy of the test results.

7. A company is planning a round of layoffs due to financial constraints and is considering offering severance packages to affected employees. It wants to ensure compliance with the ADEA and the OWBPA. What is a key requirement the company must adhere to when providing severance agreements to employees older than 40?

   A. Offer different severance terms to employees based on their age.

   B. Provide a waiver of ADEA claims in exchange for severance benefits without adequate time for review.

   C. Include a provision that employees cannot challenge the waiver in court.

   D. Allow employees at least 21 days to review the agreement and provide a 7-day revocation period.

8. An employer is conducting a job interview for a position that requires physical fitness and stamina. The candidate, who is 52 years old, expresses concern about whether age could be a factor in the hiring decision. What should the employer consider to comply with the ADEA in this situation?

   A. The employer can openly discuss age-related concerns during the interview.

   B. The ADEA allows employers to consider age as a primary factor in hiring for physically demanding positions.

   C. The employer should avoid asking any questions related to age during the interview.

   D. Age cannot be a consideration unless the candidate brings it up.

9. An employer plans to implement changes to its employee retirement benefits program, including reducing contributions to the 401(k) plan. They want to ensure compliance with the ADEA and the OWBPA. What is a key requirement they should consider when making changes to retirement benefits for older workers?

   A. Implement changes without notifying affected employees to prevent resistance.

   B. Provide clear and timely written notices about the changes, including detailed information on the impact.

   C. Offer additional benefits to older employees without notifying younger employees.

   D. Allow employees to opt out of the retirement benefits program altogether.

10. A prestigious women's college is hiring a new admissions officer. The hiring manager is considering specifying in the job advertisement that the college is seeking a female candidate because of the college's long-standing tradition of providing a women-only education. What should the college consider regarding bona fide occupational qualifications (BFOQ) when making this hiring decision?

    A. The college can specify a preference for female candidates without violating BFOQ principles.

    B. BFOQ allows the college to require that the admissions officer be a female without exceptions.

    C. The college must not specify a gender preference in the job advertisement to comply with BFOQ.

    D. BFOQ applies only to physical attributes, not gender-related preferences.

11. A private religious school is hiring a teacher for a religious studies class. The school's doctrine specifies that only individuals who adhere to the school's specific religious beliefs and practices can teach these classes. What should the school consider regarding BFOQ when making this hiring decision?
    - **A.** The school can require that the teacher adhere to its religious beliefs as a BFOQ.
    - **B.** BFOQ applies only to physical attributes and not to religious beliefs.
    - **C.** The school cannot consider religious beliefs as a BFOQ in the hiring process.
    - **D.** BFOQ allows the school to consider religious beliefs but not require adherence.
12. John, an employee, recently lost his job due to a company downsizing. He is concerned about losing his health insurance coverage. How can COBRA benefit John in this situation?
    - **A.** COBRA allows John to continue his employer-sponsored health insurance coverage at no cost for up to two years.
    - **B.** COBRA grants John an extension of his unemployment benefits.
    - **C.** COBRA enables John to purchase a new health insurance policy outside the company's plan.
    - **D.** COBRA permits John to continue his employer-sponsored health insurance coverage for a limited time by paying the premiums.
13. Samantha, an employee, is about to give birth and plans to take maternity leave. How does COBRA apply to her health insurance coverage during her leave?
    - **A.** Samantha must cancel her health insurance coverage during maternity leave.
    - **B.** COBRA requires Samantha's employer to cover all maternity-related expenses.
    - **C.** Samantha can continue her health insurance coverage under COBRA, but she must pay the full premium.
    - **D.** Samantha can continue her health insurance coverage under COBRA, with the employer covering the entire premium cost.
14. Alex, a former employee, lost his job a month ago. He just received COBRA enrollment information from his previous employer. What is the maximum time frame within which Alex must decide to elect COBRA coverage?
    - **A.** Alex has one week to decide.
    - **B.** Alex has 30 days to decide.
    - **C.** Alex has 90 days to decide.
    - **D.** Alex has one year to decide.

15. Priya is a part-time employee working for a small retail business with fewer than 50 employees. She's heard about the Patient Protection and Affordable Care Act and is wondering if it affects her. Which of the following statements is correct for Priya?

A. Priya is required to purchase health insurance through the PPACA's health insurance marketplace.

B. Priya's employer is not required to provide her with health insurance coverage under the PPACA.

C. Priya is eligible for subsidies to help her purchase health insurance through the marketplace.

D. Priya's employer must offer her a comprehensive health insurance plan that covers all medical expenses under the PPACA.

16. Which of the following is a key provision of the Patient Protection and Affordable Care Act?

A. It mandates that all U.S. citizens must purchase health insurance or face a penalty.

B. It provides subsidies to help low- and middle-income individuals and families afford health insurance coverage.

C. It requires employers of any size to offer health insurance coverage to all employees.

D. It eliminates the private health insurance industry in the United States.

17. Vicky, an employee, believes she has experienced discrimination at her workplace based on her gender. She wants to file a complaint with the appropriate federal agency. Which of the following best describes the role of the EEOC in this situation?

A. The EEOC only handles complaints related to race and ethnicity, so Vicky should contact a different agency.

B. The EEOC is responsible for investigating complaints of employment discrimination based on various protected characteristics, including gender.

C. The EEOC only provides legal representation to employees in discrimination cases.

D. The EEOC conducts immediate workplace investigations upon receiving a complaint, bypassing the need for a formal complaint.

18. You work as an HR manager for a company that frequently bids on government contracts. You want to ensure compliance with relevant labor laws, including the Walsh-Healey Public Contracts Act. Which of the following statements accurately describes the Walsh-Healey Act?

A. The Walsh-Healey Act applies only to contracts related to construction projects.

B. It requires federal contractors to pay their employees a minimum wage determined by the federal government.

C. The act covers contracts valued at $100,000 or more for the manufacturing or furnishing of materials, supplies, articles, or equipment to the federal government.

D. The act mandates that contractors provide comprehensive healthcare benefits to their employees.

19. The human resources manager at XYZ Corp. discovered that the company was improperly denying certain requested reasonable accommodations to individuals with disabilities, a violation of the ADA. She reported this to management, and shortly after, her employment was terminated. Was the HR manager's reporting of the ADA violation considered protected activity under the law?

A. No, because her reports were part of her managerial duties, not protected activity.

B. Yes, because reporting ADA violations is considered protected activity under the ADA.

C. No, because her reports did not meet all the other relevant requirements for protected activity.

D. Yes, because EEO complaints by HR managers and advisors are automatically considered protected activity.

20. A temporary custodian, Lisa, discovers that she is being paid a dollar less per hour than previously hired male counterparts in the same seasonal role. Concerned about this wage disparity, she approaches her supervisor. Which of the following statements made by Lisa would be considered protected opposition under employment law?

A. "I don't think my pay is fair, but I guess there's nothing I can do about it."

B. "I demand that you raise my pay immediately to match what the male custodians are earning!"

C. "I believe you're paying me less than the male custodians, which I think may be against the law."

D. "I'm unhappy with my pay, but I don't want to make any trouble about it."

21. Leslie, a police officer, requested light duty during her pregnancy due to medical advice against lifting more than 20 pounds. The police department denied her request, citing a policy that limited light duty to employees injured on the job. What legal challenge can be brought against the police department based on this scenario?

A. The police department can argue that its policy is justifiable based on the state law mandating payment to officers injured on the job, which outweighs any disparate impact concerns.

B. The police department can argue that its policy is not discriminatory since it applies equally to all employees, regardless of the cause of their work limitations.

C. Leslie can challenge the police department's policy based on the concept of disparate impact, asserting that it unfairly affects pregnant workers compared to nonpregnant workers with similar work limitations.

D. Leslie can challenge the police department's policy as a violation of her rights under state law, demanding that her request for light duty be granted based on her medical condition.

22. You are an HR manager for a medium-sized company with a diverse workforce. One of your employees, Sarah, recently gave birth to a baby and has returned to work after her maternity leave. She requests accommodation for nursing her child during working hours. Which of the following actions should HR take?

   A. Deny Sarah's request since the company does not have a designated lactation room, and providing accommodations would be too costly.

   B. Inform Sarah that she can breastfeed her child only during her scheduled breaks, and she must make up the time spent nursing.

   C. Evaluate the feasibility of creating a private and comfortable space for nursing mothers to express breast milk, such as a lactation room, and work with Sarah to find a suitable solution.

   D. Suggest that Sarah use a restroom for breastfeeding, as it is a private space, and it aligns with the company's budget constraints.

23. As an HR professional, you are responsible for understanding and adhering to immigration policies to ensure your organization remains compliant with the law. You've recently hired a new employee who mentions that they are a Deferred Action for Childhood Arrivals (DACA) recipient. You want to ensure that you handle their employment correctly. Which of the following statements about the administration of DACA is accurate?

   A. DACA recipients are eligible for federal financial aid for higher education.

   B. DACA recipients can apply for U.S. citizenship after five years of DACA status.

   C. DACA provides recipients with a path to permanent legal residency.

   D. DACA recipients must renew their status every two years.

24. Uzo, an employee, is considering contributing to his employer's 401(k) plan. He wants to know if ERISA sets specific contribution limits for 401(k) plans. What should he be aware of?

   A. ERISA sets uniform contribution limits for all 401(k) plans.

   B. ERISA does not specify contribution limits for 401(k) plans; they are determined by the Internal Revenue Code.

   C. ERISA allows employers to establish contribution limits at their discretion.

   D. ERISA mandates that all 401(k) plans must have a maximum annual contribution limit.

25. You are an HR manager responsible for ensuring workplace compliance with various federal regulations. One of the regulations you need to be familiar with is Executive Order 11246. Which of the following statements accurately describes the implications of Executive Order 11246 in the workplace?

   A. Executive Order 11246 requires federal contractors and subcontractors to implement affirmative action plans for all protected categories, including race, color, religion, sex, and national origin.

   B. It applies only to federal contractors that have 100 or more employees.

   C. The order mandates that federal contractors must pay all their employees a minimum wage determined by the federal government.

   D. Executive Order 11246 does not apply to workplace discrimination based on religion.

26. Daisuke has recently retired from his job and is receiving pension benefits from his former employer's defined benefit plan. He's concerned about ensuring his benefits are paid as promised. What role does ERISA play in protecting Daisuke's pension benefits?

A. ERISA guarantees that all defined benefit plans will fully fund pension benefits.

B. ERISA ensures that pension benefits are paid in full and on time, regardless of plan funding.

C. ERISA requires that employers contribute to a dedicated trust fund for each participant to secure pension benefits.

D. ERISA sets minimum funding standards that defined benefit plans must meet to ensure the financial security of pension benefits.

27. Meg is a participant in her employer's 403(B) retirement plan, which is covered by ERISA. She is considering taking out a loan from her account to cover unexpected medical expenses. What should Meg be aware of regarding loans from ERISA-covered retirement plans?

A. ERISA prohibits loans from 403(B) retirement accounts.

B. ERISA allows loans from 403(B) accounts without any restrictions or consequences.

C. ERISA permits loans from 403(B) accounts, but there are specific rules and limitations that must be followed.

D. ERISA mandates that all loans from 403(B) accounts must be approved by the Department of Labor.

28. In the landmark case of *Griggs v. Duke Power* (1971), the U.S. Supreme Court established important guidelines for employment practices. Which of the following statements accurately represents the requirements set forth by Griggs v. Duke Power?

A. The case ruled that employers must use explicit quotas to ensure equal employment opportunities for all races and ethnicities.

B. *Griggs v. Duke Power* upheld the legality of employment tests and practices that disproportionately favored one racial group over others.

C. The case determined that employers must demonstrate that their selection criteria are job-related and consistent with business necessity to avoid discrimination.

D. *Griggs v. Duke Power* eliminated all affirmative action programs in the workplace.

29. John is the owner of a small bakery in a rural town. He employs a few workers to help him with baking and serving customers. Recently, he heard about the Fair Labor Standards Act and wondered if it applies to his bakery. What should John consider regarding FLSA coverage?

A. FLSA covers employers with 20 or more employees, so John's bakery is exempt from its provisions.

B. FLSA applies to all employers, regardless of the number of employees, so John's bakery is likely covered.

C. FLSA covers employers with 50 or more employees, so John's bakery is exempt from its provisions.

D. FLSA applies to employers with 100 or more employees, so John's bakery is exempt.

30. Which of the following is key criteria for classifying employees as exempt?

A. Exempt status is solely determined by the employer's discretion without specific criteria.

B. Employees can be classified as exempt if they receive a fixed monthly salary, regardless of their job duties.

C. Exempt employees generally must meet specific job duties and salary requirements outlined by the FLSA.

D. The FLSA does not allow employers to classify employees as exempt from overtime pay.

31. Brittany works at a manufacturing plant that requires employees to undergo a security screening process before and after their shifts. The security screening involves waiting in line to have bags and personal belongings checked for unauthorized items. The employer contends that this time is not compensable, while Brittany believes it should be. Which federal law might Brittany invoke to support her claim for compensable time in this scenario?

A. Fair Labor Standards Act.

B. Occupational Safety and Health Act.

C. National Labor Relations Act.

D. Portal-to-Portal Act.

32. A small business owner is concerned about the potential financial burden of providing minimum wage to all employees as required by the FLSA. Can the small business owner request an exemption from the FLSA's minimum wage requirements?

A. Yes, the small business owner can request an exemption from the FLSA's minimum wage requirements without any limitations.

B. No, the FLSA does not allow exemptions from minimum wage requirements for any type or size of business.

C. Yes, the small business owner can request an exemption, but it is subject to approval by the Department of Labor.

D. The FLSA requires minimum wage only for full-time employees, so part-time employees can be paid below minimum wage.

33. XYZ Corporation is considering hiring interns for the summer to help with various projects. The company wants to ensure it complies with labor laws and provides a valuable experience for the interns. Which of the following statements best describes the legal considerations when employing interns in the United States?

A. Interns must always be paid at least the federal minimum wage.

B. Unpaid internships are allowed as long as the interns receive academic credit.

C. The Fair Labor Standards Act does not apply to internships.

D. Interns can perform only clerical tasks and cannot be involved in significant work that benefits the employer.

34. XYZ Corporation is expanding its workforce and needs to make precise distinctions between employees and independent contractors to ensure compliance with U.S. labor laws. To navigate this complex issue, what are the critical distinctions that set apart an employee from an independent contractor?

A. Employees have more control over the details of their work assignments.

B. Independent contractors are eligible for unemployment benefits.

C. Employees are generally subject to the company's direction and control over their work, while independent contractors maintain greater autonomy.

D. Independent contractors are entitled to the same workplace protections and benefits as employees.

35. An employee in a company located in a state where medical marijuana is legal has been using marijuana to manage a chronic medical condition under the guidance of her healthcare provider. She has not used marijuana during working hours and has never been impaired at work. However, her employer recently became aware of her medical marijuana use and is concerned about its impact on workplace safety. How should the employer typically handle this situation?

A. The employer should immediately terminate her employment since marijuana is illegal at the federal level.

B. The employer should consult state laws and legal counsel to determine how to accommodate her medical marijuana use, ensuring compliance with state and federal laws.

C. The employer should request that she provide a medical certificate confirming her medical condition and the necessity of using medical marijuana.

D. The employer should follow her state's laws, which explicitly require employers to accommodate employees' medical marijuana use if they have a valid prescription.

36. Under the Fair Labor Standards Act, which of the following provisions determines whether an employee is eligible for overtime pay?

A. The employee's job title and seniority within the company.

B. The employee's age and years of service with the employer.

C. The employee's calculated hourly wage and the number of hours worked in a workweek.

D. The employee's level of education and professional certifications.

37. Joe's elderly father is seriously ill and requires constant care. Joe wants to take time off from work to provide care and support to his father. Is he eligible for leave under the FMLA for this purpose?

A. Joe is eligible for FMLA leave to care for his father if he uses his sick leave.

B. Joe is eligible for FMLA leave to care for his father if he works for an employer with fewer than 50 employees.

C. Joe is eligible for FMLA leave to care for his father if he meets the FMLA's eligibility criteria.

D. Joe is not eligible for FMLA leave to care for his father since the FMLA covers only parents and their children.

38. Madison, an employee, has been diagnosed with a serious medical condition that necessitates frequent doctor appointments and treatments. She requires intermittent leave from work to attend these medical appointments. What are the legal considerations for tracking Madison's intermittent leave under the FMLA?

A. Madison can take intermittent leave without any specific tracking requirements under FMLA.

B. Madison must provide advance notice of each instance of intermittent leave and make a reasonable effort to schedule medical appointments to minimize workplace disruption.

C. Madison is entitled to an unlimited amount of intermittent leave under FMLA.

D. Madison's employer is responsible for tracking her intermittent leave, and she has no reporting obligations.

39. Madison has been approved for intermittent leave under the Family and Medical Leave Act because of her serious medical condition. However, Madison has not been providing proper documentation or notice for her FMLA-approved leave. What should the employer do in this situation to ensure compliance with FMLA regulations?

A. The employer should immediately terminate Madison's employment for noncompliance with FMLA documentation requirements.

B. The employer should continue allowing Madison to take intermittent leave without addressing the documentation issue.

C. The employer should engage in an interactive process with Madison to understand the reason for the lack of documentation and provide her with written notice of the deficiencies.

D. The employer should report Madison to the Department of Labor for FMLA violations.

40. Under the Family and Medical Leave Act in the United States, which statement regarding the use of accrued paid leave for FMLA leave is accurate?

A. The FMLA prohibits the use of accrued paid leave for any FMLA-related reason.

B. Employees can unilaterally decide to use accrued paid leave for FMLA purposes without following the employer's leave rules.

C. An employee must follow the employer's normal leave rules to substitute accrued paid leave for FMLA leave.

D. Accrued paid leave used for FMLA reasons is not FMLA-protected and does not count toward the employee's FMLA entitlement.

41. John, an employee, is currently taking intermittent leave under the Family and Medical Leave Act for his recurring medical treatments. Because of his absence during these treatments, his employer decides to temporarily transfer him to an alternative job that better accommodates his leave schedule and has equivalent pay and benefits. How does the employer's action align with FMLA regulations?

A. The employer is in compliance with FMLA regulations because John is being transferred to an alternative job that suits his leave schedule without consulting him.

B. The employer's action is not compliant with FMLA regulations, as the employer should not make any changes to John's job duties while he is on intermittent leave, even if it is to accommodate his medical treatments.

C. The employer is following FMLA regulations by temporarily transferring John to an alternative job that better suits his recurring periods of leave, ensuring equivalent pay and benefits.

D. The employer must terminate John's employment since his intermittent leave disrupts its operations, and FMLA does not allow for temporary job transfers.

42. To qualify for the computer employee exemption under the FLSA, which of the following criteria must be met by the employee?

A. The employee must be compensated on an hourly basis at a rate not less than $684 per week.

B. The employee's primary duty must involve administrative tasks such as managing computer systems and databases.

C. The employee's primary duty must involve applying systems analysis techniques, designing computer systems or programs, or doing related activities in the computer field.

D. The employee must have at least five years of experience in the computer field.

43. William is applying for a new job and knows that the potential employer will conduct a background check on him as part of the hiring process. What rights does William have under the FCRA concerning this background check?

A. William has the right to refuse the background check if he feels uncomfortable with it.

B. William has the right to be notified in writing and give his consent before the background check is conducted.

C. William has no rights under the FCRA when it comes to background checks for employment.

D. William has the right to request a copy of the background check report, but only after he has been hired.

44. At your place of work, the collective bargaining agreement between the labor union and employer establishes a lower overtime premium rate than the one mandated by the Fair Labor Standards Act regulations. The FLSA, on the other hand, requires a higher overtime premium rate for eligible employees. What is the likely outcome in this situation?

A. The employer is bound by the FLSA's higher overtime premium rate, and the collective bargaining agreement's lower rate is unenforceable.

B. The employer has the option to choose between the FLSA's higher overtime premium rate and the rate specified in the collective bargaining agreement.

C. The collective bargaining agreement takes precedence, and the employer is not required to comply with the FLSA's higher overtime premium rate.

D. The employer must adhere to whichever rate benefits the employees more, whether it's the FLSA rate or the rate specified in the collective bargaining agreement.

45. D'Arcy is a job applicant, and during the interview process, the employer asks her about her family's medical history, including her parents' health conditions. How should D'Arcy respond to this inquiry, considering GINA?

A. D'Arcy should provide all the requested information to the employer.

B. D'Arcy should refuse to answer the question, citing her right under GINA to keep her genetic information private.

C. D'Arcy should answer the question honestly, as GINA applies only to current employees, not job applicants.

D. D'Arcy should answer the question but request that the employer keep her family's medical history confidential.

46. Ted's employer, a large healthcare company, is planning to offer a wellness program to its employees. As part of the program, the company wants to collect genetic information from employees to assess health risks. How should Ted and his co-workers respond to this request, considering GINA?

A. Employees should willingly provide their genetic information to participate in the wellness program.

B. Employees should provide their genetic information but request that the employer keep it confidential.

C. Employees can refuse to provide their genetic information, as GINA generally prohibits the collection of genetic information for wellness programs.

D. Employees should provide their genetic information, as healthcare companies are exempt from GINA requirements.

47. In the landmark labor relations case of *NLRB v. Weingarten*, what was the central issue that led to the Supreme Court's decision, and what was the outcome?

   A. The central issue was whether an employee has the right to request union representation during a disciplinary meeting, and the outcome favored the employee's right to representation.

   B. The central issue was whether an employer can unilaterally deny an employee's request for union representation during an investigatory interview, and the outcome favored the employer's discretion.

   C. The central issue was whether an employee can request union representation only during a collective bargaining negotiation, and the outcome favored broader rights for employees to request representation.

   D. The central issue was whether a union can compel an employer to provide representation to an employee, and the outcome favored the union's right to compel representation.

48. Rosie works in the human resources department in a nonmedical company. She has access to employee records, including personal health information submitted for insurance purposes. A colleague asks Rosie if they can see a co-worker's medical records to confirm a medical condition. What should Rosie do to comply with HIPAA?

   A. Rosie should provide her colleague with access to the medical records to assist them.

   B. Rosie should inform her colleague that accessing medical records without proper authorization is a violation of HIPAA.

   C. Rosie should ask her supervisor for permission before providing access to the medical records.

   D. Rosie should request written consent from the coworker whose records are being requested.

49. What key competency is essential for an HR professional to effectively apply the Health Insurance Portability and Accountability Act (HIPAA) regulations in the workplace?

   A. Technical proficiency in healthcare administration and medical coding.

   B. Knowledge of federal labor laws and collective bargaining agreements.

   C. Strong understanding of employee benefits and retirement planning.

   D. Ability to maintain the confidentiality of protected health information (PHI) and ensure compliance with HIPAA privacy and security requirements.

50. Lisa, a manager in a nonmedical organization, is conducting a performance review for one of her employees. During the review, the employee mentions a recent medical diagnosis that has affected their performance. What should Lisa do to maintain HIPAA compliance?

   A. Lisa should share the employee's medical diagnosis with other team members to provide context for the performance issues.

   B. Lisa should document the information provided by the employee and keep it confidential within the HR department.

   C. Lisa should require the employee to provide medical documentation from a healthcare provider to verify the diagnosis.

   D. Lisa should discuss the employee's medical diagnosis openly during team meetings to promote transparency.

51. Employees at a manufacturing company have been discussing forming a union to address workplace issues. They approach their supervisor with their concerns. What should the supervisor do in accordance with the NLRA?

A. The supervisor should support the employees' unionization efforts and assist them in the process.

B. The supervisor should inform the employees that discussing unionization is not allowed in the workplace.

C. The supervisor should report the employees' unionization discussions to upper management for further action.

D. The supervisor should listen to the employees' concerns and not interfere with their right to discuss unionization.

52. A group of employees in a retail store is dissatisfied with their working conditions and believes that forming a union is the solution. They decide to hold a meeting to discuss unionization during lunch in the breakroom. Can the employer take any action regarding this meeting under the NLRA?

A. The employer can prohibit the meeting, as it is unrelated to work and takes place during their lunch break.

B. The employer can attend the meeting to monitor the employees' discussions.

C. The employer cannot interfere with the meeting, as it is a protected activity under the NLRA.

D. The employer can inform the employees that they will face consequences if they hold the meeting.

53. A construction company has a collective bargaining agreement (CBA) with its unionized workers. However, some employees refuse to pay union dues, arguing that they disagree with the union's political activities. Can the employees be compelled to pay union dues under the LMRA?

A. The employees cannot be compelled to pay union dues since they disagree with the union's political activities.

B. The employees must pay union dues as required by the CBA, regardless of their personal beliefs.

C. The employees can pay reduced union dues to avoid contributing to political activities they disagree with.

D. The employees can pay union dues only if they voluntarily choose to join the union.

54. A labor union is preparing for an election to represent employees at a manufacturing company. The union has requested a list of employee names and addresses from the company to conduct its campaign. What type of list is this?

A. Excelsior.

B. Union Membership.

C. Payroll Roster.

D. Employee Directory.

55. A labor union's leadership is being challenged by a group of members who believe that the union's financial practices are not transparent. Which federal law governs the reporting and disclosure requirements of labor unions to ensure transparency in their financial activities?

A. Wagner Act.

B. Taft-Hartley Act.

C. Landrum-Griffin Act.

D. William-Beall Act.

56. At a construction site, workers are engaged in a project that involves demolition and renovation of an old building. The site supervisor is responsible for ensuring compliance with Occupational Safety and Health Administration (OSHA) regulations. During an inspection, an OSHA compliance officer observes a potential violation related to fall protection. The officer notes that workers on elevated surfaces are not using fall protection systems such as guardrails, safety nets, or personal fall arrest systems. What type of OSHA violation is exemplified by the observed failure to use fall protection systems on elevated surfaces?

A. Serious violation.

B. Willful violation.

C. De minimus violation.

D. Other-than-serious violation.

57. In a busy office environment, Sarah, an administrative assistant, spends long hours at her computer workstation. She frequently experiences discomfort, pain, and numbness in her hands and wrists due to her job's repetitive tasks. Sarah's condition has been diagnosed as a result of ergonomic-related issues. What specific type of ergonomic-related injury is Sarah most likely suffering from?

A. Ergonomics injury.

B. Cumulative trauma disorder (CTD).

C. Osteoarthritis.

D. Simple strain.

58. Alex is an HR manager at a medium-sized company. The company is subject to the employer mandate under the ACA. The company employs 50 full-time employees. What is the minimum number of full-time employees that would trigger the employer mandate under the ACA?

A. 10 full-time employees.

B. 20 full-time employees.

C. 30 full-time employees.

D. 50 full-time employees.

59. Three companies are jointly owned, with one having an average of 20 full-time employees during the year, another having 25, and the third having 12. These three companies form an aggregated group for ACA compliance. To determine their ACA status as an Applicable Large Employer (ALE), what is the number of full-time equivalent (FTE) employees for this aggregated group for the year?

A. 20.

B. 25.

C. 12.

D. 57.

60. Makeda works for a medium-sized company and is eligible for her employer's health insurance plan. She is considering enrolling in her employer's plan but is worried about the cost. What percentage of an employee's income should an employer's health insurance plan typically not exceed to be considered affordable under the ACA?

A. 5% of the employee's income.

B. 7.5% of the employee's income.

C. 9.12% of the employee's income.

D. 15% of the employee's income.

61. ABC Company, a large manufacturing firm, is facing financial difficulties and is considering laying off a significant number of employees at its main plant. The layoffs may affect more than 500 employees, and ABC Company is unsure about its obligations under the WARN Act. What should ABC Company do in this situation?

A. ABC Company is not required to provide any notice since the layoffs are due to financial difficulties.

B. ABC Company should provide notice to all affected employees at least 60 days before the layoffs.

C. ABC Company should only provide notice if the layoffs will result in the closure of the main plant.

D. ABC Company should provide notice to the employees affected by the layoffs but only 30 days in advance.

62. A medium-sized manufacturing company plans to close one of its facilities located in a small town because of declining demand for its products. The closure will result in the termination of 150 employees. However, the company wants to delay providing notice to employees until they find suitable alternative employment for them. Can the company do this under the WARN Act?

A. Yes, the company can delay notice as long as they provide notice before the closure date.

B. Yes, the company can delay notice as long as they have a written agreement with affected employees.

C. No, the company is required to provide notice to affected employees at least 60 days before the closure.

D. No, the company can delay notice only if the closure is due to unforeseeable business circumstances.

63. Delta Consolidated Corporation (DCC) is a medium-sized company that has recently hired several employees. During the hiring process, the HR department discovered that some of the documents presented by new hires for employment verification appear to be counterfeit. What action should ABC Corporation take in accordance with the IRCA?

   A. DCC should continue employing these individuals since they have already been hired.

   B. DCC should immediately terminate the employment of these individuals without further investigation.

   C. DCC should provide a reasonable opportunity for these individuals to present valid, authentic documents.

   D. DCC should report these individuals to the local immigration enforcement authorities.

64. Piazzo Corporation is a large employer with offices in multiple states. It has a diverse workforce and is committed to complying with IRCA's requirements. What is one of the primary responsibilities of Piazzo Corporation under IRCA?

   A. Piazzo Corporation must conduct immigration status checks on all job applicants.

   B. Piazzo Corporation must report all foreign-born employees to the federal government.

   C. Piazzo Corporation must complete the I-9 Employment Eligibility Verification form for all new hires.

   D. Piazzo Corporation must verify the immigration status of employees' family members.

65. A new employee, John, has just started working at your company. He presents a receipt as his employment authorization documentation. Which of the following statements is true regarding this situation?

   A. You must accept the receipt as long as John presents it within three business days after his first day of employment.

   B. You can accept the receipt only if John's employment will last less than three business days.

   C. Accepting a second receipt at the end of the initial receipt validity period is permissible.

   D. You must reject the receipt and request List A, B, or C documentation from John.

66. ABC Manufacturing Company is a contractor that frequently bids on government contracts for the production of goods. Recently, it secured a contract with a federal agency to supply military uniforms. As part of this contract, ABC Manufacturing is subject to the Walsh-Healey Public Contracts Act. What key requirement does this act impose on ABC Manufacturing?

   A. ABC Manufacturing must ensure equal pay for all employees regardless of their roles.

   B. ABC Manufacturing must pay prevailing wages to employees working on government contracts.

   C. ABC Manufacturing must provide health insurance to all employees.

   D. ABC Manufacturing must comply with federal tax regulations related to government contracts.

67. Neha, a highly skilled software engineer from India, has been offered a job at a leading tech company in Silicon Valley. The company wants to bring her to the United States for a short-term business-related visit. Which nonimmigrant visa category would be most suitable for Neha?

A. H-1B visa.

B. L-1 visa.

C. J-1 visa.

D. B-1 visa.

68. Tiya is a manager at a retail store and is responsible for hiring new employees. She receives two job applications—one from John and one from Simone. Both applicants are equally qualified for the position. However, Tiya decides to hire John because he shares the same race as her. What action has Tiya taken, and does it comply with the Civil Rights Act of 1964?

A. Tiya has taken a lawful action as she is entitled to hire whomever she prefers.

B. Tiya has engaged in unlawful racial discrimination, violating the Civil Rights Act.

C. Tiya's decision is lawful if she can justify it based on other factors unrelated to race.

D. Tiya's decision is lawful as long as she also hires Simone for another position.

69. Ted, a transgender employee, informs his employer that he will be undergoing gender transition and will soon present as female at work. How should Ted's employer respond to this situation to comply with the Civil Rights Act of 1964?

A. The employer can terminate Ted's employment since his gender transition is a personal matter.

B. The employer should support and accommodate Ted's gender transition as required by the act.

C. The employer should transfer Ted to another department where his transition will not be noticeable.

D. The employer should ignore Ted's request and not take any action.

70. Maya is a server at a restaurant that is known for its busy weekend nights. The federal minimum wage is $7.25 per hour, and the employer pays Maya the minimum direct wage for tipped employees, which is $2.13 per hour, as per the FLSA regulations. However, Maya notices that her paychecks consistently fall short of the minimum wage, even when factoring in her tips. Which of the following best describes the violation the employer is committing under the FLSA?

A. The employer is in compliance with the FLSA since Maya is a tipped employee.

B. The employer is not in compliance because Maya's tips should be counted separately from her direct wage.

C. The employer is not in compliance because Maya's tips, when combined with her direct wage, should equal at least the federal minimum wage.

D. The employer is not in compliance because they should be paying Maya a higher direct wage than $2.13 per hour.

71. Allesandra is an employee at Weis Markets' Mifflintown, Pennsylvania store. She has been experiencing unwelcome and offensive sexual harassment from her supervisor, who frequently makes inappropriate comments, winks at her, and even kissed her face without her consent. Allesandra decides to report the sexual harassment to her employer, Weis Markets, following which the company conducts an internal investigation. After Allesandra reports the sexual harassment, the company informs her that co-workers have complained about her and, as a result, she will be required to participate in its employee assistance program (EAP). The EAP referral would involve a medical examination and disability-related inquiries, and the company confirms that it's to determine whether she should be placed on disability leave. Allesandra refuses to comply with the mandatory EAP referral. As a consequence, Weis Markets suspends her without pay and ultimately terminates her employment. Which federal laws do Weis Markets' actions in this scenario violate?

A. The Civil Rights Act of 1964 only.

B. The Americans with Disabilities Act only.

C. Both the Civil Rights Act of 1964 and the Americans with Disabilities Act.

D. Neither the Civil Rights Act of 1964 nor the Americans with Disabilities Act.

72. At PRC Industries' Reno, Nevada, facility, two Black employees endured months of racial taunts and slurs from their supervisors. Despite the employees reporting this racial harassment to multiple levels of PRC leadership, the employer failed to intervene. After escalating their complaints to a vice president, one of the harassers fired the workers via text message, which resulted in a lawsuit filed by the U.S. Equal Employment Opportunity Commission (EEOC). The lawsuit alleges violations of Title VII of the Civil Rights Act of 1964, which prohibits racial harassment and retaliation. What remedies may be enforced by the EEOC to address the employer's violation of Title VII in this case?

A. The EEOC may require the employer to issue a written warning to the supervisors involved in the harassment.

B. The EEOC may seek monetary compensation for the two former employees and require the employer to implement preventative measures.

C. The EEOC may order the company to conduct diversity training for its employees.

D. The EEOC may request the employer to issue a public apology to the two former employees.

73. Jama is a job applicant who has been deaf since birth. She communicates effectively using American Sign Language (ASL) and has never used hearing aids or cochlear implants. She applies for a position at a company, but during the interview, the employer expresses concern about her ability to communicate with co-workers and clients due to her deafness. The employer decides not to hire Jama based on these concerns. Which definition of a disability under the Americans with Disabilities Act does Jama's deafness fall under in this scenario?

A. The first prong, as Jama is substantially limited in the major life activity of hearing.

B. The second prong, as Jama has a record of an impairment that substantially limited a major life activity in the past.

C. The third prong, as the employer regards Jama as having an impairment of hearing.

D. None of the above, as Jama's deafness is not covered by the ADA.

74. An employee at a McDonald's restaurant in Northport, Alabama, has a cosmetic disfigurement known as Sturge Weber Syndrome, which manifests as a "port wine stain" covering a significant portion of her face. When she initially joined McDonald's as a cook, she was assured that she would have the opportunity for promotion to a management position based on her performance. To be eligible for a management role, employees must demonstrate proficiency in various aspects of restaurant operations, including serving customers at the front counter. However, because of her appearance, Samantha was removed from the front counter serving customers. Later, she received the news that she would never be promoted to a management position because of her appearance. Consequently, Samantha resigned from her position. In this scenario, which term best describes Samantha's departure from her job?

- **A.** Voluntary resignation.
- **B.** Involuntary termination.
- **C.** Constructive discharge.
- **D.** Early retirement.

75. Maribeth is an employee at United Management LTD, and she has been experiencing sexual harassment from her supervisor, Mark. Mark has made inappropriate comments, sent explicit messages, and created a hostile work environment for Maribeth. Maribeth decides to report the sexual harassment to her employer and initiates a lawsuit under Title VII of the Civil Rights Act of 1964. In this scenario, what steps can the company take to potentially establish the Faragher/Ellerth affirmative defense against vicarious liability in the sexual harassment case?

- **A.** Proving that the supervisor's conduct constituted a "tangible" employment action.
- **B.** Demonstrating that the supervisor's actions were unintentional and that they had no knowledge of the harassment.
- **C.** Showing that they had effective policies and complaint procedures in place and that Maribeth unreasonably failed to take advantage of these procedures.
- **D.** Asserting that Mark's behavior was a one-time occurrence and not part of a pattern of harassment.

76. ABC Corporation is in the process of selecting candidates for a software development position. They have implemented a new selection test to assess technical skills. During the validation process, ABC Corporation discovers that the test disproportionately excludes female candidates. What action should ABC Corporation take in accordance with the Uniform Guidelines on Employee Selection Procedures?

- **A.** ABC Corporation should continue using the test as it is, as long as it is job-related.
- **B.** ABC Corporation should discontinue using the test immediately to avoid potential legal issues.
- **C.** ABC Corporation should review and revise the test to reduce adverse impact and ensure job-relatedness.
- **D.** ABC Corporation should hire only male candidates to avoid further complications.

77. A company has recently hired 100 new employees for various positions, with 60 being men and 40 being women. What is the disparate impact ratio?

    A. 0.67.

    B. 0.75.

    C. 1.25.

    D. 1.50.

Key Concept Research Questions

Making the most of your study time often requires a deeper dive into key concepts that may require a contextual study approach. The following questions are designed for you to find new ways to learn about key concepts. You can find the correct answers in Appendix C.

1. What was the primary purpose of the Portal-to-Portal Act? Give examples of compensable time as defined by this amendment. Search the U.S. Department of Labor's website for more information.
2. How should HR professionals best handle the issue of medical marijuana in the workplace? Go to `SHRM.org` and click the "resources and tools" button. Search for the term "medical marijuana."
3. What are the basic tenants of the Lilly Ledbetter Fair Pay Act? View the video on YouTube titled *A Call to Act: Ledbetter v. Goodyear Tire and Rubber Co.* to learn more.

Test Your Labor Law Terminology Knowledge

The following are the labor law glossary terms you should be familiar with. Use each of these terms once to fill in the blanks in the statements that follow. You can find the correct answers in Appendix B.

- Advance notice
- Affirmative defense
- Amendments
- Arbitration
- BFOQ (Bona Fide Occupational Qualification)
- COBRA qualifying event
- Compensable time
- Confidentiality
- Hostile workplace
- Major life activity
- Modified duty
- Overtime
- Pay equity
- Prevailing wage

- Qualifying event
- Reliability
- Unconscious bias
- Unlawful discrimination
- Unionization
- Validity

1. ____________ is the process of resolving labor disputes through an impartial third party's recommendations or decisions.
2. Employees who work beyond their regular hours may be eligible for ____________ pay.
3. A ____________ is a circumstance that triggers specific benefits or protections under the law.
4. The Americans with Disabilities Act (ADA) defines a ____________ as a function that is essential to an individual's daily life.
5. The ____________ provision of the WARN Act mandates that employers provide employees with prior notification in the event of certain workplace closures or mass layoffs.
6. An ____________ is a legal argument or assertion made by a defendant in response to a plaintiff's claims.
7. ____________ occurs when individuals are treated unfairly or unequally based on protected characteristics.
8. A ____________ is a legitimate job requirement that allows for employment discrimination in certain circumstances.
9. A ____________ is an event, such as job loss, that triggers the continuation of group health insurance coverage under COBRA.
10. ____________ is the process by which employees vote to decide whether they want to be represented by a labor union.
11. When employees are unable to perform their regular job duties due to injury or illness, they may be placed on ____________.
12. ____________ refers to the concept of ensuring that employees receive equal pay for equal work, regardless of gender or other protected characteristics.
13. ____________ includes all the hours an employee is entitled to be compensated for, such as time spent working, attending meetings, and on-call time.
14. ____________ refers to the degree to which a test or measurement accurately measures what it is intended to measure.
15. ____________ is a measure of the consistency and stability of a test or measurement over time.
16. A ____________ is a work environment in which unwelcome behavior based on protected characteristics creates an intimidating atmosphere.
17. ____________ refers to biases that individuals may hold without awareness.

18. The ______________ is the minimum wage set by the government for specific jobs or projects, often in government contracts.
19. ______________ is protecting individuals' privacy.
20. Legislative ______________ involve changes or additions to existing laws or regulations.

Conclusion

Labor law compliance is crucial for organizations, and competent HR professionals play a pivotal role in ensuring it. By staying up-to-date with ever-changing legislation, HR professionals protect companies from costly legal disputes, fines, and damage to their reputation, especially in today's world of viral social media and other methods for rapid information sharing. HR teams establish fair employment practices, safeguarding against discrimination and harassment, all of which foster a positive work environment.

The PHR and SPHR exams from HRCI do not have a specific functional area set aside for U.S. labor law compliance; rather, compliance is embedded in specific content areas such as compensation and safety and health. SHRM's BASK has an entire area set aside to measure competency in this area. One of SHRM's proficiency indicators is to "maintain current working knowledge of relevant global and domestic laws." For the exams, it's important to focus *solely* on federal labor law as state-specific regulations are distractors from the correct answer and you must be proficient in the laws that are current at the time you sit for the test.

Both SHRM and HRCI note that students will be tested on the labor laws that are current at the time they sit for the exam. This principle holds even if the exam content outlines from HRCI and SHRM's Body of Applied Skills and Knowledge have not been formally updated.

It is also worth noting that what is ethical is not necessarily determined by what is legal. In the absence of a labor law, human resource professionals are tasked with advising their employers on what is right, not just what is legal.

Additional Resources

Compliance with labor laws is a significant responsibility for HR professionals at all stages of their careers. With the passage of new laws every year, staying on top of emerging legislation is part of responsibility as a business partner. If you want to study U.S. labor law in more detail, there are several reputable websites, podcasts, and videos where you can access comprehensive information and materials related to labor law.

Websites

- U.S. Department of Labor (`www.dol.gov`)

  The official website of the U.S. Department of Labor provides a wealth of information on labor laws and regulations, including the Fair Labor Standards Act, the National Labor Relations Act (NLRA), and various other employment-related laws. It offers fact sheets, guides, and compliance assistance materials.
- The Equal Employment Opportunity Commission (`www.eeoc.gov`)

  The Equal Employment Opportunity Commission (EEOC) website serves as a comprehensive resource for information related to workplace discrimination and equal employment opportunities in the United States. It provides valuable guidance to employers and employees regarding federal laws, regulations, and policies aimed at preventing discrimination based on factors such as race, gender, age, disability, and other protected class groups.
- Legal Information Institute, Cornell Law School (`www.law.cornell.edu`)

  Cornell Law School's Legal Information Institute offers a comprehensive resource for U.S. federal labor laws and regulations. It provides access to the full text of statutes and regulations, making it a valuable research tool.
- National Labor Relations Board (`www.nlrb.gov`)

  The NLRB's website offers extensive resources related to the NLRA, labor relations, and collective bargaining. It includes case decisions, publications, and educational materials.
- FindLaw (`employment.findlaw.com`)

  FindLaw offers a dedicated section on employment law, providing articles, legal guides, and resources on various labor law topics.

Podcasts

- *The Proactive Employer Podcast* with host Jonathan Segal

  This podcast discusses a wide range of employment law topics, including U.S. labor laws. It provides insights and tips for employers to stay compliant with labor regulations.
- *Employment Law This Week* with host Epstein Becker Green

  This podcast covers the latest labor and employment law developments, including changes in U.S. labor laws and regulations. It provides concise updates for HR professionals and employers.
- *Lawyer 2 Lawyer: Law News and Legal Topics* with hosts Robert Ambrogi and J. Craig Williams

  This legal podcast covers a variety of legal topics, including labor and employment law issues in the United States.

YouTube Channels

Using websites such as YouTube is a great way to break up the monotony of reading. There are several channels at www.youtube.com that focus on U.S. employment law. Log in and search for these shows by name:

- LegalEagle

  LegalEagle, hosted by attorney Devin Stone, provides legal analysis and commentary on various legal topics, including employment law. While not exclusively focused on U.S. employment laws, the channel covers relevant legal issues.

- Littler Mendelson P.C.

  Littler Mendelson is a prominent labor and employment law firm. Its YouTube channel features discussions and insights on employment law, workplace compliance, and HR topics.

Chapter 3

Business Management and Strategy

As part of his overhaul of the culture at Uber, incoming CEO Dara Khosrowshahi announced the ride-sharing company has adopted 8 new "cultural norms," replacing the 14 values first introduced by his predecessor, Travis Kalanick. Khosrowshahi said he wanted the norms to reflect the perspectives of Uber's employees, so he asked for and received more than 1,200 submissions that were voted on by employees more than 22,000 times until they settled on the final 8. Examples of how employees believed all stakeholders should act include "We build globally, we live locally;" "We are customer obsessed;" and "We celebrate differences." This collaborative approach to defining one of the core components of business strategy—the company values—signaled a change in how the company would prioritize initiatives going forward. The need for change came on the heels of the prior CEO's headline-making unethical (sometimes unlawful) behaviors, and the new CEO acknowledged this on his LinkedIn page by saying, "The culture and approach that got Uber where it is today is not what will get us to the next level." He wrote, "As we move from an era of growth at all costs to one of responsible growth, our culture needs to evolve."

Business strategy encompasses the comprehensive plan and framework that guides an organization's actions, goals, and objectives. Ubers' example shows that business strategy is not a static, one-time event, but rather a continuous process of evolution. The strategic plan is built by identifying and optimizing internal and external strengths and opportunities and mitigating weaknesses and threats to achieve sustainable growth and a competitive advantage in their respective markets.

For HR, as with all other business units, the goal is to build the people systems and structure interventions that support organizational results. For this, a department strategy is needed that aligns with business strategy. The following are the critical concepts related to human resource and business strategy that are reviewed in the practice questions:

- **Purpose of business strategy:** At its core, business strategy defines an organization's overarching vision and mission, outlining the long-term objectives and goals it aims to achieve, serving as a blueprint for decision-making, and guiding how an organization allocates its resources, manages its operations, and positions itself in the marketplace.
- **Competitive advantage and differentiation:** Organizations seek ways to distinguish themselves from competitors, whether through cost leadership, product differentiation, innovation, or customer-centric approaches. Business strategies aim to carve out unique value propositions that resonate with customers, fostering brand loyalty and market dominance.
- **Strategic planning process:** The development and execution of a successful business strategy involves a structured process. It begins with environmental scanning to understand the industry landscape, followed by setting clear goals and objectives. Strategic planning then progresses into the formulation of strategies and tactics, resource allocation, and continuous monitoring and adjustments to adapt to changing circumstances.

- **Strategic management:** Strategic management is the ongoing process of overseeing and aligning an organization's activities with its strategic goals. It involves effective leadership, resource allocation, performance measurement, and adaptation in response to internal and external changes.
- **Measuring effectiveness:** A well-crafted business strategy is only as good as its execution. The ability to translate strategic plans into actionable steps and then measure success through milestone check-ins, after-action reviews, and other methods involve competencies of project management, business acumen, and data analysis.

Real World Scenario

Transforming a Traditional Retailer: A Case Study in Business Management, Strategy, and Environmental Scanning

In the ever-evolving landscape of retail, businesses must adapt or risk becoming obsolete. This case study examines the transformation journey of ClassicThreads, a traditional brick-and-mortar clothing retailer, and underscores the critical role of environmental scanning and elements of the strategic planning process in their survival and growth.

Background and Problem

ClassicThreads had been a well-established retailer for decades, specializing in classic and timeless fashion for a loyal customer base. However, with the rise of e-commerce and fast fashion, the company faced declining sales and shrinking profit margins. It became evident that a change in business strategy was imperative.

Diagnosis

ClassicThreads initiated a comprehensive strategic analysis, incorporating environmental scanning, to assess their internal strengths and weaknesses and understand the external market forces. They identified the following key issues:

- **Outdated inventory management:** The company's inventory system was inefficient, leading to overstocking unsold items and frequent stockouts of popular products.
- **Limited online presence:** ClassicThreads had a minimal online presence, making it difficult to compete with e-commerce giants.
- **Customer demographic shift:** The core customer base was aging, and there was a need to attract a younger audience to remain relevant.
- **Skill assessment:** The HR department conducted a thorough assessment of the existing workforce to identify skills gaps and areas requiring development. This included evaluating the digital literacy of employees and their knowledge of sustainable fashion practices.

Strategies

The following strategic planning processes were implemented:

- **Environmental scanning:** ClassicThreads conducted an exhaustive analysis of market trends, competitors, and changing consumer behaviors through environmental scanning. This information informed their strategic decisions.
- **Inventory optimization:** ClassicThreads implemented modern inventory management software to optimize stock levels and introduced data analytics to forecast demand accurately. This reduced carrying costs and improved cash flow.
- **E-commerce expansion:** Recognizing the importance of e-commerce, the company launched an attractive, user-friendly online store. They also integrated an omnichannel approach, allowing customers to shop online and in store seamlessly.
- **Rebranding and marketing:** To appeal to a younger demographic, ClassicThreads underwent a rebranding process. They revamped their store layouts and marketing campaigns to align with modern tastes and lifestyles.
- **Customer engagement:** ClassicThreads leveraged social media platforms to engage with customers, gather feedback, and offer personalized shopping experiences. Loyalty programs were introduced to incentivize repeat business.
- **Customized training:** Based on the skill assessment, HR collaborated with department heads and subject-matter experts to design customized training programs. These programs included modules on e-commerce operations, sustainable fashion practices, and customer service excellence.

Results

To measure the results of their transformation efforts, ClassicThreads introduced a strategic evaluation metric, the Customer Satisfaction Index (CSI). They measured CSI through surveys, feedback forms, and online reviews. The CSI showed a significant improvement from 3.8 to 4.5 on a 5-point scale within the first year, reflecting increased customer satisfaction.

Conclusion

As can be seen with ClassicThreads, effective business management, strategic planning, environmental scanning, and performance metrics can breathe new life into a traditional retailer. By addressing critical issues, embracing technology, adapting to changing consumer preferences, and upskilling their team members (while consistently monitoring their progress), the company not only survived but thrived in a competitive marketplace. This transformation serves as a valuable lesson for businesses facing similar challenges, highlighting the importance of strategic agility and continuous evaluation in today's dynamic business environment.

Business Management and Strategy Questions

1. What is the first step in the strategic management process?
   - **A.** Implementing the strategy.
   - **B.** Evaluating performance.
   - **C.** Conducting an environmental scan.
   - **D.** Setting organizational goals.
2. Which of the following is an example of a SWOT analysis component?
   - **A.** Competitive analysis.
   - **B.** Market segmentation.
   - **C.** Product pricing.
   - **D.** Financial forecasting.
3. ABC Company is in the process of setting its HR strategic objectives for the upcoming year. The executive team wants to align HR goals with the organization's overall strategic plan. Which of the following HR strategic objectives is most aligned with a company's goal of increasing market share and expanding its customer base?
   - **A.** Implement a comprehensive employee training program to enhance skill development.
   - **B.** Reduce employee turnover by 20% through improved retention strategies.
   - **C.** Increase workforce diversity and inclusion through targeted recruitment efforts.
   - **D.** Streamline HR processes and reduce administrative costs by 15%.
4. Which of the following HR competencies is most likely to drive organizational performance outcomes?
   - **A.** HR expertise.
   - **B.** Leadership.
   - **C.** Personal integrity.
   - **D.** Business and competitive awareness.
5. What is a core element of Porter's Five Forces framework?
   - **A.** Market segmentation.
   - **B.** Competitive rivalry.
   - **C.** Employee satisfaction.
   - **D.** Marketing budget.

6. Which growth strategy involves selling existing products to new markets?
   A. Market penetration.
   B. Market development.
   C. Product development.
   D. Diversification.
7. What is a disadvantage of a cost leadership strategy?
   A. Limited pricing flexibility.
   B. High risk of imitation.
   C. Low-profit margins.
   D. Narrow target market.
8. Which of the following best describes the first step in the strategic planning process?
   A. Conducting a SWOT analysis.
   B. Setting organizational objectives.
   C. Identifying strategic alternatives.
   D. Defining the organization's mission and vision.
9. What is a key purpose of a business's mission statement?
   A. To outline specific financial targets.
   B. To communicate the company's core purpose and values.
   C. To provide product processes and procedures.
   D. To identify the market share.
10. ABC Corporation is planning to divest one of its non-core business units to focus on its core operations. As part of this divestiture strategy, what is HR's primary role?
    A. Implementing a hiring freeze during the divestiture.
    B. Managing employee communication and transition strategies.
    C. Negotiating sale terms with potential buyers.
    D. Overseeing the financial aspects of the divestiture, such as asset valuation.
11. You are the manager of a small tech startup. Your company has been primarily focused on developing software for the healthcare industry. Recently, you've noticed increased demand for your software in the education sector. What strategic approach should you consider?
    A. Maintain your current strategy as it's been successful so far.
    B. Pursue a market development strategy to enter the education sector.
    C. Focus on diversification by expanding into multiple industries.
    D. Reduce your offerings to healthcare only for cost savings.

12. You are the CEO of a retail company facing intense competition. You want to gain a competitive advantage by offering unique, high-quality products that your competitors do not have. What strategy are you most likely pursuing?

A. Cost leadership strategy.

B. Differentiation strategy.

C. Market penetration strategy.

D. Liquidation strategy.

13. You work for a multinational corporation that operates in various countries. The company is conducting a PESTLE analysis for its expansion into a new market. Which factor would be considered under the "S" category in the analysis?

A. Exchange rates.

B. Government regulations.

C. Demographic trends.

D. Technological advancements.

14. You are the manager of a manufacturing company. You notice that your competitors are using new, more sustainable materials in their products, and consumers are increasingly valuing eco-friendly options. What actions should you consider to align with this trend?

A. Continue using traditional materials for cost savings.

B. Invest in research to develop sustainable materials.

C. Ignore the trend as it may be short-lived.

D. Conduct a focus group to determine demand.

15. You are the manager of a retail chain facing a slowdown in sales due to economic recession. You want to maintain profitability by reducing costs without compromising product quality. What strategy should you consider?

A. Cost leadership strategy.

B. Differentiation strategy.

C. Market development strategy.

D. Product diversification strategy.

16. What are the advantages of conducting environmental scans as part of the strategic planning process? (Choose all that apply.)

A. Environmental scans help identify emerging opportunities and threats.

B. Environmental scans facilitate proactive adaptation to changes.

C. Environmental scans drive cost savings.

D. Environmental scans eliminate the need for internal analysis.

17. What is the primary disadvantage of relying on historical data in environmental scans?
    - **A.** It does not take into account the impact of current social trends.
    - **B.** It can lead to complacency and lack of innovation.
    - **C.** It reduces the ability to adapt to rapid changes.
    - **D.** It increases the need for scenario planning.

18. BMW and Hyundai are both automotive manufacturers, but their product offerings and brand positioning differ. BMW focuses on high-performance, luxury vehicles, while Hyundai emphasizes affordability and reliability. Which of the following statements regarding their strategies is accurate?
    - **A.** BMW and Hyundai both employ cost leadership strategies.
    - **B.** BMW and Hyundai both employ differentiation strategies.
    - **C.** BMW employs a differentiation strategy, while Hyundai employs a cost leadership strategy.
    - **D.** BMW and Hyundai have identical business strategies.

19. TaylorMade Golf's mission statement is "to be the best performance golf brand in the world." How does this mission statement influence their competitive strategy?
    - **A.** By emphasizing low-cost production to provide affordable golf equipment.
    - **B.** By focusing on creating innovative, high-performance golf products.
    - **C.** By expanding their retail presence in non-golf-related markets.
    - **D.** By partnering with other golf brands to share technology and resources.

20. Which aspect of Lego's corporate identity is reflected in their statement to be a global force for "learning through play"?
    - **A.** Vision.
    - **B.** Mission.
    - **C.** Values.
    - **D.** Brand.

21. What aspect of Tesla's corporate identity is reflected in their statement "to accelerate the advent of sustainable transport by bringing compelling mass market electric cars to market as soon as possible"?
    - **A.** Vision.
    - **B.** Mission.
    - **C.** Values.
    - **D.** Brand.

22. How can a company's mission, vision, and values influence its global strategy?

A. A company's mission, vision, and values impact a company's ability to adapt to changing markets.

B. A company's mission, vision, and values impact a company's ability to attract and retain talent that aligns with the company's culture.

C. A company's mission, vision, and values impact a company's ability to increase the effectiveness of short-term goals through the creation of long-term goals.

D. A company's mission, vision, and values impact a company's ability to navigate diverse markets and create long-term value.

23. Which of the following best defines a talent management strategy in HR?

A. Focusing on recruitment and sourcing processes.

B. Implementing policies for employee retention and engagement.

C. Providing extensive training programs for skill development.

D. Conducting performance appraisals on a quarterly basis.

24. Which of the following is a primary goal of a strategic compensation plan in HR? (Choose all that apply.)

A. Conducting a benefit utilization review.

B. Ensuring fair and equitable pay across all job roles.

C. Implementing an organization-wide salary structure to ensure pay fairness.

D. Offering bonuses to top-performing employees.

25. IKEA, a renowned furniture and home goods retailer, is known for its vision to "create a better everyday life for the many people." Which aspect of IKEA's vision statement is most prominent?

A. IKEA's aspiration to become the world's largest furniture retailer.

B. IKEA's aim to take a cost-leadership approach to its business strategy.

C. IKEA's commitment to making quality furniture accessible and affordable.

D. IKEA's focus on differentiated home furnishings.

26. Clothing manufacturer Bombas seeks to create a competitive advantage while maintaining a commitment to corporate social responsibility. Part of this initiative is to donate one pair of socks for every pair sold. This is the best example of which of the following competitive strategies?

A. A competitive cost leadership strategy by increasing their point-of-sale costs to offset the donations.

B. A competitive cost leadership strategy through strategic return-on-investment.

C. A competitive differentiation strategy through philanthropy.

D. A competitive differentiation strategy through shareholder engagement.

27. Which of the following is an example of a behavior from a company that is pursuing a differentiation strategy for developing a competitive advantage?
    - **A.** Paying higher-than-market wages.
    - **B.** Offering free shipping.
    - **C.** Seeking patents.
    - **D.** Investing in continuous improvement.

28. How can an effective customer relationship management (CRM) system contribute to a competitive advantage?
    - **A.** By decreasing the cost of engagement with customers.
    - **B.** By improving the number of quality interactions.
    - **C.** By improving customer loyalty and retention.
    - **D.** By creating customer self-service portals to reduce costs.

29. Which of the following is a common key performance indicator (KPI) used to evaluate the financial effectiveness of a business strategy?
    - **A.** Employee satisfaction.
    - **B.** Customer demographics.
    - **C.** Return on investment (ROI).
    - **D.** Office location.

30. Tabour Inc., a leading software development company, is in the process of implementing a balanced scorecard to measure its strategic outcomes effectively. They want to ensure that their measurement framework is comprehensive and aligned with their strategic goals. To measure employee-related aspects under the "Employee" perspective of the balanced scorecard, which specific methods or tools should they consider using during the implementation process?
    - **A.** Conducting a customer satisfaction survey.
    - **B.** Analyzing the number of new software features developed.
    - **C.** Calculating return on investment (ROI) from recent product launches.
    - **D.** Performing a turnover analysis.

31. In the context of evaluating business strategy results, what does the term *key performance indicators* (KPIs) refer to?
    - **A.** The specific strategies implemented by a company.
    - **B.** The financial forecasts for the next fiscal year.
    - **C.** Quantifiable metrics used to assess the success or performance of a strategy.
    - **D.** The company's market share compared to competitors.

32. A multinational technology company has recently implemented a new market entry strategy to expand into a highly competitive emerging market. After one year, the company's market share has increased, but profitability has declined due to aggressive pricing to gain market share. Customer satisfaction is mixed, with some customers praising the low prices, while others are dissatisfied with the after-sales support. What should the company conclude when evaluating the effectiveness of its market entry strategy?

A. The strategy is highly effective due to the increased market share.

B. The strategy is ineffective because profitability has declined.

C. The strategy is effective since some customers are satisfied with low prices.

D. The strategy is effective because it successfully penetrated the market.

33. A retail company has implemented a new human resources strategy aimed at reducing employee turnover and improving productivity. After six months, the turnover rate has indeed decreased, but productivity has declined significantly, and some employees have reported dissatisfaction due to increased workload and stress. What aspect of the strategy should the company reconsider when evaluating its effectiveness?

A. Employee turnover reduction, which aligns with retention objectives.

B. Productivity improvement, as it enhances operational efficiency.

C. Employee satisfaction, as it directly impacts morale and engagement.

D. The overall strategy, as both turnover and productivity need improvement.

34. Which strategic framework is often used to analyze an organization's competitive environment by assessing the bargaining power of suppliers, buyers, threat of new entrants, threat of substitutes, and competitive rivalry?

A. SWOT analysis.

B. Balanced scorecard.

C. Porter's Five Forces.

D. BCG Matrix.

35. Which of the following is the BEST example of aligning a Total Rewards strategy with a business strategy?

A. Providing employees with unlimited vacation days to promote work-life balance.

B. Offering a comprehensive wellness program to reduce healthcare costs and improve employee productivity.

C. Introducing a profit-sharing plan where employees receive a percentage of company profits based on individual and team performance.

D. Increasing the retirement age eligibility to reduce pension liabilities and align with industry standards.

36. As part of the annual strategic planning sessions, your team has been tasked with analyzing different employee groups based on their growth potential (demand for specific skills or roles) and relative market share (the company's strength in attracting and retaining talent within those segments). Which strategic framework would be best suited to help achieve this task?
   - A. McKinsey 7-S Framework.
   - B. BCG Matrix.
   - C. Blue Ocean Strategy.
   - D. SWOT analysis.

37. What is the first step an HR professional should take when conducting a pay equity analysis?
   - A. Compare job descriptions for role parity.
   - B. Interview employees for their perspectives.
   - C. Gather pay data for analysis.
   - D. Determine if discrimination has occurred.

38. What is the main difference between an HR strategy plan and an HR human capital management plan?
   - A. An HR strategy plan focuses on workforce planning and talent acquisition, while an HR human capital management plan focuses on employee development and performance management.
   - B. An HR strategy plan outlines the organization's overall approach to managing its workforce, while an HR human capital management plan specifically addresses the recruitment and retention of top talent.
   - C. An HR strategy plan emphasizes aligning HR practices with business objectives, while an HR human capital management plan prioritizes optimizing employee skills and capabilities.
   - D. An HR strategy plan encompasses the organization's long-term goals and objectives related to its workforce, while an HR human capital management plan details short-term initiatives for improving employee engagement and satisfaction.

39. Which of the following is an example of the strategic initiatives commonly included in an HR strategic plan? (Choose all that apply.)
   - A. Hosting monthly employee events.
   - B. Conducting regular performance appraisals and feedback sessions.
   - C. Analyzing external pay data.
   - D. Re-designing the employee breakroom.

40. Which aspect of an HR strategic plan is focused on ensuring that the organization has the right people, in the right roles, at the right time?
   - A. Employee retention strategies.
   - B. Talent acquisition and workforce planning.
   - C. Employee engagement programs.
   - D. Workplace diversity initiatives.

41. Which of the following HR initiatives directly contribute to compliance with federal labor laws?

- **A.** Requiring two weeks' notice from employees who quit.
- **B.** Auditing personnel files.
- **C.** Paying severance to laid-off workers older than 40.
- **D.** Adhering to hiring quotas for under-represented groups.

42. When HR professionals navigate the formal and informal structures within a work group, what is a primary reason for doing so?

- **A.** To ensure supervisors are communicating in a nondiscriminatory fashion.
- **B.** To ensure that all employees are following company policies, procedures, and rules.
- **C.** To become friends with employees to build trust.
- **D.** To build relationships and address employee concerns.

43. In the context of HR's role in navigating informal structures, what is the significance of understanding informal power dynamics within a work group?

- **A.** It allows HR to establish strict rules for employee interactions.
- **B.** It helps HR identify potential whistleblowers.
- **C.** It enables HR to leverage informal influencers to promote positive change.
- **D.** It ensures that all employees follow formal procedures at all times.

44. Penelope, a mid-level manager, has identified a project that could significantly benefit her department and the company as a whole. However, she knows that the project will require support and resources from other departments. How should Penelope navigate this situation?

- **A.** Penelope should proceed with the project independently without seeking support or resources from other departments to show that she is capable and trustworthy.
- **B.** Penelope should reach out to key stakeholders in other departments to understand their priorities.
- **C.** Penelope should take the time to build relationships with key stakeholders in other departments and then present a well-structured proposal highlighting the project's benefits.
- **D.** Penelope should not pursue the project at all to avoid getting involved in the organizational politics.

45. At Company ABC, there's a power struggle among department heads, and it's impacting decision-making and teamwork. As an HR professional, what should you consider when addressing this issue?

- **A.** Ignoring the power struggle to maintain neutrality.
- **B.** Supporting one department head to resolve the conflict quickly.
- **C.** Mediating discussions, facilitating communication, and promoting conflict resolution.
- **D.** Advocating for the removal of all department heads involved in the power struggle.

46. When creating strategic goals, which of the following considerations is MOST important for ensuring their effectiveness?

A. Setting goals that are easily achievable to gain easy but important wins.

B. Ensuring that goals are aligned with the organization's mission and vision.

C. Setting goals based on industry benchmarks and to address competitors' performance.

D. Assigning critical deadlines to create a sense of urgency.

47. Company XYZ is implementing a strategic initiative to improve customer satisfaction. To create actionable goals, they decide to set the following goal: "Increase the percentage of positive customer feedback by 15% within the next six months." What characteristic of SMART goals does this exemplify?

A. Specific.

B. Mastery.

C. Active.

D. Relatable.

48. Company ABC has recently implemented a new HR strategy aimed at improving employee engagement. What is a suitable short-term goal to help achieve this strategy within the next six months?

A. Develop a comprehensive leadership training program for all employees.

B. Increase employee retention rates by 50% over the next five years.

C. Launch a new HR software system to streamline administrative tasks.

D. Conduct quarterly employee engagement surveys and address immediate concerns.

49. Your company is developing a long-term HR strategy that aims to use advanced HR systems to support its broader business strategy of global expansion over the next five years. What is a suitable long-term goal related to HR systems in this context?

A. Implement a new HR software system within the next six months.

B. Achieve a 10% reduction in employee turnover within one year.

C. Establish an HR analytics team to provide data-driven insights over the next three years.

D. Conduct an annual employee satisfaction survey.

50. In the process of implementing a new performance management system, the HR department discovers that there is a potential incompatibility with the performance module and the company ERP system. This incompatibility could lead to data breaches. This is the BEST example of which of the following conditions?

A. Internal risks.

B. Internal threats.

C. Internal weaknesses.

D. External threats.

51. In HR project management, which of the following techniques is commonly used to prioritize tasks based on their impact and urgency?

- **A.** PERT analysis.
- **B.** Critical Path Method (CPM).
- **C.** Eisenhower Matrix.
- **D.** SWOT analysis.

52. In HR project management, which method is commonly used to evaluate and prioritize project risks by assessing their likelihood and severity?

- **A.** Fishbone diagram.
- **B.** Monte Carlo simulation.
- **C.** Pareto analysis.
- **D.** Risk matrix.

53. To build credibility and influence with other department managers, what is a key strategy that HR professionals should focus on?

- **A.** Understanding the unique challenges and objectives of each department.
- **B.** Providing unsolicited advice and recommendations to department managers.
- **C.** Maintain impartiality to ensure a fair distribution of outcomes.
- **D.** Minimizing communication with employees to respect the proper chain of command.

54. What is the primary purpose of conducting a cost-benefit analysis in business analysis?

- **A.** To determine the breakeven point for a project.
- **B.** To evaluate the financial feasibility of a project.
- **C.** To identify potential risks associated with a project.
- **D.** To allocate resources efficiently within a project.

55. The HR department implemented a new employee training program aimed at enhancing productivity. The total cost of implementing the program was $50,000, and it resulted in an estimated productivity gain of $100,000 over the course of a year. What is the ROI of the HR initiative?

- **A.** 50%.
- **B.** 100%.
- **C.** 150%.
- **D.** 200%.

56. What is a key difference between a CBA and ROI?

- **A.** CBA assesses the financial feasibility of a project, while ROI calculates the percentage increase in profits.
- **B.** CBA evaluates the costs and benefits of a project, while ROI measures the net gain or loss as a percentage of the initial investment.
- **C.** CBA is used for long-term financial planning, while ROI is primarily used for short-term financial decisions.
- **D.** CBA focuses on assessing external factors' impact, while ROI is entirely internal.

57. The company you work for is in the process of creating its HR budget for the next fiscal year. What is the first step that HR professionals should take when developing the budget?
   - **A.** Calculate changes in labor spending for the next fiscal year.
   - **B.** Estimate the total number of new hires expected in the upcoming year.
   - **C.** Analyze historical HR spending and expenses.
   - **D.** Determine the desired increase in employee salaries.

58. Your company has finalized its HR budget for the year and is now in the implementation phase. What is a crucial aspect of successfully implementing the HR budget?
   - **A.** Allocating any excess funds to employee compensation.
   - **B.** Adhering to the budget without flexibility.
   - **C.** Continuously monitoring expenses and adjusting as needed.
   - **D.** Delaying other HR initiatives until the end of the fiscal year.

59. How do you calculate the HR to FTE ratio in an organization?
   - **A.** Divide the number of part-time employees by the total number of employees.
   - **B.** Divide the number of HR employees by the total number of employees.
   - **C.** Divide the number of HR employees by the number of part-time employees.
   - **D.** Divide the number of FTEs by the total number of employees.

60. What is the best way for HR to ensure equity effectiveness in the design of human resource strategy?
   - **A.** Conducting regular pay equity audits to identify and rectify disparities.
   - **B.** Implementing comprehensive diversity training programs for all employees.
   - **C.** Utilizing blind recruitment processes to mitigate unconscious bias.
   - **D.** Establishing mentorship and sponsorship programs to support underrepresented groups.

61. When aligning HR efforts with business strategy, what is a key benefit of aligning HR practices with the company's strategic goals?
   - **A.** Reduced need for employee training and development programs.
   - **B.** Improved organizational agility and adaptability to market changes.
   - **C.** Increased reliance on standardized HR processes.
   - **D.** Elimination of diversity and inclusion initiatives to streamline HR practices.

62. What is a best practice when developing a business case for a new project or initiative?
   - **A.** Be optimistic about the benefits to gain approval from stakeholders.
   - **B.** Provide general information to keep the business case concise.
   - **C.** Clearly outline the expected costs, benefits, and risks of the project.
   - **D.** Avoid involving key stakeholders until the business case is finalized.

63. Which of the following initiatives should HR undertake to best support a company's goal to improve product quality?

A. Implementing cost-cutting measures.

B. Enhancing employee training and development programs.

C. Reducing marketing expenses.

D. Increasing office space and infrastructure.

64. In business strategy, how is BATNA typically utilized?

A. As a method for evaluating market trends and consumer behavior.

B. As a framework for assessing the financial performance of a company.

C. As a tool for analyzing potential risks associated with new ventures.

D. As a strategy for assessing alternatives and enhancing negotiation leverage.

65. What is the primary purpose of obtaining a patent under U.S. patent law?

A. To keep an invention a secret from competitors.

B. To ensure that the inventor is the only one who can monetize the invention.

C. To provide the inventor with tax benefits.

D. To encourage the sharing of inventions with the public for free.

66. The NeuroStim Pro is a cutting-edge medical device designed to treat neurological disorders and improve the quality of life for patients suffering from conditions such as Parkinson's disease, essential tremor, epilepsy, and other movement-related disorders. The device utilizes advanced technology to deliver targeted electrical stimulation to specific regions of the brain. What kind of patent would best protect this invention?

A. Design.

B. Utility.

C. Provisional.

D. Plant.

67. What is the primary focus of systems thinking in the context of business strategy?

A. Isolating business units for separate optimization.

B. Analyzing the short-term and long-term risks in evaluating business strategy.

C. Understanding the interconnectedness and relationships among various elements within an organization.

D. Maximizing immediate profits through HR systems.

68. In the context of systems thinking, which of the following best describes the concept of differentiation of units?

A. Isolating individual components for separate optimization.

B. Ignoring the interrelationships between different parts of a system.

C. Focusing solely on the short-term goals of an organization.

D. Promoting synergy and collaboration among various elements within a system.

69. The impact of the regulatory environment on a corporation's business strategy is an example of which SWOT category?

 A. Strength.

 B. Weakness.

 C. Opportunity.

 D. Threat.

70. Which growth strategy involves increasing a company's sales within their current competitive landscape?

 A. Market penetration.

 B. Market development.

 C. Product development.

 D. Diversification.

71. What factor primarily determines the bargaining power of suppliers in a market?

 A. The number of substitute products available.

 B. The level of differentiation in the industry.

 C. The concentration of suppliers relative to buyers.

 D. The size of the buyer's market share.

72. Which of the following is a KPI for a healthcare HR department? (Choose all that apply.)

 A. Employee turnover rate.

 B. Patient satisfaction scores.

 C. Nurse safety records.

 D. Revenue generated per physician.

73. A leading technology company had the opportunity to acquire a promising startup specializing in renewable energy solutions. The startup had developed innovative solar panel technology that had the potential to revolutionize the renewable energy industry. However, due to hesitation from the company's executives, the acquisition did not proceed. As a result, the startup was later acquired by a competitor, allowing them to integrate the technology into their product offerings and gain a significant competitive advantage. What was the lost strategic opportunity cost for the technology company in failing to acquire the renewable energy startup?

 A. Expanding into a new market segment.

 B. Strengthening the company's brand reputation.

 C. Securing a competitive edge in the renewable energy industry.

 D. Improving employee morale and engagement.

74. Which of the following terms are related to strategic downsizing? (Choose all that apply.)

 A. Offshoring.

 B. Layoffs.

 C. Reduction-in-force.

 D. Diversifying.

Key Concept Research Questions

Taking a deeper dive into key concepts helps to create context, and the information necessary to critically think through the questions on exam day. A bonus is that this research should also make you more knowledgeable in your work, so making the time to answer the next question is worth it.

1. Forbes research shows that 88% of consumers want choices that help them be more environmentally conscious. Many companies are responding by changing the way they do business. Nordstrom, for example, is now selling used clothing. What are at least three ways that organizations can adapt their business practices to adopt a more environmentally oriented mission, vision, or values? Take a look at the World Business Council for Sustainable Development business guide for ideas at `www.wbcsd.org/Archive/Sustainable-Lifestyles/Resources/The-Good-Life-Goals-Business-Guide`.

Test Your Business Management and Strategy Terminology Questions

The following are business management and strategy terms you should be familiar with. Use each of these terms once to fill in the blanks that follow. The correct answers are in Appendix B.

- Action plan
- BCG matrix
- Business plan
- Competitive analysis
- Cost leadership
- Differentiation
- Environmental analysis
- Evidenced-based decision-making
- Focus strategy
- Joint venture
- Kaizen
- Management
- Process flowchart
- Process improvement
- Return on investment (ROI)
- SMART goals
- Strategic alignment
- Strategic planning
- SWOT analysis
- Total Quality Management (TQM)

1. ______________ is the process of setting goals, planning, and organizing resources to achieve those goals effectively and efficiently.
2. A ______________ is a document that outlines a company's goals and strategies for achieving them.

3. _____________ is a management philosophy that focuses on continuous improvement in all aspects of the business.
4. A strategic _____________ is a detailed roadmap outlining specific goals, tasks, timelines, and responsibilities designed to implement strategic initiatives and achieve desired outcomes within an organization."
5. _____________ is a strategy that focuses on becoming the low-cost leader in an industry.
6. _____________ is a process of lining up an organization's activities and resources with its strategic objectives.
7. _____________ is a strategy that involves gaining a competitive advantage by offering unique and high-quality products or services.
8. In business analysis, the _____________ framework is used to assess the external factors that can impact an organization's strategic planning and decision-making.
9. _____________ is the process of assessing and analyzing an organization's internal strengths and weaknesses and external opportunities and threats.
10. _____________ is a framework used to evaluate a company's competitive position within its industry.
11. _____________ is a strategy that involves forming partnerships or collaborations with other companies to achieve mutual goals.
12. _____________ is a strategic approach that involves offering a limited selection of products or services in a narrow market.
13. _____________ is a systematic approach to identifying and managing an organization's key processes to achieve better efficiency and effectiveness.
14. A _____________ is a visual representation of the steps or activities in a standard operating procedure.
15. _____________ is the use of empirical data and analysis to inform strategic actions.
16. _____________ is a measurement of how well a company is using its assets to generate profits.
17. _____________ is the process of planning, organizing, directing, and controlling resources to achieve specific goals or objectives within an organization.
18. _____________ is a strategic management tool that visually represents a company's portfolio of products or business units based on their market growth rate and relative market share and is used to guide resource allocation and make strategic decisions.
19. _____________ is the process of setting specific, measurable, achievable, relevant, and time-bound goals to guide an organization's actions.
20. _________ is a comprehensive approach to improving organizational performance and customer satisfaction by integrating quality principles throughout all aspects of the business, involving all employees in continuous improvement efforts.

Conclusion

As a human resource professional, your role goes beyond the operational practice of HR systems within the life cycle of the employee. As the competitive landscape continues to evolve rapidly, it becomes even more important that you demonstrate competencies in business management and strategy, which is evidenced in the exam content. For the PHR and PHRi, it's categorized as "Business Management" and makes up 14% of the exam. In the SPHR and SPHRi, you'll see content related to "Leadership & Strategy," and this makes up the largest part of the tests at 33%. In the SHRM CP and SCP, content is related to how HR Strategy contributes to business results. While this chapter focuses on the topic of HR and Business Strategy, you will see questions in all chapters about how HR builds people, processes, and project systems to support organizational goals.

Additional Resources

When studying business strategy, it's essential to consider your specific interests and goals, strengths, and weaknesses. Consider gaps in your education or work experience and whether you're looking for introductory material or more advanced concepts. Take a practice assessment or two to really see what concepts give you the most trouble, and consider adding a few of the resources listed here to your study tool rotation.

Websites

- Harvard Business Review (HBR) (`hbr.org`)

  Harvard Business Review offers a vast collection of articles, case studies, and insights on business strategy. It covers various aspects of strategic management and leadership.

- Coursera (`www.coursera.org`)

  Coursera offers a wide range of online courses related to business strategy, strategic management, and competitive advantage. Courses are often provided by top universities and institutions.

- Strategic Management Society (SMS) (`www.strategicmanagement.net`)

  SMS offers valuable resources, including research papers, publications, and information on upcoming conferences related to strategic management.

- Strategy + Business (`www.strategy-business.com`)

  This platform from PWC provides insights into business strategy, management, and leadership through articles, reports, and expert perspectives.

- MIT Sloan School of Management, OpenCourseWare (`ocw.mit.edu/index.htm`)

  MIT Sloan offers free online course materials, including lecture notes, assignments, and readings related to strategy and management.

- Investopedia (`www.investopedia.com/financial-term-dictionary-4769738`)

  Investopedia's strategy section provides explanations and articles on various business and financial strategies. This link will take you to their dictionary, which is an excellent source to understand strategic terms.

Podcasts

- *HBR IdeaCast* hosted by Harvard Business Review

  This podcast features interviews with leading business thinkers and covers a wide range of management and strategy topics.

- *The McKinsey Podcast* hosted by McKinsey & Company

  McKinsey & Company's podcast provides insights into management and strategy by featuring conversations with McKinsey experts and business leaders.

- *The Strategy Skills Podcast* with various hosts

  This podcast focuses on strategic management and offers practical insights and tools for business leaders including videos and PowerPoint presentations for a more detailed look at strategic topics.

- *The Strategy Bridge Podcast* with various hosts

  Focused on military strategy, this podcast offers valuable insights into strategic thinking and decision-making that can be applied to business.

- *The Indicator from Planet Money* hosted by National Public Radio (NPR)

  This NPR podcast focuses on economic and business indicators, providing insights into current trends and their impact on strategy.

YouTube Channels

YouTube is a valuable platform for learning about business management and strategy. Log in to `www.youtube.com` and search and subscribe to these channels:

- Stanford Graduate School of Business

  Stanford Graduate School of Business offers videos of lectures, panel discussions, and interviews with business leaders, providing insights into management and strategy.

- The Economist

  The Economist's YouTube channel covers global economic and business news, offering analysis and discussions on various business and management topics.

- Inc.

  Inc.'s YouTube channel provides advice, tips, and success stories for entrepreneurs and business leaders, including content on strategy and management.

- Wharton School of the University of Pennsylvania

  The Wharton School's YouTube channel features lectures, discussions, and interviews related to business management, leadership, and strategy.

Talent Planning and Acquisition

A 2023 article online at Forbes Advisor noted that 86% of individuals look at company reviews and ratings before applying for a job, and more than 50% will not apply to a company with a bad reputation.[1] With turnover being high across all industries and the more modern psychological contract, the ability to attract, develop, and retain top talent has become a strategic imperative for companies across industries. This is accomplished through their HR teams.

Talent Planning and Acquisition, often referred to as talent management or workforce planning, encompasses a range of strategies and practices aimed at aligning an organization's talent needs with its strategic objectives. It involves identifying, acquiring, developing, and retaining the right talent to drive innovation, productivity, and overall organizational performance. This dynamic field has gained prominence as organizations recognize that their human capital is not merely a cost but a valuable asset that can lead to a sustainable competitive advantage.

In this review of Talent Planning and Acquisition, we will delve into these fundamental exam concepts:

- Strategies and tools used to recruit, select, and onboard qualified individuals to the team
- The critical role the employee value proposition plays in acquiring top talent
- Using job analysis and design principles to properly structure and classify jobs
- Developing the HR competencies necessary to negotiate and craft job offers
- Navigating technological resources to optimize recruiting without compromising the candidate experience
- Analyzing talent acquisition metrics such as time-to-hire and cost-per-hire

In essence, Talent Planning and Acquisition is a multifaceted discipline at the heart of modern Human Resource Management (HRM). Not only will this knowledge help you on exam day, but the practical application of the principles will help you become a strong business partner.

[1]Key HR Statistics and Trends In 2024 `https://www.forbes.com/advisor/business/hr-statistics-trends`

Real World Scenario

Square's Journey: Crafting a Culture-Centric Onboarding Solution for Rapid Growth and Remote Work Success

Square, a leading financial services and mobile payment company has gained recognition not only for its innovative products but also for its unique approach to employee onboarding and orientation. This case study explores how Square successfully integrated new hires into its organization through a structured and inclusive onboarding process.

Background and Problem

Square's rapid growth and innovative culture necessitated an effective onboarding and orientation process. The challenge was to ensure that new employees quickly understood the company's values, products, and culture while feeling welcomed and supported during their transition.

Diagnosis

These were the main problems Square aimed to address:

- **Rapid growth:** With its expanding workforce, Square needed a standardized onboarding process to maintain consistency and ensure that every employee received essential information.
- **Maintaining culture:** As Square grew, there was a concern about preserving its unique culture and values. The company wanted new hires to embrace and contribute to this culture fully.
- **Remote work:** The shift to remote work due to external factors required Square to adapt its onboarding process to integrate remote employees effectively.

Strategies

Square employed the following strategies to overcome these challenges and create a successful onboarding and orientation process:

- **Structured onboarding:** Square developed a structured onboarding program with clear schedules and milestones to ensure all new hires received consistent training.
- **Culture emphasis:** The company placed a strong emphasis on its culture and values during orientation, encouraging new employees to embody these principles.
- **Role-specific training:** Square provided specialized training tailored to each employee's role and department, ensuring they had the necessary skills and knowledge.
- **Mentorship and support:** New hires were paired with mentors who offered guidance and support during their initial days and beyond.

- **Inclusivity:** Square integrated diversity, equity, and inclusion (DEI) principles into the onboarding process to foster an inclusive environment.
- **Continuous learning:** The company promoted a culture of continuous learning, encouraging new employees to seek ongoing education and development opportunities.
- **Feedback mechanisms:** Square solicited feedback from new hires to improve the onboarding experience continually.
- **Remote adaptation:** The onboarding process was adapted to accommodate remote work, ensuring remote hires received the same level of support and engagement.

Results

The implementation of these strategies yielded several positive outcomes for Square:

- **Consistency:** The structured onboarding program ensured consistency across the organization, enabling every employee to start their journey with a clear understanding of Square's mission and values.
- **Culture preservation:** Square successfully maintained its unique culture by instilling its values in new hires from day one.
- **Remote success:** The adaptation of the process for remote work allowed Square to seamlessly integrate remote employees and maintain a sense of unity across all teams.

Conclusion

Square's approach to employee onboarding and orientation showcases the importance of a structured yet flexible process that prioritizes culture, inclusivity, and continuous learning. By addressing the challenges of rapid growth and remote work, Square has positioned itself for continued success in the competitive tech industry.

Talent Planning and Acquisition Practice Questions

1. Your company is expanding and needs to hire a software developer with expertise in a specific programming language. You've received several applications but want to ensure the candidate is genuinely skilled in that language. Which recruitment method is most appropriate in this situation?

   A. Conduct a panel interview with general questions.

   B. Use a technical skills test related to the programming language.

   C. Rely solely on the candidate's résumé and references.

   D. Hire based on the candidate's years of experience.

2. Your organization is looking to hire a marketing manager. You've narrowed down the candidates to two equally qualified individuals. One has significantly more experience, while the other is younger and may bring fresh ideas, especially in social media marketing. What should you consider when making the final decision?

   A. Hire the more experienced candidate.

   B. Hire the younger candidate for innovation.

   C. Conduct reference checks for both candidates.

   D. Get a second opinion from another manager.

3. You are part of the HR team at a fast-paced, high-volume sales department, and you've been assigned the task of conducting a comprehensive job analysis to improve team efficiency and productivity. However, the sales manager is notoriously difficult to work with and is hesitant to allocate time for the team to participate in the job analysis process. To address the sales manager's reservations and successfully conduct the job analysis, which HR competencies will be crucial?

   A. Strong organizational and project management skills.

   B. Extensive knowledge of sales techniques and strategies.

   C. Excellent negotiation and conflict resolution skills.

   D. In-depth technical expertise in the sales department's software.

4. As an HR recruiter, you are facing the daunting task of sifting through thousands of résumés received through the applicant tracking system (ATS) for a critical position in your organization. You decide to employ a statistical model that calculates a résumé suitability score for each applicant based on their qualifications, such as education, relevant experience, and skills, compared to the job requirements. The model assigns higher scores to candidates whose qualifications closely match the job criteria, allowing you to prioritize candidates with the best fit. Which statistical model is being reflected in this example?

   A. Regression analysis.

   B. Decision tree analysis.

   C. Logistic regression.

   D. Factor analysis.

5. In your role as an HR team member, you are tasked with conducting a job analysis for a key position in your organization. The goal is to identify the critical skills and qualifications required for the job. You collect data from job incumbents and subject-matter experts, including information on their education, years of experience, technical skills, and soft skills. To identify the most critical qualifications, you create a visual representation of the hierarchy of qualifications and their importance in predicting success in the role. Which statistical model is being used in this example?
   - **A.** Decision tree analysis.
   - **B.** Linear regression analysis.
   - **C.** Factor analysis.
   - **D.** T-test analysis.

6. When calculating the cost-per-hire for a new employee, which of the following expenses should be considered?
   - **A.** Only direct recruiting costs such as advertising and job board fees.
   - **B.** All direct and indirect expenses associated with the recruitment process.
   - **C.** Only the salary and benefits of the new employee.
   - **D.** Miscellaneous overhead costs not directly related to recruitment.

7. You are an HR manager at a growing company and need to calculate full-time equivalents (FTEs) for your department for accurate reporting and budgeting. Which of the following formulas should you use to calculate FTE?
   - **A.** (Total number of employees) / (Total hours in a week)
   - **B.** (Total hours worked by all employees) / (Standard hours for a full-time employee)
   - **C.** (Total number of projects) / (Total number of employees)
   - **D.** (Total hours worked by all employees) / (Average workweek hours)

8. Your company is seeking highly specialized talent with unique skills for a niche role. Which recruiting source is most appropriate for this situation?
   - **A.** Online job boards.
   - **B.** Employee referrals.
   - **C.** Headhunters or executive search firms.
   - **D.** Temporary staffing agencies.

9. When conducting a task inventory analysis, which methods can be used to gather data about job tasks and responsibilities? (Choose all that apply.)
   - **A.** Surveys and questionnaires.
   - **B.** Observations.
   - **C.** Focus groups and brainstorming sessions.
   - **D.** Interviews.

10. You are conducting an unstructured interview with a candidate for a creative role in your company. What distinguishes an unstructured interview from other types?
    A. It follows a strict set of standardized questions.
    B. It involves open-ended questions and free-flowing conversation.
    C. It is typically conducted by a panel of interviewers.
    D. It focuses on situational scenarios.

11. Which type of interview is better at assessing how aligned a candidate is with a company culture?
    A. Structured interview.
    B. Unstructured interview.
    C. Behavioral interview.
    D. Group interview.

12. When using a personality test as a selection tool in the hiring process, which of the following statements is accurate?
    A. Personality tests are the sole determinant of a candidate's suitability for a position.
    B. Personality tests cannot be used because they create a disparate impact and could discriminate against certain applicant.
    C. Personality tests can provide valuable insights when used in conjunction with other assessment methods.
    D. Personality tests should be used only for entry-level positions.

13. When considering the advantages of using chatbots or artificial intelligence (AI) during the recruiting process, which of the following statements accurately highlights a key benefit?
    A. Chatbots/AI can replace human recruiters entirely, reducing labor costs and improving efficiency.
    B. Chatbots/AI can provide instant responses to candidate inquiries, ensuring a seamless and responsive candidate experience.
    C. Chatbots/AI are immune to bias, ensuring fair and equitable evaluations of all candidates.
    D. Chatbots/AI can independently assess the cultural fit of candidates, leading to better long-term employee retention.

14. In the realm of employment categories, which statement accurately distinguishes between the various types?

A. Temporary employees are typically hired for a specific project or period and may not receive benefits, while part-time employees work fewer hours than full-time employees but may still be eligible for certain benefits.

B. Contract employees have no fixed work schedule and are often paid on an hourly basis, whereas seasonal employees are engaged only during peak periods and receive full benefits.

C. Freelancers work exclusively for a single employer and are considered full-time employees, while consultants provide specialized advice and services to multiple clients.

D. Interns are typically paid employees who have completed their formal education and have extensive industry experience, while apprentices are paid employees who have access to additional support such as housing and health benefits.

15. Why is properly classifying employees at the time of hire considered a risk management "best-practice" for employers?

A. It allows employers to avoid paying employee benefits altogether.

B. It ensures compliance with labor laws and regulations, reducing the risk of costly fines and legal disputes.

C. It simplifies payroll processing, leading to more efficient administrative practices.

D. It automatically guarantees job security for all employees.

16. You've been tasked with evaluating the efficiency of your company's recruitment process by calculating the applicant-to-interview-to-offer ratio for a recent job opening using the following data:
Number of applicants for the job: 200
Number of applicants interviewed: 40
Number of offers made: 4
What is the applicant-to-interview-to-offer ratio?

A. 5

B. 10

C. 20

D. 50

17. What is the primary goal of strategic workforce management?

A. Maximizing short-term profits.

B. Reducing employee turnover.

C. Aligning workforce with organizational goals, vision, and values.

D. Increasing employee benefits.

18. Which of the following is a key component of strategic workforce planning?

A. Reactive hiring based on immediate needs.

B. Annual performance appraisals.

C. Long-term talent development.

D. Short-term workforce adjustments.

19. Which factor is NOT typically considered in strategic workforce management?

A. Employee engagement.

B. Market competition.

C. Regulatory compliance.

D. Daily task assignments.

20. A leading electric vehicle manufacturer is focused on strategically managing its workforce to staff its new battery plant efficiently. What strategic workforce management approach should the company prioritize to ensure the success of this critical facility?

A. Hiring a large number of temporary workers for short-term cost savings.

B. Implementing a talent development program to upskill current employees.

C. Relying on external recruitment agencies for staffing needs.

D. Requesting the county government to subsidize part of their hiring effort.

21. Which of the following is NOT a primary component of an effective human capital management (HCM) plan?

A. Talent acquisition and recruitment.

B. Employee training and development.

C. Compensation and benefits management.

D. Financial accounting and reporting.

22. In the context of global employment categories, which of the following best describes an expatriate employee?

A. A local employee hired by a multinational company to work in their home country.

B. An employee who works remotely for a company based in another country.

C. An employee who is a citizen of the host country but working for a foreign company within their home country.

D. An employee who is a citizen of one country but is temporarily assigned to work in a different country by their employer.

23. Company Alpha is a global pharmaceutical company headquartered in Switzerland planning to establish an R&D center in India for innovative drug development. They have a broad search for qualified experts in their field and are considering hiring an engineer from Turkey as a third-country national. Which of the following is a significant advantage of this approach?

A. Facilitating cross-border cooperation between Swiss, Indian, and Turkish teams.

B. Simplifying the process of obtaining regulatory approvals in Switzerland.

C. Reducing the costs associated with hiring local Indian talent.

D. Ensuring strict compliance with Swiss labor laws within the Indian workplace.

24. In which phase of the business lifecycle are workforce plans most likely to focus on attracting and retaining specialized talent?

A. Startup phase.

B. Growth phase.

C. Maturity phase.

D. Decline phase.

25. A global ecommerce giant faced the challenge of developing a remote staffing plan to expand its workforce. The company wanted to ensure that remote data is properly secured, stored, and transmitted. What was a key factor the company likely considered when developing this remote staffing plan?

A. Ergonomics in home offices.

B. Business continuity plans.

C. Technological infrastructure.

D. Product recall protocols.

26. A popular fashion and lifestyle brand recognized the importance of aligning its workforce plan with its business strategy to achieve its goals effectively. The company undertook a strategic initiative to ensure this alignment. What is a key step the company most likely took to align its workforce plan with its business strategy?

A. Implementing a systematic hiring process.

B. Offering unlimited paid time off.

C. Conducting a skills gap analysis.

D. Eliminating employee training programs.

27. DEF Inc. is facing a sudden economic downturn and needs to make staffing adjustments to manage costs. What approach should they consider when developing their staffing plan during this challenging period?

A. Implementing a plan to do across-the-board layoffs.

B. Conducting skills assessments and retraining employees.

C. Freezing all hiring and promotions indefinitely.

D. Increasing salaries to retain top talent.

28. When conducting a labor market analysis, which of the following factors is typically considered part of the demand-side analysis?

A. Wage and salary trends.

B. Education and skills of the available workforce.

C. Unemployment rates and labor force participation.

D. Government regulations and labor laws.

29. In a labor market analysis, what does the term *labor force participation rate* refer to?

A. The percentage of the working age population employed.

B. The percentage of the working age population either employed or actively seeking employment.

C. The percentage of employees not yet eligible for retirement benefits.

D. The percentage of employees with disabilities in the workforce.

30. A major food delivery service wanted to optimize their staffing plan to meet the growing demand for their services in various regions. To achieve this, they decided to use labor market data as a key input. What is a likely way in which the company used labor market data to formulate their staffing plan?

A. Surveying drivers to see if paid time would increase retention.

B. Increasing the prices of their delivery services.

C. Analyzing driver availability in specific regions.

D. Eliminating customer support positions.

31. A large hospital system known for its commitment to patient care and employee well-being is hiring nurses for its expanding healthcare facilities. What employer brand strategy should the company prioritize to attract nursing candidates?

A. Offering the highest nurse-to-patient ratio in the region.

B. Promoting a supportive work environment and professional development opportunities.

C. Providing free snacks and coffee in the break rooms.

D. Featuring celebrity endorsements in their recruitment materials.

32. When aiming to attract passive talent by leveraging the employee value proposition (EVP), which of the following strategies is most likely to effectively capture the interest of potential candidates?

A. Offering the highest compensation package in the industry.

B. Creating an EVP that closely mimics competitors in the industry.

C. Transparently communicating your organization's unique EVP.

D. Conducting interviews with transparent information sharing.

33. When measuring recruiting effectiveness, which of the following metrics provides the most comprehensive assessment of the entire recruitment process?
   A. Time-to-fill.
   B. Cost-per-hire.
   C. Quality-of-hire.
   D. Offer acceptance rate.

34. Which of the following is a key difference between an employee and an independent contractor?
   A. Employees have more flexibility in choosing their work hours.
   B. Independent contractors are typically eligible for employee benefits.
   C. Employees are generally subject to tax withholding by the employer.
   D. Independent contractors have permanent job security.

35. What legal obligation do employers generally have for employees but not for independent contractors?
   A. Providing workspace and equipment.
   B. Offering training and professional development.
   C. Paying overtime for work beyond 40 hours per week.
   D. Offering retirement benefits.

36. A multinational technology company, TechGenius Inc., is assessing its recruitment process's efficiency. It wants to calculate the hiring yield ratios to evaluate various stages of its hiring funnel accurately. The company recently posted a job opening for a senior software engineer position and received a total of 500 applications. Out of those, 200 candidates were selected for the initial phone screening, 50 moved on to the technical interview round, and, eventually, 10 candidates received job offers. TechGenius Inc. filled two positions through this recruitment. What is the hiring yield ratio for the technical interview stage in this scenario?
   A. 0.20.
   B. 0.25.
   C. 0.50.
   D. 0.02.

37. Rebecca, the HR manager at a software development firm, is responsible for completing Form I-9 for all new hires. She recently hired Ted, an experienced software engineer, and asked him to complete Section 1 of Form I-9 on his first day of work. Ted, however, mistakenly filled out the form using his previous address from a different state, even though he currently resides near the company's headquarters. Rebecca noticed the error when reviewing the form. What is the appropriate course of action for Rebecca to take regarding this mistake on Form I-9?

A. Correct the mistake in Section 1 of Form I-9 and have Ted sign and date the corrected section.

B. Ask Ted to complete a new Form I-9 with the correct information and attach it to the original form.

C. Keep the incorrect information in Section 1 as it is and make a note of the error in the employee's file.

D. Request Ted to provide updated documentation to match the incorrect address on the form.

38. When considering the advantages and disadvantages of using background checks in hiring, one potential advantage is that they can help mitigate the risk of making __________________ hiring decisions.

A. Inefficient.

B. Biased.

C. Costly.

D. Swift.

39. A manager in your organization lacks the knowledge and skills to conduct effective job interviews. How should HR best support this manager?

A. Providing a standardized interview script for the manager to follow.

B. Offering a one-time training workshop on interview techniques.

C. Assigning another experienced manager to conduct interviews on the manager's behalf.

D. Providing ongoing coaching and feedback on interview performance.

40. You are in the process of staffing a new call center. The customer service representatives (CSRs) will be required to handle customer inquiries, resolve complaints, and process orders. Which selection test is most likely to be effective in hiring qualified candidates?

A. Cognitive ability tests.

B. Personality tests.

C. Emotional intelligence tests.

D. Situational judgment tests.

41. Rebecca, the HR coordinator, is assisting a remote employee named Michael with Form I-9 completion. Michael has presented a foreign passport and an Employment Authorization Document (EAD) as his List A and List C documents, respectively. The documents appear valid, but Michael is unable to physically bring them to the HR office. What should Rebecca do?

- **A.** Instruct Michael to mail the original documents to the HR office for verification.
- **B.** Use remote verification procedures to verify the documents without physical inspection.
- **C.** Request that Michael provide notarized copies of the documents.
- **D.** Inform Michael that remote verification is not permitted, and he must visit the HR office in person.

42. What is a primary advantage of using temporary staffing agencies as an alternative staffing method?

- **A.** Greater control over employee work hours.
- **B.** Reduced administrative burden for the hiring organization.
- **C.** Long-term commitment from temporary employees.
- **D.** Guaranteed permanent placement of workers.

43. You are the VP of human resources of a multinational corporation with operations in various countries. The company is undergoing a major expansion into new international markets, which involves complex market research, regulatory compliance, and local partnerships. The question of whether to utilize consultants or hire full-time employees in this global environment has become a pivotal strategic challenge. What is the primary consideration that favors choosing a consultant over hiring a full-time employee?

- **A.** When the project requires specialized expertise in local markets and regulations.
- **B.** When the company prioritizes long-term employee retention and career development.
- **C.** When the project involves day-to-day operational tasks with high consistency and predictability.
- **D.** When the company is focused on in-house knowledge transfer and intellectual property protection.

44. What is the key distinction between turnover and attrition in the context of employee departures?

- **A.** Turnover includes all employee departures, both voluntary and involuntary, while attrition specifically refers to voluntary departures.
- **B.** Turnover refers to the number of employees who leave the organization, while attrition calculates the cost associated with replacing departing employees.
- **C.** Turnover occurs when employees leave the organization voluntarily, whereas attrition encompasses all departures, including retirements, resignations, and terminations.
- **D.** Turnover is the result of a deliberate HR strategy to maintain workforce diversity, while attrition is an unplanned reduction in staff due to unforeseen circumstances.

45. What are the primary factors that affect the time-to-fill metric in recruiting?

- **A.** The number of job applicants.
- **B.** The complexity of the hiring process.
- **C.** The company's annual revenue.
- **D.** The location of the job position.

46. Heathrow Manufacturing is hiring candidates for roles that require operating heavy machinery. Safety is a top priority. What preemployment test should Heathrow Manufacturing consider?

- **A.** Credit check.
- **B.** Background check.
- **C.** Drug screening.
- **D.** Behavioral interview.

47. Leeds Healthcare is hiring medical professionals for patient care roles. They need to ensure the candidates have the necessary qualifications and credentials to provide high-quality care. What preemployment test should Leeds use to verify these qualifications?

- **A.** Personality assessment.
- **B.** Criminal background check.
- **C.** Reference check.
- **D.** Credential verification.

48. When should an employer typically conduct drug screens as part of the preemployment testing process?

- **A.** After the candidate has started working and completed the onboarding process.
- **B.** During the final interview stage to assess the candidate's honesty.
- **C.** After extending a conditional job offer but before the candidate starts working.
- **D.** Only if the candidate has a known history of substance abuse.

49. You are an HR professional tasked with creating a strategic workforce plan that aligns with your company's goals. The company is focused on expanding its market share in the next five years and wants to ensure it has the right talent in place to support this growth. How can you best demonstrate the competencies of business acumen and influence?

- **A.** Conduct a workforce analysis and present the data to senior management.
- **B.** Collaborate with department heads and other key decision-makers to understand their specific talent needs and how they relate to the company's growth strategy.
- **C.** Develop a workforce plan in isolation, focusing solely on HR-related metrics and initiatives.
- **D.** Seek external consultants to create the workforce plan independently to maintain objectivity.

50. Which legal requirement must employers typically meet when using unpaid interns in employment?

A. Providing the same benefits as regular employees.

B. Paying interns at least the minimum wage.

C. Offering internship opportunities exclusively to current employees.

D. Complying with applicable federal and state labor laws.

51. Under the Fair Labor Standards Act (FLSA), which of the following criteria must be met to classify an intern as unpaid?

A. The intern must be engaged in work that directly benefits the employer.

B. The intern's work must replace the work of regular employees.

C. The intern must receive training similar to that provided in an educational institution.

D. The intern must work full-time hours and meet a minimum experience requirement.

52. ABC Corporation is looking to hire workers for a construction project. It is considering hiring either independent contractors or employees for the job. What key factor should ABC Corporation consider when determining the classification of these workers?

A. The length of the project and whether it's short-term or long-term.

B. The worker's preference for classification as an independent contractor.

C. The worker's qualifications and experience in the construction industry.

D. The level of control and direction the company has over the workers.

53. Nelson Tech is a software development company that frequently hires freelance software developers for short-term projects. What is a potential legal risk that Nelson Tech should be aware of when classifying workers as independent contractors?

A. Offering employee benefits to independent contractors.

B. Treating all freelancers as employees to avoid misclassification.

C. Providing equipment and tools to freelancers for project work.

D. Failing to withhold taxes from payments made to freelancers.

54. What is a key consideration for employers when implementing a work-from-home policy in the workplace?

A. Providing unlimited paid time off to remote employees.

B. Maintaining a consistent work schedule for all remote workers.

C. Ensuring data security and privacy for remote work arrangements.

D. Offering onsite childcare facilities for employees.

55. What is a potential challenge for employees when working remotely under a flexible work-from-home policy?

A. Limited access to career development opportunities.

B. Increased commute times and expenses.

C. Overcoming the feeling of isolation and loneliness.

D. Difficulty in adhering to a fixed 9-to-5 work schedule.

56. As the HR manager responsible for negotiating job offers with potential candidates, you are aware of the various forms of bias that can influence these negotiations. Which form of bias should you be most cautious about to avoid unintentional discrimination?

A. Confirmation bias, where you tend to favor candidates who share your personal interests.

B. Affinity bias, which involves favoring candidates who share a similar background or characteristics with you.

C. Outcome bias, where you prioritize candidates based on their previous job outcomes.

D. Anchoring bias, where you fixate on the initial salary expectation a candidate provides.

57. Company A is acquiring Company B, and the HR team is tasked with integrating the workforce of both organizations. What is a critical staffing consideration during this merger and acquisition process?

A. Retaining all employees from both companies to maintain stability.

B. Quickly downsizing to reduce redundancy and cut costs.

C. Aligning compensation and benefits packages for all employees.

D. Delaying communication with employees until the merger is finalized.

58. AFC United is merging with AFC Premier, which has a significantly different corporate culture. What staffing strategy can help mitigate potential culture clashes during the integration process?

A. Maintaining separate workspaces and facilities for each company's employees.

B. Enforcing a strict uniform dress code to promote consistency.

C. Implementing cross-cultural training and team-building programs.

D. Reducing communication between employees from both companies.

59. You are a recruiting manager in a growing technology company. You understand the importance of providing a positive candidate experience to attract top talent. You're about to conduct interviews for a key engineering role, and you want to ensure that the candidates have a positive experience throughout the process. What is a crucial step to ensure a positive candidate experience during the interview process?

A. Conducting back-to-back interviews to expedite the process and save candidates' time.

B. Providing prompt and clear communication at each stage of the process, including updates and feedback.

C. Minimizing the number of interview rounds to reduce the candidate's time commitment.

D. Sharing detailed information about the company's history and culture only after the candidate has accepted an offer.

60. What does the principle of employment-at-will generally mean in the context of employment law?

A. Employees have a guaranteed job for life once they are hired.

B. Employers can terminate employees at any time for any reason, with exceptions.

C. Employees are required to provide two weeks' notice when quitting.

D. Employers are required to provide job security to their employees.

61. Which of the following is NOT an exception to the employment-at-will doctrine in the United States?

A. Termination based on race or gender discrimination.

B. Termination in violation of a written employment contract.

C. Termination due to poor performance or misconduct.

D. Termination based on the employee's refusal to commit an illegal act.

62. You are an HR manager at a local company known for its innovative and inclusive workplace culture. You are actively recruiting college and university students for internships and entry-level positions. How can you best promote the employer brand when using college and university recruiting sources?

A. Emphasize competitive salary packages to attract top talent.

B. Highlight the company's commitment to diversity and inclusion in recruitment materials and presentations.

C. Limit engagement to the recruiting fairs and exclude online and social media platforms.

D. Focus primarily on showcasing the company's industry awards and recognition.

63. What is one of the primary purposes of using assessment centers in the hiring process?

A. To make rapid hiring decisions based solely on résumé qualifications.

B. To provide candidates with on-the-job training opportunities.

C. To evaluate candidates' job-related skills, competencies, and behaviors.

D. To conduct reference checks with previous employers.

64. During negotiations for an employment offer, what should HR professionals consider when addressing counteroffers made by candidates?

A. Evaluating counteroffers and discussing them openly with the candidate.

B. Rejecting all counteroffers to maintain the original offer terms.

C. Immediately retracting the original offer in response to a counteroffer.

D. Avoiding any further communication with the candidate once a counteroffer is made.

65. What are some benefits of using the Cultural Orientations Indicator (COI) assessment tool in a multicultural workplace environment?

A. Enhancing cross-cultural communication and collaboration.

B. Assessing individual adaptability to new cultural environments.

C. Identifying personal strengths and weaknesses in a global context.

D. Evaluating cultural dimensions within a team.

66. You are an HR manager in a competitive organization that recently conducted interviews for a highly sought-after job position. Several candidates were interviewed, but only one candidate could be selected for the role. As the HR manager, you need to decide on the best way to handle candidates who were not selected to move on in the selection process. What is the best approach to handle candidates who were not selected for the job position?

   A. Send a polite rejection email, expressing appreciation for their interest and keeping the door open for future opportunities.
   B. Provide detailed feedback to each candidate, highlighting specific areas where their qualifications didn't align with the role's requirements.
   C. Inform candidates about the selected candidate and ask if they would like to be considered for other open positions in the company.
   D. Allow the ATS to send a form rejection email.

67. You are the HR manager for a growing tech startup, and you're overseeing the onboarding of a new software developer. On their first day, what is the most important aspect to include in the onboarding process?

   A. Assigning them to a project team and providing coding assignments immediately.
   B. Begin acclimating them to the workplace through tours and introductions.
   C. Conducting a detailed review of the company's financial statements.
   D. Giving them access to all company databases and systems.

68. What is one of the advantages of employee acculturation programs in a multinational organization?

   A. Increased employee turnover due to cultural differences.
   B. Enhanced employee engagement and retention.
   C. Simplified cross-cultural communication challenges.
   D. Reduced need for diversity and inclusion initiatives.

69. You are an HR consultant working with a startup company that is rapidly expanding its team. The CEO wants to ensure that job roles are clearly defined. Which of the following is a potential method to gather information for the job analysis process in this situation?

   A. Conducting employee satisfaction surveys.
   B. Observing employees during their lunch breaks.
   C. Interviewing employees and supervisors.
   D. Reviewing competitors' marketing strategies.

70. What is a talent planning need when downsizing due to economic challenges?

   A. Providing extensive training for all remaining employees.
   B. Reassessing workforce skills and competencies.
   C. Increasing employee compensation to retain talent.
   D. Expanding the employee benefits package.

Key Concept Research Questions

Often, making the most of your study time requires a deeper dive. The following questions are designed for you to access alternative resources to gain a more robust understanding of topics you are likely to see on test day. You can find the correct answers in Appendix C.

1. According to the Hiring and Workplace Trend 2023 report conducted by Indeed and Glassdoor, there are several demographic shifts that will continue to drive a tight labor market. What kinds of technology strategies should HR recommend addressing the competitive labor market? Access the research report at `www.glassdoor.com/research/workplace-trends-2023`.
2. As the psychological contract between employers and employees evolves in today's dynamic workforce, what strategies and approaches should human resource professionals adopt to proactively cultivate a robust employee value proposition (EVP) that aligns with changing expectations and fosters a positive employer/employee relationship?
3. Imagine a scenario where a rapidly growing technology startup is expanding its operations into a new geographic region. The company needs to recruit a specialized team of engineers and developers to spearhead this expansion. In this context, how do the human resource competencies of business acumen, analytical aptitude, and teamwork come together to effectively address the complex talent acquisition challenge and ensure the company's successful expansion into the new market? Use one of the competencies provided by SHRM's BASK to craft your answer. You can find more on this at `www.shrm.org/certification/prepare/Pages/bodyofappliedskillsandknowledge.aspx`.

Test Your Talent Planning and Acquisition Terminology

The following are the Talent Planning and Acquisition glossary of terms you should be familiar with. Use each of these terms once to fill in the blanks that follow. The correct answers are in Appendix B.

- Applicant tracking system
- Background screening
- Candidate evaluation
- Candidate relationship management (CRM)
- Candidate selection
- Career development
- Competitive compensation
- Diversity recruitment
- Employee development
- Employee referral program
- Employee separation
- Employment contract
- External hiring

- Global talent acquisition
- Internal job posting
- Job description
- Job offer
- Passive candidate sourcing
- Performance management system
- Qualifications
- Recruitment
- Recruitment technology
- Rehiring
- Résumé screening
- Skills gap analysis
- Succession planning
- Talent analytics
- Talent strategy
- Temporary staffing
- Workforce planning

1. ____________ is the process of identifying and attracting qualified candidates for job openings within an organization.
2. ____________ is a written document that outlines the skills, qualifications, and experience required for a specific role.
3. ____________ is the practice of promoting job openings within the organization to encourage current employees to apply.
4. ____________ is the assessment of an individual's qualifications, skills, and experience to determine job fit.
5. ____________ is the process of selecting the best applicant for a job from a pool of applicants.
6. ____________ is a comprehensive approach to workforce planning that aligns hiring goals with overall business goals.
7. ____________ is a written proposition given to a candidate that outlines the terms and conditions of the role including base pay, schedule, and benefits.
8. ____________ is software used to manage job postings, applications, and candidate information.
9. ____________ is the practice of evaluating an employee's performance and potential for advancement within the organization.
10. ____________ refers to the set of skills, knowledge, and abilities that a candidate possesses.
11. ____________ is the process of engaging with potential candidates and building relationships for future hiring needs.
12. ____________ is a strategy for attracting passive candidates who are not actively seeking new job opportunities.
13. ____________ is a formalized program that provides structured training and development opportunities to employees.
14. ____________ is the process of reviewing and evaluating job applications to create a shortlist of qualified candidates.

15. ____________ refers to the practice of hiring individuals on a temporary or project basis rather than as permanent employees.
16. ____________ is the practice of hiring individuals from outside the organization to fill key positions.
17. ____________ is a system that tracks and manages the performance and development of employees.
18. ____________ is the process of identifying the skills and capabilities required for future organizational success.
19. ____________ is a measure of how well an organization's recruitment efforts align with its diversity and inclusion goals.
20. ____________ is the practice of hiring individuals who have previously worked for the organization.
21. ____________ is the process of collecting and analyzing data related to talent acquisition and management.
22. ____________ is the practice of using technology, such as artificial intelligence, in the recruitment process.
23. ____________ is the strategy of recruiting talent from a global pool of candidates.
24. ____________ is the practice of offering competitive compensation and benefits to attract and retain top talent.
25. ____________ is a document that outlines the terms and conditions of employment for a new hire.
26. ____________ is the process of transitioning an employee out of the organization, either voluntarily or involuntarily.
27. ____________ is the practice of conducting background checks and verifying information provided by job applicants.
28. ____________ is a system that manages and tracks employee referrals for job openings.
29. ____________ is the process of assessing and forecasting future workforce needs.
30. ____________ is the practice of providing employees with opportunities for advancement and development within the organization.

Conclusion

Talent planning and acquisition activities are crucial for human resource business partners. These activities involve identifying, attracting, and retaining top talent to meet organizational goals effectively. HR business partners play a pivotal role in aligning talent strategies with business objectives. By proactively identifying skill gaps and future workforce needs, they ensure that the right talent is in place to drive growth and innovation. Effective talent planning also enables HR partners to mitigate risks associated with turnover and skill shortages. It enhances employee engagement, fosters a culture of continuous improvement, and ultimately contributes to the overall success and competitiveness of the organization.

The domain of "People" in SHRM's Body of Applied Skills and Knowledge accounts for 18% of the CP and SCP exams, and Talent Acquisition is only one part of this domain. Workforce Planning and Talent Acquisition makes up 14% of the PHR/PHRi exams and 17% of the SPHR/SPHRi exams. While these numbers may not seem high, it is important to realize that Talent Planning and Acquisition affects all functional areas of human resources, including organizational design, total rewards, and performance management.

Additional Resources

If you want to study talent planning and acquisition in more detail, you can explore various online resources, podcasts, and videos that offer valuable insights and information on this subject. The following are some reputable online resources to help you delve deeper into talent planning and acquisition.

Websites

- AIRS Training by ADP (`www.airsdirectory.com`)

  AIRS is a website powered by ADP that is specifically geared toward talent planning knowledge and insights.

- Society for Human Resource Management (SHRM) (`www.shrm.org/resourcesandtools/toolsandsamples/toolkits/pages/talentacquisition.aspx`)

  SHRM provides a collection of resources, articles, and tools related to talent acquisition, including best practices, templates, and guides.

- `HR.com` (`www.hr.com/en/app/guide/talentacquisitionp2oafvom.html`)

  `HR.com` offers a dedicated section on talent acquisition, featuring webinars, articles, and whitepapers on recruitment strategies and talent planning.

- Indeed Hiring Insights (`www.indeed.com/hiringlab`)

  Indeed's Hiring Lab provides research reports, data analysis, and trends related to talent acquisition, helping you stay informed about the job market.

- `Recruiter.com` (`www.recruiter.com`)

  `Recruiter.com` offers articles, webinars, and tools for recruiters and HR professionals, covering various aspects of talent acquisition.

Podcasts

- *The Chad & Cheese Podcast* with hosts Chad Sowash and Joel Cheesman

  This podcast offers a humorous take on the world of recruiting and talent acquisition. Chad and Cheese discuss industry trends, technology, and innovative recruitment strategies. Their interviews with industry experts provide valuable insights.

- *Recruiting Future* with host Matt Alder

  Recruiting Future explores the future of recruitment and talent acquisition. It features interviews with thought leaders, HR professionals, and experts who share insights into emerging trends, technology, and strategies.

- *Hiring on All Cylinders* with host Entelo

  Entelo's podcast covers various talent acquisition topics, including sourcing, employer branding, and diversity and inclusion. The show features interviews with HR and talent acquisition leaders.

- *The Talent Angle* with host Gartner

  This podcast by Gartner focuses on talent management and HR strategies. It offers insights into leadership development, employee engagement, and the future of work. The show features interviews with HR experts and executives.

- *DriveThruHR* with various hosts

  DriveThruHR covers a wide range of HR and talent acquisition topics. The podcast features HR professionals, thought leaders, and practitioners discussing recruitment trends, talent development, and workplace issues.

YouTube Channels

There are several YouTube channels (`www.youtube.com`) that focus on talent management, recruitment, and HR practices. Log in and search for these title shows:

- LinkedIn Talent Solutions

  LinkedIn Talent Solutions offers video content on various talent acquisition and HR topics. You can find webinars, interviews with industry experts, and tips for optimizing LinkedIn for recruitment.

- Indeed

  Indeed's YouTube channel provides resources for job seekers and employers. It includes videos on hiring strategies, employer branding, and insights into the labor market.

- `HR.com`

  `HR.com`'s YouTube channel features webinars, interviews, and discussions on HR and talent management. It covers a wide range of HR-related topics, including talent acquisition.

- `Recruiter.com`

  `Recruiter.com`'s YouTube channel offers video content on recruiting best practices, hiring trends, and expert insights from the recruiting industry.
- Glassdoor for Employers

  Glassdoor for Employers provides videos on employer branding, recruitment strategies, and tips for using Glassdoor in your talent acquisition efforts.
- HR Bartender

  HR Bartender, run by Sharlyn Lauby, offers HR and talent management tips, advice, and discussions on various HR-related topics.

Chapter 5 Learning and Development

Long Life Learning: Preparing for Jobs That Don't Even Exist Yet is a book by Michelle Weise that highlights some of the major challenges employers are having in keeping up with the emerging learning needs of our society. Weise makes the case that, somewhere in the very near future, an average career will span nearly 100 years, and employers are challenged with preparing, upskilling, and reskilling employees in response.

The function of learning and development (L&D) within an organization is to facilitate the acquisition of knowledge, skills, and behavioral competencies—of both the employees and the organization—to enhance performance. This is done through human, organizational, and process interventions. As HR professionals, it is crucial to have a solid understanding of how L&D activities support this growth and development to sustain organizational success, drive adaptation to changing market conditions, and increase the company's competitive position. This chapter will guide you through the fundamental concepts and practices that form the benchmarks of L&D in HR. In this chapter, we explore concepts related to the following:

- **Training needs analysis:** We will explore the process of identifying gaps in knowledge and skills within an organization, ensuring that L&D initiatives are tailored to address these needs.
- **Training methods and design:** From on-the-job training to e-learning platforms, you will gain insight into various training methodologies, instructional design methods, and their applications.
- **Adult learning theory:** Understanding how adults learn differently than children is essential. We will delve into the principles of adult learning and how they inform L&D strategies.
- **Organizational interventions:** Learn about the various types of organizational design interventions—planned changes in an organization's structure, processes, technology, and human resources that aim to enhance efficiency, effectiveness, alignment, and adaptability to achieve organizational goals and objectives.
- **Evaluation and metrics:** Discover the importance of assessing the impact of L&D programs. We will explore key evaluation methods and metrics used to gauge training effectiveness.
- **Technology in L&D:** In the digital age, technology has revolutionized the L&D landscape. Explore how HR professionals can leverage e-learning platforms, simulations, and other tech tools to enhance training outcomes.
- **Employee career development:** Career development includes both formal and informal activities that go beyond basic training. In this chapter, we will discuss strategies for continuous development and career progression, fostering a culture of lifelong learning within organizations.

Real World Scenario

Unlocking Success: How Effective Career Pathing Transformed a Company's Talent Acquisition and Retention Practices

Introduction

Career pathing and development is a powerful tool that can significantly impact an organization's ability to attract and retain top talent while improving employee engagement and business performance. This case study examines Company A's journey to implement effective career pathing strategies, highlighting the benefits it reaps and the steps taken to achieve success.

Background and Problem

Company A, a midsize technology company, faced a pressing issue: two out of three employees had recently contemplated leaving their Recognizing the importance of professional growth in retaining talent, Company A sought to implement career pathing as a solution to address these challenges.

Diagnosis

Through internal surveys and employee feedback, Company A identified that many employees were dissatisfied with the limited career development opportunities available to them. This dissatisfaction had a direct impact on employee engagement and job satisfaction, resulting in the potential loss of valuable talent—in a competitive labor market no less.

Strategies

The company's HR team banded together to create a career pathing strategy made up of these six key elements:

- **Assess business needs:** Company A initiated its career development program by conducting a comprehensive assessment of its business needs, growth goals, and anticipated skill requirements. This evaluation helped identify challenging roles to fill, succession planning needs, and emerging roles expected to be critical in the future. Clear jobs were created for each role, outlining the necessary skills and qualifications.
- **Employee goal discussions:** Regardless of where the employee was in their tenure (new or seasoned), regular discussions were held to understand their short and long-term career goals. These conversations helped align individual aspirations with the organization's growth opportunities and paved the way for creating personalized career pathways.
- **Personalized career pathways:** Career pathways were developed by identifying the intersection between employee goals and business needs. These pathways highlighted the skills, knowledge, and experience required for each stage of career advancement. The focus was not solely on vertical progression but also on lateral and dual career ladders to accommodate diverse career journeys.

- **Employee development plans:** To support career progression, tailored employee individual development plans (IDPs) were established. These plans included a mix of online courses, stretch or broadening assignments, certifications, coaching, and mentoring to bridge skill gaps. Specific development recommendations were provided to ensure alignment with individual career goals.
- **Performance monitoring:** Regular performance monitoring and assessment were integrated into Company A's practices. Two-way communication allowed for feedback exchanges, ensuring employees had the necessary support and resources to pursue their goals. Flexibility was maintained to adapt plans as needed to accommodate changing circumstances.
- **Reward for professional development:** Company A introduced a system to reward employees for achieving career milestones and professional development. Recognition, pay increases, other incentives, and promotions were offered as employees gained new skills and experiences. This provided motivation and sent a clear message that the organization values employee growth.

Results

Company A's implementation of effective career pathing strategies yielded significant results. It attracted more top talent by showcasing career progression opportunities during recruitment. Employee retention improved as individuals could visualize their future with the organization. Business performance benefited from employees' increased motivation, resulting in positive impacts on various metrics such as productivity, turnover reduction, and profitability.

Conclusion

Career pathing is a valuable tool that, when implemented effectively, can address the challenges of skill development, career advancement, and employee retention. Company A's implementation of career pathing positively impacted its ability to attract top talent by showcasing career progression opportunities during recruitment. It also improved employee retention by providing employees with a clear vision of their future within the organization and offering rewards for professional development, ultimately fostering higher engagement and satisfaction. By fostering a culture of professional growth and continuous development, organizations can futureproof their businesses while upskilling and retaining top talent.

Learning and Development Practice Questions

1. An organization is grappling with a high employee turnover rate and a lack of skilled employees in critical positions. The senior leadership team is seeking a solution to address this problem. Which of the following options aligns best with solving this organizational problem?
   - **A.** Outsource recruiting to a specialized firm to target desired talent.
   - **B.** Engage in a hiring campaign to poach talent from competitors.
   - **C.** Launch a comprehensive learning and development program to enhance employee skills and competencies.
   - **D.** Reduce the workforce to cut costs and improve efficiency.
2. Which of the following is a key principle of adult learning theory?
   - **A.** Passive learning.
   - **B.** Teacher-centered approach.
   - **C.** Self-directed learning.
   - **D.** Rote memorization.
3. According to adult learning principles, what is the significance of relevancy in the learning process?
   - **A.** It makes no difference to adult learners.
   - **B.** It enhances engagement and motivation.
   - **C.** It leads to information overload.
   - **D.** It promotes passive learning.
4. In a corporate training program, employees are encouraged to take charge of their learning by seeking knowledge and skills not only within the formal training sessions but also in their daily work experiences and interactions. They are actively encouraged to learn from colleagues, mentors, and even their own mistakes. What learning model is being applied in this corporate training program?
   - **A.** Simulation.
   - **B.** Vestibule.
   - **C.** Socratic method.
   - **D.** Everywhere model.

5. As a global HR professional with the responsibility of designing and promoting cross-cultural learning programs for your multinational organization, you need to ensure that the learning programs are culturally sensitive, effective, and aligned with the company's objectives. What competency is most critical in this situation?
   A. Conflict resolution.
   B. Communication.
   C. Business acumen.
   D. Diversity, equity, and inclusion.
6. Your organization has recently shifted its strategic focus toward digital transformation and innovation. To align learning and development strategies with this new direction, what should HR prioritize?
   A. Leadership development programs.
   B. Technical skills training.
   C. Diversity and inclusion initiatives.
   D. Employee engagement surveys.
7. Your company is expanding its global presence, opening new offices in different countries. HR has been tasked with designing training initiatives to prepare teams for global assignments. To align learning and development strategies with this expansion, what should HR consider?
   A. Cultural awareness training.
   B. CSR initiatives.
   C. Digital learning platforms.
   D. Social media advertising campaigns.
8. How can corporate learning and development programs assist in fighting corruption on global assignments?
   A. By providing specialized anti-corruption training for employees going on global assignments.
   B. By mandating company ethics training.
   C. By organizing team-building workshops to enhance employee morale during global assignments.
   D. By implementing strict travel expense policies for employees on global assignments.
9. A company is looking to identify training needs for its customer service team to improve their performance and the customer experience ratings. Which internal needs analysis technique would be the LEAST effective in this situation?
   A. Surveys.
   B. Observations.
   C. Interviews.
   D. Focus groups.

10. Which of the following learning styles is typically exhibited by an employee who prefers to learn through physical engagement and hands-on activities?

A. Auditory.

B. Visual.

C. Kinesthetic.

D. Inquisitive.

11. Which phase of the ADDIE model is primarily concerned with identifying the learning objectives, target audience, and assessment criteria?

A. Analysis.

B. Design.

C. Development.

D. Evaluation.

12. In the context of learning design and Bloom's taxonomy, which level represents the highest order of cognitive skills?

A. Application.

B. Analysis.

C. Synthesis.

D. Description.

13. In a management training program, employees have been learning about various leadership styles and their applications in the workplace. The program assigns a task where participants are required to assess different leadership styles and interpret them through real-life workplace scenarios. Which cognitive level of Bloom's taxonomy does this task primarily represent?

A. Knowledge.

B. Comprehension.

C. Application.

D. Evaluation.

14. A university is designing an online course on computer programming for beginners. They want to ensure that the course is structured in a way that learners can progressively build their skills. Which learning design model would best support this objective?

A. Constructivist model.

B. TPACK framework.

C. Gagne's Nine Events of Instruction.

D. Merrill's First Principles of Instruction.

15. In the context of instructional design and action mapping, what is the primary purpose of creating "performance-focused objectives"?

A. To define the desired learner outcomes.

B. To identify potential learning activities.

C. To list the topics to be covered in the training.

D. To assess the learners' prior knowledge.

16. Which of the following is NOT typically considered one of Kirkpatrick's levels of training evaluation?

A. Reaction.

B. Learning.

C. Implementation.

D. Results.

17. A company has just implemented a new customer service training program for its employees. It wants to evaluate the program's effectiveness in improving customer satisfaction. Which evaluation method would be most suitable for assessing this specific outcome?

A. Level 1: Reaction.

B. Level 2: Learning.

C. Level 3: Behavior.

D. Level 4: Results.

18. Which of the following is NOT a common feature of integrated training and development management solutions?

A. Tracking modules.

B. Performance appraisal.

C. Surveys.

D. Gamification.

19. A large corporation is planning to implement an integrated learning management system. They want to streamline their HR processes and enhance employee engagement. Which of the following steps should they prioritize during the implementation?

A. Conducting a thorough needs assessment.

B. Designing an organizational communication strategy.

C. Selecting a vendor based on cost-effectiveness.

D. Creating a detailed project timeline.

20. A manufacturing company has asked the HR team to design learning and development activities to enhance the research and development (R&D) team's effectiveness in sourcing global components. Which competencies are most essential for the HR team to use to accomplish this task successfully?

A. Technical skills and problem-solving.

B. Analytical aptitude and consultation.

C. Communication and leadership.

D. Creativity and innovation.

21. Which theory of organizational design and development emphasizes the importance of aligning organizational structure with the environment and focuses on adapting to external changes?

A. Contingency theory.

B. Human relations theory.

C. Scientific management theory.

D. Classical organizational theory.

22. Which of the following statements is true regarding how the design of an organization affects organizational learning?

A. A hierarchical structure with strict top-down control promotes a culture of innovation and encourages employees to freely share knowledge.

B. A matrix structure, where employees report to both functional managers and project managers, enhances cross-functional collaboration and knowledge sharing.

C. A flat organizational structure with minimal hierarchy hinders communication and knowledge transfer among employees.

D. A bureaucratic organization with rigid rules and procedures is highly conducive to fostering a culture of experimentation and adaptability.

23. A company is facing challenges with a lack of innovation and resistance to change, which has led to communication gaps and decreased productivity. What organizational design intervention should they consider?

A. Employee recognition programs.

B. Leadership training workshops.

C. Revising the organizational structure.

D. Implementing a new software tool.

24. A large manufacturing company is undergoing a significant organizational design overhaul to improve its competitiveness in the market. The leadership team believes that leadership development is crucial to the success of this transformation. In the context of organizational design interventions, what is the role of leadership development?

- **A.** Leadership development is irrelevant as organizational design primarily focuses on structural changes, not leadership capabilities.
- **B.** Leadership development should be a separate initiative, unrelated to organizational design, to avoid distractions during the transformation process.
- **C.** Leadership development is integral to the success of organizational design interventions, as it equips leaders with the skills to implement and navigate the changes effectively.
- **D.** Leadership development is necessary only for middle-level managers, while senior executives' skills remain unaffected by organizational design changes.

25. Which of the following is a key benefit of job redesign interventions?

- **A.** Decreasing employee workload.
- **B.** Increasing job satisfaction and engagement.
- **C.** Eliminating the need for performance appraisals.
- **D.** Reducing the number of job positions.

26. How can learning portals be beneficial in learning and development activities at an organization?

- **A.** Learning portals are primarily useful for delivering in-person training sessions.
- **B.** Learning portals provide a one-size-fits-all approach to training, ensuring consistency in learning outcomes.
- **C.** Learning portals offer a centralized platform for self-paced learning, access to resources, and tracking progress.
- **D.** Learning portals are designed to support compliance training.

27. A midsize healthcare facility has been experiencing delays in patient check-in and registration, leading to long wait times for patients. To address this issue, the administration has assembled a cross-functional team of staff members, including front-desk personnel, nurses, and IT specialists to analyze the problem and propose changes. The team has conducted a detailed analysis, identified bottlenecks, and suggested improvements. One of the key proposed changes is the implementation of a digital check-in system that allows patients to complete their registration online before arriving at the facility. The team believes this will significantly reduce wait times and improve the overall patient experience. What kind of intervention is being conducted in this scenario?

- **A.** Process improvement.
- **B.** Technological transformation.
- **C.** Structural reorganization.
- **D.** Employee training and development.

28. How can employee development support succession plans within an organization?

A. By offering financial incentives to top performers.

B. By providing extensive training for new hires.

C. By identifying and grooming potential future leaders.

D. By outsourcing key leadership positions to external candidates.

29. What is a fundamental aspect of change management training when engaged in organizational design interventions?

A. Convincing employees that the change is good.

B. Minimizing communication with affected stakeholders.

C. Building buy-in and support for the proposed changes.

D. Keeping change plans confidential within the leadership team.

30. At a large multinational healthcare corporation, employees often struggle to find relevant information efficiently, resulting in wasted time and resources. Over the years, they have accumulated research papers, emails, patient data, and more that can be useful in creating a strategic advantage over their main competitors. The organization's leadership is keen to harness this wealth of this knowledge for strategic decision-making. What is the primary challenge they need to tackle in this scenario?

A. Lack of access to advanced technology tools for streamlined knowledge sharing.

B. Difficulty in incentivizing employees to contribute their knowledge.

C. Overwhelming amounts of unstructured information and data.

D. Resistance from top leadership to implement knowledge management.

31. How can HR professionals benefit from the application of predictive analytics in the context of employee performance?

A. By assessing past performance to justify promotions.

B. By making informed decisions about high-potential employees or development opportunities.

C. By using judgments to evaluate employee potential.

D. By automating performance management tasks to increase efficiencies.

32. What is the primary objective of implementing a 360-degree feedback program in the workplace?

A. To exclusively focus on evaluating team dynamics.

B. To collect feedback from direct supervisors.

C. To assess only technical skills and knowledge.

D. To enhance the holistic evaluation of an individual's performance.

33. A company is undergoing a major organizational change, and employees have concerns about the process. What type of feedback program should the company implement to effectively address this need?

   A. Focus groups.

   B. An informal team meeting.

   C. A suggestion box.

   D. A 360-degree feedback program.

34. A multinational corporation with diverse learning and development (L&D) programs across different regions is looking to assess the impact of its executive leadership development initiative. The goal is to measure the program's effectiveness in driving organizational performance and strategic alignment. Which evaluation method should they prioritize for this complex assessment?

   A. Analyzing the total budget allocated to L&D programs.

   B. Conducting a comprehensive ROI analysis, considering both qualitative and quantitative metrics.

   C. Reviewing the number of employees who completed the program.

   D. Holding focus group discussions with a select group of program participants.

35. A tech startup implemented a tailored technical training program for its software engineers. The program aimed to enhance their coding skills and problem-solving abilities. The HR department wants to gauge the program's effectiveness in terms of skill improvement. Which evaluation method would provide the most objective and data-driven results?

   A. Conducting anonymous peer reviews among the engineers.

   B. Administering a series of unannounced skill assessments and coding challenges.

   C. Asking participants to rate their perceived skill improvement in a post training survey.

   D. Analyzing the startup's market share and customer satisfaction levels.

36. Billboard Basics, a major online record corporation, is experiencing a decrease in employee productivity. The HR department believes that a training program might be needed to address this issue. What type of needs assessment should Billboard Basics conduct to identify the specific training needs?

   A. Organizational needs assessment.

   B. Task analysis.

   C. Person analysis.

   D. Environmental analysis.

37. A manager consistently gives high ratings to an employee who has been with the company for many years. Despite some recent performance issues, the manager believes the employee is a valuable asset because of institutional knowledge. What type of performance appraisal bias is evident in this scenario?

   A. Similar-to-me bias.

   B. Recency bias.

   C. Leniency bias.

   D. Longevity bias.

38. A multinational corporation is facing the challenge of "brain drain" as experienced employees are leaving the organization in search of better opportunities abroad. To combat this global phenomenon, what strategies related to learning and development programs can the organization implement?

- **A.** Offer attractive retirement packages to incentivize older employees to stay.
- **B.** Create mentorship programs to facilitate knowledge transfer from experienced employees to younger talent.
- **C.** Reduce investment in learning and development to cut costs.
- **D.** Implement strict noncompete agreements to prevent employees from leaving for competing firms.

39. Taylor is an instructional designer tasked with developing a new employee training program for a software company. She wants to ensure that the training is effective and aligns with the company's objectives. Which phase of the ADDIE model should Taylor begin with in her training design process?

- **A.** Analysis.
- **B.** Design.
- **C.** Development.
- **D.** Implementation.

40. How can the use of AI in LMSs benefit from the design of training solutions?

- **A.** AI in LMS primarily replaces human trainers, reducing costs by eliminating the need for human intervention.
- **B.** AI in LMS enhances personalization by analyzing learner data to tailor training content and delivery.
- **C.** AI in LMS automates administrative tasks such as course enrollment and attendance tracking.
- **D.** AI in LMS primarily focuses on gamification, making training more entertaining.

41. In your organization, Lewis is a highly qualified team member who has expressed a desire to advance his career but has no interest in managing people directly. He is looking for a way to progress within the company without taking on leadership roles that involve team management. What approach could best address Lewis's career aspirations and needs?

- **A.** Encourage him to accept a management position, as it is the traditional path for career advancement.
- **B.** Offer him lateral moves to different departments or roles, hoping they find something of interest.
- **C.** Implement a dual career ladder system, allowing him to advance his career without becoming a people manager.
- **D.** Provide additional training and mentoring to help him develop management skills.

42. Your company is hosting a knowledge-sharing session to facilitate learning and collaboration among employees. What facilitation technique is most suitable for encouraging open discussions and idea generation during the session?

A. Implementing strict time limits for each speaker.

B. Providing all the answers in advance.

C. Encouraging active listening and asking open-ended questions.

D. Avoiding discussions and relying solely on presentations.

43. A large organization is implementing a significant change in its operations and is facing resistance from employees who are hesitant to embrace the new processes. To combat this resistance to change, what strategies related to learning and development programs can the organization implement?

A. Reduce investments in learning and development to allocate resources to other aspects of the change initiative.

B. Provide training programs that focus on the technical aspects of the change to increase employee skillsets.

C. Offer workshops and coaching sessions that help employees develop the necessary skills and mindset to adapt to the change.

D. Implement disciplinary measures to discourage resistance.

44. You are designing an online course for adult learners in a professional development program. What approach should you consider to make the course more effective based on adult learning principles?

A. Keep the content theory heavy and academic to challenge learners.

B. Provide frequent quizzes and tests to assess knowledge retention.

C. Allow learners to set their own individual development plan goals.

D. Assign mandatory assignments with clear deadlines.

45. Cian is a busy marketing manager at a fast-paced digital recording tech startup. He wants to enhance his digital marketing skills but struggles to find time for traditional lengthy training programs. What learning and development technique might be most suitable for Cian's situation?

A. In-person workshops.

B. Micro-learning modules.

C. Online courses.

D. Annual conferences.

46. As a human resources manager at a tech company, Adam is considering the use of personality assessments for various purposes. He has recently hired Jesse, a new software engineer, and Adam wants to ensure that new hires such as Jesse have the proper opportunities for growth and development within the organization. Which of the following best represents the appropriate use of personality assessments in this context?

A. For predictive hiring.

B. For workforce analytics.

C. To determine readiness for promotion.

D. For career development.

47. Celine has recently completed her bachelor's degree in computer science and has joined a tech company as an entry-level software developer. She's eager to advance her career and is seeking opportunities for continuous learning and growth. What career development technique should Celine consider?

   A. Sabbatical leave.

   B. Mentoring and coaching.

   C. Professional certification.

   D. PIP.

48. Within the dynamic environment of Instrumental Innovations, a cutting-edge technology firm, the HR department is encouraging employees to craft individual development plans (IDPs) as part of their career development. What is the overarching objective of an IDP?

   A. To provide a complete record of an employee's daily activities and job responsibilities.

   B. To chart a detailed route for employees' progression through various roles within the organization.

   C. To function as a real-time performance monitoring tool for assessing employee productivity.

   D. To furnish a comprehensive, structured framework for an employee's skill enhancement and career progression.

49. What distinguishes apprenticeships from other training methods?

   A. They require participants to complete formal classroom-based education.

   B. They are exclusively available to individuals with prior industry experience.

   C. They combine practical work experience with structured training and mentorship.

   D. They are typically shorter in duration than other training programs.

50. What does the 70/20/10 model of adult learning primarily emphasize?

   A. The importance of formal classroom training as the primary mode of learning.

   B. The idea that 70% of learning occurs through on-the-job experiences and challenges.

   C. The need for 20% of learning to come from peer interactions and group discussions.

   D. The requirement for 10% of learning to be self-directed and independent.

51. A company is facing a significant challenge in its employee learning and development programs. Despite having invested in various training initiatives, many employees are not acquiring the necessary skills and knowledge to excel in their roles. The HR department has been tasked with addressing this issue. Which of the following HR competencies will need to be used to solve this problem?

   A. Evaluating business challenges.

   B. Change management.

   C. Service excellence.

   D. Harnessing HR data analytics.

52. The HR department of a large organization is struggling with an outdated and inefficient learning and development process. Employee training programs are disorganized, and there is a lack of alignment between training initiatives and the organization's strategic goals. Many employees feel that their development needs are not being adequately addressed. To address this learning and development problem, which of the following HR competencies will need to be used to solve this problem?

A. Restructure the HR department.

B. Exchange organizational information.

C. Influence.

D. Vision.

53. A company is looking to transform into a learning organization to adapt better to changing market conditions and enhance its competitiveness. To achieve this transformation, they aim to embrace the key characteristics of a learning organization as outlined by Peter Senge. Which of the following characteristics is NOT aligned with the concept of a learning organization according to Senge's work?

A. Systems thinking.

B. Hierarchical decision-making.

C. Personal mastery.

D. Shared vision.

54. A multinational corporation is preparing an employee for a global assignment in a new country with a different culture. They want to ensure that the employee possesses the necessary cultural competency to succeed in the new environment. Which of the following characteristics of cultural competency is MOST relevant in this context?

A. Proficiency in the host country's language.

B. Extensive knowledge of the company's products and services.

C. Technical expertise in the employee's field of work.

D. Familiarity with the company's corporate policies and procedures.

55. A company is implementing a new employee training program for its sales team. The company schedules mandatory, instructor-led training sessions for all sales team members, covering product knowledge, sales techniques, and customer service. These sessions are held at specific times, and attendance is required. Which method of training is the employer using?

A. The "push" method.

B. The "pull" method.

C. The "autonomous" method.

D. The "self-paced" method.

56. A large corporation is concerned about the low retention of training among its employees. Many employees attend training sessions but seem to forget the material quickly, leading to reduced effectiveness and return on investment in training programs. Which of the following human resource competencies related to instructional design methods can enhance employee retention of training?

A. Designing successful performance management initiatives.

B. Building an effective succession plan.

C. Skill in designing engaging and interactive training materials.

D. Designing total rewards programs using incentive pay.

57. A company has recently implemented a comprehensive training program for its employees to enhance their skills and productivity. The HR department wants to evaluate the effectiveness of these training activities to ensure they align with the company's goals. Which of the following methods is MOST appropriate for measuring the impact of the training activities?

A. Count the number of training sessions conducted.

B. Survey employees to gather feedback on the training content and delivery.

C. Measure the total hours spent on training activities.

D. Monitor the number of employees who attended the training.

58. A manager in a large organization is eager to establish effective coaching and mentoring for employee development. Which of the following coaching and mentoring best practices should the manager prioritize to ensure success in the workplace?

A. Offering ad hoc coaching and mentoring without a formalized structure.

B. Matching mentors and mentees solely based on their department within the organization.

C. Implementing regular feedback and assessment mechanisms to track progress.

D. Focusing exclusively on technical skill development, ignoring personal growth and leadership skills.

59. A company is committed to fostering a culture of creativity and innovation among its employees. They want to implement learning and development (L&D) techniques that encourage these qualities in the workplace. Which of the following L&D techniques is MOST suitable for achieving this goal?

A. Conducting traditional classroom training on standard operating procedures.

B. Providing employees with opportunities to attend industry conferences.

C. Offering workshops on design thinking and brainstorming techniques.

D. Assigning mandatory online compliance training modules.

60. A large organization is seeking to optimize the movement of employees within the company to maximize talent development and retention. They want to ensure that employees have opportunities for career growth and development. Which of the following approaches to managing job movement within the organization is MOST likely to contribute to employee retention?

- **A.** Implementing a succession planning program that identifies and grooms internal candidates for key roles to ensure continuity.
- **B.** Implementing a replacement planning program that identifies potential external candidates to fill key roles when needed.
- **C.** Encouraging employees to explore lateral moves across different departments and teams to diversify their skills and experiences.
- **D.** Providing upskilling opportunities for employees to enhance their skills and competencies.

Key Concept Research Questions

Taking a deeper dive into key concepts helps to create context and the information necessary to think through the questions on exam day critically. A key bonus is that this research should also make you more knowledgeable in your work, so making the time to answer the next two questions is worth it. You can find the answers in Appendix C.

1. What are the key differences between the ADDIE, SAM, and Action Mapping models of training design, and how do they impact the instructional design process? Consider using `elearningindustry.com` for your research. Search for the key terms and see what you discover.
2. What are the key characteristics of organizational learning techniques, and how can they benefit a company's growth and development? *Harvard Business Review* is excellent research to learn more about the concept of Organizational Learning. Start at `https://hbr.org/topic/subject/organizational-learning` and see what you can learn about this important learning and development topic.

Test Your Learning and Development Terminology Knowledge

The following are the terms to use to test your knowledge on Learning and Development key terms. The correct answers are found in Appendix B.

- Active learning
- Career development
- Coaching
- Competency assessment
- Compliance training
- Development

- Development plan
- E-learning
- Evaluation
- Experiential learning
- Goal setting
- High-potential development
- Instructor-led training
- Job rotation
- Learning
- Learning culture
- Lifelong learning
- Needs assessment
- Onboarding
- Peer learning
- Progress monitoring
- Recognition
- Scenario-based training
- Self-paced learning
- Self-study
- Simulation
- Skills assessment
- Soft skills training
- Succession planning

1. ______________ is the process of acquiring knowledge, skills, and competencies to improve an individual's job performance.
2. ______________ refers to training and development programs designed to enhance employees' communication and leadership skills.
3. A ______________ is a systematic approach to identifying an organization's training and development needs.
4. ______________ is the process of helping employees acquire new skills and knowledge to improve their job performance.
5. ______________ is a learning method that involves learners participating in the learning process through discussions, activities, and problem-solving.
6. A ______________ is a document that outlines an individual's goals and growth opportunities within the organization.
7. ______________ is a strategy that involves employees learning from one another through mentoring and coaching.
8. ______________ is the use of technology platforms, to deliver training and development programs.
9. ______________ is the process of evaluating the effectiveness of training and development programs.
10. ______________ is the intentional and continuous learning mindset that individuals adopt to stay updated and relevant in their careers.
11. ______________ is the process of measuring employees' existing abilities and knowledge.
12. ______________ is a training method that emulates real life work situations to develop specific skills.
13. ______________ is the practice of providing ongoing feedback and coaching to employees to support their development.

14. ______________ is a formalized program that helps employees transition into new roles or responsibilities.

15. ______________ is a training method that involves learners accessing educational materials online on their own schedule.

16. ______________ is the process of setting specific learning objectives.

17. ______________ is a form of training that involves a facilitator delivering content to a group of learners.

18. ______________ is a systematic approach to identifying and nurturing individuals with above average skill sets or aptitudes.

19. ______________ is the process of evaluating employees' job-related knowledge, skills and abilities.

20. ______________ is the practice of providing employees with opportunities for skill development and advancement.

21. ______________ is the use of case studies and real-world examples in training and development programs.

22. ______________ is the process of identifying the skills and knowledge necessary for future roles within the organization.

23. ______________ is a model of learning and development that focuses on simulations or understanding past practices in learning.

24. ______________ is the process of creating and maintaining an environment of continuous learning within an organization.

25. ______________ is the practice of rotating employees through different roles to broaden their skills and experiences.

26. ______________ is a formalized program that prepares employees for leadership roles within the organization.

27. ______________ is the practice of measuring employees' learning progress and adjusting training accordingly.

28. ______________ is a type of training that focuses on compliance with laws and regulations.

29. ______________ is a learning method that involves learners studying and completing assignments independently.

30. ______________ is the process of acknowledging and rewarding employees for their learning and development achievements.

Conclusion

Learning and development activities are a cornerstone of effective human resource management (HRM). They play a pivotal role in nurturing a dynamic and skilled workforce, essential for organizational growth and competitiveness. L&D initiatives empower employees to acquire new skills, adapt to evolving industry trends, and contribute to innovation. These initiatives boost employee morale, engagement, and retention, fostering a positive workplace culture.

The importance of the outcomes is reflected in the SHRM and HRCI exam content. For the CP and SCP exams, L&D competencies make up part of the 18% domain of "People." On the HRCI exams, this functional area will account for 10% of the PHR and PHRi exams. In 2024, HRCI published the new exam content outlines that combine content for the SPHR and the SPHRi exams. Part of this update was the introduction of a new functional area titled "Talent Management," which makes up 23% of these senior level exams. In 2018, L&D made up only 14% of the SPHR exam, so it is worthwhile to prepare for this important functional area properly.

Additional Resources

Understanding L&D in the workplace is crucial for both employees and organizations. Casting a wide net when studying can help create context for maximum retention even past exam day. Take a deeper look at these websites, podcasts, and online videos to support your study effort.

Websites

- ATD (Association for Talent Development) (`www.td.org`)

  ATD is a professional organization dedicated to talent development and workplace learning. The website provides a wealth of resources, including articles, research reports, webinars, and tools to help you stay updated on best practices and trends in the field.

- eLearning Industry (`elearningindustry.com`)

  eLearning Industry is a comprehensive online resource for e-learning and workplace training. It offers articles, reviews, whitepapers, and guides on e-learning tools and strategies, making it a valuable source for professionals interested in digital learning and development.

- Percipio (`https://www.skillsoft.com/meet-skillsoft-percipio`)

  Formerly known as Skillsoft, this website offers research reports, webinars, and an active blog on several business topics. Use this resource to learn about compliance training, leadership, and general training solutions to broaden your understanding of business principles and L&D.

Podcasts

- *The Learning Leader Show* with host Ryan Hawk

  This podcast features insightful interviews with leaders, authors, and experts in various fields. It explores leadership, personal development, and effective learning strategies for continuous growth.
- *Learning Uncut* with hosts Michelle Ockers and Karen Moloney

  Learning Uncut is dedicated to sharing real-world stories and practical insights into workplace learning and development. It features case studies and discussions with learning professionals.
- *The Talented Learning Show* with host John Leh

  This podcast focuses on learning technology, online learning, and the business of learning. It explores e-learning trends, strategies, and best practices.
- *The eLearning Coach Podcast* with host Connie Malamed

  The eLearning Coach Podcast is a valuable resource for instructional designers and e-learning professionals. It provides tips, strategies, and interviews with experts in the field of online learning.

YouTube Channels

YouTube is a valuable platform for accessing informative content on workplace L&D. Simply go online to `www.youtube.com` and search for the following channels to find insights, tips, and discussions related to L&D:

- Chartered Institute of Personnel and Development (CIPD)

  CIPD's YouTube channel offers videos on HR, learning, and development in the workplace. It covers a wide range of HR topics, including talent management, employee engagement, and training and development.
- Learning Pool

  Learning Pool offers videos on e-learning, training, and workplace development, with a focus on digital learning solutions and best practices.
- Talentsoft: The Ins & Outs of Work

  Talentsoft's YouTube channel focuses on talent management and HR software solutions, offering insights into employee development and performance management.

Chapter 6

Total Rewards

"Culture eats strategy for lunch" is a well-known, clickable phrase often attributed to Peter Drucker. It suggests that fostering and maintaining a strong organizational culture is key to organizational success, even above strategy. But is it true? Maybe.

The truth is that most people work not because they need access to a "family" of co-workers, but because that is how they earn their living; in short, they need their paycheck and the security the wages and benefits bring. It comes down to really understanding what money can and cannot do. Behavioral sciences show that once a minimum threshold of earnings is earned, compensation loses some of its ability to motivate. Regardless, savvy HR pros know that a functional Total Rewards system addresses the many personal, organizational, and regulatory challenges that exist within the workplaces of today.

Total Rewards is a fundamental concept within the realm of human resource management (HRM) that continues to evolve. At its most basic, this functional area is concerned with paying employees their wages and benefits. At its most strategic, Total Rewards practices impact recruiting, retention, engagement, global effectiveness, and organizational design. As an HR professional preparing for the exams, you need to understand the key concepts of Total Rewards, as it not only plays an important role in shaping an organization's culture but also influences its competitiveness in the talent market.

Total Rewards represents a comprehensive approach to employee compensation and benefits, encompassing both monetary and nonmonetary elements. This holistic perspective recognizes that employee satisfaction and productivity are not solely dependent on salary but are equally affected by various other factors such as work-life balance, recognition, and a positive work environment. As you prepare, you'll want to be familiar with these Total Rewards concepts:

- **Compensation and benefits:** This core element encompasses the traditional salary and benefits package provided to employees, including base pay, increases, bonuses, incentives, health insurance, retirement plans, and the influence of the regulatory environment surrounding these practices.
- **Recognition and rewards:** Acknowledging and appreciating employee contributions is a key driver of engagement. Learning about various recognition programs and rewards systems, such as employee of the month awards or spot bonuses, is part of the process.
- **Special compensation:** Addressing issues such as executive compensation, global pay practices, and household payroll is an important competency for HR practitioners to have a firm grasp on.
- **Work-life balance:** Organizations that promote a healthy work-life balance through flexible work arrangements, paid time off, and wellness initiatives tend to have more engaged and satisfied employees.

- **Total well-being:** This emerging concept focuses on the physical, mental, and emotional well-being of employees and the wellness of communities in which companies operate. Awareness of holistic well-being programs and initiatives is becoming increasingly important as a form of corporate social responsibility and employee retention efforts that go beyond the paycheck.
- **Communication and Total Rewards strategy:** Effective communication is essential in ensuring that employees are aware of and appreciate the value of their Total Rewards package.

Real World Scenario

The Complex Environment of Executive Pay: A Case Study

The healthcare industry continues to experience high turnover among its executive leaders, primarily driven by natural attrition and also an increase in retirement decisions following years of navigating the challenges posed by the COVID-19 pandemic. This wave of departures has presented healthcare organizations with a formidable challenge: the urgent need to fill critical executive roles with capable leaders in a turbulent and uncertain time. As a result, compensation committees and other decision-makers within these organizations are compelled to reassess their compensation strategies to meet the evolving demands of the healthcare sector. In this case study of Intermountain Health of Utah (IHC), the impact that operational, financial, and societal needs can exert on compensation strategies is examined. IHC's CEO Marc Harrison and examples of the company's compensation programs provide the model for these concepts.

Background and Problem

The healthcare industry has witnessed a surge in leadership turnover, driven in part by executives opting for retirement following the enduring challenges of the COVID-19 pandemic. This trend has intensified competition among healthcare organizations in their quest to secure top executive talent. A recent survey by SullivanCotter[1] revealed that nearly 40% of healthcare organizations have ramped up efforts to recruit executives, a response to workforce dynamics and the long-overdue equity needs of teams and patient populations. Old-school "best" Total Rewards practices that rely solely upon market data do not address the layers of complexity of the healthcare landscape.

---

[1] Modern Healthcare. "Diversity, wellness incentives rise to retain care delivery execs" by Matti Gellman. August 2nd, 2021. `https://sullivancotter.com/wp-content/uploads/2021/08/Diversity-wellness-incentives-rise-to-retain-care-delivery-execs_MHC-REPRINT.pdf`

Diagnosis

This intricate landscape poses substantial challenges for compensation committees as they strive to strike a delicate balance between adhering to prevailing market norms, fulfilling corporate strategies, meeting the expectations of shareholders and stakeholders, and acting as good stewards of the communities they serve. Companies now are expected to integrate environmental, social, and governance (ESG) objectives into their executive compensation structures, extending beyond the confines of traditional market data. Furthermore, linking executive pay directly to performance presents an opportunity to establish a transparent correlation between the *efforts* of C-level executives and their high-value *rewards* packages.

Strategies and Results

As with any other business strategy, the organization built a set of initiatives outlining the response to the compensation challenges. These included the following:

Benchmarking and Market Norms

To benchmark executive compensation effectively and prevent overpayment, companies should engage in a variety of compensation package elements such as clear performance targets, claw back provisions (accountability for contract violations such as misconduct or regulatory violations), and shareholder input.

Establishing Nonfinancial Performance Targets

Companies are increasingly incorporating environmental, social, and governance (ESG) goals into executive compensation plans to align them with broader stakeholder interests and societal expectations. Examples of how IHC could have tied Harrison's Total Rewards package include the following:

Social responsibility: Harrison's commitment to reducing the number of opioids prescribed for acute pain by 40% reflects a key social goal in the fight against the opioid crisis in America.

Innovation: IHC's consistent recognition as one of the most technologically advanced hospital systems over multiple years (2016–2018) underscores its focus on innovation. Success was proven by their ability to rapidly shift thousands of workers to work remotely in a single week of March 2020.

Cost control: Achieving the top rank in the United States for providing high-quality healthcare at sustainable costs in 2016–2017 demonstrates the company's emphasis on cost control, as does their leadership in bringing low-cost generic drugs to market through R&D contributions.

Service excellence: Winning Consumer Choice Awards for hospital-level service in 2016–2017 highlights IHC's commitment to delivering exceptional healthcare services.

Environmental sustainability: The transition to remote work resulting in 18,200,000 fewer miles driven by caregivers and reduced emissions equivalent to 36 railcars of coal burned showcases the organization's improving air quality.

Leadership development: The establishment of a leadership institute focused on strategy, innovation, finances, supply chain operations, and clinician burnout addresses recruiting challenges and creates a leadership pipeline for the future.

The goal of differentiated performance targets such as those identified here is to minimize executive decision-making that is focused only on short-term results.

Short- and Long-Term Crisis Response

By aligning executive pay with crisis management and attention to longer-term risks, companies can demonstrate responsible stewardship beyond financial targets. The CEO of IHC responded to the pandemic by accelerating virtual hospital services, participating in global research, and sharing their findings with the medical community. Additionally, Harrison noted that "the COVID-19 pandemic has starkly illuminated the profound racial disparities in healthcare, and these must be rapidly addressed to achieve health equity." To address this, IHC worked on a three-year pilot project in Utah, investing $12 million and staff resources to tackle social determinants of health outlined by the CDC. The project successfully led to a 12.7% reduction in emergency department visits among participants, prompting the Utah legislature to expand the model statewide.

Total Rewards Communication

Transparent communication is a hallmark of all best pay practices. CEO Marc Harrison went public during the pandemic to address specific criticisms and rumors around physician pay. He acknowledged that many providers were facing reduced patient activity due to canceled elective surgeries. Harrison shared that in response the leadership team took measures to ensure that no provider would earn less than 85% of their base salary, a proactive measure aimed at supporting their financial stability during those challenging times.

Conclusion

Executive compensation remains a complex and evolving aspect of corporate governance. While benchmarking against peers plays a role in determining compensation levels, companies must strike a balance and consider individual corporate strategies and cultural factors. These multifaceted strategies reflect how healthcare organizations are addressing the pressing issues of rising executive compensation and the complexities of executive recruitment, all while striving to align with societal expectations and maintain responsible stewardship in the healthcare sector.

Total Rewards Practice Questions

1. Job evaluation is the process by which employers properly ________________ jobs, whereas job analysis is the process of how the work is ________________.
   - **A.** Evaluate; analyzed.
   - **B.** Value; designed.
   - **C.** Classify; performed.
   - **D.** Assign; documented.
2. When conducting surveys to gather employee feedback for refining the Total Rewards strategy, which of the following areas should HR focus on to ensure alignment with business results?
   - **A.** Employee tenure and job titles.
   - **B.** Preferred office location and workspace design.
   - **C.** Individual performance and goal-setting preferences.
   - **D.** Personal hobbies and interests outside of work.
3. What potential challenges might arise when a company strictly relies on a performance-based pay structure without any flexibility or adaptation in aligning Total Rewards with business results?
   - **A.** Decreased employee retention.
   - **B.** Failure to comply with wage and hour laws.
   - **C.** Complex compensation administration.
   - **D.** Bias in compensation-related decisions
4. `Buffer.com` is a forward-thinking social media management company known for its progressive and ethical workplace practices. The senior leadership team is discussing its compensation philosophy during an internal meeting. What is likely to be a key element of `Buffer.com`'s compensation philosophy?
   - **A.** Offering the highest salaries in the industry to attract top talent.
   - **B.** Emphasizing performance-based bonuses as the primary form of compensation.
   - **C.** Prioritizing transparency in pay structures and ensuring fairness.
   - **D.** Providing minimal benefits to maximize profitability.
5. What component of Total Rewards strategies focuses on nonmonetary benefits and programs aimed at improving employees' work-life balance and overall well-being?
   - **A.** Base salary.
   - **B.** Performance bonuses.
   - **C.** Employee benefits.
   - **D.** Stock options.

6. Which of the following is an essential consideration when designing an effective Total Rewards strategy?

   A. Ignoring employee feedback and preferences.

   B. Standardizing rewards for all employee roles.

   C. Aligning rewards with organizational goals and values.

   D. Offering only monetary rewards without nonmonetary incentives.

7. Carmy Manufacturing Company is facing a significant organizational problem with employee productivity. Despite having a skilled workforce and modern machinery, production output has been consistently below expectations. The management team has noticed that employees seem unmotivated and disengaged, resulting in lower productivity levels and increased operational costs. The company is keen to implement a new pay structure to address this challenge and improve employee performance. Which of the following pay structures is most likely to solve this challenge?

   A. Commission pay.

   B. Hourly wage.

   C. Piece-rate pay.

   D. Profit sharing.

8. According to the Fair Labor Standards Act (FLSA), when are vacation pay, sick pay, and holiday pay due?

   A. The last working day of each month.

   B. Annually on the employee's original hire date.

   C. Due dates are determined by state laws.

   D. Due on the 15th of each month.

9. Which pay structure provides employees with a percentage of the revenue or sales they generate as compensation?

   A. Hourly wage.

   B. Salary pay.

   C. Commission-based pay.

   D. Piece-rate pay.

10. Sugar Shakes is facing challenges with its current pay structure in the workplace. Employees in various departments have expressed concerns about fairness, and there are ongoing discussions about whether the existing pay structure effectively rewards performance and encourages retention. What should HR primarily consider when addressing these pay structure challenges?

    A. Implementing a one-size-fits-all pay structure to simplify administration.

    B. Conducting market research to understand industry compensation trends.

    C. Increasing the base salary for all employees to boost morale.

    D. Eliminating performance-based bonuses to reduce complexity.

11. A large manufacturing company is in the process of conducting a comprehensive job evaluation to determine the relative worth of various positions within the organization. HR has assigned a team of experienced HR professionals to examine job descriptions, observe job tasks, and interview employees to gather detailed information about the roles. They are particularly interested in understanding the unique skills, qualifications, and responsibilities associated with each position. Which of the following job evaluation methods is being used in this scenario?
    - **A.** Job content based.
    - **B.** Job ranking.
    - **C.** Point factor.
    - **D.** Market based.
12. At a board meeting, the HR department is discussing different methods used by organizations to calculate pay increases for employees. What factors are typically considered when determining pay increases?
    - **A.** Employee seniority and years of service.
    - **B.** Employee performance, market conditions, and cost of living adjustments.
    - **C.** External economic conditions.
    - **D.** Company profits and executive decisions.
13. A progressive tech startup, TechWave Innovations, is considering implementing an open leave policy for its employees. What is a key characteristic of an open leave policy?
    - **A.** Employees have unlimited paid time off with no restrictions.
    - **B.** Employees can take only unpaid leave without affecting their job security.
    - **C.** Employees can take leave only during specific seasons or holidays.
    - **D.** Employees must obtain prior approval from multiple supervisors to take leave.
14. What is one of the common challenges associated with open-leave policies in the workplace?
    - **A.** Difficulty in maintaining improved employee work-life balance.
    - **B.** Struggles in maintaining enhanced employee productivity.
    - **C.** Difficulty in managing scheduling and staffing.
    - **D.** Obstacles in streamlining communication within the organization.
15. At your large manufacturing company, a significant downsizing decision has been made due to economic challenges. As a result, several employees will be laid off. The HR department is tasked with determining the compensation approach for these employees. What is the BEST compensation method that the HR department might consider to support the workers being laid off?
    - **A.** Offering a severance package to provide financial assistance and support during their transition.
    - **B.** Increasing the salaries of the remaining employees as a gesture of goodwill.
    - **C.** Providing additional stock options to departing employees to compensate for their loss.
    - **D.** Not offering any compensation, as layoffs are a standard business practice.

16. What is one of the special considerations that employers should address when compensating domestic workers?

A. Offering company stock options and profit-sharing as part of their compensation package.

B. Providing free accommodation to domestic workers as a substitute for monetary compensation.

C. Complying with minimum wage laws and accurately tracking overtime for live-in domestic workers.

D. Paying domestic workers based on the number of tasks completed each day.

17. What does it mean when a company chooses to "match" the labor market in terms of compensation strategy?

A. Engaging in nondiscriminatory pay practices.

B. Using "comparable worth" to structure pay ranges.

C. Paying employees wages that are similar to the industry average.

D. Using consistent and fair salary ranges, regardless of the geographic location of the job.

18. What do comparable worth laws primarily aim to address in the workplace?

A. Discrimination based on age and seniority in compensation decisions.

B. Discrimination based on gender in compensation decisions.

C. Discrimination based on education and experience in hiring practices.

D. Discrimination based on physical disability in promotion opportunities.

19. Which of the following is NOT an advantage of the point factor method of job evaluation?

A. It provides a systematic and objective way to assess job values.

B. It allows for the comparison of different jobs within the organization.

C. It can help in designing fair and competitive compensation structures.

D. It can be inexpensive to administer.

20. In a company in the maturity stage of the business life cycle, several employees who have been with the organization for many years are noticing a concerning trend. New hires with little to no experience in the industry are being hired at salaries that are nearly on par with the long-tenured employees who have accumulated years of experience and expertise in their roles. These experienced employees are concerned that their pay relative to new hires is not reflecting their contributions and dedication to the company. What compensation phenomenon is being demonstrated in this scenario?

A. Wage stagnation

B. Pay equity

C. Pay compression

D. Wage discrimination

21. In a large corporation, the HR department can be tasked with conducting remuneration surveys to ensure that employee compensation is competitive in the industry. During this process, HR professionals utilize their competencies to gather and analyze data from various sources. However, a senior manager disagrees with HR's recommendations based on the survey results. Which HR competencies are HR professionals primarily using when conducting remuneration surveys, and which competency might the senior manager be relying on when disagreeing with HR's recommendations?
   - **A.** Business Acumen and Networking.
   - **B.** Vision and Influence.
   - **C.** Analytical Aptitude and Designing HR Solutions.
   - **D.** Networking and Team Building.

22. What role does addressing mental well-being play in enhancing an organization's Total Rewards package for remote workers?
   - **A.** It has no impact on employee morale or productivity.
   - **B.** It can lower absenteeism and increase engagement, enhancing Total Rewards.
   - **C.** Remote workers do not experience mental health issues, so it's irrelevant.
   - **D.** Mental well-being is easily assessed through Zoom calls, supporting Total Rewards.

23. At BrightTech Solutions, a tech company with a large and diverse workforce, the HR department has been receiving an increasing number of inquiries from employees about their compensation packages. Many employees have expressed confusion and uncertainty about the full scope of their compensation beyond their base salary, particularly in light of a major competitor announcing a relocation to the same city as BrightTech. Which of the following compensation solutions would best address the employee concerns?
   - **A.** Eliminating all nonmonetary perks and benefits to simplify the compensation structure.
   - **B.** Providing employees with a onetime bonus to compensate for the lack of transparency.
   - **C.** Implementing a comprehensive Total Rewards statement for each employee.
   - **D.** Offering employees a new set of nonmonetary perks to aid in retention.

24. What is the primary purpose of conducting a compensation program audit in the workplace?
   - **A.** To determine employee performance ratings.
   - **B.** To identify areas of potential pay disparities.
   - **C.** To establish employee job titles and descriptions.
   - **D.** To calculate employee overtime pay rates.

25. As an HR manager, you need to calculate the total value of compensation and benefits for employees at your organization. Which of the following steps should you consider when performing this calculation?
   - **A.** Include only the base salary and ignore any additional benefits.
   - **B.** Add the base salary and subtract the value of employee benefits.
   - **C.** Sum the base salary, bonuses, stock options, and the monetary value of all employee benefits.
   - **D.** Calculate the average salary across all employees without considering nonmonetary factors.

26. Employee A has an annual compensation of $75,000, and the median annual compensation within the department is $60,000. The employee burden (taxes and benefits) adds an additional 30%. Calculate the compensation ratio for Employee A.

A. 1.25.

B. 0.8.

C. 1.00.

D. 0.6.

27. When designing global pay structures, what factors should organizations consider as best practices?

A. Standardizing pay scales across all countries.

B. Adhering exclusively to local market rates.

C. Balancing headquarter consistency and local competitiveness.

D. Ignoring regional economic disparities.

28. To determine the benefits utilization rate for a specific employee benefit program, you need to calculate the ratio of employees who have used the benefit to the total number of eligible employees. Your company offers a tuition reimbursement program, and out of 150 eligible employees, 50 have used this benefit in the last year. Calculate the benefits utilization rate for the tuition reimbursement program.

A. 0.33.

B. 0.50.

C. 3.00.

D. 2.00.

29. How can an employer use their compensation philosophy to attract and retain talent effectively?

A. By offering the highest salaries in the industry.

B. By aligning compensation practices with the organization's values and goals.

C. By optimizing employee benefit programs to balance costs while maintaining competitive compensation structures.

D. By providing one-size-fits-all compensation packages.

30. Imagine a multinational corporation considering salary survey data from various regions. They want to align this data with their internal pay structure, which includes different pay grades and salary ranges. What does this leveling process involve?

A. It involves rounding salary figures to the nearest thousand for simplicity.

B. It refers to adjusting the data to align with an organization's predetermined pay structure.

C. It means collecting data from multiple sources to increase accuracy.

D. It signifies comparing the data to industry averages.

31. How should an HR professional handle compensation for hours worked above and beyond a standard workweek in a country that does not adhere to the FLSA of the United States?

A. Apply the FLSA regulations to ensure consistency in overtime pay calculations.

B. Comply with the labor laws and regulations of the specific country in which the employees work.

C. Determine overtime pay based on the policies and guidelines of the parent company, regardless of local laws.

D. Disregard overtime pay as it is not a legal requirement in countries outside the United States.

32. What does the USMCA require regarding minimum wage standards for member countries like the United States and Mexico?

A. The USMCA harmonizes minimum wage rates across member countries.

B. The USMCA establishes uniform minimum wage rates for all industries within member countries.

C. The USMCA requires each member country to maintain and enforce its own minimum wage laws within its jurisdiction.

D. The USMCA allows member countries to disregard minimum wage laws for cross-border trade.

33. How can HR professionals use "doing business in" guides to structure pay systems for international operations?

A. To set standardized pay rates across all countries.

B. To understand legal and regulatory requirements in the target country.

C. To ignore cultural norms and social expectations related to compensation.

D. To ensure compliance with minimum wage laws.

34. Which of the following is a potential drawback of tying executive compensation primarily to short-term financial performance metrics?

A. Enhanced alignment with long-term company goals.

B. Inadvertently causing unethical behavior to achieve short-term results.

C. Simplifying the administration of executive pay.

D. Reducing executive turnover.

35. Sydney, an employee at a medium-sized company, recently received her paycheck and noticed that there is a significant error in the amount. Her paycheck reflects a lower amount than what she was expecting, and it seems that some of her overtime hours are missing. Sydney is concerned about this issue and contacts the HR department for assistance. How should the HR department handle Sydney's paycheck error in this scenario?

A. Advise Sydney that a correction will be made in her next paycheck to address the error, explaining that it may take a pay cycle to process the adjustment.

B. Ask Sydney to provide evidence of the error before taking any action.

C. Promptly investigate the issue, correct the error, and ensure Sydney receives the correct payment on her next paycheck.

D. Instruct Sydney to contact the payroll department directly and resolve the issue without HR involvement.

36. HR professionals must take steps to ensure the alignment of a rewards strategy with an organization's business strategy. What is the first step that organizations should take when implementing this strategy?

A. Conducting a comprehensive employee survey.

B. Analyzing competitor compensation practices.

C. Identifying business objectives and goals.

D. Conducting a market survey.

37. Jamie Lee, a senior HR professional at a large corporation, is responsible for developing the annual budget for compensation. Her company has a diverse workforce, and she needs to ensure that the compensation budget aligns with the organization's strategic goals while remaining competitive in the labor market. What budgeting strategy should Jamie Lee employ when developing the annual budget?

A. Implement a top-down budgeting approach, where senior management sets the compensation budget without considering market data.

B. Utilize zero-based budgeting, requiring justification for each compensation expense, considering market data, and aligning with strategic objectives.

C. Base the budget solely on historical compensation expenditures, making minor adjustments for inflation.

D. Rely on a fixed percentage increase from the previous year's budget without a thorough analysis.

38. Which of the following is an example of using employee perks as an indirect form of compensation to enhance job satisfaction and employee retention?

A. Increasing the base salary for all employees.

B. Providing on-site childcare services.

C. Offering additional paid vacation days.

D. Implementing a mandatory overtime policy.

39. Cousin's Hamburgers is a restaurant retail chain in the Midwest that is facing an EEOC charge related to compensation discrimination. The charge alleges that the company pays its Hispanic employees less than their non-Hispanic counterparts for the same job roles and responsibilities, despite both groups having similar qualifications and experience. Which federal law is the charge most likely based on?

   A. Fair Labor Standards Act.

   B. Americans with Disabilities Act.

   C. Equal Pay Act.

   D. Title VII of the Civil Rights Act of 1964.

40. In a midsize company, an HR manager notices that a particular employee's compensation ratio exceeds 1.00. The HR manager investigates further to understand the reasons behind this situation. What could be a likely reason for the compensation ratio exceeding 1.00 in this scenario?

   A. The employee is new to the team.

   B. The company has a match market pay strategy.

   C. Managers are not following pay increase policies.

   D. The company is likely using a broadbanding structure.

41. How can organizations effectively use Total Rewards to manage multiple generations in the workplace, considering the diverse needs and preferences of different age groups?

   A. Providing identical rewards packages for all employees.

   B. Offering flexible work arrangements and schedules.

   C. Eliminating all nonmonetary rewards.

   D. Increasing the retirement age for all employees.

42. The director of HR at a large multinational corporation is tasked with designing a new compensation system. The corporation operates in multiple countries and regions, each with its own unique labor laws, cultural norms, and economic conditions. Additionally, the organization needs to ensure that its compensation packages remain competitive in the global talent market while also managing costs effectively. The director of HR decides to conduct a comprehensive analysis of market salary surveys, internal pay equity considerations, and cost projections before finalizing the new compensation system. They also take into account the cultural nuances and legal requirements of the various locations where the corporation operates. Moreover, they collaborate with HR teams from different regions to gather valuable insights and input into the compensation design process. What competencies is the director of HR demonstrating?

   A. Employee Relations and Diversity and Inclusion.

   B. Global Mindset and Analytical Aptitude.

   C. Talent Acquisition and Training and Development.

   D. Benefits Administration and Performance Management.

43. What is a key difference between a single-rate pay system and a time-based pay system in organizations?

A. Single-rate pay systems are based on individual performance, while time-based pay systems focus on teamwork.

B. In a single-rate pay system, employees are paid a fixed rate regardless of the number of hours worked, while time-based pay systems compensate based on hours worked.

C. Single-rate pay systems are typically used for executive level positions, whereas time-based pay systems are for entry-level employees.

D. Time-based pay systems are more prevalent in industries with variable work hours, whereas single-rate pay systems are common in manufacturing.

44. What is a commonly recommended best practice used to create wage bands in an organization?

A. Randomly assigning salary ranges to job positions.

B. Benchmarking against industry compensation data.

C. Using a fixed percentage increase for all employees.

D. Relying solely on employee negotiation for pay rates.

45. What is a key benefit of using a market-based approach to create wage bands in an organization?

A. It ensures uniform salary ranges for all job positions.

B. It allows for flexibility in responding to market changes.

C. It eliminates the need for annual performance reviews.

D. It guarantees higher salaries for all employees.

46. What are the different types of standard pay increases commonly used by organizations to adjust employee compensation?

A. Annual performance bonuses and one-time cash awards.

B. Cost-of-living adjustments (COLAs) and employee recognition awards.

C. Overtime pay and holiday bonuses.

D. Vacation pay and health insurance benefits.

47. A national healthcare organization is considering designing an incentive program to improve employee performance among healthcare professionals within their host country of Japan. They are exploring different approaches to incentivize their staff effectively. What type of incentive program would likely be more welcome and align better with the collectivist culture of the country?

A. Individual incentives, as they promote healthy competition.

B. Team-based incentives, as they reinforce collaboration and shared goals.

C. Performance-based incentives, as they cater to individual achievements.

D. Monetary incentives, as they are universally appealing.

48. In a manufacturing company, a team member is asked to work the night shift, which has fewer employees on duty and requires a different work schedule compared to the regular day shift. The company compensates the team member at a higher hourly rate for their night shift work. Which time-based differential is being demonstrated to compensate the team member?

   A. Emergency pay.

   B. Shift differential pay.

   C. Holiday pay.

   D. Premium pay.

49. What is a characteristic of voluntary benefits in the workplace?

   A. They are mandatory for all employees.

   B. Employees typically contribute to the cost.

   C. They include legally required programs.

   D. They cover basic health insurance.

50. A medium-sized manufacturing company has been grappling with the rising cost of offering healthcare insurance to its employees. The HR department is tasked with finding strategies to combat these escalating costs while ensuring that employees continue to receive adequate health benefits. What kind of strategies should HR advise to combat the rising costs of offering healthcare insurance to employees effectively?

   A. Reduce the coverage options available to employees to minimize expenses.

   B. Encourage employees to seek medical care less frequently to decrease claims.

   C. Implement wellness programs and preventive care initiatives to promote employee health.

   D. Shift the entire cost burden of health insurance onto employees.

51. The HR team at Innovative Solutions is exploring various alternative workplace benefits, including housing partnerships, to enhance employee well-being and satisfaction. What is the primary purpose of offering housing partnerships as an alternative workplace benefit?

   A. To provide employees with free housing as a perk of their compensation.

   B. To help employees find affordable housing options near the workplace.

   C. To offer employees a comprehensive healthcare package.

   D. To promote remote work opportunities.

52. Lionel, an American expatriate, has been working in Shanghai, China, on an international assignment for two years. He plans to stay for another three years before potentially moving to another international assignment. Lionel is concerned about his retirement savings and has heard that the Chinese retirement system is only for Chinese nationals. He is considering whether to continue contributing to the U.S. Social Security system or explore other retirement options. What advice should he consider for the next three years?

A. Lionel should continue paying into the Chinese retirement system to maximize his benefits.

B. Lionel should opt out of paying into the Chinese retirement system and continue contributing to the U.S. Social Security system.

C. Lionel should participate in both the Chinese retirement system and the U.S. Social Security system to maximize his retirement benefits.

D. Lionel should focus on short-term financial goals and not worry about retirement savings during his international assignment.

53. The HR team at a large company has conducted a benefits gap analysis and identified a significant issue: many of the company benefits are being underutilized by employees. This underutilization has raised concerns about the effectiveness of the benefits program. What should the HR team advise section leadership on addressing underutilized company benefits based on the benefits gap analysis?

A. Reduce the overall benefits budget to cut costs.

B. Communicate the existing benefits more effectively to employees.

C. Eliminate underutilized benefits to streamline the program.

D. Increase employee salaries instead of offering extensive benefits.

54. Which mandated workplace benefit provides eligible employees with income replacement if they involuntarily separate from their job?

A. Health insurance.

B. Retirement pension.

C. COBRA.

D. Unemployment compensation.

55. Why do family leave policies differ from country to country?

A. Family leave policies are solely determined by global organizations like the United Nations.

B. Cultural norms and societal values influence the design of family leave policies.

C. All countries adopt a universal approach to family leave policies.

D. Family leave policies are solely determined by the country's economic status.

56. Given the leave disparity in multinational companies due to varying family leave policies in different countries, what strategies can HR teams implement to address this issue and promote consistency and fairness in employee benefits across the organization?

  A. Standardize family leave policies across all countries to ensure uniformity.
  B. Provide additional leave allowances for employees in countries with less generous policies.
  C. Offer flexible leave options and supplemental benefits to bridge the gap.
  D. Encourage employees to move to countries with more favorable leave policies.

57. What are some advantages and disadvantages of implementing a tuition reimbursement program in an organization?

  A. Advantages: Enhanced employee skill development; Disadvantages: Increased organizational costs.
  B. Advantages: Attraction and retention of top talent; Disadvantages: Limited impact on employee skills.
  C. Advantages: Decreased employee morale; Disadvantages: Improved workforce diversity.
  D. Advantages: Limited impact on employee engagement; Disadvantages: potential lost talent pipeline.

58. How are health savings accounts (HSAs) in the workplace typically regulated?

  A. HSAs are regulated solely by the federal government.
  B. HSAs are subject to state-level regulations and guidelines.
  C. HSAs are not subject to any regulatory oversight.
  D. HSAs are regulated by both federal and state governments.

59. How can flexible spending accounts (FSAs) be utilized to support employee wellness in the workplace?

  A. FSAs can be used only for medical expenses and cannot contribute to employee wellness.
  B. FSAs allow employees to set aside pretax funds for eligible medical expenses and wellness-related costs.
  C. FSAs are limited to covering wellness program participation fees and cannot be used for medical expenses.
  D. FSAs provide employees with a fixed monthly wellness stipend, separate from their medical expenses.

60. What is the primary difference between an FSA and an HSA?

  A. FSAs have higher annual contribution limits than HSAs.
  B. Only individuals with high deductible health plans (HDHPs) can participate in FSAs.
  C. HSAs allow for rollover of unused funds from year to year, while FSAs typically follow a "use it or lose it" rule.
  D. FSAs are owned by the individual, providing portability, whereas HSAs are typically owned by the employer.

61. What are domestic partner benefits in the workplace primarily designed to provide?
   A. Exclusive benefits for unmarried couples older than 65.
   B. Benefits for employees' extended family members, such as parents and siblings.
   C. Coverage for employees' cohabitating partners who are not legally married.
   D. Additional benefits for employees who are legally married.

62. Which type of group incentive plan in the workplace often involves setting specific performance targets and rewards employees when those targets are met?
   A. Gainsharing plan.
   B. Team-based bonus plan.
   C. Employee stock ownership plan.
   D. Peer recognition program.

63. What is a key characteristic of an employee stock ownership plan as a group incentive plan in the workplace?
   A. Employees receive cash bonuses based on team achievements.
   B. Employees have the option to purchase company stock.
   C. Rewards are distributed equally among all employees.
   D. Participation is restricted to high-performing individuals.

64. What is an effective method for communicating information about an employer's compensation programs to employees?
   A. Sharing all details through a single email announcement.
   B. Conducting in-person group meetings with employees.
   C. Posting information in an obscure section of the company's website.
   D. Sending confidential compensation reports to individual employees.

65. What is a potential advantage of a defined contribution plan compared to a defined benefit plan?
   A. Predictable retirement income.
   B. Employer assumes all investment risk.
   C. Flexibility for employees to manage investments.
   D. Guaranteed lifetime payments for retirees.

Key Concept Research Questions

Taking a deeper dive into key concepts helps to create context and the information necessary to think through the questions on exam day critically. Doing the following research will make you more knowledgeable in your work:

1. What should small employers (fewer than 50 employees) do to comply with the Patient Protection and Affordable Care Act if they do not offer health insurance to their employees? Hint: Check out `www.healthcare.gov` and search for "exploring coverage options for small businesses." Alternatively, you can run a general Internet search for "qualified small employer health reimbursement arrangement."
2. What are the four main categories of incentive-based wellness programs covered under the Affordable Care Act? Hint: Find the final ruling in the federal register at `www.federalregister.gov`. Search for the rule titled "Incentives for Nondiscriminatory Wellness Programs in Group Health Plans."

Test Your Total Rewards Terminology Knowledge

The following are the terms to use to test your knowledge on Total Rewards key terms. The correct answers are found in Appendix B.

- Additional leave
- Base salary
- Compensation philosophy
- Disability income
- Education assistance
- Employee assistance program
- Flextime
- Healthcare reimbursement account
- Incentive compensation
- Job classification
- Job evaluation
- Longevity bonus
- Merit increase
- Noncash compensation
- Performance bonus
- Perks
- Salary range
- Stock purchase plan
- Total rewards
- Wellness program

1. ______________ is the combination of all the tools, programs, and benefits provided to employees in exchange for their work.
2. ______________ is a financial incentive program that rewards employees for meeting or exceeding performance goals.

3. ______________ is the amount of money an employee earns, typically in the form of a regular paycheck.
4. ______________ is the practice of providing employees with time off beyond their regular paid time off.
5. ______________ is a program that allows employees to purchase equity ownership in the company at a discounted price.
6. ______________ is the portion of an employee's compensation that is nonmonetary.
7. ______________ is a type of benefit that offers employees the opportunity to continue their education.
8. ______________ is a program that provides employees with alternative work hours or locations.
9. ______________ is the process of determining the value of a job within an organization.
10. ______________ is a type of insurance that provides employees with income replacement in case of an off-the-job injury often provided through additional benefits or governments.
11. ______________ is a benefit that reimburses employees for eligible healthcare expenses.
12. ______________ is a company's overarching principles and beliefs that guide how it compensates employees, including factors like market competitiveness, pay for performance, and internal equity.
13. The minimum and maximum allowable pay for a specific job or role within an organization, which helps establish a framework for compensation decisions, is called the ______________.
14. A component of compensation that rewards employees based on their performance, often in the form of bonuses, commissions, or profit-sharing plans, is known as ______________.
15. A ______________ is a pay adjustment or raise given to an employee based on their individual performance, contributions, and achievements within the organization.
16. ______________ is the process of categorizing jobs within an organization into specific groups or grades based on factors like responsibilities, skill levels, and job requirements, which can influence pay scales and structures.
17. ______________ is a benefit that offers employees access to mental health and counseling services.
18. ______________ is a financial incentive program that rewards employees for their loyalty and tenure with the organization.
19. ______________ is a benefit that provides employees with access to physical and mental health programs.
20. __________ refer to additional benefits or advantages offered to employees beyond their regular compensation.

Conclusion

The concept of Total Rewards encompasses various critical aspects of human resource management. Compensation and benefits include traditional salary and benefits packages, such as base pay, bonuses, health insurance, retirement plans, and the regulatory landscape that governs these practices. Beyond this baseline, however, is the opportunity that Total Rewards packages present to employers to influence key business outcomes. This is done in several ways. Recognition and rewards play a crucial role in employee engagement by appreciating their contributions. Special compensation considerations, such as executive pay, global pay practices, and domestic worker remuneration, and promoting work-life balance through flexible arrangements and other engagement strategies not only boost satisfaction but also enhance employee well-being.

The importance of these outcomes is reflected throughout SHRM and HRCI exam content. For the CP and SCP exams, Total Rewards benchmarks make up part of the 18% domain of "People." On the HRCI exams, this functional area will account for 15% of the PHR and PHRi exams. In the 2024 updates, Total Rewards jumped from 12% on the SPHR/SPHRi exams to 17%, implying that senior HR professionals will need to understand the strategic impact of these programs.

Having a complete understanding of these Total Rewards topics will also inform other functional areas of HR including job design, staffing, and employee engagement, not to mention the complex arena of compliance with wage and hour laws.

As you prepare for your HR exam, keep in mind that Total Rewards is not a one-size-fits-all concept; it must be tailored to the unique needs and preferences of both the organization and its employees. Both federal and state laws impact how programs are administered, although the exams will test you on your federal knowledge only.

Additional Resources

These online resources offer a combination of articles, research, best practices, and trends that can help you gain a deeper understanding of Total Rewards in the workplace reports. Depending on your specific interests and needs, you can explore these resources for more reading, listening, or watching videos to mix up your preparation activities and embed new knowledge for future application on exam day and in the workplace.

Websites

- World at Work (`www.worldatwork.org`)

  World at Work is a leading professional association focused on Total Rewards, compensation, and benefits. Their website offers valuable research reports, articles, webinars, and tools related to Total Rewards strategies and practices. While there are paywalls for premium content, free guides and reports are also available.

- Mercer (`www.mercer.com`)

  Mercer is a global consulting firm specializing in HR and Total Rewards. Their website offers research, articles, and reports on various compensation and benefits topics, helping you understand trends and best practices.

- Aon (`www.aon.com`)

  Aon's website provides insights into employee benefits, compensation, and Total Rewards strategies. You can access research papers, webinars, and tools to help you design and optimize Total Rewards programs by navigating to their "Insights" page.

- Gallagher (`www.ajg.com`)

  Gallagher's resources include articles, surveys, and reports on employee benefits, compensation, and Total Rewards. Their insights can help you navigate the complexities of reward programs in the workplace.

Podcasts

- *Paying for Good* with host Corinne Carr

  Based in the UK, this podcast provides insights into compensation, recognition, and benefits strategies through interviews with industry professionals.

- *Comp + Coffee* with various hosts

  Comp + Coffee by PayScale is a podcast dedicated to compensation professionals. It explores various aspects of compensation and Total Rewards, providing practical insights and tips.

- *The Executive Compensation Podcast* with various hosts

  This podcast, produced by Meridian Compensation Partners, focuses on executive compensation strategies for compensation committees and other compensation professionals. It features conversations with experts in the field.

YouTube Channels

YouTube is a valuable platform for accessing informative content on Total Rewards, especially if you prefer to learn by video. Log in to YouTube at `www.youtube.com` and search for the following channels to find insights, tips, and discussions related to Total Rewards:

- World at Work TV World at Work

  This leading organization in the field of Total Rewards has a YouTube channel where they share videos on various compensation and benefits topics. You can find interviews with experts, conference highlights, and educational content.

- Willis Towers Watson (WTW)

  WTW, a global HR consulting firm, provides insights into compensation, benefits, and Total Rewards on their YouTube channel. They share videos on trends, research findings, and best practices in HR.

- Aon Aon's YouTube channel

  This channel covers a range of HR and compensation-related topics, offering insights into Total Rewards strategies, benefits management, and employee engagement.

Chapter 7

Risk Management

It is not an exaggeration to say that the word of the year in the function of risk management is *polycrisis*. Polycrisis is described by the World Economic Forum (WEF) as a risk that includes known and unknown risks such as artificial intelligence, pandemics, an uncertain economy, and more. One must only have been an HR practitioner in the last several years to have firsthand experience of the multitude of risks that must be managed in the modern workplace. The range of threats must be addressed is highly diverse (employee safety, customer data privacy, supply chain disruptions), demanding a comprehensive and forward-thinking approach to risk management.

Enterprise risk management (ERM) represents a fundamental shift in how organizations perceive, assess, and mitigate risks that impact their organizations. Historically, risk management primarily focused on employee health and safety (EHS) and operational and financial risks, such as business continuity planning and theft. The contemporary business environment demands a broader and more holistic perspective. Additionally, in today's interconnected world, technology plays a central role in the evolution of ERM. It not only introduces new risks but also offers innovative tools and concepts to address them effectively. This chapter delves into the dynamic landscape of ERM concepts, which include the following:

- **Employee health and safety:** Employee health, safety, and wellness encompass the practices and measures put in place by employers to protect their workers from workplace hazards, accidents, and illnesses, promoting employee physical and mental wellness.
- **Emergency planning:** Emergency planning involves developing and implementing strategies and protocols to respond to unexpected crises and disasters effectively.
- **Regulatory compliance:** Regulatory compliance refers to the adherence to laws, regulations, and ERM industry standards such as OSHA and whistleblowing protection, ensuring that organizations operate within legal and ethical boundaries.
- **Data analytics:** By analyzing vast datasets, ERM can now provide more accurate risk assessments, anticipate emerging threats, and optimize mitigation strategies.
- **Cybersecurity:** Cybersecurity has risen to prominence as a paramount tech-driven concept in ERM. Threats such as data breaches and cyberattacks can jeopardize not only sensitive customer information but also the safety and well-being of employees and the integrity of products.

Real World Scenario

Behind the Scenes of Risk: Exploring "Billions" for Lessons in Ethical Leadership and HR

This case study delves into the dynamics of risk management as depicted in the fictional television show *Billions*. We will explore the intricate financial maneuvers, ethical dilemmas, and corporate challenges faced by the characters in the show. Additionally, we will examine the human resources (HR) issues that could have been addressed to maintain a cohesive and ethical organizational culture amid high-stakes financial dealings.

Background and Problem

Billions is a television series available on streaming services that revolves around the complex and intense world of finance, law, and power. The show primarily follows the rivalry between hedge fund manager Bobby Axelrod and U.S. Attorney Chuck Rhoades. Their confrontations involve high-stakes financial risks, legal battles, and ethical dilemmas.

Diagnosis

Risk management is at the core of the conflicts and challenges depicted in *Billions*. As characters make risky financial moves and engage in questionable ethical behavior; the organization's reputation, legal compliance, and employee morale are at stake. HR plays a critical role in addressing these issues, as does a main character who brings the psychology of performance coaching to mainstream television.

Strategies

The following are HR strategies used on the show.

Performance Coaching

Wendy Rhoades (loosely acting human resources) was a high-performance coach who served as an executive and team advisor. She focused on assisting the characters in developing mental toughness, maintaining focus, and managing stress, all of which are essential for making rational decisions in high-pressure situations. Wendy also helped the characters analyze intricate financial scenarios, assess potential risks, and select appropriate strategies. By making more informed and calculated decisions, the characters could reduce the likelihood of significant financial losses. Emotional control techniques were also taught to prevent emotional reactions from affecting judgment and causing risky behaviors.

Risk Modeling

Billions portrayed risk models as crucial tools within the world of high finance. Quantitative analysis was used to analyze historical data, market trends, and other financial indicators. These models aimed to predict potential outcomes and assess the probability of success or failure for different investment strategies. In season 6, the CEO gifted employees with health monitoring rings, failing to tell them that the rings tracked and transmitted their health for company monitoring, ostensibly to inform wellness programs. The employees rebelled, and this effort highlighted how using technology to protect assets often creates moral dilemmas.

Whistleblowing

Whistleblowing in *Billions* served as a central plot element that underscored the moral and ethical complexities of the financial world. Wendy's internal struggle and the potential consequences of her decision to expose illicit activities at her place of work to her U.S. Attorney husband contributed to the show's exploration of power, ethics, and the blurred lines between right and wrong. Her main fear—that of retaliation—echoes the very real concerns of whistleblowers in real life, one that labor law seeks to address.

Compliance Oversight

In response to a court order and other legal maneuvering, Axe Capital is forced to place a compliance officer on the payroll, through which trades area is supposed to be approved. The show highlights the challenges to the approval process and the moral justifications of behavior that are behind the success of many of the high performers.

Results

The strategies outlined here yielded both positive and negative outcomes for Axe Capital and the U.S. Attorney's office. Some legal battles were avoided, and reputational damage was mitigated, reflecting the effectiveness of these efforts. However, the persistent tension between personal ambition and ethical responsibility remained a central theme. Several characters still faced indictments, and ultimately, the company was acquired by a competitor renowned for its sustainable and ethical investment behavior.

Conclusion

There are several avenues of risk that a modern-day HR professional must navigate. They include those portrayed by this fictional television show, such as performance coaching, risk modeling, whistleblowing, ethics, and navigating the regulatory environment. ERM is, of course, more than just these items, and while fictional examples serve to highlight a few extreme examples, one need only look at the headlines to see the real-world impact of effective ERM practices.

Risk Management Practice Questions

1. Bluth Industries wants to calculate its debt-to-equity ratio (D/E ratio) as a key risk indicator (KRI) to assess its financial risk. The company's total debt is $2,000,000, and its total shareholders' equity is $4,000,000. Calculate the debt-to-equity ratio.

   A. 0.25.

   B. 0.5.

   C. 1.0.

   D. 2.0.

2. Which of the following is a key component of an effective enterprise risk management framework?

   A. Prioritizing low-impact risks.

   B. Reactive risk management.

   C. Stakeholder engagement.

   D. Overreliance on insurance.

3. In a workplace risk assessment, what does "risk probability" primarily measure?

   A. The potential consequences of a risk event.

   B. The likelihood or chance of a risk event occurring.

   C. The severity of past workplace incidents.

   D. The costs associated with risk mitigation measures.

4. What are the primary differences between SLE and ALE?

   A. SLE represents the expected loss from a single security incident, while ALE calculates the total losses over a year from all security incidents combined.

   B. SLE is used for assessing long-term risks, while ALE is employed for short-term risk evaluations.

   C. SLE measures financial losses, while ALE assesses non-financial losses such as reputation damage.

   D. SLE provides a probabilistic assessment, while ALE offers a deterministic assessment of losses.

5. You are the safety manager at Berzatto Corp., a large manufacturer of industrial restaurant equipment. The company is planning to introduce a new piece of heavy machinery to the production line. There are potential safety risks associated with the operation of this machinery. You need to assess these risks and prioritize them for mitigation. What tool would be most appropriate for evaluating and prioritizing these safety risks?

   A. A bar chart displaying the historical accident data.

   B. A risk matrix.

   C. A written report summarizing safety concerns.

   D. An employee survey on safety perceptions.

6. Which of the following is NOT a key characteristic of lobbying as a form of risk management for businesses?
   A. Shaping laws and regulations to align with business interests.
   B. Gaining access to early information on potential policy changes.
   C. Reducing reputational risks through public relations efforts.
   D. Focusing on short-term financial gains.

7. In the workplace, what type of moral hazard is characterized by employees taking undue risks due to the allure of immediate financial incentives, potentially disregarding the organization's long-term interests?
   A. Ethical hazard.
   B. Social loafing.
   C. Job security moral hazard.
   D. Supply chain moral hazard.

8. Which of the following actions best exemplifies a proactive approach to risk management in the workplace?
   A. Waiting for an incident to occur before taking any preventive measures.
   B. Conducting regular safety audits and inspections to identify potential hazards.
   C. Assigning blame to individuals responsible for accidents after they happen.
   D. Ignoring safety guidelines and hoping that luck will prevent accidents.

9. Which risk category best characterizes a scenario where a company is embarking on a groundbreaking project involving cutting-edge technology with limited industry precedents while they are grappling with the inherent uncertainties and potential challenges of this endeavor?
   A. Foreseeable risk.
   B. Inherent risk.
   C. Unforeseeable risk.
   D. Emergent risk.

10. According to CDC recommendations for employers during a pandemic, what steps should employers take to promote infection control among their workers?
    A. Offer employees unlimited sick leave to reduce workplace contagions.
    B. Provide workers with PPE such as gloves, face shields, and respirators.
    C. Shut down business operations for a minimum of two weeks during cold and flu season.
    D. Provide worker training on infection controls and access to essential supplies.

11. In strategic risk management, which type of analysis is most suitable for assessing the potential impact of geopolitical events on a multinational corporation's operations?
    A. Sensitivity analysis.
    B. SWOT analysis.
    C. Monte Carlo simulation.
    D. PESTLE analysis.

12. How can human resource leadership best prepare for outlier events that are difficult to predict but have a major impact on the organization?

A. Developing contingency plans and scenarios for various disruptive events to assess their potential impact on the workforce and business operations.

B. Identifying skillsets that can be adapted to different roles within the organization to maintain workforce flexibility.

C. Collaborating with other departments such as legal, finance, and operations to create a comprehensive response strategy that addresses HR-related issues.

D. Implementing programs to support employees' mental health and well-being during turbulent times.

13. What is the role of technology in ERM?

A. Data collection and analysis.

B. Vendor risk management.

C. Business continuity and disaster recovery.

D. Legal compliance.

14. How can correlation analysis be valuable in risk management?

A. To identify causation between risk factors.

B. To estimate the absolute probability of a specific risk event.

C. To assess the degree of association between two variables.

D. To predict the exact timing of a risk occurrence.

15. At work one busy Friday morning, right before the holiday weekend, when the operations will be closed for four days, the ERM system triggers an automated alert. The alert indicates a significant increase in machine downtime, surpassing the predefined threshold. The ERM team receives the alert simultaneously on their mobile devices and computers. They quickly access the system to gather more information. Which action should the ERM team take next?

A. The ERM team decides to ignore the alert, as the line is already scheduled to be down for the holiday.

B. The ERM team initiates a discussion with the maintenance department to investigate the cause of the increased machine downtime.

C. The ERM team escalates the alert to the executive team for further direction.

D. The ERM team turns off the automated alert system to avoid unnecessary notifications.

16. As the HR manager at your organization, it has just been brought to your attention that a certain chemical used in your production process poses a serious health risk to your employees, including severe allergic reaction and breathing trouble. What should you recommend as their HR advisor?
    - **A.** Immediately stopping the use of the chemical to protect employee health, until additional information is received.
    - **B.** Continue using the chemical to maintain current production levels, prioritizing short-term financial gains over employee health.
    - **C.** Conduct a detailed investigation to determine the financial impact of both options and make a decision based on the results.
    - **D.** Seek input from employees and follow their majority preference, regardless of the financial implications.
17. What is the primary role of HR business partners in enterprise risk management?
    - **A.** Conducting financial audits and risk assessments.
    - **B.** Developing cybersecurity protocols and strategies.
    - **C.** Identifying and mitigating human capital-related risks.
    - **D.** Managing supplier relationships and supply chain risks.
18. While expanding into a new market, a multinational corporation conducts a thorough assessment of potential risks and uncertainties, including market volatility and regulatory changes. This exemplifies which risk management principle from ISO 31000:2018?
    - **A.** The company prioritizes financial performance over risk mitigation.
    - **B.** The company relies on historical data alone to identify risks.
    - **C.** The company adopts a proactive and systematic approach to risk management, focusing on the identification and assessment of risks.
    - **D.** The company exclusively addresses risks related to product quality and safety.
19. What is a common barrier to effective risk management within organizations?
    - **A.** Excessive financial investments in risk management practices.
    - **B.** A culture that discourages open communication about risks.
    - **C.** An overreliance on external consultants for risk assessments.
    - **D.** A clear and well-documented risk management strategy.
20. What is the first step in the process of developing a business continuity plan (BCP) for a workplace?
    - **A.** Conducting a risk assessment.
    - **B.** Writing the plan document.
    - **C.** Assembling the crisis management team.
    - **D.** Communicating the plan to employees.

21. What is a key element to include in an emergency action plan (EAP) for a workplace?
   A. Emergency personnel recommendations.
   B. Employee contact information.
   C. Marketing strategies.
   D. Vendor contracts.

22. In the context of management barriers to effective risk management techniques, which HR competency is particularly important for navigating a political organization and overcoming resistance to risk management initiatives?
   A. Technical proficiency in data analysis and risk assessment.
   B. Proficiency in legal compliance and regulatory knowledge.
   C. Interpersonal skills and stakeholder engagement.
   D. Strategic planning and financial acumen.

23. What is an important best practice for employers to protect employees from workplace violence related to customer interactions?
   A. Encouraging employees to engage in physical altercations to protect themselves as necessary.
   B. Providing customer service training with an emphasis on de-escalation.
   C. Discouraging employees from interacting with angry customers.
   D. Implementing strict access controls for customers.

24. A software development company is concerned about the potential for data breaches, cyberattacks, and the major cost associated with recovery should a large-scale event occur. They want to protect their sensitive information and customer data. What risk management technique should they consider?
   A. Creating a disaster recovery plan.
   B. Purchasing cybersecurity insurance.
   C. Ignoring the risk and focusing on development.
   D. Outsourcing all IT functions.

25. How can employers use generally acceptable accounting principles (GAAP) to prevent employee theft?
   A. By implementing strict internal controls and segregation of duties.
   B. By offering higher salaries to employees to deter theft.
   C. By conducting surprise searches of employees' personal belongings.
   D. By providing financial incentives for employees who report theft.

26. A multinational energy company operates drilling rigs in politically unstable regions with a history of civil unrest. Employees working in these areas face specific risks, such as potential kidnapping, political violence, and supply chain disruptions. What is the most appropriate risk response for the company in this scenario?

A. Offering hazard pay to employees as a financial incentive.

B. Providing comprehensive security training and measures for employees.

C. Ignoring the risks due to the profitability of the drilling operations.

D. Relocating the drilling operations to a safer region.

27. What advice should the HR manager provide to senior leadership regarding the key benefits to emphasize in a business case for conducting workplace audits, including the associated costs, time investment, and support required from other managers?

A. Increased operational efficiency.

B. Enhanced employee privacy.

C. Reduced need for insurance.

D. Lower employee turnover.

28. Which of the following is a primary goal of Occupational Safety and Health Administration (OSHA) standards in the workplace?

A. Increasing workplace competition.

B. Minimizing workplace accidents and injuries.

C. Maximizing employee overtime hours.

D. Reducing employee benefits.

29. Which of the following is a key aspect of OSHA standards for hazardous chemicals in the workplace?

A. Keeping proprietary chemical information confidential.

B. Providing employees with access to safety data sheets (SDS).

C. Encouraging employees to handle hazardous chemicals without training.

D. Avoiding the labeling of chemical containers.

30. A manufacturing company is undergoing an OSHA inspection. During the inspection, the inspector observes that multiple machines lack the required safety guards. There are 10 machines in total, each missing the necessary guards. What type of OSHA violation is the manufacturing company most likely facing based on the OSHA memorandum regarding "instance by instance" (IBI) violations?

A. A single violation for machine guarding.

B. 10 separate violations for machine guarding.

C. Willful violation for machine guarding.

D. 10 repeat violations for machine guarding.

31. In fiscal year 2023, OSHA issued more than 7,000 violations of fall protection standards, making fall protection the most violated OSHA standard for the 13th consecutive year. As part of prevention efforts, a major U.S. university and OSHA have entered into a partnership agreement to prioritize worker safety and health at a construction site. Fall hazards and prevention are among the key focus areas for this partnership. What role will OSHA play as a partner in this agreement?

A. Conduct safety and health training for all construction site employees.

B. Audit monthly reports and make recommendations to reach safety goals.

C. Provide priority consideration to small contractors working on the construction site.

D. Appoint a representative to the project safety committee.

32. One Monday morning at Newport Financial Services, the AI-powered fraud detection system generates an alert related to an employee who works in the company's financial compliance department. The alert indicated that they accessed the financial transaction database outside of normal working hours and communicated via email with an external address that is not on the approved list for compliance-related discussions. What type of anomaly did the AI detect?

A. Baseline.

B. Compliance.

C. Behavioral.

D. Fraudulent.

33. Why is it important for HR to actively participate in the oversight of risk management in an organization?

A. To minimize HR department workload.

B. To ensure the exclusivity of risk management.

C. To align risk management with talent management and organizational goals.

D. To bypass the need for risk assessments.

34. HR is responsible for managing risks associated with compliance, operations, human capital, finances, and business strategy, just to name a few. Which of the following is an example of strategic risk that HR plays a key role in mitigating?

A. Cybersecurity attacks from employee negligence.

B. Supply chain disruptions.

C. Employee turnover and talent retention.

D. Changes in tax regulations affecting executive compensation.

35. A technology company employs remote workers who access company data from various locations. The company is concerned about unauthorized access and data breaches. What role will HR teams play in implementing cybersecurity measures to mitigate the risks?

A. HR teams will actively monitor and investigate potential cybersecurity threats.

B. HR teams will develop and implement cybersecurity policies and procedures.

C. HR teams will provide technical support to remote workers for cybersecurity tools.

D. HR teams will conduct regular cybersecurity training sessions for remote workers.

36. A healthcare organization manages electronic health records (EHRs) for its patients. What role will HR teams play in implementing cybersecurity measures to safeguard patient confidentiality and comply with data protection regulations in the healthcare organization?
    - **A.** HR teams will be responsible for managing and configuring encryption tools for EHRs.
    - **B.** HR teams will monitor patient data access logs for security breaches.
    - **C.** HR teams will ensure that employees receive training on data protection regulations.
    - **D.** HR teams will conduct vulnerability assessments on the organization's EHR systems.

37. An HR professional who is also part of the safety team has just been informed that an employee may have been exposed to a dangerous chemical in the workplace and has passed out on the floor. Which of the following actions should she take first?
    - **A.** Take preventive action.
    - **B.** Contain the exposure.
    - **C.** Secure immediate medical attention.
    - **D.** Contact the company insurance.

38. In a technology company, a disengaged employee named George begins accessing and copying sensitive company files, source code, and confidential information, intending to share it with a competitor who has recently offered him an executive leadership position. What type of threat does George's actions pose to the company?
    - **A.** Insider threat.
    - **B.** Phishing attack threat.
    - **C.** Copyright infringement.
    - **D.** Cybersecurity threat.

39. A manufacturing company operates a facility where employees work with heavy machinery. One day, an employee sustains a serious injury while operating a machine, resulting in a reportable injury under OSHA regulations. When does the 8- and 24-hour clock for reporting the injury to OSHA begin?
    - **A.** When the injured employee arrives at the hospital.
    - **B.** When the supervisor on duty at the time of the incident knows about the injury.
    - **C.** If the injury results in a fatality.
    - **D.** When/if the hospital confirms it is a reportable injury.

40. What is a key component of an effective crisis management plan that helps guide actions during a crisis?
    - **A.** Assigning fault to individuals responsible for the crisis.
    - **B.** Conducting an in-depth analysis of historical data.
    - **C.** Establishing clear roles and responsibilities for crisis response.
    - **D.** Avoiding communication with employees and stakeholders.

41. At a large office building, the management conducts regular fire and emergency drills to ensure the safety of employees. However, during the latest drill, many employees appeared disinterested and did not take the exercise seriously. Some continued working at their desks or chatted with colleagues, while others simply ignored the alarms and announcements. What strategies can HR employ to increase the effectiveness of safety training and ensure employees are better prepared for emergencies?

A. Implement gamified training modules that make safety training more engaging and interactive.

B. Discipline employees who do not actively participate in emergency drills to instill a sense of responsibility.

C. Reduce the frequency of emergency drills to avoid desensitizing employees to safety procedures.

D. Remove responsibilities to free up time for employees to participate in drills.

42. Lindsay, a construction worker, benefits from workers' compensation after injuring her leg on the job, covering medical expenses and providing temporary disability benefits. Tobias, an office manager at the same company with a non-work-related medical condition, relies on disability insurance for income replacement during his recovery. What is the primary difference between workers' compensation and disability insurance?

A. Workers' compensation covers only medical expenses, while disability insurance provides income replacement.

B. Workers' compensation is available to all employees, while disability insurance is accessible only to managers.

C. Workers' compensation is limited to work-related injuries, while disability insurance covers all types of disabilities.

D. Workers' compensation offers higher benefit amounts than disability insurance.

43. If an employee is injured at work and qualifies for workers' compensation benefits, what does the "exclusive remedy" principle mean?

A. Employees are allowed to sue their employer in private courts for additional damages.

B. The injured employee can choose to receive medical treatment from any healthcare provider.

C. The injured employee can opt out of workers' compensation and seek private insurance.

D. Workers' compensation is the only path for damages available to the injured employee.

44. An employee has reported experiencing workplace harassment and has formally filed a complaint with the HR department. What should be the first step in conducting a workplace investigation in response to this complaint?

A. Immediately terminate the alleged harasser to prevent further issues.

B. Begin interviewing witnesses and collecting evidence.

C. Contact the complainant and request additional information.

D. Conduct a preliminary meeting with HR and the alleged harasser.

45. An employer has received an anonymous tip alleging fraudulent activities within the finance department. The employer decides to initiate an internal investigation to determine the validity of the claim. What is a critical consideration in this scenario?

- **A.** Sharing the anonymous tip with all employees to gather more information.
- **B.** Notifying the finance department immediately to prevent any potential misconduct.
- **C.** Ensuring the investigation is conducted confidentially and discreetly.
- **D.** Ignoring the tip until concrete evidence of fraud is found.

46. In a corporate office, tensions have been rising among employees due to increased workloads and tight deadlines. Recently, there have been instances of verbal disputes and heated arguments, raising concerns about the potential for workplace violence. The HR department recognizes the need to address this issue and protect the well-being of employees. What strategies can HR implement to mitigate the risk of workplace violence and ensure the safety of workers in this scenario?

- **A.** Provide conflict resolution training and encourage open communication among employees.
- **B.** Install security cameras throughout the office to monitor employee interactions.
- **C.** Restrict employee access to common areas to minimize interactions.
- **D.** Implement strict disciplinary measures and penalties for employees involved in disputes.

47. At a real estate conference being held in a busy downtown area, attendees are required to wear a purple wristband for admission. At one point in the evening, a 65-year-old conference attendee with a significant medical history begins to feel chest pain. He drives himself to the local hospital and awaits care in triage. It is 7 p.m. on a Friday night, and a shift change has just occurred. Moments later, the patient stops breathing. The nurse who just began her shift rushes to the patient's side and notices a purple wristband. Mistaking it for a Do Not Resuscitate (DNR) band, she doesn't call the code, and the patient passes away. After the initial investigation, the HR and risk management teams are tasked with designing a preventative solution so this situation does not happen again. What should HR recommend to improve patient safety in the emergency department (ED)?

- **A.** Increase nurse training on wristband recognition to prevent similar errors in the future.
- **B.** Implement a policy where all patients must remove wristbands before entering the ED.
- **C.** Introduce a system where front-desk employees are responsible for providing the appropriate wristbands and checking for any patient-worn bands.
- **D.** Encourage healthcare providers to double-check wristband information before administering care.

48. How should HR teams address substance abuse in the workplace effectively?

- **A.** Randomly conduct drug tests on all employees to deter substance use.
- **B.** Implement a comprehensive substance abuse policy that includes testing, prevention, education, and support.
- **C.** Fire employees immediately upon discovering any evidence of substance abuse.
- **D.** Ignore the issue unless it directly affects job performance.

49. A company has a drug testing policy in place, and as part of routine screening, an employee's drug test comes up positive for a controlled substance. The employee has been a long-standing, reliable team member with no prior issues. What is the appropriate procedure for HR to follow when an employee's drug screen comes up positive for a controlled substance?

A. Immediately terminate the employee's employment due to the positive drug test result.

B. Conduct a confirmatory test to validate the initial positive result and offer the employee an opportunity to explain the result.

C. Inform the employee's immediate supervisor and colleagues about the positive result to ensure workplace transparency.

D. Place the employee on probation without further investigation due to their prior reliability.

50. Balboa Corporation, a global manufacturing company of educational kitchen equipment, has been experiencing a series of workplace accidents at its manufacturing facilities in different regions. These accidents have resulted in injuries to employees and damage to equipment, leading to increased insurance costs and a decline in overall safety morale. The company's leadership is concerned about the rising risks associated with workplace safety and the potential impact on the organization's reputation and financial stability. What is the most appropriate action for the HR leader to take to demonstrate their Consultation competency in risk management?

A. Implement immediate disciplinary actions against employees involved in accidents to set an example.

B. Conduct a thorough analysis of the workplace safety incidents, gather input from relevant stakeholders, and collaborate with the executive team to develop a comprehensive risk management plan.

C. Delegate the responsibility of addressing workplace safety concerns to the respective facility managers for regional consideration and response.

D. Recommend outsourcing risk management responsibilities to a third-party consultant to handle the situation.

51. A global software development company recently experienced a critical security breach that exposed sensitive customer data. The incident raised concerns about the company's cybersecurity practices and the potential impact on its reputation and financial stability. The CEO wants to improve the company's risk management processes to prevent future security breaches. Which risk management technique can the company effectively employ to assess the security breach incident and identify areas for improvement?

A. Conducting an annual cybersecurity training for all employees.

B. Implementing a new security software.

C. Conducting an after-action review (AAR) to evaluate the incident response and identify lessons learned.

D. Increasing the marketing and public relations budget to manage the incident's fallout.

52. Lucille is an employee at a large pharmaceutical company. Over the past few months, she has noticed some unethical practices within the company's research and development department. Specifically, she has observed data manipulation in clinical trial reports that could potentially lead to the release of a new drug without adequate safety testing. Lucille is deeply concerned about the potential risks to public health and safety. She overcomes her initial fears, decides to report these concerns, and preserves the evidence necessary to prove her claims. As an added precaution, she contacts her brother-in-law (who is an attorney) and retains his services. What protections is Lucille likely to have under whistleblowing laws?

   A. Lucille is only protected if she reports the concerns externally to regulatory agencies.

   B. Lucille is not protected because she did not immediately report the concerns to regulatory authorities.

   C. Lucille is protected as a whistleblower because she reported the concerns internally, retained evidence, and sought legal counsel.

   D. Lucille is protected as a whistleblower only if the unethical practices are proven to be true.

53. What does physical asset risk management primarily involve?

   A. Protecting digital data and information.

   B. Managing financial investments and portfolios.

   C. Identifying and mitigating threats to tangible resources like equipment and infrastructure.

   D. Ensuring employee safety through training and development.

54. Mae, an employee at a large corporation, confides in her HR department about her concerns regarding potential violence from her abusive partner, who knows where she works. In light of Mae's situation, what HR strategy can best address the risk of workplace violence resulting from intimate partner abuse and ensure the safety and well-being of employees in similar circumstances?

   A. Advise Mae to handle the situation privately without involving the workplace.

   B. Provide training to employees and managers on recognizing signs of intimate partner abuse and reporting concerns.

   C. Focus solely on Mae's work-related matters.

   D. Implement stricter security measures to prevent outside individuals from entering the workplace.

55. In a medium-sized tech company, several employees have recently reported incidents of workplace harassment. The reports include instances of offensive comments, derogatory jokes, and unwanted advances. These incidents have created an uncomfortable and hostile work environment, causing concern among employees and affecting overall morale. What is an effective employer best practice to address workplace harassment and manage the associated risks in this scenario?

A. Ignore the reports unless formal complaints are filed to avoid unnecessary drama in the workplace.

B. Conduct a thorough investigation into each reported incident, provide support to victims, and take appropriate disciplinary actions against perpetrators.

C. Ask employees to handle the issue among themselves without involving HR or management.

D. Organize a company-wide diversity and inclusion training session without addressing the specific incidents reported.

56. A small tech startup has identified a potential security vulnerability in their new mobile app, which could lead to data breaches and customer privacy concerns if not addressed. The startup's management team is discussing how to handle this risk. Which risk management strategy should the startup consider for addressing the security vulnerability in their mobile app?

A. Avoidance.

B. Acceptance.

C. Transfer.

D. Mitigate.

57. A small construction company is operating on a tight budget and has identified a potential physical workplace hazard involving using older but still functional, scaffolding equipment. While the equipment meets safety standards, there is a slightly higher risk compared to newer scaffolding systems. The construction company's management team is discussing how to handle this risk. Which risk management strategy should the construction company consider to address the potential hazard associated with the older scaffolding equipment?

A. Avoidance.

B. Acceptance.

C. Transfer.

D. Mitigate.

58. What is a potential risk of using ChatGPT in the workplace?

A. Increased likelihood of social engineering scams.

B. Decreased creativity as employees rely too heavily on AI-generated suggestions.

C. Increased likelihood of copywrite infringement.

D. Increased cost of doing business.

59. How can an employer prevent an active shooter situation in the workplace? (Select all that apply.)

- **A.** Establishing a no solicitation policy in the workplace.
- **B.** Partnering with local law enforcement to provide active shooter training for employees.
- **C.** Restricting access to the workplace by implementing keycard entry systems.
- **D.** Racial profiling employees for signs of violence.

60. Which of the following is the BEST example of corporate espionage?

- **A.** Insider trading.
- **B.** Whistleblowing.
- **C.** Industrial spying.
- **D.** Patent violations.

Key Concept Research Questions

Taking a deeper dive into key concepts helps to create context and the information necessary to critically think through the questions on exam day. A key bonus is that this research should also make you more knowledgeable in your work, so making the time to answer the next two questions is worth it:

1. A major risk management responsibility for human resource teams is the prevention of substance abuse in the workplace. What are the key elements to creating and maintaining a drug-free workplace? Access `www.samhsa.gov` and search for "components of a drug-free workplace" to get started.
2. Business continuity plans are critical to prepare for any workplace disruption—planned or unplanned. What are the key elements that should be included in a business continuity plan? The site `www.ready.gov` offers several planning toolkits for use. If you're an auditory learner, check out FEMA's YouTube channel and search for the video *Ready .gov-Business Continuity Training Part 1: What is Business Continuity Planning* to help you get started (`www.youtube.com/watch?v=XscWmBuUXMU`).

Test Your Risk Management Terminology Knowledge

The following are the terms to use to test your knowledge on risk management key terms. The correct answers are found in Appendix B.

- After action review
- Enterprise risk management (ERM)
- Financial risk management
- Insider threat

- Natural disaster
- Risk acceptance
- Risk assessment
- Risk avoidance
- Risk identification
- Risk impact
- Risk mitigation
- Risk monitoring and control
- Risk scoring
- Risk tolerance
- Risk transfer
- Supply chain risk management

1. ______________ is the process of discovering and analyzing potential events or situations that could impact an organization's objectives.
2. ______________ is the level of risk that an organization is willing to accept in pursuit of its goals and objectives.
3. ______________ is the practice of sharing risk with a third party, typically through insurance or contractual agreements.
4. ______________ is a risk management strategy that involves taking actions to reduce the likelihood or impact of a risk.
5. ______________ is a measure of the potential harm or damage that a risk event could cause.
6. ______________ is a risk management technique that allows for inherent risk to be part of the business cycle.
7. ______________ is a structured approach to evaluating and improving an organization's risk management processes.
8. ______________ is the process of collecting data and responding to risk factors on an ongoing basis.
9. ______________ is a risk management approach that seeks to identify and address risks across all levels of an organization.
10. ______________ is the process of identifying and analyzing risks associated with an organization's raw material and other sourcing activities.
11. ______________ is a risk management approach that focuses on the impact and mitigation of risks such as embezzlement or fraud associated with accounting practices.
12. ______________ is a risk management method that involves eliminating activities or situations that could lead to potential risks.
13. ______________ are structured debriefing sessions to evaluate what went well and what went wrong and identify lessons learned for future improvement.
14. ______________ is a quantitative analysis technique that assigns numerical values to risks based on their impact and probability.
15. ______________ is a security risk posed by individuals within an organization who have access to sensitive information and may misuse it.
16. ______________ refers to extreme, unpredictable events such as earthquakes, hurricanes, or floods that can disrupt normal business operations.

Conclusion

In the ever-evolving landscape of modern business, organizations face a complex array of risks that constantly threaten their most valuable assets: people, products, and physical resources. These risks span a wide spectrum, from the menace of cybersecurity threats to the disruptive forces of supply chain breakdowns, underscoring the critical need for a comprehensive and forward-thinking approach to risk management.

The Risk Management content on the SHRM exams falls within the Workplace Knowledge domain, sharing 16% of exam weight with Managing a Global Workforce, Corporate Social Responsibility, and Employment Law. The SHRM exams focus on risk assessment, prioritization, and resource management.

As with other functional areas, Risk Management changed with the 2024 HRCI content updates. It does not have its own domain and rather is represented in all functional areas. For example, in Total Rewards, an HR professional would need to understand the risks associated with legally compliant compensation systems and ethical executive compensation programs. In global workforce management, HR must understand the risks associated with expatriate assignments and compliance with country-by-country legal environments. HRCI candidates should pay close attention to navigating risks within the new exam domain, HR Information Management (PHR/PHRi) and HR Information Management, Safety and Security (SPHR/SPHRi). These are likely to include risks associated with data privacy, cybersecurity, and artificial intelligence, to name a few.

Additional Resources

While all of the activities of a human resource business partner are important, only a few come close to the weight of the responsibility for employee health and safety. This aspect of risk management along with the protection of other organizational assets makes it well worth your time to explore new online resources. To learn more about ERM, consider the following websites, podcasts, and online videos.

Websites

- Risk Management Society (RIMS) (`www.rims.org`)

  RIMS is a leading professional organization dedicated to risk management. Their website offers a wealth of resources, including articles, webinars, whitepapers, and educational events focused on ERM practices and industry insights. Navigate to their site and then select "Resources" to access their blog with lots of relevant content.

- Enterprise Risk Management Initiative (erm.ncsu.edu)

  This initiative by North Carolina State University provides valuable resources and thought leadership on ERM. Their website "library" offers research reports, case studies, webinars, and educational materials to help individuals and organizations understand and implement ERM best practices.

- The Risk Management Association (www.rmahq.org)

  RMA focuses on risk management in the financial services industry. Their website offers resources, including publications, webinars, and events, which can be valuable for those interested in financial risk management and ERM.

Podcasts

- *RIMScast* with various hosts

  The official podcast of the Risk Management Society features interviews with risk management professionals, industry experts, and thought leaders. It covers a wide range of topics, including ERM, financial risk, cybersecurity, and compliance.

- *RiskWatch* with various hosts

  Learn about various types of enterprise risk management as well as featured topics on due diligence, fiduciary responsibilities, and transparency.

- *Ask the CIO* with host Jason Miller

  This podcast tackles the branch of enterprise risk management related to technology such as the cloud and data science.

- *Risk Commentary* with host Edward Robertson

  Focused on innovation in enterprise risk management processes, this podcast features topics such as defining and framing ERM and how to implement results-driven risk management programs.

YouTube Channels

Look for YouTube channels dedicated to enterprise risk management and global risk management to round out your study efforts. Log on to www.youtube.com and surf/subscribe the following channels:

- Institute of Risk Management (IRM)

  This globally recognized institute provides videos related to enterprise risk management theories, techniques, and tools. The channel also highlights significant research in international risk management practices.

- Deloitte US

  Deloitte Risk and Financial Advisory YouTube channel covers a wide range of topics, including managing the financial risks associated with business management. They often share insights from Deloitte professionals and experts in the field. Their website is also a great resource for additional study material.

- PwC US

  PwC's YouTube channel includes videos on risk management, compliance, and ERM. You can find discussions on current risk-related issues and insights from PwC experts.

- KPMG US

  KPMG's YouTube channel features videos related to risk and ERM. They offer insights into risk management strategies, regulatory compliance, and industry trends on using data analytics in ERM.

- Protiviti

  Protiviti is a global consulting firm that provides content on risk management, internal audits, and ERM practices. They share insights from Protiviti experts and thought leaders.

Chapter 8

Employee Engagement and Retention

Employee engagement refers to the degree of emotional, physical, and mental investment that employees have with their work, colleagues, and the organization as a whole. Headlines such as "Your Business Strategy Hinges on Engagement" (Gallup, 2024) and "The Turnover Tsunami Is Real" (SHRM, 2021) have digitally screamed at HR professionals for the last several years, showing just how important employee engagement and retention have become to the success and sustainability of any organization.

Highly engaged employees are not only more productive but also more likely to stay with their current employer, fostering a sense of loyalty and dedication. The company culture also has a significant impact on "boomerang" employees—those who leave the company for other work and then decide to come back. This creates an alum talent pool built upon a company culture around engagement. Employee retention focuses on the ability of an organization to keep its talented workforce intact, reducing turnover rates and preserving institutional knowledge. Combined, they form the basis for HR to perform high-value tasks for their teams. Key topics that you will be tested on in the exams include the following:

- **Enhancing employee participation and engagement:** Supporting the implementation and communication of organizational programs aimed at boosting employee participation and engagement, including surveys, focus groups, and welfare/wellness activities.
- **Job-attitude theories:** Examining job-attitude theories and basic principles that influence employee attitudes, behavior, and job satisfaction.
- **Job design principles:** Analyzing job-design principles and techniques that organizations can use to create meaningful and fulfilling work experiences for employees.
- **Employee lifecycle phases:** Understanding the different phases of the employee life cycle, from recruitment and onboarding to development, retention, and exit.
- **Employee retention:** Exploring concepts and best practices related to employee retention, focusing on strategies to retain top talent.
- **Engagement, retention, and turnover metrics:** Measuring and evaluating retention and turnover metrics to identify trends, issues, and opportunities for improvement.

The following sections will delve deeper into the concepts of engagement and retention. By understanding and implementing these principles effectively, organizations can create workplaces where employees feel valued, motivated, and committed to achieving both personal and organizational success.

Real World Scenario

Kaiser Permanente's Employee Engagement Strategies: A Focus on Well-Being

This case study explores the dynamics of employee engagement and retention within Kaiser Permanente, one of the world's largest healthcare providers. Kaiser Permanente's commitment to employee well-being and satisfaction plays a pivotal role in its ability to deliver high-quality healthcare services. Read on to learn about how the healthcare giant employed engagement and retention strategies through their human resource systems.

Background and Problem

Kaiser Permanente operates in a highly competitive healthcare industry, where employee engagement and retention are critical for delivering excellent patient care. The organization's approach to employee well-being encompasses several initiatives aimed at creating a supportive and inclusive work environment. To attract qualified talent—and keep them—the company knew it had to take an interventionist approach to understand and act upon the drivers of engagement. Conscious disruption within the interventionist approach involves purposefully challenging conventional practices or systems to foster innovation, adaptability, and positive change within an organization.

Diagnosis

To maintain a highly engaged and satisfied workforce, Kaiser Permanente needed to implement various HR strategies to address employee well-being, work-life balance, elite benefits, and support for disabled and veteran employees. This requires balancing the motivations and needs of a diverse talent pool. The company further knew that it needed these engagement and retention strategies to align with its values, including its commitment to diversity, equity, and inclusion (DEI).

Strategies

The following are several of the initiatives delivered through the company's HR programs:

Support for Work-Life Balance

Kaiser Permanente offers a range of work-life balance programs, including online nutrition courses, healthy eating options, team wellness tools, smoking cessation support, and flexible scheduling. HR plays a crucial role in promoting these initiatives, ensuring that employees have access to resources and support to maintain a healthy work-life balance.

Elite Benefits

HR at Kaiser Permanente ensures that employees receive competitive benefits, such as ample vacation time, holiday and sick leave, and comprehensive medical, vision, mental health, and dental coverage. These benefits are essential in attracting and retaining top talent in the healthcare industry.

Support for Disabled and Veteran Employees

HR actively supports disabled employees by offering accommodations and additional assistance. This commitment to inclusivity has resulted in Kaiser Permanente's recognition as a top company in DEI and as an employer for people with disabilities. The organization also provides dedicated support to veterans and their families, facilitating their transition into the workforce. HR's role is critical in implementing these support programs effectively.

Results

Kaiser Permanente's emphasis on employee engagement and retention has yielded positive results. The organization has consistently ranked among the top companies for DEI and continues to attract and retain a diverse and talented workforce. Employee satisfaction and well-being are reflected in the high-quality healthcare services provided by the organization.

Conclusion

Employee engagement and retention are paramount in the healthcare sector, and Kaiser Permanente's proactive approach to addressing HR issues has proven effective. By prioritizing work-life balance, competitive benefits, and supporting disabled and veteran employees, they have created an inclusive work environment that fosters employee engagement and increases the tenure of qualified workers.

Employee Engagement and Retention Practice Questions

1. Which of the following is the best definition of employee engagement?
   A. The number of hours an employee spends working each week.
   B. The emotional commitment and involvement of employees toward their organization.
   C. The salary and benefits provided to employees by their organization.
   D. The level of supervision and control exerted by managers over employees.
2. How can employees increase their engagement through job crafting?
   A. By job sharing to learn new skills.
   B. By redesigning their job tasks and responsibilities to align with their strengths and interests.
   C. By taking advantage of workplace sabbatical benefits to gain industry knowledge.
   D. By attending more team-building workshops and events.
3. Which of the following best defines job satisfaction, a crucial aspect of job attitudes?
   A. The degree of positivity or negativity an employee feels toward the organization.
   B. The degree to which the employee feels loyal to their team.
   C. The degree to which the employee feels recognized and valued.
   D. The degree of commitment an employee feels toward their work.
4. As the HR manager of a medium-sized company, you've noticed a decline in employee productivity and morale over the past few months. You're concerned about the overall engagement level of your employees, and you believe it's essential to measure and address this issue to improve the work environment. Which of the following metrics will best provide the necessary information?
   A. Using employee turnover rates.
   B. Conducting employee satisfaction surveys.
   C. Monitoring employee's social media activity.
   D. Tracking the number of sick days taken.
5. In a corporate setting, HR faces the challenge of enhancing employee engagement and internal communication to boost organizational performance. They aim to understand the connections between employee engagement, perceived organizational support, the employer brand, and effective internal communication strategies. Considering their goals and challenges, what strategy should the HR team recommend to senior leadership to enhance employee engagement and internal communication?
   A. Implement a hierarchical structure to streamline communication channels.
   B. Allow employees to craft their jobs based on their individual strengths and weaknesses.
   C. Engage in a job design review to measure workflow efficiencies.
   D. Design formal feedback channels to measure and assess employee attitudes.

6. Which job design principle involves expanding an employee's tasks and responsibilities to make their job more varied and interesting?
   A. Job enrichment.
   B. Job rotation.
   C. Job enlargement.
   D. Work simplification.

7. A forward-thinking organization is in the process of designing HR programs to enhance its employees' experiences. Their focus is on creating initiatives that ensure seamless transitions during critical employee milestones. These initiatives include comprehensive onboarding, skills development, and knowledge transfer programs. Which stage of the employee life cycle is the organization primarily emphasizing?
   A. Recruitment and sourcing.
   B. Talent acquisition and selection.
   C. Talent development and retention.
   D. Talent separation and offboarding.

8. How can alternative staffing arrangements, such as flexible work hours and remote work options, impact employee engagement?
   A. They are likely to decrease employee engagement due to the isolation inherent in remote work.
   B. They lead to higher employee engagement through increased workload and productivity expectations.
   C. They can enhance employee engagement by promoting work-life balance and autonomy.
   D. They may have no immediate effect on employee engagement, as it depends on individual preferences.

9. A midsize company is facing a productivity challenge in its customer service department. The employees have been feeling overwhelmed with their workload, resulting in decreased job satisfaction and performance. In addition, some of the roles in the department have a heavy emotional burden leading to burnout, and other positions are highly routine, resulting in boredom. Which of the following options is most likely to provide a solution that improves employee morale and enhances productivity?
   A. Job sharing.
   B. Job rotation.
   C. Job enrichment.
   D. Job enlargement.

10. Which combination of strategies is most effective for increasing employee retention and job satisfaction within the first 90 days of employment?
    A. Offering competitive salaries/benefits and assigning a mentor.
    B. Establishing team building events and 360-degree feedback sessions.
    C. Implementing realistic job previews and personalized onboarding.
    D. Allowing the employee to select specific webinars and other formal training sessions.

11. In a company, the voluntary turnover rate for the year is 15%, the involuntary turnover rate is 5%, and the attrition rate is 20%. What does the attrition rate primarily represent in this context?

A. The total number of employees who left the organization in a given period.

B. The percentage of employees who left voluntarily.

C. The percentage of employees who left involuntarily.

D. The overall turnover, including both voluntary and involuntary separations.

12. You are a senior manager at a global manufacturing company looking to improve employee engagement and achieve better organizational results. You believe that utilizing engagement metrics can play a pivotal role in this endeavor. Which of the following strategies demonstrates the best use of engagement metrics to achieve organizational results?

A. Implement quarterly employee engagement surveys to collect feedback from all employees, analyze the results, and create action plans based on the feedback to address specific issues.

B. Set a fixed target for employee engagement scores and communicate it to all teams, making it a key performance indicator (KPI) for managers and employees.

C. Conduct monthly one-on-one meetings with employees to discuss their engagement levels and address any concerns without formal surveys or metrics.

D. Compare your company's engagement metrics with industry benchmarks and adjust your strategies accordingly.

13. As an HR manager at a medium-sized technology company, you are considering implementing an employee engagement survey to assess the overall engagement levels of your workforce. However, you are aware of the strategic, operational, and human relations disadvantages associated with using such surveys. Which of the following represents a strategic disadvantage?

A. Employee engagement surveys can be time-consuming to administer and analyze, requiring significant resources.

B. Conducting surveys may lead to a sense of survey fatigue among employees if they are asked to participate frequently.

C. Surveys may not capture the qualitative aspects of engagement, such as the depth of employee commitment to the organization.

D. Employees may provide biased or overly positive responses to surveys to avoid potential repercussions.

14. In an effort to measure employee engagement at a manufacturing company, HR conducted a survey with 250 employees. The survey asked participants to rate their level of engagement on a scale from 1 to 5, with 1 being "Not Engaged" and 5 being "Highly Engaged." The results were as follows:

60 employees rated their engagement as 5.

120 employees rated their engagement as 4.

40 employees rated their engagement as 3.

20 employees rated their engagement as 2.

10 employees rated their engagement as 1.

Calculate the mean engagement level of the employees based on the survey results.

A. 2.5.

B. 3.2.

C. 3.8.

D. 4.0.

15. You are an HR manager at a large multinational global security agency called Strike Inc., and the organization is facing a challenge with high turnover in one of its key departments. You decide to use HR engagement metrics to address this issue. Which of the following approaches represents the most effective use of HR engagement metrics to solve the turnover problem?

A. Analyze overall turnover rates in the department and compare them to industry benchmarks to identify the extent of the issue.

B. Conduct exit interviews with departing employees to gather insights into their reasons for leaving.

C. Implement an employee engagement survey focused on the specific department, analyzing the results to identify areas of low engagement.

D. Increase compensation and benefits for employees in the department to reduce turnover.

16. What type of motivation technique involves providing employees with opportunities to learn new skills and advance in their careers?

A. Extrinsic motivation.

B. Intrinsic motivation.

C. Peer motivation.

D. Social motivation.

17. You are a manager at a midsize software development company and are looking to increase employee motivation within your team. You decide to apply the Job Characteristics Model (JCM) to redesign their roles. Which of the following modifications aligns best with the JCM principles and is likely to increase employee motivation?

  A. Reducing the number of tasks and simplifying job roles to minimize the mental effort required for each task.

  B. Increasing the level of autonomy by allowing employees to choose their projects and set their own deadlines.

  C. Implementing a strict hierarchical structure with clear job descriptions.

  D. Introducing a performance-based bonus system where employees receive rewards based on individual productivity.

18. As an HR professional, you are tasked with improving employee engagement within your organization. One of the competencies crucial in this process is active listening. Which of the following actions best demonstrates the professional competency of listening when working on employee engagement?

  A. Conducting surveys to collect employee feedback.

  B. Holding regular one-on-one meetings with employees to discuss their concerns.

  C. Sending out email communication to employees summarizing the company's engagement initiatives.

  D. Providing generalized training sessions to employees to be consistent in the information being shared.

19. Nancy, a graphic designer at Agatha Corporation, finds her job exceptionally satisfying and fulfilling. She values the creative aspects of her work, task flexibility, her designs' impact on projects, and, most especially, when her clients acknowledge how much they love her work. Which characteristic of the Job Characteristics Model (JCM) most likely motivates Nancy in her role as a graphic designer at the company?

  A. Task Identity.

  B. Autonomy.

  C. Skill Variety.

  D. Feedback.

20. How does the Job Characteristics Model (JCM) differ from organizational commitment?

  A. The JCM focuses on employee job satisfaction while organizational commitment assesses the alignment of personal values with organizational values.

  B. The JCM emphasizes the impact of job design on motivation and job performance, while organizational commitment measures an employee's loyalty and attachment to their organization.

  C. The JCM examines the psychological contract between employees and employers, while organizational commitment evaluates the extent to which an organization provides skill development opportunities.

  D. The JCM measures the level of employee engagement in organizational decision-making, while organizational commitment assesses the fairness of promotions and salary increases.

21. The company you work for has engaged in a companywide restructuring as part of a merger and acquisition. The employees are nervous and uncertain about the new initiatives, and several indications of job dissatisfaction have come to the attention of HR. Senior leaders have challenged the HR team to create and implement a communication strategy to address the level of uncertainty with the ultimate goal to gain buy-in from the team of the changes. Considering the importance of feedback and communication in improving employee engagement, which action can HR take to achieve this outcome?
    - **A.** Conduct employee feedback surveys.
    - **B.** Hold mandatory town hall meetings.
    - **C.** Hire outside consultants as advisors.
    - **D.** Plan a state-of-the company event to communicate more information about the change and set a tone of celebration.

22. Which competency is most crucial for an HR professional to effectively communicate employee engagement data and make recommendations to senior leaders?
    - **A.** Technical HR knowledge.
    - **B.** Data analysis skills.
    - **C.** Conflict resolution skills.
    - **D.** Presentation skills.

23. At what stage in the employee life cycle can HR have the most significant impact on employee retention?
    - **A.** Within the first six months of employment.
    - **B.** After their introductory period.
    - **C.** During the recruitment phase.
    - **D.** During the performance management stage.

24. Trixie works in the marketing department and consistently seeks opportunities to influence decisions and take on leadership roles within the organization. For instance, when a critical project is at hand, Trixie actively seeks the role of project leader. She enjoys working with others, making strategic decisions, delegating tasks to the most qualified team members, and overseeing the project's outcomes. Which of McClelland's theories is best represented as Trixie's primary motivation?
    - **A.** Achievement.
    - **B.** Affiliation.
    - **C.** Power.
    - **D.** Hygiene.

25. How can the composition of cross-functional teams impact employee job satisfaction?
    - **A.** It has no influence on job satisfaction as long as team members have similar skills.
    - **B.** It can enhance job satisfaction by promoting diversity of perspectives and skills.
    - **C.** It decreases job satisfaction because cross-functional teams are often inefficient.
    - **D.** It affects job satisfaction only if all team members share the same background.

26. How do the various stages of team development (forming, storming, norming, and performing) affect team engagement and productivity?

A. Teams tend to be most engaged and productive during the forming stage.

B. Teams experience higher engagement and productivity during the storming stage.

C. Teams experience a decrease in engagement during the performing stage.

D. Teams are most engaged and productive during the performing stage.

27. In addressing the organizational challenge of improving employee engagement, how can networking as an HR competency benefit HR professionals?

A. Networking can train HR teams on how to increase employee engagement.

B. Networking gives HR teams an outlet to air their frustrations with other professionals.

C. Networking provides access to best practices, resources, and collaboration opportunities.

D. Networking is unrelated to HR's role in employee engagement.

28. What characteristics of a flat organizational structure influence employee retention?

A. Flat structures often result in increased autonomy as there are fewer layers of bureaucracy.

B. Flat structures have more hierarchical levels, creating more opportunities for career progression.

C. Flat structures lead to an increased focus on collaborative outcomes due to a focus on teamwork.

D. Flat structures are structured to be aligned with individual values.

29. What competencies must an HR professional develop in order to use technology to structure predictive attrition analysis?

A. Continuous learning to keep pace with emerging trends.

B. Business intelligence skills such as collection, cleaning, and visualization.

C. Knowledge of HR practices related to attrition trends.

D. Programming skills to run efficient queries.

30. According to Maslow's Hierarchy of Needs theory, which of the following is a lower-order need that must be satisfied before an individual can be motivated by higher-order needs in the workplace?

A. Self-actualization.

B. Esteem.

C. Safety.

D. Belonging and love.

31. Which motivation theory suggests that individuals are driven by their need for achievement, affiliation, and power in the workplace?

A. Two-Factor theory.

B. Acquired Needs theory.

C. Hierarchy of Needs theory.

D. Equity theory.

32. According to Herzberg's Two-Factor theory, which factors are considered hygiene factors that, when lacking, can lead to job dissatisfaction?

A. Recognition and achievement.

B. Salary and benefits.

C. Responsibility and advancement.

D. Work itself and personal growth.

33. According to the Expectancy theory of motivation, which of the following is a key component that influences an individual's motivation to perform a task?

A. Job security.

B. Perceived equity.

C. Self-efficacy.

D. Managerial authority.

34. How has the psychological contract in the workplace evolved in recent years?

A. It has become more rigid and rule-bound.

B. It has shifted toward greater job security and traditional benefits.

C. It has become more transactional and less reliant on loyalty.

D. It has remained unchanged over time.

35. Imagine you work for a reputable tech company known for its innovative culture. Many of the employees were initially attracted to the company because of its commitment to work-life balance and flexible schedules. However, over the past year, the company has undergone significant changes due to increased competition and financial pressures. The management has implemented a new policy to stay competitive that requires employees to go from being fully remote to a hybrid schedule of being on-site a minimum of 3 days a week. This change has left many employees feeling overwhelmed and stressed and thinking about finding another job. Which of the following HR strategies would most likely combat the threat of increased turnover?

A. Enhance employee well-being programs.

B. Call back the hybrid schedule and continue to allow remote work.

C. Introduce stay bonuses.

D. Offer more vacation days.

36. Which of the following is NOT a benefit of employee wellness initiatives designed to improve engagement and retention?

A. Reduced absenteeism.

B. Enhanced job satisfaction.

C. Increased financial well-being.

D. Improved relationships with team members.

37. How can HR use AI to predict employee turnover effectively?
    A. By deploying AI-powered chatbots for employee engagement.
    B. By monitoring employees' emails and communication.
    C. By analyzing historical HR data and using machine learning algorithms.
    D. By conducting randomized surveys throughout departments.

38. What interpersonal competency is essential for HR professionals to manage employee engagement strategies effectively?
    A. Technical expertise in HR software and systems.
    B. Active listening and empathy.
    C. Project management skills.
    D. Financial analysis proficiency.

39. In a high-stress customer service job, employees often find themselves emotionally drained from dealing with irate customers. The company decides to implement employee engagement strategies to reduce emotional labor. Which of the following should the HR team tackle first?
    A. Training and development on how to de-escalate situations.
    B. Empowering CSR's to make decisions on behalf of the customer within a reasonable limit.
    C. Clearly define the roles and responsibilities so the employees know what is expected of them.
    D. Offer flexible scheduling to reduce exposure and emotional fatigue.

40. Why are exit interviews conducted when employees leave an organization, and how do they benefit the company?
    A. Exit interviews are primarily used for legal documentation and have no direct benefit to the company.
    B. Exit interviews aim to persuade departing employees to reconsider their resignation and continue working for the company.
    C. Exit interviews provide valuable feedback to understand the reasons for departure and gather insights for improving the employee experience.
    D. Exit interviews are pointless as the employee has already decided to leave, and it's too late to change their mind.

41. Robin, a dedicated employee with 30 years of service, is approaching retirement and is considering shortening her hours to part-time. She has been a valuable team member, is highly knowledgeable in her field, and wants to continue working as long as possible so her health insurance benefits will continue. What action should HR take to support Robin at this stage of her employment?
    A. Offer her a promotion to a higher position.
    B. Encourage her to take advantage of phased retirement.
    C. Assign her more challenging projects.
    D. Provide opportunities for skill transfer and mentorship.

42. A company has a total of 100 job openings. In a given month, they successfully fill 80 of these positions with qualified candidates. What is the vacancy rate for this month?
   - A. 20%.
   - B. 40%.
   - C. 60%.
   - D. 80%.

43. Which of the following sets of strategies are most likely to improve employee retention levels while supporting business outcomes?
   - A. Career pathing, employee resource groups, and stakeholder involvement.
   - B. Competitive total rewards packages, unlimited time-off policies, and flexible scheduling.
   - C. Personalized benefits offerings, remote work schedules, and guaranteed leadership opportunities for those who express an interest.
   - D. Free lunches, housing allowances, and other corporate perks.

44. The company you work for has an assimilation program during their onboarding boot camps that includes mandatory attendance at a series of after-hours networking events, often held in restaurants with bars. The goal is for team members to get to know each other and start to build connections, particularly as some of the employees come in from out of town to attend and will be working remotely. What is a potential challenge of this assimilation approach for protected-class groups?
   - A. The events may result in limited opportunities for team building and professional networking.
   - B. The events may create feelings of exclusion for employees unable to attend due to caregiving responsibilities or other factors.
   - C. The events may lead to excessive alcohol consumption, potentially affecting employees' well-being.
   - D. The events may lead to a lack of engagement among remote employees, hindering their integration into the organization.

45. How might overly strict grooming policies adversely affect employee engagement and compliance with labor laws during the employee's life cycle?
   - A. By restricting individual expression.
   - B. By hindering creativity and alternative perspectives.
   - C. By creating barriers for employees with cultural or religious grooming practices.
   - D. By diminishing individual identities as required by law.

46. What is a key advantage of using a Net Promoter Score (NPS) question in employee engagement surveys?
   - A. NPS questions are comprehensive, covering multiple aspects of engagement.
   - B. NPS questions are easy to understand but lack depth.
   - C. NPS questions provide a simple and quantitative measure of engagement.
   - D. NPS questions are tailored to specific industries.

47. What is a key strategy to improve employee retention for remote workers?
   - **A.** Conduct daily check-ins to make sure the team member does not feel isolated.
   - **B.** Implement flexible work hours for on-site employees to avoid perceptions of inequity.
   - **C.** Offer regular virtual check-ins, support, and recognition so the employee stays connected with the team.
   - **D.** Encourage remote workers to work independently to ensure autonomy.

48. As an HR leader, what is the most effective way to collaborate with organizational leaders to create a positive employee experience?
   - **A.** Providing occasional HR reports on employee satisfaction.
   - **B.** Holding regular joint meetings with organizational leaders to discuss employee feedback and identify opportunities for improvement.
   - **C.** Developing HR policies and initiatives that address organizational issues.
   - **D.** Implementing employee experience initiatives based on HR's competencies and expertise.

49. How can predictive analytics be effectively utilized in performance management?
   - **A.** Predicting individual employee performance ratings for the next quarter to inform compensation decisions.
   - **B.** Automating the performance review process to reduce HR's workload and speed up evaluations.
   - **C.** Generating historical performance reports for employees without offering insights or recommendations.
   - **D.** Identifying performance trends and patterns to address areas needing improvement and development proactively.

50. Company XYZ is experiencing low employee morale and high turnover rates. The HR department decides to implement a comprehensive employee engagement program, which includes regular feedback sessions, career development opportunities, and recognition programs. How can these HR activities increase organizational effectiveness?
   - **A.** By giving employees greater access to HR.
   - **B.** By boosting employee morale and retention.
   - **C.** By cutting costs.
   - **D.** By focusing employees on the essential functions of the job.

51. What does the World Health Organization (WHO) define as occupational burnout in its International Classification of Diseases (ICD-11)?
   - **A.** A medical condition caused by workplace stress.
   - **B.** Feelings of exhaustion and frustration during vacations.
   - **C.** Chronic workplace stress that has not been successfully managed.
   - **D.** A temporary state of emotional distress related to work-life balance.

52. In what ways do employee engagement efforts lower the cost of goods sold?

A. By reducing the cost of raw materials and supplies.

B. By increasing employee turnover, thus reducing labor costs.

C. By improving employee morale and reducing absenteeism and errors.

D. By increasing production output and requiring fewer work hours.

53. Fill in the blank: The impact of employee engagement efforts on organizational results is largely _______.

A. Immeasurable.

B. Indirect.

C. Subjective.

D. Objective.

54. Which of the following most accurately describes the process of goal-recording in employee engagement and retention efforts?

A. Conducting manager intake to identify the greatest opportunities for employee growth.

B. Collaboratively establishing clear and measurable goals with employees.

C. Assigning development goals and typing it to incentive compensation.

D. Creating team objectives in which the employee actively contributes.

55. What is the primary difference between goal-recording and an engagement dashboard?

A. Goal-recording focuses on tracking employee progress, while an engagement dashboard measures overall workforce engagement levels.

B. Goal-recording is used for tracking financial performance, while an engagement dashboard monitors employee goals.

C. Goal-recording is a visual representation of employee engagement data, while an engagement dashboard records individual employee goals.

D. Goal-recording is a tool for conducting employee surveys, while an engagement dashboard tracks employee productivity.

56. What is an Employee Service Award?

A. A monetary bonus given to employees for excellent performance.

B. A recognition program that honors employees for their years of dedicated service to the organization.

C. A paid time-off benefit provided to employees on their work anniversaries.

D. An annual performance review conducted by the HR department.

57. How does using realistic job previews (RJPs) influence employee engagement?

A. RJPs provide employees with a clear understanding of what to expect on the job.

B. RJPs help employees predict success in the new role.

C. RJPs reveal the most challenging aspects of a job so employees can mitigate or avoid them.

D. RJPs primarily affect employee turnover, not engagement.

58. Which of the following factors is a key contributor to employee engagement in the workplace?
   - **A.** The number of vacation days provided to employees.
   - **B.** The frequency of performance appraisals conducted by managers.
   - **C.** The alignment of an employee's values with the organization's mission and values.
   - **D.** The availability of free snacks and coffee in the breakroom.

59. When is peer-to-peer recognition in the workplace most effective?
   - **A.** During annual performance reviews.
   - **B.** In highly competitive work environments.
   - **C.** When used as the sole form of recognition.
   - **D.** As a regular, ongoing practice.

60. Which of the following strategies is most likely to develop leaders in understanding the impact of employee engagement?
   - **A.** Offering cultural sensitivity training to understand engagement preferences.
   - **B.** Building engagement dashboards to measure results.
   - **C.** Coach leaders on positive relations techniques.
   - **D.** Make employee engagement results a leadership KPI.

Key Concept Research Questions

You can do additional research on key engagement and retention topics that are likely to show up on the exam. See Figure 8.1 for the main pillars of employee engagement.

The following questions are designed for you to critically think about these concepts:

1. What are the different ways human resource teams can support employee engagement?

   To learn more about the important link between engagement and performance management, review the article on Gallup Workplace titled "What is Employee Engagement and How do You Improve It." You'll find it at `www.gallup.com/workplace/285674/improve-employee-engagement-workplace.aspx` or on YouTube at `www.youtube.com/watch?v=KZjKY9I6UYE&t=11s`.

2. Employer retention efforts should be spread throughout the employee's entire life cycle. Opportunities to increase loyalty exist from the hiring process all the way through separation (including those caused by internal promotions or lateral moves) and can help sustain an alum applicant pool to draw from for future roles. Give an example of retention efforts at each stage of the employee life cycle.

   Consider examples such as those found at major recruiting source `Indeed.com` at `www.indeed.com/career-advice/career-development/how-to-retain-an-employee`.

FIGURE 8.1 The pillars of employee engagement

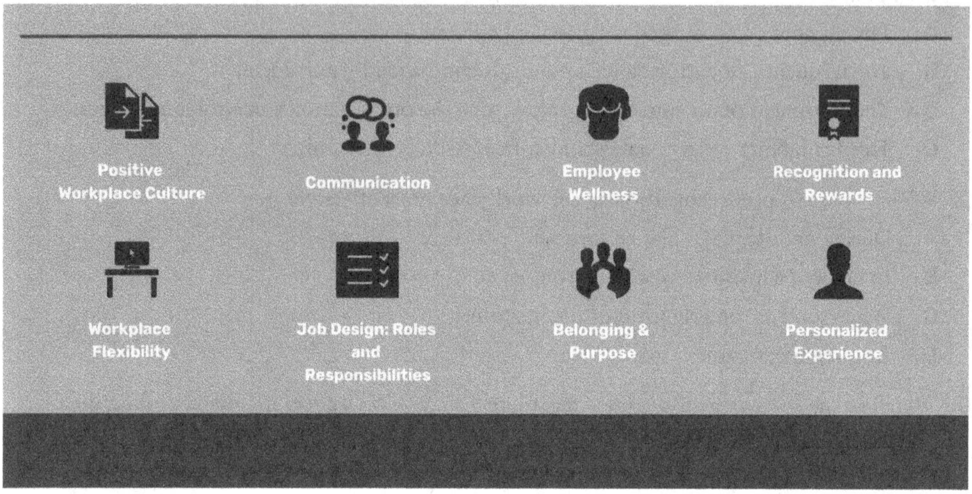

Test Your Engagement and Retention Terminology Knowledge

The following are the terms to use to test your knowledge of Engagement and Retention key terms. The correct answers are found in Appendix B.

- Culture building
- Employee connection
- Employee development
- Employee engagement
- Employee feedback
- Employee involvement
- Employee wellness
- Engagement dashboard
- Equity
- Exit interviews
- Expectancy theory
- Flexible work arrangements
- Goal alignment
- High-potential development
- Job characteristics
- Job satisfaction
- Maslow's hierarchy
- Performance appraisal
- Realistic job preview
- Self-determination theory

1. ___________ is constructive information and insights provided by employees, supervisors, or peers to assess and improve performance, communication, and overall engagement.
2. ___________ is the practice of providing candidates with an accurate and balanced portrayal of the job and work environment during the recruitment process to ensure realistic expectations.
3. ___________ is the concept of ensuring that individual and team goals are in harmony with organizational objectives, promoting a sense of purpose and direction.
4. ___________ is the active participation and engagement of employees in decision-making processes, problem-solving, and contributing to organizational success through their actions.
5. ___________ are alternative work schedules or arrangements that allow employees to balance work and personal responsibilities while maintaining high productivity.
6. ___________ is the overall level of contentment and fulfillment that employees experience in their work, often influenced by factors such as job design and organizational culture.
7. An ___________ is a visual tool or platform that provides real-time data and insights into employee engagement levels, allowing organizations to track progress and make informed decisions.
8. ___________ are programs and initiatives designed to support employees' physical, mental, and emotional well-being, promoting a healthy work-life balance.
9. ___________ is a psychological theory that suggests individuals are motivated to exert effort when they believe their efforts will lead to successful performance (expectancy), which in turn will result in desired outcomes (valence).
10. ___________ are structured conversations conducted with departing employees to gather insights into their reasons for leaving and to identify areas for organizational improvement.
11. ___________ is a theory of motivation that emphasizes the importance of autonomy, competence, and relatedness in fostering intrinsic motivation and well-being.
12. ___________ is the process of shaping and nurturing an organization's culture and shared values to create a positive and productive work environment.
13. ___________ is the concept of ensuring fairness and impartiality in all aspects of employment, including compensation, promotions, and opportunities, to promote equality among employees.
14. ___________ is the identification and cultivation of employees with the skills necessary for leadership and key roles within the organization.
15. ___________ is a psychological theory of human needs, including physiological, safety, love and belonging, esteem, and self-actualization needs.

16. ____________ is the level of emotional commitment and involvement that employees have toward their work, organization, and its goals.
17. ____________ are the specific attributes of a job, including skill variety, task identity, task significance, autonomy, and feedback, which can impact employee motivation and satisfaction.
18. ____________ is a formal process of evaluating and assessing an employee's job performance and providing feedback for development.
19. ____________ is the ongoing process of enhancing employees' skills, knowledge, and abilities through training, education, and career growth opportunities.
20. ____________ is the establishment of a strong and meaningful relationship between employees and their organization, fostering a sense of engagement and commitment.

Conclusion

Employee engagement goes beyond the traditional notions of job satisfaction. It represents a deep emotional connection between employees and their work, fostering a sense of purpose and commitment. Engaged employees are more productive, innovative, and dedicated to achieving both individual and organizational goals. They become valuable assets to any company, driving its success. Retention strategies are equally vital in today's competitive job market. Organizations must invest in initiatives that not only attract top talent but also retain it. Realistic job previews, flexible work arrangements, mentorship programs, and a strong focus on employee development all contribute to creating an environment where employees feel valued, motivated, and inclined to stay.

SHRM defines the function of Employee Engagement as follows: "Employee Engagement & Retention refers to activities aimed at retaining talent, solidifying and improving the relationship between employees and the organization, creating a thriving and energized workforce, and developing effective strategies to address appropriate performance expectations from employees at all levels."

In 2024, HRCI added this functional area to the PHR and PHRi exam content, weighing in at 17% of those exams, and removed Employee Engagement as its own functional area on the SPHR and SPHRi. That does not mean it is not important for senior-level practitioners, but rather, the content was combined with Learning and Development to form a new functional area called "Talent Management" (23% of the SPHR/SPHRi). These shifts suggest that PHR and PHRi hopefuls should pay attention to how employee engagement directly impacts operations, and SPHR/SPHRi candidates should understand engagement in the context of workforce management strategies that support business strategy.

Additional Resources

Understanding employee engagement and retention is crucial for maintaining a motivated and productive workforce. Here are some top online websites, podcasts, and YouTube channels to help you gain a deeper understanding of engagement and retention concepts.

Websites

- Gallup Workplace (`www.gallup.com/workplace`)

  Gallup is well-known for its research on employee engagement. Their website offers numerous articles, reports, and resources related to employee engagement, including the renowned Gallup Q12 employee engagement survey.
- *Harvard Business Review* (`www.hbr.org`)

  Harvard Business Review features articles and case studies on various aspects of employee engagement and retention. You can find insights into leadership, workplace culture, and strategies for retaining top talent.
- Bersin by Deloitte (`www2.deloitte.com`)

  Bersin by Deloitte offers research, reports, and articles on HR and talent management, including employee engagement and retention trends.
- *Human Resources Today* (`www.humanresourcestoday.com`)

  Human Resources Today is a platform that aggregates HR-related content, including articles, blog posts, and webinars on employee engagement and retention.

Podcasts

- *WorkLife with Adam Grant* (`www.ted.com/podcasts/worklife`)

  Organizational psychologist Adam Grant explores various aspects of work life, including employee engagement and retention. He shares research-backed advice and real-life stories to improve workplace dynamics.
- *HR Happy Hour* with various hosts (`www.hrhappyhour.net`)

  HR Happy Hour covers a wide range of HR topics, including employee engagement strategies and best practices. The hosts often interview experts and practitioners in the field.
- *Employee Cycle* with various hosts (`www.employeecycle.com/podcast`)

  Employee Cycle focuses on HR, data-driven practices, and strategies for retaining top talent. The podcast features discussions with HR leaders and practitioners who share their experiences and insights.
- *Engage for Success Radio* with various hosts (`www.engageforsuccess.org/radio-show`)

  Engage for Success is a UK-based movement promoting employee engagement. Their show discusses strategies for creating engaged workplaces and features interviews with experts.

YouTube Channels

Many students make the mistake of preparing for their exams by only reading through extensive study guides. Take a break from the reading and log on to `www.YouTube.com` to search for the following channels to complement your study efforts:

- Limeade Listening, formerly TINYpulse

  This channel explores the best practices for employee engagement and features discussions with HR experts and leaders. It offers practical insights and strategies for creating a positive workplace culture.

- Harvard Business Review

  Harvard Business Review's YouTube channel features videos on leadership, workplace culture, and employee engagement. You can find interviews with experts and summaries of HBR articles.

- Gallup Strengths Center

  Gallup's YouTube channel focuses on strengths-based development, which is closely related to employee engagement. It offers insights and resources to help individuals and teams thrive.

- Simon Sinek's "The Infinite Game" Playlist

  Anything by Simon Sinek is going to be useful to understand how HR exam content applies in the workplace. This article channel highlights Sinek's "The Infinite Game" concept as it is particularly relevant to long-term employee engagement and retention. His playlist covers this topic in depth.

Chapter 9

Employee and Labor Relations

In 2022, Twitter was featured in their own platform's headlines after its new owner, Elon Musk, gave employees an ultimatum: work long hours at high intensity or quit and receive three months' severance pay. Employees were given about 24 hours to make the decision after the edict was given. The email to staff read: "Going forward, to build a breakthrough Twitter 2.0 and succeed in an increasingly competitive world, we will need to be extremely hardcore. This will mean working long hours at high intensity. Only exceptional performance will constitute a passing grade." In similar news, Musk was also quoted in a prior year as welcoming individuals who did not have a formal degree, noting that individuals with "exceptional abilities" did not have to have a formal college degree to work at Tesla, Musk's highly successful car manufacturing company. Both examples exemplify how a company's employee relations philosophy and strategy have a significant impact on laying the foundation of individual and employee performance. Also of note is that both decrees would be managed through a company's human resource programs.

Employee and Labor Relations is the function of human resource management that focuses on cultivating a positive work environment while adhering to legal and ethical standards. This chapter explores key issues and strategies related to employee and labor relations, providing HR professionals with the knowledge and tools necessary to foster healthy workplace dynamics, ensure compliance, and effectively manage disputes. Be prepared to tackle the following key issues:

- **Promoting positive employee and labor relations:** Promoting techniques and tools for fostering positive employee and labor relations
- **Employment rights, labor law compliance, standards, and concepts:** Understanding the rights and responsibilities of employers and principles outlined by the International Labour Organization (ILO), including the tools used to remain in compliance
- **Alternative dispute resolution (ADR):** Exploring various forms of ADR, their advantages, and disadvantages as mechanisms for resolving conflicts and disputes in the workplace
- **Workplace investigations:** Discussing techniques for conducting effective workplace investigations, ensuring fairness, confidentiality, and adherence to due process
- **Progressive discipline:** Understanding the methods and approaches for implementing progressive disciplinary actions, including counseling, performance improvement plans, verbal warnings, and more
- **Labor relations:** Navigating the third-party relationships between a labor union, employer, and union members, including the organizing process, strikes and lockouts, employee complaints and grievances

This chapter will provide HR professionals with a comprehensive understanding of these critical issues and equip them with the skills needed to effectively manage employee and labor relations within their organizations, ultimately contributing to a harmonious and compliant work environment.

Real World Scenario

Southwest Airlines' Successful Labor-Management Cooperative: Achieving Positive Results

Southwest Airlines, renowned for its unique approach to labor relations, has achieved remarkable success through its cooperative engagement with labor unions. This case study delves into the positive outcomes stemming from the labor-management partnership at Southwest Airlines, emphasizing how it has contributed to the airline's competitiveness, operational consistency, and employee satisfaction.

Background and Problem

Southwest Airlines, like many companies in the airline industry, faces the challenge of balancing the needs and demands of its unionized workforce while maintaining a strong operational performance. With more than 80% of its workforce represented by unions, the company has taken a distinctive approach to labor relations, focusing on cooperation, open communication, and shared objectives.

Diagnosis

The lack of cooperation between general airlines and trade unions stems from historical grievances, differing goals, and a lack of trust. Communication breakdowns and cultural differences exacerbate the strained relationships, hindering effective collaboration. The root causes include misalignment in objectives, a trust deficit due to past conflicts, and structural barriers within the organization.

Strategies

Southwest adopted a cooperative labor-management strategy summed up by this philosophy:

> "In contract negotiations, our philosophy is to reach agreements that are rewarding for Employees, have scheduling flexibility that allow the Company to operate efficiently in a highly competitive marketplace, and provide long-term job security."[1]

[1] `https://swamedia.com/labor-relations` / Southwest Airlines.

Southwest accomplished this by adopting the following strategies:

- **Cultivating a culture of cooperation:** Southwest Airlines has prioritized building a culture of cooperation between management and labor unions. This involves promoting open communication channels, fostering trust, and emphasizing shared goals and objectives. By involving employees in decision-making processes and valuing their input, Southwest has created a sense of ownership and accountability among its workforce.
- **Proactive conflict resolution:** Southwest Airlines has implemented proactive conflict resolution strategies to address potential issues before they escalate into full-blown disputes. This includes establishing formal channels for grievance resolution, providing mediation services, and conducting regular dialogue sessions between management and union representatives. By addressing concerns in a timely and transparent manner, Southwest has been able to maintain harmony in its labor relations.
- **Transparency and information sharing:** Southwest Airlines prioritizes transparency and information sharing as key components of its labor relations strategy. Management regularly communicates with employees and union leaders regarding company performance, strategic objectives, and upcoming changes. This transparency helps build trust and credibility, reducing the likelihood of misunderstandings or conflicts arising from miscommunication.

Results

Southwest's contract negotiation and labor-relations efforts needed to be flexible enough to account for macro-level changes such as the economic and regulatory environments, while also remaining competitive to attract and keep industry talent. Southwest adopted several strategies to address these factors:

- **Positive labor relations:** The labor-management cooperative environment at Southwest has fostered positive labor relations. Employees, including union members, feel valued and respected, which has reduced the likelihood of labor actions. The result is a workforce that is more inclined toward collaboration and constructive dialogue.
- **Consistent operations:** The absence of labor strikes or disruptions has allowed Southwest Airlines to maintain consistent and reliable operations. This operational consistency is a cornerstone of the airline's reputation for on-time performance and customer service excellence.
- **Employee satisfaction:** The cooperative approach has led to high levels of employee satisfaction and morale. Satisfied employees are less likely to engage in labor disputes, strikes, or other disruptive actions. This has contributed to a more stable and motivated workforce.
- **Profit-sharing incentives:** Southwest's profit-sharing program has provided employees, including union members, with financial incentives tied to the company's success. This innovative approach aligns the interests of employees and the company, reducing the likelihood of labor conflicts and fostering a sense of shared prosperity.

- **Industry-leading performance:** Southwest Airlines consistently outperforms competitors in the airline industry. This includes industry-leading on-time performance, customer service, and financial stability. The cooperative labor relations model has played a pivotal role in achieving and maintaining this high level of performance.

Conclusion

Southwest Airlines' unique labor-management cooperative approach has yielded a multitude of positive results. The company's ability to avoid strikes, maintain positive labor relations, ensure consistent operations, boost employee satisfaction, offer profit-sharing incentives, and achieve industry-leading performance sets it apart in the airline industry. The success of this cooperative model demonstrates the benefits of collaboration and open communication between management and labor unions in achieving long-term organizational success.

Overall, Southwest Airlines' profit-sharing program serves as a powerful tool for aligning the interests of employees and the company, fostering a cooperative and harmonious labor-management relationship that benefits both parties and contributes to the airline's exceptional performance.

Employee and Labor Relations Practice Questions

1. Which of the following are critical comments to consider when conducting workplace investigations? (Choose all that apply.)
   - **A.** Considering the feelings of the individual being interviewed.
   - **B.** Ignoring pressure from executives to come to a specific outcome.
   - **C.** Guaranteeing the confidentiality of the complainant.
   - **D.** Maintaining open lines of communication.

2. What does the concept of "due process" mean in the context of workplace investigations?
   - **A.** Allowing employees to choose their investigators.
   - **B.** Protecting the rights of all individuals involved.
   - **C.** Completing investigations in a timely fashion.
   - **D.** Conducting investigations with consent of the involved parties.

3. Matilda came to the HR department complaining about a sexually explicit magazine that she found in the break room. She knew who it belonged to as the address label was on the magazine. When you, the HR manager, went to ask the employee about the situation, he was clearly embarrassed and said that he had brought in a stack of sports magazines that he was getting rid of and didn't realize the sexually explicit issue was there. There had been no other complaints about him up to that point. What is the next action you should take as part of the investigation?
   - **A.** Document the incident but take no further action.
   - **B.** Explain the situation to Matilda and determine next steps from there.
   - **C.** Discipline the employee for violating standards of conduct.
   - **D.** Continue to investigate to see if the employee has other complaints against his conduct.

4. Who do the International Labour Organization (ILO) standards primarily apply to, and who do the National Labor Relations Act (NLRA) standards primarily apply to?
   - **A.** ILO: All countries worldwide; NLRA: U.S. employers and employees.
   - **B.** ILO: U.S. employers and employees; NLRA: All countries worldwide.
   - **C.** ILO: Only member countries that ratified ILO conventions; NLRA: U.S. employers, employees, and labor unions.
   - **D.** ILO: All countries within the United Nations; NLRA: U.S. federal government employees.

5. You are an HR manager at a multinational corporation that operates in several countries. You receive a complaint from an employee in one of your overseas branches, alleging that they are not being paid a fair wage for their work, which is significantly below the local living wage. What should you do to address this issue in compliance with the International Labour Organization (ILO) standards?

   A. Ignore the complaint, as wage standards vary from country to country.

   B. Investigate the complaint to determine if the employee's claim is valid and, if confirmed, take steps to adjust their compensation to meet the local living wage.

   C. Advise the employee to seek legal assistance in their own country.

   D. Ask the employee to resign if they are dissatisfied with their current compensation.

6. Which of the following is NOT a primary responsibility of the International Labour Organization (ILO)?

   A. Promoting decent work and social justice worldwide.

   B. Providing humanitarian aid during natural disasters.

   C. Setting international labor standards.

   D. Offering capacity-building to member countries.

7. Which of the following should be included in a company's employee relations strategy?

   A. A code of conduct.

   B. Incentives for compliance.

   C. The company's policy on employee relations.

   D. The vision of what the employer hopes to accomplish.

8. A group of workers in a manufacturing plant has organized to collectively bargain for better wages, improved working conditions, and job security. They have established a formal association that represents the interests of its members in negotiations with the management of the company. This association engages in strikes, negotiations, and advocacy to protect and advance the rights of the workers. Based on the scenario described, what type of organization does this group most likely represent?

   A. Trade union.

   B. Federation.

   C. Nongovernmental organization (NGO).

   D. Workers' cooperative.

9. What is a "union card check" in the context of union organizing?

   A. A card used by management to track employee attendance.

   B. A card used by employees to request a union election.

   C. A card used by union organizers to gather support from employees.

   D. A card used to discourage employees from joining a union.

10. What is the purpose of a "strike vote" in the union organizing process?
    - A. It is used to compel employers to act in a favorable way toward the union.
    - B. It is a vote by union members to authorize a strike.
    - C. It is used to line-item strike clauses from a collective bargaining agreement during the negotiation process.
    - D. Nothing, as the union must be authorized to represent the members before they can strike.

11. What does right-to-work legislation mean in the context of labor relations?
    - A. Legislation that guarantees a job for every union member.
    - B. Legislation that prohibits unions from organizing in a workplace.
    - C. Legislation that allows employees to choose whether to join or financially support a union.
    - D. Legislation that mandates union membership for all workers.

12. A group of factory workers is on strike, demanding better working conditions and higher wages. The management of the company is considering hiring strikebreakers to continue production during the strike. What is the role of strikebreakers in this situation?
    - A. Strikebreakers are hired to put pressure on striking workers to return to work.
    - B. Strikebreakers are hired to support the striking workers and join the picket line.
    - C. Strikebreakers are hired to replace the striking workers and keep the production going.
    - D. Strikebreakers are hired to protest in sympathy with the striking workers.

13. A labor union representing employees at a manufacturing company is in negotiations with the company's management for a new collective bargaining agreement. The HR department plays a crucial role in this process. What is HR's primary responsibility in the collective bargaining agreement negotiation?
    - A. HR's primary responsibility is to lead the negotiations on behalf of the company.
    - B. HR's primary responsibility is to advocate for the union's demands and support the employees' interests.
    - C. HR's primary responsibility is to provide legal advice and ensure that the collective bargaining agreement complies with labor laws.
    - D. HR's primary responsibility is to facilitate open communication between the labor union and the employer.

14. Which of the following factors contributes to the cost of administering a labor contract in a unionized workplace?
    - A. The size of the labor union representing the employees.
    - B. The complexity of the negotiated contract terms.
    - C. The number of employees eligible for union membership.
    - D. The level of employee satisfaction with the labor contract.

15. You are an advanced HR professional working in a company with a well-established labor union. In the midst of organizational changes and restructuring, there is a complex situation emerging where teams are gatekeeping and departments are not being transparent. What approach should you adopt to effectively navigate this workplace situation while maintaining harmony within the organization?

A. Adopt a confrontational stance, aligning with one department's interests over others.

B. Maintain strict neutrality and minimize involvement in departmental politics to avoid taking sides.

C. Promote cross-departmental collaboration, encourage open dialogue, and seek common goals among teams.

D. Act as a mediator between conflicting departments, making decisions to balance their interests.

16. A company and its labor union are in negotiations for a new collective bargaining agreement. The company wants to increase production efficiency to remain competitive, while the union is concerned about job security and maintaining the current wages and benefits for its members. What bargaining approach should the parties adopt to achieve their aims?

A. Integrative negotiation.

B. Concessionary bargaining.

C. Distributive negotiation.

D. Interest based bargaining.

17. The company you work for has a hostile relationship with the labor union, and there is legitimate concern that the members will strike to settle disputes. Senior leaders have tasked HR with preparing for the possibility of a strike. Which of the following should the HR team do first?

A. Develop early warning systems.

B. Hire temporary workers as potential replacements.

C. Develop contingency plans.

D. Ask for employee feedback on a desired resolution.

18. The union members at your organization have just voted to strike, and your HR team has been tasked with creating a contingency plan that is focused on continued operations. Which of the following should be included in this plan? (Choose all that apply.)

A. Hiring strikebreakers.

B. Preparing for supply chain disruptions.

C. Protecting nonstriking employees.

D. Protecting striking workers' information.

19. In a manufacturing company, employees have gone on strike due to disputes over wages and working conditions. The management is considering its response. What would be an appropriate initial step in their strike response plan?
    - A. Hiring replacement workers immediately to avoid operational disruptions.
    - B. Confronting the striking employees to advocate the employer's position.
    - C. Initiating a dialogue with striking employees and their representatives.
    - D. Filing an unfair labor practice charge lawsuit against the striking employees and their union.

20. In response to employees' organizing efforts, an employer begins to listen to the employee complaints and document employees' concerns to understand the grievances. Management has also started to hold meetings with the employees to hear about the status of the union organizing efforts. What unfair labor practice has the employer committed?
    - A. Targeting employees who support the union.
    - B. Discriminating against employees who show interest in forming a union.
    - C. Interfering with, restraining, or coercing employees in the exercise of their rights.
    - D. None; these are reasonable efforts to communicate with the employees.

21. Which of the following is the best example of a secondary boycott?
    - A. A labor union urging its members to strike at their own workplace to achieve better working conditions.
    - B. Employees refusing to purchase products from a company that does business with their employer's supplier in support of a union strike.
    - C. A group of workers organizing a picket line outside their own workplace to protest unfair labor practices.
    - D. Workers participating in a strike to demand higher wages and improved benefits.

22. Which type of strike occurs when a union calls a strike without following the proper legal procedures or before the expiration of a labor contract?
    - A. Wildcat strike.
    - B. Sympathy strike.
    - C. General strike.
    - D. Economic strike.

23. During a period of labor conflict between the FAA and NATCA (the air traffic controllers' union), there was a work slowdown by air traffic controllers. How did this conflict and work slow down likely affect organizational results?
    - A. Organizational results remained unaffected as the conflict had no impact on operations.
    - B. Organizational results suffered due to decreased efficiency and increased operational costs.
    - C. Organizational results improved as labor negotiations led to cost-saving measures.
    - D. Organizational results fluctuated, with some departments benefiting from the conflict.

24. What approach involves employers and unions forming joint committees to regularly discuss workplace safety, productivity, and other mutual concerns?
   A. Traditional bargaining.
   B. Conflict resolution.
   C. Labor-management cooperation.
   D. Arbitration.

25. Many large companies have been successful at lawfully preventing employees from forming unions. What is the primary proactive approach in a union avoidance strategy?
   A. Actively engaging with employees to determine if there is union organizing activity occurring.
   B. Not discussing the union organizing to avoid a charge of an unfair labor practice.
   C. Employing measures to dissuade and deter unionization efforts.
   D. Collaborating with unions to address employee concerns and demands.

26. What is the main difference between a policy, a procedure, and a rule within an organization?
   A. Policies provide overarching principles, procedures outline specific steps, and rules specify consequences.
   B. Policies outline specific steps, procedures provide overarching principles, and rules specify consequences.
   C. Policies specify consequences, procedures provide overarching principles, and rules outline specific steps.
   D. Policies and procedures are set internally by the company; rules are set externally by the government.

27. Which of the following is an advantage and disadvantage of an open-door policy to prevent retaliation?
   A. Advantage: Encourages transparency; Disadvantage: May lead to a flood of minor complaints.
   B. Advantage: Creates a supportive work culture; Disadvantage: Undermines management authority.
   C. Advantage: Reduces employee stress; Disadvantage: Slows down conflict resolution.
   D. Advantage: Protects the organization from legal liability; Disadvantage: Increases employee isolation.

28. In workplace dispute resolution, when is it generally more appropriate to use mediation rather than arbitration?
   A. When a quick and legally binding decision is needed to resolve the dispute.
   B. When parties want to maintain control over the resolution process and reach a mutually agreeable solution.
   C. When a neutral third party is required to impose a final decision and settlement.
   D. When the dispute involves complex legal issues that require a formal hearing.

29. You are an HR manager in a company that has recently implemented a nonretaliation policy to protect employees who report workplace misconduct. An employee has just come forward with a complaint about their supervisor's inappropriate behavior. What actions should you consider taking to ensure compliance with retaliation prevention approaches?
    - A. Communicate with the employee to understand the complaint further and provide them with information about the nonretaliation policy.
    - B. Seek feedback from the supervisor in question to get their perspective on the issue.
    - C. Consult with legal counsel to determine the potential legal implications of the complaint.
    - D. Review the employee's performance and disciplinary history to assess their credibility.

30. What is a key positive approach for employers seeking to manage labor relations and employee concerns effectively in the workplace?
    - A. Offer to establish a committee of employees to bring up issues and concerns to management.
    - B. Actively listening to and addressing employee concerns and grievances.
    - C. Fostering a culture of open communication and trust with employees.
    - D. Encouraging employees to participate in workplace decision-making.

31. What are the primary differences between progressive discipline and positive discipline strategies?
    - A. Progressive discipline focuses on compliance and corrective action, while positive discipline emphasizes employee development and coaching.
    - B. Progressive discipline is strict, while positive discipline avoids negative consequences.
    - C. Progressive discipline involves immediate termination of employees, while positive discipline encourages leniency in policy violations.
    - D. Progressive discipline and positive discipline are essentially the same, with no significant differences between them.

32. Fill in the blank: A ________________ outlines ethical and behavioral expectations for employees, while a ________________ is a legally binding agreement negotiated between an employer and a labor union.
    - A. Code of conduct; employment contract.
    - B. Collective bargaining agreement; company policy.
    - C. Code of conduct; collective bargaining agreement.
    - D. Employment contract; company policy.

33. An employee feels they have been unfairly treated due to a violation of company policies. They decide to initiate the grievance process. What should be their first step?
    - A. File a lawsuit against the company.
    - B. Speak to their immediate supervisor informally.
    - C. Contact a labor union representative.
    - D. Submit a written grievance to HR or management.

34. Which of the following is a lawful use of an employment contract?

A. Requiring employees sign a contract as a condition of union membership.

B. Including noncompete clauses that place limits on employees from working in similar roles for competitors after leaving the company.

C. Including a clause where the employee is not entitled to overtime pay.

D. Requiring employees to sign a contract that allows the employer to terminate them at any time and for any reason.

35. Your company is downsizing as they have lost a large contract to a competitor. This requires you to lay off a number of employees. Some of those being laid off will need to transfer their knowledge of what they do to the remaining workforce. Which of the following is the best strategy to ensure a smooth transition?

A. Hold a series of town hall meetings to ask for support.

B. Add a cooperation clause into the severance agreements.

C. Offer stay bonuses.

D. Ask the transitioning workers to create standard operating procedures (SOPs), so the processes are documented for future training needs.

36. What is a potential disadvantage of progressive discipline policies in the workplace?

A. They create an atmosphere of continuous tension and distrust.

B. They offer vague and unpredictable consequences for misconduct.

C. They can limit employer action for more serious infractions.

D. They discourage open communication among employees.

37. You are the HR manager of a large manufacturing company, and it has come to your attention that an employee on the marketing team is having some attendance issues. Marie is usually punctual and productive but has been consistently arriving a few minutes late for the morning team meetings over the past two weeks. Her tardiness is not causing any major disruptions to the team's workflow, and her overall performance in other aspects of her job remains satisfactory. How should HR respond?

A. Issue Marie a verbal warning.

B. Have a discussion with Marie to find out what is causing her unusual tardiness.

C. Coach the department manager to chat with Marie to find out more about what is causing the lateness.

D. Ignore the issue as it is not affecting the team's output.

38. Which employee discipline technique is used for severe misconduct or repeated violations and involves placing the employee on unpaid leave for a specified period?

A. Termination.

B. Verbal counseling.

C. Suspension.

D. Corrective action.

39. Carl, an employee at Dreams Inc., recently filed a formal complaint with HR, alleging workplace harassment by his supervisor, Isabelle. HR initiated an internal investigation into Carl's complaint to determine its validity. During the investigation, HR found no evidence to substantiate Carl's claims of harassment, and it concluded that the complaint was without merit. Later, Carl was let go from his position as part of a business restructuring. Which of the following statements is true regarding Carl's termination?

   A. Carl's termination is wrongful because he filed a harassment complaint, and retaliation is illegal.

   B. Carl's termination is wrongful because Carl was protected as he had recently exercised his rights under the law.

   C. Carl's termination may be unlawful based on the timing of his separation.

   D. Carl's termination is wrongful because the company should have transferred him to a different department instead.

40. You are the HR manager at an employer with a policy that states that any employee who receives more than two customer complaints within a month will be subject to immediate termination. What impact does this policy have on achieving organizational results?

   A. The policy is a barrier to achieving organizational results.

   B. The policy ensures excellent customer service and employee accountability.

   C. The policy encourages open communication and collaboration among employees.

   D. The policy is unlawful and may result in a wrongful termination claim against the employer.

41. Which term best describes a process in which the parties to a dispute agree to let a neutral third-party determine the outcome, and both parties are bound by the neutral third-party's decision?

   A. Nonbinding ADR.

   B. Facilitative ADR.

   C. Evaluative ADR.

   D. Neutral ADR.

42. You are an advanced HR professional working with a business unit leader in your organization. The leader is interested in implementing a new employee recognition program to boost morale and productivity. The leader approaches you for guidance on how to proceed. What should you do in this consultative role?

   A. Provide an employee recognition program template and ask the leader to implement it as is.

   B. Collaborate with the leader to understand the specific needs and goals of the business unit and then tailor an employee recognition program accordingly.

   C. Identify external employee recognition providers and make a business case to use them.

   D. Provide the leader with training resources so they can learn more about effective recognition programs.

43. In the context of labor contract administration, which of the following is a potential cost-saving measure for employers?

A. Extensive training programs for union representatives.

B. Frequent renegotiation of contract terms.

C. Investing in technology for contract management and communication.

D. Lengthening the contract duration between negotiations.

44. Rachael is the customer service manager at a small OEM organization. She is new to her position and has realized that of her seven total employees, many seem to be arriving late. For example, of the 20 workdays this month, 6 days of work were missed due to employee absences. Before she approaches the issue, she wants to understand the nature of the problem. What is the absenteeism rate for the customer service team in October?

A. 15%.

B. 20%.

C. 30%.

D. 40%.

45. In a manufacturing facility, the use of standard operating procedures (SOPs) plays a crucial role in ensuring compliance with safety and quality standards. Which of the following statements best explains how SOPs help ensure compliance?

A. SOPs increase the complexity of tasks, making it more challenging for employees to follow guidelines.

B. SOPs provide clear and standardized instructions, making it easier for employees to understand and follow procedures.

C. SOPs are primarily used for managerial purposes and do not impact employees' compliance with safety regulations.

D. SOPs are optional, and employees can choose whether or not to follow them.

46. In your organization, employees have recently learned that a colleague who performs similar work as them is receiving significantly higher compensation. This discovery has led to feelings of dissatisfaction and demotivation among some employees. Which aspect of equity theory is evident in this situation?

A. Overpayment inequity.

B. Underpayment inequity.

C. Overpayment equity.

D. Underpayment equity.

47. Which type of HR system is essential for effectively managing employee relations within an organization?

A. Payroll management system.

B. Talent acquisition system.

C. Employee portals.

D. Performance management software.

48. Which of the following is NOT a key element to a strategic labor strategy?

- **A.** Employee training and development programs.
- **B.** Labor cost analysis and optimization.
- **C.** Workforce planning and forecasting.
- **D.** Union negotiations and collective bargaining.

49. A union has recently successfully been organized at the company where you work. Rather than being an adversarial relationship, management wants to work collaboratively so that the union, the company, and the team members are all successful. Which of the following structures should you recommend?

- **A.** A management-led committee.
- **B.** A labor cooperative.
- **C.** A federation.
- **D.** A wage board.

50. Which of the following describes a key difference in collective bargaining practices between the United States and many other countries?

- **A.** In other countries, collective bargaining is mandatory for all industries.
- **B.** In the United States, collective bargaining primarily occurs at the industry level.
- **C.** In other countries, sectoral bargaining is common, involving multiple companies within an industry.
- **D.** In the United States, enterprise-level bargaining is rare, with unions negotiating only at the national level.

51. In what ways are employee relations and employee engagement similar HR functions?

- **A.** Both focus on hiring and recruiting top talent.
- **B.** Both involve managing and improving workplace relationships.
- **C.** Both are heavily focused on labor law compliance.
- **D.** Both revolve around workplace safety and satisfaction.

52. Which of the following measures of positive employee relations is most likely to motivate older workers?

- **A.** Offering flexible work schedules and phased retirement options.
- **B.** Implementing a performance-based pay structure.
- **C.** Providing extensive training and development opportunities.
- **D.** Introducing a casual dress code policy.

53. Which of the following is an example of an employee relations strategy at the onboarding stage of the employee life cycle?

- **A.** Conducting a 90-day review.
- **B.** Providing new employees with a comprehensive benefits package.
- **C.** Offering orientation sessions that emphasize company culture and values.
- **D.** Accelerated training and development.

54. Which of the following does NOT need to be included in any employee relations strategy?

A. Crisis management.

B. Employee feedback.

C. Employee recognition.

D. Sourcing strategy.

55. How do organizational lobbying efforts affect the labor relations function of human resources?

A. They help get favorable political candidates elected to office.

B. They can influence labor laws and regulations.

C. Lobbying leads to decreased costs of doing business in certain communities.

D. They lead to decreased unionization rates within the workforce.

56. What is negligent hiring in the context of employee relations?

A. A hiring process that thoroughly screens and selects the best candidates.

B. A second-chance program that gives jobs to individuals convicted of a crime.

C. Failing to conduct proper background checks or due diligence before hiring an employee.

D. A process that emphasizes diversity and inclusion in recruitment.

57. What is one of the key benefits of implementing employee involvement strategies in employee relations?

A. Decreased employee job satisfaction.

B. Reduced employee turnover.

C. Decreased workplace conflicts.

D. Lower employee productivity.

58. Which of the following is not an example of an employee involvement strategy designed to solicit employee feedback?

A. Self-directed work team.

B. Focus groups.

C. Staff meetings.

D. Employee surveys.

59. What role does homogeneity typically play in ethical international human resource management (IHRM)?

A. Homogeneity enhances ethical decision-making by promoting diverse perspectives within multinational teams.

B. Homogeneity can lead to ethical challenges as it may create a lack of cultural sensitivity and understanding.

C. Homogeneity in IHRM ensures consistency in ethical practices across diverse cultural contexts.

D. Homogeneity has no significant impact on ethical considerations in IHRM.

60. What is one of the key tensions in a global employee relation in a shared service structure?
   A. The tension between employee engagement and productivity.
   B. The tension between talent retention and corporate structure.
   C. The tension between corporate structures and local practices.
   D. The tension between linguistic and cultural relationships.

Key Concept Research Questions

Taking a deeper dive into key concepts helps to create context, the information necessary to critically think through the questions on exam day. A bonus is that this research should also make you more knowledgeable in your work, so making the time to answer the next two questions is worth it. You can find the answers in Appendix C.

1. What are the main reasons that employees form unions?

   Consider using the largest federation in the United States, the AFL-CIO, to understand the reasoning behind why employee join unions. Find them at `https://aflcio.org`.

2. What are strategies employers can use to help avoid union organization?

   Staying union-free is a strategic initiative that is just as important as other business strategies. This is of particular interest for industries that are regularly targeted by unions, such as big-box retail and manufacturing. Take a look at the positive employee relations strategies outlined at `https://projectionsinc.com/unionproof/staying-union-free-strategies` to help answer this question.

Test Your Employee and Labor Relations Terminology Knowledge

The following are the terms to use to test your knowledge on Employee and Labor Relations key terms. You can find the correct answers in Appendix B.

- Arbitration
- Code of conduct
- Collective bargaining agreement
- Due process
- Employee complaint process
- Employee participation
- Employee relations
- Employee rights
- Good faith bargaining
- Grievance procedures
- Labor dispute resolution
- Labor-management cooperation
- Mediation
- Positive employee relations
- Retaliation
- Standard operating procedures
- Strikes
- Trade union
- Union election
- Workplace policies

1. __________ is the process of resolving disputes between labor unions and employers through a neutral third party's binding decision.
2. A __________ is a set of ethical guidelines and rules that define acceptable behavior and expectations within an organization.
3. A __________ is a legally binding contract that outlines terms and conditions of employment negotiated between a labor union and an employer.
4. __________ is the fair and impartial treatment and procedures that ensure employees' rights are protected during disciplinary actions or disputes.
5. The __________ is a formal system within an organization for addressing and resolving employee concerns, grievances, or disputes.
6. __________ is the practice of involving employees in decision-making processes that affect their work and the organization.
7. __________ is the management of interactions and relationships between employers and employees to create a positive and productive work environment.
8. __________ are the legal protections and entitlements granted to employees in the workplace, often related to fair treatment, wages, and working conditions.
9. __________ is a sincere and honest negotiation process between labor unions and employers to reach agreements in a fair and cooperative manner.
10. __________ are structured and formalized steps for addressing and resolving employee complaints or disputes within an organization.
11. __________ is the process of resolving conflicts and disagreements between labor unions and employers to maintain workplace harmony.
12. __________ are collaborative efforts between labor unions and employers to address common workplace issues and challenges.
13. __________ is a facilitated negotiation process where a neutral third party helps labor unions and employers reach a mutually acceptable agreement.
14. __________ are strategies and practices used by employers to foster a harmonious and cooperative relationship with employees and labor unions.
15. __________ is the adverse actions taken by employers against employees in response to their exercise of legally protected rights or actions.
16. The __________ are established and documented step-by-step guidelines that dictate how specific tasks or processes should be performed within an organization.
17. __________ are an organized work stoppage by employees, often initiated by a labor union, to press for specific demands or negotiate better terms.
18. __________ is an organization formed by workers in a specific industry or trade to collectively represent their interests in negotiations with employers.
19. __________ is the formal process where employees vote to determine whether they want to be represented by a labor union.
20. __________ are the written rules and regulations that govern behavior, expectations, and procedures within an organization.

Conclusion

The elements of effective communication, fair treatment, and conflict resolution are all part of effectively managing relationships in the workplace. This includes examining the union-organizing and collective bargaining processes, all essential for cultivating a harmonious and productive workplace.

The context of labor relations has remained relatively stable throughout exam changes over the years. This domain continues to focus on the relationships within the workplace: relationships between the employer and employee, and the relationship between an employer, a union, and a union member. There were some changes, however. While the 2018 HRCI exams allocated a significant 39% of content to this domain, the 2024 PHR/i updates have reallocated this to 20%, emphasizing the more compliance-related aspects. For senior HR leaders, the SPHR/i subject has transitioned from a dedicated, separate functional area to becoming part of the new Talent Management functional area.

In the SHRM CP and SCP exams, Employee and Labor Relations find their place within the Organization domain, mirroring content like the HRCI exams. For seasoned professionals, the focus extends beyond compliance to consultative competencies, empowering them to act as advisors and cultivate meaningful relationships with external resources.

Additional Resources

If you want to study employee and labor relations in more detail, there are several reputable online resources, podcasts, and videos designed to help you learn using a variety of learning styles.

Websites

- U.S. Department of Labor (DOL), Office of Labor-Management Standards (OLMS) (`www.dol.gov/agencies/olms`)

  The DOL's OLMS provides a wealth of information on labor relations, union activities, and compliance with labor laws. It offers various reports, guides, and resources related to labor-management relations in the United States.

- National Labor Relations Board (NLRB) (`www.nlrb.gov`)

  The NLRB is responsible for enforcing the National Labor Relations Act (NLRA) and oversees labor relations in the private sector. The website includes educational materials, case decisions, and publications related to labor law.

- Cornell University's ILR School, Labor and Employment Law Program (`www.ilr.cornell.edu/labor-and-employment-law-program`)

  Cornell's ILR School offers online courses and resources that cover various aspects of labor and employment law, including collective bargaining, labor relations, and workplace conflict resolution.

- American Bar Association (ABA), Section of Labor and Employment Law (www.americanbar.org/groups/labor_law)

  The ABA's Labor and Employment Law Section provides valuable insights and resources related to labor and employment law, including publications, webinars, and events.

Podcasts

- *Labor Relations Today* by Constangy, Brooks, Smith & Prophete, LLP (www.constangy.com/newsroom-podcasts)

  This podcast discusses various labor and employment law topics, including labor relations, union organizing, and collective bargaining. It features legal experts sharing insights and analysis.
- *The Culture Factor* hosted by the Human Capital Institute (HCI) (www.hci.org/resources?type=91)

  This podcast by HCI explores the role of company culture in employee engagement and retention. It features interviews with HR professionals, authors, and thought leaders.
- *Culture First Podcast* by Culture Amp (www.culturefirst.com/podcast)

  Culture Amp's podcast focuses on building a positive workplace culture, which is closely tied to employee engagement and retention. It features conversations with HR and culture experts.

YouTube Channels

Accessing exam content using multiple learning styles is a beneficial way to create new pathways to recall. Subscribe to the following channels on www.YouTube.com to stay up-to-date on important Employee Relations content:

- HR Bartender

  HR Bartender, hosted by Sharlyn Lauby, offers HR insights, including employee relations, leadership, and workplace culture. The channel includes informative videos and discussions.
- The Spiggle Law Firm

  This law firm provides interesting and informative videos on the history of employment law and enforcement agencies (such as the EEOC) and general labor relations. It offers legal perspectives and updates on labor-related issues.
- Employment Law This Week by Epstein Becker Green

  Employment Law This Week is a video series that covers the latest developments in labor and employment law. It provides legal insights and updates on key employment issues.

- [illegible]
- [illegible]

Podcasts

[illegible]

Chapter 10

Ethical Practice and Corporate Social Responsibility

The World Bank regularly holds anticorruption forums to help educate leaders on the role they play in ethical and humane business practices. Highlights of the 2023 sessions included the emerging and important role that private organizations have on ensuring fair treatment, ensuring transparency, and fighting corruption in the communities where we live and work. The 2023 forum also featured leaders speaking on the need to restore trust, meaning that there is much to repair and prevent in terms of organizational unethical behaviors. Cue human resources.

In HR, ethical behavior and personal and professional integrity contribute to building trust, fostering a positive workplace culture, and ensuring the compliance of HR practices with legal and ethical standards. While employees are expected to act in a trustworthy manner, organizations themselves are charged with acting in the interest of all stakeholders. This is often accomplished through the lens of corporate social responsibility initiatives.

There are opportunities for applying ethical best practices throughout the life cycle of the employee and in business strategy itself. The key factors covered in this chapter include the following:

- **Corporate governance:** Ensuring that there are clear structures and processes in place for ethical decision-making at the highest levels of the organization.
- **Ethical business principles including conflicts of interest and bias:** Implementing policies and practices to identify and mitigate conflicts of interest and bias in hiring, promotions, and decision-making.
- **Corporate social responsibility (CSR):** Engaging in CSR initiatives that consider the social, environmental, and economic impacts of business decisions, such as supporting sustainability and community development.
- **HR competencies:** HR professionals should demonstrate personal and professional integrity in all HR functions, including recruitment, employee relations, and compliance.

The practice questions in this chapter will cover various aspects of ethical behavior and corporate social responsibility in the context of human resources. You will be tested on your knowledge of these key factors and how they influence HR practices and organizational behavior as a whole.

Real World Scenario

REI's Commitment to Ethical Practices: A Focus on Well-Being

REI, a prominent outdoor retailer, is celebrated not only for its top-tier outdoor gear but also for its extensive commitment to ethical employment and corporate practices. In this case study, we will explore how REI's steadfast dedication to ethical principles has molded its employment and corporate practices and the numerous commendable outcomes it has achieved.

Background and Problem

Founded in 1938, REI, or Recreational Equipment, Inc., has grown into one of the United States' largest outdoor retail cooperatives. The company's extensive range of outdoor products is matched only by its unwavering devotion to advocating for environmental sustainability and ethical business practices. REI operates as a consumer cooperative, with its customers functioning as owners. Its mission transcends the pursuit of profits, extending to a commitment to the outdoors and the environment.

Diagnosis

REI's ethical employment and corporate practices were established to harmonize its business operations with its core values. The company identified these two main challenges:

- **High turnover:** As with many retail enterprises, REI grappled with high employee turnover rates, resulting in escalated hiring costs and a detrimental impact on employee morale and customer service.
- **Ethical sourcing:** As an outdoor retailer, REI faced the challenge of ensuring the ethical sourcing of its products, including concerns regarding supply chain labor practices and environmental consequences.

Strategies

To confront these challenges and uphold its commitment to ethical principles, REI implemented a multifaceted array of strategies.

- **Employee engagement and well-being:** REI embarked on a journey to enhance employee engagement and well-being by offering competitive compensation, comprehensive benefits, and opportunities for outdoor experiences. This approach aimed to diminish turnover rates while bolstering employee morale.
- **Ethical sourcing and sustainability:** The company made ethical sourcing a top priority by forging partnerships with suppliers dedicated to fair labor practices and environmental sustainability. REI also championed eco-friendly products and initiatives aimed at reducing its carbon footprint.

- **Community engagement:** REI actively engaged with local communities by organizing volunteer events, supporting outdoor education programs, and advocating for the protection of natural spaces. This demonstrated the company's commitment to giving back to the communities it serves.

Results

REI's commitment to ethical employment and corporate practices generated a host of beneficial outcomes.

- **Reduced turnover:** By investing in employee well-being and engagement, REI managed to significantly curtail employee turnover, resulting in substantial cost savings and a more dedicated and satisfied workforce.
- **Ethical reputation:** REI's emphasis on ethical sourcing, sustainability, and community engagement elevated its reputation as a socially responsible company. Customers were drawn to the company's transparency and dedication to ethical values, further enhancing its image as a responsible retailer.
- **Community impact:** REI's community engagement initiatives, including volunteerism and support for outdoor education, had a positive impact on local communities. This not only strengthened its ties with customers but also contributed to the preservation of natural spaces.

Conclusion

REI's ethical employment and corporate practices have demonstrated that a large company can prioritize employee well-being, ethical sourcing, environmental sustainability, and community engagement while remaining profitable and competitive in the market. By aligning its business operations with its core values, REI has created a profoundly positive impact on both its employees and the outdoor industry.

Ethical Practice and Corporate Social Responsibility Questions

1. At the organization you work for, the CEO is accountable to the board of directors and shareholders. She has a generous executive compensation agreement, where her annual bonus is tied directly to the company's stock price. Which of the following control is most likely to prevent conflicts of interest in the CEO's decision-making?
   - **A.** Quarterly reporting.
   - **B.** Board oversight.
   - **C.** GAAP.
   - **D.** An ethical code of conduct.
2. A recent report in the United States announced that many major car brands were at high risk of working with overseas businesses that were guilty of human rights violations. The car manufacturers are facing public scrutiny and potential legal action due to findings involving unethical practices and violations of environmental and social standards. What aspect of corporate social responsibility is most likely to be under review?
   - **A.** Failing to comply with an NGO.
   - **B.** Issues with supply chain transparency.
   - **C.** Lack of compliance with FLSA standards.
   - **D.** Violations of ILO standards.
3. One of the largest and most significant cyberattacks in history occurred in 2017, when hackers exploited a vulnerability in a major credit reporting agency's website software, gaining access to sensitive personal information of approximately 147 million Americans. This breach exposed individuals' Social Security numbers, birth dates, addresses, and, in some cases, credit card information, leading to widespread concerns about identity theft and cybersecurity. The CFO and two other executives sold a combined $1.8 million in company stock in the days following the company's discovery and before public disclosure of the breach. What ethical duty, if any, did company executives who knew about the data breach have regarding stock sales?
   - **A.** They should have gained approval from the board of directors to sell their stock.
   - **B.** They had an obligation to inform all "covered insiders" not to sell any stock until the breach information was made public.
   - **C.** They should have waited to sell their stock until the SEC gave them clearance to do so.
   - **D.** They had no ethical duty regarding stock sales.
4. Mary, an HR professional, discovers that a colleague has been engaged in fraudulent activities within the organization. What should Mary do in this situation?
   - **A.** Confront her colleague directly.
   - **B.** Report the misconduct to higher management or ethics hotline.
   - **C.** Ignore the misconduct to avoid confrontation.
   - **D.** Cover up her colleague's actions to protect the team's reputation.

5. What is the primary purpose of a code of ethics in human resource management?
   A. To eliminate unethical behavior from the workplace.
   B. To establish a legal framework for HR practices.
   C. To guide ethical behavior and decision-making.
   D. To prevent fraudulent activity.

6. What is the primary purpose of an "opt-in" policy in the workplace regarding data collection for employee benefits?
   A. To automatically enroll employees in benefit programs.
   B. To allow employees to choose whether they want to participate in benefit programs.
   C. To require employees to participate in all available benefit programs.
   D. To provide benefits to employees without their consent.

7. As the HR manager, you recently discovered a discrepancy in employee payroll that resulted in all team members being overpaid by one full day. Instead of ignoring the error or attempting to cover it up, you promptly notify the employees and senior leadership and work with payroll to schedule a repayment plan by the employees. Which of the following is the best example of personal integrity?
   A. Admitting the mistake.
   B. Writing a policy to prevent the error from occurring again.
   C. Training colleagues to ensure they understand the importance of accurate payroll.
   D. Protecting the integrity of the team by taking the blame.

8. What is a common barrier to personal integrity for HR professionals and leaders in the workplace?
   A. Prioritizing the interests of shareholders over ethical considerations.
   B. Fearing negative consequences as a result of being honest.
   C. Avoiding legal responsibilities to protect personal interests.
   D. Having a rigid, inflexible approach to ethical dilemmas.

9. Carlos often evaluates employees' performance based on their punctuality and attendance rather than their actual job performance. He frequently overlooks other aspects of their work. What type of bias is Carlos displaying?
   A. Availability bias.
   B. Confirmation bias.
   C. Performance bias.
   D. Horn bias.

10. What is a key strategy for human resource teams to become a trusted and credible business partner within an organization?
   A. Minimizing communication with employees to maintain neutrality.
   B. Focusing on administrative tasks and paperwork.
   C. Aligning HR strategies with the overall business goals.
   D. Avoiding collaboration with other departments to maintain independence.

11. Kinsey, an HR manager, is aware of a potential company restructuring that might result in layoffs. Some employees have heard rumors about this, and a local news reporter has contacted her for information. What action should Kinsey take to use appropriate discretion when communicating with company stakeholders?

- **A.** Share all the details with the news reporter to ensure transparency.
- **B.** Immediately inform all employees about the potential restructuring to address their concerns.
- **C.** Refuse to comment on the matter with the news reporter and communicate only what has been officially announced internally.
- **D.** Share speculative information with employees to prepare them for possible changes.

12. Which of the following is a key characteristic of a well-structured code of ethics?

- **A.** A description of the consequences for failing to act in an ethical manner.
- **B.** An anonymous reporting mechanism.
- **C.** A definition of how whistleblowers are protected under the law.
- **D.** A company code of conduct.

13. Mark, an IT supervisor, is asked by his manager to delete incriminating emails related to a regulatory violation. What ethical risk does Mark face in this situation?

- **A.** Insider trading.
- **B.** Data breach.
- **C.** Falsifying records.
- **D.** Cybersecurity violations.

14. What is a fundamental ethical consideration in total rewards activities?

- **A.** Offering higher compensation to employees with more experience.
- **B.** Ensuring piece rate pay is consistent across all departments.
- **C.** Keeping accurate payroll records.
- **D.** Ensuring transparency in how total rewards are determined and communicated.

15. Which ethical control can help foster accountability and transparency in the workplace?

- **A.** Promoting a culture of zero tolerance for ethical violations.
- **B.** Providing limited access to information for employees to protect confidentiality.
- **C.** Implementing an anonymous whistleblower hotline.
- **D.** Restricting access to employee personnel files.

16. In one of your company's overseas subsidiaries, Rosie, a mid-level manager, became aware that the CEO bribed a local official to win a contract for services. Feeling morally obligated to act, Rosie decides to file an ethical complaint within the company. Which of the following is NOT a primary responsibility of an ethics officer in response to this complaint?

- **A.** Conducting an impartial and thorough investigation into the alleged ethical violations.
- **B.** Protecting the identity of the whistleblower.
- **C.** Reporting the ethical complaint to the local authorities for legal action.
- **D.** Ensuring that the company's policies and procedures are followed throughout the investigation.

17. In the context of ethical use of company assets, what should employees prioritize when faced with asset-related decisions?
   A. Maximizing personal financial gain as a perk of employment.
   B. Minimizing reporting of asset usage to protect the company from oversight.
   C. Aligning asset utilization with the organization's goals and policies.
   D. Discouraging personal use of personal devices within the workplace.

18. Edgewater Inc., a pharmaceutical company, has been engaging in unethical practices by inflating drug prices in a low-income region, making essential medications inaccessible to the local population. How might this unethical corporate behavior affect the community stakeholders?
   A. It may bring a well-needed spotlight on the need for healthcare in the region.
   B. It could increase profits for the company shareholders.
   C. It might result in negative publicity for the organization.
   D. It is likely to worsen public health outcomes and exacerbate poverty.

19. Which of the following is an example of a corporate social responsibility (CSR) initiative related to environmental sustainability?
   A. Offering stock options to employees.
   B. Reducing carbon footprints.
   C. Ensuring supply chain humane practices.
   D. Supporting local charities.

20. A major frozen vegetable producer designed an incentive program to reward line workers in the quality control department. The company implemented a piece rate pay system that gave employees an incentive for every bug removed from the line. The inadvertent result was that employees began to bring bugs and plant them on the quality line to earn the additional pay. What does this situation highlight about the ethical considerations of incentive pay?
   A. Incentive pay systems can effectively motivate employees to improve their performance.
   B. Monetary rewards do not necessarily improve ethical outcomes.
   C. Piece-rate pay should be based on objective data.
   D. Employees are inherently dishonest.

21. What are the primary differences between legal obligations and ethical responsibilities?
   A. Legal obligations are enforceable by law and can result in penalties for noncompliance, while ethical obligations are moral principles and guidelines that may not have legal consequences.
   B. Legal obligations are based on secular beliefs, while ethical obligations are religious principles derived from philosophy.
   C. Legal obligations are universal and apply to all individuals, while ethical obligations vary from person to person.
   D. Legal obligations are concerned with personal values and beliefs, while ethical obligations pertain to societal norms and regulations.

22. When considering business ethics in the design of corporate strategy, which of the following is a fundamental ethical principle to prioritize?

A. Maximizing short-term profits for shareholders.

B. Pursuing aggressive competitive tactics to gain market dominance.

C. Balancing the interests of stakeholders while maintaining integrity and transparency.

D. Focusing on cost-cutting measures to increase profitability.

23. In a healthcare setting, a group of nurses is concerned about a hospital's policy that seems to prioritize cost-cutting over patient care. They believe that this policy compromises patient safety and well-being. What best represents ethical advocacy in this scenario?

A. The nurses used the hospital's whistleblower hotline to report wrongdoing.

B. The nurses gathered evidence of the policy's negative impact on patient care and presented their findings to hospital administrators.

C. The nurses anonymously leaked information to the media to raise public awareness about the hospital's policy.

D. The nurses lodged a complaint with the hospital board of directors of corporate wrongdoing.

24. What does the "stakeholder theory" emphasize in corporate social responsibility?

A. CSR efforts should address the interests of all stakeholders, not just shareholders.

B. Focusing on environmental sustainability is a key responsibility for responsible organizations.

C. Maximizing profits for shareholders should be the priority for corporate leadership.

D. Gathering feedback from the community will improve stakeholder outcomes.

25. What are the three Ps of the triple bottom line theory?

A. Product, price, and production.

B. People, planet, and profit.

C. Performance, production, and public relations.

D. People, process, and policies.

26. A retail company donates a portion of its profits to support local community development projects, sponsors educational programs for underprivileged children, and actively engages in recycling and waste reduction efforts in its stores. These initiatives are in line with which aspect of the triple bottom line?

A. Compliance with ILO standards.

B. Acting as good faith community partners.

C. Focusing on environmental sustainability.

D. Enhancing social responsibility.

27. What is the initial step in the corporate social responsibility strategic process?
    - **A.** Gathering feedback from experts.
    - **B.** Conducting a stakeholder analysis.
    - **C.** Announcing CSR intentions to the public to gain support.
    - **D.** Calculating ROI for CSR activities.

28. How can senior HR leaders effectively communicate a vision for organizational culture that aligns corporate behavior with organizational values?
    - **A.** By leveraging emails for regular communication of ethical highlights.
    - **B.** By hosting open forums and dialogues with employees to discuss culture and values.
    - **C.** By surveying employees about how inclusive the company is.
    - **D.** By training middle managers on how to behave in an ethical manner.

29. What role does empathy play in a company's CSR strategy?
    - **A.** Empathy can weaken the objectivity of a CSR strategy.
    - **B.** Empathy should drive CSR initiatives for maximum impact.
    - **C.** Empathy is a strong predictor for employee involvement in CSR initiatives.
    - **D.** Empathy plays no role in a company's CSR success or failure.

30. A multinational food and beverage company is facing public criticism for its excessive use of single-use plastic packaging, contributing to environmental pollution. In response, the company announces a new initiative to reduce plastic waste, including transitioning to recyclable packaging and investing in waste reduction technologies. Which stage of the CSR strategic management process does this scenario represent?
    - **A.** CSR goal setting and planning.
    - **B.** CSR stakeholder engagement.
    - **C.** CSR implementation and action.
    - **D.** CSR reporting and communication.

31. What is the best way for senior HR leaders to audit a company's ethical business practices?
    - **A.** Conducting regular ethical audits.
    - **B.** Relying on employee self-reporting to gauge ethical business practices.
    - **C.** Outsourcing ethical audits to third-party consultants to minimize bias.
    - **D.** Conducting one-time ethical audits without ongoing monitoring and follow-up as conditions regularly change.

32. When designing ethical training programs for employees, what should be a fundamental component to ensure effectiveness and behavioral change?
    - **A.** Including legal training on compliance regulations.
    - **B.** Incorporating real-world ethical dilemmas and case studies.
    - **C.** Emphasis on company policies and procedures.
    - **D.** Standardizing the content to ensure consistent information is learned.

33. Which of the following are key characteristics of a human resource professional acting as an ethical agent?

A. Modeling fairness and equity in making HR decisions.

B. Maximizing company profits.

C. Ensuring employee benefits are in alignment with employee needs.

D. Not discriminating in decisions about promotions.

34. A technology conglomerate with operations across the globe develops a CSR strategy that aligns its initiatives with global sustainability targets such as the United Nations sustainable development goals (SDGs). The company implements consistent sustainability practices and reporting across all its subsidiaries worldwide. What type of CSR program is this scenario indicative of?

A. A globally integrated CSR program.

B. A locally responsive CSR program.

C. A compliant CSR program.

D. An independent CSR program.

35. What is one of the positive outcomes of employee volunteerism programs for organizations?

A. Improved productivity.

B. Enhanced corporate profits.

C. Increased job satisfaction.

D. Improved corporate social responsibility image.

36. Which of the following is a NOT a challenge to successfully measuring CSR initiatives?

A. Lack of a universally accepted framework.

B. Difficulty in defining impact.

C. Lack of standardized data.

D. Lack of objective data to measure ROI.

37. What is a potential drawback of employee volunteerism programs in terms of employee diversity and inclusion?

A. Increasing feelings of favoritism if an employee's preferred charity is not supported.

B. Fostering a culture of individualism versus collectivism.

C. Unintentionally excluding certain groups of employees.

D. Decreasing overall employee engagement.

38. How can an organization utilize an ESG rating as part of their corporate social responsibility program?

A. An ESG rating provides objective data to use for marketing purposes to attract customers and investors.

B. ESG ratings are mainly utilized to measure financial performance and are unrelated to CSR efforts.

C. An organization can use its ESG rating to improve their greenhouse gas emissions.

D. ESG ratings are useful for nonprofit organizations to comply with grant requirements that have CSR clauses.

39. What is the primary difference between sustainability and social responsibility in the context of corporate practices?

A. Sustainability primarily focuses on financial profitability, while social responsibility prioritizes environmental conservation.

B. Sustainability centers on long-term environmental impact, while social responsibility is concerned with philanthropic initiatives.

C. Sustainability encompasses environmental and economic considerations, while social responsibility extends to ethical treatment of employees and communities.

D. Sustainability is exclusively related to product quality, while social responsibility pertains to customer satisfaction.

40. Which of the following is not considered a stakeholder in traditional CSR initiatives?

A. Investors.

B. Customers.

C. Governments.

D. Communities.

41. As an HR professional, you recognize that it is difficult to anticipate and plan for every possible ethical dilemma that can arise in the workplace. Which of the following is a best practice that can be used navigate ethics in the workplace?

A. Ethical frameworks.

B. Evidenced-based decision-making.

C. Availability heuristics.

D. Labor law compliance.

42. How does an HR professional's ability to be authentic play an important role in creating and supporting an ethical culture?

A. Authenticity is a main driver to setting the direction of corporate behavior.

B. Authenticity helps HR professionals maintain personal integrity.

C. Authenticity is essential for making difficult decisions.

D. An HR professional's authenticity is not relevant to creating an ethical culture.

43. As the HR manager of a large corporation committed to CSR, the company allocates a significant portion of its profits to community development programs, with a particular focus on improving the well-being of economically disadvantaged communities. The CSR initiatives are designed to ensure that the benefits of corporate success are distributed in a way that prioritizes the needs of the least advantaged members of society. This corporate behavior is an example of which of the following?

A. Procedural justice.

B. Duty-based ethics.

C. Moral high ground.

D. Rawls' theory of justice.

44. Imagine you work for a multinational corporation with a strong commitment to corporate social responsibility (CSR). The company's CSR initiatives include implementing fair wage policies, providing equal opportunities for career advancement, and investing in educational programs in underprivileged communities. The aim is to ensure that the benefits of the company's success are shared in a way that promotes economic equity and reduces disparities. This corporate behavior is an example of which of the following?

A. Goodwill.

B. Absolutism.

C. Distributive justice.

D. Categorical imperative.

45. In the context of CSR initiatives, a key characteristic of a libertarian view of distributive justice is:

A. Minimal government intervention.

B. Voluntary government oversight.

C. Involuntary government oversight.

D. Mediated oversight through an NGO.

46. Which of the following words best describes ethical Total Rewards administration?

A. Competitive.

B. Nondiscriminatory.

C. Transparent.

D. Humane.

47. Which of the following statements best describes the role of employer ethical behavior in workers' compensation claims?

A. The employer has a general duty to keep employees safe from harm.

B. The employer has a moral imperative to protect worker safety.

C. The employer has a responsibility to return the injured worker as close to "whole" as possible.

D. The employer must pay for an injured worker's treatment for as long as necessary.

48. What is the main difference between a fiduciary responsibility and ethical behavior?

A. Fiduciary responsibility is legally mandated, while ethical behavior is voluntary.

B. Ethical behavior requires financial expertise, while fiduciary responsibility does not.

C. Fiduciary responsibility focuses on social responsibility, while ethical behavior centers on legal obligations.

D. Ethical behavior is primarily concerned with financial matters, while fiduciary responsibility involves moral decision-making.

49. To whom does the doctrine of "do no harm" best apply?

A. Consultants.

B. Employees.

C. Attorneys.

D. All professionals.

50. Camilla, a 35-year old tech worker, has recently been laid off from her job and heard from her former co-workers that the company promoted a team member who was willing to be paid less for the same work. Which of the following did the employer violate?

A. Title VII of the Civil Rights Act of 1964.

B. The Duty of Good Faith and Fair Dealing.

C. The Doctrine of At-Will Employment.

D. The Equal Pay Act.

51. Which of the following scenarios best represents a "common good" approach to ethical decision-making?

A. A company prioritizes short-term profits so that all employees get their annual bonus.

B. An organization focuses on their responsibility to all stakeholders.

C. A CEO orients his decision-making to maximize profits for shareholders.

D. A business pursues social justice marketing tactics to reach a more diverse customer.

52. Which of the following is NOT an ethical consideration when evaluating the company's supply chain?

A. Ensuring fair labor practices and workers' rights.

B. Minimizing environmental impact and sustainability.

C. Maximizing profits and cost-effectiveness.

D. Preventing child labor and exploitative working conditions.

53. What distinguishes social mores from ethical behaviors?

A. Social mores are universal moral principles, while ethical behaviors are culturally specific norms.

B. Social mores are based on universal moral principles, while ethical behaviors are culturally specific norms.

C. Social mores are culturally specific norms, while ethical behaviors are grounded in universal moral principles.

D. Social mores and ethical behaviors are interchangeable terms with the same meaning.

54. Which of the following statements best reflect the need for recognizing an ethical situation when it arises?

A. Having a strong sense of personal integrity.

B. Seeing when an employee is visibly upset about an issue.

C. Having inside knowledge to the intent behind a decision.

D. Understanding when a decision will violate an unwritten agreement.

55. When using personality assessments in the workplace, what is the primary ethical consideration for employers?

A. Selecting assessments that are most cost-effective for the organization.

B. Ensuring that external consultants administer the assessments to maintain objectivity.

C. That the assessments are reliable predictors of behaviors.

D. That the assessments are not psychological in nature, but rather job-related.

56. Which of the following best characterizes the virtue approach to ethical decision-making?

A. Prioritizing the greatest good for the greatest number of people.

B. Focusing on adherence to established rules and regulations.

C. Emphasizing the development of behavioral traits and moral attitudes.

D. Maximizing personal benefit and self-interest.

57. What can HR do to address corruption risks when doing business in other countries?

A. Collaborate with local law enforcement to investigate potential corruption cases.

B. Implement a robust anti-corruption compliance program and train employees on ethical conduct.

C. Ignore corruption risks to maintain good business relations with foreign partners.

D. Encourage employees to engage in corrupt practices to navigate foreign business environments.

58. A standard for employee investigations is the best example of which of the following?

A. An internal ethics control.

B. An employment contract clause.

C. An HR best practice.

D. A response to unethical behaviors.

59. What are the two main components of an effective code of conduct for employees?

A. Expected standards of behaviors for the employee and the employer.

B. Values-based and rules-based standards for behavior.

C. Legal and ethical principles of behaviors.

D. The company's vision and values.

Key Concept Research Questions

The ability to critically think on exam day and beyond requires taking a deeper dive into key topics. Take the time to understand the ideas behind the following two questions:

1. It is not unusual for there to be competing demands between company results and corporate ethics. Many organizations rely on statistical analysis to guide decision-making, and that can come at a significant cost. One such example is Ford Motor Company that, in the 1970s, put profit before people when faced with a design challenge on their low-cost Ford Pinto. The company used statistical analysis to estimate incident probability and made the decision to keep the rear placement of the vehicle's gas tank, even though they knew it could burst into flame in low-impact rear-end collisions. The result was serious injury and death and a reputational hit that took the Pinto completely off the market. Search online for the case study on the Ford Pinto. I like the one at `https://philosophia.uncg.edu/phi361-matteson/module-1-why-does-business-need-ethics/case-the-ford-pinto`. Think about the ways in which the company failed to account for the indirect costs of the design of the gas tanks that caused significant injury and loss of life. What mechanisms could the company have put in place to avoid the situation described in the case study?
2. One of the most difficult elements of corporate social responsibility initiatives is knowing what to focus on. There are so many stakeholders with (sometimes) competing demands that it can be overwhelming for organizations to pick a specific area(s) to focus on. Think about the mission, vision, and values at your current or former place of work or educational institution. Take a look at the evidenced-based information of Our World in Data at `ourworldindata.org`. Click Browse by Topic and take some time to get a better understanding of the various CSR issues to consider. What CSR initiative is most in alignment with the company's purpose?

Test Your Ethical Practice and Corporate Social Responsibility Terminology Knowledge

The following are the terms to use to test your knowledge on Ethical Practice and Corporate Social Responsibility key terms. The correct answers are found in Appendix B.

- Authenticity
- Compliance
- Conflict of interest
- Consistency
- CSR policy
- CSR reporting
- Deontological ethics
- Environmental stewardship

- Ethical controls
- Ethics
- ESG rating agencies
- Employee welfare
- Good faith and fair dealing
- Honesty
- Integrity
- Morals
- Moral imperative
- Political pressure
- Privacy
- Self-dealing
- Social responsibility
- Transparency
- Triple bottom line
- Unconscious bias
- Utilitarian ethics

1. __________ is the right to personal space, confidentiality, and control over one's personal information.
2. __________ occurs when an individual in a position of trust or authority uses their influence for personal gain, often at the expense of others or the organization they serve.
3. __________ refers to the study of moral principles and values that guide human behavior and decision-making.
4. __________ involves the disclosure of an organization's social and environmental performance, including its efforts to address corporate social responsibility issues, to stakeholders and the public.
5. A __________ outlines an organization's commitment to ethical and socially responsible practices, including its goals, strategies, and initiatives to benefit society and the environment.
6. __________ is the principle that requires individuals and organizations to act honestly, fairly, and in good faith when engaging in transactions or negotiations.
7. __________ are the beliefs and values that influence an individual's ethical decision-making and behavior.
8. __________ includes openness and the disclosure of information, enabling stakeholders to understand and assess the actions, decisions, and operations of individuals or organizations.
9. __________ are responsible for evaluating companies based on their environmental, social, and governance practices.
10. A __________ arises when an individual or entity's personal or financial interests potentially interfere with their ability to make impartial decisions or act in the best interests of others.
11. __________ involves taking responsibility for the sustainable and ethical management of natural resources and ecosystems, ensuring their protection and preservation for future generations.

12. __________ is an ethical theory that focuses on maximizing overall happiness and minimizing harm when making decisions, often by evaluating actions based on their consequences.
13. __________ is the obligation of individuals and organizations to contribute positively to society by addressing social and environmental issues and promoting ethical practices.
14. __________ involves adhering to laws, regulations, and established standards. It ensures that individuals and organizations act within legal boundaries and follow prescribed guidelines.
15. __________ is the adherence to strong moral and ethical principles.
16. __________ is the automatic and unintentional beliefs or prejudices that people hold, often based on stereotypes, which can influence their judgments and actions.
17. __________ is an organization's efforts to ensure the well-being and satisfaction of its employees, encompassing fair treatment, benefits, and a safe working environment.
18. __________ is the influence exerted by entities, individuals, or groups to manipulate or affect decision-making in favor of their interests or agenda.
19. __________ is the quality of being genuine and true to one's values, beliefs, and principles. In the context of business and ethics, it implies sincerity and honesty in actions and communications.
20. __________ is an ethical theory that emphasizes the importance of moral principles and duties in determining the rightness or wrongness of actions, regardless of the consequences.
21. __________ is the act of being truthful and straightforward in one's actions, communications, and dealings. It is a fundamental ethical principle.
22. __________ are mechanisms, policies, and procedures implemented by organizations to promote ethical behavior and prevent ethical violations among their employees and stakeholders.
23. The __________ is a framework that evaluates an organization's performance based on economic, social, and environmental dimensions, emphasizing the importance of sustainability.
24. __________ is the practice of maintaining uniformity in actions, decisions, and behaviors over time. It is essential for building trust and reliability.
25. A __________ is a principle or duty that is considered obligatory and necessary to uphold, often without exception.

Conclusion

HR professionals are entrusted with vital ethical and corporate social responsibility (CSR) responsibilities. They must champion integrity, fairness, and transparency in the workplace, fostering an ethical culture. Advocating for diversity and inclusion contributes to CSR and reduces inequalities. Engaging with stakeholders through ethical practices builds trust. HR leaders should exemplify ethical behavior, promoting it throughout the organization. Staying informed about evolving ethical issues and measuring the impact of ethical and CSR initiatives are essential for adapting and demonstrating positive outcomes.

It's clear that both SHRM and HRCI emphasize the importance of ethical practices in the field of human resources. SHRM incorporates ethical practice as part of its leadership competencies, highlighting the significance of personal and professional integrity aligned with company values. On the other hand, HRCI recognizes the importance of ethics in various areas, including talent management, workforce planning, talent acquisition, and corporate social responsibility.

Furthermore, HRCI underscores the ongoing commitment to ethical awareness by requiring certificants to fulfill an ethics credit as part of their recertification process. This requirement reflects the evolving landscape of workplace ethics and the role that HR professionals play in upholding and promoting ethical behavior.

Additional Resources

These online resources cover a range of topics related to help you learn more about ethical HR practices, including codes of ethics, diversity and inclusion, ethical leadership, and creating a culture of integrity in the workplace. Whether you are an HR professional, manager, or interested in ethics within organizations, these resources can help you promote and uphold ethical standards in HR practices.

Websites

- The Ethics Centre, HR and People Management (`https://ethics.org.au/ethics-in-your-organisation/hr-and-people-management`)

  The Ethics Centre offers resources and articles specifically focused on ethical HR practices. It covers topics such as diversity and inclusion, ethical leadership, and employee rights.

- Ethics and Compliance Initiative (ECI) (`www.ethics.org`)

  ECI provides research, tools, and resources related to ethics and compliance in the workplace. While not HR-specific, their insights can be applied to HR practices.

- Ethical HR Management, CIPD (Chartered Institute of Personnel and Development) (www.cipd.org/uk)

  CIPD offers resources on ethical HR management, including articles, guides, and case studies. It explores the ethical challenges HR professionals may face.
- Institute of Business Ethics (IBE) (www.ibe.org.uk)

  IBE is a UK-based organization dedicated to promoting ethical business practices. Their website offers research reports and guidance on ethics in HR and the workplace.

Podcasts

- *Honest HR Podcast* hosted by SHRM

  The Honest HR Podcast discusses various HR topics, including ethics, diversity, and inclusion. It offers insights into maintaining ethical standards in HR. It can be found on Various Podcasting platforms, including Apple Podcasts and SHRM's website.
- *EthicalVoices* (www.ethicalvoices.com)

  Ethical Voices focuses on ethical issues in communications and public relations but often touches on HR and leadership topics. It features interviews with ethics experts.
- *Inclusive AF Podcast* (www.inclusiveafpodcast.com)

  This podcast discusses diversity, equity, and inclusion, which are closely related to ethical HR practices. It features discussions on creating inclusive workplaces.

YouTube Channels

While these YouTube channels may cover a range of HR and business-related topics, they often include content related to ethical HR practices, leadership, and workplace ethics. Explore their playlists and videos to find content that aligns with your interests and learning goals in the realm of ethical HR practices. Log onto www.youtube.com and search for the channel names. Subscribe and get notified for new content.

- Global Ethics Solutions

  This channel offers discussions and insights on business ethics, including topics related to HR, such as ethical decision-making and corporate social responsibility.
- The Ethics Centre

  The Ethics Centre channel explores ethics in a more holistic and global context to help individuals understand the framework from which ethical based decisions should be made and the issues that should be considered.

Chapter 11

Managing a Global Workforce

The need for coffee to start the day as an HR practitioner is near universal. Yes, that's an exaggeration; however, in many countries, coffee is truly a way of life. Brazil is the world's largest producer of coffee, and as such there are more than 8 million people engaged in the processing of the crop from seed to cherry to drying to roasting and eventually to the consumer. Benefits such as paid rest, workers' compensation, and family leave are granted to the employees as a direct result of cooperative labor agreements. Human rights, environmental sustainability, and other issues are all part of the work of this globally consumed product.

International human resource management (IHRM) is the strategic approach and management of an organization's human resources when operating across international borders, encompassing the planning, deployment, and coordination of HR policies and practices to effectively manage a diverse global workforce. It involves addressing unique challenges related to cross-cultural management, compliance with international labor laws, and optimizing HR strategies to support the organization's global expansion and objectives. Key exam objectives covered in this chapter include the following:

- **Global organizational structures:** This refers to the various ways in which multinational companies organize their operations worldwide.
- **HR structures for global work:** HR structures for global work entail designing human resource departments and practices that can effectively support and manage a global workforce.
- **Employee life cycle:** Staffing, total rewards, performance management, and more must be understood and practiced in a global context and should include cultural sensitivity and awareness.
- **Labor laws and social norms:** Complying with country laws and adapting to social norms are also part of the role of global HR practitioners.

The practice questions in this chapter will cover these aspects in more detail to help you understand key concepts for exam day.

Real World Scenario

International HR Practices in Fast Food Leads to Success

With more than 40,000 fast-food restaurants worldwide, McDonald's has achieved unparalleled success in the global market, making it the largest fast-food restaurant chain in terms of revenue. They serve more than 70 million customers daily and operate in more than 100 countries. McDonald's is responsible for developing a quick service restaurant (QSR) production line that prioritizes efficiency, predictability, standardization, and control. This case study explores the key global workforce management practices that have contributed to McDonald's international success.

Background and Problem

The company's success in different countries can be attributed to its remarkable ability to adapt to diverse cultures and markets. However, the challenge lies in maintaining a consistent global brand while catering to local preferences. The problem is to strike the right balance between standardization and adaptation, ensuring that they can thrive in various cultural contexts.

Strategies

- **Cultural adaptation and workforce diversity:** McDonald's values a diverse workforce and actively promotes a culture of inclusion and respect. By recognizing and embracing the unique perspectives and talents of its global employees, they have created a collaborative and innovative work environment that reflects the diverse customer base they serve. Additionally, the company invests in cultural sensitivity training and development programs to ensure that employees worldwide understand and appreciate the differences in cultural norms and practices, fostering a harmonious and inclusive workplace.
- **Corporate social responsibility:** The company has made a commitment to act in a socially responsible manner in all aspects of their business. One example is at their flagship restaurant in Bogotá, Columbia. McDonald's has implemented sustainability practices that focus on reducing environmental impact. This includes efforts to minimize waste through recycling programs, energy-efficient restaurant design, and sourcing local ingredients when possible to reduce carbon emissions associated with transportation.
- **Talent localization and global mobility:** This retail restaurant understands the importance of having local talent in key positions to better connect with customers and navigate the complexities of different markets. The company strategically identifies and promotes local leaders who possess a deep understanding of the culture, market trends, and consumer preferences. Moreover, they offer global mobility opportunities to their employees, enabling them to gain international experience and contribute to the company's success in different regions. This approach not only enhances employees' skills but also strengthens the company's global workforce.

- **Employee training and development:** McDonald's invests significantly in employee training and development programs to ensure that its workforce is equipped with the skills and knowledge required for their roles. These programs are standardized globally, providing consistent training materials and guidelines.

  Furthermore, the company tailors some training elements to specific regions or countries, addressing local needs and cultural nuances. This dual approach helps the teams maintain a high level of operational consistency while allowing for adaptation to local workforce requirements.

- **Communication and feedback channels:** Headquarters fosters open communication channels between its corporate resources and regional offices, as well as between management, frontline employees, and franchisees. This two-way communication ensures that important messages are conveyed effectively and that feedback from employees is heard and considered.

  In addition, the company encourages the sharing of best practices and ideas across regions, allowing for continuous improvement and knowledge sharing among its global workforce. This collaborative approach strengthens the sense of belonging and engagement among employees.

- **Employee benefits and well-being:** Leadership understands that employees are their most valuable asset, and they prioritize their well-being and benefits. McDonald's offers competitive compensation packages, health and wellness programs, and opportunities for career advancement.

  Moreover, the company adapts its benefits offerings to meet local legal requirements and cultural expectations, ensuring that employees receive relevant and meaningful support wherever they are located. This approach reinforces employee loyalty and satisfaction, contributing to the company's global workforce retention.

Results

Through its culturally sensitive approach, this organization has fostered strong customer loyalty and achieved impressive market penetration in diverse countries. The company's focus on digital innovation and sustainability has kept it competitive in an increasingly digital and socially conscious world. The business continues to evolve its strategies, adapting to changing global consumer demands while staying true to its core values and brand promise.

Conclusion

With its California origins, McDonald's has had international success and serves as a valuable lesson for businesses aiming to expand globally. The success of McDonald's is built upon its ability to strike a balance between maintaining a global brand identity and catering to local tastes, acting with cultural awareness and a global mindset while prioritizing social responsibility. This is a testament to the value of international best practices in human resources worldwide.

Global Human Resource Management Practice Questions

1. What is a characteristic of a greenfield investment in global operations?
   - **A.** It involves acquiring an existing facility or business in a new market.
   - **B.** It requires starting a new operation from the ground up.
   - **C.** It primarily relies on partnering with an established local business.
   - **D.** It is a strategy used to revitalize an underperforming subsidiary.
2. A multinational corporation is considering expanding its presence in a foreign market. The corporation decides to purchase an existing factory in that market and renovate it for its operations. What type of investment is this?
   - **A.** Brownfield investment.
   - **B.** Greenfield investment.
   - **C.** Joint venture investment.
   - **D.** Offshore investment.
3. What is a key advantage of a joint venture as a method of structuring global operations?
   - **A.** Full control and autonomy over operations.
   - **B.** Sharing risks and costs with a local partner.
   - **C.** No need for local market knowledge or expertise.
   - **D.** Faster market entry compared to other methods.
4. A multinational corporation is expanding into several new countries. What organizational structure is most suitable for managing its global workforce in this situation?
   - **A.** Centralized structure.
   - **B.** Decentralized structure.
   - **C.** Matrix structure.
   - **D.** Flat structure.
5. What is a benefit of a decentralized organizational structure for managing a global workforce?
   - **A.** Enhanced global consistency.
   - **B.** Faster decision-making at the local level.
   - **C.** Streamlined communication across regions.
   - **D.** Reduced need for local adaptations.

6. Which of the following factors is NOT typically considered a significant influence on global mobility?
   A. Economic opportunities.
   B. Cultural diversity.
   C. Political stability.
   D. Language homogeneity.

7. What defines a multinational corporation?
   A. A company that operates in the United States and one other country.
   B. A company that does business in multiple countries of the EU.
   C. A company that conducts business in multiple countries.
   D. A company that is owned by the government.

8. Which of the following is a primary motive for multinational corporations to expand internationally?
   A. Improving global profits.
   B. Engaging in CSR activities.
   C. Building new environmental footprints.
   D. Accessing new markets and resources.

9. What is a subsidiary in the context of multinational corporations?
   A. A company's main headquarters.
   B. A business entity that is partially owned by a parent company.
   C. A competing multinational corporation.
   D. A government regulatory agency.

10. Which of the following global forces has a significant impact on how business is structured in the modern world?
    A. Technological advancements.
    B. Language diversity.
    C. Geopolitical events.
    D. The cost of travel.

11. Which of the following best represents the value HR teams can bring to global strategy in the context of talent acquisition?
    A. Effectively managing the local cost of labor through compensation benchmarks.
    B. Aligning individual workforce goals with global business strategy.
    C. Facilitating the adoption of change management techniques to increase transition efficiencies.
    D. Building leadership pipelines to prepare the workforce for expatriate assignments.

12. Which of the following is a primary responsibility of a global HR manager?

A. Coordinating expatriate travel.

B. Adapting policies for cultural and legal context.

C. Conducting global wage surveys.

D. Driving CSR strategy.

13. Which of the following best describes the mindset necessary for global leaders?

A. They accept contradictions.

B. They are able to remain consistent in the application of home-country norms.

C. They value stability.

D. They believe diverse cultures are better than American cultures.

14. Which of the following is not a factor of a global mindset for an HR professional?

A. Language diversity.

B. Cultural sensitivity.

C. Personal adaptability.

D. Global awareness.

15. What are the fundamental elements of the four strategies described by J. Stewart Black, Allen J. Morrison, and Hal B. Gregersen that can help develop a global mindset?

A. To emphasize individualism, cultural intelligence, adaptability, and flexibility in a global context.

B. To promote a U.S. federal, state, global, and localized approach to HR practices.

C. To highlight the importance of talent, technology, training, and teams in building a global mindset.

D. To prioritize the use of global best practices in talent management, compensation, risk management, and technology.

16. What is the primary purpose of including jurisdiction clauses in global employment contracts?

A. To specify the country where disputes related to the contract will be resolved.

B. To standardize contract terms across international locations.

C. To protect the employer's ability to take legal action in case of disputes.

D. To comply with local labor laws and regulations.

17. Which global staffing approach involves hiring host-country nationals to manage subsidiaries in their respective countries?

A. Ethnocentric approach.

B. Polycentric approach.

C. Geocentric approach.

D. Regiocentric approach.

18. A multinational corporation sends employees from the headquarters to work in key positions in their foreign subsidiaries. Which staffing approach is being utilized?

- **A.** Geocentric approach.
- **B.** Ethnocentric approach.
- **C.** Polycentric approach.
- **D.** Regiocentric approach.

19. Which of the following best define the HR competencies necessary to operate within a multinational company?

- **A.** Business and competitive awareness.
- **B.** Communication and listening.
- **C.** Networking and relationship building.
- **D.** Negotiation and conflict management.

20. A multinational corporation offers differential compensation packages to employees in different countries based on the market conditions where they are situated. Which compensation strategy is being employed?

- **A.** Global compensation strategy.
- **B.** Standardized compensation strategy.
- **C.** Localization compensation strategy.
- **D.** Equalization compensation strategy.

21. What is the potential drawback of a standardized global compensation strategy?

- **A.** Difficulty in complying with local regulations.
- **B.** Inability to attract top talent.
- **C.** Inconsistency in employee pay.
- **D.** Increased administrative complexity.

22. An employee from a multinational company based in France has been relocated to their subsidiary in Brazil for six months to provide specialized training to the local team. What type of expatriate assignment is this?

- **A.** Short-term assignment.
- **B.** Commuter assignment.
- **C.** Permanent transfer.
- **D.** Repatriation assignment.

23. A multinational corporation is considering offshoring its customer service operations to a country with a lower cost of labor. However, the country has a reputation for high levels of corruption. What ethical consideration should the company address?

- **A.** Lobbying the local government(s) for change.
- **B.** Implementing a strong anti-corruption policy and compliance measures.
- **C.** Adopting a secondary set of practices to adapt to the cultural norms.
- **D.** Minimizing transparency to avoid detection of corrupt activities.

24. A multinational corporation is offshoring its software development to a country known for its strong intellectual property protections. What should the company consider as part of its ethical guidelines to protect its intellectual property?
    - **A.** Rely on patents to protect proprietary information.
    - **B.** Ensuring all employees sign nondisclosure agreements.
    - **C.** Align company policy with local norms.
    - **D.** Create a comprehensive IP strategy.

25. Which of the following is not a challenge to managing global assignments?
    - **A.** Taking into consideration the impact a global assignment has on the expatriating employee.
    - **B.** Managing conflicting expatriate allegiances to the home country and host country.
    - **C.** Ensuring equity between differing compensation and cost of living standards.
    - **D.** Making sure the expatriate has a global employment contract.

26. How can participating in global assignments positively impact a team member's career path?
    - **A.** By exposing them to diverse experiences that can drive cultural awareness back at headquarters.
    - **B.** By improving their knowledge and application of global business practices.
    - **C.** By increasing their earnings potential upon return from an expatriate assignment.
    - **D.** By protecting them from career opportunities that may not serve their personal career interests.

27. What does the cultural integration model emphasize in the context of international human resource management (IHRM)?
    - **A.** The cultural integration model highlights the importance of balancing global integration and local responsiveness in managing a multinational workforce to effectively address cultural diversity.
    - **B.** The cultural integration model focuses primarily on imposing a standardized set of HR practices across all international locations to create uniformity within the organization.
    - **C.** The cultural integration model primarily emphasizes the exclusion of cultural diversity in favor of a homogenous organizational culture.
    - **D.** The cultural integration model focuses on aligning HR practices with the dominant culture of the organization's headquarters, irrespective of local cultural nuances.

28. XYZ Corporation, a multinational organization with teams operating in various countries, recognizes the importance of cultural awareness among its team members. They are planning a training program to enhance cultural sensitivity and understanding of differences in culture. In selecting a cultural awareness model for their training, which model should XYZ Corporation consider?
    - **A.** Kotter's eight-step model.
    - **B.** Lewin's management model.
    - **C.** Cultural integration model.
    - **D.** Hofstede's dimensions theory.

29. What is a primary objective of HR when conducting market surveys to design global pay structures?

A. To maintain consistent pay rates regardless of market conditions.

B. To align compensation with local market competitiveness.

C. To match home country rates to avoid discriminatory pay practices.

D. To lag headquarter rates based on lower costs of living in other areas.

30. What is the main advantage of using an outside consultancy to benchmark global pay data over the use of local governments as a data source?

A. Access to comprehensive industry data.

B. Unbiased neutral perspectives.

C. Cost efficiencies and time savings.

D. Alignment with local regulatory environments.

31. What is a crucial consideration when implementing an HRIS system for managing a global workforce?

A. Restricting access to the HRIS to company headquarters for security purposes.

B. Ensuring the HRIS supports multiple languages and currencies.

C. Using paper-based records for redundancy.

D. Keeping all HR data stored on local servers for access on demand.

32. Which of the following is NOT a key consideration for the use of technology in managing a global workforce?

A. Compliance with government regulations of the Internet in host countries.

B. The environmental impact of the choice of technology.

C. The adaptability of interfaces to local capabilities.

D. The time zone of the host country location.

33. A multinational corporation has operations in several countries, each with its own set of workplace discrimination laws. An employee working in one of these countries feels they have experienced workplace discrimination. What should the organization consider when addressing this issue?

A. Ignore the complaint as different countries have varying standards for discrimination.

B. Apply the workplace discrimination laws of the home country to the employee's case.

C. Seek legal counsel to advise on the validity of the discrimination claim.

D. Comply with the workplace discrimination laws of the specific country in which the employee works.

34. Which of the following is NOT a characteristic of cross-cultural competency?

A. Effective cross-cultural communication skills.

B. Ability to enforce a standardized approach across all cultural contexts.

C. Cultural sensitivity and empathy toward individuals from diverse backgrounds.

D. Understanding of cultural norms and practices in different regions.

35. Which of the following protects an expatriate from dual taxation?
   A. International Labour Organization.
   B. North American Free Trade Agreement.
   C. Totalization agreements.
   D. The United States-Mexico-Canada Agreement.

36. Under what circumstances does the foreign law defense apply to an alleged discrimination case involving a U.S. corporation or its foreign affiliate employing U.S. citizens abroad?
   A. It must be impossible to comply with both the U.S. law and the foreign law.
   B. The foreign law violated must be the law of the country where the employee works.
   C. Compliance with U.S. law must "cause" a violation of foreign law, and the conduct must be governed by a law of the foreign country, not merely a custom or preference.
   D. The defense must result from a law of a foreign country, and the foreign law violated must be the law of the country where the employee works.

37. A 60-year-old U.S. citizen is working in Puerto Rico for a newspaper that is a subsidiary of an American corporation. Under the laws of the Commonwealth of Puerto Rico, an employer must retire an employee at the age of 60. The newspaper informs the employee that he will be involuntarily retired due to the Puerto Rican law. The employee files a charge of age discrimination with the Equal Employment Opportunity Commission. The newspaper responds, claiming that their action is lawful under the foreign law defense. Which of the following statements is true?
   A. The newspaper's action is not protected under the foreign law defense.
   B. The newspaper's action is protected under the foreign law defense.
   C. The employee is not protected because they needed to file the charge in Puerto Rico.
   D. The employee is not protected because they do not meet the minimum age requirement under the ADEA.

38. How do the rules of the European Union affect global workforce mobility?
   A. Facilitates global mobility by providing a unified visa and work permit for all non-EU citizens within its borders.
   B. Promotes global mobility by allowing non-EU citizens to work freely in any EU member state.
   C. Enhances global mobility through the Schengen Agreement, allowing for passport-free travel within the Schengen Area.
   D. Regulates global mobility by imposing strict quotas on the number of non-EU workers allowed in EU member states.

39. Which of the following metric is most valuable when managing global assignments?
   A. Time to fill rates.
   B. Turnover rates.
   C. Expatriate failure rate.
   D. Bonus payout percentages.

40. What is a key characteristic of risk audits when managing global assignments?

A. They are conducted as part of the HR due diligence process.

B. They primarily focus on assessing the employee's performance during the assignment.

C. They involve a comprehensive evaluation of potential risks and challenges before and during the assignment.

D. They are focused on the financial risk related to compensation packages.

41. Which of the following approaches to global compensation strategies is characterized by tailoring the offerings to the unique needs of the expatriate and the assignment?

A. Equalized.

B. Ad hoc.

C. Balance sheet.

D. Differential.

42. Which of the following characteristics is particularly necessary for a transnational leader?

A. Synergistic learning.

B. Home country policy awareness.

C. Multilingual.

D. Business acumen.

43. Fill in the blank: The ____________ approach to identifying global leaders is characterized by filling leadership roles based on clearly defined needs and responsibilities.

A. Managed development.

B. Functional excellence.

C. Local responsiveness.

D. Collaborative.

44. Which of the following employee attitudes is most likely to be found in organizations in countries with planned economies?

A. Employees feel that quick returns are the most competitive way to do business.

B. Employees believe that less government interference in their right to work, the better.

C. Employees prefer individual rewards, such as performance-based pay.

D. Employees collectively own and benefit from shared efforts.

45. Which of the following statements best describes the elite cohort approach to the selection of high-potential leaders within global cultures?

A. The elite cohort approach emphasizes selecting leaders from top universities and then grooming them over time for managerial roles.

B. The elite cohort approach focuses on hiring talent recruited from elite universities and given leadership positions right away.

C. The elite cohort approach prioritizes promoting leaders based on their years of experience within the organization.

D. The elite cohort approach advocates for the rotation of leaders across various countries.

46. Which of the following must be included when calculating the total labor costs of staffing an offshore location?

A. Severance packages for expatriate workers due to low retention rates.

B. Direct wages, benefits, and local tax obligations.

C. Cost of tax equalization needs.

D. The cost of expanded government-sponsored work-life benefits.

47. Which of the following best represents an international labor law in the area of learning and development?

A. A priority to be placed on multilingual global executives.

B. The equalization of home country and host country educational degrees where appropriate.

C. The requirement that all employees must translate compliance-related training into the local language.

D. The expectation that employers will pay a payroll tax to government-sponsored training programs.

48. What culture-related problems are generally associated when MNEs use third-country nationals to staff open positions?

A. Language barriers and communication difficulties.

B. Lack of familiarity with local market conditions.

C. Resistance from the home country's workforce.

D. Difficulty in adapting to host country's customs and norms.

49. Which of the following best defines a works council?

A. A formal labor organization representing employees' interests in collective bargaining.

B. A committee of senior executives responsible for HR policies and practices.

C. A group of employees selected by management to oversee workplace safety.

D. A representative body of employees within an organization responsible for addressing workplace issues and facilitating communication between employees and management.

50. Which IHRM approach to managing the union/MNE relationship is characterized by overall decision-making control belonging to local management?

A. Hands off by headquarters.

B. Guide and advise based on impact of the issues.

C. Adhere to a globally aligned response strategy.

D. Integrate practices where necessary and be hands off when possible.

51. Which of the following is a reason that unions have difficulty trusting multinational enterprises?
   - A. Unions believe MNEs can force workers in one country, faced by competition from union workers in other countries, to make concessions to keep their jobs.
   - B. Unions believe that MNEs do not follow proper safety protocols and standards.
   - C. Unions believe that the cost to administer a collective bargaining agreement is more expensive in MNEs.
   - D. Unions believe that it is more difficult to organize strikes and other work stoppages across borders.

52. What is the first approach senior HR leaders should take when an employment practice that is illegal in the home country is acceptable in the host country?
   - A. Follow the home country practice.
   - B. Follow the host country practice.
   - C. Research to understand why the practice is acceptable.
   - D. Consider that the practice is a violation of a human right.

53. A large international corporation in China has experienced significant growth, and as a result, their employees enjoy above-market-range compensation and benefits packages. How can HR help to motivate these workers beyond financial rewards?
   - A. Implement a more competitive compensation structure.
   - B. Offer flexible work arrangements and work-life balance initiatives.
   - C. Upgrade titles to signify seniority.
   - D. Publicly praise the high-performing workers.

54. In a rapidly growing international economy, what is a key challenge that organizations often face when developing their workforce?
   - A. Managing a surplus of skilled workers.
   - B. Ensuring consistency in hiring practices.
   - C. Sourcing qualified candidates from around the world.
   - D. Maintaining low employee turnover rates.

55. Which of the following statements best describes culture context in egalitarian countries?
   - A. There is high power distance between management and employees.
   - B. Many unions are required by the governments.
   - C. Employees are seen as stakeholders.
   - D. Works councils have low degrees of influence.

56. Which of the following statements best describes the cultural context of ethical absolutism?
   - A. Ethical principles are determined by the cultural norms and values of a specific group.
   - B. Ethical principles are universally applicable and do not vary across cultures.
   - C. Ethical flexibility is encouraged, allowing individuals to adapt principles to their specific culture.
   - D. Ethical relativism is the primary guiding principle in ethical absolutist cultures.

57. When conducting business negotiations over a meal in China, leaving some food on your plate as a sign of satisfaction with their hospitality and the meal represents which of the following elements of cultural awareness?

  A. Proper etiquette.

  B. American manners.

  C. Corporate bonding.

  D. Honesty and integrity.

58. In international business, understanding cultural etiquette is essential for successful global interactions. Which of the following is an example of cultural etiquette that varies between countries? (Choose all that apply.)

  A. The use of handshakes as a common greeting.

  B. Exchanging business cards with both hands.

  C. Scheduling meetings at a precise time.

  D. Using email for business communication.

59. Which of the following is NOT a reason that international trade with Africa can be difficult?

  A. Lack of predictability in the labor market.

  B. Political instability.

  C. Unfriendly business climate.

  D. Unqualified labor force.

60. Which of the following is an HR trend as the result of a shift to free-market policies in countries other than the United States?

  A. Cultural pride and loyalty have decreased.

  B. Wage suppression has become normalized.

  C. The responsibility for retirement plans has shifted from the government to individuals.

  D. The organization of unions has continued to decline.

61. In a country focused on free trade to increase economic prosperity, where on the flexibility-security nexus are they most likely to be found?

  A. High flexibility and low security.

  B. High flexibility and high security.

  C. Low flexibility and low security.

  D. Low flexibility and high security.

62. Which of the following properly characterizes European labor laws?

  A. European labor laws tend to be more relaxed than those of the United States.

  B. European labor laws focus on protecting employee health and wellness.

  C. European labor laws are closely tied to government-sponsored labor unions.

  D. European labor laws tend to be more comprehensive than U.S. labor laws.

63. What is the main difference between global HR systems and international HRM policies and practices?

- **A.** Systems align with organizational strategy, whereas policies and practices can vary by country.
- **B.** Systems are centralized practices, whereas policies and procedures are regionally unique.
- **C.** Systems focus on IHRM staffing, whereas policies and practices focus on compliance with global labor law.
- **D.** Systems speak to HR technology, whereas policies and practices focus on individual behaviors.

64. When designing expatriate crisis management plans, what should be the first step HR takes?

- **A.** Identifying boots-on-the ground security consultants.
- **B.** Conducting risk assessments of host countries.
- **C.** Developing communication protocols.
- **D.** Assembling a crisis response team.

65. What is the benefit of developing an international human resources website specifically for global workers?

- **A.** Streamlined engagement and cohesion.
- **B.** Administrative support like differences in number of characters in names and global address protocols.
- **C.** Improved enterprise-wide system integration.
- **D.** Ability to monitor local market conditions.

66. Which of the following is a major challenge when managing globally?

- **A.** Management techniques that work in one country often do not work in other countries.
- **B.** Employees of some countries have stronger work ethics than others.
- **C.** It can be difficult applying headquartered policies in nondiscriminatory ways.
- **D.** Many counties have hostile business climates.

67. Which difference in international HR practices highlights the role of labor unions?

- **A.** Staffing.
- **B.** Business management.
- **C.** Employee relations.
- **D.** Risk management.

68. What is the main difference between countries with planned economies versus countries with market economies?

- **A.** Government control dictates production and distribution in planned economies, while market forces of supply and demand determine these aspects in market economies.
- **B.** Planned economies prioritize individual entrepreneurship and competition, while market economies focus on central planning and state ownership of key industries.
- **C.** Planned economies encourage free-market principles and minimal government intervention, while market economies emphasize state control and regulation of economic activities.
- **D.** Market economies promote equitable distribution of wealth and resources through central planning, while planned economies rely on market mechanisms for resource allocation.

Key Concept Research Questions

Understanding the nuanced layers of international human resource practices and managing a global workforce requires much more than rote memorization. Taking the time to do quality research can help understand the larger environment of practice, which is the goal of researching the following question.

1. Part of a job of global human resource professionals is to manage the visa requirements of individual countries. Pick a country and research their visa guidelines using a website such as `www.visaguide.world`. Answer the following questions about your country of choice:
   a. Who is required to obtain a visa?
   b. How long is a visa valid for work?
   c. What limitations, if any, are on the use of visa while in the host country?

Test Your Global HR Management Terminology Knowledge

The following are the terms to use to test your knowledge on Global Human Resource Management key terms. You can find the correct answers in Appendix B.

- Ad hoc
- Cultural intelligence
- Cultural etiquette
- Expatriate
- Foreign law defense
- Global competencies
- Global mindset
- Global mobility
- Host country
- International human resource management (IHRM)
- Immigration specialist
- International trade
- Multinational enterprise (MNE)
- Repatriation
- Reverse mentorship
- Social mores
- Tax equalization
- Travel advisory
- Work visa
- Works council

1. __________________ is the strategic management of human resources in multinational corporations operating across borders, involving the coordination of HR practices, policies, and procedures to effectively manage a diverse workforce in different cultural, legal, and economic contexts.

2. ________________ is a legal document issued by a host country's government that allows foreign nationals to reside and work within its borders for a specified period, subject to certain conditions and restrictions.
3. ________________ is a professional who provides expertise and assistance in navigating immigration laws, regulations, and procedures for individuals or organizations seeking to relocate employees or individuals to another country.
4. ________________ is the country in which a multinational corporation or individual conducts business operations or resides, typically different from the home country.
5. ________________ is the ability to understand, communicate, and effectively interact with people from different cultural backgrounds, including awareness of cultural norms, values, beliefs, and behaviors.
6. A ________________ is characterized by openness, adaptability, and awareness of global trends, cultures, and business practices, enabling individuals to effectively navigate and succeed in diverse international environments.
7. ________________ is the exchange of goods, services, and capital between countries, facilitated by agreements, tariffs, regulations, and economic policies.
8. ________________ is the process of returning an expatriate employee to their home country after completing an overseas assignment, involving logistical, cultural, and professional adjustments.
9. ________________ is an individual who resides and works outside their home country for a temporary period, often employed by a multinational corporation in a foreign location.
10. A ________________ is a legal strategy used by multinational corporations to address allegations or legal actions arising from their operations in foreign countries, typically involving compliance with local laws and regulations.
11. ________________ is the movement of individuals or talent across borders for employment or business purposes, encompassing expatriate assignments, international transfers, and cross-cultural experiences.
12. ________________ is the customary rules and behaviors governing social interactions and conduct in specific cultural contexts, including norms related to communication, dress, manners, and customs.
13. ________________ are the skills, knowledge, and attributes that enable individuals to effectively operate and succeed in global or multicultural environments, including cross-cultural communication, adaptability, and cultural sensitivity.
14. ________________ are the accepted norms, customs, and behaviors within a society, influencing social interactions, relationships, and cultural practices.
15. ________________ is a compensation strategy used by multinational corporations to ensure that expatriate employees do not experience significant differences in tax liabilities between their home and host countries, typically involving reimbursement or adjustments to account for tax variations.

16. ________________: A company that operates business activities in multiple countries, with subsidiaries, branches, or affiliates located in different geographic regions.
17. A ________________ is a professional development approach in which younger or less experienced employees provide guidance, insights, and skills to older or more senior colleagues, often related to technology, social trends, or cultural perspectives.
18. ________________ describes something done or arranged on an impromptu or temporary basis, without prior planning or formal structure.
19. A ________________ is official guidance or warnings issued by governments or international organizations regarding potential risks, safety concerns, or travel restrictions in specific countries or regions.
20. A ________________ is a representative body composed of employees elected or appointed to represent their interests and negotiate with management on issues related to employment conditions, workplace policies, and labor rights, commonly found in European countries.

Conclusion

International HRM is, in its most basic form, the life cycle of an employee with a global twist. Understanding the business environment in which the company is competing, along with the corporate structure, drives HR decision-making in all of the key areas, such as staffing, performance management, and total rewards.

The SHRM exams highlight various aspects of managing a global workforce, encompassing HR structures, immigration and mobility, best practices for international assignments, and methods for moving work offshore. These competencies emphasize the need for HR professionals to possess a deep understanding of global HR management, including legal and operational considerations.

The 2024 integration of the international PHRi and SPHRi exams with the general PHR and SPHR content outlines by HRCI underscores the universal importance of global competencies across HR roles and levels. While no longer delineated as a separate functional area, the global dimension is woven throughout each of the other exam domains, mirroring the comprehensive nature of managing a global workforce.

As HR professionals, recognizing and mastering global HR management equips us to navigate the complexities of a global workforce, comply with legal requirements, and drive organizational success on a global scale.

Additional Resources

Understanding global issues can be a daunting task for an average practitioner, but well worth the investment of time and brain power. Trying to read about complex topics, such as immigration and politics can make retention difficult, so taking the time to access the material in other ways such as through websites, podcasts, and videos, is vital for retention.

Websites

- Deloitte Insights, Global Human Capital Trends Special Report (`www2.deloitte.com/us/en/insights/focus/human-capital-trends/2021/human-capital-trends.html`)

  This report from Deloitte discusses how the employer-employee relationship is changing in response to global conditions, which is good knowledge for understanding the landscape upon which these global workforce issues are being laid out.

- The World Bank, Jobs and Development (`www.worldbank.org/en/topic/jobsanddevelopment`)

  The World Bank's Jobs and Development portal provides research, reports, and data related to employment and workforce development in various countries. It offers insights into labor market dynamics worldwide.

- United States Department of State, Travel Advisories (`travel.state.gov/content/travel/en/traveladvisories/traveladvisories.html`)

  This website provides current travel advisories to areas around the globe. It includes travel information for special considerations country by country, including faith-based travel and LGBTQ+ travelers; the kind of documents required based on the purpose of travel; and how to handle crises abroad.

Podcasts

- *World Affairs* (`worldaffairs.org/podcasts`)

  This podcast discusses global issues, geopolitics, and international business. It can provide insights into the global workforce's impact on international relations.

- *HCI Podcast* by Human Capital Institute (`https://ivy.fm/podcast/human-capital-institute-podcasts-70256?tag=global-workforce`)

  This podcast provides a broad look at the issues affecting the global workforce including the candidate experience and global HR trends.

- *Planet Money* by the National Public Radio (NPR) (`www.npr.org/podcasts/510289/planet-money`)

  This engaging podcast explores the economic forces shaping the world and how business gets done. Search for episodes related to the economy and the global labor market and find content related to coffee shop unionization, the effect of poverty in under-developed countries, and labor issues in MNEs.

YouTube Channels

Videos are an excellent way to take your learning on the go. While there are hundreds of channel options on the topic of HR, be selective about the experts you access on global affairs to ensure you are getting an unbiased perspective. Log into `www.youtube.com` and search for the following channels to find insights, tips, and discussions related to international HRM:

- The International Labour Organization (ILO)

  The ILO's YouTube channel provides a unique view into the personal stories from work across the globe and shares insights into important issues such as green jobs, workplace violence, and the need for international standards.

- World Economic Forum

  Hear about critical global economic topics for the leading international organization committed to reviewing issues such as international trade, politics, and academic trends shaping the future labor market.

Chapter 12

Diversity, Equity, and Inclusion

In 2022, the Society for Human Resource Management (SHRM) validated research around the competency of diversity, equity, and inclusion (DEI). SHRM defined DEI as "the KSAOs needed to create a work environment in which all individuals are treated fairly and respectfully, have equal access to opportunities and resources, feel a sense of belonging, and use their unique backgrounds and characteristics to contribute fully to the organization's success." While research continues to emerge in this important area, it is clear that effective human resource management involves championing these initiatives throughout the organization.

Just as there is a life cycle for the employee, there is also a business life cycle. All businesses travel through four stages: infancy, growth, maturity, and decline. Interestingly enough, this cycle also applies to specific business units and strategic initiatives such as DEI, as shown in Figure 12.1. This can create challenges and misalignment of resources as some parts of the organization are in their maturity stage: well-resourced, understood, and, in some cases, entrenched. This is compared to relatively young initiatives that are often under-resourced, uncertain, and changing at a rapid pace as organizations learn what works and what doesn't work. In the context of DEI, it is safe to say that the domain has yet to reach its maturity stage, and much is still being studied and worked out.

The effective implementation of DEI initiatives has emerged as a critical benchmark of organizational excellence. To achieve this, organizations must adopt a holistic approach, integrating DEI principles into their policies, practices, and culture. This approach extends beyond mere compliance with legal requirements; it is about creating an inclusive environment where every individual feels valued, respected, and empowered to contribute their unique perspectives and talents.

- **Creating a diverse and inclusive culture:** HR professionals should be capable of fostering an environment where diversity is valued and inclusion is encouraged. This involves implementing strategies, such as executive sponsorship, leadership buy-in, and employee resource groups.
- **Ensuring equity effectiveness:** HR professionals need to ensure that policies and practices within the organization are equitable, addressing disparities related to gender, race, age, abilities, and other factors. This may involve conducting hiring and pay audits, promoting pay transparency, and monitoring diversity at all organizational levels.

FIGURE 12.1 The diversity life cycle

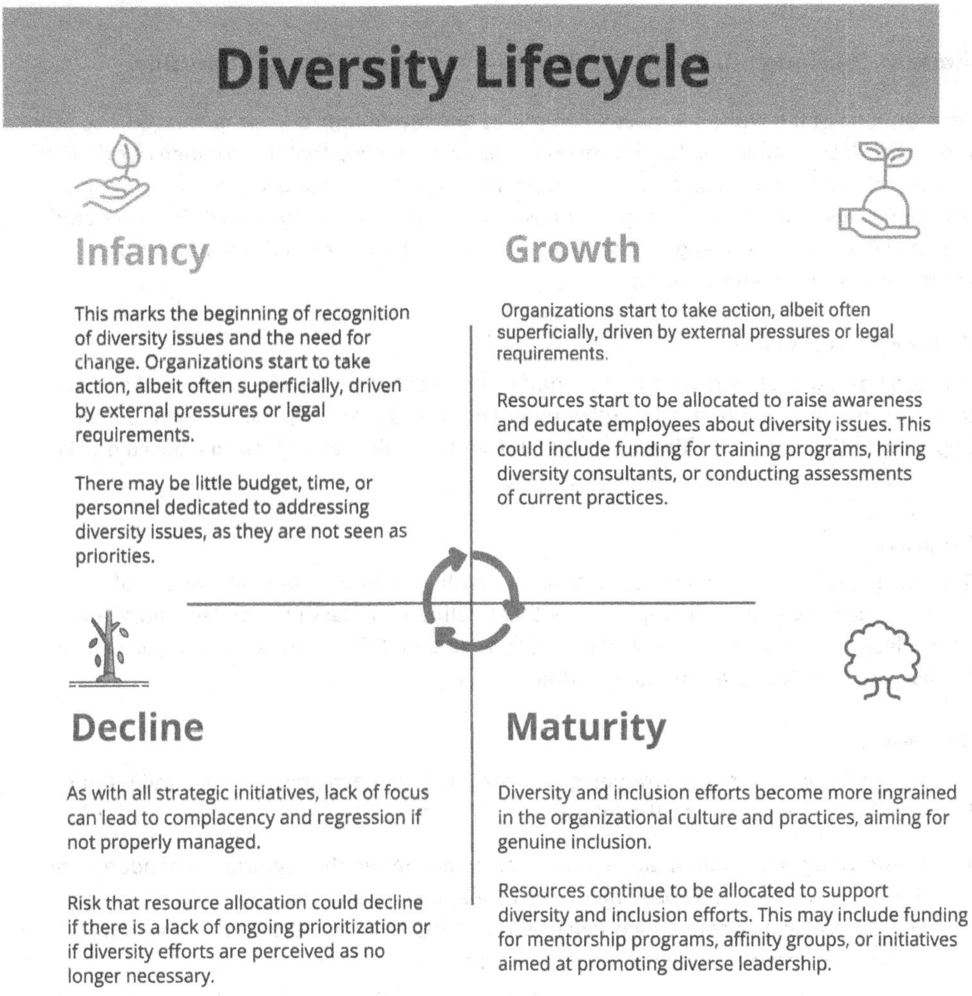

- **Connecting DEI to organizational performance:** HR professionals should understand how DEI initiatives can positively impact organizational performance. They should be able to measure and analyze DEI metrics, such as gender and race diversity, retention rates for diverse employees, and external stakeholder diversity.

In addition to these competencies, HR professionals should have a deep understanding of the various barriers to DEI success, including conscious and unconscious bias, stereotypes, and microaggressions. They should also be familiar with techniques to measure and increase equity, such as using the SHRM Empathy Index and conducting diversity surveys.

Real World Scenario

Amazon Responds to Social Media Pressure: Managing DEI Scrutiny

Amazon, one of the world's largest e-commerce and technology companies, faced a social media backlash in June 2020 when several employees alleged that the company's efforts to address diversity, equity, and inclusion were insufficient. The backlash emerged as part of a broader movement for racial justice following the killing of George Floyd. This case study explores the events, challenges, and strategies related to Amazon's DEI initiatives and its response to social media criticism.

Background and Problem

Amazon has a global workforce and a significant impact on various industries. Like many large corporations, it has faced scrutiny regarding its DEI practices. The company's initial approach to DEI was met with skepticism, and some employees organized a social media campaign to demand more meaningful change.

Diagnosis

The social media backlash against Amazon primarily revolved around allegations of systemic racism within the company, unequal treatment of Black employees, and a perceived lack of transparency and accountability regarding DEI initiatives. Employees and the public called for concrete actions to address these issues.

Strategies

Amazon adopted several key strategies to contain the backlash and prevent similar issues from occurring. They included the following:

- **Acknowledgment and engagement:** Amazon recognized the importance of addressing the concerns raised on social media and engaged in open dialogue with employees and the public. The company publicly acknowledged the need to confront systemic racism and committed to listening to feedback.
- **Investment in DEI:** To address the shortcomings in its DEI efforts, Amazon pledged to invest in initiatives aimed at promoting racial equity within the organization. This included committing funds to support organizations focused on racial justice.
- **Transparency and accountability:** Amazon committed to increased transparency in its DEI initiatives and published data on the diversity of its workforce. The company also emphasized accountability by setting goals and tracking progress in addressing racial disparities.

Results

As a result of the social media backlash and the subsequent engagement and commitments made by Amazon, the company took several concrete actions:

- **Increased transparency:** Amazon released data on the diversity of its workforce, including race and gender representation.
- **Financial commitment:** The company pledged funds to support organizations working on racial justice and equity.
- **Continued dialogue:** Amazon engaged in ongoing conversations with employees and stakeholders to address DEI concerns.
- **Reevaluation of DEI initiatives:** The company reviewed its existing DEI programs and policies to ensure they aligned with its commitment to racial equity.

Conclusion

The social media backlash against Amazon served as a catalyst for the company to reevaluate and strengthen its DEI initiatives. It highlighted the importance of open dialogue, transparency, and accountability in addressing systemic issues related to diversity, equity, and inclusion within organizations. While challenges remain, Amazon's response to the backlash demonstrates its commitment to making meaningful changes to promote racial equity in the workplace.

Diversity, Equity, and Inclusion Practice Questions

1. Which of the following best describes the differences between the terms *diversity* and *equity*?
   - **A.** Diversity is the process of recognizing advantages and barriers that create unequal starting places, while equity is the range of human differences.
   - **B.** Diversity refers to recognizing and valuing differences among individuals, while equity pertains to addressing and mitigating inequalities.
   - **C.** Diversity is the act of making a person part of a group or collective, while equity involves creating an inclusive work environment.
   - **D.** Diversity is the act of valuing human differences, while equity adjusts employment treatment based on a person's unique circumstances so that the end result is equal.

2. What is the best way for HR professionals to address inclusivity during the performance management stage of the employee life cycle?
   - **A.** Conduct employee surveys to gather feedback about the company's inclusivity practices.
   - **B.** Provide equal opportunities for professional growth and development to all employees.
   - **C.** Ensure equal pay for equal performance.
   - **D.** Exclude diversity and inclusion considerations from the performance management process to ensure unbiased evaluations.

3. During a team meeting icebreaker, Kathy was asked to share three "fun facts" about herself. She shared that when she was a teenager, she competed in a Rubik's Cube competition and won by solving the 3×3 puzzle in less than two minutes! Kathy is of Asian descent, and her manager, Howie, made a comment that she "must really be from China," despite Kathy being born and raised in the same city as Howie. This comment makes Kathy feel uncomfortable and singled out. What is an appropriate response for Kathy to address the microaggression she experienced from her manager?
   - **A.** Ignore the comment and chalk it up to typical ignorance.
   - **B.** Privately address the issue with Howie after the meeting, expressing how the comment made her feel.
   - **C.** Share her feelings about the microaggression on social media to raise awareness within the company.
   - **D.** Immediately report the incident to HR and request a formal investigation.

4. A leading tech company is committed to promoting diversity and inclusion in the workplace. Recently, the company has noticed a lack of representation and engagement among employees with disabilities, particularly in leadership roles. The HR department has been tasked with finding a solution to address this issue and ensure that employees with disabilities feel included and empowered within the organization. Which of the following actions should HR recommend?
   - **A.** Employee resource groups.
   - **B.** Employee focus groups.
   - **C.** Whistleblower hotlines.
   - **D.** Written policies with training for leaders.

5. Which of the following statements highlights a major barrier to the implementation of successful equity initiatives?
   - **A.** Lack of executive sponsorship.
   - **B.** Employees' diverse perspectives and experiences.
   - **C.** Transparent and inclusive communication.
   - **D.** Adequate funding and resources.

6. Which of the following is one of the organizational benefits to DEI efforts?
   - **A.** A psychologically safe workplace.
   - **B.** A sense of personal belonging and acceptance.
   - **C.** Equitable compensation packages.
   - **D.** Reduced attrition.

7. What was one of the major disadvantages of the COVID-19 pandemic as it relates to an organization's DEI efforts?
   - **A.** A disproportionate number of women left the workforce.
   - **B.** High-risk older individuals were left without adequate protections.
   - **C.** There was inequity in the groups who were eligible for remote work.
   - **D.** White-collar workers faced higher numbers of unemployment.

8. How should organizations craft effective DEI initiatives?
   - **A.** By implementing diversity quotas to ensure equal representation.
   - **B.** By conducting a one-time DEI training for all employees.
   - **C.** By engaging in ongoing dialogue, assessment, and inclusivity efforts.
   - **D.** By updating their assimilation policies to be more inclusive.

9. Several individuals got together and began discussing their salaries and work schedules. It was discovered that many employees who held similar jobs have significantly different pay rates. They brought it to the attention of their managers, and their managers referred them to the HR department. How should HR respond to their concerns?
   - **A.** Discipline employees for sharing their pay information, which is against company policy.
   - **B.** Conduct a pay audit to see if there is a pattern of discriminatory practices.
   - **C.** Explain to employees that salaries are based on more factors than just the job descriptions, such as education and experience.
   - **D.** Call the labor attorney for advice.

10. How can organizations connect diversity efforts to organizational results in a meaningful way?
    - **A.** By being open about the success or failure of DEI initiatives with the team.
    - **B.** By being clear on the relationship between DEI efforts and performance.
    - **C.** By holding quarterly state-of-the-company meetings to share outcomes.
    - **D.** By rewarding team members who model desired behaviors.

11. After a series of DEI intervention activities, it was brought to HR's attention that there is a perception of a lack of equity in the workplace. Upon investigation, HR found that there was indeed a disparity in many of the HR programs. What should HR professionals do first to increase equity in the HR systems?
    - **A.** Audit the workplace to evaluate the effectiveness of DEI initiatives.
    - **B.** Hold focus groups to gather feedback about how well or poorly the DEI efforts are working.
    - **C.** Invest in hiring practices that make equity a priority.
    - **D.** Train managers on unconscious bias and other forms of inequitable behaviors.

12. Which of the following metrics should be prioritized to understand the impact of an organization's hiring practices on DEI goals?
    - **A.** Turnover in the first 90 days of employment.
    - **B.** Rate of promotion based on demographic data.
    - **C.** Equitable salaries in employment offers.
    - **D.** Diversity of the applicant pool.

13. A company is committed to improving its DEI effectiveness. Which metric can help them assess whether their DEI initiatives are positively impacting employee retention?
    - **A.** Employee engagement survey scores.
    - **B.** Number of job applications received.
    - **C.** Total revenue generated in the past year.
    - **D.** Employee attendance records.

14. Which of the following strategies is most likely to improve DEI outcomes for LGBTQ+ employees?

A. Engage in social media campaigns sharing the company's inclusivity efforts.

B. Symbolically show support through company logos and participation in Pride activities.

C. Explicitly prohibit targeted or discriminatory treatment of LGBTQ+ team members.

D. Avoid calling attention to these characteristics to protect privacy and avoid charges of unequal treatment.

15. What is a key element to building a DEI strategic initiative?

A. Taking it as seriously as other strategic initiatives.

B. Appointing a DEI officer.

C. Hiring external DEI consultants.

D. Enforcing government regulations regarding anti-discrimination laws.

16. In 2022, the U.S. Congress passed the CROWN Act, making it unlawful for employers to discriminate against protected-class workers based on their natural hair texture and style. This is an example of which of the following PESTLE forces that must be considered when developing DEI strategies?

A. Political and economic.

B. Social and legal.

C. Environmental and social.

D. Political and legal.

17. How can employers strategically use their DEI initiatives to respond to the threat of substitutes being brought to market?

A. By outsourcing production to reduce costs and offer more competitive pricing.

B. By expanding their product lines to include a wider variety of options.

C. By emphasizing their commitment to DEI in marketing campaigns to build a loyal customer base.

D. By forming alliances with substitute product providers to share resources and market jointly.

18. How can HR partner with business leaders to improve equity in outcomes in the communities where they operate?

A. Collaborate on DEI initiatives.

B. Support community engagement programs.

C. Enhance employee volunteer programs.

D. Implement sustainable business practices.

19. Imagine a company that wants to ensure equity for its multigenerational workforce. What step could they take to promote this equity?
   A. Implement age-based promotions.
   B. Offer flexible work hours and remote options.
   C. Conduct cultural sensitivity training.
   D. Provide gender-specific benefits.

20. How can staffing programs effectively support an organization's DEI efforts?
   A. Involve peers in the interviewing process.
   B. Implement blind recruitment practices to reduce bias.
   C. Exclude over-represented groups from recruitment initiatives.
   D. Base hiring decisions on technical qualifications for the job.

21. What is one of the main challenges to the use of mentorship programs to develop a diverse and inclusive workplace?
   A. Over-reliance on individual perspectives and experiences.
   B. The potential for groupthink and promotion of reverse stereotypes.
   C. Lack of diverse mentors in senior roles.
   D. The presence of institutional and systemic bias in the workplace.

22. At a workplace with several new mothers, what is the most suitable accommodation to support lactation needs?
   A. Designate a shared bathroom for expressing breast milk.
   B. Provide a private and comfortable lactation room.
   C. Encourage mothers to express milk in their cubicles.
   D. Suggest mothers use a public break area for lactation needs.

23. An employee consistently downplays their accomplishments and feels they don't deserve their achievements, often fearing being exposed as a fraud. What personal barrier is this employee experiencing in the context of DEI?
   A. Confirmation bias.
   B. Imposter syndrome.
   C. Stereotype threat.
   D. Anchoring bias.

24. You are currently helping to recruit for an open marketing position. One of the managers is concerned about a potential hire as she appears to be about childbearing age, and the manager would like your team to continue recruiting to find other qualified, older candidates who are likely to be more committed to their work over time. When you tell the manager that kind of thinking is discriminatory, she brushes it off, assuring you that it can't be discrimination because she is also a woman and is asking for an older candidate. What form of bias did the manager display?

   A. Micro-aggression.

   B. Age-based bias.

   C. Stereotype bias.

   D. Same-sex bias.

25. An organization is committed to improving equity. What tool can they use to assess the experiences and perspectives of their employees from diverse backgrounds?

   A. An annual diversity report.

   B. An empathy index survey.

   C. An organizational hierarchy analysis.

   D. A random sampling audit.

26. Which of the following is NOT an example of a tangible diversity target?

   A. Increasing procurement from women-owned or minority-owned businesses by 15% in the coming year.

   B. Reducing the gender pay gap within the company by 10% over the next two years.

   C. Collecting and analyzing inclusivity efforts over the next 12 months.

   D. Launching three new ERGs focused on various dimensions of diversity within the organization.

27. How can mentoring be an effective tool to support DEI initiatives in the workplace?

   A. By exclusively pairing mentees with mentors from the same background.

   B. By offering one-size-fits-all mentoring programs to avoid stereotyping.

   C. By providing diverse mentor-mentee pairings and tailored guidance.

   D. By limiting mentoring programs to high-potential employees.

28. Which of the following are essential competencies for HR professionals seeking to act as diversity advocates at their place of work?

   A. Relationship building and negotiation.

   B. Global mindset and communication.

   C. Listening and conflict management.

   D. Business acumen and personal integrity.

29. An HR manager is tasked with assessing the effectiveness of their organization's DEI initiatives. Which metric would be most relevant to measure retention and inclusivity?
    A. Employee satisfaction surveys.
    B. Number of employees in leadership positions.
    C. Employee attendance rates.
    D. Employee training completion rates.

30. How can organizations effectively measure and increase equity in their workplace culture?
    A. By conducting regular audits of diversity levels.
    B. By relying on the empathy index.
    C. By avoiding the use of reports and assessments.
    D. By focusing on organizational hierarchy.

31. An organization is committed to resolving pay inequity among its employees. What initiative should they prioritize to address this issue effectively?
    A. Conducting regular diversity audits.
    B. Implementing transparent pay structures.
    C. Increasing the salary of diverse employees.
    D. Ignoring pay disparities to avoid conflicts of interests.

32. What is a key initiative that organizations can take to resolve inequity related to career advancement and promotion opportunities?
    A. Establishing a hierarchical structure.
    B. Implementing a matrix structure.
    C. Shifting to a cross-functional structure.
    D. Developing self-directed work teams.

33. An organizational leader is holding a team meeting and notices that a team member seems withdrawn and disengaged. What is the most empathetic and inclusive action for the leader to take?
    A. Assume that the team member is having a rough day and allow them their privacy.
    B. Use humor to draw the employee out of their disengagement.
    C. Privately check in with the team member to understand their concerns.
    D. Remind the team member that their input is valuable and failing to participate can lead to negative perceptions about their commitment.

34. A leader in an organization is reviewing employees eligible for promotion. They notice that an employee, despite a continuous record of excellent performance, has been consistently passed over for promotions. The individual's demographics are underrepresented in the organization. What should the leader do to promote inclusivity and equity?
    A. Continue promoting other candidates based on seniority.
    B. Offer the underrepresented employee a promotion.
    C. Review the promotion process for potential biases and barriers.
    D. Talk to the employee to find out if they even want to be promoted.

35. A leader is responsible for a diverse team, and they want to foster a more inclusive work environment. What action should the leader take to promote inclusivity and empathy within the team?

A. Gather feedback from the team to identify their specific needs.

B. Allow similar groups to work together in pods to encourage collaboration.

C. Discourage conversations about diversity to avoid potential conflicts.

D. Promote a culture of competition so that individuals do their best work.

36. How can managers distinguish between performance issues and DEI differences when addressing workplace challenges?

A. By aligning individual employee performance with the job responsibilities.

B. By ensuring that qualified individuals are hired for the roles.

C. By conducting open conversations with under-performing employees to understand the root cause of any performance issues.

D. By not discussing protected information with the employee to avoid the perception of stereotyping.

37. How can meetings within organizations be structured to be more inclusive?

A. By asking the more extroverted team members to let others have a say.

B. By using feedback exercises such as affinity diagrams to allow for shared insights.

C. By rewarding individuals who speak up.

D. By encouraging active participation from all individuals in meetings, even the introverts.

38. Which of the following is an example of interpersonal risk-taking as an HR professional competency?

A. Advocating for a new diversity and inclusion initiative in a meeting with senior leaders, despite knowing that it may face resistance.

B. Sticking to established HR practices and not challenging the status quo.

C. Avoiding difficult conversations with employees about performance issues.

D. Asking for alternative viewpoints during employee conflict resolution.

39. Which of the following is the best definition of allyship in the workplace?

A. Forming alliances with like-minded promoters of diversity at work.

B. Taking actions to support and advocate for colleagues from underrepresented groups.

C. Externally networking with potential DEI resources.

D. Positively branding the organization as a diverse place to work.

40. In a multigenerational workplace, what is a key factor that contributes to psychological safety?

A. Offering flexible benefits based on preferred lifestyle choices.

B. Developing reverse mentoring programs to support upskilling.

C. Promoting healthy competition among different generations.

D. Disciplining team members who discriminate based on age.

41. Which of the following is an example of diversity training needs at an organizational level?
 A. Employees have low cultural sensitivity skills.
 B. HR hiring practices are resulting in bias.
 C. The company supply chain is purchasing from vendors with unfair labor practices.
 D. There is a lack of women in leadership.

42. What should be the approach for an organization that is facing staffing challenges as the result of an aging workforce?
 A. Implement an age-based retirement policy to encourage older employees to retire early.
 B. Develop a comprehensive succession planning program to ensure a smooth transition of knowledge and skills.
 C. Hire younger employees exclusively to replace older workers.
 D. Offer incentives for older employees to continue working beyond retirement age.

43. Which of the following best describes executive sponsorship of DEI initiatives?
 A. Executive accountability for DEI outcomes.
 B. Company donations to organizations such as the NAACP or PFLAG.
 C. Inclusive marketing ad campaigns.
 D. The authorization for an employee resource group.

44. In a team meeting, Mabel, an employee, consistently speaks assertively, is quick to share her ideas, and often takes the lead during discussions. On the other hand, Oliver, another employee, tends to be quieter, prefers to listen more, and takes time to process information before contributing. Which layer of diversity does this best represent?
 A. Internal.
 B. External.
 C. Personality.
 D. Preferences.

45. Which of the following is a key tenant to Gardenswartz and Rowe's Four Layers of Diversity model at the organizational level?
 A. Recognizing the importance of individual personality traits in decision-making.
 B. Acknowledging that external dimensions of diversity matter in an organization.
 C. Valuing the uniqueness of each individual, considering all layers of diversity.
 D. Promoting diversity based on internal dimensions like age and gender.

46. What is the primary difference between an employee resource group and a diversity council?
 A. The level of leadership involvement and decision-making authority.
 B. The focus on internal diversity and external community engagement.
 C. The frequency of meetings and events organized.
 D. The size and membership requirements of the group.

47. When forming an employee resource group, it is most important that the members _______.

A. Are under-represented in the workplace.

B. Self-select.

C. Have strong peer influence.

D. Consider themselves advocates.

48. Which of the following is the most important characteristic of allyship in a company's DEI work?

A. Compassion.

B. Advocacy.

C. Courage.

D. Action.

49. During a job interview, an employee, who is one of the interviewers, consistently interrupts and dismisses a female candidate's responses while giving uninterrupted time and more consideration to male candidates' answers. The employee does not seem to be aware that she is doing it. This is an example of which of the following?

A. Rudeness.

B. Stress interview.

C. Same-sex harassment.

D. Unconscious bias.

50. Why is it important to use employees' preferred gender pronouns?

A. It creates a climate of inclusiveness.

B. It is the polite thing to do.

C. It is required by law.

D. The customers demand it.

51. In the context of DEI, mentoring most closely aligns with which of the following efforts?

A. Allyship.

B. Coaching.

C. Teaching.

D. Developing.

52. Empowerment, humility, accountability, and courage are all characteristics of which of the following DEI principles?

A. Mentoring.

B. Allyship.

C. Psychological safety.

D. Education.

53. Which of the following strategies can help accommodate neurodiverse individuals in the workplace and promote a more inclusive environment?
    A. Providing sensory-friendly workspaces and lighting adjustments.
    B. Implementing consistency in work tasks and routines.
    C. Providing training so that neurodiverse employees can adapt to the existing culture.
    D. Minimizing communication channels and options to reduce distractions.

54. At a team meeting, the manager notices that two employees, Belinda and Charlotte, both attended the same prestigious university. The manager, who is also an alumnus of that university, immediately strikes up a conversation with them about their experiences, asking about professors and shared memories while largely ignoring the contributions and experiences of other team members who did not attend the same university. In subsequent team discussions and project assignments, Belinda and Charlotte consistently receive more attention, praise, and opportunities for advancement, creating a sense of exclusion and disadvantage for their colleagues who did not share the same alma mater. What kind of bias is being illustrated here?
    A. Social comparison.
    B. Affinity.
    C. Halo effect.
    D. Unconscious.

55. Which of the following leadership theories is most likely to result in ingroup/outgroup bias?
    A. Theory X and Theory Y.
    B. Acquired Needs Theory.
    C. Two Factor Theory.
    D. Leader-Member Exchange Theory.

56. The additional workload of individuals identified to champion organizational DEI efforts is which of the following?
    A. Cultural taxation.
    B. Discrimination.
    C. Bias.
    D. Unfair treatment.

57. Grooming policies are most likely to result in what kinds of behaviors from protected class employees?
    A. Masking.
    B. Covering.
    C. Quiet quitting.
    D. Defensiveness.

58. What is the main distinction between unlawful discrimination and microaggressions?

A. Unlawful discrimination involves intentional and illegal actions that harm individuals based on protected characteristics, while microaggressions are unintentional and subtle behaviors or comments that reflect biases.

B. Unlawful discrimination is overt and easily identifiable, whereas microaggressions are covert and difficult to detect.

C. Unlawful discrimination pertains to macro-level systemic biases, while microaggressions focus on individual-level biases.

D. Unlawful discrimination is a term used for discrimination in the workplace, while microaggressions are specific to discrimination in social settings.

59. What is the purpose of creating quiet or prayer rooms in the workplace?

A. Compliance with religious anti-discrimination laws.

B. Creating an inclusive space for all religions to practice their faith.

C. Improved productivity due to improved morale.

D. Creating quiet spaces for diverse individuals to meditate, pray, or calm sensory overload.

60. What tool should HR professionals use to measure the degree to which positions with similar responsibilities (such as janitors and maids) are comparably compensated?

A. HR audits.

B. Diversity audits.

C. Adverse impact formulas.

D. Pay equity reports.

61. What are implicit biases in the workplace?

A. Conscious attitudes and stereotypes that guide decision-making.

B. Unconscious attitudes or stereotypes that influence behavior without awareness.

C. Deliberate efforts to promote diversity and inclusion.

D. Equal opportunities provided to all employees without any bias.

62. What are explicit biases in the workplace?

A. Unlawful discriminatory behaviors.

B. Unconscious behaviors based on stereotypes.

C. Microaggressions.

D. Stereotypes.

63. Which of the following examples best represents the diversity dividend?

A. A company hires employees from diverse backgrounds to meet diversity quotas.

B. An organization fosters an inclusive culture, resulting in increased innovation and profitability.

C. A business faces legal consequences for not complying with diversity and inclusion regulations.

D. An organization conducts mandatory diversity training for its employees.

64. What are the main differences between equity and equality?

A. Equity focuses on fairness in how people are treated, while equality aims to ensure everyone has the same rights and opportunities.

B. Equity and equality are two terms that mean the same thing.

C. Equity is about treating everyone the same, while equality emphasizes fairness.

D. Equity is required by federal law, whereas equality is up to individual states to enforce.

65. Physical characteristics are the best examples of which of the following types of diversity?

A. Protected.

B. Legacy.

C. Experiential.

D. Observable.

Key Concept Research Questions

Preparing for an exam requires critical thinking skills to interpret question context. For this reason, it is useful to understand key topics on a deeper level. Take the time to answer the following questions to aid in your understanding of DEI.

Research from a report titled "Together Forward at Work" by the Society for Human Resource Management (SHRM) states, "Despite years of financial and strategic investments in diversity, equity and inclusion, U.S. companies have notable numbers of workers who express concerns and discomfort about fundamental issues of racial equality in the workplace. This manifests in the workers' perceptions of discrimination and incivility, as well as the inability to have conversations on the topic of race. Further, the data show significant gaps in beliefs between Black and white U.S. workers, including—and perhaps even more concerning—those in the HR function."

On the SHRM exams, you will be tested on competencies related to HR's ability to create a diverse and inclusive culture, as well as being charged with ensuring equity effectiveness. Take a deeper look into these exam competencies by downloading the SHRM Body of Applied Skills and Knowledge (BASK). You can find this at `www.shrm.org`. Use it to answer the following questions:

1. What are the competencies necessary for HR professionals to be more successful at creating a diverse workforce?
2. What can HR professionals do to overcome the lack of meaningful results from current DEI practices? Consider taking a look at the full Together Forward @Work at `www.shrm.org/topics-tools/news/inclusion-equity-diversity/report-companies-going-motions-dei` for key insights.

Test Your DEI Terminology Knowledge

The following are the terms to use to test your knowledge of DEI key terms. You can find the correct answers in Appendix B.

- Accommodation
- Advocacy
- Bias training
- Cultural awareness
- Discrimination
- Diversity
- Diversity audits
- Diversity goals
- Diversity training
- Employee feedback
- Equality
- Equity
- Equity audit
- Equity policies
- Inclusion
- Inclusion dialogue
- Inclusion policies
- Neurodiversity
- Physical accessibility
- Reporting channels

1. __________ are organizational guidelines and rules designed to promote fairness and equal opportunities for all members, particularly those from marginalized groups.
2. __________ are organizational policies that promote and promote a sense of belonging in individuals from diverse backgrounds and perspectives.
3. __________ are assessments conducted to measure the level of diversity within an organization and identify areas for improvement.
4. __________ are an assessment or analysis of an organization's policies, practices, and procedures to identify and rectify any potential disparities in treatment or opportunities.
5. __________ are conversations and discussions aimed at addressing diversity and inclusion issues, fostering understanding, and promoting positive change.
6. __________ are mechanisms within organizations for employees to report incidents of discrimination, harassment, or other concerns related to diversity and inclusion while ensuring confidentiality and a safe reporting environment.
7. __________ ensures that spaces and facilities are designed and equipped to accommodate individuals with disabilities, making them accessible to all.
8. __________ is the act of actively supporting and promoting the interests and rights of marginalized or underrepresented groups, often through campaigning, lobbying, or raising awareness.
9. __________ is input provided by employees regarding their experiences, concerns, and suggestions related to workplace diversity and inclusion.
10. __________ is the state of being equal in terms of rights, opportunities, and treatment for all individuals, regardless of their background or characteristics.
11. __________ are training programs designed to educate individuals about prejudices they may hold, with the aim of reducing discriminatory behavior.
12. __________ is the recognition and acceptance of the natural variation in neurological differences among individuals, including conditions such as autism, ADHD, and dyslexia.
13. __________ is a practice of modifying the work environment, policies, or procedures to enable individuals with disabilities to perform their job tasks effectively.
14. __________ are educational programs aimed at increasing awareness and understanding of diversity issues, with the goal of creating more inclusive environments.
15. __________ is unfair treatment or prejudice against individuals or groups based on factors such as race, gender, age, or other characteristics, resulting in unequal opportunities or outcomes.
16. __________ is the practice of providing fair and just treatment and opportunities to individuals, taking into account their unique needs and circumstances to achieve equality.
17. __________ are specific objectives set by organizations to promote and achieve diversity within their workforce or community.

18. __________ is an understanding and appreciation of different cultural backgrounds, values, and perspectives, often necessary for fostering diversity and inclusion.

19. __________ is the presence of a variety of different backgrounds, perspectives, and experiences within a group, organization, or community.

20. __________ is the practice of creating an environment where all individuals feel valued, respected, and included, regardless of their differences.

Conclusion

DEI is not merely a buzzword; it is an ethical necessity and a strategic advantage in today's diverse and interconnected world. As you pursue your certification or continue your HR career, fostering diversity, equity, and inclusion is key to shaping a brighter and more inclusive future for organizations and society.

For PHR and PHRi candidates, DEI is notably emphasized in the Employee and Labor Relations domain, highlighting its importance in workplace relations and compliance. The SPHR and SPHRi certification places a substantial focus on DEI within the Leadership & Strategy and Talent Management domains, acknowledging DEI's strategic significance in organizational success.

On the SHRM exams, DEI is a central competency with three subcompetencies, illustrating its comprehensive nature. SHRM recognizes that DEI initiatives profoundly impact an organization's social, ethical, and legal behaviors, solidifying its status as a core HR competency.

As HR professionals, staying attuned to the evolving DEI landscape is essential, as it not only enhances exam readiness for the PHR/i, SPHR/i, or SHRM certifications but also equips practitioners to drive meaningful change in their organizations.

Additional Resources

The following online resources offer a variety of tools, articles, guides, and research to help individuals and organizations understand and implement effective DEI initiatives in the workplace. Whether you are an HR professional, a manager, or simply interested in promoting diversity, equity, and inclusion, these resources provide valuable insights and guidance.

Websites

- Diversity, Equity, and Inclusion Resources by SHRM (www.shrm.org/resourcesandtools/tools-and-samples/toolkits/pages/diversityandinclusion.aspx)

  The Society for Human Resource Management provides a comprehensive toolkit with articles, templates, and resources to help organizations develop and implement effective DEI initiatives.
- Diversity, Equity, and Inclusion Toolkit by Catalyst (www.catalyst.org/research/diversity-equity-and-inclusion-toolkit)

  Catalyst offers a toolkit with resources, reports, and guides to support women in the workplace. It includes practical advice and research on inclusive leadership.
- The Racial Equity Tools (www.racialequitytools.org)

  This resource provides more than 4,500 tools and resources to help individuals and organizations advance racial equity and inclusion. It includes articles, worksheets, and training materials.
- The Center for the Study of Social Policy - Advancing Equity and Inclusion Series (https://cssp.org)

  This series offers resources and guides on advancing equity and inclusion, particularly in the context of social policy and human services.

Podcasts

- *"Still Processing"* Hosted by Wesley Morris and J Wortham (www.nytimes.com/column/still-processing-podcast)

  This New York Times podcast shines a light on many of the most compelling social issues around DEI that go beyond the workplace.
- *"Race at Work"* Hosted by Porter Braswell (www.podchaser.com/podcasts/race-at-work-with-porter-brasw-1536471)

  Hear from business and other leaders on their personal experiences around race in the workplace.
- *"The Will to Change"* Hosted by Jennifer Brown (www.jenniferbrownspeaks.com/podcasts)

  A diverse podcast in and of itself, the show covers issues such as second chance programs, trauma associated with lack of DEI initiatives, and many other broader issues surrounding DEI.

YouTube Channels

While these YouTube channels may not focus exclusively on DEI initiatives, they often include content related to diversity, equity, and inclusion in the workplace. Explore their playlists and videos at `www.youtube.com` and subscribe to their content that aligns with your interests and learning goals related to DEI.

- The Conference Board

  The Conference Board's channel covers various business and HR topics, including diversity and inclusion in the corporate world. It features discussions with industry leaders.

- The Diversity Movement

  The Diversity Movement's channel focuses on diversity, equity, and inclusion, offering informative videos on creating inclusive workplaces.

- DiversityInc

  DiversityInc's channel features videos on diversity and inclusion in the workplace. It includes interviews, panel discussions, and insights from DEI experts.

Chapter 13

Workforce Analytics and Technology

In December 2021, U.S. mortgage company Better.com fired 900 workers over Zoom. "If you're on this call, you're part of the unlucky group being laid off," the CEO told the workers. To add insult to injury, it was effective immediately. Just half a year later, United States–based Carvana let 2,500 workers go in a similar manner, some during group Zoom calls, some via email. Almost simultaneously, the CEO of Swedish company Klarna announced 700 job cuts in a prerecorded message, after which workers had to wait up to 48 hours for an email telling them whether they were part of the affected group. Layoffs are an unfortunate but necessary part of the business cycle; how HR handles them is a choice. These mass virtual layoffs generated bad publicity, left staff angry, and are excellent examples of when HR's use of technology is counterproductive. This highly visible situation shines a light on some of the pitfalls of living in such a globally connected time and place, and is but one of the many aspects of technology that HR seeks to influence. These other technology aspects include the following:

- **Workforce analytics:** Analyzing the workforce involves utilizing data to optimize various aspects of workforce management, such as recruitment, retention, and performance. This data is used by HR to identify trends in employee performance, forecast future staffing needs, and develop targeted strategies for talent management and retention.
- **Qualitative and quantitative statistical analysis:** Methods for analyzing data entails examining both numerical and non-numerical data to derive meaningful insights into organizational processes and employee behaviors. This measures the effectiveness of training programs, helps to evaluate employee satisfaction, and informs evidenced-based decisions to enhance organizational effectiveness.
- **HR technology:** HR technology such as HR information systems (HRISs) and applicant tracking systems (ATSs) facilitates efficient management of employee data, streamlines recruitment processes, and enhances overall HR operations. HR technology, including HRISs and ATSs, is leveraged by HR professionals to streamline administrative tasks, track employee progress, and improve communication and collaboration within the organization.
- **Data privacy and security:** HR is responsible for ensuring the confidentiality and integrity of employee data, complying with regulations, and implementing measures to prevent unauthorized access or breaches. The goal of these efforts is to protect sensitive employee, customer, and other organizational information from breaches or unauthorized access.

- **Artificial intelligence (AI):** AI in HR refers to the integration of artificial intelligence technologies to automate tasks, improve decision-making processes, and personalize employee experiences through data-driven insights and predictive analytics. AI can help automate routine tasks such as résumé screening, provide personalized learning and development recommendations, and enhance the recruitment process through predictive analytics and candidate matching algorithms.

Real World Scenario

Streamlining HR Data Systems

Contributed by James Galluzzo, III, SPHR, PMP, Lieutenant Colonel, United States Army (Retired)

In 2022, the United States Department of Defense was ranked as the second largest employer in the world. Its oldest branch, the Army, has its roots in the American Colonial Era. Established in 1775 at the beginning of the Revolutionary War, it predates even the founding of the country. Older institutions tend to grapple with entrenched technology systems due to historical legacy, inertia, and risk aversion. Migration challenges, budget constraints, and fear of disruption hinder updates. Strategic planning is crucial for successful modernization and overcoming barriers to adapt to evolving technological landscapes.

Background and Problem

Comprised of nearly 1,000,000 service members serving on active duty, the Army Reserves, and the National Guard, the U.S. Army had multiple HRIS platforms, including legacy systems nearly 30 years old. The systems were costly to maintain, could not readily share data across platforms, and did not meet compliance requirements established by Congress for auditability. This fragmentation in HRIS platforms led to inefficiencies in personnel management, hindering the Army's ability to integrate and manage its vast workforce effectively. The lack of compliance jeopardized the Army's accountability and transparency, necessitating modernization efforts to align with evolving standards and streamlined operations.

Diagnosis

The Army had previously attempted a single comprehensive system that would also integrate with other military services, but that system was not implemented due to cost and other delays. However, from its initial concept and foundation, the Army looked to create the Integrated Personnel and Pay System – Army (IPPS-A). It was clear that from this baseline the Army required a robust framework to be implemented.

Strategies

The Army embarked on the design of a commercial, off-the-shelf (COTS) system using a modified program based on PeopleSoft from Oracle. This approach allowed for minimal customization to keep costs lower. The developed system also is visible in real time across all three Army components and could subsume legacy platforms that were obsolete. The programs were designed to provide enough data points that, when combined with built-in data visualization tools, could produce a reliable, common operating picture that met compliance requirements and allowed Army leaders to make informed decisions regarding their workforce.

Results

The IPPS-A system went live across the full Army force in 2023 and continues to develop. The use of the Agile program methodology allows for the rapid delivery of improvements and enhanced capabilities, dramatically reducing the time to deliver to the end user. The Army has also adopted some private-sector HR terminology, replacing military jargon inside the system to be more aligned to best HR practices.

Conclusion

The United States Army's endeavor to modernize its HRIS platforms highlights the importance of technological evolution within vast organizational frameworks. Addressing legacy systems and compliance gaps presents an opportunity for enhanced operational efficiency, data integrity, and mission preparedness. Through deliberate modernization strategies, the Army has demonstrated the capacity to navigate evolving operational landscapes on both a macro and micro level while upholding its commitment to excellence and accountability in serving the people of the United States.

Workforce Analytics and Technology Practice Questions

1. What is the primary goal of workforce analytics?
   - A. To reduce employee turnover.
   - B. To optimize workforce productivity.
   - C. To increase customer satisfaction.
   - D. To lower operating costs.
2. Which of the following is an example of an HR benchmark in a manufacturing environment?
   - A. Product defect rate.
   - B. Energy consumption per unit.
   - C. Units produced per hour.
   - D. Supplier out-of-stocks.
3. When building a business case to argue the merits of investing in an expensive data modeling software program, what role does a cost-benefit analysis play?
   - A. It details the costs associated with the plan.
   - B. It describes how the plan will be funded.
   - C. It considers the cost of potential data security breaches.
   - D. It showcases the return on investment over time.
4. Which of the following is a common challenge in workforce analytics implementation?
   - A. Lack of quality data.
   - B. Employee resistance to change.
   - C. Too much data to analyze.
   - D. Lack of employee insights.
5. The company you work for has a turnover rate hovering around 32%. You have been tasked with creating a business case for the use of analytics to understand the reasons employees are leaving and how to prevent future turnover. Which of the following combinations of analytics would be most useful?
   - A. Descriptive and predictive.
   - B. Predictive and prescriptive.
   - C. Prescriptive and descriptive.
   - D. Diagnostic and prescriptive.

6. Which of the following components should HR include in a request for a new applicant tracking system proposal?
   - A. Desired features and functionality.
   - B. Budget and pricing information.
   - C. Proprietary details of use.
   - D. Marketing and advertising strategies.

7. Which of the following is an advantage of the use of commercial off-the-shelf (COTS) collaboration software in the workplace?
   - A. Enhanced security measures.
   - B. Improved internal communication.
   - C. Streamlined collaboration with all stakeholders.
   - D. Reduced employee workload.

8. A large multinational corporation is struggling with the verification of international educational and work experience credentials during its hiring process. The company often encounters difficulties in validating the authenticity of qualifications from various countries, leading to inefficiencies and potential hiring of unqualified candidates. Which of the following processes will best improve efficiencies without compromising quality outcomes?
   - A. Manual verification by HR team.
   - B. Outsourcing verification to a third-party service.
   - C. Implementing artificial intelligence for verification.
   - D. Utilizing blockchain for credential verification.

9. How can Natural Language Processing (NLP) benefit HR teams in managing employee feedback and communications effectively?
   - A. NLP can automatically generate employee feedback without HR intervention.
   - B. NLP can translate all employee communications into a single language for ease of understanding.
   - C. NLP can analyze and interpret employee feedback, emails, and chat interactions for insights.
   - D. NLP can replace HR personnel in conducting employee surveys and interviews.

10. The company you work for has recently implemented an AI-powered employee promotion recommendation system to assist HR in identifying high-potential candidates for managerial positions. The system analyzes employee performance data, including job performance, attendance, and project completion rates, to make promotion recommendations. In an unrelated audit, your HR team discovers that the algorithm consistently favors men for promotion despite similar or even superior qualifications and performance by female employees. What is the most likely reason for this bias?
    - A. The AI algorithm has a bug or technical error.
    - B. The historical data used to train the AI system reflects past discriminatory promotion practices within the organization.
    - C. There is a lack of diversity in the HR team responsible for overseeing the AI system.
    - D. The AI algorithm is too complex for HR to understand and manage effectively.

11. Which of the following is NOT a blockchain capability when it comes to human resource management practices?

A. Secured record-keeping.

B. Enhanced privacy and confidentiality.

C. Real-time payroll processing.

D. Decentralized identity verification.

12. You have been tasked with explaining the security features of blockchain technology to convince the executive team to adopt this costly new technology. The executive team is struggling to grasp the technology's most basic purpose. Which of the following provides the simplest and most accurate definition of blockchain security features?

A. It is a digital identity.

B. It is an enhanced password.

C. It is a digital fingerprint.

D. It is a CAPTCHA-like feature.

13. One morning, as employees start their workday, they receive an email with the subject line: "Urgent: Verify Your Account Information." The email appears to be from the company's IT department and claims that employees' accounts need immediate verification due to a security breach. It includes a link to a login page that looks almost identical to the company's actual login portal. This is the best example of what kind of cybersecurity attack?

A. Hacking.

B. Phishing.

C. Ransomware.

D. Social engineering.

14. What is the main difference between social engineering and hacking?

A. Social engineering involves manipulating individuals, while hacking involves exploiting technical vulnerabilities.

B. Social engineering focuses on unauthorized access, while hacking focuses on psychological manipulation.

C. Social engineering is a form of hacking, while hacking is a form of cybercrime.

D. Social engineering is legal, while hacking is illegal.

15. The statement "All employees accessing the company's network remotely must adhere to strict security protocols, including the use of multi-factor authentication and encrypted connections, to ensure the confidentiality and integrity of corporate data" belongs to which of the following technology management policies?

A. Personal use policy.

B. Social media.

C. Internet messaging.

D. Offsite network access.

16. What is the primary objective of a Bring Your Own Device (BYOD) policy in the workplace?

A. To establish guidelines for employees using their personal devices for work purposes.

B. To ensure that all employees use the same company-owned devices.

C. To prohibit employees from using their personal devices for work.

D. To restrict internet access on personal devices.

17. As a best practice, what is the role of human resources when it comes to data backup and recovery?

A. HR plays no role in data backup and recovery; it is the responsibility of IT departments.

B. HR supports data backup procedures and managing data recovery efforts.

C. HR is responsible for physically storing backup tapes and drives.

D. HR is responsible for troubleshooting technical issues during data recovery.

18. What does "scale" refer to in the context of microlearning?

A. The size of individual microlearning modules.

B. The ability to efficiently deliver content to a large number of learners.

C. The duration of a microlearning session.

D. The depth and complexity of microlearning topics.

19. Which of the following is NOT an important consideration when designing microlearning content for employees?

A. Accessibility.

B. Gamification.

C. Mass appeal.

D. Personalization.

20. The company you work for has asked you to design a DEI survey, the results of which will serve to inform strategic initiatives over the next 5 years. Which of the following elements is the most critical to the survey design?

A. Obtaining informed consent.

B. Selecting the proper mode.

C. Pre-testing the survey for validation.

D. Clearly defining the objectives.

21. What is the primary purpose of validating a workplace assessment tool or survey?

A. To verify that the survey measures what it intends to measure accurately.

B. To confirm that the survey has a high response rate.

C. To comply with the Uniform Guidelines on Employee Selection Procedures (UGESP).

D. To compare the survey results to industry benchmarks.

22. At a large retail corporation, the HR department has been quietly analyzing vast amounts of historical employee data to uncover patterns and insights to enhance their hiring and retention strategies. They have been examining factors, such as employee performance, work hours, training programs, and demographics to identify key traits and practices associated with high-performing and long-tenured employees. This information is then used to create tailored hiring criteria and development programs, ultimately leading to more successful and satisfied employees. Which of the following activities is HR engaged in?

A. Statistical analysis.

B. Data Reporting.

C. Data mining.

D. Trend Analysis.

23. In a busy healthcare clinic, the administrative team has been struggling with errors and inconsistencies in patient records. They've noticed that some patients have duplicate entries with slightly different information, while others have missing or outdated details in their files. This has led to confusion during appointments, billing discrepancies, and delays in providing appropriate medical care. What action should HR recommend?

A. Hiring a dedicated IT team to manage large quantities of data.

B. Invest in cloud storage to increase capacity.

C. Train employees on proper knowledge management techniques and storage.

D. Manage the process of data cleansing as a strategic initiative.

24. In a rapidly growing technology company, the Human Resources (HR) department faces a significant challenge in analyzing and presenting employee trends effectively. With a diverse workforce and multiple office locations worldwide, HR needs to provide insights to senior management on talent acquisition, employee engagement, and retention strategies. However, their current reports are overwhelming, filled with rows and columns of numbers, making it challenging for the leadership team to extract meaningful insights. What HR competencies will be necessary to translate this information into easily understandable insights?

A. Project Management skills.

B. Data Visualization skills.

C. Communication skills.

D. Presentation skills.

25. How does integrating HR systems facilitate better talent management and workforce planning?

A. By focusing on data security and confidentiality.

B. By centralizing HR data and providing real-time analytics.

C. By increasing ESS capabilities.

D. By eliminating the need for HR personnel in talent management.

26. Which of the following HR tasks are best suited to automation?

A. Payroll processing.

B. Employee onboarding.

C. Performance evaluations.

D. Workplace conflict resolution.

27. In a dynamic and data-driven corporate environment, the Human Resources (HR) department has taken on a new role as data advocates. The company has recognized the importance of leveraging data to make informed decisions regarding talent management, employee engagement, and overall organizational performance. What role does continuous improvement play in being effective data advocates?

A. Continuous improvement ensures that HR professionals have the most up-to-date data analysis tools.

B. Continuous improvement helps HR maintain employee morale and engagement.

C. Continuous improvement allows HR to track data trends but doesn't impact advocacy efforts.

D. Continuous improvement enables HR to adapt and enhance data-driven initiatives to better serve the organization's goals and objectives.

28. Which of the following is the responsibility of a senior HR leader but not necessarily HR Generalists in the context of data advocacy? Choose all that apply.

A. Promotes the use of HR metrics to understand organizational performance.

B. Demonstrates an understanding of the use of data to inform business decisions.

C. Maintains working knowledge of data collection methods.

D. Maintains objectivity when interpreting data.

29. Which of the following is an advantage of the use of cloud-based software in HR technology management?

A. Scalability.

B. Accessibility.

C. Limited customization.

D. Data security.

30. Fill in the blank: __________ is characterized by using research and best practices to build strategies to achieve organizational results.

A. Data analysis.

B. Evidenced based decision-making.

C. Peer reviews.

D. Validation studies.

31. Which approach is consistent with evidence-based decision-making when addressing workplace challenges?
    A. Using an employee suggestion system to gather feedback.
    B. Seeking input from a diverse group of employees.
    C. Relying on senior leadership to guide objectives.
    D. Collaborating with legal experts to maintain legally defensible practices.

32. You are tasked with presenting the annual financial performance of your company to the board of directors. Which communication approach is most effective?
    A. Delivering a narrative that uses storytelling and visualizations to highlight key insights.
    B. Sharing a spreadsheet with graphical representation of financial data.
    C. Providing a written report for reference after the presentation.
    D. Send the raw data via email so the participants can come prepared to the meeting.

33. Which of the following is NOT an internal source of information HR teams may use to develop HR initiatives?
    A. Employee wellness programs.
    B. Performance reviews.
    C. Benchmarking.
    D. Focus groups.

34. What is a key consideration when conducting an external scan to understand data utility needs in the workplace?
    A. Being mindful of data privacy regulations to access desired data sources.
    B. Obtaining data from reputable and legitimate sources for credibility and accuracy.
    C. Focusing on key competitors in your market to ensure the data is strategically relevant.
    D. Finding free or low-cost resources to align with company budget requirements.

35. What is one of the primary challenges organizations may face when implementing AI in human resource applications?
    A. Difficulty finding AI talent for the HR department.
    B. Overemphasis on scalability at the expense of security.
    C. Inability to integrate AI systems with existing HR software.
    D. AI's limited capacity to handle routine HR tasks.

36. When considering the challenges of using AI in human resource applications, what issue may arise when there is a significant gap in human relations experience within the implementation team?
    A. Overemphasis on security at the expense of scalability.
    B. Difficulty finding AI talent for HR applications.
    C. Inability to align AI initiatives with organizational goals.
    D. Challenges in understanding and addressing the nuanced needs of employees.

37. Which of the following HR practices are employee self-service technologies most suited to support?

   A. Compliance on legal matters.

   B. Employee coaching.

   C. Updates to sensitive personnel data.

   D. Tracking major life events.

38. In which of the following scenarios is HR most likely going to demonstrate the competency of negotiation?

   A. Implementing a new process or technology.

   B. Interpreting workforce data.

   C. Predicting workforce trends.

   D. Dealing with a data security breach.

39. In the HRIS selection process, what should HR consider after identifying the organization's HR needs and requirements?

   A. Finalizing the contract with a preferred HRIS vendor.

   B. Assessing the scalability and integration capabilities of HRIS systems.

   C. Conducting employee training on the selected HRIS system.

   D. Launching the implementation of the HRIS system without further evaluation.

40. The HR department of the global company you work for is considering implementing a new HRIS system to enhance data analytics, facilitate global workforce management, and ensure compliance with international labor laws and regulations. As the HR manager, you're tasked with creating a compelling business case for the HRIS implementation. What key considerations should you address to make a strong case?

   A. Emphasize the potential reduction in administrative workload for HR staff.

   B. Highlight the cost of implementing the HRIS system and potential short-term budgetary impact.

   C. Focus on the need for advanced features and functionalities to stay competitive in the industry.

   D. Outline how the HRIS system aligns with the organization's international expansion strategy, compliance goals, and long-term growth.

41. How is SaaS commonly utilized in HR technology?

   A. To manage payroll and employee benefits.

   B. To develop in-house HR software solutions.

   C. To maintain on-premises HR databases.

   D. To conduct in-person HR training sessions.

42. What is the primary purpose of an ATS in HR technology?

A. To support compliance-related tasks.

B. To manage and streamline the recruitment process.

C. To track the software used on company devices.

D. To comply with regulatory requirements for hiring.

43. Fill in the blank: A __________ is a digital platform that provides access to educational content, resources, and tools, often used for training, skill development, and knowledge sharing.

A. Website.

B. Learning portal.

C. Intranet.

D. Learning machine.

44. In a manufacturing facility, employees are required to wear smartwatches that track their movements and provide real-time feedback. What is the employer most likely utilizing this technology for?

A. Monitoring personal social media accounts.

B. Enhancing employee productivity and safety.

C. Collecting data on employee break times.

D. Measuring employee stress levels.

45. What is one of the potential risks associated with using wearable technology, such as smart clothing, in the workplace?

A. Decreased employee morale.

B. Decreased work productivity.

C. Privacy and data security concerns.

D. Increased workplace injuries.

46. What is the greatest risk associated with the use of VPNs in the workplace?

A. Increased internet bandwidth consumption.

B. Increased vulnerability to social engineering.

C. Increased system crashes.

D. Decreased storage capacity.

47. Which of the following is the least effective technique used by employers to protect employee information?

A. Policies.

B. Passwords.

C. Tiers.

D. Data keys.

48. When analyzing RFPs for the acquisition of new technology, how should the criteria be considered?

A. Assessing the alignment of timelines.

B. Ordered from price, highest to lowest.

C. Weighed in order of component importance.

D. Considered by level of post-implementation support.

49. Which needs should be prioritized when selecting HR technology?

A. Compliance with record-keeping requirements.

B. How the technology supports organizational strategy.

C. Who will own the technology.

D. How the technology will be stored.

50. In what ways can the IT department be a strong business partner for HR when selecting an HRIS?

A. IT will have the final say in what software HR should select.

B. IT can provide the necessary integration support with enterprise-wide systems.

C. IT will support HR in the purchasing process.

D. IT will serve as the expert on how to best secure confidential employee data.

51. What is a potential advantage of using AI in the hiring process? Choose all that apply.

A. Increased efficiency in screening candidates.

B. Enhanced objectivity in candidate evaluation.

C. Filtering candidates who distrust AI or feel negatively about the prospective employer.

D. Improved time to hire metrics.

52. What are the likely outcomes of the digital monitoring of employees? Choose all that apply.

A. Increased employee stress levels.

B. Increased productivity and efficiency through performance tracking.

C. Increase in employee counterproductive behaviors.

D. Improved compliance with company policies and regulations through monitoring.

53. In a cutting-edge corporate environment, a team of employees works under the guidance of a newly introduced anthropomorphized robot supervisor named ARI (Artificial Intelligence Response Interface). ARI, equipped with advanced AI capabilities, is responsible for evaluating employee performance and delivering feedback. How might the use of a robot supervisor for delivering performance feedback impact the workplace dynamics?

A. Increase employee engagement and motivation through personalized feedback tailored to individual strengths.

B. Elicit feelings of mistrust and resentment among employees, leading to decreased morale and productivity.

C. Foster a collaborative work culture by providing constructive criticism in a non-threatening manner.

D. Enhance communication and transparency within the organization by standardizing feedback delivery processes.

54. Which of the following best describes the role of descriptive statistics in the workplace?

A. Predicting future trends and outcomes based on historical data.

B. Summarizing and presenting data to provide insights into the current state of affairs.

C. Evaluating the impact of interventions and initiatives on employee performance.

D. Conducting hypothesis tests to determine causation between variables.

55. In a survey of employee satisfaction conducted at a company, the following ratings (on a scale of 1 to 5) were recorded: 4, 3, 5, 2, 4, 4, 3, 4, 5, 3, 3, 2, 4, 5. What is the mode of the employee satisfaction ratings?

A. 2.

B. 3.

C. 4.

D. 5.

56. In a survey of employee satisfaction conducted at a company, the following ratings (on a scale of 1 to 5) were recorded: 4, 3, 5, 2, 5, 4, 5. What is the mean of the employee satisfaction ratings?

A. 2.

B. 3.

C. 4.

D. 5.

57. A company is implementing a new employee assessment tool designed to measure various job-related competencies, such as problem-solving skills and teamwork abilities. To evaluate the concurrent validity of the new assessment tool, the company administers it to current employees and compares their assessment scores with their performance ratings from their supervisors. What is the primary purpose of evaluating the concurrent validity of the new employee assessment tool?

A. To assess the long-term predictive validity of the tool in predicting future job performance.

B. To determine whether the tool accurately measures the intended competencies by comparing it with an established criterion.

C. To evaluate the reliability of the assessment tool by comparing scores obtained from different administrations.

D. To examine whether the assessment tool measures unique aspects of job performance not captured by other existing measures.

58. Which of the following is a benefit of automating unemployment claims processing? Choose all that apply.

A. To reduce processing time and streamline efficiency.

B. To comply with documentation requirements of laws that vary from state to state.

C. To enhance data security and confidentiality.

D. To improve the likelihood of winning unemployment appeal.

59. After a reduction in force, what technology need becomes a priority for optimizing remaining workforce operations?

A. Revoking security clearances and other access to company assets.

B. Managing the company reputation through strong social media messaging.

C. Holding the meetings with affected workers with compassion.

D. Integrating AI-powered chatbots for streamlined employee support services.

60. Which of the following best defines evidenced-based decision-making in the workplace?

A. Making decisions based on intuition and gut feelings.

B. Relying on precedent and case law to make decisions.

C. Utilizing empirical evidence and data analysis to inform decisions.

D. Following traditional best practices to guide behaviors.

61. Which of the following statements best reflects a challenge faced by global organizations regarding the use of the internet?

A. Global organizations enjoy unrestricted access to all websites and software tools regardless of geographical location.

B. Global organizations must adhere to standardized internet regulations across all regions to ensure seamless operations.

C. Global organizations encounter obstacles in accessing certain websites and utilizing specific software due to regional restrictions and censorship policies.

D. Global organizations are immune to internet restrictions as they possess specialized access privileges.

62. Which of the following factors is most crucial for a global organization when selecting collaboration software?

A. Scalability to accommodate diverse teams across different geographical locations.

B. Integration with a limited number of third-party applications to minimize complexity.

C. Compatibility with a single language to facilitate uniform communication.

D. Exclusivity to a specific region to ensure regulatory compliance.

63. Which of the following options accurately describes how multiple hiring sites within a company can electronically enroll in E-Verify for employment verifications? Choose all that apply.

A. Each site can enroll separately, sign its own Memorandum of Understanding (MOU), and create cases for its newly hired employees.

B. One site may create cases for all of their sites.

C. Enrollment in E-Verify is automatic for all hiring sites within the company.

D. The company must designate a single representative to enroll all sites in E-Verify and manage case creation centrally.

64. The company you work for is in the early stages of completing a merger and acquisition. You have been tasked with managing the due diligence process. Which of the following best represents the use of technology throughout this process?
   - **A.** Converting personnel files to digital formats.
   - **B.** Analyzing HR and other systems for integration capability.
   - **C.** Automating HR audits to verify compliance with labor laws.
   - **D.** Staying organized with project management software.

65. The company you work for has recently switched to a mobile time card app. In an audit, it was discovered that employees were clocking in on their phones without actually being on-site at the start of their shift. Which technology solution should HR recommend?
   - **A.** Implement geofencing technology in the mobile time card app to restrict clock-ins to specific on-site locations.
   - **B.** Introduce biometric authentication features in the mobile time card app to verify employees' identities before allowing clock-ins.
   - **C.** Enable real-time GPS tracking within the mobile time card app to monitor employees' locations and ensure on-site presence during clock-ins.
   - **D.** Integrate the mobile time card app with the company's access control system to verify employees' physical presence on-site before allowing clock-ins.

66. Which of the following best describes a potential benefit of implementing biometrics in the workplace?
   - **A.** Enhanced privacy protection by minimizing the reliance on traditional identification methods.
   - **B.** Improved employee convenience with faster and seamless authentication processes.
   - **C.** Enhanced security by providing a unique and difficult-to-forge authentication method.
   - **D.** Streamlined administrative processes with reduced paperwork and documentation requirements.

67. Which of the following best defines asset management in Human Resource Management Systems?
   - **A.** Asset management refers to tracking and managing financial investments within the Human Resource Management System.
   - **B.** Asset management involves managing the organization's physical and intangible assets, including equipment, software licenses, and intellectual property.
   - **C.** Asset management primarily focuses on employee performance evaluations and talent development.
   - **D.** Asset management entails managing employee benefits and compensation packages electronically.

68. At a large corporation, several employees have recently fallen victim to identity theft, resulting in financial losses and compromised personal information. The company is concerned about preventing such incidents in the future and ensuring compliance with regulations like General Data Protection Regulation (GDPR). What action could the company take to prevent identity theft in the workplace and comply with the GDPR?

- **A.** Provide employees with free antivirus software for their personal devices.
- **B.** Implement a clear desk policy to ensure sensitive documents are securely stored.
- **C.** Conduct regular phishing awareness training sessions for employees.
- **D.** Encrypt all personal data collected and stored by the company.

69. Which of the following would be considered a data controller by definition of the General Data Protection Regulation (GDPR)? Choose all that apply.

- **A.** A third party.
- **B.** A private entity.
- **C.** A public organization.
- **D.** A self-employed person.

70. An employee is going into a disciplinary meeting and turns on his phone to record the session. The company has a strict "no recording" policy in place. How should HR handle this situation?

- **A.** Allow the employee to make the recording.
- **B.** Prohibit the employee from making the recording.
- **C.** HR should turn on their recorder as well.
- **D.** Neither party should record the meeting.

Key Concept Research Questions

When taking an important exam, "context" refers to the specific circumstances, conditions, and background information that surround and influence the subject matter, in this case, the world of Human Resources. This means that getting ready for test day means understanding more than just foundational knowledge. Take some time to work into your study plan extra research into the following key topics related to Workforce Analytics and Technology.

1. As noted in many other chapters, company culture has a significant impact on how HR practices are received by the team. What role does culture play on the effectiveness of AI initiatives in the workplace? Take advantage of the wealth of resources from HR automation expert Ben Eubanks and his case study on this very topic. Find it at `https://lhra.io/wp-content/uploads/2024/01/LHRA-Case-Study-Report-Company-Culture-Age-of-AI.pdf` or browse his website for even more relevant insights on the role of technology in the important work of HR (`https://lhra.io`).

2. Storytelling with data has become an important skill for all business professionals when making a business case for HR and other strategic initiatives. Storytelling in HR involves using visualizations and narratives to convey insights about employee performance, engagement, and organizational trends, facilitating informed decision-making and enhancing communication between HR professionals and stakeholders. Figure 13.1 illustrates the do's and don'ts of storytelling using data.

What are the critical components of bringing data to life through storytelling? Check out the storytelling tips found at `www.storytellingwithdata.com/makeovers` to help understand this important communication skill for HR leaders.

FIGURE 13.1 HR Storytelling

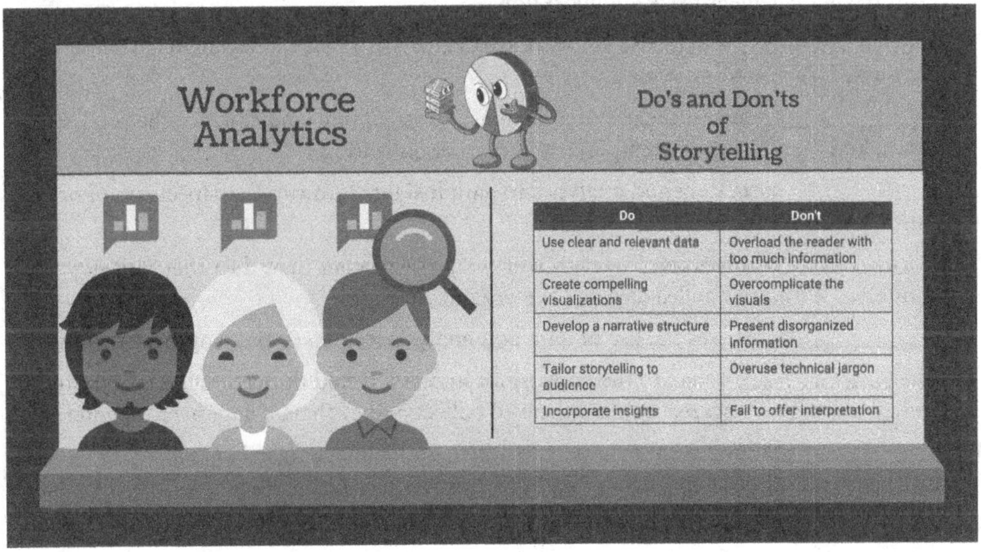

Test Your Workforce Analytics and Technology Terminology Knowledge

The following are the terms to use to test your knowledge on Workforce Analytics and Technology key terms. The correct answers are found in Appendix B.

- Applicant Tracking System (ATS)
- Employee collaboration platform
- Employee engagement score
- Employee self-service (ESS)
- HR process automation
- HRIS

- Internet of Things (IoT)
- Onboarding technology
- People analytics
- Remote work technology
- Retention analytics
- Survey tool
- Talent analytics
- Time and attendance system
- Workforce utilization

1. ____________ system is used by organizations to manage the recruiting process.
2. An ____________ is a digital platform that facilitates communication among employees within an organization such as Slack or Microsoft Teams.
3. ____________ involves using technology to increase the efficiencies of various human resource management tasks and workflows.
4. An ____________ is database software that helps HR professionals manage employee data and HR-related processes.
5. ____________ refers to the use of a database to streamline and enhance the process of hiring and integrating new employees into an organization.
6. ____________ uses data and analytics to gain insights into various aspects of an organization's workforce.
7. ____________ enables employees to work at a place other than the office and stay connected with their colleagues and the organization.
8. ____________ involves the use of data and analysis to understand employee turnover.
9. The ____________ refers to the network of interconnected devices, sensors, and objects embedded with software, enabling them to collect and exchange data over the internet.
10. ____________ allows team members to access and manage their HR-related information and tasks through a digital platform.
11. A ____________ is used to collect feedback and data from employees.
12. ____________ involves the use of data and analytics to gain insights into employee's skills and abilities to make strategic decisions.
13. A ____________ is a system used to track employee attendance and working hours.
14. ____________ involves the analysis of employee efficiencies.
15. ____________ involves rating the overall job satisfaction, loyalty and investment of employees in their jobs.

Conclusion

In today's data-driven workplace, the operational and strategic management of human resources has undergone significant transformations. While in the past HR systems have struggled to keep up with the rapid evolution of business practices, technology has helped bridge the gap, provided HR knows how to leverage the benefits and minimize the disadvantages. Workforce analytics and technology have emerged as indispensable tools for organizations seeking to optimize their workforce, drive informed decision-making, and enhance overall operational efficiency.

The 2024 SPHR/i exam content update introduced dedicated functional areas highlighting the significance of data privacy, security, and the digital transformation of corporate strategy and HR initiatives. This underscores the imperative for HR professionals to navigate the challenges and opportunities presented by the rapid digitization of workplaces. The PHR/i exams were also updated with a new HR Information Management functional area, with emphasis on the operational aspects driven by HR Information Systems (HRIS), data analytics, and cybersecurity. These competencies reflect the practical skills and knowledge required to effectively manage HR data and technology.

On the SHRM exam, the focus on Analytical Aptitude underscores the importance of being a data advocate, gathering data, conducting data analysis, and making evidence-based decisions. This competency aligns with the growing demand for HR professionals who can harness data-driven insights to inform strategic decision-making within organizations.

Additional Resources

These online resources offer a wealth of information and educational materials for individuals interested in workforce analytics and technology. Whether you're an HR professional or a business leader, these resources can help you stay updated on the latest trends and best practices in utilizing data and technology for workforce management.

Websites

- HR Tech Outlook (`www.hrtechoutlook.com`)

  HR Tech Outlook provides insights articles, whitepapers, webinars, and resources related to HR technology and workforce analytics. It covers emerging trends and technologies in HR.

- HR Valley (`www.hrtechvalley.org/hr-analytics-academy`)

  Based out of the University of Zurich, HR Valley's mission is to "elevate humans in the future of work." Their website offers news, insights and events about HR tech and other workforce trends.

- Workforce Institute by Kronos (www.workforceinstitute.org)

  The Workforce Institute provides research reports, articles, and webinars on workforce management, analytics, and technology. It offers insights into workforce trends and technology solutions.

Podcasts

- *"People Analytics"* Hosted by Sean Boyce (https://podcasts.apple.com/us/podcast/people-analytics/id1498112650)

  Built for HR practitioners and talent acquisition professionals, this podcast interviews leaders in the industry on multiple analytics topics.

- *"Analytics on Fire"* Hosted by BI Brainz AOF (https://bibrainz.com/podcast)

  This podcast focuses on analytics and data-driven decision-making, including workforce analytics. It covers topics like data visualization, predictive analytics, and data strategy.

- *"HR Examiner"* Various Hosts (www.hrexaminer.com/category/hrexaminer-radio)

  HR Examiner provides updates and insights on HR technology trends, including workforce analytics tools and solutions. It covers the latest developments in HR tech.

- *"HR Data Labs"* Hosted by Salary.com (https://hrdatalabs.com/podcast)

  HR Data Labs explores HR data, analytics, and technology. It includes discussions on using data to drive HR decisions and improve workforce outcomes.

YouTube Channels

While there may not be YouTube channels exclusively dedicated to workforce analytics and technology, you can find valuable content related to these topics on various HR and analytics-related channels. Here are two www.youtube.com channels to subscribe to:

- Visier People Analytics

  Visier's YouTube channel focuses on people analytics, workforce planning, and HR data insights. It includes webinars, expert interviews, and discussions on data-driven HR.

- Data with Decision

  This YouTube channel offers tips and downloads on data visualization best practices using MS Office Suite.

Chapter 14

Human Resource Competencies

Did you know? According to a *Forbes* study, 75% of employees said that they have experienced overall job burnout, 45% say they are burned out by organizational changes, nearly 38% quit within their first year of employment, and 40% of those separations occur within the first 90 days. With an average HR:FTE ratio of 1.4 HR for every 100 employees, these stats make for a busy HR desk![1]

HR professionals play a pivotal role in shaping the success of organizations. The field of HR is not merely about recruitment and payroll management; it encompasses a wide array of responsibilities, from strategic workforce planning to talent development and from ensuring compliance to fostering a workplace culture that promotes diversity, equity, and inclusion. To excel in this multifaceted role, HR professionals need to possess a set of competencies that go beyond basic administrative skills. This chapter delves into the HR competencies identified by the exam bodies of knowledge, including the following:

- **Leadership competencies:** Effective leaders demonstrate strong vision and inspire others through clear communication of goals. They empower their teams by fostering a culture of trust, collaboration, and accountability.
- **Interpersonal competencies:** Individuals with strong interpersonal skills build rapport easily, communicate effectively, and resolve conflicts diplomatically. They demonstrate empathy, active listening, and adaptability in diverse social and professional settings.
- **Business competencies:** Professionals proficient in business competencies understand market dynamics, financial principles, and strategic planning. They leverage analytical thinking, problem-solving skills, and innovation to drive organizational growth and success.

Figure 14.1 presents a visual look at the SHRM competencies you must be prepared to tackle on test day and beyond.

[1] Forbes Advisor Key HR Statistics and Trends In 2024 sourced at `www.forbes.com/advisor/business/hr-statistics-trends`

FIGURE 14.1 SHRM Body of Knowledge competencies

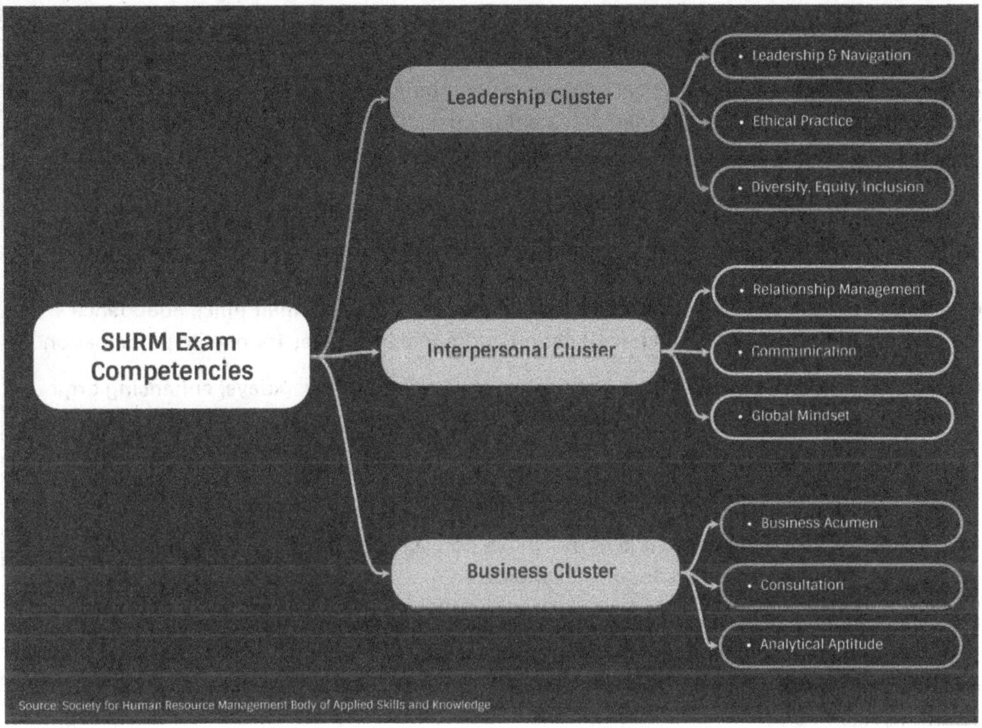

Real World Scenario

Hybrid at Will

Envoy Workplace is a software company that digitalizes streamlined workplace logistics. Each year they publish research pulled from their thousands of customers to understand workplace trends. In March 2020, workplaces were shut down in response to the COVID-19 pandemic. Fast-forward four years, and return-to-office (RTO) is still not at 100%. Envoy coined the term *hybrid at will* to capture the various ways employers are responding to the desire of employees for remote work. It defines the idea that in addition to traditional hybrid schedules, such as two to three days on-site per week, employees are being allowed to schedule their on-site days "at will."[2] This case study delves into the dynamics of this and other hybrid workplace strategies, focusing on the adoption rates, challenges, and effective solutions employed by organizations to engage employees in returning to the office.

[2] At Work the 2023 Workplace Trends Report sourced from `https://envoy.com/workplace-trends-reports/workplace-trends-report-2023`

Background and Problem

The advent of hybrid work models has revolutionized traditional office dynamics. However, as companies transition to this new norm, they face the challenge of encouraging employees to return to the physical workplace voluntarily. Despite the popularity of hybrid work, only 15% of workplace leaders have enforced a 100% in-office requirement, leaving the majority of companies navigating the complexities of hybrid work adoption.

Diagnosis

The survey revealed four predominant hybrid work policies:

- **Hybrid at-will:** 56% of companies allow employees to choose their office attendance days, offering flexibility but necessitating additional incentives for on-site participation.
- **Hybrid split-week:** 11% enforce specific on-site and remote workdays, enhancing organizational planning but potentially limiting employee autonomy.
- **Hybrid manager-scheduling:** 8% empower managers to determine team on-site days, prioritizing collaboration but risking inconsistency across teams.
- **Hybrid mix:** 25% adopt a blend of the above policies, balancing flexibility, planning, and collaboration benefits for all stakeholders.

88% of companies resort to incentives to motivate employees to return to the office, with popular strategies including food programs, social events, company-wide gatherings, enhanced office amenities, and environmental enhancements.

Strategies

To optimize hybrid workplace engagement, companies are employing multifaceted strategies:

- **Incentive programs:** Offering attractive incentives such as food and beverage provisions, social events, and enhanced office amenities to create an inviting workplace atmosphere.
- **Technology investments:** Leveraging technology to facilitate seamless remote collaboration, videoconferencing, and space booking, ensuring a smooth transition between remote and on-site work.
- **Physical workspace enhancements:** Reconfiguring office spaces to accommodate hybrid work needs, creating collaborative zones, meeting rooms, and additional workstations to support both remote and in-office teams.

Results

The implementation of these strategies has yielded promising results:

- **Increased engagement:** 85% of workplace leaders report positive outcomes from incentive programs, with employees exhibiting heightened enthusiasm toward returning to the office.

- **Enhanced workplace experience:** Investments in technology and physical workspace improvements have fostered a conducive environment for collaboration, productivity, and employee well-being.
- **Adaptive organizational culture:** Companies are evolving their culture to align with hybrid work dynamics, fostering a sense of purpose, value, and belonging among employees.

Conclusion

There are several competencies necessary for an HR professional to navigate these hybrid policies. They include the following:

- **Change management:** HR leaders must be adept at guiding organizations through the transition to hybrid work, managing resistance to change, and fostering a culture of adaptability and resilience among employees.
- **Communication skills:** Effective communication is essential for HR leaders to articulate the rationale behind hybrid work policies, address employee concerns, and ensure clarity regarding expectations for remote and in-office work.
- **Technology proficiency:** HR leaders need to be well-versed in digital tools and platforms used for remote collaboration, communication, and performance management, enabling them to leverage technology to support hybrid work arrangements effectively.
- **Flexibility and adaptability:** Given the dynamic nature of hybrid work, HR leaders must demonstrate flexibility and adaptability in responding to evolving employee needs, organizational priorities, and external factors influencing the workplace environment.
- **Empathy and emotional intelligence:** Understanding and empathizing with the diverse experiences and challenges faced by employees in a hybrid work setting is crucial for HR leaders to foster a supportive and inclusive work culture.
- **Strategic Thinking:** HR leaders should possess strategic thinking skills to anticipate future trends, proactively identify opportunities for improvement in hybrid work practices, and align HR initiatives with organizational goals and objectives.
- **Leadership and Influence:** HR leaders need to demonstrate strong leadership capabilities to inspire confidence, build trust, and influence stakeholders at all levels of the organization in support of hybrid work initiatives.

The hybrid work landscape presents both challenges and opportunities for organizations seeking to optimize employee engagement. By adopting a tailored approach encompassing incentives, technology investments, and physical workspace enhancements, companies can create an environment conducive to hybrid work success. However, the key lies not only in incentivizing employees but also in cultivating a workplace culture that prioritizes collaboration, creativity, and purpose to ensure sustained employee enthusiasm for choosing the office over remote work options.

Human Resource Competencies Practice Questions

1. Why is it important for HR leaders to possess business acumen?
   - **A.** To focus on HR processes and policies that protect the company from risk.
   - **B.** To reduce employee turnover.
   - **C.** To align HR strategies with overall business goals.
   - **D.** To enforce strict adherence to labor laws.
2. Your HR team has grown proficient at designing recognition and rewards programs that acknowledge and celebrate employees who exemplify the organization's values and contribute significantly to achieving its goals. This is the best example of which HR competencies? (Choose all that apply.)
   - **A.** Supporting the company vision.
   - **B.** Navigating the organization.
   - **C.** Implementing HR initiatives that support organizational development.
   - **D.** Relationship building.
3. The marketing department of a company is planning to launch a new advertising campaign. They need to hire additional creative professionals for this project. Which role does human resources play in supporting the marketing department in this situation?
   - **A.** Equally distributing the workflow to understand the new job requirements.
   - **B.** Identifying potential advertising channels.
   - **C.** Conducting interviews and hiring creative professionals.
   - **D.** Using social media to communicate the company brand.
4. The research and development (R&D) department of a technology company is working on a highly confidential project. They need to hire a team of researchers with specialized skills. How can HR assist the R&D department in maintaining confidentiality during the hiring process?
   - **A.** Implement strict NDAs with candidates.
   - **B.** Conduct background checks on all current R&D employees.
   - **C.** Tell the candidates of the need for discretion.
   - **D.** Threaten candidates with legal action should they disclose sensitive information.
5. What is the primary function of HR within an organization?
   - **A.** Engaging employees to increase retention.
   - **B.** Managing employee recruitment, training, and development.
   - **C.** Improving company efficiencies through people and process management.
   - **D.** Supporting organizational results through people management strategies.

6. The finance department of a company is restructuring its cost allocation methods. They need to gather data on employee salaries, benefits, and overhead costs. How can HR assist the finance department in this process?
   - A. By providing financial investment advice.
   - B. By generating financial reports for shareholders.
   - C. By supplying payroll and benefits data.
   - D. By managing the company's budget and expenses.
7. What is the primary goal of active listening?
   - A. To use your influence to affect positive change.
   - B. To provide timely solutions.
   - C. To understand and empathize with others.
   - D. To navigate the politics and silos of the workplace culture.
8. In a conflict-resolution scenario, what should an HR professional prioritize?
   - A. Making sure relationships stay positive.
   - B. Maintaining neutrality and fairness.
   - C. Following company policies related to the issues.
   - D. Offering the solution to end the conflict.
9. The production department of a manufacturing company is experiencing a high employee turnover rate on the factory floor, leading to disruptions in production schedules. What can HR do to support the production department?
   - A. Develop a new product line to improve efficiency.
   - B. Provide additional training for production employees.
   - C. Manage employee performance evaluations.
   - D. Set production quotas for the next quarter.
10. Which of the following is an example of a closed-ended question in an HR interview?
    - A. "Tell me about your work experience."
    - B. "What are your long-term career goals?"
    - C. "How did you handle a difficult co-worker in the past?"
    - D. "Did you complete your last project on time?"
11. During a performance appraisal meeting, an employee becomes emotional and starts crying. What should the HR professional do first?
    - A. Prioritize empathy and emotional support.
    - B. Be quiet and allow the employee a moment to compose themselves.
    - C. Continue discussing the appraisal without addressing the emotions.
    - D. End the meeting and reschedule for another day.

12. In a scenario where an employee's performance is deteriorating, what action should HR take first?
   A. Follow the company's written policies to ensure fairness.
   B. Discuss the situation with the employee's manager.
   C. Have a one-on-one discussion to understand the reasons.
   D. Change the company's performance criteria to be more flexible.

13. Which interpersonal skill is vital for HR professionals when conducting diversity and inclusion training?
   A. Conflict resolution.
   B. Cultural sensitivity.
   C. Influence.
   D. Global mindset.

14. During a team-building workshop, an HR facilitator asks participants to share personal stories. What is the likely purpose of this activity?
   A. To build trust and camaraderie among team members.
   B. To create a more personalized approach to performance management.
   C. To judge participants' storytelling skills.
   D. To identify potential weaknesses that will need to be developed.

15. In which HR scenario is assertiveness a valuable interpersonal skill?
   A. Negotiating employee benefits packages.
   B. Conducting exit interviews.
   C. Disciplining an employee for misconduct.
   D. Sending company-wide email updates.

16. In written workplace communication, what should be the primary focus to ensure clarity and professionalism?
   A. Using appropriate technical jargon to increase credibility.
   B. Keeping the message as concise as possible.
   C. Including personal anecdotes for engagement.
   D. Use a more formal style to reduce misunderstandings.

17. The HR manager at your place of work has been recently hired, and she is still unfamiliar with the president/CEO's management style. The president recently directed her to contact his adult children (who are passive stakeholders) to gather their input on what is most important for the upcoming health insurance renewals. The HR manager does as he asks but disregards the children's input because she is more experienced than they are and has a better understanding of how health insurance packages should be structured. Which of the following competencies is the HR manager displaying a lack of?
   A. Situational awareness.
   B. Collaboration.
   C. Professional integrity.
   D. Navigating the organization.

18. What are the primary differences between consensus and commitment when navigating workplace conflict?

- **A.** Consensus involves finding a compromise, while commitment entails one party yielding to the other.
- **B.** Consensus focuses on alignment of opinions, while commitment centers on shared dedication to a common goal.
- **C.** Consensus seeks to avoid conflict, while commitment addresses conflict head-on.
- **D.** Consensus relies on authoritative decision-making, while commitment promotes democratic conflict resolution.

19. When should the "compromise" conflict-management technique be employed?

- **A.** When one party wants a quick resolution.
- **B.** When one party is willing to give in entirely.
- **C.** When there is no urgency to resolve the conflict.
- **D.** When both parties are equally invested in the outcome.

20. What is a key advantage of using alternative dispute resolution (ADR) techniques such as mediation or arbitration in the workplace?

- **A.** The outcomes are more costly than litigation.
- **B.** They provide legally binding resolutions.
- **C.** They promote open and effective communication.
- **D.** They involve judges and formal court proceedings.

21. You are a manager negotiating a salary increase with an employee. The employee has expressed concerns about their current financial situation. Which negotiation technique involves understanding and acknowledging the employee's perspective before presenting your offer?

- **A.** Principled bargaining.
- **B.** Positional bargaining.
- **C.** Perspective taking.
- **D.** Win-lose negotiation.

22. The training manager at your organization has been tasked with conducting the company's annual DEI training. While she is committed to the task and highly professional, you notice that during the training sessions she frequently interrupts participants, provides overly lengthy explanations to questions, and shares too many personal anecdotes to make her points. The participants' body language indicates that they are not comfortable with her interruptions, and they often simply stop actively participating. Which of the following characteristics of emotional intelligence is she missing?

- **A.** Cultural sensitivity.
- **B.** Relationship management.
- **C.** Self-management.
- **D.** Self-awareness.

23. You're attending a professional conference in your field. During a networking event, you strike up a conversation with a fellow attendee. What is the best way to initiate a connection that can lead to building a professional network?

A. Quickly exchange business cards and move on to meet more people.

B. Share personal anecdotes and hobbies to establish rapport.

C. Ask about their professional background and interests.

D. Commiserate about the conference's organization and logistics.

24. What is an effective way for HR senior leaders to create opportunities for their teams to build relationships with other department leaders?

A. Hosting mandatory cross-departmental meetings.

B. Coordinating volunteer efforts and ask HR to lead different teams.

C. Organizing cross-functional projects and initiatives.

D. Coordinating company events and seat the HR team with different leaders.

25. As an HR professional, you're looking to build a network of mentors and advisors. Which action is most likely to help you achieve this goal?

A. Post on your LinkedIn or other social media networks that you are looking for a mentor.

B. Find a mentor within your organization so that you gain internal insights to help your career.

C. Hire an external coach to help you develop your generalist skills.

D. Attend HR-specific events and actively engage with participants.

26. Part of your responsibility as an HR generalist is to process weekly payroll. The managers are responsible for auditing and approving employee time cards, but several of them don't get to it by the deadline, leaving you to complete them so that the payroll cutoff is not missed. What is your best approach in this scenario?

A. Talk to your HR manager about hiring a payroll specialist.

B. Conduct a training session with the managers on the expectations and how to properly submit time cards.

C. Set a "soft" deadline of the day before so if managers are late, you still make the cutoff.

D. Do nothing, as this is simply part of the job.

27. Which team structure encourages team members to have equal authority and responsibility in decision-making?

A. Hierarchical team structure.

B. Flat team structure.

C. Functional team structure.

D. Autocratic team structure.

28. What is a potential challenge of cross-functional teams in organizations?

A. Compromised communication and collaboration.

B. Limited diversity of skills and perspectives.

C. Unhealthy alliances and silos.

D. Difficulty in coordinating different functional areas.

29. Which factor is crucial for the success of virtual teams in organizations?

A. Limited reliance on technology for communication.

B. Frequent face-to-face meetings.

C. Strong team cohesion.

D. High degrees of autonomy in decision-making.

30. In a focus group discussion, a facilitator observes that the conversation is veering off-topic and becoming unproductive. What facilitation skill should the facilitator use to refocus the discussion?

A. Allow the group to continue discussing the topics to encourage creative problem-solving.

B. Introduce additional off-topic questions and then work to get them back on track.

C. Gently guide the discussion back to the main topic.

D. Put unrelated issues in a "parking lot" and get the team back to the agenda.

31. It has come to your attention through informal channels that many managers are frustrated by the number of weekly meetings they are required to attend. They say that meetings are time wasters and much of the content could be accomplished via emails or a quick phone call. Which of the following responses best demonstrates the problem-solving competency of an HR professional?

A. Champion a strategic efficiency initiative to review the efficacy of company meetings.

B. Conduct a survey among managers to gather their feedback and suggestions on improving meeting efficiency.

C. Create a policy that restricts the number and duration of meetings for managers, requiring approval for any new meetings.

D. Let the managers know that you don't have control over the meeting cadence, so they will need to problem-solve among themselves.

32. Which persuasive communication technique involves using emotional appeals to connect with your audience?

A. Logos.

B. Facial expressions.

C. Pathos.

D. Body language.

33. Non-HR managers are struggling to explain a complex HR procedure to their team members. What approach can help them simplify and convey the information more effectively?

A. Provide the managers with a technical HR glossary.

B. Conduct the training on behalf of the manager so they know you support them.

C. Coach the managers on breaking down the procedure into simple steps.

D. Suggest the managers enroll in webinars and other training to gain better insights into HR.

34. You are a senior HR professional tasked with addressing C-suite executives about a sensitive HR issue. How should you approach this communication?

A. Send those who need to know an email to document the conversation.

B. Provide all the details of the issue, including confidential information.

C. Share high-level information, emphasizing potential risks and solutions.

D. Use humor to lighten the atmosphere and ease tension.

35. In which of the following scenarios is sending an email the best way to communicate?

A. When providing documents or forms.

B. When sharing good news or celebrating employee milestones.

C. When there is an interpersonal but nonserious situation in the group.

D. When there is no time available to communicate in a more personal way.

36. In addition to traditional HR responsibilities, which of the following statements best describes an HR professional's competency of competitive awareness?

A. Competitive awareness refers to HR professionals' expertise in payroll management and compensation structures.

B. Competitive awareness involves HR professionals staying updated on industry trends, labor market conditions, and competitor practices.

C. Competitive awareness means HR professionals are skilled in conflict resolution and employee relations.

D. Competitive awareness focuses on HR professionals' ability to manage employee benefits and retirement plans effectively.

37. Which data source is the most credible resource for human resource professionals to remain competent as strategic partners?

A. Social media headlines.

B. Labor law newsletters.

C. HR networking groups.

D. Websites that end in `.org`, `.edu`, or `.gov`.

38. What is the primary difference between the nominal group and Delphi facilitation techniques?

- **A.** The Delphi technique involves face-to-face meetings, while the nominal group technique relies on anonymous feedback.
- **B.** The nominal group technique involves a panel of experts, while the Delphi technique involves brainstorming.
- **C.** The Delphi technique uses ranking and voting, while the nominal group technique uses open discussion and consensus building.
- **D.** The primary difference is that the nominal group technique is used for decision-making, while the Delphi technique is used for problem-solving.

39. In a large corporation, the HR department is analyzing employee turnover rates over the past year to identify potential retention strategies. They calculate the average turnover rate as 15% for the year. However, they notice that there is a wide variation in turnover across different departments, with some experiencing rates as low as 5% and others as high as 30%. What statistical principle is the HR department likely applying in this scenario?

- **A.** Regression analysis.
- **B.** Analysis of variance.
- **C.** Simple random sampling.
- **D.** Descriptive statistics.

40. A small startup company is interested in understanding the relationship between employee performance scores and the number of training hours employees have completed. They collect data from 50 employees and calculate the correlation coefficient, which is found to be 0.75. What does this correlation coefficient value indicate?

- **A.** There is a strong positive linear relationship between performance scores and training hours.
- **B.** There is no relationship between performance scores and training hours.
- **C.** There is a strong negative linear relationship between performance scores and training hours.
- **D.** There is a moderate positive linear relationship between performance scores and training hours.

41. Which HR competency is essential for effectively connecting diversity, equity, and inclusion initiatives with organizational performance?

- **A.** Employee relations.
- **B.** Strategic planning.
- **C.** Personal integrity.
- **D.** Conflict management.

42. In facilitation, what is the purpose of a warmup or ice breaker?

- **A.** To introduce the meeting content in a fun and energizing way.
- **B.** To help the participants start to like each other more.
- **C.** To build psychological safety within the group.
- **D.** To warm up critical thinking skills.

43. Package delivery service UPS made headlines when the drivers' union negotiated up to $170,000 in total rewards by the end of the five-year contract. What likely role did HR play in these negotiations?

A. Supporting negotiations between the drivers' union and UPS management.

B. Analyzing the cultural impact of proposed compensation changes.

C. Ensuring compliance with labor laws and regulations during negotiations.

D. Developing strategies to address driver retention and satisfaction concerns.

44. Popular fast-food chain restaurant Wendy's announced a plan to introduce "dynamic pricing" to their menus. This means that the price of their menu items can change depending on factors such as geographic location, weather, and time of day. The rollout of this new program came under harsh criticism, and the company found itself having to clean up some of the reputational damage the poor messaging created. Which of the following elements of leadership competencies likely contributed to this failed marketing initiative?

A. Lack of clear communication with stakeholders.

B. Poor conflict-management skills.

C. Inadequate ability to deliver messages.

D. None, as HR was not likely to be involved in marketing initiatives.

45. Retail giant Walmart offers several in-house certificate programs on topics such as frontline manager leadership, people and business leadership, data science, software development, and project management. By bringing the training in-house and shortening the time it takes to complete the programs, corporate aims to fill the predicted 100,000 job openings they will have over the next three years. HR likely played a significant role in designing and implementing this strategic initiative. Which of the following competencies were necessary for their HR teams to act as strategic business partners in this scenario? (Choose all that apply.)

A. Negotiation.

B. Business acumen.

C. Vision.

D. Influence.

46. As the HR leader of a company transitioning back from remote work to a hybrid model, you encounter resistance from some employees who have grown accustomed to the flexibility of working from home. Your goal is to effectively manage this transition and ensure a smooth return to the office while addressing employee concerns. Which competency is crucial for the HR leader to demonstrate when managing the transition of employees back from remote work to a hybrid model? (Choose all that apply.)

A. Proficiency in graphic design software to create visually appealing communication materials.

B. Ability to lead conversations around office redesign to prepare for a hybrid work model.

C. Strong change management skills to guide employees through the transition process.

D. Expertise in technology solutions to protect confidential data during the transition.

47. Which of the following can be a source of conflict in hybrid work structures? (Choose all that apply.)

A. Role ambiguity.

B. Face-time bias.

C. Unsafe working conditions.

D. Gender discrimination.

48. What is the primary responsibility for HR leaders under the No Surprises Act of 2021?

A. Ensuring compliance with annual prescription drug data reporting requirements.

B. Negotiating lower premiums for employee health insurance plans.

C. Implementing new employee wellness programs.

D. Enforcing workplace safety regulations.

49. In which of the following ways can HR leaders perform their fiduciary responsibilities in health plan administration. (Choose all that apply.)

A. Negotiating the lowest costs for prescription drug coverage.

B. Asking for details on the spread between a drug cost and charges to the employer plan.

C. Simplifying pricing structures to aid in employee understanding.

D. Demanding transparency from their health plan administrators.

50. A lawsuit filed against a major Fortune 500 company alleges that they overpaid for prescription drug coverage under their employee health plan. The company negotiated terms that paid more than 250 times the retail cost for a 90-day supply of one drug. The lawsuit also alleged that the company incentivized plan members to use a specific mail-in pharmacy, despite the mail order costs being routinely higher than other pharmacies. In this example, how was the fiduciary duty of the company allegedly breached?

A. By failing to audit drug price costs on behalf of plan members.

B. By lack of oversight of the cost of routine prescription medications.

C. By overcharging premiums for employee health insurance.

D. By costing their ERISA plans and their employees millions of dollars in alleged drug overpayments.

51. Which of the following best describes the role of a Center of Excellence (CoE) in designing HR services?

A. CoEs focus on administrative tasks within HR departments.

B. CoEs are responsible for overseeing employee relations and conflict resolution.

C. CoEs specialize in providing expertise and best practices in specific HR areas, such as talent acquisition or learning and development.

D. CoEs primarily handle payroll processing and benefits administration.

52. What do decentralization, HRIS, and HR:FTE ratio have in common?

A. They are all drivers of HR system digitization.

B. They are all elements of an HR department structure.

C. They are all functions of an HR CoE.

D. They are all necessary for managing a remote workforce.

53. Which of the following are examples of navigating the organization as an HR competency? (Choose all that apply.)

A. HR collaborates with department heads and middle managers to address resistance to a new performance evaluation system, dealing with conflicting interests and building consensus for its implementation.

B. HR strategically networks with influential stakeholders across various departments to gather support for a diversity and inclusion initiative, leveraging relationships to ensure its successful integration into organizational culture.

C. HR conducts annual market wage surveys to ensure the company is competitive in its respective markets, ensuring compliance with state and federal regulations.

D. HR partners with the marketing department to identify the employee value proposition and champions the initiative to market the company as an employer of choice.

54. Why is the competency of navigating the organization important for skilled HR professionals?

A. To understand the organizational structure and dynamics, facilitating effective collaboration and communication within the company.

B. To navigate complex organizational politics and relationships, ensuring HR initiatives are successfully implemented.

C. To adapt HR strategies and practices to align with the organization's goals and values, fostering organizational effectiveness.

D. To establish credibility and influence with key stakeholders, gaining support for HR initiatives, and driving organizational change.

55. Why is the competency of critical evaluation important for skilled HR professionals?

A. To assess the effectiveness of HR policies and practices in achieving organizational goals.

B. To identify areas for improvement within the HR function and propose strategic solutions.

C. To evaluate the credibility and relevance of HR research and data before making decisions.

D. To critically analyze feedback and performance metrics to inform talent management strategies.

56. A report in Employee Benefits News discovered that 47% of younger workers are getting better advice from ChatGPT than they are from their managers. What approach should HR take to address this reality? (Choose all that apply.)
    - A. Implement training programs for managers to improve their mentoring and coaching skills.
    - B. Introduce ChatGPT as a supplementary resource for managers to support their employees.
    - C. Foster a culture of open communication and feedback between employees and managers.
    - D. Conduct surveys to understand the specific needs and preferences of younger workers regarding guidance and support.

57. Which of the following benefits are most likely to retain the younger workforce? (Choose all that apply.)
    - A. Flexible scheduling.
    - B. Mental health benefits.
    - C. Competitive salaries.
    - D. Student loan support.

58. The cost of offering employees various health and wellness benefits has been steadily increasing over the last several years. The leadership team has come to the HR department for advice on how to cut costs. Which of the following strategies should HR recommend to demonstrate the competency of designing HR solutions and data gathering?
    - A. Conduct a utilization review.
    - B. Partner with the insurance broker to uncover strategies.
    - C. Research trusted networking sites to identify cost reduction/savings strategies.
    - D. Recommend dropping the most expensive plans.

59. You are an HR manager at a shipyard in the United States, facing retention challenges among employees. Despite offering competitive salaries, some workers are leaving the company, causing disruptions in operations. Upon investigation, you discover that one of the primary reasons for attrition is the demanding nature of the work environment and the lack of opportunities for career advancement. How should you address this retention issue?
    - A. Increase salaries and benefits to match or exceed industry standards.
    - B. Implement flexible work schedules to accommodate employees' personal needs.
    - C. Establish a career development program offering training and advancement opportunities within the company.
    - D. Implement an over-hiring strategy to offset the high turnover rates.

60. Which of the following best describes the concept of building an employee pipeline in the tech sector?
    - A. Visiting colleges for recruiting events.
    - B. Community mentorships on the company's products and services.
    - C. Mentoring middle school students on STEM skills.
    - D. Attending military job fairs for transitioning personnel.

61. As an HR manager, you have sole responsibility for human resources at your organization with approximately 100 employees. There has been a rise in "no call, no shows" on the production line, and several employees are showing up late or leaving early. Despite your advice, the department manager does not want to engage in disciplinary action because it is "too difficult to find qualified people right now." Which of the following actions should you take?

- **A.** Follow through on the current attendance policies with verbal warnings and write-ups to maintain consistency and fairness for the other employees.
- **B.** Listen to the department manager and take a step back as he is responsible for his own department.
- **C.** Ask the manager to attend compliance and other policy training so he understands the risks associated with his approach.
- **D.** Work with the manager to create a replacement plan for employees not following policy.

62. Fill in the blank: An __________-based ERG is a voluntary, employee-led organization within a company that provides support, resources, and advocacy for individuals who share a common identity, background, or interest.

- **A.** Action.
- **B.** Evidenced.
- **C.** Inclusive.
- **D.** Affinity.

63. The DEI initiatives at your place of work are not generating the desired results because the state in which you are headquartered is considering bills that limit the reach of DEI initiatives. There have been reports of consumer backlash against the company for being "too woke." Senior leadership is considering lowering the strategic priority of DEI. What competencies will the HR leader need to demonstrate to advocate for these important initiatives?

- **A.** Negotiation and conflict management.
- **B.** Influence and vision.
- **C.** Political savvy and navigating the organization.
- **D.** DEI and interpersonal skills.

64. Quizlet, a global online learning platform, has a dedicated HR team whose mission is to find ways to connect engagement initiatives with the company's business strategy and values. As such, all team members—remote and headquartered—are required to attend two-day training events at a University of California campus and take courses taught by university professors. The goal is to connect the employees' passion for learning with the company's purpose. What competencies are best exemplified by the employee engagement team?

- **A.** Training and development.
- **B.** HR innovation.
- **C.** Business acumen.
- **D.** Relationship building.

65. As the HR manager of a company transitioning to a remote work model, you notice instances of proximity bias affecting the performance review process. Some managers tend to favor employees who are physically present in the office, leading to unfair evaluations and disparities in recognition and advancement opportunities. Your goal is to adjust the performance review system to mitigate any elements of this bias that negatively affect the process. What action should the HR manager take to accomplish this?

   A. Implement a policy requiring remote employees to provide weekly progress reports to ensure visibility and accountability.

   B. Conduct training sessions for managers on recognizing and mitigating biases in performance evaluations, emphasizing the importance of evaluating outcomes rather than physical presence.

   C. Establish a quota system for in-office and remote employees to ensure equal opportunities for recognition and advancement.

   D. Restructure the performance review criteria to prioritize objective measures of productivity, quality of work, and achievement of goals, regardless of physical location.

Key Concept Research Questions

Understanding the nuanced layers of human resource competencies requires much more than rote memorization. Taking the time to do quality research can help understand the larger environment of practice, which is the goal of researching the following question.

1. To ensure that certified HR professionals consistently maintain their competence and ethical standards, both HRCI and SHRM have specific criteria for recertification. These requirements encompass ongoing professional development, adherence to a code of ethics, continuing education credits at regular intervals, or you can choose to recertify by exam. Most would prefer to avoid that last option, so staying on top of your continuous education is important. Figure 14.2 shows an example of the types of courses you can take to meet the recertification requirements, as well as a sample training dashboard.

   Research the specific requirements for the exam you are studying for. The best place to start is `www.hrci.org` for the PHR/i and SPHR/i exams or `www.shrm.org` for the SHRM-CP and SHRM-SCP exams.

FIGURE 14.2 Microlearning dashboard

Test Your Human Resource Competencies Terminology Knowledge

The following are the terms to use to test your knowledge on HR competencies key terms. You can find the correct answers in Appendix B.

- Advocacy
- Business acumen
- Change management
- Competitive awareness
- Conflict management
- Data advocacy
- Evaluating business results
- Growth mindset
- Influence
- Leadership
- Listening
- Networking
- Negotiation
- Personal integrity
- Professional integrity
- Relationship management
- Service excellence
- Strategic alignment
- Teamwork
- Vision

1. _______________ is the ability to inspire and guide others toward achieving common goals and objectives.
2. _______________ is the ability to create a clear and compelling long-term direction for an organization or team.
3. _______________ is the power to affect the thoughts, behavior, and decisions of others.
4. _______________ is the quality of being honest and ethical in one's personal actions and decisions.
5. _______________ is the commitment to upholding ethical standards and principles in one's profession.
6. _______________ is the skill of effectively building and maintaining positive relationships with others.
7. _______________ is the practice of expanding professional connections to enhance career opportunities and knowledge.
8. _______________ is the art of reaching mutually beneficial agreements through communication and compromise.
9. _______________ is the ability to collaborate effectively with others to achieve shared goals.
10. _______________ is the skill of resolving disputes and disagreements in a constructive and productive manner.

11. _____________ is the act of paying close attention to and understanding what others are saying.
12. _____________ is the belief in one's ability to learn and grow throughout life.
13. _____________ is the act of advocating for or promoting a cause, idea, or solution.
14. _____________ is the understanding of how organizations operate and make decisions in the competitive marketplace.
15. _____________ is the awareness of the competitive landscape and the strengths and weaknesses of rivals.
16. _____________ is the alignment of an organization's activities and resources with its strategic goals.
17. _____________ is the process of assessing and analyzing business outcomes to inform decision-making.
18. _____________ is the management of organizational transitions and adaptations to achieve desired results.
19. _____________ is the commitment to providing outstanding and exceptional service to customers or stakeholders.
20. _____________ is the advocacy for the value and importance of evidenced-based decision-making.

Conclusion

In March 2020, when workplaces shut down due to the COVID-19 pandemic, there was much uncertainty in world. The post-pandemic world is not the same. Issues such as employee safety, hybrid work, remote work, and retention challenges share a common theme: the solutions run through HR.

The ability to be a trusted business partner must go beyond the days of compliance and event planning. The competencies necessary to perform the work of HR are well-outlined through SHRM's model of competency clusters of Leadership, Interpersonal, and Business. Competencies covered in this chapter include Leadership, Ethical Practice and Diversity, Equity and Inclusion, Relationship Management, Communication, having a Global Mindset, Business Acumen, Consultation Skills, and Analytical Aptitude. The knowledge domains of People, Organization, and Workplace are all covered in other chapters.

When the Society for Human Resource Management decided to launch its own certification exam, it represented a pivotal shift in how the practice of human resources was perceived. SHRM's primary criticism of the PHR, SPHR, and other exams offered by the Human Resource Certification Institute (HRCI) was that they were rooted in knowledge versus competencies. Knowledge refers to the information and facts one possesses, while competencies encompass the practical skills, abilities, and application of that knowledge in real-world situations. SHRM launched its own exams more than 10 years ago, and it features a comprehensive list of competencies HR professionals should be able to perform. While the competencies aren't explicitly identified as part of HRCI's PHR and SPHR body exams, they are still critical components of human resource best practices and, thus, should be thoroughly understood for success on exam day and on the job. The good to come from this situation is that—just as in the real-world practice of HR, there are many ways of approaching the same goal. Both agencies seek to validate that HR practitioners can demonstrate practical capabilities and understand universal competencies that the modern business world has indicated it values. In short, the combination of these knowledge, skills, and abilities over time makes you a stronger HR professional, regardless of which exam you choose to pursue.

Additional Resources

These online sources provide a wealth of information and resources for understanding and improving relationship skills and other human competencies in the workplace. Whether you are a manager, team member, or aspiring leader, these platforms can help you enhance your interpersonal and leadership skills for professional success.

Websites

- Society for Human Resource Management, Body of Applied Skills and Knowledge (BASK) (`www.shrm.org/credentials/certification/exam-preparation/bask`)

  If you have not already done so, download a copy of SHRM's BASK to review the competencies and subcompetencies that you will be tested on.
- Sandrareed.co partnered with MindEdge Learning (`https://catalog.mindedge.com/sandrareed`)

  I have partnered with MindEdge to provide courses in multiple domains of human resources and business. Most programs are approved for re-certification credits for HRCI and SHRM.
- Psychology Today (`www.psychologytoday.com`)

  Psychology Today offers a section dedicated to workplace psychology and interpersonal skills. It includes articles, blogs, and resources on building effective relationships at work.
- Forbes' Leadership (`www.forbes.com/leadership`)

  Forbes' Leadership section covers various leadership and relationship skills. It features articles, insights, and expert opinions on effective communication, team dynamics, and leadership competencies.

Podcasts

- *Harvard Business Review on Leadership* hosted by HBR (`https://hbr.org/2023/05/podcast-hbr-on-leadership`)

  This podcast features current thought leaders and insights on issues such as leadership, innovation, purpose, and active listening. There is an in-depth archive to draw from as well.

- *New Here* hosted by Harvard Business Review (`https://hbr.org/2023/09/podcast-new-here`)

  Another relevant podcast from the experts at *Harvard Business Review*, this podcast claims to be "the young professionals guide to work and how to make it work for you." Find topics related to new careers, motivation, workplace etiquette, and more.

- *Dear HBR* hosted by Harvard Business Review (`https://hbr.org/2018/01/podcast-dear-hbr`)

  One more from the leaders at HBR, this show features answers to some of the more snarled workplace dilemmas, such as giving remote feedback, handling sexism in the workplace, and coaching problem employees.

YouTube Channels

While YouTube channels dedicated exclusively to relationship skills and human competencies in the workplace may be limited, you can find valuable content related to these topics on various self-improvement, leadership, and personal development channels. Here are some `www.youtube.com` channels that offer insights into improving interpersonal skills and building competencies for the workplace:

- Science of People

  This channel provides evidenced-based but practical methods to build the social skills necessary to work with people.

- GreggU

  This channel offers free videos to help you improve your business competencies, such as mentoring, cultural intelligence, and personality.

- Brendon Burchard

  Known as a subject-matter expert in creating and maintaining high-performance teams, Brendon Burchard's short videos are about how to succeed in life and work.

Chapter 15

Leadership

One of the earliest industrial-organizational (I/O) field studies on leadership occurred at Western Electric in the 1920s and 30s. In a study initially designed to explore the effect of lighting on employee productivity, researchers inadvertently discovered the Hawthorne effect. This refers to the phenomenon where individuals modify their behavior simply in response to being observed or studied. Lighting and other environmental conditions were less important than the awareness of being observed had on the employees' levels of output. This revelation highlighted the importance of considering social and psychological factors in understanding human behavior in organizational settings. It also gave leaders a choice: they could drive employee outcomes through micro-management, or through positive interactions.

Are leaders born or made?

Questions like that make leadership one of the most studied topics in organizational settings, right up there with the topics of job satisfaction and employee engagement. What scholars have found is that leadership is not so easily defined by one question. However, as with most things HR related, there is a framework of best practices that define the functional role of leadership within an organization. Leadership encompasses a spectrum of skills, behaviors, and attitudes that extend beyond traditional notions of authority and hierarchy. It goes beyond the boundaries of job titles and formal positions, emphasizing that leadership is not confined to a select few at the top of an organization. Instead, it is a quality that can be cultivated, developed, and exhibited at every level of an organization. Throughout this chapter, we explore concepts related to the following:

- **The role of leaders:** Examining the responsibilities, attributes, and influence of individuals in guiding and developing others within an organization.
- **Traditional leadership theories:** Analyzing classical approaches and models that have shaped the understanding of leadership over time.
- **Team and structural factors:** Evaluating how team dynamics and organizational structures impact leadership effectiveness and effective decision-making.
- **Leadership development:** Exploring strategies and processes for nurturing and enhancing leadership skills and capabilities.
- **Leadership competencies:** Identifying the essential skills, qualities, and behaviors that effective leaders at all stages of their careers possess and develop.
- **Leading in human resources:** Focusing on leadership within the context of HR management, addressing issues related to people, processes, and projects.

Leadership and business expert Patrick Lencioni said, "If you could get all the people in an organization rowing in the same direction, you could dominate any industry, in any market, against any competition, at any time."[1] This will require the leadership skills to align business strategy and HR strategy to produce organizational results through people.

Real World Scenario

Harmony Among the Trees: A Tale of Three Leaders

In the enchanted forest of Dasos, a community of woodland creatures thrives under the guidance of various animal leaders. Among them are the wise phoenix, the cunning wolf, and the independent cat, each embodying a distinct leadership style.

Background and Problem

Due to a long dry spell, the Dasos forest has been facing a crisis of dwindling food supplies. With resources becoming scarce, tensions rise among the woodland creatures, threatening the harmony they once enjoyed. The community seeks leadership to navigate through these challenging times and find sustainable solutions to ensure their survival.

Diagnosis

The Council of Elders convenes to discuss the best course of action. They identify three potential leaders among them: Sophia the phoenix, Luc the wolf, and Matilda the cat, each representing transformational, transactional, and laissez-faire leadership styles, respectively.

Strategies

All three identified leaders embraced different strategies to address the challenges.

- **Sophia the Phoenix:** Sophia rallies the woodland creatures, inspiring hope and resilience in the face of adversity. She encourages innovation and collaboration, urging the community to explore new ways to procure food and adapt to changing circumstances. Sophia leads by example, demonstrating perseverance and determination as she guides her peers toward shared solutions.
- **Luc the Wolf:** Luc adopts a structured approach to address the food shortage. He establishes clear objectives and rewards and punishments for those who contribute or don't contribute to the collective effort of finding food. Luc implements a system of distribution, ensuring that resources are allocated efficiently based on merit and adherence to the established guidelines. His leadership instills discipline and accountability among the woodland creatures, fostering a sense of order amid chaos.

[1] Lencioni, Patrick. *The Five Dysfunctions of a Team.* Jossey-Bass, San Francisco, 2002

- **Matilda the Cat:** Matilda takes a more hands-off approach, trusting in the innate abilities of her fellow creatures to find solutions independently. She offers guidance when sought but otherwise encourages autonomy and self-reliance among the community members. Matilda believes in the importance of freedom and flexibility, allowing individuals to explore alternative methods of procuring food according to their own instincts and preferences.

Results

Under the guidance of Sophia, Luc, and Matilda, the Dasos forest community rises to the challenge and overcomes the food shortage crisis. Through collective effort, innovation, and strategic resource management, they discover new sources of sustenance and adapt to the changing environment. The leadership styles of the phoenix, the wolf, and the cat complement each other, contributing to the resilience and cohesion of the woodland community.

Conclusion

All leadership styles have merit, and whether leaders are born or made is less important than the natural tendencies embraced and applied by each unique leader. From Sophia, her transformational leadership style encourages collaboration and empowers individuals to embrace change and pursue collective goals with renewed vigor. Luc exemplifies the efficacy of transactional leadership in setting clear objectives, establishing accountability, and incentivizing performance. Matilda's laissez-faire leadership underscores the value of autonomy, trust, and adaptability. Successful organizations thrive not only through singular leadership styles but also through the integration of diverse approaches. By embracing transformational vision, transactional efficacy, and laissez-faire flexibility, businesses can navigate uncertainties, foster innovation, and empower their teams to achieve sustainable growth and success in the face of evolving challenges.

Leadership Practice Questions

1. What is the role of leadership within the organization?
   - A. To maximize profits for shareholders.
   - B. To provide direction and guide the team toward common goals.
   - C. To manage employees' day-to-day tasks.
   - D. To engage in continuous improvement to streamline efficiencies.
2. In a weekly one-on-one meeting, a team member expresses frustration about their workload. As a leader, what should you do?
   - A. Offer to take on some of their workload.
   - B. Offer them training to develop better time management skills.
   - C. Listen and ask them what they believe a solution should be.
   - D. Listen and tell them you will not assign any more work to them.
3. As a leader, you want to build trust within your team. Which of the following scenarios best demonstrates an effective way to build trust?
   - A. You frequently delegate tasks but rarely follow up with your team members, knowing that they prefer autonomy.
   - B. You communicate openly about the challenges and changes within the organization, even when the news is not entirely positive, and actively seek input and feedback from your team.
   - C. You make friends with your team, knowing about their personal lives and following each other on social media.
   - D. You maintain a professional distance from your team members, avoiding personal conversations or interactions outside of work-related matters.
4. As a senior manager in your organization, you are tasked with developing and managing workplace practices that align with the organization's vision, mission, and values. Which scenario demonstrates effective implementation of these practices to shape and reinforce organizational culture?
   - A. You encourage employees to stay focused on their individual targets without considering broader organizational values and sustainability goals.
   - B. You provide opportunities for employees to voice concerns anonymously.
   - C. You prioritize cost-cutting measures to save the company money.
   - D. You create a rigid set of rules and procedures to protect employees from unethical situations.

5. A leader wants to improve team morale and cohesion. What interpersonal skills should they focus on developing?
   A. Relationship-building and communications.
   B. Business acumen and team building.
   C. Conflict management and negotiation.
   D. Empathy and diversity.
6. Which of the following is a characteristic of leadership on a self-directed work team?
   A. No formal leadership, as the team members direct themselves.
   B. Hierarchical leadership with formal job tasks.
   C. Team leadership, with each member responsible for their assigned role.
   D. Minimal leadership, with established timelines and targets.
7. Which of the following is a characteristic of leadership within a matrix organizational structure?
   A. Centralized decision-making with little collaboration between functional and project managers.
   B. Balancing the demands and priorities of both functional managers and project managers.
   C. A strict hierarchy where project managers have authority over functional managers.
   D. A complete separation of roles and responsibilities between functional and project leaders.
8. The university you work for prides itself on its history, having been an institution in their community for more than 100 years. The school is well-funded and difficult to get into, and a tenured professorship is coveted as a career success. What is the most likely leadership structure at the university?
   A. A highly decentralized structure with significant faculty autonomy.
   B. A top-down hierarchical structure with emphasis on administrative control.
   C. An egalitarian structure with shared leadership among faculty and administration.
   D. A leadership structure based on student input and decision-making.
9. You work for a large real estate brokerage that has its residential, commercial, and rental functions as separate business units. Each unit has its own functional departments, including human resources, accounting, and finance. Which of the following leadership structures is most likely in place?
   A. Divisional.
   B. Hierarchical.
   C. Functional.
   D. Flat.

10. Which of the following characteristics of emotional intelligence is most likely to be useful for leaders in managing difficult conversations?

A. The ability to hide one's emotions.

B. The ability to regulate one's emotions.

C. The ability to recognize one's emotions.

D. The ability to manage others' emotions.

11. In which of the following scenarios should a leader use the constructive discipline over more formal feedback approaches?

A. When an employee consistently arrives late to work but is otherwise a strong performer.

B. When a team member makes a mistake that does not reflect a pattern of behavior.

C. When a team member has failed to follow company policy, but their teammates also do not always follow policy.

D. When a team member engages in disrespectful behavior, but the other person did not seem to be bothered by it.

12. What are the primary characteristics of self-discipline and self-motivation?

A. The primary characteristic of self-discipline is setting clear goals, whereas the primary characteristic of self-motivation is perseverance.

B. The primary characteristic of self-discipline is consistency, whereas the primary characteristic of self-motivation is external rewards.

C. The primary characteristic of self-discipline is time management, whereas the primary characteristic of self-motivation is delegation.

D. The primary characteristic of self-discipline is patience, whereas the primary characteristic of self-motivation is isolation.

13. Despite the inherent uncertainties in a business opportunity, a senior leader decided to invest significant company resources into the initiative. While the decision could lead to significant rewards for the company if successful, it also carries the possibility of failure. Which of the following leadership competencies does this best represent?

A. Courage.

B. Business acumen.

C. Strategic thinking.

D. Risk-taking.

14. Which leadership theory emphasizes that effective leaders possess a unique set of traits that distinguish them from nonleaders?

A. Situational leadership theory.

B. Transformational leadership theory.

C. Trait theory of leadership.

D. Contingency theory.

15. Sophie has a software developer, Luc, who is highly experienced and motivated. Luc has a strong track record of delivering exceptional results and takes initiative in team projects. Sophie takes a hands-off leadership approach, providing support and resources while allowing Luc the autonomy to make decisions and take the lead on complex projects. Conversely, another team member, James, has decent technical skills but tends to be inconsistent in his commitment and enthusiasm for the job. Sophie closely monitors James's progress and adapts her leadership style as needed. Which leadership style is Sophie employing?
    - **A.** Charismatic leadership theory.
    - **B.** Path-goal leadership theory.
    - **C.** Authentic leadership theory.
    - **D.** Laissez-faire leadership theory.

16. Carl possesses strong technical skills, seems to be easy to get along with, and may eventually want to achieve a leadership role within the organization. Where does Carl fall on the situational leadership matrix?
    - **A.** M1.
    - **B.** M2.
    - **C.** M3.
    - **D.** M4.

17. In a situation with an employee who has "high commitment, variable competence" on the situational leadership model, which of the following is the most effective leadership approach?
    - **A.** Telling.
    - **B.** Selling.
    - **C.** Delegating.
    - **D.** Participating.

18. According to the contingency theory of leadership, what is the primary factor that determines the most effective leadership style?
    - **A.** The leader's charisma and personality.
    - **B.** The situational context and circumstances.
    - **C.** The leader's ability to inspire and motivate.
    - **D.** The team's willingness to follow.

19. Which leadership theory is focused on the dynamic of the relationship between the leader and the follower?
    - **A.** LMX.
    - **B.** Path-goal.
    - **C.** Situational.
    - **D.** Servant.

20. John is the CEO of a nonprofit organization dedicated to providing educational opportunities to underprivileged children. He is known for his compassionate and servant leadership approach. One day, he observes that his team is feeling overwhelmed due to a sudden increase in workload. John decides to take action. In this scenario, how does John demonstrate servant leadership?

   A. John takes the group out for a well-deserved day of team-building exercises to relieve their stress.

   B. John organizes a meeting to discuss the challenges and stressors and to group problem solve.

   C. John sends an email to his team thanking them for their contributions and reminding them of the importance of the company mission.

   D. John gives each of them an additional day of PTO as a reward for their extra efforts.

21. Which of the following statements about laissez-faire style of leadership is most accurate? (Choose all that apply.)

   A. Laissez-faire is considered a more hands-off leadership approach.

   B. Laissez-faire is considered a more hands-on leadership approach.

   C. Laissez-faire is considered a lazier leadership approach.

   D. Laissez-faire is considered an empowering leadership approach.

22. In the leader-member exchange (LMX) theory of leadership, leaders develop different relationships with various subgroups within their team. They have higher-quality exchange with some team members, involving them in decision-making and offering them more responsibilities, while maintaining a more transactional relationship with others. How should leaders respond to team members who feel excluded as the result of this style of leadership?

   A. Leaders should maintain the status quo and continue with their higher-quality exchanges with select team members.

   B. Leaders should address the concerns of excluded team members, explain the reasons behind the differences in relationships, and work to improve relationships with all team members.

   C. Leaders should dismiss the concerns of excluded team members as they are a natural outcome of the leader-member exchange theory.

   D. Leaders should include the other members to avoid claims of favoritism.

23. Mark is a leader in a manufacturing company that operates in a highly dynamic and competitive industry. He has noticed that the effectiveness of his leadership style varies depending on factors, such as the company's financial stability, the experience level of his team members, and the current market conditions. Mark believes that there is no one-size-fits-all leadership approach and that the best leadership style depends on the unique circumstances and possibilities that arise. Which leadership theory best aligns with Mark's belief in adapting his leadership style to the specific contingencies of the situation described in the scenario?

   A. Trait theory of leadership.

   B. Path-goal leadership theory.

   C. Contingency theory of leadership.

   D. Transformational leadership theory.

24. Which of the following is the most important characteristic of a leader in a high-performance culture?

A. Emphasis on results.

B. Centralized decision-making.

C. Strict organizational structure.

D. Employee involvement.

25. What is a potential advantage of the autocratic leadership style?

A. High employee morale and job satisfaction.

B. Enhanced creativity and innovation within the team.

C. Quick decision-making and efficiency.

D. Equal distribution of decision-making power among team members.

26. What is a key similarity between transformational and autocratic leadership styles in the workplace?

A. Both styles emphasize employee empowerment.

B. Both styles are characterized by high control and strict rules.

C. Both styles are well-received by followers.

D. The styles are actually interchangeable.

27. Fill in the blank: Transactional leadership is most clearly defined by a ________ style.

A. Quid pro quo.

B. Passive.

C. Assertive.

D. Charismatic.

28. In which of the following leadership roles would a transactional leadership style be most effective?

A. Manufacturing line lead.

B. Nursing manager.

C. Project manager.

D. HR manager.

29. A large multinational corporation is planning to implement a leadership development program to prepare its employees for future leadership roles. They want to foster a culture of continuous learning and growth within the organization. What type of leadership development program is most suitable for achieving this goal?

A. A one-time, intensive leadership training workshop.

B. A mentorship program pairing junior employees with senior leaders.

C. A coaching program focused on improving specific leadership skills.

D. An annual leadership conference featuring external speakers.

30. A midsize tech company wants to provide leadership development opportunities for its remote workforce, spread across different time zones. Which type of leadership development program should the company consider to accommodate this distributed workforce effectively?

A. In-person leadership workshops at the company's headquarters.

B. An online leadership training platform with self-paced modules.

C. Weekly virtual team meetings with leadership discussions.

D. An annual leadership retreat at a remote location.

31. What is a primary benefit of incorporating experiential learning into a leadership development program?

A. Reduced program costs.

B. Enhanced theoretical knowledge.

C. Improved application of leadership skills in real-world scenarios.

D. Increased program duration.

32. In a leadership development program, which component focuses on helping individuals recognize their strengths, weaknesses, and areas for growth?

A. Mentoring.

B. Self-assessment.

C. Team-building exercises.

D. Online courses.

33. Which of the following best describes a 360-degree feedback process often used in leadership development programs?

A. A process of selecting leaders based on their qualifications.

B. A process where participants receive feedback from their peers, subordinates, and supervisors.

C. A process of ranking leaders based on their performance.

D. A process of assessing leadership potential through psychological tests.

34. Which technique is commonly used to identify high-potential employees for leadership development within an organization?

A. Promoting employees based on seniority.

B. Relying on external hiring for leadership positions.

C. Succession planning and talent reviews.

D. Career development modeling.

35. What is a key benefit of providing leadership development opportunities to employees within an organization?

A. Decreased employee turnover.

B. Reduced need for performance evaluations.

C. Increased operational efficiency.

D. Simplified organizational structure.

36. What is a common approach to building a leadership pipeline that involves rotating high-potential employees through different roles and departments?

A. Succession planning.

B. Skills assessment.

C. Job enrichment.

D. Task specialization.

37. Which of the following is NOT a common barrier to leadership effectiveness in a diverse workplace?

A. Overemphasis on bottom-up communication.

B. Lack of transparency in decision-making.

C. Misalignment of organizational resources.

D. Absence of diverse mentors.

38. An HR manager must make a hiring decision for the leader of a remote work team. Which of the following candidates should she choose?

A. David, a candidate with strong communication and collaboration skills.

B. Mindy, a candidate with strong technical and problem-solving abilities.

C. Lisa, an adaptable leader with excellent project management skills.

D. Eric, a strategic thinker with strong conflict resolution skills.

39. You are managing a remote team, and one team member frequently reports feeling overwhelmed and stressed. What steps should you take to address this issue and support the team member's well-being?

A. Redistribute the team member's work to others.

B. Talk to senior leaders about their unreasonable productivity expectations.

C. Schedule more check in meetings.

D. Ignore the issue as it is likely temporary.

40. What is the primary difference between succession and replacement planning?

A. Succession planning focuses on internal candidates, while replacement planning relies on external hires.

B. Succession planning is a long-term strategy, while replacement planning is a short-term strategy.

C. Succession planning is primarily used for entry-level positions, while replacement planning is for senior management roles.

D. Succession planning is focused on employee development, while replacement planning is concerned with filling vacancies.

41. How is leadership succession planning a form of employee engagement?

A. It involves promoting employees based on seniority, which boosts morale.

B. It increases employee commitment by providing leadership opportunities.

C. It focuses on replacing current leaders with external hires, creating diversity.

D. It is unrelated to employee engagement efforts.

42. In response to a regional economic downturn, EveryMart, a retail chain specializing in electronics and appliances, has decided to pivot to a cost-leadership strategy. What could be a critical role for the HR department in supporting this strategic shift?

A. HR should lead the effort in managing employee layoffs to decrease labor costs.

B. HR should organize employee morale-boosting events to maintain a positive workplace atmosphere.

C. HR should advocate for product price cuts to increase sales.

D. HR should engage in workflow analysis to determine where redundancies may exist.

43. In their consultative role, how can human resource leaders support other organizational leaders?

A. By partnering with the leaders to understand their HR challenges.

B. By ensuring HR policies are in compliance with labor laws.

C. By hiring qualified workers to fill key leadership positions.

D. By engaging employees to increase retention.

44. Which of the following best represents the human resource competency of relationship-building with other organizational leaders?

A. Facilitating difficult interactions with their employees.

B. Acting with personal and professional integrity in the execution of their responsibilities.

C. Promptly responding to work assignments and other requests.

D. Making diversity, equity, and inclusion important strategic HR initiatives.

45. In their consultative role, how can human resource leaders support organizational leaders in talent acquisition?

A. By conducting interviews and making hiring decisions.

B. By providing market analysis and candidate recommendations.

C. By training line managers on the recruitment process.

D. By conducting accurate market wage surveys to build competitive job offers.

46. Which of the following best characterizes the nature of service excellence as a senior leader's professional competency?

A. Responding promptly to the requests of stakeholders.

B. Identifying larger system needs and issues.

C. Identifying early-stage risks in organizational problem-solving.

D. Maintaining service quality with HR vendors.

47. You are an HR professional tasked with implementing a new performance management system, but some department heads are resistant to the change. How can you effectively manage this initiative despite pushback from these leaders?

  A. Proceed with the implementation without involving the resistant department heads.
  B. Ask other organizational leaders to advocate for the needed changes.
  C. Abandon the initiative to avoid conflicts with department heads.
  D. Seek input and feedback from the resistant department heads and incorporate their suggestions where feasible.

48. What is considered a best practice when it comes to assessing leader performance in the workplace?

  A. Relying on self-assessments provided by the leaders.
  B. Conducting 360-degree feedback assessments.
  C. Evaluating leaders based on employee reviews.
  D. Evaluating leaders based on their tenure.

49. Which of the following is the least effective measurement when evaluating CEO and other senior leader results?

  A. Financial performance and profit margins.
  B. Employee satisfaction and engagement.
  C. Social media popularity and followers.
  D. Market share and competitive positioning.

50. What is a potential drawback of relying solely on quantitative metrics for evaluating leader performance?

  A. Quantitative metrics provide a subjective assessment of leadership skills.
  B. Quantitative metrics may be too broad to capture all aspects of leadership effectiveness.
  C. Quantitative metrics are universally applicable to all leadership roles.
  D. Quantitative metrics are the most time-consuming method of evaluation.

51. In which of the following areas are managers most likely to fail when leading project management initiatives that require multitasking and working with diverse personalities?

  A. Technical expertise.
  B. Time management.
  C. Communication skills.
  D. Budget management.

52. What is a crucial element to consider when building diverse leadership development programs?

  A. Maintaining a one-size-fits-all approach for all participants.
  B. Tailoring the programs to meet the specific needs and backgrounds of participants.
  C. Selecting participants who may not have traditional backgrounds of success.
  D. Focusing on technical skill development.

53. What is an important factor in retaining high-potential employees within an organization?

- **A.** Offering expatriate opportunities for accelerated career growth career paths.
- **B.** Providing a flexible and inclusive work environment.
- **C.** Leading the markets in pay rates.
- **D.** Providing tuition reimbursement.

54. You are a manager leading a team of diverse individuals with varying levels of experience and skills. Some team members are new to the company, while others have been with the organization for years. You need to guide them effectively to achieve their goals. Which people management technique is most appropriate in this situation?

- **A.** Delegating.
- **B.** Mentoring.
- **C.** Directing.
- **D.** Coaching.

55. You are a senior manager introducing a new sustainability initiative within your organization. To encourage employees to adopt eco-friendly practices, you personally start using recyclable materials and reducing waste in your own work. Which influence technique are you demonstrating?

- **A.** Forming coalitions.
- **B.** Rational persuasion.
- **C.** Personal appeal.
- **D.** Leading by example.

56. What is a key distinction between the personal appeal and rational persuasion influence techniques?

- **A.** Personal appeal relies on logical arguments, while rational persuasion focuses on building personal relationships.
- **B.** Personal appeal involves presenting data and evidence, while rational persuasion emphasizes emotional connections.
- **C.** Personal appeal appeals to relationships and trust-building, while rational persuasion relies on logical arguments and evidence.
- **D.** Personal appeal and rational persuasion are interchangeable terms with no discernible differences.

57. What advantage does leading by example have over forming coalitions as an influence technique?

- **A.** Leading by example can build trust and credibility more effectively.
- **B.** Leading by example is less time-consuming.
- **C.** Leading by example allows for collective decision-making.
- **D.** Leading by example requires less emotional intelligence.

58. Fill in the blank: In Fiedler's contingency theory of leadership, leaders change conditions to be more ________.

A. Productive.

B. Favorable.

C. Compliant.

D. Diverse.

59. What impact does high-power distance have on the relationship between leaders and their teams?

A. Increases trust and collaboration between leaders and teams.

B. Decreases mistrust and miscommunication.

C. Has no significant impact on the relationship.

D. Depends on other contextual factors.

60. Which of the following is a shared characteristic between contingency theory and the job characteristics model?

A. The tasks of the job themselves have an impact on organizational situations.

B. The degree of power distance is equal to the degree of employee satisfaction.

C. Employees are expected to follow a clear hierarchy.

D. Leaders adapt their behaviors to the requirements of the job.

61. A prominent CEO in the tech sector is known for his hands-on leadership approach and pushes the boundaries of innovation at his companies. This is coupled with his visionary outlook on the future of technology and humanity. What is his likely leadership style?

A. Transformational.

B. Autocratic.

C. Charismatic.

D. Laissez-faire.

62. Steve Jobs was known for his high involvement and end-to-end control to ensure quality and ensure his vision was fulfilled on each product line. Jobs was also known for his demanding and sometimes abrasive demeanor, as well as his ability to inspire and motivate his teams to achieve greatness. Which of the following most appropriately defines his leadership style?

A. Transformational and transactional.

B. Creative and innovative.

C. Authoritarian and autocratic.

D. Visionary and charismatic.

63. What kind of leadership competencies are required to succeed in a third-party logistics organization? (Choose all that apply.)

A. Strategic planning and supply chain management expertise.

B. Strong communication and negotiation skills.

C. Ability to adapt to changing market conditions and technologies.

D. Effective team leadership and conflict resolution abilities.

64. Which of the following statements best describes the importance of self-awareness as a leadership competency?

   A. Self-awareness allows leaders to understand their strengths and weaknesses, enabling them to leverage their strengths and work on areas for improvement effectively.

   B. Self-awareness fosters better communication and relationships with team members, as leaders are able to recognize and regulate their own emotions, leading to a more positive and collaborative work environment.

   C. Self-awareness enhances a leader's ability to adapt to different situations and challenges, as they have a clear understanding of how their behaviors and decisions impact others and the organization as a whole.

   D. Self-awareness promotes authenticity and integrity in leadership, as leaders who are self-aware are more likely to align their actions with their values and remain true to themselves, earning the trust and respect of their team members.

65. It's been brought to your attention as the senior HR leader that the company is struggling to absorb the pay increases of the last two years, as productivity gains did not offset the increased labor costs. In the meantime, employees are beginning to ask their managers when their next pay increases are scheduled. The executive team has asked for your advice on how to best handle the increases. Which of the following strategies should you suggest?

   A. Upskilling workers to give them a clear path to advancement.

   B. Hiring a sales force to drive revenue growth.

   C. Freezing pay increases until the market changes.

   D. Laying off labor surplus to decrease labor costs.

Key Concept Research Questions

Understanding the content of the HR exams is dependent on experience, not only knowledge. For this reason, it is helpful to look at key concepts through the lens of application by using the Internet to do some research on the following questions:

1. The role of emotional intelligence in leadership involves the ability to understand, manage, and leverage emotions effectively, both in oneself and others, to inspire, motivate, and guide individuals and teams toward shared goals and success. What are three to four primary characteristics of emotional intelligence in leaders? Harvard Business School online has an excellent resource to help you understand this issue at `https://online.hbs.edu/blog/post/emotional-intelligence-in-leadership`.

2. The lack of a leadership pipeline is a challenge many organizations are facing today, and they are looking to their HR teams to provide solutions. How can HR leaders design and advocate for effective leadership development programs that cultivate talent, foster growth, and drive organizational success? Take a look at an article from Harvard Business Review on evidenced-based ways to design these programs at `https://hbr.org/2023/02/what-makes-leadership-development-programs-succeed`.

Test Your Leadership Terminology Knowledge

The following are the terms to use to test your knowledge on leadership key terms. You can find the correct answers in Appendix B.

- Authentic
- Autocratic
- Behavioral
- Contingency
- Development
- Democratic
- Laissez-faire
- Leader-member exchange (LMX)
- Path-goal
- Servant
- Situational
- Trait
- Transactional
- Transformational
- Visionary

1. ______________ leadership is one where leaders make decisions independently without seeking input from team members.
2. ______________ leadership is an approach where leaders actively involve team members in decision-making and problem-solving.
3. ______________ is a passive leadership tyle where the leader is likely to delegate and be hands-off.
4. ______________ leadership focuses on nurturing and supporting team members, often associated with coaching and mentoring.
5. ______________ leadership is an approach that emphasizes setting clear expectations and providing rewards or punishments based on performance.
6. Leadership ______________ involves cultivating skills, behaviors, and attitudes to empower individuals to effectively guide and inspire others toward shared goals and objectives.
7. ______________-based leadership is a model that suggests leaders have certain innate characteristics that make them effective leaders.
8. ______________ theory proposes that effective leadership depends on the match between a leader's style and the situational demands.
9. ______________ theory of leadership emphasizes the importance of leader-member relationships, task structure, and positional power.
10. ______________ leadership is a theory that emphasizes the leader's ability to adapt to various environments, events, and leadership styles.

11. ______________ leadership emphasizes observable actions and interactions when establishing vision and directing others.
12. ______________ is the ability of a leader to create a shared purpose and align team members with that purpose.
13. ______________ is a leadership theory that proposes that leaders are effective when they are seen as role models by their followers.
14. ______________ leadership suggests that leaders are most effective when they come from a place of their true selves and act with personal integrity.
15. The __________ theory of leadership suggests that effective leaders create clear goals, removes obstacles, and provides support and guidance to followers, ultimately enhancing their motivation and performance.

Conclusion

It has been said that people don't leave organizations, they leave managers, which sums up the importance of effective leadership in a nutshell. It's not only about productivity and results; it's also about motivating individuals to reach their full potential. So much of what has been covered in this book up to this point has revolved around organizational behavior and the behavior of employees. The bridge between both characteristics is effective leaders.

Leadership defies simple categorization such as "are they born or made." Rather, it encompasses a complex interplay of skills, behaviors, and attitudes that extend far beyond traditional notions of authority and hierarchy.

Leadership exists at every level of the organization, and in some cases, informal leaders carry more influence than those with formal titles. In fact, leadership is inherent in the role of all HR professionals, and for this reason it is a prominent domain on the SHRM and HRCI exams.

For the SHRM CP and SCP, leadership is an independent cluster with the subcompetencies of Leadership and Navigation, Ethical Practice, and Diversity, Equity, and Inclusion driving the bulk of exam content. The SHRM Body of Applied Skills and Knowledge (BASK) also focuses on many of the inter-personal competencies covered in this chapter.

On the PHR and PHRi exams, the concept of leadership is found in the first domain of Business Management, which accounts for 14% of exam content. On the SPHR and SPHRi exams, Leadership and Strategy is the first exam domain, and it accounts for 33% of the test—the highest of all domains. Understanding leadership is important not only to serve your organizations and teams but for your own professional development as well.

Additional Resources

These online resources offer a wealth of information and practical tools to help you learn more about leadership and enhance your leadership skills. Whether you're a seasoned leader or just starting your leadership journey, these platforms can provide valuable insights and guidance.

Websites

- Center for Management and Organization Effectiveness (`https://cmoe.com/resources/articles-and-tools`)

  The Center for Management and Organization Effectiveness offers several articles and tools with insights into the relevant leadership topics of the day.

- Center for Creative Leadership (`www.ccl.org`)

  CCL offers a range of leadership resources, including articles, research reports, and webinars. It focuses on leadership development, leadership assessment, and leadership coaching.

- Leadership Now (`www.leadershipnow.com`)

  Leadership Now provides articles and book summaries on leadership topics. It offers a collection of leadership quotes, book recommendations, and leadership development resources.

Podcasts

- *The Leadership Podcast* with various hosts (`www.theleadershippodcast.com`)

  This podcast explores leadership from various angles, including leadership principles, strategies, and insights from successful leaders.

- *The Learning Leader Show* hosted by Ryan Hawk (`www.learningleader.com/podcast`)

  Dubbed by *Forbes* magazine as the "most dynamic leadership podcast of all time," Hawk features interviews with leaders from various fields. It explores their leadership journeys and the lessons they've learned.

- *Tilted: A Lean In Podcast* (`https://leanin.org/tilted-podcast-season-2/leadership`)

  While only two seasons are available, there are several fascinating interviews on issues related to gender and organizational cultures.

- *The Leader's Panel* (`www.theleaderspanel.com`)

  The Leader's Panel features discussions with leaders from various industries, sharing their leadership experiences and advice.

- *Jocko Podcast* hosted by Jocko Willink (`https://jockopodcast.com/all-episodes`)

  Leadership lessons from the battlefield are taught by retired Navy Seal Jocko Willink. He interviews several successful leaders beyond the military as well to talk about how to be successful in life and work.

YouTube Channels

These `www.youtube.com` channels cover a wide range of leadership topics and offer diverse perspectives on leadership development. Whether you're a current leader looking to improve your skills or someone aspiring to become a better leader, you can find valuable content on these channels.

- Stanford Graduate School of Business

  The mission of Stanford Graduate School of Business is to "create ideas that deepen and advance our understanding of management and with those ideas to develop innovative, principled, and insightful leaders who change the world." Their channel features guest interviews and speakers on the relevant business and leadership challenges of the day.

- Nordic Business Forum

  The Nordic Business Forum is a business conference held annually in the Nordic region, featuring top speakers, thought leaders, and executives who share insights and strategies on leadership, innovation, and entrepreneurship. Their channel includes behind-the-scenes clips and interviews with keynote speakers.

- London Business Forum

  The London Business Forum is a renowned platform offering inspiring events, workshops, and resources designed to empower professionals with practical skills, insights, and strategies for success in today's dynamic business landscape. Their YouTube channel highlights topics such as how to build your brand and the "80-minute MBA."

Chapter 16

Organizational Development and Design

In its simplest form, human resource management is about the development and design of HR systems that support organizational strategies. The HR systems are built around the life cycle of employees, and practitioners are charged with implementing and evaluating the effectiveness of their work to support outcomes at all stages. In short, HR systems support organizational health, and organizational health is influenced by how it is designed.

Organizational development and organizational design are two distinct but interrelated concepts within the realm of organizational management. Organizational *development* focuses on enhancing the overall effectiveness and performance of an organization through interventions aimed at improving processes, structures, culture, and employee capabilities. It involves initiatives such as leadership development programs, team-building exercises, change management strategies, and cultural transformation efforts. Organizational *design* primarily concerns the deliberate arrangement of an organization's structures, roles, processes, and systems to achieve its strategic objectives and optimize efficiency and effectiveness. This involves decisions about the division of labor, hierarchy, communication channels, workflow optimization, and resource allocation. While organizational development focuses on human aspects such as skills development and cultural change, organizational design deals with structural aspects such as roles, processes, and systems. Despite their differences, both organizational development and organizational design aim to enhance organizational performance and adaptability in dynamic environments. This chapter covers the human resources and organizational theories that drive development and design, including the following:

- **Corporate structure and restructuring:** Corporate structures refer to the formal arrangement of roles, responsibilities, authority, and communication channels within an organization, defining how tasks are divided, coordinated, and controlled to achieve strategic objectives.
- **BOD/governance:** BOD/governance pertains to the system of oversight, decision-making, and accountability within an organization, led by a board of directors (BODs), responsible for setting strategic direction, ensuring compliance, and safeguarding stakeholders' interests.
- **Change management:** Change management encompasses processes and strategies aimed at preparing, guiding, and supporting individuals, teams, and organizations through transitions, ensuring successful adoption of new initiatives, technologies, or ways of working while minimizing resistance and disruption.

- **Culture:** Culture represents the shared values, beliefs, norms, and behaviors that characterize an organization, influencing how members interact, make decisions, and perceive their environment.
- **Organizational theories:** Critical organizational development theories such as change management and scientific management offer frameworks and principles for understanding and addressing organizational challenges, emphasizing aspects such as systematic change processes and scientific approaches to optimizing work processes and productivity.
- **Organizational health:** Organizational health refers to the overall well-being and effectiveness of an organization, encompassing factors such as employee engagement, communication, alignment with strategic goals, adaptability to change, and resilience in the face of challenges, indicating its capacity for sustained success and growth.

Real World Scenario

Dutch Railways Use of the Internet of Things as an Organizational Restructuring Tool

The Dutch Railways System, managed by ProRail, serves as a major transportation network in the densely populated region of Randstad in the Netherlands. With increasing ridership and aging infrastructure, ProRail faced significant challenges in maintaining operational efficiency. To address these issues, ProRail turned to the Internet of Things (IoT) technology to optimize railway operations and enhance overall performance.

Background and Problem

The Netherlands, home to more than 17 million residents and numerous multinational organizations such as Unilever and Royal Dutch Shell, relies heavily on public transportation. This is particularly true in the densely populated Randstad region that includes Amsterdam, The Hague, and Rotterdam. With forecasts projecting a 40% increase in ridership over the next decade and aging infrastructure posing challenges, ProRail confronted the urgent need to modernize its operations. Traditional solutions like building additional tracks were deemed insufficient for addressing the complexities of the railway system's demands, necessitating innovative approaches.

Strategies

The IoT refers to the interconnected network of devices and objects, similar to how modern smart homes operate, where household appliances and equipment are linked to a network, enabling real-time data sharing. Recognizing the potential of IoT technology, ProRail embarked on a journey to leverage data generated by IoT sensors to revolutionize railway operations. By harnessing this data, ProRail aimed to gain insights into railway conditions and operations that were previously unattainable through human analysis alone. This data-driven approach enabled ProRail to focus on improved safety and efficiencies and to be mindful of the lack of land to build new tracks for increased capacity. The data collected from the sensors drove many organizational interventions aimed at optimizing train schedules, conducting preventative maintenance, and enhancing overall operational efficiency.

Additionally, ProRail explored the use of algorithms to analyze data and predict potential safety hazards, such as trespassing incidents on railway tracks. The organization aimed to transition from relying on external data sources to establishing its own data collection and analysis capabilities, with the ultimate goal of elevating train transport on a European scale.

Results

The implementation of IoT technology and data analytics yielded significant results for ProRail. By leveraging IoT sensor data, the organization successfully optimized train schedules, improved equipment maintenance, and enhanced safety measures. The ability to predict and prevent potential disruptions, such as trespassing incidents, contributed to the overall reliability and efficiency of the railway system. Furthermore, ProRail's efforts to establish internal data collection capabilities marked a significant step toward achieving its vision of becoming a data-driven organization.

Conclusion

The integration of IoT technology not only addressed operational challenges but also served as a key organizational restructuring technique for the Dutch Railways System. By leveraging data-driven approaches, particularly through IoT sensor data and analytics, ProRail optimized its operations and positioned itself for future growth and innovation. As the organization continues to expand its capabilities in data analytics and IoT, it will enhance operational efficiency as well as transform its organizational structure to become more agile, responsive, and data-driven in navigating the challenges of modern railway management.

Organizational Development and Design Practice Questions

1. Which of the following is the primary distinction between organizational design and organizational development?
   - **A.** Organizational design focuses on improving structures and processes, while organizational development concentrates on enhancing employee skills and capabilities.
   - **B.** Organizational design prioritizes strategic planning, while organizational development emphasizes cultural transformation.
   - **C.** Organizational design aims to optimize efficiency and effectiveness, while organizational development aims to improve employee morale and motivation.
   - **D.** Organizational design emphasizes hierarchical arrangements, while organizational development emphasizes flat organizational structures.
2. Which of the following activities is likely to take place as part of an organizational re-design? (Choose all that apply.)
   - **A.** Job restructuring.
   - **B.** Leadership training.
   - **C.** Changed span of control.
   - **D.** Team building activities.
3. Which of the following is most likely to occur as a result of adjusting a manager's span of control?
   - **A.** Redistributing a manager's responsibilities.
   - **B.** Demoting a manager due to low performance.
   - **C.** Changing the manager's direct supervisor.
   - **D.** Changing the department's structure to a cross-functional team.
4. Which of the following are likely to be associated with job restructuring? (Choose all that apply.)
   - **A.** Layoffs.
   - **B.** Refined job descriptions.
   - **C.** New hires.
   - **D.** Updated workflows and reporting channels.
5. Which of the following best describes the role of task specialization in organizational restructuring?
   - **A.** Task specialization involves consolidating job roles to increase employee versatility.
   - **B.** Task specialization entails dividing complex tasks into smaller, specialized components.
   - **C.** Task specialization focuses on promoting cross-functional training to diversify employee skills.
   - **D.** Task specialization emphasizes reducing employee autonomy to streamline decision-making processes.

6. As the company you work for transitions to a hybrid work model, it decides to overhaul its office layout. Which of the following best reflects the objective of this workspace redesign?
   A. With the aim of maximizing individual focus, the company plans to create designated quiet zones in the office to minimize disruptions.
   B. In response to the need for seamless collaboration between remote and in-office employees, the company intends to redesign the workspace layout to facilitate communication and teamwork across both settings.
   C. Seeking to reduce expenses associated with office space, the company plans to implement a hot-desking system to accommodate fewer employees physically present in the office.
   D. To ensure effective supervision, the company will implement fixed seating arrangements based on hierarchy, enabling managers to oversee their teams more closely.
7. Amidst a period of significant growth and restructuring, a multinational corporation seeks to enhance organizational clarity and communication. Which of the following best represents the primary purpose of implementing an organization chart?
   A. The organization chart is primarily utilized to streamline employee performance evaluations and promotions.
   B. The organization chart serves as a visual representation of the company's hierarchy and reporting relationships, aiding in clarifying roles and responsibilities.
   C. The organization chart is primarily employed to track inventory levels and optimize supply chain management.
   D. The organization chart is utilized to enforce strict adherence to corporate policies and procedures across all departments.
8. When is the use of automation as a strategic intervention most appropriate in an organization's operations?
   A. When there is a need to enhance employee autonomy and decision-making capabilities.
   B. When the organization aims to reduce costs associated with labor-intensive tasks.
   C. When the goal is to foster a collaborative work environment and promote teamwork.
   D. When the organization seeks to prioritize traditional manual processes over technological advancements.
9. Which of the following is a characteristic of a sole proprietorship as a business legal structure?
   A. Limited liability protection.
   B. Separate legal entity.
   C. Multiple owners.
   D. Full personal liability.
10. In a partnership, how is the income taxed?
   A. It is not subject to taxation.
   B. It is taxed at corporate tax rates.
   C. It is taxed at individual tax rates for each partner.
   D. It is taxed at a fixed rate determined by the government.

11. A multinational organization (MNE) is MOST likely to have which of the following business structures?

A. LLC.

B. Corporation.

C. Sole proprietorship.

D. Global.

12. In a cross-functional organizational structure, what is the primary role of HR?

A. Managing within a traditional hierarchy.

B. Facilitating interdepartmental communication and collaboration.

C. Building broadband wage ranges.

D. Creating blended job descriptions and cross-training programs.

13. In a matrix organizational structure, which of the following is likely to be the biggest challenge for HR professionals? (Choose all that apply.)

A. Ensuring clear lines of authority and accountability.

B. Facilitating effective communication between multiple reporting lines.

C. Managing conflicts arising from dual reporting relationships.

D. Implementing standardized performance evaluation metrics.

14. What is the primary objective of corporate governance?

A. Balance the interests of shareholders and leadership.

B. Increase employee satisfaction.

C. Minimize environmental impact.

D. Maximize shareholder returns.

15. What is the primary distinction between shareholders and stakeholders in a business context?

A. Shareholders own a portion of the company, while stakeholders have no financial ownership.

B. Shareholders are employees of the company, while stakeholders are external to the organization.

C. Shareholders are concerned with profit maximization, while stakeholders prioritize ethical and social considerations.

D. Shareholders have voting rights in corporate decisions, while stakeholders do not.

16. A large manufacturing company is planning to build a new factory in a small town. The factory is expected to create hundreds of jobs and boost the local economy. Which group of stakeholders is likely to be most concerned about this project?

A. Shareholders of the manufacturing company.

B. Local residents and community members.

C. Competing manufacturing companies.

D. The company's board of directors.

17. A technology company is considering outsourcing its customer support services to a third-party provider to reduce costs. Which group of stakeholders is likely to have concerns about this decision?
    - **A.** Industry analysts and market competitors.
    - **B.** Corporate governance boards and regulatory agencies.
    - **C.** Research and development teams within the company.
    - **D.** Environmental sustainability organizations.

18. What is an ethical best practice in corporate governance regarding CEO compensation?
    - **A.** Providing generous stock options to the CEO.
    - **B.** Tying CEO compensation to long-term performance.
    - **C.** Offering a fixed, nonvariable salary to the CEO.
    - **D.** Keeping CEO compensation details confidential.

19. Which of the following is the primary role of an HR professional in corporate governance?
    - **A.** Ensuring compliance with labor laws and regulations.
    - **B.** Developing executive employment contracts.
    - **C.** Hiring the board of directors.
    - **D.** Safeguarding ethical conduct and fostering a culture of integrity.

20. Which of the following is not a priority for HR when complying with the Brown Act?
    - **A.** Ensuring transparency in board meetings.
    - **B.** Providing notice of meetings to the public and interested stakeholders.
    - **C.** Facilitating closed-door negotiations between the board and external parties.
    - **D.** Recording accurate minutes of board meetings.

21. Which financial report primarily provides a snapshot of a company's financial position at a specific point in time?
    - **A.** Income statement.
    - **B.** Balance sheet.
    - **C.** Cash flow statement.
    - **D.** Statement of retained earnings.

22. As the HR director of a medium-sized company, you are reviewing the financial statements and notice a significant increase in overtime expenses for the past quarter. What is a possible HR-related explanation for this increase in overtime expenses?
    - **A.** Employees are taking more vacation days.
    - **B.** The company has implemented flexible work hours.
    - **C.** There is a shortage of skilled workers, leading to longer work hours.
    - **D.** Employees are using their sick leave entitlement more frequently.

23. At a small manufacturing firm, suspicions arise regarding an employee, Ricky, who handles accounts receivable, as discrepancies in financial records become apparent. After further investigation, it appears that he has been granting himself additional vacation days and then cashing out his time. This is likely the result of which of the following gaps in company management?

A. A manager who is not paying proper attention to financial statements.

B. Lack of conducting a background check when hiring Ricky.

C. Failing to have the proper internal controls.

D. Poor policies, procedures, and rules.

24. What is the primary focus of organizational structures in a business?

A. Facilitating information flow and data integration.

B. Defining roles, hierarchy, and reporting relationships.

C. Optimizing business processes and workflows.

D. Managing technological infrastructure and resources.

25. What is the central purpose of organizational systems in a business context?

A. Establishing clear lines of authority and reporting.

B. Defining job descriptions and responsibilities.

C. Managing and optimizing operational processes.

D. Promoting employee engagement and motivation.

26. Which of the following best describes the role of organizational structures in decision-making within a business?

A. Defining the processes and tools for data analysis.

B. Establishing a hierarchy of authority and responsibility.

C. Managing and optimizing supply chain operations.

D. Promoting team collaboration and creativity.

27. In a large multinational corporation, the executive leadership team is responsible for making high-level strategic decisions and setting the overall direction of the company. At the same time, various departments, such as marketing, finance, and operations, operate independently and have their own decision-making authority within their domains. What aspect of organizational design is this scenario highlighting?

A. A centralized organizational structure.

B. A flat organizational structure.

C. A functional organizational structure.

D. A matrix organizational structure.

28. In a tech startup, teams are organized around specific projects, and employees report to multiple team leaders simultaneously. Each team has autonomy in decision-making related to their project goals, and employees collaborate across teams as needed. What aspect of organizational design is evident in this scenario?

A. A centralized organizational structure.

B. A flat organizational structure.

C. A functional organizational structure.

D. A matrix organizational structure.

29. A manufacturing company is divided into distinct departments, each responsible for a specific function, such as production, finance, and sales. The company also uses an enterprise resource planning (ERP) system that consolidates data and processes across all departments, enabling seamless information flow and decision-making. What aspect of organizational design is exemplified in this scenario?

A. A centralized organizational structure.

B. A flat organizational structure.

C. A functional organizational structure.

D. An integrated systems approach.

30. A multinational technology company, Tech Innovations Inc., is undergoing a significant organizational redesign to adapt to changing market dynamics and enhance operational efficiency. As part of this restructuring process, several departments are merged, and new reporting relationships are established. The company aims to streamline decision-making processes and improve collaboration between teams. However, the organizational redesign has been met with resistance from some employees who are apprehensive about the changes and uncertain about their roles in the new structure. Which of the following training and development approaches should HR recommend?

A. Leadership development.

B. Change management initiatives.

C. Market wage reviews.

D. Team-building exercises.

31. ABC Corporation, a leading manufacturing company, is preparing to implement significant changes to its production processes to improve efficiency and reduce costs. The management team understands the importance of effectively managing these changes to ensure successful implementation. They decide to adopt Lewin's theory of change management to guide the process. As ABC Corporation embarks on implementing changes to its production processes, what initial step in Lewin's theory of change management should the management team prioritize to prepare employees for the upcoming transitions?

A. Assessing the effectiveness of the current production processes.

B. Identifying key performance indicators to measure the success of the changes.

C. Creating a sense of urgency and highlighting the need for change among employees.

D. Stabilizing the organizational chart to position for future changes.

32. Which of the following is a step that can be taken to anchor change within an organization? (Choose all that apply.)

A. Establish feedback systems.

B. Create reward systems.

C. Identify barriers to change.

D. Breaking down the status quo.

33. Ricardo Corporation, a global technology company, is undergoing a significant organizational transformation to adapt to evolving market demands and enhance competitiveness. The CEO, recognizing the importance of effective change management, decides to implement John Kotter's eight-step model for change to guide the process. However, as the transformation progresses, employees express concerns about feeling excluded from the decision-making process and unheard regarding their perspectives on the changes. Which aspect of Kotter's model should Ricardo Corporation prioritize to address the employees' concerns and ensure their active involvement in the change process?

A. Create a sense of urgency.

B. Build a guiding coalition.

C. Generate short-term wins.

D. Enable action by removing barriers.

34. Which of the following is a potential challenge associated with John Kotter's change management model?

A. Lack of clarity in the steps involved.

B. Overemphasis on employee involvement.

C. Insufficient attention to the end result.

D. Too much dependence on a few leaders.

35. Which of the following best describes the primary focus of the ADKAR change management model?

A. Providing detailed instructions for implementing change initiatives.

B. Ensuring a smooth transition for organizational leaders.

C. Supporting employees throughout the change process.

D. Promoting rapid changes to meet organizational goals.

36. According to the Kubler-Ross change curve, what role does empathy and communication play in embedding the change within an organization?

A. Empathy and communication are secondary to other employee needs when embedding change.

B. Empathy and communication are the most important factors to unfreeze the current state.

C. Without empathy and communication, the change is likely to fail.

D. Without empathy and change, employees will feel left out of the transformation.

37. A manager is using an unconscious personal approach with an employee by finding connections they share related to a proposed change at the company. This closely follows which change model?

A. Nudge.

B. Kotter.

C. Bridges.

D. ADKAR.

38. In 2022, Elon Musk made a highly publicized, successful takeover bid for the social media giant Twitter (rebranded as X). In his early days at the helm, Musk let go more than half of the employees, eventually rehiring some of them in that first year. Issues such as limited resources, lack of cultural alignment with the new leadership, and threat of substitutes drove many of Musk's early decision-making. Which of the following change management issues is best highlighted by the Twitter example?

A. The importance of immediately implementing change to achieve rapid results.

B. The necessity of carefully balancing the speed of change with resource limitations and organizational needs.

C. The effectiveness of delaying change to allow for thorough planning and consideration.

D. The importance of maintaining the status quo to avoid disruption.

39. What is the primary focus of Frederick Taylor's theory of scientific management?

A. Maximizing employee satisfaction.

B. Enhancing workplace democracy.

C. Increasing productivity and efficiency.

D. Promoting employee autonomy.

40. Which of the following best characterizes the chaos theory of management?

A. Emphasizing strict hierarchical structures and centralized decision-making processes.

B. Advocating for rigid adherence to predetermined plans and strategies.

C. Acknowledging the unpredictability and complexity of organizational systems.

D. Focusing on linear cause-and-effect relationships in management practices.

41. At New York Apartment Corporation, the CEO is responsible for establishing clear lines of authority and communication channels within the organization. Each department head knows to whom they report, and employees understand their roles and responsibilities within their respective departments. The CEO emphasizes the importance of unity of command and scalar chain, ensuring that instructions flow from top management down through the hierarchy without confusion. Which characteristic of Henri Fayol's administrative theory is exemplified in the preceding scenario?

A. Unity of command.

B. Scalar chain.

C. Span of control.

D. Division of labor.

42. Which approach to managing multinational corporations aligns most closely with Howard V. Perlmutter's ethnocentric orientation?

 A. Allowing subsidiaries in different countries high levels of autonomy and decision-making authority.

 B. Integrating global and local perspectives to make key decisions based on a worldwide viewpoint.

 C. Emphasizing the values, interests, and beliefs of the parent company's home country in decision-making.

 D. Promoting a cohesive corporate culture across different regions to enhance global efficiency.

43. How might Perlmutter's ethnocentric principle conflict with principles of global organizational design that emphasize localization, responsiveness, and empowerment of local subsidiaries?

 A. By promoting standardized practices and policies across different regions to reflect the dominant culture and practices of the parent company's home country.

 B. By encouraging decentralized decision-making and autonomy among local subsidiaries to adapt to diverse market conditions and cultural differences.

 C. By fostering a cohesive corporate culture across different regions to enhance global efficiency and alignment with organizational goals.

 D. By prioritizing uniformity and centralization in decision-making processes, limiting responsiveness to local market conditions and cultural differences.

44. A tech startup experiences rapid growth and expansion, resulting in challenges related to role ambiguity and overlap among employees. To address this issue, the company introduces a new organizational structure that clearly defines roles, responsibilities, and reporting relationships. What type of organizational intervention is exemplified in this scenario?

 A. Employee wellness program implementation.

 B. Performance appraisal system overhaul.

 C. Change in leadership structure.

 D. Structural redesign and clarification.

45. How can an organization's culture impact the likelihood of its employees considering unionization? (Choose all that apply.)

 A. An organizational culture that encourages open communication and employee empowerment may discourage unionization.

 B. An organizational culture characterized by strict hierarchy and centralized decision-making often fosters increased interest in unionization.

 C. Organizational culture plays no role in employees' decisions to unionize; it depends on individual employee preferences.

 D. An organizational culture promoting innovation and adaptability usually leads to reduced interest in unionization.

46. The company you work for has an institutional dress code requiring employees to wear business suits, allowing for business casual wear on Fridays. Which of Schein's three layers of culture does this policy represent?

A. Symbols.

B. Beliefs.

C. Artifacts.

D. Unconscious values.

47. According to Geert Hofstede's research, which cultural dimension focuses on the extent to which a society values assertiveness, achievement, and material success in the workplace?

A. Individualism versus collectivism.

B. Masculinity versus femininity.

C. Power distance.

D. Long-term versus short-term orientation.

48. How can HR leverage Hofstede's theory of power distance to design organizational interventions?

A. Implementing hierarchical structures within the organization to reflect cultural preferences for high power distance.

B. Conducting cultural sensitivity training to help employees understand and navigate power dynamics in diverse workplace environments.

C. Encouraging open communication channels and transparency to reduce perceived power distance and promote collaboration.

D. Offering mentorship programs to support employees in developing skills and confidence to navigate power dynamics effectively.

49. At Mertz Mercantile Inc., employees are encouraged to work independently, take initiative, and prioritize personal goals and achievements. Teamwork is valued, but employees are expected to take ownership of their tasks and outcomes. Decision-making is decentralized, allowing individuals to have autonomy in their roles and responsibilities. Feedback is given on an individual basis, and recognition is often based on individual performance rather than team accomplishments. Which characteristic of individualism in organizational culture is most prominently displayed?

A. Decentralized decision-making.

B. Emphasis on teamwork.

C. Collective responsibility for outcomes.

D. Group-based recognition and rewards.

50. Which of the following is an example of an organizational-level strategic intervention?

A. Launching a new advertising campaign.

B. Offering employee training programs.

C. Restructuring the company's top management team.

D. Adjusting product pricing.

51. Which strategic intervention approach emphasizes employee involvement, problem-solving, and continuous improvement to drive organizational change?

A. Top-down leadership approach.

B. Total quality management (TQM).

C. Outsourcing strategy.

D. Market expansion strategy.

52. Company VII, a leading technology firm, has identified a need to improve innovation and employee creativity. They decide to implement a strategic intervention to foster a culture of innovation. What approach would be most suitable for Company VII?

A. Instituting a top-down leadership structure.

B. Implementing regular employee performance appraisals.

C. Launching an innovation lab where employees can collaborate on new ideas.

D. Reducing employee benefits to allocate resources for innovation.

53. The company you work for is going through a major organizational restructuring. The HR department is tasked with managing the transition, which involves changes in reporting structures and job roles. To navigate the political framework effectively during this transformation, what should HR professionals prioritize?

A. Maintaining a strictly neutral stance and avoiding any involvement in office politics.

B. Focusing on implementing the restructuring plan without considering employee concerns.

C. Building relationships with key stakeholders, understanding their interests, and addressing concerns.

D. Implementing strict policies to eliminate any political discussions within the organization.

54. At Company ABC, a manufacturing firm, the production department has been experiencing significant delays in delivering products to customers. Upon investigation, it is discovered that there are inefficiencies in the production process due to the adoption of new technology, resulting in bottlenecks and delays. In response to this issue, the HR department proposes an upskilling initiative to prepare the employees for the production changes. What human-process organization intervention strategy is being proposed by the HR department?

A. Techno-structural.

B. Job enrichment.

C. Cross-training.

D. Workforce planning.

55. At the company where you work, employee engagement surveys indicate low morale, high turnover rates, and dissatisfaction with communication and decision-making. What organizational intervention strategy is most appropriate for addressing the identified challenges?

   A. Techno-structural intervention to upgrade outdated technology systems.

   B. Job enrichment initiative to provide employees with more challenging and rewarding tasks.

   C. Cross-functional training program to improve collaboration and teamwork among departments.

   D. Leadership development program to enhance the leadership skills of mid-level managers.

56. In a large corporation, the organizational design team is responsible for restructuring departments and optimizing workflows to enhance efficiency and productivity. It includes a manager from each functional business unit. Due to unexpected circumstances, a key member of the team is temporarily unable to fulfill their role on the design team, so the HR manager was asked to fill in. What should the HR manager prioritize to ensure the continuity of the organizational design process?

   A. Conducting employee engagement surveys to gather feedback on potential restructuring initiatives.

   B. Collaborating with department heads to identify pain points and inefficiencies within their teams.

   C. Reviewing organizational charts and analyzing workflow data to identify areas for improvement.

   D. Facilitating cross-functional meetings to ensure alignment and buy-in for proposed organizational changes.

57. Which of the following options best translates the statement "Our comprehensive talent acquisition strategy incorporates AI-driven ATS platforms to streamline candidate sourcing, leveraging data analytics for predictive hiring models that optimize time-to-fill and enhance quality of hire" into simplified terms without changing the context?

   A. "We use advanced technology to find and hire the right people faster."

   B. "Our hiring process is more efficient thanks to AI and data analysis."

   C. "We employ cutting-edge tools to speed up hiring and improve candidate quality."

   D. "We're making our hiring process better and faster with technology and data."

58. Lucy, a senior HR leader, presents a business case for a talent development program aimed at enhancing leadership capabilities. She analyzes employee retention data and identifies talent gaps to align the program with strategic goals. By quantifying the potential impact on revenue growth and ROI, Lucy demonstrates the program's value in driving business success. Her fluency in business language secures buy-in from senior leadership. What strategy did Lucy use to gain buy-in for the talent development program?

   A. Analyzing market trends.

   B. Translating the program's impact into financial value.

   C. Implementing technology solutions.

   D. Focusing on employee satisfaction.

59. Which competency is essential for HR professionals to effectively communicate organizational change to a geographically dispersed team?

A. Active listening.

B. Technical expertise.

C. Conflict resolution.

D. Business acumen.

60. The organization you work for has decided to implement a new performance management system to improve employee performance, development, and overall organizational effectiveness. The HR department is tasked with leading this change initiative. Recognizing the complexity of implementing a new performance management system, the HR professional reviews literature, case studies, and industry reports to understand successful strategies, potential pitfalls, and emerging trends in performance management. This is the best example of which of the following HR competencies?

A. Seeking competing points of view.

B. Soliciting feedback.

C. Interpreting and understanding context.

D. Clarifying ambiguity.

61. What is the best step for an HR professional to take when they need to create board-level communication on organizational change?

A. Conduct extensive research on organizational change theories and practices, and then present multiple options to the board for consideration.

B. Develop a comprehensive briefing that outlines the rationale, objectives, anticipated impacts, and strategies for managing the change, tailored to the board's perspective and concerns.

C. Delegate the task to a communications specialist within the HR team, providing them with necessary resources and guidance.

D. Schedule individual meetings with each board member to discuss the proposed organizational change in detail, gathering their input and addressing any concerns before presenting it collectively to the board.

62. Which of the following scenarios best exemplifies the role of conflict management as an HR competency when redesigning jobs as part of a broader organizational restructuring initiative?

A. During the job redesign process, the HR manager encounters resistance from employees who feel anxious about the changes. The manager listens attentively to their concerns, facilitates open dialogue, and collaboratively works toward solutions that address employees' needs while aligning with organizational objectives.

B. The HR department conducts observations to understand the necessary job design changes and makes recommendations to the leaders about what needs to be changed.

C. The HR team encounters disagreements among department heads regarding the allocation of job responsibilities in the redesigned structure. The HR manager advocates for leadership development training to help the leaders grow accustomed to the changes.

D. As part of the job redesign process, the HR manager imposes changes without considering the potential impact on employee workloads and job satisfaction. When employees express frustration and dissatisfaction, the HR manager holds a focus group with the intention of explaining how the change will benefit the team.

63. How does the design of an organization contribute to ethical decision-making?

   A. Implementing clear and transparent organizational policies and procedures that guide ethical behavior and decision-making.

   B. Fostering a culture of accountability and integrity from top leadership down to all levels of the organization.

   C. Establishing mechanisms for employees to report ethical concerns confidentially and without fear of retaliation.

   D. Offering regular ethics training and workshops to employees to enhance their awareness and understanding of ethical principles and dilemmas.

64. What organizational intervention strategy is most likely to address lack of diversity within teams?

   A. Human process.

   B. Change management.

   C. Cultural interventions.

   D. Training and development.

65. What organizational intervention strategy can HR use to overcome a poor employer brand?

   A. Implementing employee advocacy programs to promote positive experiences and improve employer reputation.

   B. Revamping the recruitment process to ensure alignment with the company's values and culture.

   C. Conducting regular employee satisfaction surveys and taking actions to enhance employer brand perception.

   D. Offering professional development opportunities and fostering a supportive work environment to attract and retain top talent.

66. Which of the following methods is commonly used to measure organizational health?

   A. Employee satisfaction surveys.

   B. Financial performance analysis.

   C. Customer feedback evaluation.

   D. Market share comparison.

67. Which of the following methods is best used to measure the success of total quality management interventions?

   A. 360-degree feedback.

   B. Key performance indicators.

   C. Continuous monitoring.

   D. Balanced scorecards.

68. Which of the following evaluation methods is best used to measure the success of leadership development initiatives? (Choose all that apply.)

A. Return on investment.

B. 360-degree feedback.

C. Pre- and post-training assessments.

D. Employee surveys.

69. In what ways can HR best optimize the use of total rewards systems to support organizational development initiatives?

A. Aligning total rewards with organizational goals and values to reinforce desired behaviors and outcomes.

B. Implementing performance-based incentives and recognition programs to motivate employees toward achieving organizational objectives.

C. Conducting regular audits and assessments of total rewards programs to ensure competitiveness and alignment with industry standards.

D. Increasing transparency and communication about total rewards offerings to enhance employee engagement and satisfaction.

70. What risk management best practices should HR follow when designing global organizational development (OD) initiatives?

A. Conducting thorough risk assessments to identify potential challenges and cultural differences in different regions.

B. Establishing clear communication channels and feedback mechanisms to address concerns and ensure alignment across diverse global teams.

C. Implementing robust compliance measures to adhere to local regulations and international laws in each operating region.

D. Offering cross-cultural training and development programs to foster cultural competence and sensitivity among employees involved in global OD initiatives.

Key Concept Research Questions

The ability to critically think on exam day and beyond requires taking a deeper dive into key topics. Take the time to understand the ideas behind the following two questions:

1. Think about your current organization or a company that you have worked for in the past. Select one of the challenges you experienced from the following list (circle one):

- Lack of teamwork
- Task redundancies
- Poor leadership
- Outdated technology
- Lack of communication
- Unsafe working conditions
- Wasted time
- Lack of diversity
- Low morale
- Poor company reputation

Which organizational intervention strategy would be or would have been most useful in solving that challenge? Consider using the following link to learn more about intervention strategies to support the results: `www.mindtools.com/aiydadc/organization-design`.

2. What role does HR play in influencing effective organizational design structures and strategies to optimize employee performance, job satisfaction, and overall organizational success in today's dynamic business environment? Try `www.scholar.google.com` to access a vast collection of scholarly articles, research papers, and studies on organizational design, HR practices, and organizational performance. Use keywords related to organizational design, employee performance, job satisfaction, and organizational success to retrieve relevant articles and studies that address the question.

Test Your Organizational Development and Design Terminology Knowledge

The following are the terms to use to test your knowledge on organizational development and design key terms. You can find the correct answers in Appendix B.

- Automation
- Centralized
- Change management
- Flat organization
- Functional
- Matrix
- Organic
- Organization chart
- Organizational design
- Organizational development
- Phased implementation
- Project-based
- Restructuring
- Span of control
- Structure
- Task specialization
- Team building
- Total quality management
- Training and development
- Workspace redesign

1. ______________ is the process of structuring an organization to achieve its goals and objectives effectively.
2. ______________ is the arrangement of tasks, roles, and responsibilities within an organization.
3. ______________ is a type of organizational structure where authority and decision-making are from the top down.

4. A ______________ is an organizational structure that combines elements of both functional and divisional structures.
5. A ______________-based structure where teams are organized around specific projects or tasks and disband when the project is completed.
6. A ______________ defines clear reporting relationships and lines of authority in an organization.
7. A ______________ structure groups employees and tasks based on their similarity, such as accounting and human resource departments.
8. A ______________ is an organizational design approach that focuses on reducing hierarchy and increasing employee autonomy.
9. ______________ is the extent to which tasks within an organization are divided into smaller, specialized jobs.
10. ______________ is an intervention aimed at improving communication and collaboration among different parts of the organization.
11. ______________ is an intervention that involves changing how the organization functions to improve its efficiency and effectiveness.
12. ______________ is a change management approach that involves gradually implementing changes in an organization.
13. An ______________ approach to organizational design is one that emphasizes flexibility and adaptability.
14. ______________ is the use of technology to streamline organizational processes and improve efficiency.
15. ______________ is an intervention aimed at reducing helping employees and other stakeholders accept changes within an organization.
16. ______________ is a type of intervention aimed at improving the skills and capabilities of employees.
17. ______________ is a type of intervention that involves changing the physical layout of the workplace.
18. __________ refers to the number of direct reports a manager has.
19. __________ is the systematic process of enhancing an organization's effectiveness and performance through planned interventions aimed at improving processes, structures, culture, and employee capabilities.
20. _________ is a comprehensive approach to management that focuses on continuous improvement, customer satisfaction, and the involvement of all employees in achieving organizational excellence.

Conclusion

Human resource management revolves around the design and development of HR systems that align with organizational strategies and support the entire employee life cycle. Practitioners are tasked with implementing and evaluating these systems to ensure their effectiveness in driving organizational outcomes at every stage.

Organizational development and organizational design are two interconnected concepts that play independent roles in enhancing organizational performance. Organizational development focuses on improving processes, structures, culture, and people, while organizational design involves deliberate decisions regarding structures, roles, processes, and systems to achieve strategic objectives. Ultimately, the study of human resource management and becoming strategic business partners allow HR teams to drive organizational effectiveness and adaptability and become the employer of choice.

Becoming strategic business partners through the administration of OD concepts is threaded throughout all of the HR exams. In 2024, HRCI completely eliminated the "knowledge" requirements from their exam content outlines. This included theories of change management, leadership, and culture. However, this fundamental knowledge is critical for understanding and applying the concepts covered in this chapter. The SHRM exams are a bit more direct in their BASK, with the "Organization Knowledge" domain covering many of the competencies inherent in organizational development and design. This includes the structure of HR, organizational effectiveness, workforce management, employee and labor relations, and technology management, all examples of the types of interventions described in OD theory.

Additional Resources

These online resources cover a wide range of topics related to organizational design, from traditional structures to innovative approaches like design thinking. They offer valuable insights, courses, and articles to help you understand and apply effective organizational development and design principles.

Websites

- Organizational Design Community (`www.orgdesigncomm.com`)

  The Organizational Design Community provides resources, articles, and discussions related to organizational design. It's a valuable platform for connecting with experts in the field.

- IDEO U, Leading for Creativity (www.ideou.com)

  IDEO U offers several reasonably priced courses and free resources around creativity including leading and problem-solving. These resources cover strategy and innovation principles and how they can be applied to organizational design.

- Mind Tools, Organizational Design and Structure (www.mindtools.com/aiydadc/organization-design)

  Mind Tools is a think-tank website that offers resources on many organizational design and other business related topics.

Podcasts

- *The Human and Organizational Performance Podcast* hosted by Andy Baker and Matt Florio (www.hoppodcast.com)

  This podcast delves into human and organizational performance, covering aspects of organizational design, leadership, and performance improvement.

- *Org Design Podcast* hosted by Amy Springer, Tim Brewer, and Damian Bramanis (https://player.fm/podcasts/Amy-Springer,-Tim-Brewer-and-Damian-Bramanis)

  The *Org Design Podcast* focuses on organizational design and transformation. It features interviews with experts and leaders who share their experiences and insights.

- *WLEI- Lean Enterprise Institute Podcast* (https://lei.podbean.com)

  This podcast discusses lean principles and their application in organizational design and improvement.

- *Unpacking Organizations: The Practitioners Podcast* hosted by Rupert Morrison and Shradha Prakash (www.orgvue.com/resources/podcast/unpacking-organizations-the-practitioners-podcast)

  This weekly podcast delves into organizational design concepts, offering insights and strategies for designing more adaptive and systematic organizations.

YouTube Channels

These YouTube channels offer a variety of perspectives on organizational design, from industry experts and thought leaders. You can find case studies, interviews, and practical insights to help you understand and apply effective organizational design principles. Log in to www.youtube.com and search and subscribe the following channels:

- Business School 101

  This channel explores key business concepts and theories and is taught by U.S.-based professors.

- Bain & Company

  Bain & Company's channel covers a range of business topics, including organizational design and transformation. It features interviews and insights from Bain experts.
- Center for Humane Technology

  This channel discusses ethical technology design and its impact on organizations and society. It offers perspectives on designing technology for the betterment of organizations.
- Patrick Lencioni

  The author of several organizational development and design books, Lencioni is the master of thought leadership in the realm of organizational health.

Appendix A

Answers to Review Questions

Chapter 2: U.S. Labor Law

1. C. Subscribing to a reputable HR industry newsletter that provides regular updates on federal labor laws is the best option. This approach allows Anna to stay consistently informed about changes in labor laws as they occur. By subscribing to such a newsletter, Anna can proactively monitor any changes or developments in federal labor laws, ensuring that her company remains compliant. Relying solely on the company's legal department (Option A) is not the best approach because legal departments may not always provide real-time updates on labor laws, and HR professionals should be proactive in staying informed about legal changes that may affect their organization. Attending an annual HR conference (Option B) can be beneficial for professional development, but it may not provide the regular and up-to-date information needed to stay current on federal labor laws. Reviewing federal labor laws on an ad hoc basis when specific issues arise (Option D) is not the best approach because it lacks a proactive and systematic method for staying current.

2. B. Organizing group workshops or training sessions is the best method for Emily to effectively coach employees on their rights and responsibilities. This approach allows her to deliver consistent information to a larger audience simultaneously. Option A may be time-consuming and impractical, especially in larger organizations. Written handbooks, as suggested in Option C, are a useful supplementary resource, but relying solely on a handbook for coaching may result in employees not fully engaging with the material or having questions left unanswered. While emails can be a helpful way to communicate information (Option D), they are not sufficient for coaching employees on their rights and responsibilities.

3. B. The best approach for the business is to conduct a detailed assessment of its specific compliance needs and budget constraints before selecting external resources. By assessing its compliance needs and budget constraints, the company can identify its priorities and allocate resources effectively. Option C may be insufficient for ensuring comprehensive compliance, as labor laws can be complex and subject to change. Hiring a large consulting group or multiple specialists (Options A and D) can be a viable option but is most likely cost-prohibitive for smaller organizations on a budget.

4. B. Denying Eleanor's request for a temporary modification of her work schedule to attend prenatal appointments would likely be considered a violation of the Pregnancy Discrimination Act. The PDA prohibits discrimination on the basis of pregnancy, and this includes the denial of reasonable accommodations related to pregnancy, such as allowing time off for prenatal medical appointments. Options A and C are not violations because reassigning tasks or additional breaks to accommodate pregnancy-related limitations can be a reasonable accommodation. Option D is not a violation because offering a promotion (which Eleanor declines) does not constitute pregnancy discrimination.

5. C. The case resulted in a settlement between the Equal Employment Opportunity Commission (EEOC) and Verizon, with both parties agreeing to resolve the matter through mediation. In many employment discrimination cases, parties opt for settlement to avoid the uncertainty and costs associated with litigation. Settlements often involve negotiated agreements to address the issues raised in the lawsuit, which may include policy changes, financial compensation, or other remedies.

6. C. Chidi's employer is prohibited from requesting or requiring him to take a polygraph test in this situation. The Employee Polygraph Protection Act generally prohibits private employers from requesting or requiring employees to take polygraph tests, regardless of the reason. There are specific exemptions under the EPPA for certain industries, such as security services, but these exemptions are subject to various conditions and restrictions, and they do not apply to all employees in those industries. Option A is incorrect because Chidi's employer cannot unilaterally require him to take a polygraph test, even if it is related to workplace security. Option B is incorrect because the EPPA does not permit polygraph tests based solely on reasonable suspicion of employee involvement in wrongdoing. Option D is incorrect because providing a copy of the test results is not a sufficient condition to make a polygraph test legally required under the EPPA.

7. D. Under the Older Workers Benefits Protection Act (OWBPA), when offering severance agreements to employees older than 40, employers must provide them with at least 21 days to review the agreement and a 7-day revocation period to change their minds without forfeiting their benefits. Options A, B, and C are incorrect because they would violate the Age Discrimination in Employment Act (ADEA) and OWBPA requirements by discriminating based on age and impeding the validity of the waiver.

8. C. The employer should avoid asking any questions related to age during the interview. The ADEA prohibits age discrimination in hiring, and employers should avoid asking questions related to age during the interview process. Age should not be a determining factor unless a specific exemption applies (e.g., a bona fide occupational qualification). Options A, B, and D are incorrect because they do not align with the ADEA principles of age-neutral hiring.

9. B. Under the OWBPA, employers must provide clear and timely written notices to employees about changes to retirement benefits, including detailed information on the impact of the changes. This ensures transparency and compliance with ADEA requirements. Options A, C, and D are incorrect because they do not align with the notification and information requirements of the OWBPA.

10. C. BFOQ allows certain exceptions based on specific job requirements, but specifying a gender preference in a job advertisement, in this case, would likely not meet the BFOQ criteria. BFOQ is generally limited to cases where a particular characteristic (such as gender) is essential to performing the job's duties. In most cases, providing education to female students does not require a specific gender for the admissions officer role. The Court of Appeals for the Fifth Circuit held that "discrimination based on sex is valid only when the essence of the business operation would be undermined by not hiring members of one sex exclusively" (source: EEOC CM 625.4).

11. A. BFOQ can apply to certain job roles in religious institutions where adherence to specific religious beliefs or practices is essential to perform the job duties. In this case, for a religious studies class in a private religious school, it may be considered a valid BFOQ to require that the teacher adheres to the school's religious beliefs to effectively convey the teachings and values of the faith.

12. D. COBRA allows eligible employees, like John, to maintain their employer-sponsored health insurance coverage for a limited period (typically up to 18 or 36 months) after job loss or other qualifying events by paying the premiums. It does not provide coverage at no cost, grant unemployment benefits, or offer new health insurance policies.

13. C. Under COBRA, employees like Samantha have the option to continue their employer-sponsored health insurance coverage during maternity leave, but they must pay the full premium cost during the leave period. COBRA does not require the employer to cover maternity-related expenses.

14. B. Under COBRA, individuals like Alex generally have 30 days from the date they receive COBRA enrollment information to decide whether to elect COBRA coverage. Failing to make a decision within this time frame may result in losing the opportunity to continue coverage.

15. B. Priya's employer is not required to provide her with health insurance coverage under the PPACA. The PPACA mandates that employers with 50 or more full-time equivalent employees must offer affordable health insurance coverage to their full-time employees. However, for businesses with fewer than 50 full-time equivalent employees, there is no requirement to provide health insurance coverage to employees under the PPACA. Options A and C are incorrect because Priya is not required to purchase health insurance through the PPACA's health insurance marketplace, and she may not be eligible for subsidies if her income is above certain thresholds. Option D is incorrect because the PPACA does not require employers to offer comprehensive health insurance plans that cover all medical expenses.

16. B. The PPACA includes provisions for providing subsidies to eligible individuals and families to make health insurance purchased through the health insurance marketplace more affordable. These subsidies are designed to assist low- and middle-income individuals in paying their health insurance premiums and, in some cases, out-of-pocket costs. Option A is incorrect because the PPACA had an individual mandate at one point, but it was effectively eliminated in 2019. Option C is incorrect because the PPACA mandates that only larger employers (those with 50 or more full-time equivalent employees) are required to offer health insurance coverage to their full-time employees. Option D is incorrect because the PPACA does not eliminate the private health insurance industry but rather regulates and reforms it to expand access and improve coverage options.

17. B. The EEOC enforces federal laws that prohibit discrimination based on race, color, religion, sex (including pregnancy, gender identity, and sexual orientation), national origin, age (40 or older), disability, or genetic information. Employers with 15 or more employees (20 in age discrimination cases), as well as labor unions and employment agencies, are subject to these laws. They cover various work situations, such as hiring, firing, promotions, harassment, training, wages, and benefits, ensuring equal opportunities for all employees and job applicants regardless of their protected characteristics.

18. C. The Walsh-Healey Act applies to contracts valued at $100,000 or more for the manufacturing or furnishing of materials, supplies, articles, or equipment to the federal government. This act establishes labor standards, working conditions, and other requirements for such contracts. The Walsh-Healey Act does not apply exclusively to construction projects, thus eliminating Option A. Option B is partially incorrect. While the Walsh-Healey Act sets labor standards for federal contractors, it does not directly mandate a specific minimum wage. Option D is incorrect because the act focuses on labor standards and working conditions but does not mandate the provision of healthcare benefits by federal contractors.

19. B. Under the ADA, reporting violations of the law, such as improperly denying reasonable accommodations to individuals with disabilities, is considered protected activity. It does not matter whether the reporting is part of the individual's managerial duties; as long as the report pertains to unlawful company actions and meets other relevant requirements for protected activity, it is protected under the ADA.

20. C. In this scenario, Lisa's statement in Option C conveys her belief that there may be a violation of employment laws (gender-based pay discrimination) by paying her less than male custodians. This expression of concern about potential legal violations is considered protected opposition under employment law. Lisa does not need to make aggressive demands (Option B) or passively accept the situation (Option A); simply expressing her belief that the company might be breaking the law qualifies as protected opposition. Option D is nonspecific and does not address the issue directly, making it less likely to be considered protected opposition.

21. C. In this scenario, the best answer is that Leslie can challenge the police department's policy on the grounds of disparate impact, as it disproportionately affects pregnant officers. Options A and B are not true, and there is not enough information to know if Option D is true in Leslie's state.

22. C. The ACA requires employers to provide nursing mothers with a private and comfortable space (other than a restroom) for expressing breast milk. Employers should evaluate the feasibility of creating such a space and work with the employee to find a suitable solution. Option A is incorrect because the ACA requires employers to provide reasonable accommodations for nursing mothers, and cost considerations alone should not be a basis for denial. Option B is incorrect because the law mandates that nursing mothers should have reasonable break times and a private space to express breast milk. Option D suggesting that Sarah use a restroom does not provide a private and comfortable space as required by the law.

23. D. DACA recipients must renew their status every two years to maintain their eligibility for work authorization and protection from deportation. It's crucial for HR professionals to be aware of the renewal process and ensure that employees maintain their valid DACA status to continue their employment legally. DACA recipients are not eligible for federal financial aid for higher education. Additionally, DACA recipients cannot apply for U.S. citizenship solely based on their DACA status (Option B), and DACA does not provide recipients with a path to permanent legal residency (green card) or citizenship (Option C).

24. B. ERISA does not set specific contribution limits for 401(k) plans. Instead, the contribution limits are determined by the Internal Revenue Code. Employees like Uzo should refer to the IRC and the plan documents for specific contribution limits.

25. A. Executive Order 11246, signed by President Lyndon B. Johnson in 1965, requires federal contractors and subcontractors who hold contracts exceeding certain monetary thresholds and have 50 or more employees to take affirmative action to prevent discrimination and provide equal employment opportunities to individuals regardless of race, color, religion, sex, or national origin. Option B is incorrect because the order applies to federal contractors and subcontractors that meet specific monetary thresholds, not just those with 100 or more employees. The order does not mandate a specific minimum wage for federal contractors (Option C), and 11246 explicitly prohibits discrimination based on religion among other protected categories (Option D).

26. D. ERISA sets minimum funding standards that defined benefit plans must meet to ensure the financial security of pension benefits. Options A, B, and C are not true.

27. C. ERISA allows loans from 403(B) retirement accounts, but there are specific rules and limitations that participants must adhere to. Loans from such accounts must comply with ERISA regulations and the terms of the individual retirement plan. The other statements are not true.

28. C. *Griggs v. Duke Power* established the principle that employers must demonstrate that their selection criteria, including tests and practices, are job-related and consistent with business necessity to avoid discriminatory employment practices. This decision aimed to prevent employment practices that had a disparate impact on certain protected groups, even if the intent to discriminate was not explicit. Options A, B, and D are untrue statements.

29. B. FLSA applies to employers making more than 500,000 in sales or engaged in interstate commerce (which is practically every company based on legal precedent interpretation), regardless of the number of employees they have. Even small businesses like John's bakery are generally covered by FLSA. Options A, C, and D are not true.

30. C. To classify employees as exempt from overtime pay under the FLSA, specific criteria must be met, including both job duties and salary requirements. Exempt status is not solely determined by the employer's discretion, and employees must meet the FLSA's criteria for exemption.

31. D. The Portal-to-Portal Act clarifies what constitutes compensable time under the Fair Labor Standards Act. It specifies that time spent on activities that are "preliminary" and "postliminary" to the principal activities an employee is hired to perform is generally not compensable. However, if the security screening is integral and indispensable to the employee's principal activities, it may be considered compensable time under the FLSA. The Portal-to-Portal Act amended the FLSA, making Option A not the best choice. Option B, OSHA, primarily focuses on workplace safety and health regulations. Option C, the NLRA, protects employees' rights to engage in collective bargaining and organize.

32. B. The FLSA does not allow exemptions from minimum wage requirements for any type or size of business. All employees, regardless of the business's size, are entitled to receive at least the federal minimum wage.

33. B. Unpaid internships can be legally offered if they meet specific criteria outlined by the Department of Labor. One of the common criteria is that the intern receives academic credit for their work, demonstrating that the internship has an educational focus. Option A is incorrect because interns are not always required to be paid at least the federal minimum wage. Option C is incorrect because the FLSA can apply to internships in certain circumstances, particularly when interns are considered employees and not meeting the criteria for unpaid internships. Option D is incorrect because interns can engage in meaningful work and contribute to projects, provided that their work aligns with the educational purpose of the internship and meets the criteria established by the Department of Labor.

34. C. The primary distinction between employees and independent contractors under U.S. labor laws is the degree of control and direction exercised by the hiring entity. Employees are typically subject to the company's direction and control over their work, while independent contractors maintain greater autonomy in how they perform their work. Both employees and

independent contractors may have some degree of control, but the key lies in who exercises control over the broader aspects of the work relationship, so Option A is not the best choice. Independent contractors are typically not eligible for unemployment benefits (Option B). Independent contractors are not entitled to the same workplace protections and benefits as employees (Option D).

35. B. The handling of medical marijuana use in the workplace can vary significantly depending on the state's laws, and it must also consider federal laws. In states where medical marijuana is legal, employers often need to balance the rights of employees with medical conditions against concerns related to workplace safety and compliance with federal law. Option A is incorrect because immediate termination may not be necessary or legally justified, as state laws and circumstances vary. Option C is a possible step an employer might take to gather more information, but it should be done in accordance with applicable laws and regulations. Option D is a distractor specific to California, where state law does offer some protections for employees with medical marijuana prescriptions, but the specific state is not mentioned in the question.

36. C. Under the FLSA, eligibility for overtime pay is primarily determined by an employee's calculated hourly wage and the number of hours worked in a workweek. If an employee earns less than the threshold wage and works more than 40 hours in a workweek, they are generally entitled to overtime pay. The employee's job title and seniority within the company (Option A) are not factors considered in the FLSA for determining overtime eligibility. The employee's age and years of service with the employer (Option B) are also not criteria used to determine overtime eligibility under the FLSA. The employee's level of education and professional certifications (Option D) are not factors considered under the FLSA.

37. C. The FMLA allows eligible employees to take leave to care for a seriously ill family member, including a parent, if they meet the eligibility criteria. This criteria includes the size of the employer (50 or more employees within a 75-mile radius) and how long the employee has been with the company (worked for their employer for at least 12 months and have worked at least 1,250 hours in the 12-month period immediately preceding the leave request).

38. B. Under FMLA, employees taking intermittent leave are generally required to provide advance notice of each instance of leave if it is foreseeable, and they should make a reasonable effort to schedule medical appointments in a way that minimizes workplace disruption. This ensures that both the employer and employee can plan for the intermittent leave. While FMLA allows for intermittent leave for qualifying medical conditions (Option A), employees are typically required to provide notice to their employer for each instance of leave and follow the employer's established procedures. Madison is not entitled to an unlimited amount of intermittent leave under FMLA (Option C). Madison's employer is responsible for tracking her intermittent leave, but Madison also has reporting obligations (Option D).

39. C. When an employee like Madison is not providing proper documentation for FMLA-approved leave, the employer should engage in an interactive process to understand the reasons behind the deficiency. This can include discussing the importance of documentation, providing written notice of the deficiencies, and giving Madison an opportunity to rectify the situation. Employers should follow FMLA's requirements for notice and documentation. Terminating Madison's employment immediately (Option A) for noncompliance with FMLA documentation requirements is not the appropriate initial step. Allowing Madison to continue taking intermittent leave without addressing the documentation issue (Option B) may not be following FMLA regulations, nor does it protect the employer from potential abuse. Reporting Madison to the Department of Labor for FMLA violations, as in Option D, is not a viable option.

40. C. FMLA provides job protection, not wage replacement. If the employee wants to be paid by using accrued leave, they must adhere to the employer's normal leave rules and procedures. This ensures that the use of paid leave is in compliance with both the employer's policies and FMLA regulations (Option A). The FMLA allows employees to use accrued paid leave, such as vacation or sick leave, for FMLA-related reasons if they choose to do so (Option B). Employees cannot unilaterally decide to use accrued paid leave for FMLA purposes without following the employer's leave rules (Option D). Accrued paid leave used for FMLA reasons is FMLA-protected and counts toward the employee's FMLA entitlement.

41. C. FMLA regulations allow employers to temporarily transfer employees to alternative jobs that better accommodate recurring periods of leave while maintaining equivalent pay and benefits. This is done to minimize disruptions to both the employer's operations and the employee's ability to take FMLA leave (Option A). The employer cannot unilaterally transfer an employee like John to an alternative job under FMLA without consulting and considering the employee's rights (Option B). While the employer should generally not make significant changes to an employee's job duties during FMLA leave, accommodating the employee's medical treatments by temporarily transferring them to an alternative job is an acceptable practice (Option D). Terminating John's employment due to intermittent leave would not be following FMLA regulations.

42. C. To qualify for the computer employee exemption, the employee's primary duty must involve applying systems analysis techniques, designing computer systems or programs, or engaging in related activities within the computer field. The tasks listed in the criteria match the types of duties that would qualify an employee for this exemption (Option A). To qualify for the computer employee exemption, the employee can be compensated on either a salary or fee basis or, if compensated on an hourly basis, at a rate not less than $27.63 an hour. The $684 per week figure mentioned in the regulations refers to the minimum salary threshold, not an hourly rate (Option B). The primary duty of an employee seeking the computer employee exemption must involve specific tasks related to computer systems, programming, or analysis, not general administrative tasks (Option D). The number of years of experience in the computer field is not a specific requirement for the computer employee exemption under FLSA regulations.

43. B. Under the Fair Credit Reporting Act, employers are generally required to provide written notice to job applicants and obtain their consent before conducting a background check for employment purposes. William has the right to be informed and give his consent before the background check takes place.

44. A. In most cases, employer agreements and policies must meet or exceed the minimum standards set by federal labor law. If a collective bargaining agreement offers less benefit or protection than the FLSA, the FLSA's provisions take precedence. The FLSA provides minimum standards that cannot be waived or reduced by collective bargaining agreements. Therefore, the employer must adhere to the FLSA's higher overtime premium rate. Options B, C, and D are false.

45. B. The Genetic Information Nondisclosure Act (GINA) prohibits employers from requesting genetic information, including family medical history, from employees and job applicants. D'Arcy has the right to refuse to answer such questions to protect her genetic privacy.

46. C. The Genetic Information Nondisclosure Act (GINA) generally prohibits employers from collecting genetic information, even for wellness programs. Employees have the right to refuse to provide their genetic information in such situations.

47. A. In *NLRB v. Weingarten*, the central issue was whether an employee has the right to request union representation during a disciplinary meeting or investigatory interview with their employer. The outcome of the case established that employees do have the right to request such representation.

48. B. The Health Insurance Portability and Accountability Act (HIPAA) regulations apply to the protection of personal health information (PHI) regardless of the workplace setting. Rosie should inform her colleague that accessing medical records without proper authorization is a violation of HIPAA and that only authorized personnel can access such records.

49. D. HR professionals handling health-related information must be competent in maintaining the confidentiality of protected health information (PHI) and ensuring compliance with the Health Insurance Portability and Accountability Act (HIPAA) privacy and security requirements. HIPAA regulations mandate strict privacy standards, and HR professionals play a critical role in ensuring that these standards are upheld within their organizations (Option A). While technical proficiency in healthcare administration and medical coding may be valuable in certain healthcare-related HR roles, it is not the central competency needed to apply HIPAA regulations (Option B). Knowledge of federal labor laws and collective bargaining agreements is important for HR professionals, but it is not directly related to HIPAA regulations (Option C). Strong understanding of employee benefits and retirement planning is essential for HR professionals but does not specifically address the core competency required for HIPAA compliance.

50. B. The Health Insurance Portability and Accountability Act (HIPAA) requires the protection of an employee's medical information and privacy. Lisa should document the information provided by the employee but keep it confidential within the HR department and only share it with those who have a legitimate need to know, such as HR personnel and higher management involved in the performance review process. Sharing such information with others without authorization would violate HIPAA. HR may request additional documentation for items such as reasonable accommodation through the interactive dialogue process but cannot compel or require an employee to provide such documentation.

51. D. Under the National Labor Relations Act (NLRA), employees have the right to engage in discussions and activities related to unionization without interference or intimidation from their employer. The supervisor should not interfere with their right to discuss unionization and should respect their concerns.

52. C. Under the NLRA, employees have the right to engage in discussions related to unionization during non-working hours, such as breaks or after work. The employer cannot interfere with or prohibit such meetings, as they are protected activities.

53. B. Under the LMRA, employees covered by a CBA are typically required to pay union dues or agency fees as a condition of employment, even if they disagree with some of the union's activities or political positions. These fees are often used to cover the costs of bargaining and administering the CBA. The Supreme Court has ruled that states and public sector unions cannot compel workers to pay dues. While the example in this question is of a private-sector employer, the law and court challenges are in flux and should be monitored for changes.

54. A. An Excelsior list, also called an Eligible Voter List, contains the names and addresses of eligible voters (employees) who may participate in the election. This list must be provided to the union by the employer within a reasonable period after an election has been approved. Options B, C, and D are incorrect answers.

55. C. The Landrum Griffin Act, also known as the Labor Management Reporting and Disclosure Act (LMRDA), establishes reporting and disclosure requirements for labor unions to ensure transparency in their financial activities. It also outlines the rights of union members to access information about their union's finances and leadership elections. The Wagner Act (Option A), also known as the National Labor Relations Act (NLRA), protects the rights of employees to engage in collective bargaining and form labor unions. The Taft-Hartley Act (Option B), formally known as the Labor Management Relations Act (LMRA), regulates the activities and power of labor unions, including provisions to counterbalance some of the powers granted to unions by the Wagner Act. William-Beall (Option D) were the supporters of the Employee Retirement Income Security Act (ERISA), which regulates employer pension plans.

56. A. A serious violation is one where there is a substantial probability of death or serious physical harm resulting from a workplace hazard that the employer knew or should have known about (Option B). A willful violation is the intentional and knowing disregard for, or indifference to, OSHA standards and regulations, demonstrating a clear lack of concern for employee safety and health. The example of lack of fall protection in the question could be willful if there was an indication that the employer ignored the standard (Option C). A de minimus violation is a technical violation that does not have a direct impact on employee safety or health, and it does not result in a penalty or citation but requires correction by the employer (Option D). An other-than-serious violation is a violation of OSHA regulations that has a direct relationship to job safety and health but is not classified as serious.

57. B. Cumulative trauma disorder (CTD), also known as repetitive strain injury (RSI), is characterized by injuries that develop over time due to repetitive movements and poor ergonomics. Sarah's symptoms of discomfort, pain, and numbness in her hands and wrists align with CTD. Ergonomics Injury (Option A) is a general term that does not describe a specific type of injury. It refers to injuries related to the design and setup of the workspace, including issues like poor posture and inadequate equipment. While Sarah's symptoms are related to ergonomics, they are better categorized as a specific type of ergonomic-related injury. Osteoarthritis (Option C) is a degenerative joint disease that may not be directly related to Sarah's symptoms. Simple strain (Option D) is a general term for a minor injury resulting from overexertion or excessive use of muscles or tendons and is not specific enough to be the best answer.

58. D. Under the ACA, the employer mandate applies to employers with 50 or more full-time employees or the equivalent in full-time employee equivalents (FTEs). Employers with fewer than 50 full-time employees are generally not subject to the mandate.

59. D. To calculate the average number of FTE employees for the aggregated group, you need to add the full-time employees' counts for each company together (20 + 25 + 12 = 57) and consider this total when determining their ACA status as an ALE for the year.

60. C. Under the Affordable Care Act (ACA) in 2023, an employer's health insurance plan is considered affordable if the employee's share of the premium for self-only coverage does not exceed 9.12% of their income and is adjusted annually. If the cost exceeds this threshold, the employee may be eligible for premium tax credits through the Health Insurance Marketplace. For the purposes of the exam, you must be familiar with the threshold for the year in which you sit for your test.

61. B. Under the Worker Adjustment and Retraining Notification (WARN) Act, a notice is required when a business with 100 or more full-time workers (not counting workers who have less than 6 months on the job and workers who work fewer than 20 hours per week) is laying off at least 50 people at a single site of employment or employs 100 or more workers who work at least a combined 4,000 hours per week and is a private for-profit business or private nonprofit organization.

62. C. Under the Worker Adjustment and Retraining Notification (WARN) Act, employers are generally required to provide notice at least 60 days before a plant closing or mass layoff. Delaying notice for the purpose of finding alternative employment is not an exemption under the act.

63. C. Under the Immigration Reform and Control Act (IRCA), employers should not immediately terminate employees if their employment eligibility documents appear to be counterfeit. Employers are required to provide a reasonable opportunity for employees to present valid, authentic documents to establish their work eligibility.

64. C. One of the primary responsibilities of employers under the Immigration Reform and Control Act (IRCA) is to complete and retain the I-9 Employment Eligibility Verification form for all new hires. This form is used to verify the identity and employment eligibility of employees.

65. A. Employers must accept a receipt in place of List A, B, or C documentation if the employee presents one. When John presents the original replacement document, cross out the word "Receipt," then enter the information from the new documentation into the Additional Information field in Section 2, and initial and date the change. Accepting a second receipt at the end of the initial receipt validity period is not allowed.

66. B. The Walsh-Healey Public Contracts Act requires contractors, such as ABC Manufacturing, to pay its employees working on government contracts the prevailing minimum wage and fringe benefits as determined by the U.S. Department of Labor. This act aims to ensure fair wages and working conditions for employees on government-funded projects.

67. D. The B-1 visa is typically used for temporary business visitors like Neha, allowing individuals to enter the United States for purposes such as attending meetings, conferences, negotiations, or training, without engaging in long-term employment or labor activities. The H-1B visa (Option A) is typically used for highly skilled workers, including professionals in fields like software engineering; Neha will need an H-1B if she goes to work full-time in the United States. The L-1 visa (Option B) is a nonimmigrant visa category used when multinational companies need to transfer employees from a foreign office to a U.S. office, typically for managerial, executive, or specialized knowledge positions. The J-1 visa (Option C) is a non-immigrant visa program designed for cultural exchange and international educational opportunities in the United States, covering various categories, including research scholars, au pairs, and participants in work and travel programs.

68. B. The Civil Rights Act of 1964 prohibits discrimination in employment based on race, color, religion, sex, or national origin. Tiya's decision to hire John based on his race is a clear violation of this act, as employment decisions should be based on qualifications and merit, not race.

69. B. The Civil Rights Act of 1964, as interpreted by courts and agencies, prohibits discrimination based on sex, which includes gender identity and transgender status. Employers are required to support and accommodate employees undergoing gender transitions.

70. C. In this scenario, the employer is not in compliance with the FLSA because, according to the regulations, the employer must ensure that tipped employees like Maya receive at least the full federal minimum wage ($7.25 per hour) when their direct (or cash) wages and the tip credit amount are combined. If Maya's tips and direct wages do not add up to at least $7.25 per hour, the employer must make up the difference to meet the minimum wage requirement.

71. C. Weis Markets' actions in this scenario violate both the Civil Rights Act of 1964 (Title VII) and the Americans with Disabilities Act. Title VII prohibits workplace sexual harassment, and in this case, the supervisor's unwelcome and offensive sexual comments and actions constitute harassment. The ADA prohibits requiring employees to undergo medical examinations or answer questions that are likely to reveal whether they have disabilities unless it is job-related and consistent with business necessity. In this scenario, the mandatory EAP referral involving medical examination and disability-related inquiries is not consistent with business necessity and violates the ADA. Additionally, the company's retaliation against Allesandra for refusing to comply with the referral and the interference with her ADA rights further violates the ADA.

72. B. In this scenario, the EEOC has filed a lawsuit against the employer for violating Title VII by allowing racial harassment and retaliation to occur without taking appropriate action. To address this violation, the EEOC may seek monetary compensation (such as the $400,000 awarded to the two former employees in the consent decree) and require the employer to implement preventative measures, including written policies and procedures, a comprehensive complaint process, and training for all employees and managers. Options A, C, and D do not fully address the remedies that the EEOC is likely to enforce in this case.

73. A. In this scenario, Jama's deafness falls under the first prong of the ADA's definition of disability. According to the ADA, individuals with an impairment of hearing are considered to have a disability if they are substantially limited in hearing or another major life activity. Jama's deafness substantially limits her in the major life activity of hearing, as she has been deaf since birth and does not use hearing aids or cochlear implants. Therefore, she meets the first prong of the ADA's definition of disability.

74. C. Samantha's departure from her job, where she felt compelled to resign because she was told she would never be promoted due to her appearance, is an example of constructive discharge. Constructive discharge occurs when an employer makes the working conditions so intolerable that an employee feels forced to resign. In this case, Samantha's treatment at work, which led to her resignation, is considered a constructive discharge as it was the result of discrimination based on her appearance.

75. C. To establish the Faragher/Ellerth affirmative defense against vicarious liability in a sexual harassment case involving "intangible" employment actions (such as a hostile work environment), an employer can demonstrate that they had effective policies and complaint procedures in place and that the victim unreasonably failed to take advantage of these procedures. This shows that the employer made efforts to prevent and promptly correct any harassment and that the victim did not cooperate in resolving the issue through the available channels. The other options do not directly pertain to the affirmative defense criteria established in the Faragher and Ellerth cases.

76. C. According to the Uniform Guidelines on Employee Selection Procedures, when a selection procedure disproportionately excludes a particular group, employers should review and revise the procedure to reduce adverse impact while maintaining its job-relatedness.

77. B. The disparate impact ratio, calculated as `(Number of Women Hired / Total Hires) / (Number of Men Hired / Total Hires)`, resulted in a value of 0.75. This means that women were hired at a rate of 75% compared to men. A disparate impact occurs when one group is hired at a significantly lower rate than another group. In this scenario, the hiring rate for women is 75% of the hiring rate for men, indicating a potential imbalance in the hiring process that may warrant further examination for possible discrimination or bias.

Chapter 3: Business Management and Strategy

1. C. The first step in the strategic management process is to conduct an environmental scan to assess the external and internal factors that may affect the organization's strategy. This information is crucial for making informed strategic decisions. The other options are steps that come later in the process in the following order: scan the environment, set organizational goals, implement the strategy, and evaluate performance.

2. A. A SWOT analysis is a strategic planning tool that evaluates an entity's strengths, weaknesses, opportunities, and threats (SWOT) to inform decision-making and enhance organizational performance. Competitive analysis is part of the "Opportunities and Threats" component of a SWOT analysis, which focuses on external factors affecting a business.

3. A. By investing in employee training and skill development, the company can ensure that its workforce is equipped with the necessary skills and knowledge to meet the evolving needs of the market and serve an expanding customer base effectively. This initiative can lead to improved product quality, better customer service, and increased competitiveness, all of which contribute to achieving the organization's overarching goal. Option B is incorrect as while reducing turnover can have positive impacts on employee morale and organizational stability, it may not directly contribute to market expansion or customer acquisition. Option C is incorrect as it also may not directly contribute to the company's goal of increasing market share and expanding its customer base. Option D is incorrect because cost reduction is more of a process efficiency initiative as opposed to a growth effort.

4. D. Business and competitive awareness as a competency involves understanding the broader business context in which HR operates, including industry trends, market dynamics, and

competitive pressures. HR professionals with strong business and competitive awareness can align HR strategies and practices with organizational goals, anticipate future challenges, and capitalize on emerging opportunities. Option A is incorrect as it may not directly drive organizational performance outcomes on its own; it is the application of this expertise within the broader business context that truly impacts organizational performance. Options B and C are both important competencies for HR professionals; however, they do not directly drive organizational performance outcomes to the same extent as competencies more closely linked to business strategy and execution.

5. B. Porter's Five Forces framework assesses the competitive intensity and attractiveness of an industry. Competitive rivalry is one of the five forces, along with the threat of new entrants, the threat of substitutes, the bargaining power of buyers, and the bargaining power of suppliers.

6. B. Market development involves selling existing products to new markets. This involves extensive market research, understanding the needs and preferences of new customer segments, and adapting marketing strategies to effectively penetrate and capture these markets. Option A is incorrect as market penetration involves selling existing products in existing markets. Option C is incorrect as product development involves creating new products or modifying existing ones to cater to existing markets. Option D is incorrect as diversification involves entering entirely new markets with new products or services that may be unrelated to the company's current offerings.

7. B. A cost leadership strategy involves achieving a competitive advantage by offering products or services at a lower cost than competitors while maintaining satisfactory quality. One disadvantage of a cost leadership strategy is that it can be easily imitated by competitors, leading to increased competition and potential margin erosion. The other options are not associated with cost leadership.

8. D. Defining the organization's mission and vision lays the foundation for the strategic planning process. The mission statement articulates the organization's purpose, its reason for existence, and what it aims to achieve, while the vision statement outlines the desired future state or long-term goals. These statements provide clarity and direction for all subsequent strategic decisions and actions. Option A is incorrect because conducting a SWOT analysis typically occurs after defining the organization's mission and vision and involves analyzing internal strengths and weaknesses as well as external opportunities and threats. Option B is incorrect as setting organizational objectives usually follows the establishment of the mission and vision, as objectives are derived from the organization's overarching purpose. Option C is incorrect because identifying strategic alternatives comes later in the strategic planning process as it involves generating and evaluating different courses of action to achieve those objectives.

9. B. A mission statement serves as a guiding light for the organization, articulating its fundamental reason for existence and the principles that guide its actions. By clearly defining the company's core purpose and values, the mission statement aligns the efforts of employees, stakeholders, and customers toward a common vision. Option A is incorrect as financial targets may be part of a business's strategic plan or objectives but are not the primary purpose of a mission statement. Option C is incorrect because mission statements are not intended

to outline product processes and procedures. Option D is incorrect because identifying market share is a component of strategic planning and market analysis but is not the primary purpose of a mission statement.

10. B. Effective communication and transition strategies can help minimize disruption and ensure the well-being of employees during a significant organizational change. Option A is incorrect because HR's primary focus should be on managing the transition for existing employees, and a hiring freeze may be counter-productive to the primary initiative. Option C is incorrect because negotiating sale terms with potential buyers is the responsibility of the organization's legal and business development teams, not HR. Option D is incorrect as although HR may provide information about employee-related costs, the financial aspects of a divestiture, such as asset valuation and financial due diligence, are managed by the finance and accounting teams.

11. B. In this scenario, market development is the most suitable strategy as it involves selling existing products (software) to new markets (education sector). Options A and D suggest maintaining the status quo or limiting your offerings, which may not capitalize on the opportunity. Option C could be too risky as a startup as it is unrelated to your current expertise.

12. B. Pursuing a differentiation strategy involves offering unique and high-quality products to distinguish your company from competitors. Option A focuses on low-cost operations, while Option C aims to increase market share without necessarily emphasizing product differentiation. Option D is not relevant to gaining a competitive advantage.

13. C. PESTLE stands for Political, Economic, Social, Technological, Legal, and Environmental factors. In a PESTLE analysis, the "S" category stands for Social factors, which include demographic trends, cultural norms, and societal changes. The other options represent other elements of PESTLE forces. Political factors encompass a range of elements including government policies, regulations, stability, and political influences. Technological factors focus on advancements, innovations, and developments in technology. Legal factors encompass legal regulations, laws, and compliance requirements that businesses must adhere to in their operations. Environmental factors address environmental considerations, such as climate change, sustainability practices, natural resource availability, and ecological concerns.

14. D. By conducting a focus group or market research, the manufacturing company can gather valuable insights into consumer preferences, attitudes, and purchasing behavior regarding sustainable materials. By identifying and responding to consumer preferences for eco-friendly options, the company can better align its products with market trends, enhance its competitiveness, and meet the evolving needs of environmentally conscious consumers. Option A is incorrect because continuing to use traditional materials for cost savings does not align with the trend of consumers valuing eco-friendly options. Option B should be undertaken based on the results from the focus group to minimize risk. Option C is incorrect as ignoring the trend as it may be short-lived is a risky strategy that may result in missed opportunities and loss of market relevance.

15. A. Pursuing a cost leadership strategy can help maintain profitability by reducing costs while maintaining product quality. Option B focuses on offering unique products, which may not be suitable in a recession. Options C and D involve expanding or introducing new products to different markets, which might not address the immediate cost reduction goal.

16. A, B. By conducting environmental scans, organizations can stay informed about changes in their external environment, such as market trends, regulatory developments, and technological advancements. This allows them to identify emerging opportunities that they can capitalize on and potential threats that they need to mitigate, enabling more effective strategic planning and decision-making. This proactive approach enables them to adapt their strategies, operations, and resources in a timely manner, increasing their resilience and competitiveness in dynamic markets. Option C is incorrect as environmental scans do not drive cost savings, but in fact, they require investment in resources such as time, personnel, and tools for data collection and analysis. Option D is incorrect because both internal and external analyses complement each other in the strategic planning process, providing a holistic understanding of the organization's strategic position and options.

17. B. Historical data primarily reflects past events and trends, which may not accurately represent current or future market conditions. Organizations that rely too heavily on historical data may become overly focused on replicating past successes or maintaining the status quo, rather than proactively seeking out new opportunities or adapting to changing circumstances. This can stifle innovation and agility, making the organization vulnerable to competitors and market disruptions. Option A is incorrect because historical data can still provide some insight into past social trends, but its limitation lies more in its inability to accurately predict or capture emerging trends and shifts in consumer behavior. Option C is incorrect as organizations can still adapt to rapid changes by supplementing historical data with real-time information and dynamic analysis. Option D is incorrect because historical data does not inherently increase the need for scenario planning. Scenario planning is a strategic tool used to explore various future possibilities and their potential implications, regardless of whether historical data is used in environmental scans.

18. C. BMW's focus on high-performance, luxury vehicles represents a differentiation strategy, as it seeks to differentiate its products based on quality, features, and brand image. In contrast, Hyundai's emphasis on affordability and reliability aligns with a cost leadership strategy, as it aims to provide value to customers through cost-effective production.

19. B. To be the best performance golf brand in the world, TaylorMade would need to focus on creating innovative and high-performance golf products that set them apart from competitors. Option A is incorrect as the mission statement implies a focus on quality and performance rather than low-cost production. Option C is incorrect because their primary goal is to excel in the golf industry, so expanding into unrelated markets would be a diversion from their core mission. Option D is incorrect as the mission statement itself does not explicitly mention partnerships or resource-sharing.

20. A. Lego's statement reflects their long-term aspirations and overarching goal to be a global force for learning through play in the future. Option B is incorrect as a company's mission statement defines its core purpose and how it plans to achieve its goals. Option C is incorrect because a company's values represent the principles and beliefs that guide an organization's behavior and decision-making. Option D is incorrect as a brand encompasses various elements that contribute to a company's identity, including its logo, reputation, and messaging.

Lego's statement is more forward-looking and focused on their future impact rather than their mission, values, or brand.

21. B. A company's mission statement defines its core purpose and how it plans to achieve its goals. Tesla's statement reflects their mission because it describes their primary objective and how they intend to fulfill it. Option A is incorrect as a company's vision statement outlines its long-term aspirations and overarching goals. Option C is incorrect as company values represent the principles and beliefs that guide an organization's behavior and decision-making. Option D is incorrect because a company brand encompasses more than its internal mission, vision, or values, but also its external reputation and customer expectations.

22. D. A clear and compelling mission, vision, and values provide a guiding framework for decision-making and behavior across diverse geographic regions. By aligning global operations with its fundamental purpose, aspirations, and guiding principles, a company can effectively navigate diverse markets, drive sustainable growth, and create long-term value for stakeholders worldwide. Option A does not capture the full extent of their influence on global strategy, thus making it incorrect. Option B is incorrect as it focuses more on human resources management than on the broader impact of mission, vision, and values on global strategy. Option C is incorrect because this option is unclear and somewhat contradictory. It seems to suggest that a company's mission, vision, and values impact its ability to increase short-term results by setting long-term goals.

23. B. Talent management involves more than just recruitment; it encompasses strategies for nurturing and retaining valuable employees within an organization. Implementing policies for employee retention and engagement focuses on creating a positive work environment, providing opportunities for growth, and fostering a sense of belonging, which are essential for retaining top talent. Options A, C, and D are incorrect as talent management involves a holistic approach that includes strategies for employee engagement, development, and retention, not just hiring, training, or performance management training.

24. A, B, D. Including a benefit utilization review as a primary goal of a strategic compensation plan aligns with ensuring that the organization's benefits offerings are effectively utilized by employees. By reviewing benefit utilization, HR can assess the effectiveness of the benefits package in meeting employees' needs and adjusting it accordingly. Ensuring fair and equitable pay across all job roles is a fundamental goal of any strategic compensation plan. It involves analyzing and adjusting compensation structures to eliminate disparities based on factors such as gender, race, or job level. Including offering bonuses to top-performing employees as a primary goal of a strategic compensation plan acknowledges the importance of recognizing and rewarding exceptional performance. Option C is incorrect as salary structures may vary across the organization based on legitimate factors such as education, experience, and job responsibilities. A single salary structure does not allow for those variables or flexibility in hiring and rewarding performance.

25. C. IKEA's commitment to making quality furniture accessible and affordable is the most prominent aspect of its vision statement. The vision, "to create a better everyday life for the many people," emphasizes accessibility and affordability, which are core principles of IKEA's business model. This vision reflects IKEA's mission to offer well-designed, functional home furnishings at prices that are accessible to a wide range of consumers. Option A is incorrect as the vision focuses more on the company's purpose and values, emphasizing the goal of creating a better everyday life for consumers, rather than explicitly stating a desire for market dominance. Option B is incorrect because it is not the central theme of its vision statement. While affordability is emphasized, IKEA's vision extends beyond simply pursuing cost leadership to encompass broader goals related to improving everyday life for its customers. Option D is incorrect as the vision emphasizes accessibility and affordability rather than differentiation as the primary goal of IKEA's business model.

26. C. By donating one pair of socks for every pair sold, Bombas differentiates itself from competitors through philanthropy. This approach enhances the brand's image, appeals to socially conscious consumers, and creates a unique selling proposition in the market. It aligns with a competitive differentiation strategy, where the company focuses on offering unique and socially responsible products or services to stand out from competitors.

27. C. Seeking patents allows a company to protect its unique innovations and technologies, thereby differentiating its products or services from competitors in the market. By obtaining patents, a company can prevent competitors from replicating its offerings, creating a barrier to entry and establishing a unique selling proposition that enhances its competitive advantage. Options A is incorrect as it is not a direct behavior associated with developing a competitive advantage through differentiation. Option B is incorrect because it is too narrow a strategy to create or sustain a long-term advantage. Option D is incorrect as continuous improvement efforts are common across various competitive strategies and are aimed at improving overall performance rather than creating a distinct market position based on uniqueness or exclusivity.

28. A. By reducing the time and resources required to interact with customers, companies can improve efficiency, allocate resources more effectively, and lower operational costs. This cost advantage can translate into lower prices for customers, higher profit margins, or additional investments in product innovation or customer experience enhancements, all of which can contribute to a competitive advantage. Option B is partially correct, as an effective CRM system can indeed improve the quality of interactions with customers by providing personalized and timely communication, but this alone may not necessarily lead to a competitive advantage because it does not directly address the cost side of the equation or provide a distinct advantage over competitors. Option C is incorrect because the system itself cannot provide a sustainable advantage if competitors can replicate similar efforts. Option D is incorrect because effective CRM systems encompass a broader range of capabilities beyond self-service portals, including data management, analytics, and automation, which can contribute to a competitive advantage in various ways beyond cost reduction.

29. C. Return on investment (ROI) is a common KPI used to measure the financial effectiveness of a business strategy. It assesses the profitability and efficiency of the strategy. Options A, B, and D are not used as KPIs for evaluating the overall effectiveness of a business strategy.

30. D. Employee turnover analysis involves tracking metrics related to employee retention, resignation rates, and turnover reasons. This method provides insights into employee satisfaction, engagement, and organizational culture, which are critical factors for achieving strategic goals related to workforce effectiveness and productivity. Option A is incorrect because they measure the customer-related aspects of the balanced scorecard. Option B is incorrect as this metric focuses more on operational performance and product development activities rather than employee engagement, satisfaction, or turnover. Option C is incorrect because ROI calculations primarily focus on financial outcomes and profitability metrics rather than employee-related metrics.

31. C. Key performance indicators (KPIs) are quantifiable metrics that organizations use to measure the success or performance of their strategies and objectives.

32. B. While the increase in market share may seem positive, the decline in profitability and mixed customer satisfaction suggest that the strategy may not be effective in the long term. Option A is incorrect because market share alone does not guarantee success if it negatively impacts profitability. Option C is incorrect because satisfaction among some customers does not necessarily reflect overall strategy effectiveness. Option D is incorrect because successful market penetration should consider profitability and long-term sustainability.

33. C. Dissatisfied employees are more likely to experience decreased motivation and productivity, as well as higher turnover rates, so focusing on this element of strategy will drive the other outcomes. Option A is incorrect as it may not necessarily lead to improved productivity if other factors such as workload or employee morale are not addressed. Option B is incorrect because it's important to recognize that focusing on productivity without considering other factors such as employee satisfaction and workload balance can lead to negative outcomes, such as increased stress and burnout among employees. Option D is incorrect because recognizing that turnover and productivity need improvement does not provide specific guidance on which aspect of the strategy to reconsider. It's important to identify the root causes of the issues and assess how each component of the strategy contributes to or detracts from the desired outcomes.

34. C. Porter's Five Forces is a strategic framework that assesses an organization's competitive environment by examining the bargaining power of suppliers and buyers, the threat of new entrants, the threat of substitutes, and competitive rivalry.

35. C. Introducing a profit-sharing plan directly aligns the Total Rewards strategy with business strategy by linking employee compensation to the company's financial performance. This approach can boost motivation, foster teamwork, and drive performance improvements. Option A is incorrect because it might be seen more as a perk for employee satisfaction rather than a direct alignment with business outcomes. Option B is incorrect because although it addresses employee well-being, it doesn't directly tie into business outcomes or financial objectives in the same way that profit-sharing or performance-based incentives might. Option D is incorrect because it's more of a financial management decision than a direct alignment of Total Rewards with business strategy.

36. B. The BCG Matrix, developed by the Boston Consulting Group, is specifically designed for portfolio analysis, helping organizations assess their various business units or products based on market growth rate and relative market share. It is well-suited for analyzing different employee groups based on growth potential (market growth rate) and relative market share (strength in attracting and retaining talent), making it the most appropriate choice for the task described in the question. Option A is incorrect because it is a model used for organizational effectiveness and alignment, focusing on seven internal elements such as strategy, structure, systems, style, staff, skills, and shared values. While it can be valuable for assessing internal alignment within the organization, it doesn't specifically address the analysis of employee groups based on growth potential and relative market share. Option C is incorrect as the Blue Ocean Strategy is a strategic approach focused on creating uncontested market space by making competition irrelevant and therefore, not directly applicable to the analysis of employee groups. Option D is incorrect because a SWOT analysis is a strategic planning tool used to identify strengths, weaknesses, opportunities, and threats related to a specific business situation or project.

37. A. Before conducting a pay equity analysis, it is essential for HR professionals to ensure that job descriptions are accurate and reflect the responsibilities and requirements of each role. By comparing job descriptions, HR can identify any discrepancies or differences in job roles that may influence compensation disparities. Option B is incorrect as it is not the first step in a pay equity analysis. Job description comparison and data gathering are prioritized to establish a foundation for the analysis. Option C is incorrect because without ensuring role parity first, the pay data analysis may be skewed or inaccurate. Option D is incorrect as discrimination determination comes later in the process, based on the findings of the analysis.

38. C. HR strategy focuses on aligning HR practices, policies, and initiatives with business objectives to support organizational goals and drive performance. Human capital management specifically emphasizes optimizing the skills, capabilities, and potential of employees to enhance organizational effectiveness and competitiveness. While HR strategy takes a broader organizational perspective, human capital management delves deeper into managing and developing the workforce to maximize its value to the organization.

39. B, C. Strategic initiatives in an HR strategic plan focus on actions that directly impact organizational goals and objectives, such as talent management, performance improvement, and HR technology implementation. Regular performance appraisals initiatives contribute to performance management and employee development, aligning employee goals with organizational objectives and fostering a culture of continuous improvement. By analyzing external pay data, organizations can benchmark their compensation practices against industry standards and market trends, ensuring they remain competitive in attracting and retaining top talent. Options A and D are incorrect because they are considered more tactical or operational rather than strategic.

40. B. Talent acquisition involves attracting and hiring top talent to fill critical roles within the organization, while workforce planning involves forecasting future talent needs and developing strategies to meet those needs. Option A is incorrect because employee retention strategies focus on efforts to retain existing employees within the organization and does not directly address the aspect of ensuring that the organization has the right people, in the right roles, at the right time. Option C is incorrect because employee engagement programs are designed to improve employee satisfaction, motivation, and commitment to the organization, not determine fit. Option D is incorrect because workplace diversity initiatives do not specifically address the aspect of ensuring that the organization has the right people, in the right roles, at the right time.

41. B. Auditing personnel files ensures that the organization is compliant with federal labor laws related to record-keeping and documentation requirements. Federal labor laws such as the Fair Labor Standards Act (FLSA) and the Equal Employment Opportunity (EEO) laws have specific requirements regarding record-keeping, including employee personnel files. Conducting regular audits helps ensure that the organization maintains accurate and up-to-date records in compliance with these laws.

42. D. The primary reason for HR professionals to navigate the formal and informal structures within a work group is to build relationships with employees and address their concerns. By understanding the dynamics within the work group, HR professionals can effectively identify

and address employee concerns, foster open communication, and promote a positive work environment. Option A is incorrect because HR's role in addressing discrimination involves investigating complaints, providing training on diversity and inclusion, and enforcing anti-discrimination policies and procedures. Option B is incorrect because HR's role in ensuring compliance involves providing training, monitoring adherence to policies, and addressing noncompliance through corrective action. Option C is incorrect as HR professionals should maintain a professional relationship with employees while focusing on their responsibilities related to employee relations, conflict resolution, and organizational effectiveness.

43. C. Understanding informal power dynamics helps HR identify key influencers who can positively impact the workplace culture and facilitate change. Options A and D do not recognize the potential benefits of informal structures, and Option B is not the primary focus of understanding informal power dynamics.

44. C. Building relationships and understanding the priorities of key stakeholders in other departments would allow Penelope to navigate the political climate effectively. By presenting a well-structured proposal highlighting the project's benefits, she is more likely to gain support and resources. Option A is incorrect because ignoring the need for support and resources from other departments may lead to the project's failure and could isolate Penelope within the organization. Option B skips the crucial step of relationship-building before understanding others' priorities. It's important to establish trust and rapport before making requests. Option D is incorrect as avoiding a project due to organizational politics may result in missed opportunities for the company and hinder Penelope's career growth.

45. C. HR professionals should consider mediating discussions, facilitating communication, and promoting conflict resolution when addressing a power struggle among department heads. This approach helps navigate the political framework while promoting collaboration and resolving conflicts.

46. B. By aligning goals with the organization's mission and vision, employees understand how their efforts contribute to the broader strategic objectives, fostering cohesion, motivation, and alignment throughout the organization. Option A is incorrect because such goals may not necessarily contribute to the organization's long-term success or strategic objectives. Option C is incorrect because basing strategic goals on external factors may not fully capture the unique context, capabilities, and strategic priorities of the organization. Option D is incorrect because deadlines should be realistic and feasible, allowing sufficient time for planning, execution, and adaptation as needed.

47. A. The goal of "Increase the percentage of positive customer feedback by 15% within the next six months" is specific because it clearly outlines what needs to be achieved. It is not broad, unmeasurable, or irrelevant, as it provides a clear target (15% increase) within a specified time frame (next six months) related to the organization's strategic initiative to improve customer satisfaction.

48. D. Conducting quarterly employee engagement surveys and addressing immediate concerns is a suitable short-term goal to achieve the HR strategy of improving employee engagement within six months. It allows for continuous feedback and action. Options A, B, and C do not align with the short-term timeframe or the specific objective of improving engagement.

49. C. Establishing an HR analytics team to provide data-driven insights aligns with the long-term goal of using advanced HR systems to support global expansion. It reflects a strategic approach to leveraging HR systems for the organization's broader business strategy. Options A, B, and D are important but do not directly address the use of HR systems in the context of long-term global expansion.

50. A. Internal risks are those that arise from within the organization and may include factors such as organizational structure, processes, technology, or personnel. Option B is incorrect because the term *threats* typically refers to intentional actions or events that could harm an organization's assets or objectives and is reflected in a SWOT analysis as an external factor, not an internal one. Option C is incorrect because while the potential incompatibility between systems could be considered a weakness if it exposes vulnerabilities in the organization's data security measures, the primary concern in this scenario is the risk posed by the incompatibility rather than the weakness itself. Option D is incorrect as external threats are risks originating from outside the organization that have the potential to negatively impact its operations or objectives. Examples of external threats include economic downturns, changes in regulatory requirements, and actions by competitors.

51. C. The Eisenhower Matrix, also known as the Urgent-Important Matrix and the Tyranny of the Urgent, is a prioritization framework that categorizes tasks into four quadrants based on their urgency and importance. Tasks are classified as urgent and important, important but not urgent, urgent but not important, or neither urgent nor important. This technique helps individuals and teams prioritize tasks effectively by focusing on what matters most and managing time efficiently. Option A is incorrect as Program Evaluation and Review Technique (PERT) analysis is a project management tool used to estimate the time required to complete tasks and identify the critical path of a project. Option B is incorrect as the Critical Path Method (CPM) is another project management tool used to identify the longest path of dependent activities in a project, determining the minimum project duration. Option D is incorrect because Strengths, Weaknesses, Opportunities, Threats (SWOT) analysis is a strategic planning tool used to identify and analyze internal strengths and weaknesses as well as external opportunities and threats facing an organization.

52. D. A risk matrix, also known as a probability-impact matrix, is a common method used in project management to evaluate and prioritize project risks. It involves plotting risks on a matrix based on their likelihood (probability) and impact (severity). Risks are typically categorized into high, medium, or low priority based on their position in the matrix. Option A is incorrect as a Fishbone diagram, also known as a cause-and-effect diagram, is a visual tool used to identify and organize potential causes of a problem or effect. Option B is incorrect as a Monte Carlo simulation is a quantitative risk analysis technique used to model the probability distribution of possible outcomes in a project by running multiple simulations using random variables. Option C is incorrect as Pareto analysis, also known as the 80/20 rule, is a technique used to prioritize problems or issues based on the principle that roughly 80% of effects come from 20% of causes.

53. A. Building credibility and influence with other department managers requires HR professionals to understand the unique challenges, goals, and objectives of each department. By gaining insight into the specific needs and priorities of different departments, HR professionals can tailor their approach and provide valuable support and solutions that align with the department's objectives. This demonstrates empathy, collaboration, and a commitment to helping departments achieve their goals, thereby enhancing credibility and influence. Option B is incorrect because providing unsolicited advice and recommendations to department

managers may not always be well-received and can come across as intrusive or presumptuous. Option C is incorrect as building credibility and influence requires actively engaging with department managers, understanding their needs, and providing valuable support and solutions tailored to their specific challenges and objectives. Option D is incorrect because minimizing communication with employees may hinder HR professionals' ability to understand the needs and concerns of different departments and effectively support them.

54. B. The primary purpose of conducting a cost-benefit analysis is to evaluate the financial feasibility of a project by comparing the costs and benefits associated with it. This analysis helps decision-makers assess whether the benefits outweigh the costs.

55. B. To calculate ROI, you use the following formula:

```
ROI = (Gains from the project - Investment Cost) /Investment
Cost * 100
```

Plugging in the numbers, would result in the following:

```
($100,000 - $50,000) / $50,000 * 100 =
$50,000 / $50,000 * 100 =
1 * 100 =
100
```

A positive ROI of 100% demonstrates that the initiative generated a substantial return relative to its cost, making it an effective investment for the HR department.

56. B. A key difference between cost-benefit analysis (CBA) and return on investment (ROI) is that CBA assesses the costs and benefits of a project, helping determine its financial feasibility, while ROI measures the net gain or loss as a percentage of the initial investment, focusing on profitability.

57. C. The first step in creating an HR budget is to analyze historical HR spending and expenses. This helps HR professionals understand past patterns and allocate resources effectively. Options A, B, and D are activities that come after data analysis.

58. C. By regularly tracking expenses and comparing them to budgeted amounts, HR can identify variances, analyze the reasons behind them, and take corrective actions as necessary. This proactive approach helps ensure that the HR budget remains aligned with organizational goals, optimizes resource allocation, and minimizes the risk of overspending or underspending. Option A is incorrect as the allocation of excess funds should be based on strategic priorities and organizational needs, which may include investing in employee compensation, training and development, benefits, or other initiatives. Option B is incorrect because unexpected events or changes in business conditions may necessitate adjustments to the budget throughout the year. Option D is incorrect because budgetary decisions should be made based on strategic priorities and the needs of the organization, rather than arbitrary timing.

59. B. To calculate the HR to FTE ratio, you divide the number of HR employees by the total number of employees in the organization. This ratio helps assess the HR department's staffing level relative to the entire workforce.

60. A. Conducting regular pay equity audits involves systematically reviewing and analyzing compensation data to identify any discrepancies or inequalities in pay based on factors such as gender, race, or other protected characteristics. By regularly auditing pay practices, HR can proactively address any disparities and ensure that compensation is fair and equitable for all employees. Option B is incorrect because while diversity training programs can be beneficial for raising awareness and fostering inclusivity within the workplace, they may not be sufficient on their own to ensure equity effectiveness in HR strategy design. Option C is incorrect because blind recruitment processes, which involve removing identifying information from job applications to mitigate unconscious bias, do not directly address disparities in pay that may already exist within the organization. Option D is incorrect as mentorship and sponsorship programs can be instrumental in providing support and opportunities for career advancement to underrepresented groups. But they do not directly address pay equity issues.

61. B. One key benefit of aligning HR efforts with business strategy is improved organizational agility and adaptability to market changes. When HR practices are closely aligned with strategic goals, the organization can respond more effectively to shifts in the business environment.

62. C. A best practice when developing a business case is to clearly outline the expected costs, benefits, and risks of the project. This transparency allows stakeholders to make informed decisions. Options A, B, and D are not recommended as they can lead to poor decision-making.

63. B. HR can provide the most support in improving product quality by enhancing employee training and development programs. Well-trained and skilled employees are better equipped to produce high-quality products, adhere to quality standards, and continuously improve processes to meet quality objectives. Options A, C, and D are incorrect because they do not directly address the goal of improving product quality.

64. D. BATNA stands for "Best Alternative to a Negotiated Agreement" and refers to the alternative course of action that a party can take if negotiations fail to reach a satisfactory agreement. It helps parties understand their options and strengthens their position in negotiations by providing a fallback plan if negotiations fail.

65. B. The primary purpose of obtaining a U.S. patent is to ensure that the inventor is the only one who can monetize the use of the invention, granting them exclusive rights to their invention for a limited period of time. Option A is incorrect because the primary purpose of obtaining a patent is not to keep an invention a secret but rather to disclose the invention to the public in exchange for exclusive rights. Option C is incorrect because patents themselves do not provide direct tax benefits. However, inventors may derive financial benefits from their patents through licensing, selling, or using their inventions in a way that generates income, which can have tax implications. Option D is incorrect because patents are primarily intended to provide inventors with exclusive rights to their inventions, giving them the opportunity to profit from their creations or control their use.

66. B. A utility patent is the most appropriate choice for protecting the NeuroStim Pro invention. Utility patents cover new and useful processes, machines, articles of manufacture, or compositions of matter. The NeuroStim Pro is a functional medical device that falls under the category of utility patents because it involves a novel and useful process (the technology and methodology behind the stimulation). Option A is incorrect because a design patent protects the ornamental and aesthetic aspects of an invention, such as the product's unique visual design or appearance. In the case of the NeuroStim Pro, the emphasis is on its advanced technology and functionality, not its visual design. Option C is incorrect because a provisional

patent is not a stand-alone patent but a temporary placeholder that allows inventors to establish a priority date for their invention. It does not grant patent protection on its own. Option D is incorrect because plant patents are not applicable to medical devices like the NeuroStim Pro or any other technology unrelated to plant breeding.

67. C. Systems thinking seeks to identify, analyze, and leverage the interconnectedness and relationships among various elements within an organization, such as processes, departments, stakeholders, and resources. It acknowledges that changes or decisions in one part of the system can have ripple effects throughout the entire organization. Option A is incorrect because systems thinking emphasizes rather than isolates the interdependence of different parts of an organization. Option B is partially correct in the sense that systems thinking does consider both short-term and long-term impacts. However, the primary focus of systems thinking is not just about risk analysis but also about understanding the broader relationships and dynamics within the organization. Option D is incorrect as while HR systems may play a role in business strategy, the primary focus of systems thinking is not just on maximizing immediate profits.

68. A. Differentiation of units in systems thinking involves the process of breaking down a complex system into its individual components or units. These individual components are then analyzed, optimized, or improved separately to enhance their performance. The idea is to understand each component in detail and how it contributes to the overall system's function. Option B is incorrect. Differentiation of units in systems thinking does not involve ignoring the interrelationships between different parts of a system. Instead, it acknowledges the interdependencies among components but focuses on breaking them down into manageable units for analysis and improvement. Option C is incorrect as differentiation of units does not exclusively concentrate on short-term objectives. Option D is incorrect because the concept of differentiation of units is more concerned with analyzing and optimizing individual components before considering how they can work together synergistically.

69. D. Threats in a SWOT analysis refer to external factors or conditions that have the potential to harm a corporation's performance or disrupt its business strategy. The impact of the regulatory environment on a corporation's business strategy often falls into this category because regulatory changes or restrictions can pose significant challenges and risks to a company's operations and profitability. Option A is incorrect because strengths refer to internal, positive attributes or capabilities of a corporation that give it a competitive advantage. Option B is incorrect because weaknesses also pertain to internal factors that hinder a corporation's performance or competitiveness. Option C is incorrect as opportunities usually relate to external factors that a corporation can exploit to its advantage.

70. A. Market penetration is the growth strategy that involves increasing a company's sales within their current competitive landscape. This strategy focuses on selling more of the existing products or services to the current customer base or capturing a larger share of the current market. Option B is incorrect as market development involves expanding into new markets or market segments with existing products or services. Option C is incorrect because product development focuses on introducing new products or services to existing markets. Option D is incorrect as diversification is a growth strategy that involves entering new markets or industries with new products or services that may be unrelated to the company's existing offerings.

71. C. The concentration of suppliers compared to buyers is a key determinant of supplier bargaining power. When there are fewer suppliers relative to buyers, suppliers tend to have more power to dictate terms, prices, and conditions. Option A is incorrect because when there are many substitutes for a product, buyers have more options and thus greater bargaining power. Option B is incorrect as it is more closely associated with competitive rivalry among existing firms rather than the bargaining power of suppliers. Option D is incorrect because supplier power is more directly tied to the concentration of suppliers relative to buyers and their ability to control the market.

72. A, B, C. Employee turnover rate is a key performance indicator (KPI) for a healthcare HR department because it measures the percentage of employees who leave the organization within a specified period. High turnover can indicate issues with recruitment, retention, morale, or workplace culture, which are critical areas for HR management in healthcare settings. Option B is another HR KPI as monitoring patient satisfaction scores is important for healthcare HR departments to ensure that staff members are meeting patient needs and delivering high-quality care. Option C is correct because monitoring nurse safety records helps identify and address potential hazards, improve workplace safety protocols, and promote a healthy work environment. Option D is incorrect because this metric is more closely related to financial performance and operational efficiency rather than HR-specific functions such as recruitment, retention, or workforce management.

73. C. By acquiring the startup with innovative solar panel technology, the company could have positioned itself as a leader in the renewable energy sector. This would have provided numerous benefits, including access to new revenue streams, differentiation from competitors, and increased market share in the growing renewable energy market. Failing to seize this opportunity resulted in the company missing out on the chance to establish a strong presence and gain a competitive edge in a strategically important industry. Option A is incorrect as the primary lost opportunity was not the expansion itself but rather the failure to secure a competitive edge within that segment. Option B is incorrect because acquiring the renewable energy startup may have enhanced the company's brand reputation; however, the primary missed opportunity was not related to brand reputation but rather to gaining a competitive edge in the renewable energy industry through access to cutting-edge technology and market leadership. Option D is incorrect as employee morale and engagement do not directly relate to the strategic opportunity cost in this scenario.

74. A, B, C. Offshoring, layoffs, and reduction-in-force (RIFs) are all related to strategic downsizing. Offshoring refers to the practice of relocating business operations or processes to a different country, often to take advantage of lower labor costs, favorable regulatory environments, or access to specific skills or markets. Layoffs refer to the termination of employees' employment due to reasons such as workforce reduction, cost-cutting measures, or organizational restructuring. RIFs is a broader term that encompasses various methods used by organizations to reduce their workforce intentionally. Both layoffs and RIFs are strategic decisions made by companies to adjust their workforce size in response to changing business conditions, economic factors, or strategic priorities. Option D is incorrect because diversifying involves expanding a company's product lines, services, or markets to reduce risk and achieve growth opportunities; it is not related to strategic downsizing.

Chapter 4: Talent Planning and Acquisition

1. B. The best approach is to assess the candidate's actual skills related to the required programming language. A technical skills test provides a practical evaluation of their abilities, ensuring they meet the specific requirements of the position. A panel interview with general questions (Option A) does not directly assess the candidate's programming language skills and may not provide a reliable evaluation. Depending solely on a résumé and references may not validate the candidate's programming language expertise adequately (Option C), and while experience is valuable (Option D), it doesn't objectively guarantee proficiency in the specific language required. It is important to note that to be compliant with nondiscrimination laws enforced by the Equal Employment Opportunity Commission (EEOC), all tests must be valid, reliable predictors of future success that do not adversely affect protected class groups.

2. C. References can provide insights into their work ethic, teamwork, and overall fit for the organization, helping you make an informed decision (Option A). While experience is valuable, it should not be the sole determinant if other factors are relevant. Option B would be unlawful, and age alone is not a reliable indicator of innovative thinking (Option D). While another's opinion is useful, it would be enhanced with relevant reference data.

3. A. Strong organizational and project management skills are essential for planning and executing a job analysis, especially when faced with resistance from a difficult manager. These competencies will help ensure that the process runs smoothly and efficiently (Option B). While knowledge of sales techniques and strategies is valuable, it doesn't directly address the HR competencies needed to handle the sales manager's resistance and successfully complete the job analysis (Option C). Excellent negotiation and conflict resolution skills are important HR competencies but may not be the primary focus when dealing with the sales manager's reluctance to allocate time for the analysis (Option D). In-depth technical expertise in the sales department's software may be useful but is not the primary requirement for conducting a job analysis and managing the sales manager's concerns.

4. A. In this example, HR is using regression analysis to create a résumé suitability score based on various qualifications and job requirements. It allows HR to quantify the fit between candidates' qualifications and job criteria, making it a suitable choice. Decision tree analysis (Option B) is a statistical method used for classification and prediction. It is typically employed when you need to make decisions or predictions based on multiple input variables. Logistic regression (Option C) is a statistical model used primarily for categorical outcomes, such as predicting whether an event will occur (e.g., whether a candidate will be hired). Factor analysis (Option D) is a statistical technique that does not directly apply to the creation of a résumé suitability score based on qualifications and job requirements.

5. A. Decision tree analysis is a statistical technique used for classification and prediction by creating a visual tree-like structure to represent the hierarchy of attributes. It helps HR identify the most critical qualifications for the job. Linear regression analysis (Option B) is used to model the relationship between variables and predict a continuous outcome, making it less suitable for creating a visual representation of qualification importance. Factor analysis (Option C) identifies latent factors within a dataset, which may not directly apply to assessing the hierarchy of qualifications for job performance. T-test analysis (Option D) is typically used for comparing means of two groups and may not be the most appropriate method for visually displaying the hierarchy of qualifications in this context.

6. B. When calculating the cost-per-hire, it's crucial to consider all direct and indirect expenses associated with the recruitment process. This includes not only advertising and job board fees but also HR staff salaries, applicant tracking system (ATS) costs, recruitment agency fees, travel expenses for interviews, background checks, and any other expenses incurred during the hiring process. Options A and C are too narrow, and the costs of Option D are not directly related to recruitment.

7. B. The formula (Total hours worked by all employees) / (Standard hours for a full-time employee) accurately calculates FTE. It takes into account the actual hours worked by all employees and divides it by the standard hours for a full-time employee to determine how many full-time equivalents are contributing to the workload.

8. C. Headhunters and executive search firms specialize in identifying and recruiting candidates with specific skills and expertise, making them ideal for finding highly specialized talent for niche roles. While online job boards (Option A) are a common recruiting source, they may not be the most effective for highly specialized roles. Employee referrals (Option B) rely on the network of current employees and may not be suitable for finding highly specialized talent. Temporary agencies (Option D) are typically used for short-term staffing needs and may not have adequate focus on specialized roles.

9. A, B, C, D. All of the listed methods (surveys/questionnaires, observations, focus groups/brainstorming sessions, and interviews) can be used in combination to conduct a comprehensive task inventory analysis. Each method has its strengths and weaknesses, and using multiple methods can provide a more accurate and well-rounded understanding of job tasks and responsibilities.

10. B. Unstructured interviews are characterized by open-ended questions that allow for a more natural and free-flowing conversation, enabling the interviewer to explore various aspects of the candidate's qualifications and personality. Option A describes a structured interview, which uses a predetermined set of standardized questions. The panel interviews mentioned in Option C can be structured or unstructured, but the presence of multiple interviewers does not define an unstructured interview. Option D is more characteristic of situational interviews, not unstructured interviews.

11. C. Behavioral interviews focus on past behavior and ask candidates to provide examples of how they have handled specific situations or challenges in the past. This helps assess their ability to apply their past experiences to future roles. Properly phrased questions can assess how aligned a person is with the company values (Option A). Structured interviews follow

a predetermined set of standardized questions and do not necessarily focus on past behavior (Option B). Unstructured interviews are characterized by a more conversational style that may or may not focus on behaviors (Option D). Group interviews involve multiple candidates being interviewed simultaneously and do not necessarily focus on past behavior.

12. C. Personality tests can offer valuable insights into a candidate's traits and behavioral tendencies. However, they are most effective when used alongside other assessment methods, such as interviews, reference checks, and skills assessments, to form a comprehensive evaluation of a candidate's suitability for a position and to ensure legal defensibility (Option A). Personality tests are a valuable tool in the hiring process, but they should not be the sole determinant of a candidate's suitability (Option B). Personality tests are permitted provided they don't create disparate impact and are properly validated to predict future success on the job for which they are applying (Option D). The appropriateness of using personality tests should be determined based on the specific job requirements and the organization's hiring goals, rather than being limited to entry-level positions.

13. B. One of the significant advantages of using chatbots or artificial intelligence (AI) in recruiting is its ability to provide immediate responses to candidate questions and inquiries. This responsiveness enhances the candidate experience, making the recruitment process more efficient and user-friendly (Option A). While these tools can assist in certain aspects of the recruiting process, they cannot replace human recruiters entirely, especially when it comes to relationship-building with candidates (Option C). Chatbots/AI can help reduce some forms of bias by following predefined criteria consistently. However, they may also inherit biases present in the data used to train them. Eliminating bias in recruiting requires ongoing monitoring and intervention by human recruiters to ensure fairness and equity (Option D). While chatbots and other forms of AI can assist in evaluating certain aspects of candidates, assessing cultural fit often requires human judgment and understanding organizational culture, which chatbots may not possess.

14. A. Temporary employees are hired for a specific project or period and may not receive full benefits. Part-time employees work fewer hours than full-time employees but may still be eligible for certain benefits, depending on the employer's policies (Option B). Contract employees may have fixed work schedules, and seasonal employees are not necessarily engaged on an hourly basis, nor do they always receive full benefits (Option C). Neither freelancers nor consultants are considered full-time employees (Option D). Interns are typically students or recent graduates who gain work experience, often without pay (provided the company follows Department of Labor guidelines), and while apprenticeships are another type of "earn while you learn" program, they do not necessarily come with special benefits beyond what a regular employee is offered.

15. B. Properly classifying employees at the time of hire is essential to comply with labor laws and regulations. Misclassifying employees can lead to costly fines, penalties, and legal disputes (Option A). Properly classifying employees is not about avoiding employee benefits but rather ensuring that employees receive the benefits they are entitled to based on their employment status (Option C). While proper classification may have administrative benefits, the primary purpose is to adhere to legal requirements, not simplify payroll processing (Option D). Job security depends on various factors, including performance and business needs, and is not solely determined by employment classification.

16. B. To calculate the applicant-to-interview-to-offer ratio, divide the number of applicants interviewed by the number of offers made:

$$\text{Applicant} - \text{to} - \text{interview} - \text{to} - \text{offer ratio} = (\text{Number of applicants interviewed}) / (\text{Number of offers made})$$

$$= 40 / 4 = 10$$

The applicant-to-interview-to-offer ratio is 10, meaning that, on average, 10 applicants were interviewed for every job offer made during this recruitment process. This ratio helps assess the efficiency of the selection process.

17. C. The primary goal of strategic workforce management is to align the workforce with the long-term goals and objectives of the organization, as well as the company vision and values. This involves ensuring that the right people with the right skills are in place to support the organization's strategic initiatives at both a job and cultural level. Option A is incorrect because it focuses on short-term profits, which may not always be aligned with long-term success. Option B is relevant but not the primary goal, as reducing employee turnover is one of the strategies used to achieve the primary goal of alignment. Option D is unrelated to the core objective of strategic workforce management.

18. C. Strategic workforce planning involves identifying and developing talent for the long-term needs of the organization. Option A is incorrect because it represents a reactive approach, whereas strategic workforce planning is proactive. Option B is related to performance management but is not a key component of strategic workforce planning. Option D is about short-term adjustments, which are not the focus of strategic workforce planning.

19. D. Strategic workforce management focuses on long-term planning and alignment with organizational goals. Daily task assignments are typically part of operational management and are not the primary concern of strategic workforce management. Options A, B, and C are all relevant factors in strategic workforce management. Employee engagement, market competition, and regulatory compliance are key considerations when making strategic decisions related to the workforce.

20. B. Implementing a talent development program to upskill current employees not only improves the skills of the existing workforce but also fosters employee loyalty and reduces turnover. This approach aligns with long-term goals and ensures a workforce that is well prepared to support the plant's operations. Hiring a large number of temporary workers for short-term cost savings, as suggested in Option A, may lead to workforce instability and can negatively impact quality and productivity in the long run. Option C, relying solely on external recruitment agencies, can limit the company's control over the recruitment process and may not ensure that the plant's workforce is aligned with the company's strategic goals. Option D, requesting the county government to subsidize part of their hiring effort, does not resolve a long-term strategic staffing need.

21. D. An effective human capital management (HCM) plan primarily focuses on managing and optimizing an organization's human resources. The key components of an HCM plan include talent acquisition and recruitment (Option A), employee training and development (Option B), and compensation and benefits management (Option C). These components are directly related to the management and development of an organization's workforce.

22. D. An expatriate employee, as described in Option D, refers to an individual who is a citizen of one country but is temporarily assigned or transferred by their employer to work in a different country. This temporary assignment typically involves specific job duties, often for a limited duration, and may include relocation to a foreign country. Expatriates are often used by multinational companies to bring in specialized skills or knowledge from their home country to support operations or projects in another country. Option A is incorrect because it describes a local employee in their home country, not an expatriate. Option B describes a remote worker but does not necessarily involve cross-border employment. Option C describes a situation where a local employee is working for a foreign company within their home country, which is not the typical definition of an expatriate.

23. A. Hiring an engineer from Turkey as a third-country national can promote cross-border cooperation and knowledge sharing between the Swiss, Indian, and Turkish teams, contributing to a more diverse and collaborative research and development environment. Option C discusses cost reduction, which is not true, as the cost of hiring outside the host country can be significantly more expensive. Option D mentions ensuring compliance with Swiss labor laws, which is not an advantage of hiring a third-country national.

24. A. During the startup phase of the business lifecycle, workforce plans often prioritize attracting and retaining specialized talent. Startups require specific expertise and skills to develop and launch new products or services. The growth phase (Option B) typically involves scaling up the workforce but may not require as much specialization as the startup phase. Option C is incorrect because the maturity phase often emphasizes stability and efficiency rather than specialized talent acquisition. The decline phase (Option D) is usually characterized by downsizing or restructuring rather than attracting specialized talent.

25. C. Developing a remote staffing plan for data storage and transmission would require the company (and HR working with the IT department) to ensure that its remote employees have access to secure and efficient technology for handling data properly. This may include the design of employee portals, enhanced security measures, encryption protocols, and policies outlining the use of personal devices to complete work tasks. Option A is a consideration for home offices; however, the question is focused on data security, not employee safety. Options B and D would have been more appropriate answers if the question was focused on disaster recovery as opposed to data security.

26. C. To align a workforce plan with a business strategy, conducting a skills gap analysis is a critical step. This involves evaluating the current skills and competencies of the workforce against the skills required to achieve the business objectives. By identifying any gaps in skills and knowledge, the company can develop targeted training and hiring plans to bridge those gaps and ensure they have the right talent to execute their strategy effectively. Option A is incorrect because a systematic hiring process is effective only if it is targeting the necessary roles identified through the gap analysis (Option B). While offering benefits like paid time off is important, it is not a direct step to aligning the workforce plan with the business strategy. Eliminating training programs (Option D) would hinder employee development and could create skill gaps, which goes against the concept of aligning the workforce with the business strategy.

27. B. During an economic downturn, a strategic approach is to assess employee skills and consider retraining them for different roles or to acquire new skills. Option A, implementing a plan to do across the board layoffs, should be a last resort as it can harm morale and

long-term productivity. Option C, freezing all hiring and promotions indefinitely, may hinder growth opportunities and employee development. Option D, increasing salaries, may not be financially viable during a downturn and may not address the root cause of the staffing issue, which is aligning skills with organizational needs.

28. A. In a labor market analysis, the demand-side analysis focuses on factors that relate to the employers' perspective and their requirements for labor. Option A, wage and salary trends, is typically considered part of the demand-side analysis. Employers need to understand current wage and salary trends in the labor market to make informed decisions about compensation packages and remain competitive in attracting talent. Options B and C are part of the supply-side analysis. Government regulations and labor laws (Option D) can be relevant but are generally considered as external environmental factors and not part of the demand-side analysis specifically.

29. B. The labor force participation rate measures the proportion of the working-age population that is either currently employed or actively looking for work. It provides insights into the extent to which people are engaged in the labor market. Option A is incorrect as the labor force participation rate does not solely measure the percentage of the working-age population that is employed. It includes both employed individuals and those who are actively seeking employment. In Option C, retirement benefits are important in labor market analysis, but the labor force participation rate does not directly relate to retirement eligibility. Option D is incorrect as the labor force population rate is not specifically about disabilities in the workforce.

30. C. To optimize their staffing plan, the company would likely use labor market data to analyze driver availability in specific regions. By examining data on the number of potential delivery drivers in various areas, they can make informed decisions about where to allocate resources, expand their services, or run promotions to attract more drivers in areas with high demand. This data-driven approach helps them match supply and demand effectively. Option A does not specifically address the strategic perspective of regional supply and demand factors. Option B is incorrect because pricing strategies are related to revenue generation but not necessarily tied to labor market data. Option D, reducing customer support positions, would not typically be a direct result of using labor market data for staffing optimization, and it may negatively impact customer service.

31. B. The company should prioritize promoting a supportive work environment and professional development opportunities to attract nursing candidates. Nurses often value workplaces that prioritize their well-being and provide opportunities for growth. Option A is important but may not be the primary factor that motivates nurses to choose an employer. Option C may be a nice perk but is not a core factor for most nursing candidates. Option D, celebrity endorsements, may not effectively communicate the hospital's commitment to patient care and employee well-being, which are more relevant factors for nursing candidates.

32. C. Passive candidates, who are not actively seeking new opportunities, may be enticed by a compelling employee value proposition (EVP) that highlights the distinctive benefits and values your organization offers. Being transparent about your EVP can pique the interest of potential candidates and motivate them to explore opportunities within your company. Option A may grab the attention of some passive candidates, but it may not be sufficient to engage them in a meaningful way if other aspects of your EVP are not appealing (Option

B). Passive candidates are often looking for unique and authentic employee value propositions that align with their career goals and personal values, so a copycat EVP may fail to capture the attention of these candidates. Option D is a viable strategy but does not address the question about the employee value proposition, which is what the question was asking.

33. C. While various metrics can help assess different aspects of recruiting effectiveness, quality-of-hire provides the most comprehensive assessment of the entire recruitment process. Quality-of-hire measures the overall success of a new hire in terms of their job performance, alignment with the organization's goals, and long-term potential within the company. Option A focuses on the speed of filling job vacancies and may not necessarily reflect the quality of the candidates hired. Option B focuses on the financial efficiency of the recruitment process but does not directly address the quality or long-term impact of the hires. Option D provides information about candidates' willingness to accept job offers but does not assess their performance or contribution after joining the organization.

34. C. One of the key differences between employees and independent contractors is that employers are responsible for withholding taxes, such as income taxes and Social Security, from employees' paychecks. Independent contractors are responsible for paying their own taxes. Option A is incorrect because employees often have less flexibility in choosing their work hours compared to independent contractors. Regarding Option B, independent contractors are typically not eligible for employee benefits such as health insurance or retirement plans from the hiring organization (Option D). Independent contractors do not have permanent job security and are usually hired on a project or contract basis.

35. C. Employers generally have a legal obligation to pay overtime to employees who work more than 40 hours per week, as mandated by labor laws like the Fair Labor Standards Act (FLSA). Independent contractors, on the other hand, are not eligible for overtime pay as they are not considered employees under these laws. Option A is incorrect because employers may provide a workspace and equipment to both employees and independent contractors as necessary for the job. Option B is incorrect because offering training and professional development can apply to both employees and independent contractors, depending on the arrangement. Option D is incorrect because offering retirement benefits is not a legal obligation though it is a common employee benefit.

36. B. The hiring yield ratio for a specific stage in the recruitment process is calculated by dividing the number of candidates who successfully pass that stage by the number of candidates who entered that stage. In this case, the number of candidates who moved on to the technical interview round is 50, and the number of candidates who entered that stage is 200. Hiring yield ratio = Number of candidates in technical interview / Number of candidates selected for initial phone screening, which in this case, is: 50 / 200 = 0.25.

37. B. When there is an error in Section 1 of Form I-9, it is generally best to have the employee complete a new form with the correct information. The new form should be attached to the original form to maintain a clear record of the correction. Correcting the mistake in Section 1 (Option A) is not recommended as it could potentially raise issues with accuracy and compliance. Option C is not sufficient to rectify the mistake on Form I-9. Option D could lead to further inaccuracies and potential compliance issues.

38. B. Option B, biased, is the correct answer. Background checks can assist in reducing biased hiring decisions by providing an objective and standardized method of assessing candidates' qualifications and suitability for a position. These checks can help ensure that hiring decisions are made based on verifiable information rather than subjective judgments, ultimately contributing to fair and equitable hiring practices. Background checks (Option A) do not affect the efficiencies of the hiring process and may in fact slow the process down and increase the cost to hire, making Options C and D incorrect also.

39. D. Providing ongoing coaching and feedback on interview performance is the most effective way to support a manager who lacks interview skills. This approach allows HR to address the specific needs and challenges of the manager over time, helping them improve their interviewing abilities. It also ensures that the manager can adapt and refine their interview techniques based on real-world feedback, leading to more successful and informed hiring decisions. Options A, B, and C do not provide the same level of continuous support and development as ongoing coaching and feedback.

40. D. Situational judgment tests are the most likely to provide a comprehensive assessment of a candidate's suitability for the role of a customer service representative in a busy call center. These tests simulate real-world scenarios that candidates are likely to encounter in the job, such as handling customer inquiries, resolving complaints, processing orders, and adhering to company policies. Situational judgment tests directly measure a candidate's capacity to excel in the specific challenges and responsibilities of the CSR role, making them a suitable choice for this comprehensive assessment. While cognitive ability tests (Option A) assess general problem-solving skills, and personality tests (Option B) and emotional intelligence tests (Option C) provide insights into interpersonal traits, situational judgment tests focus on job-specific competencies critical for success in this role.

41. B. If an employer is an E-Verify member in good standing, in certain situations, remote verification procedures are allowed for Form I9, where the employee can present their documents to a trusted representative via videoconferencing. Rebecca should use these remote verification procedures to verify Michael's documents without the need for physical inspection. It is not necessary to have the original documents physically mailed (Option A). Option C, notarized copies, is not the preferred method for verification. Option D is incorrect because remote verification procedures are permitted.

42. B. One of the primary advantages of using temporary staffing agencies is the reduced administrative burden for the hiring organization. These agencies handle tasks such as recruitment, payroll, and benefits administration, allowing the organization to focus on its core activities. Option A is incorrect because temporary employee hours are not generally directly affected by the employer of record. Option C is incorrect as temporary employees are typically not committed to long-term positions and may actually be less committed to the team. Option D is incorrect because temporary staffing agencies do not guarantee permanent placements.

43. A. In a global environment, consultants can provide valuable insights and knowledge about specific markets, including regulatory nuances, cultural understanding, and local customer behaviors, which are critical for successful market entry. While employee retention is essential (Option B), it may not be the primary consideration when deciding between a consultant and a full-time employee for addressing the complexities of international expansion (Option C). Operational tasks with high consistency and predictability may be suitable for full-time

employees, but this may not be the primary consideration for the complex challenges of international expansion (Option D). Intellectual property protection and knowledge transfer are important consideration if the question were about IP. In the context of market expansion, it is less relevant than the correct answer.

44. A. Turnover is a broad term that encompasses all employee departures, including both voluntary resignations and involuntary terminations. Attrition, on the other hand, specifically refers to voluntary departures where employees choose to leave the organization. While turnover does involve the number of employees leaving, Option B, attrition, is more about the natural reduction in staff size over time. Turnover includes both voluntary and involuntary departures, making Option C incorrect. Neither turnover nor attrition is typically linked to maintaining workforce diversity or unplanned reductions in staff, so Option D is incorrect.

45. B. The complexity of the hiring process is a primary factor that affects the time-to-fill metric. A lengthy, multistep hiring process with numerous interviews, assessments, and approvals can significantly extend the time it takes to fill a position (Option A). More applicants may increase the time if there's a need to review all applications, but it's not the primary driver (Option C). The company's annual revenue may influence the budget and resources available for recruiting, it's not a direct determinant of the time it takes to fill a job (Option D). Positions in remote or less accessible locations may take longer to fill, but it's a subcomponent to the complexity of the hiring process.

46. C. A drug screen helps identify individuals who may pose a safety risk due to drug use. Options A and B, credit and background checks, are important for other aspects of a candidate's history but do not directly assess drug impairment. Option D, a behavioral interview, is valuable for assessing a candidate's behavior and past experiences but may not be as effective as a drug screen in determining a safe workplace.

47. D. To verify the qualifications and credentials of medical professionals, DEF Healthcare should use credential verification as a preemployment test. This ensures that candidates have the necessary licenses, certifications, and qualifications to provide patient care. Options A and C, personality and reference assessments, focus on other aspects of a candidate's suitability but do not verify credentials. Option B, a criminal background check, is important for safety but does not directly assess qualifications and credentials.

48. C. Employers typically conduct drug screens after extending a conditional job offer but before the candidate starts working. This allows employers to assess whether the candidate meets the job requirements while maintaining compliance with legal and privacy considerations. Option A is incorrect because conducting drug screens after the candidate has started working can lead to complications and legal issues. Option B is incorrect because drug screens are not primarily used to assess a candidate's honesty. Option D is incorrect because drug screens are not limited to candidates with known histories of substance abuse; they are typically a standard part of the preemployment process for all candidates.

49. B. Collaborating with department heads and other key decision-makers is the best approach. By understanding their specific talent needs and how they relate to the company's growth strategy, you can ensure that the workforce plan is well-aligned with the organization's goals and that key stakeholders are engaged and supportive (Option A). Conducting a workforce analysis and presenting data to senior management may be the final outcome, but it requires input from stakeholders described in the correct answer (Option C). Developing a workforce plan in isolation, focusing solely on HR-related metrics and initiatives, may lead to a plan that doesn't effectively address the broader business needs and goals of the company (Option D). Seeking external consultants to create the workforce plan independently may provide valuable insights, but it may lack the depth of understanding of the company's internal dynamics and goals that an internal HR professional can bring.

50. D. Employers must comply with applicable federal and state labor laws when using unpaid interns, including adhering to guidelines outlined by the Fair Labor Standards Act (FLSA). Options A and B are incorrect because unpaid interns are not entitled to the same benefits as regular employees, and they can be unpaid as long as specific criteria are met. Option C is incorrect because offering internships exclusively to current employees would limit the pool of potential interns and is not a legal requirement.

51. C. According to the FLSA, to classify an intern as unpaid, one of the key criteria is that the intern must receive training similar to that provided in an educational institution. Options A and B are incorrect because the work performed by unpaid interns should not primarily benefit the employer or replace the work of regular employees. Option D is incorrect because working full-time hours and meeting experience requirements are not specific criteria for unpaid internships under the FLSA.

52. D. The key factor ABC Corporation should consider when determining whether to classify workers as independent contractors or employees is the level of control and direction the company has over the workers. If the company exerts significant control over how the work is performed and the worker's daily tasks, they are more likely to be considered employees. Options A, B, and C are incorrect because they are not the primary factors in determining worker classification. While the length of the project may be a consideration, it does not solely determine classification. Worker preference and qualifications are also relevant but do not override the control and direction factor.

53. A. Offering employee benefits, such as health insurance or retirement plans, to independent contractors can create legal risks as it may blur the distinction between employees and contractors. It is essential for Nelson Tech to avoid treating independent contractors in a manner that suggests an employer/employee relationship, including offering traditional employee benefits. Options B and C are incorrect because treating all freelancers as employees or providing equipment does not address the legal risk associated with misclassification. Option D is incorrect because it is generally the responsibility of independent contractors to handle their own tax obligations.

54. C. Data security and privacy are crucial considerations when implementing a work-from-home policy. Employers must take measures to protect sensitive company information and maintain compliance with data protection regulations. Options A, B, and D are incorrect because while paid time off, work schedules, and childcare facilities may be relevant to remote work policies, data security and privacy are the primary concern in this context.

55. C. One potential challenge for employees working remotely is the feeling of isolation and loneliness, as remote workers may miss the social interactions and camaraderie of an office environment. Options A, B, and D are less common challenges under a flexible work-from-home policy. Limited access to career development opportunities (Option A) can vary depending on the organization's policies, and remote work often reduces commute times and expenses (Option B). Flexible work arrangements typically allow employees to adapt their work schedules (Option D) so may or may not be true, depending on the worker.

56. B. Affinity bias involves favoring candidates who share similar backgrounds, characteristics, or traits with you, potentially leading to discrimination and a lack of diversity in hiring.

Confirmation bias (Option A) can lead to favoring candidates who align with your personal interests, but it is less likely to be a prevalent form of bias in job offer negotiations compared to other biases (Option C). Outcome bias, which prioritizes candidates based on their previous job outcomes, may not necessarily result in discrimination but could lead to overlooking candidates with potential (Option D). Anchoring bias, where you fixate on the initial salary expectation a candidate provides, can impact salary negotiations but is generally less associated with unlawful discrimination.

57. C. One of the critical staffing considerations during a merger and acquisition is aligning compensation and benefits packages for all employees to ensure fairness and equity. Option A is incorrect because retaining all employees without considering redundancy or alignment of compensation and benefits may not be feasible or strategic. Option B is incorrect because rapid downsizing without careful evaluation can lead to a loss of valuable talent and expertise. Option D is incorrect because effective communication with employees should start early in the merger process to reduce uncertainty and foster engagement.

58. C. To mitigate potential culture clashes during a merger, implementing cross-cultural training and team-building programs can help employees from both companies understand and adapt to each other's corporate cultures. Option A is incorrect because maintaining separate workspaces may perpetuate division rather than integration. Option B is incorrect because enforcing a strict uniform dress code is not an effective strategy for addressing deeper cultural differences. Option D is incorrect because reducing communication between employees can exacerbate cultural misunderstandings and hinder integration efforts.

59. B. Providing prompt and clear communication at each stage of the process, including updates and feedback, is crucial to ensuring a positive candidate experience. Effective communication demonstrates respect for candidates and keeps them informed throughout the process, reducing anxiety and uncertainty (Option A). Conducting back-to-back interviews may expedite the process, but it can be overwhelming for candidates and may not necessarily contribute to a positive experience (Option C). While minimizing the number of interview rounds can save the candidate's time, it should not come at the expense of thorough assessment. A balance between a reasonable number of rounds and comprehensive evaluation is essential (Option D). Providing insights into the company's values and culture earlier in the process can help candidates make informed decisions and align themselves with the company's ethos, contributing to a positive experience.

60. B. Employment at will means that employers can terminate employees at any time for any reason, with certain exceptions such as unlawful discrimination or retaliation. Option A is incorrect because it suggests guaranteed job security, which is not the case with employment at will. Option C is incorrect because employment at will works both ways in that neither the employer nor employee is required to give notice upon separation. Option D is incorrect because employment at will does not require employers to provide job security.

61. C. Termination based on poor performance or misconduct is generally not an exception to the employment-at-will doctrine. However, employers must still adhere to applicable employment laws and may need to follow disciplinary processes and documentation. Options A, B, and D are exceptions to employment at will. Termination based on race or gender discrimination (Option A) is prohibited by federal antidiscrimination laws. Termination in violation of a written employment contract (Option B) breaches the terms of the contract. Termination based on the employee's refusal to commit an illegal act (Option D) is not protected under employment at will and may be considered wrongful termination.

62. B. Highlighting the company's commitment to diversity and inclusion is a highly effective way to promote the employer brand. College and university students often prioritize inclusive workplace environments, making it an attractive aspect of your brand (Option A). While competitive salary packages are important, focusing solely on compensation may not effectively promote the employer brand (Option C). Limiting engagement to recruiting fairs and excluding online and social media platforms can be a missed opportunity. Utilizing various channels, including online and social media, allows you to reach a wider audience and reinforce your employer brand consistently (Option D). While industry awards and recognition can be compelling, they should not be the sole focus when promoting the employer brand. Students are often more interested in aspects such as company culture, career development, and values.

63. C. The primary purpose of using assessment centers in the hiring process is to evaluate candidates' job-related skills, competencies, and behaviors through various assessment methods such as simulations, exercises, and interviews. This helps employers gain insights into how candidates are likely to perform in specific roles and make informed hiring decisions. Options A, B, and D are incorrect because assessment centers are not primarily used for rapid hiring decisions, on-the-job training, or conducting reference checks; their focus is on assessing candidate capabilities and suitability for a particular role.

64. A. HR professionals should consider evaluating counteroffers made by candidates and discussing them openly. It's important to understand the candidate's motivations and whether any adjustments to the offer are reasonable and feasible. This approach allows for a collaborative negotiation process and can lead to mutually beneficial agreements. Options B, C, and D are incorrect because they do not promote effective negotiation and may result in missed opportunities or a breakdown in communication with the candidate.

65. A. The Cultural Orientations Indicator (COI) is designed to enhance cross-cultural communication and collaboration by helping individuals and teams understand their cultural preferences and potential areas of cultural friction. It aids in improving interactions and teamwork in diverse environments (Option B). The Cross-Cultural Adaptability Inventory is a separate assessment tool focused on assessing individual adaptability to new cultural environments (Option C). The Self-Assessment for Global Endeavors would be a better tool to use to help individuals identify personal strengths and weaknesses in a global context (Option D). While the COI assesses cultural orientations at an individual level, it is not primarily designed to evaluate cultural dimensions within a team.

66. A. Sending a polite rejection email that expresses appreciation for their interest and keeps the door open for future opportunities is a realistic and considerate approach. It maintains a positive candidate experience and leaves the possibility for them to apply for other roles (Option B). Providing detailed feedback is valuable but may not always be feasible or appropriate for every candidate, especially if there were many applicants (Option C). Informing

candidates about the selected candidate and offering consideration for other open positions is a reasonable approach, but it may not always be possible, especially if there are no immediate openings (Option D). An auto-reply rejection email can leave rejected candidates with a bad impression of the company, with the lack of personal attention potentially keeping them from applying to other roles they may be better suited for.

67. B. On the first day of onboarding, the most important aspect is to help the new employee feel welcomed and familiarize them with their work environment and colleagues. This fosters a sense of belonging and sets a positive tone for their integration into the company. Assigning coding assignments (Option A) should be done after the new employee has received basic orientation. Reviewing financial statements (Option C) is typically not relevant on the first day. Giving access to company systems (Option D) should follow proper security protocols and training as opposed to automatically on the first day.

68. B. One of the advantages of employee acculturation programs is that they can enhance employee engagement and retention. When employees feel supported and integrated into the organizational culture, they are more likely to stay with the company. Employee acculturation programs aim to reduce employee turnover by addressing cultural differences (Option A), but they don't increase turnover. While they may simplify cross-cultural communication (Option C), they don't eliminate all challenges. Employee acculturation programs are part of, but not a replacement for, diversity and inclusion initiatives (Option D).

69. C. In this scenario, conducting interviews with employees and supervisors is a potential method to gather information for the job analysis process. These interviews can provide insights into job duties, responsibilities, and required skills (Option A). Conducting employee satisfaction surveys focuses on employee attitudes rather than job analysis. Observing employees during lunch breaks (Option B) is not a relevant method for gathering job-related information (Option D). Reviewing competitors' marketing strategies is unrelated to the job analysis process.

70. B. Reassessing workforce skills and competencies is a potential talent planning need during downsizing, especially when the organization needs to adapt to changing economic conditions. Understanding the skills needed to meet evolving demands is crucial. Providing extensive training for all remaining employees (Option A) may not be necessary for all roles, increasing employee compensation (Option C) might not be feasible during financial challenges, and expanding the benefits package (Option D) may not align with cost-cutting objectives.

Chapter 5: Learning and Development

1. C. A comprehensive learning and development program aims to enhance the skills and competencies of existing employees, helping to retain them and fill critical positions with skilled internal candidates. It provides a holistic approach to solving both the turnover and skills gap issues. Option A does not directly address the high employee turnover rate or provide a solution to retaining existing employees. Option B does not focus on retaining existing employees or developing their skills and competencies and may not be a long-term solution to the problem. Option D does not address the problem of a lack of skilled employees in critical positions, and it can even exacerbate the turnover issue by causing insecurity among employees.

2. C. Self-directed learning is a fundamental principle of adult learning. Adults are more motivated to learn when they have control over their learning process and can set their own goals and pace (Option A). Passive learning is a teaching method where students receive information without actively engaging in the learning process, often leading to limited comprehension and retention (Option B). A teacher-centered approach is an instructional method where the teacher takes the central role in delivering information with less emphasis on student participation and autonomy, which are characteristics of adult learning (Option D). Rote memorization is the process of learning information through repetition and memorizing without necessarily understanding the underlying concepts.

3. B. Relevancy is crucial in adult learning because when adults perceive the content as relevant to their needs and goals, they are more engaged and motivated to learn. Options A, C, and D are not elements of relevancy in adult learning principles.

4. D. The Everywhere model of adult learning is where employees are encouraged to learn from various sources and experiences, both formal and informal, in their everyday work environment (Option A). Simulation involves creating artificial environments or scenarios to mimic real-life situations for learning (Option B). Vestibule training is a type of instructional method that simulates a real work environment by creating a controlled, enclosed space where employees can practice and learn specific job tasks or procedures. The Socratic method (Option C) is a teaching and questioning technique named after the ancient Greek philosopher Socrates, characterized by a series of open-ended questions aimed at stimulating critical thinking and inquiry.

5. B. Communication is the correct choice because it is essential for conveying ideas, understanding cultural nuances, and ensuring that the learning programs are clear and well-received by employees across different cultures (Option A). Conflict resolution is important, but in this scenario, the primary challenge requires effective communication to bridge cultural differences and convey the program's value (Option C). While an understanding of business principles is valuable, it is not the central competency needed here (Option D). Without clear and effective communication, it would be challenging to create learning programs that are necessary to underpin an organization's DEI efforts.

6. B. Digital transformation and innovation often require employees to acquire new technical skills and adapt to technological changes (Option A). Leadership development programs may not be the top priority when the organization is focusing on digital transformation and innovation (Option C). Diversity and inclusion initiatives are not the primary focus when the organization is undergoing a shift toward digital transformation and innovation (Option D). Employee engagement surveys do not directly align with the immediate need to prepare the workforce for digital transformation and innovation.

7. A. HR needs to ensure that employees are equipped with the skills and awareness necessary to work effectively in diverse cultural settings when expanding globally (Option B). Corporate social responsibility (CSR) initiatives are secondary to ensuring a culturally aware workforce to be prepared for global expansion (Option C). Digital learning platforms may not be the immediate priority until the content has been identified and teams have been dispersed (Option D). Social media advertising campaigns are unrelated to aligning learning and development strategies with global expansion.

8. A. Providing specialized anti-corruption training equips employees with knowledge and skills to identify, prevent, and report corrupt practices, making it an effective way to combat corruption on global assignments (Option B). Generalized ethics training would not be more effective than specialized training focused on corruption prevention (Option C). Team-building workshops do not directly address corruption concerns on global assignments (Option D). Implementing strict travel expense policies is relevant for financial accountability but not sufficient to combat corruption in all aspects of global assignments.

9. D. Focus groups may not be as effective as other techniques in this scenario because they typically involve group discussions and may not yield detailed or individualized insights into training needs for the customer service team (Option A). Surveys can be an effective needs analysis technique as they allow the collection of quantitative data from a large number of employees to identify common training needs and preferences (Option B). Observations involve directly observing employees' behavior and interactions, making it a valuable technique for understanding their performance and training needs (Option C). Interviews provide an opportunity for in-depth discussions with employees to gather qualitative insights into their training needs, preferences, and challenges.

10. C. Kinesthetic learners are individuals who learn by physically engaging with their environment, often through hands-on activities and movement. Kinesthetic learners might excel in a training program that includes interactive simulations or practical exercises (Option A). Auditory learners prefer to learn through listening and verbal communication (Option B). Visual learners learn best through visual aids like images, charts, or diagrams (Option D). "Inquisitive" is not a recognized primary learning style.

11. A. The Analysis phase of the ADDIE model is focused on gathering information, identifying learning objectives, understanding the target audience, and determining assessment criteria. It is the initial phase where the foundation for the training program is established (Option B). In the Design stage of the ADDIE model, instructional designers create a detailed plan for the learning program (Option C). During the Development stage, the actual learning materials and course content are created based on the design specifications developed in the previous stage (Option D). In the Evaluation stage, the effectiveness of the learning program is assessed through various means, including formative evaluation for ongoing improvement and summative evaluation to measure the program's overall impact and achievement of learning objectives.

12. C. Synthesis is the highest order in Bloom's taxonomy, where learners create new ideas, concepts, or products by combining existing knowledge and elements (Option A). Application, represented in the middle of Bloom's taxonomy, involves using knowledge and understanding to solve problems or complete tasks (Option B). Analysis, also a higher-order cognitive skill, entails breaking down complex information into components to examine patterns and relationships (Option D). Description, sometimes referred to as "knowledge," is the lowest level and involves recalling or stating facts without any application, analysis, or synthesis of information.

13. C. Participants are applying their knowledge and understanding of leadership styles to assess and address real-life workplace scenarios (Option A). Knowledge would involve simply recalling facts or information about leadership styles without applying them to real workplace scenarios, which is not the primary focus of this task (Option B). Comprehension would involve understanding the concepts and information about leadership styles, but the task goes beyond comprehension by requiring participants to apply that understanding to workplace situations (Option D). Evaluation would involve making judgments and drawing conclusions about the effectiveness of leadership styles in specific workplace situations, which goes beyond the primary task of applying knowledge in this scenario.

14. D. Merrill's First Principles of Instruction emphasize problem-solving, activation of prior experience, demonstration, and application. This model aligns well with the objective of designing a course where learners progressively build their programming skills (Option A). The constructivist model emphasizes active learning and knowledge construction by learners; it may not provide as structured a progression as Merrill's model for a beginners' programming course (Option B). The Technological Pedagogical Content Knowledge (TPACK) framework focuses on the integration of technology, pedagogy (child learning principles, versus andragogy, adult learning principles), and content knowledge by educators (Option C). Gagne's model is a systematic approach to instructional design, but it may not inherently address the specific goal of structuring a course for progressive skill building.

15. A. The primary purpose of creating performance-focused objectives in action mapping is to define the specific, measurable outcomes that learners are expected to achieve by the end of the training or learning experience (Option B). Identifying potential learning activities is not the primary purpose of performance-focused objectives (Option C). Listing the topics to be covered does not capture the specific performance outcomes learners are expected to achieve (Option D). Assessing learners' prior knowledge is a separate step in the instructional design process.

16. C. Kirkpatrick's four-level evaluation model consists of the following levels: Reaction, Learning, Behavior, and Results. Implementation is not one of the standard levels in this model. The levels in the model are designed to assess the effectiveness of training programs at various stages, from learner reactions to the ultimate impact on organizational results.

17. D. Level 4 evaluation in Kirkpatrick's model, Results, assesses the ultimate impact of training on organizational goals and outcomes. In this scenario, the company is interested in evaluating the program's effectiveness in improving customer satisfaction, which is an organizational result (Option A). Level 1 evaluates learner reactions and feedback, such as satisfaction with the training experience (Option B). Level 2 assesses what participants have learned during the training (Option C). Level 3 evaluates changes in behavior or performance following training.

18. D. While gamification is a growing area for learning and development delivery, it is still fairly uncommon as a standard module. Typical modules that are included in a robust learning management system include modules to track training, performance appraisals, and conduct surveys, such as those used to measure employee engagement (Options A, B, and C).

19. A. Conducting a thorough needs assessment is crucial during the implementation of an integrated LMS as it helps identify the specific training and development needs of the organization, aligning the LMS with those needs. Option B is important, but understanding the organization's learning needs should precede communication planning. Option C should follow the needs assessment phase, as the choice of vendor should align with the identified needs. Option D should come after conducting a needs assessment to ensure that the timeline aligns with the identified requirements.

20. B. Analytical aptitude is crucial for HR to assess the R&D team's current capabilities and needs, and consultation skills are essential for collaborating with the R&D team to tailor learning activities to their specific requirements. Option A is not as relevant as the correct answer. Regarding Option C, analytical aptitude and consultation take precedence over communication and leadership because they directly address the task of designing effective learning and development activities. Creative solutions mentioned in Option D may be part of the training design, but only after the needs assessment has been analyzed and the management team consulted to understand the training targets.

21. A. Contingency theory emphasizes that organizational design and structure should be contingent upon and adapted to the specific external environment in which an organization operates. It acknowledges that there is no one-size-fits-all approach and that the design should vary based on the circumstances (Option A). Human relations theory emphasizes the importance of social interactions and employee satisfaction in enhancing productivity and organizational performance (Option B). Scientific management theory focuses on optimizing efficiency and productivity by scientifically analyzing and standardizing work processes (Option C). Classical organizational theory explores principles of organizational structure and management, including concepts like hierarchy, specialization, and formalized processes.

22. B. A matrix structure encourages cross-functional collaboration by having employees report to both functional managers and project managers, facilitating the sharing of diverse knowledge and expertise, which can enhance organizational learning. Option A is incorrect because a hierarchical structure with strict top-down control often stifles innovation and may discourage employees from freely sharing knowledge due to fear of repercussions. Option C is incorrect because a flat organizational structure typically promotes communication and knowledge transfer among employees, rather than hindering it. Option D is incorrect because a bureaucratic organization with rigid rules and procedures tends to inhibit experimentation and adaptability, making it less conducive to organizational learning.

23. C. By revising the organizational structure, the company can address the communication gaps and decreased productivity that may be driving the lack of innovation and overall resistance to change caused by the current design. Viable solutions may include implementing structural interventions that decrease the layers of management to improve communication or reworking jobs to streamline efficiencies. Option A is incorrect because employee recognition programs may not directly solve the problem of communication gaps and decreased productivity resulting from an ineffective organizational structure. Workshops, outlined in Option B, do not necessarily address the overall communication challenges described. Option D, implementing new software tools such as Slack or Teams, can be helpful for improving communication but does not necessarily address the productivity issue.

24. C. Leadership development is integral to the success of organizational design interventions because it equips leaders with the skills and knowledge needed to implement and navigate the changes effectively, inspire their teams, and align their actions with the new organizational structure and goals. Option A is incorrect because leadership development plays a crucial role in organizational design interventions by enabling leaders to effectively lead and manage the changes. Option B is incorrect because leadership development should be closely aligned with organizational design efforts to ensure that leaders have the necessary skills to lead during the transformation. Option D is incorrect because leadership development should not be limited to middle-level managers; it should encompass leaders at all levels of the organization to ensure a cohesive and effective implementation of the new design.

25. B. Job redesign interventions aim to improve job satisfaction and engagement by modifying job roles to make them more meaningful, challenging, and aligned with employee skills and interests. Option A is incorrect as they do not necessarily aim to decrease employee workload although some responsibilities may shift to increase efficiencies. In Option C, job redesign interventions are primarily focused on restructuring job roles and responsibilities, not on eliminating performance appraisals. Option D is incorrect as job redesign interventions do not always aim to reduce the number of job positions within an organization.

26. C. Learning portals serve as a centralized platform where employees can engage in self-paced learning, access a wide range of learning resources (such as courses, videos, and documents), and track their progress. This promotes flexibility and convenience in the learning process. Option A is incorrect as learning portals are typically used for online and self-paced learning rather than in-person training sessions. Option B is incorrect as learning portals can offer a range of learning materials and resources that cater to different learning styles and individual needs, allowing for more personalized learning experiences. Option D is incorrect as learning portals are versatile and can be used for various types of training and development activities, not just compliance training.

27. A. The healthcare facility is addressing delays in patient check-in and registration by analyzing the current process, identifying bottlenecks, and proposing changes. The implementation of a digital check-in system is part of the process improvement to reduce wait times and enhance the patient experience. Option B is incorrect as while the intervention includes the implementation of a digital check-in system, the primary focus is on improving the check-in process itself rather than undergoing a full technological transformation of the entire organization. Option C is incorrect as the question does not describe a significant restructuring of the organizational hierarchy or reporting relationships. In Option D, the primary goal is to improve the patient check-in process through process redesign and the implementation of a digital system, not train the team.

28. C. Employee development plays a crucial role in supporting succession plans by identifying and nurturing individuals within the organization who have the potential to assume leadership roles in the future. It involves providing them with the necessary training, mentoring, and experience to prepare them for these higher-level positions. Option A focuses on financial incentives, Option B focuses on new hires (not succession planning for existing employees), and Option D suggests outsourcing leadership positions, which is not in line with internal succession planning efforts.

29. C. In change management training, the fundamental goal is to build buy-in and support among employees and stakeholders for the proposed changes. In Option A, change management is not solely about convincing employees that a change is "good" (some changes aren't from the employee perspective) but rather about helping them understand and accept the rationale behind the change and how it can benefit both the organization and individuals. Option B suggests minimizing communication (which is counterproductive). Option D implies secrecy rather than transparency, which is not recommended in change management.

30. C. The overwhelming amounts of unstructured information and data such as research papers, emails, and patient data suggests that knowledge management is the primary challenge that needs to be tackled. To harness this wealth of knowledge effectively, the organization must ensure that the data can be organized, categorized, and made accessible to employees who need it. In Option A, the core issue is the unstructured nature of the existing information and

data, not the tools themselves. Option B can be addressed once the information is better organized and accessible. Option D is incorrect as resistance from top leadership to implement knowledge management is not the primary challenge mentioned in the scenario.

31. B. Predictive analytics can analyze historical data to identify employees who are likely to excel in future roles or who may need additional support. HR professionals can use this information to make strategic decisions about promotions, leadership development, and talent management. Option A is incorrect because predictive analytics focus on forecasting future performance based on historical data rather than justifying past promotions. Option C is incorrect because relying solely on subjective judgments can introduce bias and inaccuracies into the evaluation process. Option D focuses on automation, which is a benefit of AI but does not directly address the core aspect of using predictive analytics to enhance employee performance management.

32. D. The primary goal of a 360-degree feedback program is to gather feedback from a variety of sources, including supervisors, peers, subordinates, and sometimes even customers or clients, to provide a comprehensive and well-rounded assessment of an individual's performance. Option A is incorrect as the primary goal of a 360-degree feedback program is not limited to assessing team dynamics, nor is it limited to direct supervisors as suggested in Option B. A 360-degree feedback program aims to assess a wide range of competencies and behaviors, not just technical skills and knowledge, so Option C is not the best answer.

33. A. Any organizational intervention will require varying degrees of change management techniques. When the change is major, as suggested in the question, multiple focus groups are the most effective method to gather feedback that is meaningful enough to inform decisions. Option C is limited in its ability to identify the scope of any concerns. The effectiveness of Option B can vary based on the facilitation and participation, and feedback programs (Option D) are used for performance evaluations, not to gather feedback on organizational change interventions.

34. B. For a complex evaluation of the impact of an executive leadership development program on organizational performance and strategic alignment, a comprehensive return on investment (ROI) analysis is most appropriate. This should consider both qualitative and quantitative metrics to provide a holistic view of the program's effectiveness, which often will include Option C. Options A and D may provide limited insights and do not address the full scope of the assessment.

35. B. To assess the effectiveness of the technical training program objectively and measure skill improvement, administering unannounced skill assessments and coding challenges provides the most data-driven results. This method directly tests the acquired skills. Options A, C, and D rely on subjective assessments and external factors, which may not provide an accurate measure of skill enhancement.

36. C. In this scenario, Billboard Basics is dealing with a decrease in employee productivity, which suggests that the issue may be related to specific employees or groups. A person analysis is the appropriate type of needs assessment to identify individual or group-level training needs. It focuses on evaluating the knowledge, skills, and performance of employees to determine whether training is required. Option A looks at broader organizational goals and objectives. Option B is used to break down specific job tasks and identify the skills and knowledge required for those tasks and is most useful when used in conjunction with the person analysis. Option D examines external factors that could impact an organization, such as industry trends or market conditions.

37. D. Longevity bias, also known as seniority bias, is the tendency to favor employees with longer tenure because they have been with the company for a longer time, often giving the perception that they have more value over lesser-tenured colleagues. Option A, similar-to-me bias, occurs when a manager gives higher ratings to employees who share similar characteristics or backgrounds with them. Option B, recency bias, is the tendency to give more weight to recent performance or events when evaluating an employee's performance. Option C, leniency bias, occurs when a manager consistently rates employees more favorably or provides higher ratings than they deserve, regardless of their actual performance.

38. B. Brain drain refers to the emigration of highly skilled and educated individuals from one country or organization to another, leading to a loss of valuable talent and expertise in the origin country or organization. Creating mentorship programs allows experienced employees to pass on their knowledge and expertise to younger talent. This helps retain critical knowledge within the organization and ensures a smoother transition when older employees eventually retire. Option A does not address the need to transfer knowledge and skills to the younger workforce and falls under the functional umbrella of Total Rewards, not L&D. Option C may lead to a further loss of talent and exacerbate the brain drain problem. Option D does not address the root causes of brain drain and may negatively impact the organization's reputation and employee morale.

39. A. In the ADDIE model (Analysis, Design, Development, Implementation, and Evaluation), the first phase is analysis. Taylor should begin with the analysis phase to assess the training needs, identify objectives, and understand the learners' requirements. This phase sets the foundation for designing an effective training program. Option B comes after the analysis phase and involves creating the actual training content. Options C and D are subsequent phases in the ADDIE model and should follow the analysis and design phases.

40. B. Artificial intelligence in a learning management system can analyze learner data, including past performance, preferences, and learning styles, to customize training content and delivery methods. This personalization can lead to more effective and engaging training experiences for individual learners (Option A). Human trainers play a crucial role in providing guidance and support that AI cannot replicate (Option C). AI also enhances the learning experience, recommends content, and supports learners (Option D). AI in LMS offers a wide range of capabilities beyond gamification.

41. C. A dual career ladder system allows employees to advance their careers within the organization without transitioning into people management roles. This approach recognizes and supports individuals who excel in their specialized roles and want to continue growing in their areas of expertise. Option A is incorrect as forcing Lewis into a management position when he has no interest in managing people may lead to job dissatisfaction and reduced performance. The lateral moves to different departments or roles offered in option B may not guarantee career progression and could lead to a lack of focus (Option D). In Option D, the team member may not want to utilize management skills in their career path, so training could add to dissatisfaction and reduced performance.

42. C. Encouraging active listening and asking open-ended questions fosters an environment where participants are more likely to engage in open discussions, share their thoughts, and generate new ideas. Open-ended questions invite diverse perspectives and encourage critical

thinking, leading to a more collaborative and interactive knowledge-sharing session. In Option A, strict time limits for each speaker can stifle creativity and impede open dialogue. Option B is incorrect as providing all the answers in advance can limit the opportunity for participants to engage in discussions, share their perspectives, and generate new ideas. Avoiding discussions as offered in Option D limits the opportunity for participants to actively engage with the content, ask questions, and exchange ideas.

43. C. Offering workshops and coaching sessions that help employees develop the necessary skills and mindset to adapt to the change is an effective strategy. These programs address both the technical and human elements of resistance, helping employees feel more confident and capable of embracing change. Option A can exacerbate resistance to change as employees may feel unsupported and ill-equipped to adapt to the new processes. Regarding Option B, employees not only need technical skills but also support in developing the right mindset and emotional readiness to embrace the change fully. Option D can damage employee morale and engagement and actually increase the resistance to the change initiative.

44. C. Adult learners often value autonomy and self-directed learning. Allowing them to set their own learning goals aligns with adult learning principles and helps motivate and engage learners. Option A may overwhelm learners. Option B may be seen as too controlling. Option D may not respect adult learners' diverse schedules and priorities.

45. B. Micro-learning involves short, focused, and easily digestible learning modules that are ideal for individuals with limited time. Cian can access these modules whenever he has a few minutes to spare, making it a practical choice for her busy work life. Option A often requires a significant time commitment and may not be the best choice for someone like Cian, who has limited time because of his busy schedule. Option C also typically demands a substantial time commitment and may not be feasible for Cian's schedule. Annual conferences (Option D) can be beneficial for networking and exposure to industry trends but are not typically designed for in-depth skill development.

46. D. Personality assessments can help identify an individual's strengths, weaknesses, and preferences, which can be valuable for tailoring career development plans and opportunities. Using personality assessments for career development ensures that employees like Jesse receive the support and resources they need to grow within the organization. In Option A, certain personality assessments can be used during the hiring process to predict how well a candidate may fit; however, Jesse has already been hired. Option B doesn't directly address the specific career development needs of an individual employee. Option C is incorrect as personality assessments are not the primary tool used for assessing readiness for promotion.

47. B. Mentoring and coaching are effective career development techniques for newcomers like Celine. They involve a more experienced colleague or mentor providing guidance, feedback, and support to help the individual develop their skills and advance in their career. Option A, sabbatical leave, typically involves extended time off from work, which may not align with Celine's goal of advancing her career immediately after completing her bachelor's degree. Option C may be more appropriate after Celine has gained more practical experience. Option D, a performance improvement plan (PIP), is typically implemented when an employee's performance is below expectations and needs improvement.

48. D. The overarching objective of an individual development plan (IDP) is to furnish a comprehensive, structured framework for an employee's skill enhancement and career progression. An IDP empowers employees to set specific goals, identify areas where they need to acquire or enhance skills, and plan the steps necessary to achieve these goals, thus facilitating their personal and professional growth. Option A may be a component of an IDP but is not its primary objective, which is focused on development. Option B is also not the primary purpose of an IDP. Option C is more about development and skill enhancement than real-time performance evaluation.

49. C. Apprenticeships are distinguished by their combination of practical work experience with structured training and mentorship. Apprentices work alongside experienced professionals while receiving formal training and mentorship, allowing them to learn and develop their skills on the job. Option A is not true because apprenticeships are primarily focused on practical work experience. Apprenticeships are often designed to accommodate individuals with varying levels of experience, including those with little to no prior industry exposure, thus making Option B incorrect. Option D is not true as the duration of apprenticeships can vary widely depending on the industry and the specific program, and they are not necessarily shorter than other training programs.

50. B. The 70/20/10 model of adult learning primarily emphasizes that 70% of learning occurs through on-the-job experiences and challenges such as hands-on, practical experiences in their work environment, 20% comes from exposure through social media or online platforms, and just 10% occurs through formal learning activities such as classroom training. Options A, C, and D are incorrect.

51. D. Advising on HR solutions is the most relevant competency needed to solve the problem. It involves providing recommendations and solutions related to learning and development programs. In this scenario, the HR department needs to analyze the current programs, identify their shortcomings, and provide effective solutions to improve employee learning and development outcomes. Option A may not directly address the learning and development challenges. The primary issue is related to learning and development effectiveness rather than large-scale organizational change, making Option B incorrect. In Option C, service excellence focuses on providing high-quality HR services to employees and does not directly address the learning and development challenges.

52. D. HR professionals need a clear vision for how to revamp and improve the training programs to align them with organizational goals and meet employee development needs effectively. Developing a vision for the future of learning and development is essential to drive the necessary changes and improvements. Option A is a significant organizational change that may or may not be necessary to improve learning and development processes. Option B does not directly address the specific learning and development challenges faced by the HR department. Per Option C, while influence may play a role in implementing changes, the critical factor is having a clear vision for how to improve the learning and development process.

53. B. Hierarchical decision-making is not aligned with the concept of a learning organization. Learning organizations typically encourage a more decentralized and participative decision-making approach that involves employees at various levels in decision-making processes (Option A). Systems thinking involves understanding and addressing the complex interconnections within an organization and its environment (Option C). Personal mastery

emphasizes the importance of individual and collective learning and growth within the organization (Option D). Shared vision is a core component where all members of the organization align around a common vision and work together to achieve it.

54. A. Proficiency in the host country's language is the most relevant characteristic of cultural competency when preparing an expatriate for a global assignment. Being able to communicate effectively with local colleagues, clients, and partners is crucial for building relationships and understanding the local culture. Option B is more related to the employee's job responsibilities and may not directly address cultural competency. Option C does not specifically address cultural competency. Option D is not the primary characteristic of cultural competency needed for adapting to a new cultural environment.

55. A. The employer in this scenario is using the "push" method of employee training, where training content is pushed onto employees through mandatory, scheduled, and instructor-led sessions. This approach is characterized by the organization's control over the training content and the timing of the sessions. The "pull" method (Option B), the "autonomous" method (Option C), and the "self-paced" method (Option D) are incorrect because they do not accurately describe the training approach in the given scenario. In the "push" method, employees do not have the autonomy to choose when and what to study, as it is determined by the employer.

56. C. By designing training materials that are engaging and interactive, employees are more likely to retain the material as it captures their attention and encourages active participation. Option A is incorrect as performance management does not directly address the issue of training retention. Option B is incorrect as succession planning primarily deals with identifying and developing future leaders within the organization, not instructional design. Option D is not directly related to the problem of low retention of training materials.

57. B. Surveying employees to gather feedback on the training content and delivery is the most appropriate method for measuring the impact of training activities. It allows for assessing the relevance, effectiveness, and satisfaction of employees with the training. Feedback can provide insights into whether the training is meeting its objectives and where improvements may be needed. Option A does not assess the quality or effectiveness of the training. Option C does not provide insights into the impact or effectiveness of the training on employees' skills or performance. Option D does not provide a comprehensive view of the training's effectiveness.

58. C. Implementing regular feedback and assessment mechanisms to track progress is a key best practice. It allows for continuous improvement and ensures that coaching and mentoring relationships are achieving their intended goals and objectives. Option A can lead to inconsistency and may not provide a clear framework for employee development. In Option B, effective pairings should consider the skills, experiences, and goals of both parties to ensure a productive partnership. And in Option D, effective coaching and mentoring programs should address both technical and soft skills to support holistic employee development.

59. C. Offering workshops on design thinking and brainstorming techniques is the most appropriate L&D technique for encouraging creativity and innovation. These workshops can equip employees with the skills and mindset to generate innovative ideas, solve problems creatively, and approach challenges from different perspectives. Option A is not the most suitable technique for encouraging creativity and innovation in the workplace. Option B may not directly foster creativity and innovation within the organization. Option D does not directly contribute to fostering creativity and innovation in the workplace.

60. A. Implementing a succession planning program is the most likely approach to contribute to employee retention. It identifies and develops internal talent, giving employees clear career growth paths and opportunities to take on critical roles in the organization, which can enhance their commitment and motivation to stay (Option B). Replacement planning is primarily geared toward quickly filling key roles but does not provide internal employees with long-term development paths. Options C and D are both focused on skill development without a clear development path within the organization to maximize alignment with organizational needs.

Chapter 6: Total Rewards

1. B. Job evaluation is the process of assigning a monetary value or price to a job based on its relative worth within the organization. It helps employers determine the appropriate compensation for each job. Job analysis, on the other hand, involves the detailed examination of a job's tasks, responsibilities, and requirements. It is primarily concerned with designing or defining the content and structure of a job.

2. C. Gathering input on individual performance and goalsetting preferences directly relates to aligning the Total Rewards strategy with business results. Understanding how employees prefer to be recognized and rewarded based on their performance and goals allows HR to tailor the rewards system to motivate and engage employees in achieving business objectives. Employee tenure and job titles (Option A) are more relevant to HR management practices than rewards strategy. Office location and workspace design (Option B) are not typically considered within the scope of Total Rewards strategy although remote work can be a factor. Hobbies and interest outside of work (Option D) are not directly tied to aligning rewards with business results.

3. A. A strict, inflexible performance-based pay structure can lead to decreased employee retention because it may not account for various factors affecting employee performance including complexity of outcomes, key performance indicators, supply chain failures, poor leadership, and employee pay preferences. This directly impacts business results as loss of qualified talent inhibits the achievement of goals and contributes to a low-performance culture. Option B is incorrect as the performance-based pay systems are legal. Compensation administration (Option C) does not address the challenges of alignment with business results but rather is an example how an HR department is structured for service delivery. Option D is often based on strict performance standards, which ideally will limit subjectivity and thus bias into compensation systems.

4. C. A key element of Buffer.com's compensation philosophy is likely to be prioritizing transparency in pay structures and ensuring fairness. `Buffer.com` is known for its ethical behaviors, and this extends to its compensation practices. Option A is not a typical element of a compensation philosophy unless the question had noted operating in a highly competitive environment. There is no information in the question to indicate that performance-based pay (Option B) is a critical structural element to their work. Option D is unlikely to be true in a progressive company that values ethical treatment of their team.

5. C. Employee benefits, such as health insurance, wellness programs, flexible work arrangements, and childcare support, are key components of Total Rewards strategies that aim to enhance employees' work-life balance and overall well-being. These nonmonetary benefits contribute to employee satisfaction and engagement. Options A, B, and D primarily pertain to monetary compensation elements.

6. C. Designing an effective Total Rewards strategy requires aligning rewards with organizational goals and values to ensure that employee efforts contribute to the achievement of business objectives. This alignment helps foster a sense of purpose and engagement among employees. In Option A, gathering and considering employee feedback and preferences is a critical part of effective total reward strategy design, so ignoring the feedback is not wise. Option B is incorrect as customization and differentiation based on employee roles and contributions are often essential to designing an effective strategy. Option D is incorrect because a balanced approach that includes both monetary and nonmonetary incentives is typically more effective in motivating and engaging employees.

7. C. Piece-rate pay compensates employees based on the number of units or pieces they produce. It directly links compensation to output, providing a strong incentive for employees to work efficiently and produce more. Option A is incorrect as commission pay is typically used for sales roles where employees earn a percentage of the sales they generate. Option B is incorrect as hourly wages do not directly tie compensation to performance or output, which may not address the motivation and engagement issues contributing to low productivity. Option D is incorrect as profit sharing involves distributing a portion of the company's profits among employees and does not provide the direct and immediate link between individual performance and compensation that piece-rate pay does.

8. C. Vacation pay, sick pay, and holiday pay are matters of agreement between the employer and the employee (or the employee's representative). Their computation and due dates are not regulated by the FLSA but are determined through agreements and, in some cases, by state laws.

9. C. Commission-based pay rewards employees with a percentage of the revenue or sales they generate. This structure is commonly used in sales and business development roles, where compensation is directly tied to their sales performance. Option A is incorrect as hourly wage pays employees based on hours worked, not sales or revenue generated. Option B is incorrect as salary pay provides a fixed amount of compensation, not a percentage of sales or revenue. Option D is incorrect as piece-rate pay compensates employees based on the number of units or pieces produced, not sales or revenue.

10. B. By understanding the compensation practices in the industry, HR can identify areas where the existing pay structure may need adjustments to address fairness concerns and align with market rates. Option A is incorrect as a one-size-fits-all pay structure is unlikely to address fairness concerns or align compensation with industry standards. Option C is incorrect as it may not necessarily address concerns about fairness or performance-based rewards nor is it practical from a business perspective. Option D is incorrect as eliminating performance-based incentives may demotivate employees who rely on such rewards to recognize their efforts.

11. A. HR is conducting a thorough analysis of job content, focusing on the specific duties, responsibilities, qualifications, and skills required for each position. This method aims to assess jobs based on their content rather than ranking them or comparing them to market benchmarks. Option B is incorrect as job ranking involves ordering jobs based on their perceived value or importance within the organization. It doesn't involve a detailed analysis of job content as in the scenario described. Instead, it simplifies jobs into a hierarchy based on overall significance. Option C is incorrect as point factor job evaluation is a method that assigns numerical values (points) to various factors, such as skills, responsibility, and working conditions, to determine a job's relative worth. Option D is incorrect as market-based job evaluation involves comparing jobs to external market data, such as industry salary surveys, to determine their value based on prevailing market rates.

12. B. When determining pay increases, employee performance is often a key factor, ensuring that high-performing individuals are rewarded. Market conditions help organizations stay competitive with industry pay standards, and cost of living adjustments address inflation and maintain the real value of earnings. Option A is incorrect as seniority and years of service present a limited approach that does not take into account other important factors such as performance or external economic conditions. Option C is incorrect as pay decisions are typically based on more specific and measurable criteria, such as data on the company's financial performance, employee contributions, and external market salary benchmarks. Option D does not consider factors noncompany factors related to pay increases, including individual company performance and external market conditions.

13. A. A key characteristic of an open leave policy is that employees have unlimited paid time off with no restrictions. This policy encourages flexibility and trust within the workplace, allowing employees to manage their own time off without rigid limitations. Options B, C, and D are not typical factors associated with open leave policies.

14. C. One of the common challenges of open leave policies is the complexity they can introduce into managing employee schedules and ensuring adequate staffing levels. With employees taking time off as needed, it can be challenging for employers to maintain smooth operations and meet workload demands. Option A is a potential benefit of open leave policies. When managed effectively, open leave policies can contribute to employee well-being and, subsequently, productivity (Option B). While communication (Option D) may be important for implementing and managing such policies, it is not typically considered a significant challenge in itself.

15. A. The HR department might consider offering a severance package to provide financial assistance and support to the laid-off employees during their transition. Severance packages typically include a financial payout, continuation of benefits, and other support to help departing employees. Options B and C are impractical in the face of the economic challenges being addressed as they may increase costs in the short and long term. Option D is incorrect as severance packages are a standard way to provide support to laid-off employees, manage risks, and potentially leave room for re-recruiting members when the economy recovers.

16. C. Complying with minimum wage laws and accurately tracking overtime is a critical special consideration for employers of domestic workers, as it ensures compliance with labor laws and avoids wage and hour violations. Option A is incorrect as it is not a typical consideration

for domestic workers who by definition are not working for large corporations. Option B is incorrect as it should not be a substitute for complying with minimum wage and overtime laws. Option D is incorrect as hourly wages provide a more consistent and fair approach to compensation, making them more legally defensible should the need arise.

17. C. When a company chooses to "match" the labor market in terms of compensation strategy, it means they are aligning their wages with what is prevalent in the industry. This ensures that their compensation packages are competitive and attractive enough to retain and attract talent. Option A is incorrect because it refers to compliance with pay equity and other non-discriminatory practices. Option B is incorrect as "comparable worth" refers to the principle of evaluating and compensating jobs based on the similarities in knowledge skills and abilities, not the external market. Option D is incorrect because adjusting salary ranges based on geographic location is a common practice to account for differences in cost of living, so strictly adhering to consistent ranges regardless of location may not effectively match the labor market in terms of compensation strategy.

18. B. Comparable worth laws primarily aim to address discrimination based on gender in compensation decisions. These laws seek to rectify wage disparities that may exist between predominantly female and predominantly male job categories, even if the jobs do not have identical titles or descriptions.

19. D. Implementing and maintaining the point factor method can involve costs associated with developing the evaluation system, training evaluators, and ongoing maintenance. Therefore, it is not considered a cost-effective or inexpensive method of job evaluation. Option A is incorrect because the point-factor method ensures a structured and unbiased evaluation of job roles based on predetermined criteria. Option B is also an advantage as the point factor method enables organizations to compare various job roles and determine their relative worth, aiding in compensation decisions. In Option C, by objectively assessing job values, organizations can design compensation structures that are fair and competitive in the job market.

20. C. Pay compression occurs when there is minimal difference in compensation between employees with different levels of experience, skills, or seniority. This can lead to morale issues and challenges in retaining experienced talent. Option A is incorrect as wage stagnation refers to a situation where the average or real wages of workers remain relatively flat or show minimal growth. Option B is incorrect because pay equity is the principle of ensuring that individuals are paid fairly and equally for performing jobs of equal value, regardless of their gender, race, or other non-job-related factors. Option D is incorrect as wage discrimination is the unfair or differential treatment of individuals in terms of compensation based on protected-class characteristics such as gender, race, and age, rather than their qualifications or job performance.

21. C. HR professionals primarily use their analytical aptitude to gather and analyze compensation data, and they apply their competency in designing HR solutions to recommend changes or adjustments to compensation structures based on survey results. Option A is incorrect because remuneration surveys focus on data analysis and solution design rather than business relationships. Option B is incorrect as these competencies are related to leadership and organizational strategy but are not directly involved in survey data analysis. Option D is incorrect because these competencies are more related to building relationships and fostering collaboration among employees rather than the specific task of analyzing survey data.

22. B. Addressing mental well-being can lead to improved morale, lower absenteeism, and increased engagement among remote workers, ultimately enhancing the organization's Total Rewards package. Option A disregards the widely recognized relationship between addressing mental well-being and its potential influence on employee morale and productivity. Option C makes a broad and inaccurate assumption that remote workers do not experience mental health issues, which is not a valid generalization and can vary widely among individuals. Option D does not account for the complexity of mental health assessment in a workplace setting.

23. C. Total rewards statements provide a clear and comprehensive breakdown of an employee's total compensation package, including base salary, bonuses, benefits, stock options, and other components. This solution directly addresses the issue of confusion and uncertainty regarding compensation and can aid employees in understanding the total value of their compensation when comparing it to other offers. Option A would not address the employee concerns and may lead to decreased job satisfaction. It does not provide clarity about their total compensation. Option B, potentially appreciated by employees, does not solve the issue of long-term compensation transparency. Option D would not provide the transparency needed to address employee concerns about their compensation beyond base salary.

24. B. Conducting a compensation program audit primarily serves to identify areas of potential pay discrimination or pay disparities within an organization. It helps ensure that compensation practices are fair and compliant with legal requirements.

25. C. To calculate the total value of compensation and benefits for employees accurately, it's essential to consider all elements of compensation, including base salary, bonuses, stock options, and the monetary value of all employee benefits. This comprehensive approach ensures that you capture the complete picture of what employees receive as part of their compensation package.

26. A. To calculate the compensation ratio, divide the employee's total annual compensation by the median annual compensation for all employees:

```
Compensation Ratio = Employee's Annual Compensation / Median Annual
Compensation
Compensation Ratio = $75,000 / $60,000 = 1.25
```

The compensation ratio for Employee A is 1.25, indicating that their annual compensation is 1.25 times higher than the median compensation for all employees in the organization. This ratio provides insights into how an employee's pay compares to the median within the organization and does not require employee burden to be factored in.

27. C. Organizations should aim to strike a balance between maintaining global consistency in compensation practices and ensuring local competitiveness. This approach acknowledges that while some consistency is necessary for equity and governance reasons, adapting to local market conditions is crucial for attracting and retaining talent. Option A fails to consider variations in cost of living, labor markets, and economic conditions in different regions, potentially leading to issues with talent attraction and retention. Option B does not account for the need for global consistency and alignment with the organization's overall compensation strategy. Option D is incorrect as acknowledging and addressing regional disparities is essential to designing equitable and competitive global pay structures that consider the economic realities of different countries and regions.

28. A. To calculate the benefits utilization rate, divide the number of employees who have used the benefit by the total number of eligible employees:

```
Benefits Utilization Rate = (Number of Employees Using Benefit) / (Total
Number of Eligible Employees)
Benefits Utilization Rate = 50 / 150 = 0.33
```

The benefits utilization rate for the tuition reimbursement program is 0.33, which means that 33% of eligible employees have used this benefit in the last year. This ratio helps assess how effectively a benefit program is being utilized within the organization.

29. B. An employer can use their compensation philosophy to attract and retain talent effectively by aligning compensation practices with the organization's values and goals. This approach ensures that compensation is not only competitive but also reflective of the company's culture and strategic objectives, making it more appealing to employees who share those values and want to contribute to the organization's mission. Option A may not be sustainable for the organization in the long term. Option C is incorrect as cutting benefits can negatively impact employee morale, job satisfaction, and retention. Option D may not effectively address the diverse needs and preferences of the workforce, potentially leading to talent attraction and retention challenges.

30. B. Leveling salary survey data means making adjustments to the raw survey data to ensure that it aligns with the organization's established pay structure, job grades, or compensation philosophy. This process helps in making the survey data relevant and usable for the organization's specific needs, such as maintaining internal equity.

31. B. When dealing with overtime pay, HR professionals should always adhere to the labor laws and regulations of the country where the employees are located. Overtime regulations vary widely from one country to another, so it is crucial to follow local laws to ensure legal compliance.

32. C. The US- Mexico-Canada agreement (USMCA) expects each member country to have laws and regulations that establish and enforce minimum wage standards within their respective territories. It emphasizes that the agreement does not harmonize or establish uniform minimum wage rates across member countries but rather ensures that each country enforces its own minimum wage laws. This approach promotes compliance with minimum wage standards while allowing each country to determine its specific minimum wage rates according to its domestic laws.

33. B. "Doing business in" guides provide crucial information about labor laws, tax regulations, employment contracts, and other legal and regulatory requirements in the target country. HR professionals can use this information to ensure that pay systems comply with local laws and regulations. Option A is incorrect as these guides do not promote standardized pay rates. Option C is incorrect because HR professionals should use the guides to gain insights into local customs and expectations related to compensation to design pay systems that align with local culture. Option D is incorrect as the usefulness of guides extends beyond just ensuring compliance with minimum wage requirements.

34. B. Tying executive compensation primarily to short-term financial performance metrics can potentially encourage unethical behavior as executives may prioritize achieving short-term results at the expense of long-term sustainability and ethical conduct in pursuit of their bonuses. Options A, C, and D are not drawbacks.

35. C. HR should work with the payroll department to correct the error and ensure that Sydney receives the correct payment on her next paycheck. It's essential to rectify payroll mistakes promptly to maintain employee trust and ensure fair compensation. While Option A acknowledges the error and provides a plan for correction in the next paycheck, it does not prioritize the urgency of resolving the issue. Option B, immediate investigation and resolution, should be the priority before requesting evidence from the employee; evidence may be part of the initial investigation. Option D is not recommended because HR should play a role in facilitating the resolution of paycheck errors to ensure consistency and fairness in addressing such issues.

36. C. The first step in implementing a Total Rewards strategy, according to Robert L. Heneman's approach, is to identify business objectives and goals. This step ensures that the rewards strategy aligns with the overall business strategy and objectives. By understanding the organization's business direction, HR can develop a Total Rewards program that supports and reinforces these goals. Options A, B, and D all come later in the process.

37. B. Zero-based budgeting requires a thorough justification for each compensation expense, considering market data to ensure competitiveness and alignment with the organization's strategic objectives. This approach encourages a more strategic and cost-effective allocation of resources. Option A may not be responsive to changing conditions and could lead to an imbalanced budget. Option C may not account for changing market conditions and may result in an outdated and inefficient budget. Option D lacks the strategic analysis needed to develop an effective compensation budget.

38. B. Providing on-site childcare services is an example of using employee perks as an indirect form of compensation to enhance job satisfaction and employee retention. It supports employees' work-life balance and can be a valuable benefit that contributes to job satisfaction and retention. Options A and C are not considered perks, and Option D, in addition to not being a perk, may negatively impact job satisfaction and retention.

39. D. The charge against Cousin's, alleging pay disparities between Hispanic and non-Hispanic employees for similar job roles and qualifications, is most likely based on Title VII of the Civil Rights Act of 1964. Title VII prohibits employment discrimination based on race, color, religion, sex, or national origin, including compensation discrimination. Option A primarily addresses minimum wage, overtime, and child labor standards. Option B addresses discrimination based on disabilities, and Option C primarily deals with gender-based pay discrimination.

40. C. When managers do not adhere to pay increase policies or guidelines, it can lead to some employees receiving higher pay increases than others, potentially causing their compensation ratio to exceed 1.00. A compensation ratio exceeding 1.00 means that an individual's actual compensation is higher than the reference point or benchmark used for comparison. Option A is not typically a direct factor in causing a compensation ratio to be above the benchmark. A match strategy would indicate that the company pays at or close to the market midpoint, making option B incorrect. Option D is incorrect because broadbanding is a compensation strategy that reduces the number of salary grades or pay levels within an organization to create broader salary bands. This would actually increase the spread between range minimum and maximum, making an out-of-range score less likely.

41. B. To effectively manage multiple generations in the workplace, organizations should consider offering flexible work arrangements and schedules. This approach accommodates the diverse needs and preferences of different age groups, as it allows employees to balance work and personal responsibilities in ways that suit them best. Option A does not account for pay preferences that are present amongst different generations. Option C is not a recommended strategy, as nonmonetary rewards are important for employee engagement, and Option D does not consider the individual choices and circumstances of employees from different generations.

42. B. The director is considering the diverse global context in which the multinational corporation operates, including differences in labor laws, cultural norms, and economic conditions. They are conducting a comprehensive analysis of market salary surveys, internal pay equity considerations, and cost projections. This demonstrates their ability to use data-driven insights to make informed decisions about compensation structures, balancing competitiveness, and cost-effectiveness.

43. B. In a single-rate pay system, employees are paid a fixed rate regardless of the number of hours worked, while time-based pay systems compensate based on hours worked. This statement correctly highlights the primary distinction between these pay systems. In a single-rate system, employees receive a predetermined rate of pay, while time-based systems tie compensation to the number of hours worked.

44. B. A common method used to create wage bands in an organization is benchmarking against industry compensation data. This involves comparing the organization's salary ranges to data from similar companies in the industry to ensure competitiveness and market alignment. Option A is not a recommended method and lacks the rationale of market competitiveness. Option C refers to a method of annual salary increases and is not related to creating wage bands. Option D can lead to inconsistent compensation practices.

45. B. One of the key benefits of using a market-based approach to create wage bands in an organization is that it allows for flexibility in responding to market changes. This approach enables the organization to adjust salary ranges to remain competitive in the external job market. Option A aims to align with external market data, which can vary by job position. Option C is not accurate, as performance reviews are typically separate from wage band creation. Option D is incorrect as salaries are determined by market conditions and internal compensation policies and should not be guaranteed in the absence of an explicit employment contract.

46. A. These are common types of pay increases based on an employee's performance or exceptional contributions. Annual performance bonuses are typically tied to an employee's yearly performance evaluation, while onetime cash awards may be granted for specific achievements or special recognition. Option B is incorrect because they are adjustments to employee salaries to keep pace with inflation and changes in the cost of living. Employee recognition awards are typically onetime acknowledgments of outstanding performance and are not considered standard pay increases. Option C are not standard pay increases but rather forms of additional compensation. Option D is incorrect because neither vacation pay nor benefits are types of pay increases.

47. B. Collectivism as defined by Geert Hofstede's culture model exist in countries such as Japan. These cultures place a strong emphasis on teamwork and mutual support. Team-based incentives encourage employees to work together and align with the cultural values of cooperation and group success. Options A and C are more in alignment with individualistic cultures, and Option D does not best address the nature of collectivism in compensation practices.

48. B. Shift differential pay is an additional compensation provided to employees who work during nonstandard shifts, such as night shifts or weekends. It is meant to compensate employees for the inconvenience and potential health impacts of working at unusual hours. Option A is typically provided to employees in extraordinary situations, such as responding to emergency calls or working during crisis events. Option C is extra compensation provided to employees who work on designated holidays. Option D is a general term for extra compensation provided for various reasons, including overtime, night shifts, and holiday work.

49. B. Voluntary benefits in the workplace are typically optional, and employees often have the choice to participate in these programs. The employees may also contribute to the cost of these benefits, such as through payroll deductions. Voluntary benefits are not mandatory, making Options A and C incorrect. Option D can encompass a wide range of offerings beyond basic health insurance, including supplemental insurance, wellness programs, or financial planning services.

50. C. Promoting employee health through wellness programs and preventive-care initiatives can lead to healthier employees who require fewer medical interventions. This approach can help control long-term healthcare costs while maintaining employee well-being. Option A is not a recommended strategy as it may lead to employees seeking alternative employment with better benefits. Option B can have serious health consequences and is not an ethical or effective strategy to combat rising healthcare costs. Option D may result in employees being unable to afford health insurance. This approach can lead to negative consequences for both employees and the organization.

51. B. The primary purpose of offering housing partnerships as an alternative workplace benefit is to help employees find affordable housing options near the workplace. Housing partnerships may involve collaborations with local housing providers or initiatives to assist employees in securing housing within a reasonable distance from their workplace, thus reducing commuting stress and improving work-life balance. Option A is incorrect as such partnerships typically aim to assist employees in finding suitable housing but do not necessarily provide it for free. Option C is not directly related to housing partnerships. Option D is incorrect because housing partnerships primarily focus on addressing housing-related challenges for employees who choose to work on-site.

52. B. Since the Chinese retirement system may not be applicable to expatriates like Lionel, he should consider continuing to pay into the U.S. Social Security system, which can provide retirement benefits even for expatriates working abroad. This option ensures that he maintains contributions to a retirement plan that is relevant to his situation. Option A may not provide retirement benefits for expatriates like Lionel, nor will Option C. Option D can be detrimental to long-term financial security.

53. B. Underutilization of benefits often stems from a lack of awareness or understanding among employees. HR should advise senior leadership to improve communication and education about the existing benefits. This can help employees make informed choices and utilize the benefits available to them. Reducing the benefits budget (Option A) is incorrect as it may negatively impact employee satisfaction and retention. Option C is incorrect because outright elimination of benefits can be unpopular and may not address the problem of underutilization. Option D is incorrect because improving benefits communication is a more targeted approach to addressing the issue without necessarily increasing overall compensation costs.

54. D. Unemployment compensation is a mandated workplace benefit that provides eligible employees with income replacement during periods of temporary unemployment. This benefit is typically funded by employers and administered by state-government agencies. Options A, B, and C are not related to income replacement due to unemployment.

55. B. Family leave policies vary because they are influenced by the cultural norms, societal values, and historical context of each country. These factors shape how countries approach family leave, including its duration, eligibility criteria, and benefits. Option A is incorrect as the United Nations does not dictate specific policies for each country. Option C is incorrect because there is no universal approach to family leave. Option D is incorrect because cultural and societal values, as well as political considerations, also significantly influence these policies.

56. C. To address leave disparities effectively, HR teams can provide flexible leave options that allow employees to tailor their benefits to their specific needs while adhering to local regulations. Additionally, offering supplemental benefits or allowances for employees in countries with less generous policies can help bridge the gap and provide equitable support. Option A can be challenging to achieve due to the varying legal and cultural contexts in different countries. Option B may create disparities within the organization itself and be costly and difficult to implement uniformly. Option D is not a practical or fair solution.

57. B. Advantages of implementing a tuition reimbursement program include attracting and retaining top talent. However, it accurately acknowledges that it may have a limited impact on employee skills, as the effectiveness of such programs can vary. Option A is generally not true as tuition reimbursement programs are often cost-effective investments when viewed from an ROI perspective. Option C is incorrect as tuition reimbursement programs are typically seen as employee benefits that can boost morale. Option D inaccurately suggests that tuition reimbursement programs have a limited impact on employee engagement.

58. D. HSAs are subject to regulations and oversight by both federal and state governments. Federal regulations primarily cover the eligibility and tax-related aspects of HSAs, while state regulations may come into play regarding taxation and specific rules related to health insurance plans and benefits.

59. B. FSAs offer a tax advantaged way for employees to allocate funds for both medical expenses and certain wellness-related costs. This can include expenses related to wellness programs, preventive care, and other eligible wellness initiatives.

60. C. The primary difference between a health savings account and a flexible spending account is that HSAs allow for the rollover of unused funds from year to year, while FSAs often have a "use it or lose it" provision where unused funds are forfeited.

61. C. The primary purpose of domestic partner benefits is to offer benefits, such as health insurance, to employees' partners with whom they are cohabitating, even if they are not legally married. Option A is incorrect as domestic partner benefits are designed to extend benefits to employees' partners, regardless of marital status. Option B is incorrect because these benefits typically focus on providing coverage for an employee's domestic partner, not extended family members. Option D is false.

62. A. A gainsharing plan in the workplace often involves setting specific performance targets, and employees receive rewards when those targets are met. It encourages employees to work together to achieve efficiency and productivity improvements. Option B is a general term for plans that reward teams, but it does not necessarily require specific performance targets like gainsharing. Option C involves employees owning company stock but does not typically tie rewards to performance targets. Option D focuses on employee recognition but does not necessarily involve performance targets and rewards.

63. B. An employee stock ownership plan (ESOP) allows employees to have the option to purchase or receive company stock as part of their compensation. This provides employees with a sense of ownership in the company, aligning their interests with the company's performance. Option A is not a characteristic of ESOP but may apply to other group incentive plans. Option C is not typical for ESOPs, as the allocation of stock may vary based on factors such as tenure or salary. Option D is also not characteristic of ESOPs, as they are generally open to a broader group of employees and not limited to high performers.

64. B. Conducting in-person group meetings with employees is an effective method for communicating information about compensation programs. It allows for interactive discussions, provides opportunities for employees to ask questions, and fosters a more engaging and transparent communication process. Option A may not be as effective, as important details can be lost or misunderstood in written communication. Option C is not effective because employees may not easily find or access the information, leading to confusion. Option D is not an appropriate method for communicating general information about compensation programs, as it is more tailored to individual compensation discussions.

65. C. One potential advantage of a defined contribution plan is the flexibility it offers employees to manage their own investments within the plan. Employees can choose how to invest their contributions, providing them with control over their retirement savings. Option A is a characteristic of defined benefit plans, not defined contribution plans. Option B is not an advantage but a disadvantage of defined contribution plans, as the investment risk is shifted to employees. Option D is a characteristic of defined benefit plans, not defined contribution plans.

Chapter 7: Risk Management

1. B. The debt-to-equity ratio (D/E Ratio) is calculated as follows:

   ```
   D/E Ratio = Total Debt / Total Shareholders' Equity
   ```

   In this scenario, the total debt is $2,000,000, and the total shareholders' equity is $4,000,000. Plugging these values into the formula, we have this:

   ```
   D/E Ratio = $2,000,000 / $4,000,000 = 0.5
   ```

   The debt-to-equity ratio of 0.5 indicates that for every dollar of shareholders' equity, the company has $0.50 of debt. This KRI can be used to assess its financial risk. A higher D/E ratio is risky for many reasons, including interest rates, debt restructuring costs, and decreased ability to be competitive in the market.

2. C. Stakeholder engagement is a key component of an effective ERM framework because it involves communication and collaboration with internal and external stakeholders to gather insights, assess risk tolerance, and align risk management strategies with organizational objectives. Prioritizing low-impact risks may lead to over-looking larger problems at the expense of smaller one (Option A). Proactive risk management is preferred over reactive approaches (Option B). Option D Overreliance on insurance is not a comprehensive risk management strategy and may not address all types of risks (Option D).

3. B. Risk probability is primarily concerned with assessing the likelihood or chance that a particular risk event will occur within a given timeframe. It quantifies the probability of an adverse event happening. This metric helps organizations understand how likely it is for a specific risk to materialize, allowing them to prioritize their risk management efforts accordingly. Option A focuses on the potential consequences or impact of a risk event, not its likelihood of occurring. Option C is not the primary focus of risk probability assessment. Option D is related to risk management but not directly to risk probability assessment.

4. A. Single loss expectancy (SLE) represents the expected loss from a single security incident, while annual loss expectancy (ALE) calculates the total losses over a year from all security incidents combined.

5. B. A risk matrix is a valuable tool for evaluating and prioritizing risks in a workplace. It combines two critical dimensions of risk: likelihood (probability) and severity (impact), allowing for appropriate risk planning and prioritizing. Option A doesn't provide a systematic way to assess the risks associated with the new machinery. Option C lacks a structured approach for quantifying and prioritizing risks. Option D may not provide a quantitative assessment of specific risks associated with the new machinery.

6. D. Focusing on short-term financial gains is not a key characteristic of lobbying as a form of risk management. In Option A, businesses engage in lobbying to influence legislation and regulations to mitigate risks associated with adverse governmental actions. In Option B, gaining

early access allows businesses to prepare for and adapt to regulatory shifts, reducing the risk of being caught off guard. In Option C, public relations efforts can help businesses manage their public and political influence, mitigating reputational risks.

7. C. In job security moral hazard, employees believe their job security is guaranteed, which can lead them to take risks or engage in behavior that may harm the organization. They do so because they perceive that the negative consequences of their actions won't directly affect their employment status, which can result in complacency, a lack of motivation to improve, or a disregard for company policies. Option A is incorrect as an ethical hazard is a broader concept referring to ethical situations of which there are many types beyond moral hazard. Option B is incorrect as social loafing occurs when individuals within a group reduce their effort or contribution, believing their actions won't be individually identified or rewarded. Option D is incorrect because a supply chain moral hazard pertains to situations in supply chain management where suppliers or partners engage in unethical or risky behavior.

8. B. By identifying and mitigating hazards in advance, organizations can prevent accidents and create a safer work environment for their employees. Waiting for an incident to occur before taking action means that the organization is not actively identifying and mitigating risks in advance, which can lead to avoidable accidents and losses (Option A). Option C reflects a blame-oriented and reactive approach to risk management. Ignoring safety guidelines and relying on luck is not a proactive or responsible way to manage workplace risks (Option D). It greatly increases the likelihood of accidents and harm to employees.

9. D. Emergent risk are situations where new and unexpected risks may emerge as a result of the company's innovative project with cutting-edge technology. These risks are not easily foreseen or anticipated due to the lack of industry precedents. Emergent risks often exist in environments that are volatile, uncertain, complex, and ambiguous (VUCA), so building a process to predict and respond to risks is crucial. Options A and C are incorrect because the company is dealing with uncertainties and potential challenges that are not easily foreseeable due to the unique nature of their project yet not quite unforeseeable as they are aware that risk is likely. Option B is incorrect as inherent risks are those that are known or expected from the start.

10. D. The CDC recommends that by educating workers on proper hygiene practices and ensuring they have necessary tools for a hygienic workplace, employers may actively promote infection control. Option A does not directly address infection control in the workplace, as it focuses on absenteeism rather than preventive measures. Option B, while important, is not the primary recommendation for infection control in the workplace according to CDC guidelines. Option C is not practical and goes beyond CDC recommendations for infection control, potentially causing significant economic and operational disruptions.

11. D. PESTLE analysis is a qualitative method used to assess the impact of various external factors, including geopolitical events, on an organization's operations. It helps identify and understand the political, economic, social, technological, environmental, and legal factors that can affect strategic objectives. Sensitivity analysis (Option A) and Monte Carlo simulation (Option C) are primarily used for assessing financial and quantitative (measurable) aspects of risk. SWOT analysis (Option B) is a broader strategic tool that considers both internal and external factors but may not focus specifically on geopolitical events.

12. A. Developing contingency plans and scenarios is the best answer because this approach involves creating a framework for response, identifying key risks, and formulating strategies to mitigate those risks. Option B focuses more on workforce adaptability rather than proactive planning and preparedness for outlier events. Option C emphasizes collaboration without highlighting the importance of contingency planning and scenario development, which are crucial for preparedness. Option D addresses the response to an outlier event rather than proactive preparation and planning for such events.

13. A, B, C, D. Technology supports various facets of ERM, including data analysis, vendor risk management, business continuity, and legal compliance. Technology enables organizations to collect and analyze vast amounts of data to identify potential risks and vulnerabilities, making it a crucial aspect of ERM. It also assists in assessing and managing risks associated with third-party vendors and suppliers, ensuring compliance and security measures are in place. Technology plays a vital role in developing and testing business continuity and disaster recovery plans, safeguarding critical systems and data, and aids in complying with labor laws through documentation and other record-keeping requirements.

14. C. Correlation analysis is used in risk management to assess the degree of association or relationship between two variables. It helps in understanding whether changes in one variable are related to changes in another variable and the direction (positive or negative) of that relationship. Correlation analysis (Option A) does not establish causation; it only identifies associations. Correlation analysis (Option B) does not provide absolute probabilities but rather measures the strength and direction of the relationship. Correlation analysis (Option D) does not predict the exact timing of risk occurrences but focuses on relationships between variables.

15. B. The ERM team should initiate a discussion with the maintenance department to investigate the cause of the increased machine downtime. In the context of risk management, when an automated alert is triggered due to a significant increase in machine downtime, the appropriate action is to investigate the cause. This allows the ERM team to identify and address potential risks and vulnerabilities in a proactive manner, contributing to effective risk management within the organization.

16. A. The ethically responsible choice is to stop using the chemical until the risk is understood as it prioritizes employee health and safety over short-term financial considerations. While it may involve a high initial cost, this decision aligns with the ethical duty of care toward employees. Investigation could include updated Safety Data Sheets (SDS) and updated OSHA recommendations. Option B is ethically problematic as it prioritizes cost savings over employee health and safety. Option C is partially correct as a cost-benefit analysis is a valid approach in decision-making, but in this scenario, the immediate health risk to employees should take precedence over financial considerations. Option D is incorrect as in cases involving health risks, the organization has a duty to protect employees, and their preferences should not outweigh the imperative to ensure their safety.

17. C. HR business partners play a crucial role in identifying and mitigating human capital-related risks within an organization. This includes addressing issues related to talent acquisition, employee retention, workforce planning, compliance with labor laws and regulations, and other HR-related matters that can impact the overall risk profile of the enterprise. Option A typically falls under the purview of financial and audit departments, not HR business partners. Option B typically falls under the responsibility of IT and cybersecurity professionals, and Option D is more closely associated with procurement and supply chain management teams.

18. C. The multinational corporation is actively assessing potential risks and uncertainties associated with its market expansion, which aligns with the risk management principle of ISO 31000:2018. Option A suggests that the company places a higher emphasis on achieving financial objectives rather than adequately addressing and managing risks in its market expansion. Option B implies that the company solely uses past data and experiences to identify risks, potentially overlooking emerging or unique risks associated with the new market. Option D indicates that the company focuses solely on risks associated with the quality and safety of its products, potentially neglecting other critical risks in its market expansion, such as regulatory or market-specific risks. Options A, B, and D are not in alignment with the ISO standards.

19. B. A culture that discourages open communication about risks is a common barrier to effective risk management within organizations. When employees are afraid to report potential risks or are met with resistance when doing so, it hinders the identification and mitigation of risks. Option A relates to the misallocation of resources. Relying on external consultants can be beneficial (Option C), but it is not typically considered a significant barrier. Option D is actually a facilitator of effective risk management, providing guidance and direction for risk mitigation efforts.

20. A. The first step in developing a business continuity plan (BCP) is to conduct a thorough risk assessment. This involves identifying potential risks and their impact on the organization, which serves as the foundation for designing an effective BCP. Options B, C, and D typically come later in the planning process.

21. B. In case of emergencies, it is essential to have access to up-to-date contact information to notify and communicate with employees effectively. Emergency personnel recommendations (Option A) are typically part of the action employers should take to prevent emergencies from happening, and marketing strategies (Option C) and vendor contracts (Option D) are more related to business planning rather than emergency preparedness.

22. C. Interpersonal skills and stakeholder engagement are crucial HR competencies for navigating a political organization when it comes to risk management. Effective risk management often involves convincing stakeholders, including senior management and employees, to buy into and support risk mitigation initiatives. Building relationships, communicating effectively, and engaging stakeholders can help overcome resistance and foster a culture of risk awareness. Options A, B, and D do not specifically address the management barriers associated with navigating a political organization and overcoming resistance to risk management initiatives, which requires more of an interpersonal and engagement-focused approach.

23. B. Providing customer service training that focuses on de-escalation techniques is a crucial best practice for protecting employees from workplace violence related to customer interactions. This training equips employees with the skills to defuse tense situations and minimize the risk of violence. Encouraging physical altercations (Option A) is unsafe and can lead to legal issues. Options C and D are not a practical solution in most workplaces.

24. B. In this scenario, the most appropriate risk management technique is to purchase cybersecurity insurance. This insurance can help the company mitigate the financial impact of data breaches and cyberattacks. Option A is important but does not directly address the financial aspects of a cyber incident. Option C is not advisable as cybersecurity is a critical concern in today's business environment. Option D may not be necessary and could potentially introduce additional risks.

25. A. Employers can use the generally acceptable accounting principles (GAAP) by implementing strict internal controls and segregation of duties within their financial processes. GAAP emphasizes the importance of controls and separation of responsibilities to prevent fraudulent activities, including employee theft. Option B is impractical and not directly related to GAAP. Option C can raise privacy and legal concerns, and Option D may be a good practice but is not a direct application of the principles.

26. B. The most appropriate risk response is to provide comprehensive security training and measures for employees. Given the specific risks associated with politically unstable regions, it is crucial to prioritize the safety and well-being of employees by equipping them with the knowledge and tools to mitigate these risks. Hazard pay (Option A) alone may not sufficiently address safety concerns and could incentivize employees to take unnecessary risks. Option C is not a responsible approach, as it neglects employee safety and legal obligations. Option D may not always be feasible or cost-effective and should be considered after thorough risk assessment and mitigation efforts.

27. A. Increased operational efficiency because workplace audits can identify inefficiencies and areas for improvement in processes, ultimately leading to a more streamlined and efficient operation. Workplace audits (Option B) are not primarily conducted for enhancing employee privacy but rather for assessing compliance, safety, and efficiency. Audits (Option C) do not directly reduce the need for insurance. The primary purpose of audits is not to directly lower turnover but to ensure compliance and operational effectiveness (Option D).

28. B. The primary goal of OSHA standards is to minimize workplace accidents and injuries, ensuring the safety and health of employees. Options A, C, and D are incorrect because OSHA focuses on workplace safety and does not address issues related to competition, employee overtime hours, or benefits.

29. B. OSHA requires employers to provide employees with access to safety data sheets (SDS) for hazardous chemicals in the workplace. This information helps employees understand the potential hazards of chemicals they work with and how to safely handle them. Options A, C, and D are not in compliance with OSHA standards and may compromise employee safety.

30. B. The manufacturing company is most likely facing 10 separate violations for machine guarding, as per the OSHA memorandum regarding "instance by instance" (IBI) violations. OSHA's updated policy allows for separate violations to be issued for each instance of noncompliance. Since there are 10 machines without the required guards, each instance is considered a separate violation. OSHA's new policy allows for violations to be issued per instance or per employee when appropriate (Option A). While the lack of safety guards is a serious concern, the scenario does not provide information to suggest that the violation was willful (Option C). This classification does not apply in this scenario because it does not involve a prior citation for the same violation (Option D).

31. B. As a partner to these kinds of agreements, OSHA will participate in quarterly meetings, serve as a resource and liaison, and assist with safety and health training and auditing monthly reports to make recommendations to achieve safety goals. Options A, C and D are the responsibility of the university, not OSHA.

32. C. Behavioral anomalies involve deviations from an individual's or system's typical behavior patterns. In this case, the employee's behavior deviates from usual and acceptable patterns. Option A is incorrect as baselines are not a typical type of deviation, and this option is not as specific as the correct answer. Option B is incorrect as compliance anomalies typically pertain to violations of regulatory or internal compliance policies, such as money laundering, insider trading, or improper data handling. Option D is incorrect as the term *fraudulent* specifically refers to activities involving deception or dishonesty intended to gain financial or personal benefits illegally. In this scenario, the AI has detected behavioral anomalies that may or may not lead to fraudulent activities. The alert serves as an indicator for further investigation to determine if fraud is involved.

33. C. It is essential for HR to be an active participant in the oversight of risk management to ensure alignment between risk management activities and talent management strategies, as well as overall organizational goals. HR plays a critical role in identifying and addressing human capital-related risks and ensuring that risk management efforts support the achievement of business objectives.

34. B. Supply chain disruptions pose a strategic risk to organizations as they can impact the ability to deliver products or services, affecting revenue, customer satisfaction, and overall business continuity. HR can collaborate with other departments to identify alternative suppliers, cross-train employees, and develop contingency plans to minimize the impact of supply chain disruptions on strategic objectives. Option A is incorrect as it is more representative of an operational risk. Option C is incorrect as it is an example of a human capital/workforce risk. Option D is incorrect as it is a better example of a compliance risk.

35. B. HR teams are responsible for creating and enforcing cybersecurity policies and procedures that govern the behavior of remote workers and help protect company data. HR's primary role is not active monitoring and investigation (Option A). This responsibility often falls under the IT or cybersecurity departments. Technical support for cybersecurity tools is typically handled by IT or specialized cybersecurity teams, rather than HR (Option C). While HR teams may be involved in organizing training sessions, the primary responsibility for conducting cybersecurity training often falls to cybersecurity or IT teams (Option D).

36. C. HR teams often oversee and coordinate training programs to ensure that employees are educated about data protection regulations and compliance requirements. While HR teams may have administrative tasks related to cybersecurity, such as access management, the specific management and configuration of encryption tools typically fall under the IT or cybersecurity departments (Option A). Option B and Option D are tasks typically completed by IT or cybersecurity experts, rather than HR.

37. B. In a situation involving potential exposure to a dangerous chemical, the immediate priority is to contain the exposure to prevent further harm. This may involve removing the affected employee from the source of exposure, isolating the area, or shutting down processes if necessary. Before addressing the root cause of the exposure for prevention, it's crucial to ensure the immediate safety of the affected employee and others in the vicinity by containing the exposure (Option A). Securing immediate medical attention is important, but it should typically occur after the exposure is contained to prevent further harm to the affected employee and others; this may be done concurrently where possible (Option C). Option D is not the immediate action required when an employee's safety is at risk due to chemical exposure.

38. A. Insider trading involves the theft or unauthorized acquisition of confidential business information or trade secrets with the intent to benefit a competing organization. It poses significant risks to a company's competitive advantage, intellectual property, and overall security. Phishing attacks (Option B) typically involve deceptive email messages or communications aimed at tricking individuals into revealing sensitive information like login credentials or financial details. Copyright infringement (Option C) refers to the unauthorized use or reproduction of copyrighted material, such as literary, artistic, or software works. While George's actions involve copying company files and source code, they go beyond copyright infringement. The term *cybersecurity threat* (Option D) is a broader category that encompasses various types of threats and attacks in the cyber realm.

39. B. The 8- and 24-hour OSHA reporting rule mandates that employers in the United States report work-related fatalities to OSHA within 8 hours and report severe injuries, including hospitalizations, amputations, and eye losses, within 24 hours of becoming aware of the incident. Compliance with these reporting requirements is essential to ensure prompt investigation and prevention of workplace accidents and illnesses.

40. C. A key component of an effective crisis management plan is to establish clear roles and responsibilities for crisis response. This ensures that employees know their roles and can act swiftly and cohesively during a crisis. Option A is not the primary focus during a crisis, and Option B is not central component for immediate crisis response. Option D is counterproductive; effective communication is crucial during a crisis.

41. A. To increase the effectiveness of safety training and engage employees, implementing gamified training modules is a widely recognized strategy. Gamification (simulated fire evacuations, virtual reality fire extinguisher use) adds an element of fun and competition to learning, making it more interactive and engaging for employees. This approach can help employees better retain safety procedures and respond more effectively during emergencies. Punishment may lead to resistance, fear, or resentment among employees, and it is unlikely to foster a positive safety culture (Option B). Infrequent drills may lead to a lack of readiness and increased risks (Option C). Option D is impractical and does not address the lack of engagement at its root cause.

42. C. The primary difference is that workers' compensation is specifically designed to cover work-related injuries, while disability insurance provides coverage for disabilities regardless of their origin, including non-work-related injuries and illnesses. Option A is not accurate because both workers' compensation and disability insurance can provide income replacement. Accessibility to disability insurance is not solely based on job titles like "manager" (Option B). Benefit amounts can vary depending on policy terms and regulations in different locations (Option D).

43. D. The "exclusive remedy" principle in workers' compensation means that workers' compensation benefits are typically the sole legal remedy available to an injured employee. In most cases, the injured employee cannot sue their employer for additional damages.

44. C. The first step in conducting a workplace investigation in response to a harassment complaint is to contact the complainant and request additional information. This step involves gathering details about the alleged incident, the individuals involved, and any witnesses. Option A could lead to legal issues if not based on thorough investigation. Option B typically follows the initial contact with the complainant. Option D may come later in the process but is not the first step.

45. C. Maintaining confidentiality is essential to protect the integrity of the investigation and prevent potential retaliation against the whistleblower. Option A can compromise confidentiality and may not be appropriate Option B could also interfere with the investigation, especially if any finance department employees are involved. Employers should take all tips seriously and investigate as necessary (Option D).

46. A. The most effective strategy for HR to mitigate the risk of workplace violence is to provide conflict resolution training and encourage open communication among employees. This approach addresses the root cause of tension and disputes by equipping employees with the skills to resolve conflicts in a nonviolent manner. Open communication channels also allow employees to express concerns and grievances, reducing the likelihood of unresolved issues escalating into violence. Option B may help monitor employee interactions, but it does not address the underlying causes of workplace tension and does not promote a positive workplace culture. Option C is an extreme measure that may further isolate employees and negatively impact workplace morale and productivity. Option D may be necessary in some cases but does not address the underlying cause or positive company culture.

47. C. HR should recommend a human process intervention to ensure that wristbands are correctly assigned at the point of entry, reducing the chances of errors like the one described in the scenario. Option A may not address the root cause of the problem effectively as errors can and do occur, so a systems-based safety approach is necessary. Option B may not be practical and may be less effective than the correct answer. Option D may not be sufficient to prevent errors if the wristbands are initially assigned incorrectly.

48. B. Addressing substance abuse in the workplace requires a thoughtful and comprehensive approach such as implementing a policy that covers prevention, education, and support. Option A may be invasive and potentially counterproductive unless there are specific reasons to suspect substance abuse or if drug testing is required by law for certain safety-sensitive positions. Firing employees immediately upon discovering evidence of substance abuse may not be the most effective or compassionate approach (Option C). A more constructive approach is to offer support and resources for employees facing substance abuse issues. Substance abuse can have a negative impact on an employee's overall well-being and the safety of other team members, so ignoring the issue is inadvisable and irresponsible (Option D).

49. B. The appropriate procedure when an employee's drug screen comes up positive for a controlled substance is to conduct a confirmatory test to validate the initial positive result. This is typically done to rule out false positives or errors in the initial screening. Additionally, it is important to offer the employee an opportunity to explain the result, which may include providing information about any legitimate medications they are taking that could have caused the positive result. This approach ensures fairness and due process for the employee. Option A may lead to wrongful termination claims if there was a false positive or if there are legitimate explanations for the positive result. Option C violates the employee's privacy rights. Option D is premature and does not follow due process.

50. B. The most appropriate action for the HR leader to demonstrate their Consultation competency in risk management is to conduct a thorough analysis of the workplace safety incidents, gather input from relevant stakeholders, and collaborate with the executive team to develop a comprehensive risk management plan. This approach aligns with the definition of the Consultation competency, which involves understanding the organization's needs and providing guidance to address complex issues like workplace safety effectively.

51. C. The most appropriate risk management technique is to conduct an after-action review (AAR) to evaluate the incident response and identify lessons learned. AAR is a valuable tool for analyzing past events, such as security breaches, to assess what went well and where improvements are needed. It helps organizations learn from their experiences and enhance their risk management strategies. Option A does not specifically address the need to assess and identify areas for improvement. Implementing a new security software without assessing the breach's impact is a reactive approach that may not be based on a thorough understanding of the incident's root causes (Option B). Option D does not directly address risk management or the need to evaluate and learn from the incident.

52. C. In many whistleblowing laws and policies, employees are protected when they report concerns internally, as long as the disclosure aligns with ethical and legal standards. Lucille's actions in reporting the concerns within the company, retaining evidence, and seeking legal counsel are indicative of responsible whistleblowing behavior that typically qualifies for protection under relevant laws and policies. She is not required to report concerns externally to regulatory agencies to be protected as a whistleblower, as internal reporting is often a recognized and protected avenue for raising concerns (Option A). She is not automatically disqualified from protection because she did not immediately report to regulatory authorities (Option B). Many whistleblowing laws recognize the value of addressing issues internally before considering external reporting. Lucille's protection as a whistleblower does not depend solely on the unethical practices being proven true at the initial stage of reporting (Option D). Whistleblower protection often involves an investigation or due process to assess the validity of the claims.

53. C. Physical asset risk management primarily focuses on the identification and mitigation of threats and vulnerabilities related to tangible resources, such as equipment, infrastructure, and property. This process aims to minimize the potential impact of adverse events on an organization's physical assets and operations.

54. B. In Mae's situation and for addressing the risk of workplace violence stemming from intimate partner abuse, the most effective HR strategy is to provide training to employees and managers on recognizing signs of such abuse and reporting concerns. This strategy not only empowers employees to identify potential threats but also allows for a supportive and safe workplace environment for individuals like Mae. Option A is not a recommended approach, as the workplace can play a crucial role in ensuring her safety and well-being. Option C may not provide the necessary support and protection in situations involving intimate partner abuse. Option D can address some aspects of workplace safety, and may also be necessary in this scenario, but may not specifically target the underlying issue of intimate partner abuse among employees.

55. B. The most effective employer best practice is to conduct a thorough investigation into each reported incident, provide support to victims, and take appropriate disciplinary actions against perpetrators. This approach demonstrates a commitment to a safe and respectful workplace, ensures that reported incidents are taken seriously, and helps prevent further harassment. Option A can perpetuate a hostile work environment and potentially expose the company to legal liability. Option C does not provide adequate protection for victims and could lead to retaliation or escalation of the harassment. Option D should complement, not replace, the specific actions needed to address reported incidents of workplace harassment.

56. D. Mitigation involves taking proactive steps to reduce the likelihood or impact of the risk, such as implementing security patches or updates to strengthen app security. Avoiding the security vulnerability may not be practical, as it may be challenging to eliminate it entirely (Option A). While some risks can be accepted, security vulnerabilities that could lead to data breaches are typically not suitable for acceptance due to potential legal, financial, and reputational consequences (Option B). Transferring the risk to an insurance company may not be a sufficient response as addressing security vulnerabilities requires direct action by the organization, making transfer less applicable in this context (Option C).

57. B. Acceptance involves acknowledging the risk but choosing not to take any specific actions to address it, often because the cost of mitigation or replacement outweighs the potential risk. Avoiding the use of scaffolding equipment may not be practical as it is essential for the construction work (Option A). While risk transfer can be an option, it may not directly address the risk associated with the older scaffolding equipment (Option C). While mitigation may be suitable for some risks, the construction company may opt for acceptance in this scenario due to budget constraints and the equipment's continued functionality (Option D).

58. B. Over-reliance on AI-generated suggestions can stifle innovation and creativity among employees. Creativity often thrives on human interaction, brainstorming, and diverse perspectives, which may be hindered if employees depend excessively on AI. Options A and C are incorrect because both risks are not inherent to the use of AI tools, such as ChatGPT, but rather the result of improper use or without security measures in place. Proper training and guidelines can mitigate the risk of social engineering and copyright infringement risks in the workplace. Option D is incorrect because if used effectively, ChatGPT could potentially reduce certain costs by streamlining processes, improving efficiency, and providing quick access to information.

59. B, C. Collaborating with law enforcement agencies allows employers to leverage expert knowledge and resources in developing effective active shooter training programs. Law enforcement can provide valuable insights into recognizing warning signs, responding to threats, and implementing strategies to mitigate the risk of an active shooter situation. Limiting access to the workplace through keycard entry systems can prevent unauthorized individuals, including potential threats, from entering the premises. By controlling who enters the workplace, employers can enhance security measures and reduce the likelihood of an active shooter gaining access to the premises. Option A is incorrect because while workplace policies can contribute to overall safety and security, they are not specific measures aimed at addressing the threat of an active shooter. Instead, active shooter prevention strategies should focus on proactive measures such as training, access control, and threat assessment. Option D is incorrect because racial profiling is discriminatory and unethical. Effective threat assessment should be based on behavior, actions, and observable indicators of potential violence rather than race or ethnicity.

60. C. Industrial espionage often includes tactics such as hacking, infiltration, or bribery to obtain sensitive information about products, strategies, or technologies. This activity is unethical and illegal, as it undermines fair competition and can cause significant harm to the targeted company. Option A is incorrect because insider trading occurs when individuals with privileged access to confidential information use it for personal financial gain, rather than targeting competitors or other companies to obtain trade secrets or proprietary information.

Option B is incorrect as whistleblowing refers to the act of exposing illegal, unethical, or fraudulent activities within an organization to authorities or the public. Whistleblowers often act in the public interest to promote transparency, accountability, and ethical conduct within organizations. Option D is incorrect because patent violations occur when a company or individual infringes on the intellectual property rights of another party by manufacturing, using, selling, or distributing a patented invention without permission. While patent violations can involve unlawfully using proprietary technology or innovations developed by competitors, they are not necessarily indicative of corporate espionage.

Chapter 8: Employee Engagement and Retention

1. B. The emotional commitment and involvement of employees toward their organization is the most accurate definition of employee engagement. It encompasses the extent to which employees are passionate about their work, feel a strong sense of belonging to the organization, and are motivated to contribute their best efforts. Option A does not capture the emotional commitment and involvement that characterize engagement. Option C is incorrect as engaged employees may value their compensation, but engagement is about much more than an employee's total rewards package. Option D pertains to management practices and control mechanisms and does not capture the nature of engagement.

2. B. When employees proactively modify their tasks and responsibilities to align with what they are good at and passionate about, they are more likely to be engaged in their work. This approach allows them to find greater satisfaction and motivation in their jobs, leading to increased engagement. Option A is incorrect; while job sharing can promote knowledge exchange and collaboration, it may not necessarily lead to increased engagement as job crafting focuses more on personalizing one's own role rather than sharing it with others. Option C is incorrect because sabbatical benefits typically involve taking extended leaves from work to pursue personal or professional development activities, such as travel or further education, and are not related to job crafting. Option D is incorrect because attending team-building workshops and events may contribute to improved teamwork and communication but is not directly related to job crafting.

3. D. Job satisfaction is defined as the degree to which an employee feels content, fulfilled, and committed to their job tasks and environments. It is often confused with another other job attitude, organizational commitment. Option A is incorrect as it describes organizational commitment, not job satisfaction. Organizational commitment is about an employee's feelings of loyalty and attachment to the organization as a whole, rather than their satisfaction with their specific job or work tasks. Option B is incorrect because job satisfaction encompasses a broader perspective that includes satisfaction with the job itself, not just team dynamics. Option C is incorrect because it represents a component of job satisfaction rather than its primary definition. Job satisfaction is a more comprehensive measure that includes overall feelings about the job, work tasks, colleagues, and the work environment.

4. B. Creating and administering surveys that ask employees about their job satisfaction, work conditions, relationships with colleagues and supervisors, and overall engagement is one of the most effective ways to measure employee engagement because it directly captures employees' perceptions and feelings about their workplace. While high turnover rates (Option A) can be a sign of low employee engagement, it doesn't provide a comprehensive understanding of the reasons behind the turnover. Option C is incorrect as it raises significant ethical and privacy concerns. Monitoring social media activity is not in and of itself unlawful and can provide limited insights into employee sentiments. However, it can violate employees' privacy rights and lead to legal issues. Option D is incorrect as it's not a direct measure of engagement; employees may take sick days for various reasons beyond job satisfaction.

5. D. Designing formal feedback channels is the most appropriate strategy for achieving the HR team's goals of enhancing both employee engagement and internal communication. By promoting a culture of openness and responsiveness, HR can identify areas where improvements are needed and take proactive steps to enhance communication and engagement. Option A is incorrect as it can lead to rigid communication pathways and may restrict open and transparent communication; also, it will not address the broader goal of understanding the connections between employee engagement, perceived organizational support, the employer brand, and effective internal communication strategies. Option B is incorrect as it does not directly address internal communication strategies. Option C is incorrect as it primarily pertains to job design and workflow optimization, which may not comprehensively address the goals of understanding the broader connections mentioned in the scenario.

6. C. Job enlargement is the job design principle that involves expanding an employee's tasks and responsibilities horizontally to make their job more varied and interesting. It aims to provide employees with a broader range of activities, reducing monotony and potentially increasing motivation. Option A, job enrichment, involves enhancing the depth and complexity of an employee's tasks to increase job satisfaction and engagement. Option B, job rotation, entails moving employees through different roles or departments to broaden their skills and experiences. Option D, work simplification, is a job design principle that focuses on reducing unnecessary complexity and inefficiency in tasks, which is the opposite of job enlargement.

7. C. The organization's emphasis on comprehensive onboarding, skills development, and knowledge transfer programs indicates a primary focus on talent development and retention. This stage of the employee life cycle is characterized by efforts to nurture and grow existing talent within the organization, ensuring their continued engagement and commitment. Option A is incorrect as it involves identifying and attracting potential candidates. Option B is incorrect as it refers to the processes of hiring and selecting new employees. Option D refers to employee separations such as through promotions or voluntary/involuntary terminations.

8. C. Alternative staffing arrangements, such as flexible work hours and remote work options, can enhance employee engagement by promoting work-life balance and autonomy. When employees have the flexibility to manage their work schedules and work from locations of their choice, it often leads to higher job satisfaction and engagement. Option A is incorrect because while remote work can have challenges related to isolation, it is not necessarily a guaranteed outcome. Many employees thrive in remote work environments, and the impact

on engagement depends on various factors, including company culture, communication strategies, and individual preferences. Option B is incorrect as it is not necessarily true. High workload and unrealistic expectations can lead to burnout and decreased engagement if not managed effectively. Option D is incorrect because individual preferences are only one factor; the benefits of promoting work-life balance and autonomy are well-documented in improving engagement levels.

9. A. Implementing job sharing would allow two employees to share the responsibilities of a single customer service role, distributing the workload in a way that is more equitable and that can lead to decreased emotional labor and boredom. This option also provides for cross-training, further enhancing department productivity. Option B is incorrect as job rotation involves employees changing roles for cross-training, and while job rotation can provide variety, it does not directly address the issue of workload, job satisfaction, burnout, or boredom. Options C and D are incorrect as adding depth or increasing responsibilities increases their workload, potentially exacerbating the issue of overload rather than solving it.

10. C. Implementing realistic job previews and personalized onboarding is the most effective combination of strategies for increasing employee retention and job satisfaction within the first 90 days of employment. Realistic job previews provide candidates with a clear understanding of the job, its challenges, and its expectations, helping them make informed decisions about whether it's the right fit for them. Personalized onboarding tailors the initial training and integration process to the individual employee, making them feel valued and supported from the start. This combination helps set realistic expectations and ensures a smoother transition into the organization, leading to higher job satisfaction and retention. Option A is incorrect as salary and benefits are important, but they may not have an immediate impact on job satisfaction during the initial period. Assigning a mentor is beneficial, but it may not address the need for a clear understanding of the job and personalized onboarding that is crucial in the early days of employment. Option B is incorrect because team building and feedback sessions often require more time and involvement from the employee, which might not be practical during the initial onboarding period. Option D is incorrect because in the early stages of employment, employees may not have a clear understanding of their training needs, and they might benefit more from a structured onboarding process that includes personalized elements like realistic job previews.

11. D. The attrition rate represents the overall turnover in the organization, including both voluntary and involuntary separations. Option A is incorrect because it lacks the specificity of the correct answer, which in this scenario is that attrition is the combined effect of employees leaving either voluntarily or involuntarily.

12. A. Implementing quarterly employee engagement surveys to collect feedback, analyzing the results, and creating action plans based on the feedback is the best strategy. This approach actively involves employees in the process, gathers valuable feedback, and allows for targeted improvements. It ensures a data-driven approach to addressing specific engagement issues, leading to better organizational results. Option B is incorrect as it can be counterproductive by creating pressure to achieve a numerical target without addressing underlying issues. Option C is incorrect because it lacks the systematic approach of collecting data and analyzing trends that is essential for effective engagement improvement; without formal surveys or metrics, it may be challenging to identify and address root causes of low engagement consistently. Option D is incorrect as benchmarks lack the action-oriented approach of the correct answer; benchmarking should complement a comprehensive engagement strategy but not replace it.

13. C. Option C is correct as it highlights the limitation of surveys in capturing the qualitative aspects of engagement, such as the depth of employee commitment to the organization. This is a strategic concern because it means that the survey results may not provide a comprehensive understanding of the underlying factors affecting employee engagement, which could impact strategic decision-making. Option A is incorrect because it represents more of an operational or resource-related disadvantage rather than a strategic one. Option B is also more of an operational challenge as it focuses on the practical aspect of survey administration rather than the strategic implications of survey limitations. Option D is a concern related to the reliability of survey data and the organization's culture of feedback, but it is not a specific strategic disadvantage associated with the use of engagement surveys.

14. C. To calculate the mean (average) engagement level, you need to sum the individual ratings and divide by the total number of employees.

$$\left(60^{*}5+120^{*}4+40^{*}3+20^{*}2+10^{*}1\right)/250=$$

$$\left(300+480+120+40+10\right)/250=950/250=3.8$$

The average engagement level is 3.8.

15. C. Implementing an employee engagement survey focused on the specific department and analyzing the results to identify areas of low engagement is the most effective approach. This method allows you to gather data directly related to employee engagement within the troubled department. By identifying the root causes of low engagement, you can take targeted actions to address specific issues, potentially reducing turnover. Option A is incorrect as it may provide a high-level view of the problem but lacks the depth of insight needed to develop targeted solutions. Option B is incorrect as it doesn't proactively measure and address engagement issues before employees decide to leave. Option D is incorrect because making such changes without collecting engagement metrics may not be the most cost-effective or strategic solution, as other factors may be contributing to the turnover.

16. B. Intrinsic motivation refers to motivation that comes from within an individual. When employees are provided with opportunities to learn new skills and advance in their careers, they are often intrinsically motivated. They find satisfaction, enjoyment, and a sense of personal growth in these opportunities, which drive their motivation to excel and achieve. Option A is incorrect as extrinsic motivation involves external factors or rewards, such as money, recognition, or promotions, that influence an individual's behavior or performance. Option C is incorrect as peer motivation refers to the influence and motivation that individuals derive from their peers or colleagues. It involves encouragement, support, and inspiration from co-workers. Option D is incorrect as social motivation typically refers to motivation driven by social interactions, relationships, or the desire for social recognition, none of which is present in the scenario.

17. B. The Job Characteristics Model suggests that jobs can be made more motivating by increasing the core job dimensions, including skill variety, task identity, task significance,

autonomy, and feedback. Allowing employees to choose their projects and set their own deadlines enhances their autonomy and control over their work, making the job more meaningful and motivating. Option A is incorrect as reducing the number of tasks and simplifying job roles may lead to less variety and challenge in the work, which contradicts the JCM's principle of increasing skill variety and task identity to enhance motivation. Option C is incorrect as it reduces employee autonomy and decreases the job's motivating potential. Option D is incorrect as the JCM focuses on job design rather than incentive systems.

18. B. Holding regular one-on-one meetings with employees to discuss their concerns, actively listening to their feedback, and taking action based on their input shows a commitment to understanding and addressing employee needs and concerns. This approach fosters trust and open communication, which are vital for improving engagement. Option A is incorrect as active listening involves not only collecting feedback but also engaging in meaningful conversations to understand employee perspectives and work collaboratively on solutions. Option C is incorrect as it is a one-way communication approach that may not effectively address employee concerns or engage them in the process. Active listening involves two-way communication and responsiveness to employee input. Option D is incorrect as active listening entails understanding the unique needs and preferences of employees and tailoring initiatives accordingly.

19. D. The characteristic of the Job Characteristics Model (JCM)that is most likely motivating Nancy in her role is feedback. Nancy mentions how feedback from colleagues and clients helps her continuously improve her work, indicating that receiving feedback is a motivating factor for her job satisfaction. Option A is incorrect as task identity is a characteristic in the JCM that refers to the extent to which a job allows employees to complete a whole and identifiable piece of work. It involves seeing a clear beginning and end to a task. Option B is incorrect as autonomy in the context of work refers to the degree of independence and control an employee has over their tasks, decision-making, and work processes within their job. Option C is incorrect as skill variety is a component of the JCM and represents the diversity of skills and abilities required to perform a job.

20. B. The Job Characteristics Model (JCM) primarily focuses on how job design elements (e.g., skill variety, task identity) impact an employee's motivation and job performance. It is concerned with aspects of the job itself. In contrast, organizational commitment measures an employee's loyalty, attachment, and identification with their organization, reflecting their dedication to the organization as a whole. Option A is incorrect as the JCM does consider employee job satisfaction, but it is not the primary focus. Organizational commitment is more about loyalty and alignment with organizational values. Option C is incorrect as the JCM examines job design rather than the psychological contract, and it focuses on motivation rather than skill development opportunities. Option D is incorrect as the JCM is not primarily concerned with employee engagement in decision-making but rather with the impact of job characteristics. Organizational commitment is more related to perceptions of fairness and loyalty toward the organization.

21. A. Employee feedback surveys allows employees to express their thoughts anonymously, providing honest feedback about their dissatisfaction and concerns. Analyzing the survey results helps HR identify specific issues and areas of improvement, enabling them to tailor the communication strategy effectively. Option B is incorrect as while holding employee meetings is important for communication, mandatory meetings could create resistance and potentially increase employee anxiety. Option C is incorrect as external consultants may lack the understanding of the company's culture, values, and specific employee concerns. Option D is incorrect because it may be tone deaf. While celebrating the company's achievements and setting a positive tone is important, it's vital to address immediate employee concerns and uncertainties through more focused communication strategies, such as surveys, meetings, and open channels, before planning celebratory events to ensure that employees are informed, engaged, and receptive to the message of celebration.

22. B. The most crucial competency in this context is data analysis skills. HR professionals need the ability to collect, analyze, and interpret employee engagement data to derive meaningful insights. This competency enables them to present actionable recommendations to senior leaders based on empirical evidence. Option A is incorrect as it primarily pertains to understanding HR policies, regulations, and procedures. Option C is incorrect as conflict resolution skills are more relevant to resolving workplace disputes and issues rather than analyzing and communicating employee engagement data. Option D is incorrect as the ability to analyze data is more important because it forms the basis for making informed recommendations. Presentation skills complement data analysis skills but are not the most crucial competency in this context.

23. A. HR can have the most significant impact on employee retention within the first six months of employment, often referred to as the onboarding stage. During this time, effective onboarding processes, training, and support can set the tone for an employee's experience, help them integrate into the company culture, and increase their likelihood of staying with the organization long-term. Option B is incorrect because while HR's efforts to support and engage employees after their introductory period is important, it is often more effective to address retention concerns and establish a positive work experience earlier in the employee life cycle. Option C is incorrect as the recruiting stage as retention efforts come into play after an employee has been hired. Option D is incorrect because by the time an employee reaches the performance management stage, their decision to stay or leave the organization is often influenced by earlier experiences, including onboarding and initial work experiences.

24. C. McClelland's Acquired Needs theory suggests that an individual's motivation is influenced by their needs for achievement, affiliation, and power, which are acquired through life experiences and socialization. In this example, Trixie's behavior aligns with McClelland's theory of the need for power, as she is driven by her desire to exert influence and control within the workplace and is less concerned with external rewards or job security. Option A is incorrect as the need for achievement involves a strong desire to excel and accomplish challenging tasks, which is not the primary motivator for Trixie, as she seeks influence and control over projects rather than just personal success. Option B is also part of McClelland's theory of motivation, but it refers to a motivation to build close relationships and connections with others. Option C is incorrect as hygiene factors are external things like working conditions and salary and are part of Frederick Herzberg's theory of motivation, not David McClelland's.

25. B. Cross-functional teams that bring together individuals with diverse backgrounds and skills often lead to increased job satisfaction due to the exposure to different perspectives and collaborative learning. Options A, C, and D are incorrect as they do not accurately reflect the impact the composition of teams has on employee engagement.

26. D. In the context of team development, the performing stage is characterized by high levels of team engagement and productivity. During this stage, team members have resolved conflicts, established clear norms, and are effectively working together to achieve their goals, resulting in peak performance. Option A is incorrect as in the forming stage, teams are just coming together and may not have established effective working relationships yet, so engagement and productivity are typically lower. Option B is incorrect as the storming stage is characterized by conflicts and challenges as team members establish their roles and working dynamics. Engagement and productivity can be lower during this stage. Option C is incorrect as the opposite is true; the highest levels of engagement and productivity are typically achieved in the performing stage when the team is operating at its best.

27. C. Networking in the context of HR allows professionals to connect with peers, industry experts, and organizations, providing access to a wealth of knowledge, best practices, and resources related to employee engagement. It facilitates collaboration and the sharing of valuable insights and tools to enhance HR's ability to support and improve employee engagement within their organization. Option A is incorrect as it is not primarily a training mechanism. Option B is incorrect because in networking, HR professionals typically focus on constructive discussions, problem-solving, and collaboration rather than just venting frustrations. Option D is incorrect as networking plays a significant role in HR's ability to gather knowledge, best practices, and resources that can directly contribute to enhancing employee engagement, making it a relevant and valuable competency.

28. A. Flat organizational structures typically have fewer layers of management compared to hierarchical organizations. With fewer layers of bureaucracy, employees in flat structures often have more autonomy and decision-making authority. This increased autonomy can positively influence employee retention because it allows employees to take ownership of their tasks, make decisions related to their work, and have a greater sense of control over their roles. Option B is incorrect as flat organizational structures do not inherently provide more hierarchical levels for career advancement. In fact, career progression may be limited in flat organizations due to the flatter hierarchy. Option C is incorrect as the emphasis on collaboration can vary depending on the organization's culture, goals, and priorities. Option D is incorrect because organizational structures, including flat structures, are primarily designed to facilitate the efficient functioning of the organization and achieve its objectives, rather than being specifically structured to align with individual employees' values.

29. B. Data analytics skills are fundamental to collecting business intelligence used to structure predictive attrition analysis effectively. HR professionals need to be proficient in collecting relevant employee data, cleaning and preparing it for analysis, and creating meaningful visualizations to communicate their findings. These skills are essential for data-driven decision-making, as they enable HR professionals to work with the data necessary for attrition analysis, ensure its quality, and present insights clearly to stakeholders. Option A is incorrect as continuous learning applies more broadly to staying updated on emerging trends, new technologies, and evolving HR practices. Option C is incorrect as an HR professional can have knowledge of attrition trends but still lack the ability to handle data effectively for predictive modeling. Option D is incorrect as predictive attrition analysis involves a broader range of skills.

30. C. According to Maslow's Hierarchy of Needs, physiological and safety needs are lower-order needs that must be satisfied before individuals can be motivated by higher-order needs like belongingness, esteem, and self-actualization. Options A, B, and D are all higher-order needs in Maslow's theory.

31. B. David McClelland's Acquired Needs theory suggests that individuals have three primary needs—achievement, affiliation, and power—that drive their behavior in the workplace. Option A, Herzberg's Two-Factor theory, suggests that there are hygiene factors (external factors like working conditions and salary) that, when lacking, can lead to job dissatisfaction, and motivational factors (internal factors like achievement and recognition) that, when present, can lead to job satisfaction and motivation. Option C, Maslow's Hierarchy of Needs theory, categorizes human needs into a hierarchy, with physiological needs at the base (e.g., food and shelter) and self-actualization needs at the top (e.g., personal growth and fulfillment), suggesting that individuals must satisfy lower-level needs before higher-level ones become motivators in the workplace. Option D, Equity theory, asserts that individuals in the workplace compare their input (e.g., effort, skills) and output (e.g., rewards, salary) ratios with those of others and seek fairness or equity in these comparisons, leading to feelings of satisfaction or dissatisfaction depending on the perceived fairness of the exchange.

32. B. Frederick Herzberg's Two-Factor theory suggests that salary and benefits, along with other factors like working conditions and company policies, are hygiene factors that, when lacking or inadequate, can lead to job dissatisfaction (dissatisfiers). Satisfiers or motivators are internal factors that, when present and effective, can lead to job satisfaction and motivation. Herzberg identified five specific motivational factors: achievement, recognition, work itself, responsibility, and advancement. These factors are related to the nature of the work and how it fulfills individuals' psychological needs for growth and self-fulfillment.

33. C. The Expectancy theory suggests that an individual's motivation to perform a task is influenced by their belief in their ability to accomplish it (self-efficacy), the expectation that their efforts will lead to desired outcomes, and the value they place on those outcomes.

34. C. In recent years, the psychological contract has shifted toward a more transactional nature, where employees and employers focus on mutually beneficial agreements and less on long-term loyalty. The psychological contract in the workplace refers to the unwritten expectations and obligations between employees and employers that influence attitudes, behaviors, and the employment relationship. Options A and B are incorrect because the psychological contract has become more fluid and less secure. Option D is incorrect as it does not acknowledge the changing nature of the psychological contract, which has gone from a "job-for-life" mentality to a journey of multiple employers and the development of new skill sets.

35. A. Enhancing employee well-being programs is the most effective strategy to combat the threat of increased turnover in this scenario. By investing in well-being programs, the company can provide employees with resources and support to cope with the new work arrangement. This can include mental health support, stress management workshops, and initiatives to improve work-life balance. Option B is incorrect as it may not be the most practical solution given the company's need to stay competitive in a changing market. Option C is incorrect as stay bonuses do not address the root cause of employees' stress and dissatisfaction, which is the change in the work arrangement. While it may temporarily reduce turnover, it may not lead to long-term employee satisfaction or improved well-being. Option D is incorrect because it doesn't provide a sustainable solution to the problem and may be impractical for a company that is facing increased competition.

36. D. Employee wellness programs tend to concentrate on individual health and well-being rather than interpersonal relationships within teams. Although better well-being may

indirectly lead to improved teamwork, it is not the primary goal of such initiatives. Option A is a well-documented benefit of employee wellness initiatives. These programs often lead to healthier employees who are less likely to take sick days or personal leave due to health-related issues. Option B is also a common and significant benefit of employee wellness initiatives. By promoting well-being, reducing stress, and creating a positive work environment, these programs aim to increase job satisfaction among employees. While not the primary focus, some employee wellness initiatives may include elements such as financial wellness workshops or resources (Option C); improving employees' financial health can indirectly contribute to engagement and retention by reducing financial stress.

37. C. HR can use AI to predict employee turnover effectively by analyzing historical HR data, such as employee performance, attendance, engagement, and previous turnover patterns. Machine learning algorithms can then identify trends and patterns that may indicate potential turnover risks. This approach is ethical, is data-driven, and respects employee privacy. Option A is incorrect because it addresses the use of AI in the workplace, but chatbots are not the primary tool for predicting turnover. Option B is incorrect as it is invasive and ethically questionable. It may violate privacy regulations and employee trust, making it an ineffective and inappropriate method for predicting turnover. Option D may not be effective for predicting turnover, as employees may not provide honest responses due to concerns about job security or reprisals.

38. B. HR professionals need to listen to employees' concerns, understand their needs, and empathize with their experiences to create engagement initiatives that resonate with the workforce. This enables HR to develop strategies that address employees' specific concerns, leading to higher levels of engagement and job satisfaction. Options A, B, and C are not specific to interpersonal competencies.

39. B. Empowering CSRs to make decisions within reasonable limits should be the first priority because it provides employees with the autonomy and authority needed to handle irate customers effectively, which can lead to a reduction in emotional labor and improved job satisfaction. Option A is incorrect because while training and development on de-escalation skills are essential; employees can more effectively apply these skills when they also have the authority to make decisions. Option C is limited as without the authority to act, employees may still struggle to address irate customers effectively. Option D is a valuable strategy but may not be realistic from a business perspective and may create more burden on employees due to under-staffing or an increased workload.

40. C. Exit interviews are a crucial tool for understanding why employees choose to leave and for collecting feedback that can help the organization enhance its practices, policies, and overall employee experience. Option A is incorrect as while exit interviews can serve as a record of an employee's departure, their primary purpose is to collect feedback and insights that can be used to enhance the organization's practices and culture. Option B is incorrect as it does not reflect the primary goal of the exit interview. Option D is incorrect as it is not necessarily true. While it may be too late to persuade the exiting employee to stay, properly administered interviews can provide valuable feedback to aid in decision-making and retention efforts for other workers.

41. D. As Robin is approaching retirement, providing opportunities for skill transfer and mentorship is a crucial employee engagement need. This option recognizes that Robin's extensive knowledge and experience can be valuable to the organization and her colleagues. By involving her in skill transfer and mentorship activities, the company can leverage her expertise, make her feel appreciated, and help her transition smoothly into retirement while contributing to the development of other employees. Talking with the team members and assessing their goals and then seeking to align them with business needs is important to understanding the proper engagement approach. Options A and C are not suitable engagement strategies for someone looking to reduce her hours. Option B does not address her desire to stay employed or properly address her health insurance needs.

42. A. To calculate the vacancy rate, you need to find the proportion of unfilled positions to the total positions. In this case, there are 100 job openings in total, and 80 of them have been filled. To find the vacancy rate, you subtract the filled positions from the total positions and then divide by the total positions:

$$\text{Vacancy Rate} = (\text{Total Positions} — \text{Filled Positions}) / \text{Total Positions}$$

$$\text{Vacancy Rate} = (100 — 80) / 100$$

$$\text{Vacancy Rate} = 0.2 \text{ or } 20\%$$

A higher vacancy rate suggests potential retention challenges and leads to increased workloads and decreased job satisfaction for existing employees (indication of future turnover). Monitoring and addressing the vacancy rate prompts organizations to implement retention strategies, enhancing the employee experience and fostering loyalty.

43. A. Career pathing helps employees see a clear trajectory for growth within the organization, making them more likely to stay. Employee resource groups foster a sense of belonging and inclusion, which can enhance retention. Community involvement can strengthen an employee's bond with the company and contribute positively to retention. Option B is incorrect as while competitive total rewards packages are important for retention, they may not align with the achievement of business results, especially if the company is over-paying for labor or the benefits are under-utilized. Option C is incorrect as personalized benefits and remote work schedules can enhance work-life balance, but guaranteed leadership opportunities for all employees may not be practical nor desirable for all team members. Option D is incorrect as while these perks may provide short-term satisfaction, they do not address the long-term factors that contribute to retention and may not be practical from a business perspective.

44. B. A potential challenge of this assimilation approach for protected-class groups is that the mandatory after-hours networking events may create feelings of exclusion for employees unable to attend due to caregiving responsibilities or other protected factors. This exclusion can negatively affect their engagement and integration into the organization. Options A and D are incorrect as they do not specify a protected-class characteristic. Option C is incorrect because while the events are held in bars and restaurants, the scenario does not specify that alcohol is being served.

45. C. Overly strict grooming policies can adversely affect employee engagement by creating barriers for employees with cultural or religious grooming practices; the primary issue is about potential discrimination or exclusion based on cultural, religious, or personal grooming practices. These policies may lead to feelings of exclusion and discomfort among affected employees, potentially resulting in lower engagement levels. Options A, B, and D are incorrect because grooming policies allow individual expression, creativity, and unique identification for some team members.

46. C. A key advantage of using a Net Promoter Score (NPS) question in employee engagement surveys is that NPS questions provide a simple and quantitative measure of engagement. NPS asks employees a single question, typically, "On a scale of 0 to 10, how likely are you to recommend this company as a place to work?" Employees' responses are then categorized into Promoters Passives and Detractors. The NPS score is calculated by subtracting the percentage of Detractors from the percentage of Promoters. This simplicity and quantitative nature make NPS an efficient and easy-to-understand measure of employee engagement. Option A is incorrect because NPS focuses on a single question that measures overall likelihood to recommend the company but does not delve into specific aspects or dimensions of engagement, such as job satisfaction, work-life balance, or career growth. Option B is incorrect as while NPS questions are easy to understand, a lack of depth is a disadvantage to collecting meaningful feedback. The simplicity of the question allows for a quick and straightforward measure, but it may not provide the depth of insight into the specific drivers of engagement that other survey questions might offer. Option D is incorrect because NPS questions are not inherently tailored to specific industries but rather are a standardized measure used across various industries and sectors to gauge customer and employee loyalty and satisfaction.

47. C. Remote workers may feel isolated due to physical separation from the team, and maintaining regular communication and providing support help them stay connected with their colleagues and the organization. This sense of connection and support can contribute to higher retention rates. Option A is incorrect because daily check-ins may lead to a perception of micromanagement rather than support. Option B is incorrect because implementing flexible work hours for on-site employees does not address the specific needs and challenges faced by remote workers. Option D is incorrect because encouraging remote workers to work independently to ensure autonomy is important, but it does not directly address the need for regular communication, support, and connection that remote workers may require to improve retention.

48. B. The most effective way for HR leaders to collaborate with organizational leaders to create a positive employee experience is by holding regular joint meetings. These meetings allow for open discussions about employee feedback, identification of pain points, and the joint development of strategies for improvement. Collaborative discussions ensure that both HR and organizational leaders have a shared understanding of employee needs and can work together to address them effectively. Options A, C, and D are each in their own ways one-directional. When problem-solving for employee engagement, it is essential to engage organizational leaders in discussions and decision-making to allocate resources to root-cause issues. Collaboration ensures that employee experience initiatives align with the overall strategic direction of the organization.

49. D. Predictive analytics can be effectively used in performance management by identifying performance trends and patterns within the organization. This enables proactive measures to address areas needing improvement and development. By analyzing historical data, organizations can make informed decisions to enhance overall performance. Option A is incorrect as predicting individual employee performance ratings for the next quarter is a challenging task, and while analytics can provide insights, predicting individual ratings with accuracy is complex and subject to various factors. Option B is incorrect as predictive analytics goes beyond automation and focuses on data analysis to provide valuable insights and recommendations for improving performance. Option C is incorrect as predictive analytics aims to provide actionable insights and recommendations based on historical data, making it a more valuable tool in performance management than simply generating historical reports without analysis.

50. B. Implementing HR activities such as regular feedback sessions, career development opportunities, and recognition programs can boost employee morale and retention. This, in turn, leads to increased productivity and reduced recruitment costs, contributing to organizational effectiveness. Option A is incorrect as the effectiveness of HR activities depends on their impact on employee morale, retention, and productivity, rather than simply increasing access to HR services. Option C is incorrect because the primary objective of employee engagement efforts can increase the cost of labor, not decrease it. Option D is incorrect because the scenario described goes beyond engagement at the job level; rather, it focuses on engagement throughout the life cycle of the employee.

51. C. The WHO defines occupational burnout in its ICD-11 as chronic workplace stress that has not been successfully managed, characterized by feelings of exhaustion, increased mental distance from one's job, and reduced professional efficacy. This definition highlights the significance of addressing workplace stress and its impact on individuals' well-being and job performance.

52. C. Employee engagement efforts can lead to improved morale and job satisfaction, resulting in reduced absenteeism and lower error rates. When employees are engaged and motivated, they are more likely to be present at work, make fewer mistakes, and be more efficient, ultimately contributing to cost savings and improved product quality. Option A is incorrect as there are other factors that more directly contribute to the cost of raw materials such as economic and political forces. Option B is incorrect because, in reality, high turnover rates can lead to increased costs associated with recruitment, training, and lost productivity due to turnover. Option D is partially correct because engaged employees may be more productive and efficient, but the relationship between employee engagement and production output is not always straightforward. Additionally, reducing work hours without careful consideration of productivity and operational needs may not always be feasible or advisable.

53. B. The impact of employee engagement efforts on organizational results is often indirect. Employee engagement influences factors such as morale, productivity, retention, and customer satisfaction, which, in turn, affect organizational performance and results. These effects are not always immediately visible but are important for long-term success. Options A and C are incorrect because it is not accurate to say that the impact is immeasurable or subjective. Organizations often use various metrics and assessments to gauge the effects of engagement efforts, even if some aspects are less tangible. Option D is incorrect as employee engagement efforts may lead to objective outcomes, such as increased revenue, reduced turnover, or improved customer satisfaction. However, not all the effects are purely objective, as they may also include subjective elements like employee morale and job satisfaction.

54. B. Collaboratively setting clear and measurable goals with employees ensures that they are aligned with the organization's objectives, motivates employees, and enhances their

engagement and commitment. Option A is incorrect because goal-recording involves defining, setting, and monitoring goals collaboratively with employees, not just with their manager. Option C is incorrect as assigning development goals and linking them to incentive compensation is related to performance management not the process of setting and tracking goals. Option D is incorrect as goal-recording is primarily concerned with individual employee development goals and progress tracking.

55. A. The primary difference between goal-recording and an engagement dashboard is that goal-recording pertains to individual or team goals, tracking progress toward those goals, and ensuring alignment with organizational objectives. In contrast, an engagement dashboard provides a holistic view of workforce engagement, usually through metrics and data that indicate the overall level of engagement across the organization. Options B, C, and D are not true.

56. B. An Employee Service Award is a recognition program that acknowledges and honors employees for their loyalty and dedicated service to the organization, typically awarded on milestones such as work anniversaries. Option A is incorrect as it is a performance award rather than a reward for tenure. Option C is incorrect as it is a voluntary fringe benefit, not a service award. Option D is incorrect as it is a form of performance feedback.

57. A. Realistic job previews (RJPs) influence employee engagement by providing employees with a clear understanding of what to expect on the job. When employees have realistic expectations about their roles and work environments, they are more likely to be satisfied with their jobs and engage more effectively. Option B is incorrect as an RJP's primary purpose is not to predict success but to provide a realistic view of the job. Option C is incorrect because their primary goal is not to highlight challenges for employees to mitigate or avoid. Option D is incorrect because RJPs can influence both employee engagement and turnover by helping potential employees make informed decisions about whether to accept a job offer.

58. C. Employee engagement is significantly influenced by the alignment of an employee's personal values and beliefs with the mission and values of the organization. When employees feel that their work is meaningful and in sync with their own principles, they are more likely to be engaged and motivated. Options A, B, and D are not primary factors in determining employee engagement.

59. D. Peer-to-peer recognition is most effective when it is integrated into the workplace as a regular and ongoing practice. Continuous acknowledgment and appreciation among colleagues help create a positive and motivating work culture. Option A is incorrect because peer-to-peer recognition should not be limited to annual performance reviews; it is valuable throughout the year to foster a culture of appreciation. Option B is incorrect as it is not limited to competitive contexts and can benefit workplaces of all types. Option C is incorrect because relying solely on peer-to-peer recognition may not be sufficient for comprehensive employee motivation and engagement.

60. C. Coaching leaders on positive relationship techniques is most likely to develop leaders in understanding the impact of employee engagement. Effective leadership involves understanding and fostering positive relationships with employees, which can significantly impact their engagement and overall performance. Option A is incorrect as engagement is based on many factors, not just cultural preferences. Option B is incorrect because dashboards do not develop a leader's understanding of why engagement matters or how to improve it. Option D is incorrect as making employee engagement results a leadership key performance indicator (KPI) can help hold leaders accountable for engagement initiatives, but it does not directly develop their understanding of the impact of employee engagement on the organization.

Chapter 9: Employee and Labor Relations

1. A, B, D. When conducting workplace investigations, it's crucial to consider the emotions and sensitivities of the individuals involved. This fosters trust and cooperation, leading to more meaningful and accurate information being shared during the interview process. Workplace investigations must remain impartial and free from undue influence, including pressure from executives or other higher-ups. Open communication is essential during workplace investigations to ensure that all relevant parties are informed of the process, their rights, and any developments. Option C is incorrect as the focus of an impartial investigation is to gather the relevant information necessary to render a decision and protect the rights of all involved. It may be impossible to guarantee confidentiality, as an impartial investigation may require sharing information with appropriate parties involved.

2. B. Due process is the fair and impartial treatment and procedures guaranteed to individuals by law, ensuring their rights are protected. This includes having a neutral investigator who is not biased toward any party involved. Due process ensures that all parties are treated fairly, that they have the opportunity to present their side of the story, and that the investigation is conducted objectively. Option A is incorrect as allowing employees to choose their investigators could potentially lead to conflicts of interest or biases in the investigation process. Option C is incorrect because rushing through an investigation to meet strict timeframes can compromise the quality and integrity of the process. Option D is incorrect as conducting investigations with the consent of the involved parties may not always be required for due process, especially in cases where serious misconduct or legal violations are involved. Due process often involves investigating complaints or concerns even if some parties involved do not consent to the investigation.

3. B. When faced with a situation like this, it's essential to first communicate with Matilda and explain what was discovered during the initial conversation with the employee. This ensures transparency and helps Matilda understand that the employee's actions may have been unintentional. After discussing the situation with Matilda, HR can determine the next steps based on her response, concerns, and preferences. This approach respects Matilda's feelings and allows her to have a say in the resolution process. Option A is incorrect because it does not address Matilda's concerns or provide a resolution to the situation. Ignoring the issue and taking no further action may leave Matilda feeling unheard and unsatisfied. Option B is incorrect as disciplining the employee without further investigation and understanding Matilda's perspective is premature and may not be warranted in this case. Option D is incorrect

because while it's important to take complaints seriously, it is also important to consider the rights of the accused and use discretion in proceeding accordingly.

4. C. The ILO standards primarily apply to member countries that have ratified specific ILO conventions and agreements. These standards are international in scope and are not applicable to all countries worldwide. The NLRA primarily applies to employers, employees, and labor unions within the United States, regulating labor relations and practices specific to the United States.

5. B. The correct course of action is to investigate the complaint and ensure that the employee is paid a fair wage in compliance with local living wage standards. The ILO emphasizes the importance of fair wages, and employers should adhere to these standards to promote decent work and fair labor practices. Options A, C, and D do not align with ILO standards and best practices.

6. B. Option B is incorrect as providing humanitarian aid during natural disasters is not a primary responsibility of the ILO. One of the primary responsibilities of the ILO is to promote decent work and social justice worldwide. This includes addressing labor-related issues such as workers' rights, employment opportunities, and social protection. The ILO is also responsible for setting international labor standards and conventions that member countries are encouraged to adopt and implement to improve labor conditions globally. Capacity building under the ILO refers to a strategic process aimed at strengthening the ability of governments, employers, workers, and other stakeholders to effectively address labor-related challenges, implement labor standards, and promote decent work practices.

7. D. A company's employee relations strategy should begin with a clear vision of what the employer hopes to achieve in terms of employee relations and workplace culture. Option A, B, and C are incorrect as an employee relations strategy encompasses a broader set of objectives and initiatives beyond a code of conduct, compliance incentives, or statement of policy. A comprehensive strategy should address all aspects of the employer-employee relationship, including communication, engagement, conflict resolution, and more.

8. A. Trade unions are specifically formed by workers to engage in collective bargaining with employers, negotiate labor agreements, and represent the interests of their members in employment-related matters. Option B is incorrect as a federation is an umbrella organization that represents multiple trade unions or labor organizations. It does not directly engage in negotiations or advocacy but provides a platform for affiliated unions to collaborate. Option C is incorrect as NGOs are independent organizations focused on various social, environmental, or humanitarian issues. They do not primarily represent workers in labor negotiations. Option D is incorrect because a workers' cooperative is a business entity owned and operated by its employees. It does not necessarily engage in collective bargaining or advocacy for workers' rights; its primary purpose is to provide employment and generate income for its worker-owners.

9. C. A union card check is a process where employees sign authorization cards to indicate their support for union representation. This process is used before the establishment of a union to determine sufficient interest from an eligible pool of employees. If a majority of members show interest, the employer may voluntarily recognize the union or it goes to a formal vote.

10. D. In the union organizing process, prior to the union being officially recognized as the representative body for the workers, the union does not have the legal authority to conduct a strike vote. The union's legitimacy and ability to negotiate on behalf of the workers are contingent upon being officially recognized through a certification or election process. Therefore, until the union gains this authorization, its members cannot vote for strike action.

11. C. Right-to-work legislation refers to laws that give employees the choice of whether to join or financially support a union. In states with right-to-work laws, employees cannot be required to join a union or pay union dues or fees as a condition of employment. This legislation ensures that workers have the freedom to make their own decisions regarding union membership or financial support. Option A is incorrect as this legislation does not guarantee every union member a job. Option B is incorrect because unions can still organize and represent workers in right-to-work states. Option D is incorrect because right-to-work laws do not mandate union membership for all workers.

12. C. Strikebreakers are often brought in by companies to take the jobs of striking workers and maintain operations during a strike. Options A, B, and D are not the role of strikebreakers.

13. D. In the context of collective bargaining agreement negotiations, HR plays a critical role in facilitating open and constructive communication between the two parties, helping to bridge differences, and working toward mutually acceptable terms. Mediation is essential for achieving a fair and effective labor agreement. Option A is incorrect as HR does not lead the union negotiations on behalf of the company. Negotiations are led by representatives from the company's management, and HR assists in the process but does not take the lead in union negotiations. Option B is incorrect because HR does not advocate for the union's demands or solely support the employees' interests. Option C is incorrect because HR should be careful of providing legal advice on matters beyond the scope of HR's knowledge or expertise.

14. B. The complexity of the negotiated contract terms is a significant factor contributing to the cost of administering a labor contract. Complex contract terms may require more time and resources for interpretation, enforcement, and compliance, leading to higher administrative costs. Option A is incorrect as the size of the labor union may impact negotiation dynamics and representation but does not directly contribute to the cost of administering the labor contract. Option C is incorrect as the number of employees eligible for union membership can affect the size of the bargaining unit and the scope of the contract, but it does not directly influence the administrative cost. Option D is incorrect because it is not a factor that directly determines the cost of administering a labor contract. Administrative costs are more closely related to the contract's complexity and the resources needed for its management.

15. C. Advanced HR professionals should promote cross-departmental collaboration, encourage open dialogue, and seek common goals among teams to mitigate workplace political issues and foster a harmonious working environment. Option A is incorrect because adopting a confrontational stance and favoring one department's interests over others can exacerbate the political situation and harm organizational harmony. Option B is incorrect as maintaining strict neutrality without actively addressing political issues may not be an effective approach to resolve conflicts or improve collaboration. Option D is not the primary role of HR professionals in this context.

16. D. Interest-based bargaining, also known as principled negotiation, focuses on identifying and addressing the underlying interests, needs, and concerns of both parties rather than solely focusing on positions or demands. In this scenario, where the company aims to increase efficiency and the union is concerned about job security and maintaining current wages and benefits, interest-based bargaining allows both parties to explore creative solutions that address these underlying interests while preserving their respective priorities. Option A is incorrect as integrative negotiation typically requires a high level of cooperation and trust between parties. In this scenario, where there may be conflicting interests between the company and the union regarding production efficiency and job security, achieving integrative solutions may be challenging without first addressing underlying concerns. Option B is incorrect as concessionary bargaining involves one party making significant concessions to the other, often as a result of power imbalances or external pressures. This approach tends to focus on giving up specific demands or benefits to reach an agreement, which may not be suitable in this scenario where both parties have important interests to protect. Option C is incorrect as distributive negotiation, also known as positional bargaining, involves a fixed amount of resources that parties compete to claim for themselves. It tends to result in win-lose outcomes, where gains for one party come at the expense of the other.

17. C. Contingency plans outline the organization's strategy for maintaining operations, ensuring safety, and addressing the needs of both striking and nonstriking employees. Option A is incorrect as while early warning systems are important for monitoring and detecting early signs of labor unrest, they should not be the first step in this situation. Early warning systems can complement the contingency planning process by providing ongoing monitoring and data to inform decision-making. Option B is incorrect as before hiring replacements, the HR team should have a comprehensive plan in place that considers legal and ethical considerations, employee safety, communication strategies, and other factors. Option D is incorrect as given the immediate concern about the potential strike, the HR team should focus on developing contingency plans and addressing the strike's potential impacts.

18. A, B. When union members vote to strike, one strategy for maintaining operations is to hire strikebreakers or replacement workers to perform the tasks typically carried out by striking employees. This helps the organization to continue its operations and mitigate the impact of the strike on productivity. Strikes can disrupt normal business operations and impact the supply chain. It's essential for the HR team to prepare for potential disruptions by working with purchasing and other leaders to identify alternative suppliers, manage inventory levels, and establish contingency plans to ensure a continuous flow of materials or goods. Options C and D are incorrect as they do not directly relate to creating a contingency plan focused on continued operations during a strike. These options are relevant in other contexts.

19. C. Initiating a dialogue with striking employees and their representatives is an appropriate initial step in a strike response plan. Communication and negotiation can help identify the underlying issues, potentially resolve disputes, and promote a constructive path forward. Option A is incorrect as a first step as it can escalate the situation and hinder productive dialogue. Option B is incorrect as it is counterproductive and can escalate tensions. It is not a recommended approach to handling strikes. Option D is incorrect as there is not enough information to determine if an unfair labor practice has occurred.

20. C. The actions described in the scenario, such as documenting employees' concerns and holding meetings to inquire about the status of union organizing efforts, may be seen as interference with, restraint of, or coercion of employees in the exercise of their rights under labor laws. While it is generally acceptable for an employer to communicate with employees and listen to their concerns, there is a fine line between lawful communication and interference with employees' rights under labor laws. In this scenario, the employer's actions, such as documenting employees' concerns and holding meetings about the union-organizing efforts, could be perceived as interference or coercion. Option A is incorrect as targeting employees who support the union involves specific adverse actions against union supporters, whereas the scenario focuses on broader communication efforts. Option B is incorrect because retaliation against employees who show interest in forming a union involves punitive actions against those employees.

21. B. A secondary boycott occurs when individuals or a group of employees take action against a secondary business or entity that has a relationship with the primary target of a labor dispute (usually the employer). In this case, employees refusing to purchase products from a company that does business with their employer's supplier is an example of a secondary boycott because the action is directed at a secondary business entity (the supplier's customer) to support a union strike against their primary employer. Option A, C, and D are incorrect because they are primary strike actions, not a secondary boycott.

22. A. A wildcat strike is an unauthorized strike initiated by union members without following the legal procedures or the expiration of the labor contract. Option B is incorrect because a sympathy strike, also known as a secondary strike, occurs when one group of workers strikes in support of another group of workers who are involved in a labor dispute. Option C is incorrect a general strike is a widespread and coordinated work stoppage involving employees across various industries. Option D is incorrect because an economic strike is a labor action undertaken by employees to demand better wages, benefits, or working conditions, with the primary goal of improving their economic circumstances.

23. B. The labor conflict and work slowdown likely had a negative impact on organizational results. Decreased efficiency and increased operational costs, caused by flight delays and disruptions, would have negatively affected the organization's performance.

24. C. Labor-management cooperation is an approach where employers and unions collaborate and form joint committees to discuss workplace issues, foster communication, and work together to improve productivity, safety, and other shared concerns. Option A is incorrect as traditional bargaining refers to the negotiation process between employers and labor unions to reach agreements on issues such as wages, working conditions, and employment terms through formal bargaining sessions. Option B is incorrect because conflict resolution involves the methods and strategies used to address and resolve disputes, conflicts, or disagreements between employers and employees, often with the goal of finding mutually acceptable solutions. Option D is incorrect because arbitration is a dispute resolution process in which a neutral third party, an arbitrator, makes binding decisions to settle conflicts between employers and unions when they cannot reach an agreement through negotiation or other means.

25. A. Actively engaging with employees to determine if there is union-organizing activity occurring is a proactive and lawful approach in a union avoidance strategy. Employers can stay

informed about employee concerns and sentiments, which allows them to address issues and prevent unionization efforts from gaining traction. It is essential to respect employees' rights and engage in open and constructive communication. Option B is incorrect because employers have the right to communicate with employees about unions and their rights, but they must do so without engaging in unfair labor practices. Not discussing the topic altogether may not be effective in addressing employee concerns and can lead to mistrust. Option C is incorrect because employing measures to dissuade and deter unionization efforts can involve actions that may be considered unfair labor practices and are often unlawful. Option D is incorrect because collaborating with unions to address employee concerns and demands is more relevant to labor-management relations when a union is already present in the workplace.

26. A. Policies are high-level documents that provide overarching principles and guidelines, often setting the framework for how an organization should operate. Procedures, on the other hand, outline specific steps or processes that need to be followed to achieve a particular task or goal. Rules are associated with specifying consequences or actions to be taken when certain behaviors or conditions are violated. Understanding these distinctions is essential for effective governance and management within an organization.

27. A. An advantage of an open-door policy is that it encourages transparency, as employees feel comfortable reporting concerns without fear of retaliation. However, a potential disadvantage is that it may lead to a flood of minor complaints, which can overwhelm HR or management if not managed effectively. Option B is incorrect because an open-door policy can create a supportive work culture but does not undermine management authority; it can enhance management's ability to address concerns effectively. Option C is incorrect because an open-door policy can reduce employee stress by providing a channel to report concerns, but it should ideally speed up conflict resolution rather than slowing it down. Option D is incorrect as an open-door policy can help protect the organization from legal liability by addressing issues proactively, but it should not increase employee isolation; it should promote communication and support.

28. B. Mediation is generally more appropriate when parties involved in a dispute want to maintain control over the resolution process and work together with the assistance of a neutral mediator to reach a mutually agreeable solution. In mediation, the mediator helps facilitate communication and negotiation between the parties, but the final decision and settlement are determined by the parties themselves. Options A, C, and D are incorrect as they describe situations where arbitration may be more appropriate. Arbitration is often chosen when parties need a quick and legally binding decision imposed by a neutral third party. Arbitration allows for a more structured and formal process, making it better suited for complex legal matters.

29. A. In situations where an employee raises a complaint, it is important to maintain open communication with the employee to understand the complaint better and provide them with information about the nonretaliation policy. This approach demonstrates a commitment to addressing the issue while protecting the employee. While Options B, C, and D may have their merits in specific situations, they do not address the immediate need to ensure compliance with retaliation prevention approaches and create a safe environment for the employee.

30. C. Fostering a culture of open communication and trust with employees is a key positive approach for employers seeking to manage labor relations and employee concerns effectively in the workplace. When employees feel they can openly communicate with their employer and trust that their concerns will be heard and addressed, it can lead to improved labor relations, higher employee morale, and increased job satisfaction. Option A is incorrect because asking employees to form a committee is an unfair labor practice. Option B is incorrect because it represents a specific action rather than an overarching approach, making C the more comprehensive answer. Option D is incorrect because encouraging employees to participate in workplace decision-making is also a specific versus comprehensive approach and may not be feasible for all decisions.

31. A. Progressive discipline is a strategy that focuses on ensuring compliance with company policies and addressing performance or behavior issues through corrective actions. It often involves a sequence of steps, such as verbal warnings, written warnings, and possible termination. In contrast, positive discipline emphasizes coaching, employee development, and a supportive approach to address issues, with the goal of helping employees improve their behavior and performance rather than just punitive measures.

32. C. A code of conduct outlines ethical and behavioral expectations for employees, promoting good workplace behavior and adherence to company values. A collective bargaining agreement is a legally binding contract negotiated between an employer and a labor union, addressing terms and conditions of employment, such as wages, hours, and working conditions. Company policy refers to a set of documented rules, guidelines, and procedures that an organization establishes to regulate various aspects of its operations, including employee behavior, work processes, and compliance with legal and ethical standards. An employment contract is a legally binding agreement between an employer and an employee that outlines the terms and conditions of employment, including job responsibilities, compensation, benefits, working hours, and termination conditions.

33. D. When an employee believes they have been unfairly treated due to a violation of company policies, the first step in the grievance process is to submit a written grievance to the HR department or relevant management personnel. This written grievance should outline the details of the issue, including what policies were violated and the desired resolution. Option A is incorrect because the grievance process is often an internal mechanism that allows for the resolution of disputes before resorting to legal action. Option B is incorrect because while speaking to their immediate supervisor informally can be a way to address concerns, initiating the formal grievance process (as noted in the question) involves submitting a written complaint to HR or management. Option C is incorrect because contacting a labor union representative is not the first step in addressing internal company policy violations. Union representatives may become involved at later stages if the employee is part of a union, but the initial step is usually to submit a written grievance internally.

34. B. Including noncompete clauses in an employment contract is a lawful use of such contracts. Noncompete clauses are designed to protect a company's legitimate business interests by preventing employees from immediately working for competitors or starting their own competing businesses after leaving the company. However, the enforceability of noncompete clauses varies by jurisdiction, and they must be reasonable in scope and duration to be legally valid. Option A is incorrect because depending on the circumstances, employees

have the legal right to join or refrain from joining a union, and such agreements may violate labor laws, nor is it a typical use of an employment contract. Option C is incorrect because including a clause where the employee is not entitled to overtime pay is not a lawful use of employment contracts and subject to regulation by the Fair Labor Standards Act. Option D is incorrect because requiring employees to sign a contract that allows the employer to terminate them at any time and for any reason is generally lawful in "at-will" employment states in the United States. However, it may not be lawful in other jurisdictions or in cases where specific employment protections apply, such as employment contracts for a specified duration or collective bargaining agreements.

35. B. A cooperation clause in a severance agreement is a contractual provision that requires the departing employee to cooperate with the employer or the company in various ways, even after their employment has ended. The specific terms of a cooperation clause can vary depending on the agreement, but it often includes transition assistance, confidentiality, and nondisparagement. Option A is incorrect, as holding meetings alone may not guarantee the active cooperation and participation of the exiting employees in training their replacements. Option C is incorrect as this option doesn't directly address ensuring a smoother transition by actively involving exiting employees in training their replacements. Option D is incorrect as the concern is about the cooperation and willingness of the exiting employees to train their replacements.

36. C. A potential disadvantage of progressive discipline policies in the workplace is that they can limit employer action for more serious infractions. Progressive discipline involves a series of escalating consequences for employee misconduct, starting with mild interventions like verbal warnings and progressing to more severe measures like suspensions or termination. In cases of serious misconduct, waiting for progressive steps may not be appropriate, and immediate action may be necessary. Option A is incorrect as progressive discipline policies, when applied correctly, are designed to create a structured and fair approach to addressing employee misconduct. Option B is incorrect because well-defined progressive discipline policies should offer clear and predictable consequences for misconduct, not vague or unpredictable ones. Option D is incorrect because progressive discipline policies can promote transparency and communication by outlining the consequences of misconduct and the steps employees can take to address issues.

37. C. In this scenario, the most appropriate course of action is to involve the department manager in addressing the issue with Marie. The department manager, who directly supervises Marie, can have a one-on-one discussion with her to understand the reasons behind her recent tardiness. This approach allows for a collaborative and supportive conversation while involving the immediate supervisor, who is often best positioned to address such matters. Option A is premature and overly punitive for the situation described. Option B is incorrect because the department manager is the immediate supervisor and should take the lead in understanding the reasons behind the tardiness and providing guidance or support. HR may take on a coaching role for the supervisor at this stage, but not take the lead role. Option D is not a proactive or effective approach to managing employee performance or attendance concerns.

38. C. Suspension is used for serious misconduct or repeated violations and involves placing the employee on unpaid leave as a disciplinary measure. Termination in Option A is incorrect because it refers to the formal and permanent end of an individual's employment with an organization, often due to various reasons, including performance issues or violations of workplace policies. Option B is incorrect because verbal counseling is an informal and private conversation between an employee and a supervisor aiming to address specific work-related concerns, provide feedback, and discuss potential improvements or corrective actions. Option D is incorrect because corrective action is a broader set of actions aimed at addressing and rectifying employee performance or behavioral issues.

39. C. Carl's termination may be unlawful because of the timing of his separation. It is not unusual for employers to use alternative reasons such as "business restructuring" as a mask for questionable or possibly unlawful workplace actions. If not related to Carl's complaint, the termination due to business restructuring is a separate and legitimate reason for letting an employee go. Options A and B are incorrect because there is not enough information in the scenario to know if Carl's termination is not wrongful in this context. Option D is incorrect because the decision to transfer an employee to a different department should be based on valid reasons such as employee qualifications and may not always be the appropriate solution, especially in the context of business restructuring.

40. A. This policy, which immediately terminates employees with more than two customer complaints, can create a culture of fear, uncertainty, and low morale among employees. This, in turn, can hinder employee engagement, collaboration, and overall job satisfaction, ultimately affecting organizational results negatively. Option B is incorrect because its punitive nature can have unintended consequences, including negative impacts on employee morale and relations, which can, in turn, affect the organization's results. Option C is incorrect because the policy may create an environment where employees are hesitant to interact with customers or provide feedback due to the fear of immediate termination. Option D is incorrect because policies related to performance expectations are not in and of themselves unlawful, even though it might not be a best practice.

41. C. Evaluative alternative dispute resolution (ADR) is a process in which a neutral third party is permitted to offer opinions, predictions, or even decisions. In this approach, the neutral person evaluates the legal or factual aspects of a party's case and provides assessments that may influence the final resolution. Both parties agree to be bound by the neutral's evaluation or decision. Option A is incorrect because nonbinding ADR involves a process where the neutral may offer an opinion, but neither party is bound by that opinion. Option B is incorrect because facilitative ADR involves a process where the neutral helps the parties communicate directly with each other and stimulates discussion about the issues and mutual gains. Option D is incorrect because neutral ADR is not a recognized term.

42. B. In a consultative role, it is important to collaborate with the business unit leader to understand the specific needs, goals, and dynamics of the business unit. Employee recognition programs should be tailored to the unique characteristics and objectives of the organization or business unit. By working closely with the leader, you can create a program that addresses the specific challenges and objectives of the unit. Option A is incorrect because providing a one-size-fits-all employee recognition program template without considering the unique needs of the business unit may not be effective in boosting morale and productivity. Option C is incorrect because until the leader and HR have a clear understanding of the recognition program objectives, this would be premature to offer as a solution. Option D is incorrect because

finding a training program to enhance the leader's knowledge of effective employee recognition is not an example of an active consultative role of an HR professional.

43. C. Modern technology solutions can streamline contract administration, improve communication between parties, and reduce administrative overhead by automating tasks such as document storage, compliance tracking, and reporting. Options A, B, and D are incorrect because they are not cost-savings measures but rather an investment in enhancing labor management.

44. C. Calculating the absenteeism rate of a department is important because it provides valuable insights into the overall health and productivity of that department. As a new manager, it is useful to Rachael to understand the facts of the problem before she engages in problem solving to address underlying issues. To measure the absenteeism rate, use the formula (*Number of Absences / Number of workdays*). You can then multiply the total by 100 to get a percentage. For Rachael, the formula would be as follows:

```
(6/20)*100 = 30%
```

Rounded up, the absenteeism rate for the team is 30%.

45. B. Standard operating procedures (SOPs) are designed to provide clear and standardized instructions for performing tasks and processes. By doing so, SOPs simplify complex processes and make it easier for employees to understand and follow the established procedures. This clarity reduces the likelihood of errors, improves consistency, and enhances compliance with safety and quality standards. Option A is incorrect because SOPs are not intended to increase the complexity of tasks but rather to simplify them through standardized instructions. Option C is incorrect because SOPs are not just for managerial purposes; they are essential tools for ensuring that employees understand and adhere to safety and quality standards. Option D is incorrect because SOPs are established guidelines and procedures that employees are expected to follow to ensure consistency and compliance with standards.

46. B. Underpayment inequity occurs when individuals feel they are receiving less compensation or rewards than they deserve compared to others in similar roles. In this situation, employees are experiencing dissatisfaction and demotivation because they believe they are underpaid compared to their colleague, indicating underpayment inequity. Option A is incorrect as overpayment inequity occurs when an individual believes they are receiving more compensation or rewards than they deserve compared to their colleagues, which is not what the scenario describes. Option C is incorrect as it implies that employees are satisfied with their higher compensation compared to their colleague, which contradicts the feelings of dissatisfaction and demotivation described in the situation. Option D is incorrect because underpayment equity implies that individuals are satisfied with their compensation because they believe it is fair in relation to their colleagues. This option does not align with the scenario.

47. D. Performance management software plays a crucial role in managing employee relations by enabling organizations to set goals, provide feedback, conduct performance appraisals, and address any performance-related issues. It helps in aligning employee goals with organizational objectives and fostering open communication, making it an essential tool for effective employee relations. Options A, B, and C are important HR systems but do not reflect the primary function for managing employee relations.

48. A. While employee training and development are crucial components of HR and talent management, they are not considered key elements of a strategic labor strategy. A strategic labor strategy primarily focuses on managing labor costs, workforce planning, labor relations, and negotiations, whereas training and development fall under broader HR functions (Options B, C, and D).

49. B. A labor cooperative, also known as a labor-management cooperative (LMC), is designed to enhance communication, improve workplace conditions, and achieve common goals through cooperation. Option A is not recommended because it lacks balanced representation with both union and management voices, potentially leading to an adversarial perception and not adequately representing union interests. In the worst case, it is an unfair labor practice. Option C is incorrect because a federation is a group of unions or labor organizations working together for broader objectives. Option D is incorrect because a wage board is a group that may be convened to make recommendations on wage-related matters, such as minimum wage rates in specific industries.

50. C. In other countries, such as those in Europe, sectoral bargaining is common, where unions negotiate agreements that cover entire industries or sectors, involving multiple employers and workers. This approach contrasts with enterprise-level bargaining, where negotiations occur between individual companies and their employees, which is more common in the United States. Option A is incorrect as some countries may have laws mandating collective bargaining or recognizing unions as representatives of workers, but this is not universally true across all countries outside the United States. Option B is incorrect because in the United States, negotiations take place between individual employers and unions representing their employees, rather than across entire industries. Option D is incorrect because it misrepresents the bargaining practices in the United States; unions negotiate at various levels, including the local, regional, and national levels, depending on the context and industry.

51. B. Both functions share the common goal of fostering positive interactions in the workplace. Employee relations is centered around managing and improving workplace relationships, resolving conflicts, and maintaining a positive work environment. Employee engagement focuses on enhancing the quality of relationships between employees and the organization, which includes improving morale, motivation, and job satisfaction. Options A, C, and D are not accurate descriptions of the similarities between employee relations and employee engagement.

52. A. Older workers often value flexibility as they approach retirement age. This measure allows them to balance work and personal commitments and gradually transition into retirement, which can be motivating. Option B is incorrect because older workers may have different priorities, such as work-life balance and retirement planning, which may not be as influenced by performance-based incentives. Option C is incorrect as it may not specifically target the motivations of older workers at their particular career stage. These workers may have different priorities than emphasis on skill development beyond keeping their talents up-to-date, such as with new software programs or company policies. Option D, a casual dress code policy, is unlikely to be a primary motivator for older workers, as their motivation tends to be driven by factors related to their career stage, financial security, and work-life balance.

53. C. Orientation sessions that highlight company culture and values are an example of an employee relations strategy at the onboarding stage. Such sessions help new employees understand and align with the organization's culture, which contributes to a positive employee-employer relationship. Option A is partially correct as it can be part of an

organization's overall onboarding process; however, the correct answer is better aligned with the employee relations aspect of the question. Option B is incorrect because it is not specifically an employee relations strategy. Option D is incorrect because accelerated training and development may be part of the onboarding process to help employees quickly acquire the necessary skills, but it is not primarily an employee relations strategy.

54. D. A sourcing strategy, often associated with talent acquisition or recruitment, is not a direct part of an employee relations strategy. Employee relations strategies focus on managing and improving the relationship between the organization and its current workforce. They include plans and protocols to effectively address and manage crises (such as labor disputes, accidents, or emergencies) to maintain a positive employee-employer relationship during challenging times (Option A), employee feedback to improve communication and engagement and foster a positive workplace culture (Option B), and employee recognition and appreciation to boost morale, motivation, and overall job satisfaction (Option C).

55. B. Organizational lobbying efforts influence labor laws and regulations, potentially shaping the labor relations landscape. This can impact how organizations manage their relationships with employees, unions, and other labor-related matters. Option A is incorrect because organizational lobbying efforts may aim to influence political candidates, but their primary impact on the labor relations function is related to influencing labor laws and regulations, not directly tied to election outcomes. Option C is incorrect as lobbying efforts can have various economic effects on businesses, but they are not directly related to the labor relations function of human resources. Option D is incorrect as lobbying can influence labor-related laws and regulations, but its effects on unionization rates depend on various factors, including the specific goals of the lobbying efforts and the dynamics within the workforce.

56. C. Negligent hiring refers to the practice of not conducting appropriate background checks or due diligence when hiring an employee. It can result in hiring individuals who may pose risks to the organization or other employees due to their criminal history or other relevant factors. Negligent hiring can lead to legal and safety issues for the employer. Options A, B, and D are not accurate descriptions of the concept of negligent hiring.

57. B. When employees feel more engaged and connected to their work and the organization through involvement strategies, they are less likely to leave their jobs voluntarily. This results in lower turnover rates, which can save organizations recruitment and training costs and contribute to a more stable and experienced workforce. Option A is incorrect because job satisfaction is likely to increase as the result of employee involvement strategies, not decrease. Option C is incorrect because while employee involvement strategies can contribute to better conflict resolution and management, they do not necessarily guarantee a reduction in workplace conflicts, such as inter-personal or conflicts with management. Option D is incorrect as the primary benefit of involvement strategies, particularly in the context of employee relations, is often related to employee retention and satisfaction rather than product quality directly.

58. A. A self-directed work team is not primarily designed to solicit employee feedback. Instead, self-directed work teams are groups of employees responsible for managing their own tasks and making decisions related to their work processes. Focus groups, staff meetings, and surveys (Options B, C, and D) involve small groups of employees who provide input, opinions, and insights on specific topics or issues.

59. B. Homogeneity refers to the quality of being uniform or similar in composition, nature, or characteristics. Homogeneity, or the absence of diversity in terms of cultural backgrounds and perspectives, can result in a limited awareness of cultural nuances and differences. This lack of understanding can lead to ethical challenges, misinterpretations, and potential ethical dilemmas when managing a diverse international workforce. Option A is incorrect as it presents the opposite effect of what homogeneity typically does. Option C is incorrect because homogeneity does not ensure consistency in ethical practices across diverse cultural contexts. In fact, it may lead to ethical challenges because ethical practices may not consider the cultural differences and specific needs of diverse groups. Option D is incorrect because homogeneity can have a significant impact on ethical considerations in IHRM.

60. C. A key tension in global employee relations within a shared service structure is the alignment or potential conflict between the corporate structures and policies of a company and the local practices and legal parameters in different regions. Balancing these two aspects is essential for successful global employee relations. Options A, B, and D are not examples of primary tensions in a shared service model.

Chapter 10: Ethical Practice and Corporate Social Responsibility

1. D. The most effective ethical control to prevent conflicts of interest in the CEO's decision-making is a well-defined ethical code of conduct. This code outlines the principles, values, and standards of behavior expected from all employees and can require the CEO to disclose any situation where her personal financial interests may conflict with the best interests of the company and its shareholders. Option A is incorrect as it is not primarily an ethical control but rather a financial reporting requirement that helps shareholders and the board of directors track the company's performance. Option B is incorrect as board oversight is not a control mechanism by itself but rather a governance practice. Option C is incorrect as the Generally Accepted Accounting Principles (GAAP) is a set of accounting standards that guide financial reporting, not an ethical control for executive decision-making.

2. B. In the scenario described, the corporate social responsibility (CSR) scrutiny is most likely related to supply chain sourcing. Lack of transparency and oversight in the supply chain can lead to issues such as labor law violations, unethical practices, and environmental and social standards in the supply chain, and is a common focus in CSR assessments and investigations. Option A is incorrect as a nongovernmental organization (NGO) is a nonprofit entity that operates independently from government authorities, including the United States, and the question does not suggest a group such as this is involved in the audits. Option C is incorrect as the businesses are located overseas, and the Fair Labor Standards Act (FLSA) is a U.S. labor law. Option D is incorrect as while violations of International Labor Organization (ILO) standards are certainly a significant concern in cases of labor law violations and CSR, the scenario suggests a broader set of issues that extend to unethical practices and violations of environmental and social standards. The ILO applies only to member states, which is not a factor mentioned in the scenario.

3. B. The Equifax data breach of 2017 offers several key insights into corporate ethical behaviors, especially in response to a crisis. Issues under scrutiny were a lack of proper internal controls, failing to secure customer information and failing to notify customers of the breach in a timely manner. In the context of a significant data breach involving sensitive personal information, company executives who were aware of the breach had an ethical duty to inform all "covered insiders" not to sell any stock until the breach information was made public. This ethical duty is rooted in the need for transparency and fairness in stock trading during a sensitive period.

4. B. In this situation, Mary should report the misconduct to higher management or an ethics hotline. Reporting unethical or fraudulent activities is essential to maintain the integrity and ethical standards within an organization. It helps ensure that the issue is properly investigated and addressed, promoting transparency and accountability. Option A is incorrect as confrontation could potentially escalate the situation and may not be the most effective way to address the issue or protect the organization's interests. Option C is incorrect because ignoring the misconduct to avoid confrontation could allow fraudulent activities to continue unchecked, potentially causing harm to the organization and its stakeholders. Option D is incorrect as it goes against the principles of integrity and transparency.

5. C. The primary purpose of a code of ethics in human resource management is to guide ethical behavior and decision-making within the workplace. It provides a set of principles and standards that employees, including HR professionals, should follow to ensure ethical conduct in their interactions, decisions, and practices. While it aims to eliminate unethical behavior, its primary function is to serve as a moral compass and framework for ethical conduct. Option A is incorrect as it is not possible to eliminate ethical threats from the workplace. Option B is incorrect as a code of ethics is distinct from a legal framework for HR practices. Option D is incorrect as fraud prevention is often addressed through more detailed policies and procedures within an organization's overall governance framework.

6. B. An "opt-in" policy gives employees the choice to participate in benefit programs voluntarily. Option A is incorrect because it implies automatic enrollment, which is associated with "opt-out" policies. Option C is incorrect because it enforces participation, which is contrary to the purpose of an "opt-in" policy. Option D is incorrect because it suggests benefits are provided without consent, which is not the case with "opt-in" policies.

7. A. Admitting the mistake is the best example of personal integrity in this situation. It demonstrates honesty and transparency, as the HR manager takes responsibility for the error and promptly informs both the employees and the senior leadership. This action aligns with ethical principles and upholds personal integrity. Options B and C are incorrect because personal integrity is primarily about individual ethical behavior and decision-making, and writing a policy or conducting training are more of a procedural or organizational response to the issue. Option D is incorrect as taking the blame for an error that was not personally committed is not the best example of personal integrity. Personal integrity involves taking responsibility for one's own actions and decisions, not assuming blame for others' mistakes.

8. B. A common barrier to personal integrity for HR professionals and leaders in the workplace is the fear that honesty and transparency may lead to negative consequences. This fear can deter individuals from speaking up about ethical concerns, admitting mistakes, or reporting

wrongdoing. Personal integrity often involves the courage to uphold ethical principles even when it involves facing challenges or potential backlash. Option A is incorrect as this option represents a specific ethical dilemma rather than a barrier to personal integrity as a whole. Option C is incorrect as avoiding legal responsibilities to protect personal interests is a specific issue related to negative consequences mentioned in the correct answer. Option D is incorrect because a rigid, inflexible approach to ethical dilemmas is not a barrier to personal integrity, and while it may not be appropriate in every circumstance, it is likely to support ethical outcomes as a whole.

9. A. Carlos is displaying availability bias. He is overemphasizing the importance of punctuality and attendance because these aspects are readily available and easy to recall when evaluating employees, even though they may not be the most relevant or comprehensive indicators of job performance. Option B is incorrect because confirmation bias involves seeking information that confirms preexisting beliefs or opinions. Option C is incorrect because the term *performance bias* is not a commonly recognized cognitive bias. Option D is incorrect because horn bias is a form of cognitive bias where an evaluator excessively emphasizes an employee's negative traits or behaviors.

10. C. One of the key strategies for human resource teams to become a trusted and credible business partner within an organization is to align HR strategies with the overall business goals. This involves understanding the organization's objectives and tailoring HR initiatives, such as recruitment, training, and talent management, to support those goals. Option A is incorrect because effective communication with employees is essential for engagement, productivity, and addressing their needs and concerns. Maintaining neutrality does not mean avoiding communication but rather ensuring fairness and transparency in interactions. Option B is incorrect because focusing solely on administrative tasks and paperwork limits HR's role to transactional activities and does not contribute to becoming a trusted business partner. Option D is incorrect because collaboration and cross-functional partnerships are essential for HR to understand the needs of different departments, align strategies, and contribute to the organization's success.

11. C. Kinsey should exercise discretion by refusing to comment on the matter with the news reporter. External communication, especially with the media, should be limited to what has been officially announced by the company. This ensures that accurate and authorized information is shared and prevents the spread of rumors or unverified details. Option A is incorrect as while transparency is important, it should be balanced with the need to protect the organization's interests and ensure that accurate information is disseminated through official channels. Options B and D are incorrect because premature communication can lead to anxiety, confusion, and misinformation. HR should follow the company's communication plan and share information when it is officially confirmed.

12. B. An anonymous reporting hotline is a key component of a company code of ethics that is most likely to prevent unethical behavior from occurring. The availability of such a hotline encourages employees to speak up when they witness unethical actions, thereby deterring potential wrongdoing and promoting a culture of ethics and accountability within the organization. Options A, C, and D are incorrect because they are more about setting the standards for ethical behaviors without providing a mechanism for taking action.

13. C. In this situation, Mark faces the ethical risk of falsifying records. Deleting incriminating emails related to a regulatory violation is a form of falsifying records, as it involves altering or concealing information to misrepresent the true state of affairs. Option A is incorrect as insider trading refers to trading securities based on material nonpublic information related to a company's stock. Option B is incorrect as a data breach involves unauthorized access to or disclosure of sensitive information. Option D is incorrect because cybersecurity violations may encompass various unethical actions related to IT security, but this scenario specifically revolves around altering records.

14. D. A fundamental ethical consideration in total rewards activities is ensuring transparency in how total rewards (compensation, benefits, incentives, etc.) are determined and communicated to employees. Transparency promotes fairness, trust, and alignment with organizational values. Employees should understand how their rewards are calculated and why they receive specific compensation and benefits. Options A and B are incorrect because there are many other factors to consider beyond work experience when it comes to setting pay rates, and pay practices do not have to be consistent across departments as long as they are based on job-related factors and not protected characteristics. Option C is incorrect because accurate payroll records a specific operational aspect of total rewards activities rather than the fundamental ethical consideration.

15. C. Implementing an anonymous whistleblower hotline is the correct option to foster accountability and transparency in the workplace. By providing a confidential and anonymous channel for reporting, it encourages employees to speak up about unethical practices, misconduct, or violations of company policies. Option A is incorrect as it alone may not be sufficient to foster accountability and transparency and should be complemented by mechanisms like the whistleblower hotline to encourage reporting and address issues effectively. Option B is incorrect because it addresses a different aspect of ethics, focusing on safeguarding sensitive data rather than encouraging reporting or accountability, and can inhibit transparency if the practice is too rigid. Option D is incorrect as it doesn't actively encourage employees to report ethical violations or enhance transparency in the organization.

16. C. While it is important for the ethics officer to ensure that any illegal activities are reported to the appropriate authorities, this is not considered a primary responsibility of an ethics officer within the company. Their primary focus is on addressing ethical concerns internally and ensuring compliance with company policies and ethical standards. Ethics officers are tasked with investigating ethical complaints to determine their validity and taking appropriate action to address any unethical behavior within the organization. Whistleblowers need to be protected from potential retaliation or harm, and their identity must be kept confidential to encourage reporting of ethical violations. They must ensure that the investigation is conducted in accordance with the company's established policies and procedures to maintain fairness and transparency.

17. C. The ethical use of company assets entails responsibly utilizing resources such as company funds, equipment, and intellectual property in a manner consistent with organizational objectives and policies, while avoiding actions such as embezzlement or unauthorized sharing of proprietary information. Employees should prioritize aligning asset utilization with the organization's goals and policies. This means that employees should use company assets in a

manner that supports the company's objectives and follows its established policies and guidelines. Option A is incorrect because it should not involve personal enrichment at the expense of the organization. Option B is incorrect as it can lead to unethical behavior and potentially illegal activities. Transparency and accountability in reporting asset usage are essential for ethical conduct. Option D is incorrect because discouraging personal device use within the workplace is not practical and is not necessarily the most effective method to protect the company from unethical use of assets.

18. D. Unethical corporate behavior such as inflating drug prices in a low-income region can have severe consequences for the community stakeholders. It can also exacerbate poverty by placing a financial burden on individuals who are already economically disadvantaged. Option A is incorrect because awareness of issues should be brought about in ways that do not cause additional harm to the affected communities. Option B is incorrect as it focuses on the potential financial benefits for company shareholders and doesn't address the harm caused to the community stakeholders. Option C is incorrect as it focuses on the impact to the organization, not to the community stakeholders.

19. B. Reducing carbon footprints involves taking actions to minimize the environmental impact of a company's operations by decreasing greenhouse gas emissions. This can include measures such as adopting energy-efficient technologies, using renewable energy sources, implementing waste reduction programs, and promoting sustainable transportation. Option A is a financial incentive or compensation strategy rather than an environmental initiative. Option C is incorrect because it primarily addresses ethical and social concerns related to labor and human rights, not environmental sustainability. Option D is incorrect as it is a form of philanthropy as a CSR initiative, not environmental sustainability.

20. B. The correct answer is Option B because this situation highlights a limitation of using monetary rewards as a means to improve ethical behavior. Ethical behavior depends on various factors, including the design of incentive programs and the alignment of incentives with ethical principles. Option A is incorrect because it suggests that incentive pay systems can effectively motivate employees to improve their performance in all situations, and this specific case demonstrates that they can also lead to unintended ethical issues if not designed properly. Option C is incorrect as it implies that piece-rate pay based on objective data is the solution, which would not have avoided the unethical behaviors. Option D is incorrect because it makes a blanket assumption that employees are inherently dishonest. The problem in this situation is with the design of the incentive system, not the inherent honesty or dishonesty of the employees.

21. A. Legal obligations are those duties and responsibilities that are mandated by the law and are enforceable through legal mechanisms. Noncompliance with legal obligations can lead to penalties, fines, or legal consequences. On the other hand, ethical obligations are based on moral principles and guidelines, and while they guide behavior and decision-making, they are not enforced by law and may not have legal consequences. Option B is partially correct because legal obligations are based on secular beliefs; however, ethical obligations are influenced by various sources, not just religion. Option C is incorrect because it oversimplifies the distinction by implying that legal obligations are universal, while ethical obligations vary widely from person to person. Legal obligations can also vary from one jurisdiction to another, and ethical obligations may be shared by individuals within a particular community or profession. Option D is incorrect because it inaccurately portrays legal obligations as concerning personal values and beliefs.

22. C. Balancing the interests of stakeholders while maintaining integrity and transparency is a fundamental ethical principle in designing corporate strategy. This approach acknowledges the importance of not only delivering value to shareholders but also considering the well-being and concerns of employees, customers, suppliers, communities, and other stakeholders. Option A is incorrect because prioritizing the maximization of short-term profits for shareholders can lead to unethical decision-making, such as neglecting the interests of other stakeholders or engaging in actions that harm the company's reputation. Option B is incorrect because pursuing aggressive competitive tactics to gain market dominance can sometimes involve unethical behavior, such as unfair competition or anticompetitive practices. Option D incorrect because focusing on cost-cutting measures to increase profitability may lead to unethical decisions, such as compromising product quality or disregarding the welfare of employees and suppliers.

23. B. Ethical advocacy refers to the act of raising concerns and making a business case for change. By presenting their evidence to the hospital administrators, the nurses are attempting to engage with the institution's decision-makers in a constructive manner to advocate for patient safety and well-being. Option A is incorrect because while using the hospital's whistleblower hotline may be a way to report wrongdoing, it doesn't necessarily represent ethical advocacy. Option C is incorrect because anonymously leaking information to the media could potentially violate confidentiality and harm the institution's reputation without necessarily leading to internal improvements. Option D is incorrect because lodging a complaint with the hospital board of directors is a formal action but may not be considered ethical advocacy on its own. Ethical advocacy involves presenting evidence and engaging with relevant parties within the organization to address ethical concerns constructively.

24. A. Corporate social responsibility (CSR) initiatives should address the interests of all stakeholders, not just shareholders. CSR involves a company's commitment to ethical and responsible practices that benefit not only its investors (shareholders) but also employees, customers, the environment, local communities, and other relevant stakeholders. Option B is not correct because the environment represents only one stakeholder, and the stakeholder theory applies to all stakeholders. Option C is incorrect because it suggests that the sole priority of corporate leadership should be maximizing profits for shareholders; but maximizing profits at the expense of social and environmental responsibilities is not aligned with contemporary CSR practices. Option D is not directly related to the question and does not address the primary concept of the stakeholder theory.

25. B. The triple bottom line (TBL) framework is used to evaluate a company's performance in terms of its social, environmental, and financial impacts. People represents the social aspect, focusing on the well-being of employees, communities, and stakeholders. Planet represents the environmental aspect, emphasizing sustainable and responsible environmental practices. Profit represents the financial aspect, indicating the company's economic performance. The TBL framework encourages organizations to consider and balance these three dimensions in their decision-making processes.

26. D. The initiatives described in the scenario are aligned with enhancing social responsibility. These actions reflect the company's commitment to making a positive social impact on its community and stakeholders. Social responsibility in the context of the triple bottom line (TBL) refers to a company's efforts to address and improve its social and ethical practices, including philanthropic initiatives and community engagement. Option A is incorrect because it this concept does not capture the broader scope of social responsibility initiatives mentioned in the scenario, such as community development and educational programs. Option C is incorrect because the initiatives described in the scenario primarily emphasize social responsibility efforts, such as community support and education, rather than environmental sustainability. Option B is incorrect because it does not encompass the full range of actions described, which include donating profits and sponsoring educational programs.

27. B. Conducting a stakeholder analysis is the initial step in the corporate social responsibility (CSR) strategic process. This step involves identifying and analyzing the various stakeholders who are affected by or have an interest in the company's operations so that organizations can prioritize issues, set goals, and develop CSR initiatives that align with stakeholder interests, making their efforts more meaningful and impactful. Option A is incorrect as expert feedback may be sought at various stages to inform CSR strategies, but it usually comes after conducting a stakeholder analysis to ensure that the identified experts are aligned with stakeholder interests. Option C is incorrect as companies usually engage in public communication once they have a clear understanding of their CSR objectives and strategies. Option D is incorrect as it involves evaluating the impact and effectiveness of CSR initiatives after they have been implemented.

28. B. Senior HR leaders can effectively communicate a vision for organizational culture that aligns corporate behavior with organizational values by hosting open forums and dialogues with employees. This approach fosters direct engagement and two-way communication, allowing employees to participate in discussions about culture and values. It promotes transparency, trust, and alignment between the organization's vision and the input and perspectives of its employees. Option A is incorrect because it is a one-way communication method that may not provide the same level of engagement, discussion, and employee input as open forums and dialogues. Option C is incorrect because it focuses more on assessing inclusivity rather than directly communicating a vision for organizational culture. Option D is incorrect because it is more related to training and development than communication strategies.

29. C. Empathy plays a significant role in a company's corporate social responsibility (CSR) strategy by serving as a strong predictor for employee involvement in CSR initiatives. When employees feel that the organization genuinely cares about social and environmental issues and demonstrates empathy toward communities and causes, they are more likely to engage actively in CSR activities. Empathy fosters a sense of connection, purpose, and motivation among employees, leading to increased participation and support for CSR efforts. Option A is incorrect because empathy, when appropriately applied, enhances the understanding of stakeholder perspectives and ethical considerations, leading to more informed and ethical CSR decisions. Option B is incorrect as while empathy is a crucial factor, CSR strategies should also consider organizational goals, stakeholder interests, and ethical principles for maximum impact. Option D is incorrect as a lack of empathy can hinder the effectiveness of CSR efforts, especially when it comes to employee engagement and stakeholder relationships.

30. C. The scenario represents the CSR implementation and action stage. In response to the criticism and environmental concerns, the company takes tangible steps to reduce plastic waste by transitioning to recyclable packaging and investing in waste reduction technologies. This stage involves putting CSR plans into action. Option A involves defining the social and environmental objectives and strategies that an organization intends to pursue as part of its CSR efforts. Option B refers to the process of actively involving and collaborating with various internal and external stakeholders, such as employees, customers, communities, and investors, in shaping and implementing CSR initiatives. Option D involves the transparent disclosure of a company's CSR activities, impact, and progress toward CSR goals to internal and external stakeholders, aiming to build trust and accountability.

31. A. Senior HR leaders can best audit a company's ethical business practices by conducting regular ethical audits. These audits should involve a systematic and thorough examination of the organization's ethical policies, practices, and behaviors. They aim to assess compliance with established ethical standards, identify potential ethical issues or violations, and provide recommendations for improvement. Ethical audits help senior HR leaders ensure that the company's ethical practices align with its values and that any shortcomings are addressed. Option B is incorrect because relying on employee self-reporting may not provide an accurate picture of the organization's ethical practices, as employees may be hesitant to report ethical violations, and some violations may go unreported. Option C is incorrect as senior HR leaders should actively participate in the audit process to have a firsthand understanding of the organization's ethical practices and to be actively involved in addressing any issues. Option D is incorrect as conducting one-time ethical audits without ongoing monitoring and follow-up is insufficient for maintaining and improving ethical business practices.

32. B. When designing ethical training programs for employees, incorporating real-world ethical dilemmas and case studies should be a fundamental component to ensure effectiveness and behavioral change. Real-world scenarios allow employees to engage with practical ethical challenges they may encounter in their roles. By analyzing and discussing these scenarios, employees can develop a deeper understanding of ethical decision-making, empathy, and ethical behavior. This approach helps bridge the gap between theory and practice, making the training more impactful in promoting ethical conduct in the workplace. Option A is incorrect as it primarily focuses on legal requirements and may not necessarily lead to behavioral change related to ethical decision-making. Option C is incorrect because policies and procedures provide guidelines, but ethical training should go beyond them to promote a deeper understanding of ethics. Option D is incorrect as effective ethical training should focus on engaging participants, fostering critical thinking, and encouraging discussions about ethical dilemmas, which can lead to behavioral change beyond standardized content delivery.

33. A. One of the key characteristics of a human resource professional acting as an ethical agent is modeling fairness and equity in making HR decisions. Ethical HR professionals prioritize fairness by ensuring that hiring, promotions, compensation, and other HR decisions are made impartially and without discrimination. They serve as role models for ethical conduct within the organization. Option B is incorrect because the primary role of an HR professional, as an ethical agent, is not to focus on maximizing company profits. Option C is incorrect because ensuring employee benefits alignment with employee needs is a valid HR concern, but it is not a key characteristic of an HR professional acting as an ethical agent. Ethical agents primarily focus on issues related to fairness, equity, and ethical conduct in HR practices. Option D is only partially correct in that not discriminating in decisions about promotions is indeed a key characteristic of an ethical HR professional, but it does not encompass the full range of ethical responsibilities of HR professionals.

34. A. The scenario describes a CSR program that aligns its initiatives with global sustainability targets such as the United Nations sustainable development goals (SDGs) and implements consistent sustainability practices and reporting across all its subsidiaries worldwide. This aligns with the concept of a globally integrated CSR program, which aims to address global sustainability challenges on a unified and consistent basis across the organization's global operations. Option B is incorrect because a locally responsive CSR program emphasizes tailoring its actions and initiatives to address specific community or regional needs, taking into account the local context and challenges. Option C is incorrect because it does not capture the comprehensive nature of the CSR program described in the scenario. Option D is incorrect because the example emphasizes the alignment of initiatives across all subsidiaries, suggesting a coordinated and integrated approach rather than an independent one.

35. D. When organizations actively engage in employee volunteerism and support community initiatives, it reflects their commitment to social and environmental responsibility. This commitment enhances their reputation and image as socially responsible and ethical entities, which can be appealing to customers, investors, and stakeholders. A positive CSR image can contribute to building trust, brand loyalty, and positive public perception of the organization. Option A is incorrect because volunteerism can actually decrease productivity if employees are paid to take time away from work to volunteer. Option B is incorrect as the goal of employee volunteerism programs are usually more aligned with social and community benefits rather than financial gains. Option C is incorrect as it pertains to the satisfaction that comes from the work itself, not company behaviors or culture.

36. C. Gaining buy-in for company CSR initiatives can be tricky due to the several barriers of measurement. These barriers include a lack of universally accepted practices and standardized data, as well as defining impact that may take years or decades to understand, such as reducing carbon emissions. There are several financial key performance indicators that can help companies understand the return-on-investment of their strategic CSR initiatives.

37. C. One potential drawback of employee volunteerism programs in terms of employee diversity and inclusion is that they can unintentionally exclude certain groups of employees. This exclusion can occur if the volunteer opportunities or charitable causes selected by the company do not resonate with or accommodate the interests, backgrounds, or abilities of all employees. For example, if volunteer activities are primarily geared toward physical tasks that may be difficult for individuals with disabilities, it can inadvertently exclude them from participating. Option A is incorrect because it does not directly relate to the drawback of employee volunteerism programs in terms of diversity and inclusion. Option B is incorrect because it describes a different potential consequence of employee volunteerism programs, which is the impact on organizational culture (individualism versus collectivism) and does not address the potential drawback related to diversity and inclusion. Option D is incorrect because it also does not specifically address the drawback related to diversity and inclusion, which is the focus of the question.

38. C. ESG ratings assess an organization's performance in any one or combination of three parameters: environmental, social, and governance. Reducing greenhouse gas emissions is one example of how an employer may analyze these ratings and identify specific areas where it needs to improve its sustainability and ethical practices. This information can guide the organization's CSR initiatives, helping it focus on addressing weaknesses and enhancing its overall CSR program. Options A and D are incorrect because they do not reflect the primary purpose of ESG ratings in CSR initiatives. Option B is not true.

39. C. Sustainability is a broader concept that involves considerations related to environmental preservation and economic viability. It emphasizes the responsible use of resources, reducing environmental impact, and ensuring the long-term viability of business operations. Social responsibility extends beyond environmental and economic aspects to include ethical treatment of employees, support for communities, and responsible engagement with society at large. Option A is incorrect as sustainability is not just about financial profitability; it also includes environmental and social dimensions. Option B is incorrect because social responsibility goes beyond philanthropic initiatives to include the broader considerations of all stakeholders including the communities where work is performed, the environment, the customers, and the employees. Option D is incorrect because sustainability is not exclusively related to product quality or customer service; it encompasses broader aspects such as environmental and economic considerations.

40. C. Governments are not considered stakeholders in traditional corporate social responsibility (CSR) initiatives. While governments play a regulatory role in overseeing businesses and may require compliance with certain social and environmental standards, traditional CSR initiatives focus on addressing the concerns and interests of the shareholders, customers, and communities in which the company operates. Companies often aim to provide returns to their investors while also engaging in responsible and ethical practices, striving to meet customer expectations, and engaging in socially responsible practices to enhance their reputation. Additionally, companies often engage in activities that benefit the local community, such as supporting local causes, improving infrastructure, or providing jobs.

41. A. Ethical frameworks provide a structured and systematic approach to addressing ethical dilemmas. HR professionals can use ethical frameworks to evaluate the situation, consider various ethical principles and theories, and arrive at a well-reasoned and ethical decision. Option B is incorrect as evidence-based decision-making involves using data and empirical evidence to inform decisions and improve outcomes. Option C is incorrect as availability heuristics refer to mental shortcuts where individuals rely on readily available information; relying on availability heuristics can lead to biased and potentially unethical decisions, as it may not consider all relevant factors or ethical principles. Option D is incorrect because just because something is not illegal does not make it ethical.

42. B. An HR professional that is authentic creates and supports an ethical culture because they are able to be role models that influence others in the company to follow ethical practices. This contributes to the development of an ethical culture where integrity is valued. Option A is incorrect because ethical culture is influenced by a combination of factors, including leadership, organizational values, policies, and employee behavior. Option C is incorrect because while authenticity can be helpful in making difficult decisions by ensuring that HR professionals act in accordance with their values, it is not the primary reason for authenticity in the context of creating an ethical culture. Option D is incorrect because authenticity is highly relevant in the context of ethical culture development.

43. D. The corporate behavior described aligns with John Rawls' theory of justice. Rawls's theory emphasizes the importance of fairness in the distribution of benefits and opportunities within a society. In this scenario, the company's commitment to allocating profits to community development programs that prioritize the needs of the least advantaged members of society reflects the principles of Rawls' theory, as it aims to benefit those who are most disadvantaged. Option A is incorrect as procedural justice focuses on the fairness and transparency of decision-making processes. Option B is incorrect because duty-based ethics, also known as deontology, emphasizes moral duties and obligations. Duty-based ethics often involves adhering to moral duties regardless of the consequences, which is not explicitly addressed in this scenario. Option C is incorrect because "moral high ground" is not a recognized ethical theory or concept in the context of justice theories or CSR.

44. C. Distributive justice is concerned with the fair distribution of benefits and burdens in society, ensuring that resources and opportunities are allocated equitably to reduce inequalities. In this scenario, the company's commitment to fair wages, equal opportunities, and educational programs reflects the principles of distributive justice, as it aims to distribute benefits in a way that promotes economic fairness. Option A is incorrect as it refers to the intention or motivation behind one's actions. The scenario involves more than just good intentions; it involves concrete actions aimed at achieving distributive justice. Option B is incorrect because absolutism in ethics refers to the belief in moral absolutes, where certain actions are considered inherently wrong, regardless of the context or consequences which the scenario does not describe. Option D is incorrect because the categorical imperative is a concept that emphasizes moral principles that apply unconditionally, which is not what is described in the scenario.

45. A. A key characteristic of a libertarian view of distributive justice is the belief in minimal government intervention in economic affairs. Libertarians argue that individuals and businesses should have the freedom to make their own economic decisions without excessive government regulation or oversight. Option B is incorrect as the libertarians generally prefer limited government involvement in economic and social affairs, favoring individual freedom and voluntary interactions over government-imposed regulations. Option C is incorrect because involuntary government oversight directly contradicts the libertarian perspective. Option D is incorrect because although nongovernmental organizations (NGOs) might play a role in certain libertarian approaches to governance, the emphasis is typically on minimizing government involvement rather than transferring oversight to nongovernmental entities.

46. C. Ethical Total Rewards administration requires transparency, meaning that the processes and decisions related to rewards and benefits are clear, open, and easily understood by employees. Option A is incorrect because competitiveness focuses more on the market competitiveness of salaries and benefits rather than the ethical considerations related to administration. Option B is incorrect as it captures the more legal aspect of total rewards rather than ethical responsibility of total rewards programs. Option D is incorrect as ethical administration includes more traditional aspects, such as fairness, transparency, and adherence to legal and moral standards.

47. C. In the context of workers' compensation claims, employer ethical and legal behavior includes ensuring that injured workers receive appropriate medical care, rehabilitation, and support to help them recover and return to work as closely to their pre-injury state as

possible. This reflects the ethical obligation to treat injured employees fairly and compassionately. Options A and B are partially correct as it is true that employers have a duty to provide a safe workplace and protect workers. However, these statements apply prior to an employee being injured, and the question asks specifically about a workers' compensation claim, which occur only if an employer has been injured on the job. Option D is incorrect because this option oversimplifies the issue. The duration of coverage may vary depending on factors such as the severity of the injury and legal requirements, and medical care is often capped as part of a settlement claim when necessary.

48. A. Fiduciary responsibility is a legal obligation, often tied to a specific role or profession (such as fiduciary duty in finance or legal responsibility in healthcare). Ethical behavior, on the other hand, is a broader concept that involves personal or organizational values and principles and is not always legally mandated. The other options are untrue.

49. D. The doctrine of "do no harm" applies universally to all professionals, guiding their ethical conduct and decision-making. Regardless of the specific profession, professionals have a fundamental obligation to prioritize the well-being and safety of the individuals and communities they serve. Upholding the principle of nonmaleficence is essential for maintaining trust, preserving reputation, and fulfilling the duty of care owed to clients, customers, patients, or stakeholders.

50. B. The employer's decision to promote a team member who was willing to be paid less for the same work, while laying off Camilla, may be seen as a violation of the duty of good faith and fair dealing. This duty implies that employers should act honestly and fairly in their dealings with employees, including decisions related to promotions and compensation. Option A is incorrect as Camilla is under the age of 40, so amendments to the Civil Rights of 1964 do not apply. Option C is partially correct as the doctrine of at-will employment pertains to the general principle that either the employer or the employee can terminate the employment relationship at any time for any reason; the duty of good faith and fair dealing is an exception to that doctrine. Option D is incorrect because we do not have enough information to know if Camilla was discriminated against based on her gender.

51. B. The "common good" approach to ethical decision-making involves considering the well-being and interests of all stakeholders, including employees, customers, communities, and the environment. This approach seeks to create a balance that benefits everyone involved and promotes a broader sense of responsibility. Option A is incorrect because it focuses on internal stakeholders (employees) without considering broader societal or environmental well-being. Option C is incorrect as it primarily benefits one specific stakeholder group (the shareholders) and may not consider the broader welfare of all stakeholders. Option D is incorrect because this scenario specifically focuses on marketing tactics to reach a diverse customer base, which is a business strategy. It may promote social justice but does not directly represent a "common good" approach that considers the welfare of all stakeholders comprehensively.

52. C. Maximizing profits and cost-effectiveness is a business consideration but not necessarily an ethical one in isolation. While businesses aim for profitability, ethical supply chain evaluations prioritize responsible and ethical practices over pure profit maximization. Options A, B, and D—ensuring fair labor practices and workers' rights, minimizing environmental impact and sustainability, and preventing child labor and exploitative working conditions—are all ethical considerations related to ensuring humane and fair treatment of workers.

53. C. Social mores represent the culturally specific norms and conventions that guide behavior within a particular society, while ethical behaviors are grounded in universal moral principles that transcend cultural boundaries. While there is often overlap between the two, ethical behaviors provide a deeper and more enduring foundation for evaluating the rightness of actions, even when they diverge from prevailing social norms. Options A, B, and D are not true statements.

54. A. Recognizing an ethical situation often begins with an individual's own personal integrity. When someone has a strong sense of personal values and ethics, they are more likely to recognize when they are facing an ethical dilemma or situation in which ethical principles may be at risk. Option B is incorrect as ethical situations are more about the alignment of actions with moral and ethical principles, which may not always be visibly tied to an employee's emotional state. Option C is incorrect because it does not directly reflect the need for recognizing ethical situations. Ethical situations can arise from various circumstances, including decisions made with or without full transparency. Option D is incorrect as ethical situations can involve a broader range of scenarios, and in some cases, it could be necessary to violate an unwritten agreement without it necessarily being an unethical decision.

55. C. The primary ethical consideration when using personality assessments in the workplace is ensuring that the assessments are reliable and valid predictors of behaviors, traits, or competencies relevant to the job. Using assessments that lack predictive accuracy can lead to unfair treatment of employees. Option A is incorrect as cost-effectiveness is a practical consideration rather than an ethical consideration. Option B is incorrect because objectivity can be achieved internally as well, not just by the use of consultants. Option D is incorrect because personality assessments are rooted in psychological principles, and it is more important that they accurately measure what they are intended to measure and predict behavior in a valid and reliable manner.

56. C. The virtue approach to ethical decision-making focuses on cultivating virtuous behavioral traits, such as honesty, courage, integrity, and compassion, as the foundation for ethical behavior. It emphasizes the importance of developing morally admirable qualities. Option A is incorrect as it describes the utilitarian approach to ethics, which focuses on maximizing overall happiness and well-being by prioritizing actions that benefit the greatest number of people. Option B is incorrect because it reflects a deontological approach to ethics, where ethical decisions are based on strict adherence to established rules, duties, or principles. Option D is incorrect as it represents an egoistic or self-centered approach to decision-making, where actions are primarily driven by personal benefit and self-interest.

57. B. HR's role is to proactively address corruption risks by implementing anti-corruption compliance measures and educating employees about ethical conduct when conducting business in other countries. This approach aligns with legal requirements and ethical standards. Option A may be necessary in some cases but it is the responsibility of law enforcement agencies and not HR. HR's role is to prevent corruption within the organization. Option C is not a responsible approach and goes against ethical and legal standards. Option D is unethical and illegal; HR should never encourage or tolerate corrupt practices.

58. A. A standard for employee investigations serves as an internal ethics control because it helps ensure that investigations into employee misconduct or unethical behavior are conducted consistently, fairly, and in alignment with ethical principles and organizational values. It helps

maintain ethical standards within the organization. Option B is incorrect as a standard for employee investigations is not a clause within an employment contract. Instead, it is a broader organizational procedure or policy. Option C is incorrect because conducting employee investigations is considered an HR best practice, but the standard for employee investigations involves establishing consistent procedures and controls for conducting investigations, making it broader in scope than just an HR best practice. Option D is incorrect because the standard for employee investigations is a preventive measure rather than a direct response.

59. B. An effective code of conduct typically consists of two main components. Values-based standards define the ethical principles and values that employees should uphold, promoting a culture of integrity, honesty, and respect. Rules-based standards specify the specific rules, policies, and guidelines that employees must follow, including legal requirements, compliance rules, and organizational policies. Option A is incorrect because the question focuses on employee conduct, not employer conduct. Option B represents a component of the rules-based standards, and Option D represents a component of the values-based standards, making them both only partially correct.

Chapter 11: Managing a Global Workforce

1. B. A greenfield investment in global operations involves starting a new operation or building a new facility from scratch in a foreign market. This means that the investing company creates its presence in the new market without acquiring existing assets or businesses. Option A is incorrect as it describes a brownfield investment, which involves acquiring an existing facility or business in a new market. Options C and D are not true.

2. A. A brownfield investment involves purchasing and renovating an existing facility or property in a foreign market for the purpose of expanding or establishing operations. A greenfield investment (Option B) involves starting a new operation or building a new facility from the ground up in a foreign market, without acquiring existing assets. Option C is incorrect as a joint venture investment involves collaborating with a local partner or another entity to establish a new business entity in a foreign market. Option D is incorrect as an offshore investment refers to investing in financial assets or activities in foreign countries to take advantage of tax benefits or financial opportunities.

3. B. A key advantage of a joint venture as a method of structuring global operations is that it allows for sharing risks and costs with a local partner. When two or more entities enter into a joint venture, they pool their resources, expertise, and financial investments. This shared responsibility helps distribute the risks and costs associated with entering and operating in a foreign market, making it a less burdensome endeavor for each party involved. Option A is incorrect as the primary advantage of a joint venture is not full control and autonomy but rather collaboration and risk-sharing. Option C is incorrect as partnering with a local entity does not eliminate the need for understanding the local market, its dynamics, and consumer behavior. Option D is incorrect as the speed of market entry in a joint venture can vary and is not necessarily faster than other methods, such as acquisitions or greenfield investments.

4. C. When a multinational corporation is expanding into several new countries, a matrix organizational structure is often the most suitable for managing its global workforce. In a matrix structure, employees report to both a functional manager (based on their expertise or department) and a regional or country manager (based on their geographic location). Option A is incorrect because a centralized organizational structure concentrates decision-making authority at the top of the organization and may lack the flexibility needed to address local variations and preferences effectively. Option B is incorrect because a decentralized structure delegates decision-making authority to individual country or regional units, which may result in a lack of coordination and consistency across the organization. Option D is incorrect because a flat organizational structure is characterized by minimal layers of management and a focus on simplicity and informality and may not provide the necessary mechanisms for managing a complex global workforce.

5. B. In a decentralized structure, decision-making authority is distributed to individual country or regional units. This empowers local managers to make decisions that are most relevant without waiting for approval from a centralized headquarters. Option A is incorrect because a decentralized structure may lead to variations and differences in practices and policies across different regions or countries. Option C is incorrect because decentralized structures can sometimes result in fragmented communication across regions. While local decision-making may be faster, it can also lead to less centralized oversight and coordination. Option D is incorrect because a decentralized structure often requires local adaptations rather than a reduction.

6. D. The concept of "language homogeneity" implies a lack of linguistic diversity, where one dominant language is spoken uniformly across a region or country. However, in the context of global mobility, linguistic diversity or proficiency in multiple languages is often valued as it facilitates communication, cultural integration, and opportunities for collaboration across borders. Economic opportunities often play a significant role in driving global mobility as individuals may seek better job prospects, higher salaries, or investment opportunities in other countries. Cultural diversity can be a significant factor influencing global mobility as individuals may be attracted to experiencing different cultures, traditions, and ways of life. Political stability is a crucial factor in global mobility as it provides a safe and secure environment for individuals and businesses to operate in. Regions characterized by political instability often experience lower levels of mobility due to safety concerns and uncertainties. Hence, political stability is typically considered a significant influence on global mobility.

7. C. A multinational corporation, often referred to as an MNC or multinational enterprise (MNE), is a company that conducts business operations in multiple countries. These operations can include subsidiaries, branches, or affiliates in different nations. It may have headquarters in one country (home country) while operating in several others (host countries), and the business activities can range from trade and investment to the provision of goods and services on a global scale. Option A is incorrect because the term multinational corporation implies a more extensive global presence beyond just two countries. Option B is incorrect because MNCs are not limited to the EU. Option D is incorrect because a multinational corporation is a privately owned entity, and government ownership is not a defining characteristic of multinational corporations.

8. D. When MNCs expand their operations to other countries, they often seek to tap into new consumer markets to increase their customer base and revenue. Additionally, they may aim to access new sources of raw materials, labor, or technology that can enhance their production capabilities and competitiveness. Option A is incorrect because while improving global profits is an outcome of international expansion, it is not a primary motive by itself. Option B is incorrect because CSR activities may be undertaken as part of their global operations, but they are usually secondary to economic and strategic motives. Option C is incorrect because building new environmental footprints is not a primary motive for MNCs to expand internationally.

9. B. Subsidiaries are local entities that are owned or controlled, either wholly or partially, by a parent company based in another country. They operate under the authority and guidance of the parent company while maintaining a degree of autonomy in their operations. Option A is incorrect as it describes the headquarters or central office of a company, not a subsidiary. Option C is incorrect as it is not specifically related to subsidiaries. Option D is incorrect as subsidiaries are private entities owned by corporations and are not governmental regulatory agencies.

10. A. Technological innovations, especially in the fields of communication, information technology, and automation, have transformed the way businesses operate globally. Businesses now rely on advanced communication tools, digital platforms, cloud computing, data analytics, and automation to streamline operations, expand into new markets, collaborate with remote teams, and reach a global customer base. These technological advancements influence organizational structures, supply chain management, customer engagement, and overall business strategies. Option B is incorrect as it is not a global force that directly shapes how business structures are organized. Option C is incorrect as geopolitical events can have significant impacts on international business, including trade policies, regulations, and market stability, but they do not dictate the fundamental structure of organizations. Option D is incorrect because travel costs are managed as part of business expenses but do not dictate structural changes.

11. D. Building leadership pipelines is a valuable contribution that HR teams can make to a global strategy, especially in the context of talent acquisition. Expatriate assignments often require leaders and skilled professionals to work in foreign locations. HR can identify and develop high-potential employees who can take on these roles, ensuring that the organization has a pool of talent ready for international assignments. Option A is incorrect as it primarily falls under compensation and benefits management, not talent acquisition. Option B is incorrect because this option is related to employee development and performance rather than preparing leadership pipelines for expatriate assignments. Option C is incorrect as this option is more about change management in general and does not directly relate to talent acquisition.

12. B. One of the primary responsibilities of a global HR professional is to adapt HR policies and practices to the cultural and legal contexts of different countries and regions where a multinational corporation operates. Global HR professionals must ensure that HR policies are compliant with local labor laws, customs, and cultural norms. This includes considerations related to hiring practices, compensation structures, benefits, and employee relations. Option A is incorrect because it is not the primary responsibility of a global HR professional and is a task that may be delegated to compensation specialists or teams within HR. Option D is incorrect as while HR may play a role in supporting CSR initiatives related to employee well-being, diversity and inclusion, and ethical conduct, HR serves in a support role similar to the one they play with any other strategic initiative.

13. A. Global leaders often operate in diverse and complex environments with differing cultural norms, values, and perspectives. To be effective, they need to embrace ambiguity, tolerate contradictions, and navigate situations where multiple viewpoints coexist. Option B is incorrect as adaptability and cultural sensitivity are important attributes for global leaders, and they should be willing to adjust their approaches to align with local customs and practices. Option C is incorrect as global leaders should not overly prioritize stability at the expense of innovation and adaptation. Option D is incorrect as leaders should not hold a belief that one culture is inherently better than another. Instead, they should appreciate the diversity of cultures and recognize that each culture has its own strengths and values.

14. A. Language diversity is a valued skill but is not a primary factor to having a global mindset. A global mindset for HR professionals is more focused on understanding and addressing cultural differences, adapting HR practices to diverse environments, and having a broad global perspective. In Option B, HR professionals with a global mindset need to be aware of and sensitive to cultural differences to create inclusive and effective HR practices in diverse international settings. In Option C, HR professionals must be able to adapt HR policies and practices to different cultural and legal contexts to ensure that they are effective and compliant in diverse locations. In Option D, HR professionals need to have a broad global perspective and be aware of international issues, trends, and opportunities to effectively manage a global workforce and anticipate challenges in a globalized environment.

15. C. The 4Ts strategic framework, proposed by Black, Morrison, and Gregersen, is designed to emphasize the importance of talent, technology, training, and teams in building a global mindset within organizations. This framework recognizes that to succeed in the global business environment, organizations need to focus on developing and leveraging talent, adopting relevant technology, providing training to enhance global competencies, and building effective global teams. Options A, B, and D do not reflect the 4Ts.

16. A. Including a jurisdiction clause allows organizations to specify the legal jurisdiction in the country where any disputes or legal matters arising from the employment contract will be resolved. It provides clarity and predictability in case of disputes and ensures that both parties know where legal proceedings will take place. Option B is incorrect as jurisdiction clauses primarily address the legal aspects of dispute resolution rather than standardizing contract terms. Option C is incorrect as it is not the primary purpose of including jurisdiction clauses, although it may be a secondary benefit. Option D is incorrect because jurisdiction clauses specifically address the legal venue for dispute resolution and are not directly related to ensuring compliance with labor laws and regulations.

17. B. The polycentric approach to global staffing involves hiring host-country nationals (local individuals from the country where the subsidiary is located) to manage subsidiaries in their respective countries. In the polycentric approach, the belief is that individuals from the host country have a better understanding of local culture, business practices, and market conditions, making them suitable for managing local operations effectively. Option A is incorrect because the ethnocentric approach involves filling key management positions with employees from the parent company's home country. Option C is incorrect because the geocentric approach involves selecting the most qualified individuals, regardless of their nationality, to manage subsidiaries. Option D is incorrect because a regiocentric approach is a variation that involves hiring managers from a specific region to manage subsidiaries within that region.

18. B. In the ethnocentric approach, key management positions are filled by employees from the parent company's home country, and they are transferred to foreign subsidiaries to oversee operations. This approach assumes that individuals from the home country are best suited to manage subsidiaries worldwide, regardless of their location. Option A is incorrect because the geocentric approach involves selecting the most qualified individuals for key positions, regardless of their nationality. Option C is incorrect because the polycentric approach involves hiring host-country nationals to manage subsidiaries in their respective countries. Option D is incorrect because the regiocentric approach involves hiring managers from a specific region to manage subsidiaries within that region.

19. A. HR competencies necessary to operate within a multinational company often include business and competitive awareness. Understanding the company's industry, market, competitors, and global business environment is essential as they need to align HR strategies with the company's overall business goals and stay aware of competitive challenges. Options B, C, and D are important general competencies for HR professionals but are less critical than an awareness of the business and competitive landscape to support the unique structural and operational needs of an MNE.

20. C. In a localization approach, compensation packages are tailored to the specific country or location where employees work. Localization takes into account factors such as cost of living, labor market conditions, and local compensation norms. Options A and B are incorrect because they involve standardizing compensation practices across multiple countries or regions; the approaches aim to maintain consistency in compensation packages for employees regardless of their location. Option D is incorrect because an equalization compensation strategy involves adjusting compensation for employees working in different countries to ensure that they receive a consistent standard of living or purchasing power, often by providing additional benefits or allowances.

21. A. When a multinational corporation employs a one-size-fits-all approach to compensation across different countries or regions, it may face challenges in adhering to the complex and varied labor laws, tax regulations, and other legal requirements in each location. Option B is incorrect because a standardized global compensation strategy may not necessarily lead to an inability to attract top talent. In some cases, standardized compensation packages may be competitive and attractive to potential employees. Option C is incorrect because a standardized global compensation strategy aims to maintain consistency in employee pay across different countries or regions. Option D is incorrect because increased administrative complexity is a common challenge associated with customized or localized compensation strategies rather than standardized ones.

22. A. Short-term assignments are of relatively short duration, often ranging from a few months to a year, and are intended for specific projects or tasks. Option B is incorrect because a commuter assignment involves an employee who lives in one location but commutes to another location on a regular basis, such as daily or weekly. Option C is incorrect because a permanent transfer involves an employee being permanently relocated to a different location, often with the intention of taking up a long-term position in the new location. Option D is incorrect because repatriation refers to the process of bringing an expatriate employee back to their home country or headquarters after completing an international assignment.

23. B. When a multinational corporation considers offshoring its operations to a country with a reputation for high levels of corruption, the ethical consideration it should address is implementing a strong anti-corruption policy and compliance measures. By having robust anti-corruption policies and compliance measures in place, the company can mitigate the risk of engaging in corrupt activities, protect its reputation, and uphold ethical standards. Option A is incorrect because it may not be within the immediate control of the multinational corporation, and it may not be the corporation's primary responsibility to change the entire political and legal landscape of the foreign country. Option C is incorrect because adopting secondary practices to adapt to cultural norms should not involve compromising ethical standards, especially when it comes to corruption. Option D is incorrect because minimizing transparency to hide corrupt activities is an unethical approach and can lead to legal and reputational risks for the company.

24. D. A comprehensive IP strategy involves a well-thought-out plan for identifying, protecting, managing, and enforcing intellectual property rights across all aspects of the business. An IP strategy ensures that the company's IP assets, including software, are adequately protected, and it helps prevent unauthorized use or theft of proprietary information. Option A is incorrect because while patents can be part of an IP protection strategy, relying on patents is not a comprehensive approach. Patents have limitations, including limited duration and the requirement to disclose information publicly. Option B is incorrect because although nondisclosure agreements (NDAs) help protect proprietary information, they should be part of a broader IP strategy that includes measures for securing, registering, and enforcing IP rights. Option C is incorrect because a comprehensive IP strategy should prioritize the protection of the company's proprietary information and rights, even if they differ from local norms.

25. D. Ensuring that the expatriate has a global employment contract is not a challenge in managing global assignments. Global employment contracts are designed to facilitate international assignments and are a tool used to manage global assignments effectively. Taking into consideration the impact a global assignment has on the expatriating employee (Option A) is a significant challenge in managing global assignment and involves addressing the employee's well-being, career development, family support, and cultural adjustment to ensure a successful assignment. Option B is another challenge as expatriates may feel torn between loyalty to their home country and host country, which can impact their performance and effectiveness. This challenge requires careful management and support. Option C is a challenge because organizations must ensure that expatriates are compensated fairly and equitably in their host countries to maintain their standard of living. This involves addressing differences in compensation and cost of living.

26. B. Global assignments often involve working in different countries or regions, which provides individuals with exposure to international business practices, cross-cultural communication, and global market knowledge. This experience can significantly enhance their understanding of global business and improve their ability to apply this knowledge, which is a valuable asset in many career paths. Option A is incorrect because the impact is more directly related to improving knowledge and skills applicable to global business practices, not necessarily cultural awareness at headquarters. Option C is incorrect as while expatriate assignments can come with financial incentives, such as higher salaries or benefits, they are the result of the impact to the career path, making Option B the better answer. Option D is not true.

27. A. The cultural integration model emphasizes the need for organizations to find a balance between standardizing global HR practices and adapting them to local cultures to ensure effective cultural integration. Option B is incorrect because the cultural integration model does not advocate for complete standardization but the opposite. Option C is incorrect because the model does not promote the exclusion of cultural diversity but rather aims to manage and integrate cultural differences effectively within a multinational organization. Option D is incorrect because the cultural integration model takes into account both the dominant culture of the organization and the local cultural nuances.

28. D. Geert Hofstede's theory is specifically designed to help individuals understand and compare different cultures based on various dimensions, such as power distance, individualism versus collectivism, masculinity versus femininity, uncertainty avoidance, and long-term versus short-term orientation. It provides a framework for understanding cultural differences and can be an effective tool for cultural awareness training in a multinational organization. Option A is incorrect as Kotter's model is primarily focused on managing organizational change and does not specifically address cultural awareness training. Option B is incorrect as Lewin's model is also geared toward organizational change and does not have a specific focus on cultural awareness training. Option C is incorrect as cultural integration models focus on the process of merging cultures during significant transitions and is not focused on cultural awareness.

29. B. One of the primary objectives of HR when conducting market surveys to design global pay structures is to align compensation with local market competitiveness. It means ensuring that the organization's pay rates are competitive with what other employers in the same geographic area are offering. This helps attract and retain top talent and ensures that employees are compensated fairly in their respective markets. Option A is incorrect because global pay rates should be balanced with the need to align compensation with local market competitiveness to attract and retain talent effectively. Option C is incorrect as the focus should be on adapting compensation to local market conditions to remain competitive. Option D is incorrect because while cost of living adjustments may be considered, the primary goal is still to align compensation with local market competitiveness to ensure that employees are fairly compensated in alignment with local conditions.

30. A. Access to comprehensive industry data is one of the primary advantages of using an outside consultancy for global pay benchmarking. Consultancies often collect and analyze pay information from a wide range of organizations within a specific industry, allowing for more accurate and relevant industry benchmarking comparisons. Option B is incorrect because while consultancies aim to provide unbiased and neutral data, local governments can also offer an unbiased perspective as well. The primary advantage of consultancies lies in their ability to collect industry-specific data rather than neutrality. Option C is incorrect as it may actually be more costly to use consultancies than in-house resources or government agencies. Option D is incorrect because employers are liable for any mistakes a consultancy makes, and consultancies alone are not guaranteed to be in alignment with the local regulatory environment; this would be an advantage of a government resource, but not a consultancy.

31. B. When implementing an HRIS system for managing a global workforce, an important consideration is ensuring that the system supports multiple languages and currencies. It allows employees to interact with the system in their preferred language and ensures that compensation and financial data can be accurately managed in various currencies. Option A is incorrect because restricting access to the HRIS to company headquarters may not be the most practical approach when managing a global workforce. While security is important, it's essential to provide access to the HRIS to authorized users across different locations to support HR processes effectively. Option C is incorrect because using HRIS systems are designed to replace paper-based processes with digital and automated solutions, improving efficiency, accuracy, and accessibility of HR data. Relying on paper records may introduce inefficiencies and increase the risk of errors. Option D is incorrect because keeping all HR data stored can lead to data fragmentation and accessibility challenges, especially when employees and HR professionals are distributed across multiple locations.

32. D. The time zone of the host country location is not a key consideration when using technology to manage a global workforce. Time zones primarily impact scheduling and coordination of activities but do not directly relate to the choice or implementation of technology solutions. Option A, compliance with government regulations, particularly those related to the Internet and data privacy, is crucial to ensure that your technology solutions align with local laws and regulations. Assessing the environmental impact of technology choices (Option B) is important in today's sustainability-focused world. Organizations are increasingly concerned with the ecological footprint of their infrastructure and aim to make environmentally responsible decisions. Option C, ensuring that technology interfaces can adapt to local capabilities, such as network infrastructure and device compatibility, is important for seamless integration and user experience in different regions.

33. D. When addressing a workplace discrimination complaint from an employee working in a different country, the organization should comply with the workplace discrimination laws and regulations of the specific country in which the employee is employed. This ensures that the organization operates within the legal framework of the host country and upholds its obligations to prevent and address workplace discrimination. Option A is incorrect because ignoring a discrimination complaint is not an appropriate or ethical response. Option B is incorrect because different countries have their own legal frameworks for addressing workplace discrimination, and it is essential to comply with the laws of the specific country in which the employee works to ensure legal and ethical compliance. Option C is incorrect because it is important to conduct a thorough and impartial investigation into the claim before seeking legal counsel should it become necessary.

34. B. Cross-cultural competency does not involve enforcing a single, standardized approach across all cultural contexts. Instead, it emphasizes adaptability and flexibility to accommodate and respect diverse cultural norms and practices. Cross-cultural competencies require effective communication skills, understanding and valuing cultural differences and the experiences of individuals from diverse backgrounds, and helping individuals navigate cultural differences and interact respectfully with people from diverse backgrounds.

35. C. Totalization agreements, also known as Social Security Agreements or Social Security Totalization Agreements, protect expatriates from dual taxation related to Social Security contributions. These bilateral agreements are established between the United States and certain foreign countries to ensure that workers who move between countries for employment are not dual-taxed. Option A is incorrect because the International Labour Organization (ILO) primarily focuses on promoting and protecting workers' rights and labor standards globally, not taxation issues. Options B and D are incorrect because the North American Free Trade Agreement (NAFTA) has been replaced by the United States-Mexico-Canada Agreement (USMCA), which includes provisions related to trade and investment but does not directly address dual taxation issues.

36. A. The foreign law defense is a legal argument that can be invoked to justify noncompliance with U.S. laws in cases involving American entities when enforcing U.S. law would violate the laws of the foreign country where the activity occurs. The foreign law defense applies when it is impossible to adhere to U.S. labor law and foreign law simultaneously. The conduct in question must violate a law, not just be a custom or preference. Options B, C, and D are false.

37. A. The newspaper's action is not protected under the foreign law defense. Puerto Rico is an unincorporated territory of the United States, and the provisions of the Age Discrimination in Employment Act (ADEA) extend to Puerto Rico. Therefore, the ADEA pre-empts the Puerto Rican law requiring retirement at the age of 60. Options B, C, and D are false.

38. C. The Schengen Agreement is a significant aspect of how the EU affects global mobility. It allows for passport-free travel within the Schengen Area, which includes most EU member states and some non-EU countries. This agreement has simplified travel within the region and has made it easier for both EU citizens and non-EU citizens to move across borders for tourism, business, and other purposes. It's important to note that the ability to work freely in the EU is subject to individual member states' immigration policies and work permit requirements for non-EU citizens. Options A, B, and C are untrue.

39. C. The expatriate failure rate is the most valuable metric when managing global assignments. It measures the percentage of expatriates or employees on international assignments who do not successfully complete their assignments or who return prematurely. Expatriate failure can be costly for organizations, both financially and in terms of talent management. A high expatriate failure rate may indicate issues with assignment preparation, cultural adaptation, or job fit. Options A and B are incorrect because time-to-fill and turnover rates are metrics used in talent acquisition strategies not specific to the management of global assignments. Time-to-fill and turnover rates apply to all employees, not just those on international assignments. Option D is incorrect because a bonus payout percentages metric is relevant for compensation management but is not specifically related to the management of global assignments.

40. C. A key characteristic of risk audits when managing global assignments is that they involve a comprehensive assessment of potential risks and challenges before and during the assignment. These audits aim to identify and mitigate various types of risks such as cultural, legal, operational, and security risks that may impact the success of the international assignment. Option A is incorrect as the question specifically asks about risk audits in the context of global assignments. Risk audits encompass a broader evaluation of potential risks and challenges beyond what is covered in HR due diligence, making option A less accurate. Options B and D are incorrect because the primary focus of risk audits when managing global assignments is not on assessing the employee's performance or being focused on the financial risk related to compensation packages, but rather a more holistic view of the risks throughout the employee assignment life cycle.

41. B. The "ad hoc" approach to global compensation strategies is characterized by tailoring compensation offerings to the unique needs of the expatriate and the specific assignment. This approach allows flexibility in designing compensation packages that take into account factors such as the host country's cost of living, the individual expatriate's circumstances, and the nature of the assignment. It involves a customized and adaptable approach to compensation. Options A and C are incorrect as the "equalized" and "balanced sheet" approaches involve maintaining expatriate compensation at a level equal to or similar to what they would receive in their home country, regardless of the specific circumstances of the host country or the individual assignment. Option D is incorrect as the "differential" approach refers to providing additional compensation, such as hardship or location-specific allowances, to expatriates in challenging or high-cost locations.

42. A. The word *synergistic* refers to a situation where the combined or cooperative efforts of two or more elements result in a more effective outcome than their individual actions or contributions. Synergistic learning involves the ability to adapt, learn from different cultural perspectives, and facilitate cooperation among team members from various backgrounds. Transnational leaders who embrace synergistic learning can leverage the diverse talents and ideas of their teams to achieve global objectives. Option B is incorrect because it is not a characteristic particularly different or necessary for a transnational leader; they should prioritize skills and qualities that enable them to excel in diverse and international settings. Option C is incorrect as transnational leaders can excel even if they are not multilingual, as long as they possess other skills such as cultural sensitivity and the ability to facilitate communication among diverse teams. Option D is incorrect as business acumen is a valuable characteristic for any leader, including transnational leaders, and it is not unique to transnational leadership.

43. B. The functional excellence approach to identifying global leaders is characterized by filling leadership roles based on clearly defined needs and responsibilities. In this approach, individuals are selected and promoted into leadership positions based on their specific expertise, skills, and qualifications related to the functional areas or domains where leadership roles are required. It emphasizes the importance of having leaders who excel in their respective functional roles. Option A is incorrect as the managed development approach focuses on the systematic development and grooming of leaders within the organization, often through structured programs and initiatives. Option C is incorrect as the local responsiveness approach pertains to adapting business strategies and practices to meet the specific needs and expectations of local markets or regions. Option D is incorrect as the collaborative approach emphasizes teamwork, cooperation, and collective decision-making within the organization and is not a typical approach to identifying future leaders.

44. D. In countries with planned economies, collective ownership and shared efforts are often central principles. Employees may have a sense of collective responsibility and ownership over the organization's goals and outcomes. They are more likely to work together toward common objectives rather than focusing solely on individual rewards or competition. Option A is incorrect as in countries with planned economies, where the government exerts significant control over economic activities, quick returns and competition may not be prioritized. Option B is incorrect because employees may not necessarily advocate for less government interference in their right to work but rather expect the government to provide stability and security in employment. Option C is incorrect as performance-based pay systems, which focus on individual achievements and incentives, are more common in market-driven economies where competition and individualism are emphasized.

45. A. In the elite cohort approach, organizations identify and select high-potential individuals from prestigious universities or educational backgrounds. These individuals are then provided with developmental opportunities and training to groom them for future managerial or leadership positions. The focus is on identifying and nurturing talent early in their careers. Option B is incorrect as it describes the elite political approach for identifying talent. Options C and D are not true statements.

46. B. Direct wages refer to the basic compensation paid to employees for their work, while benefits encompass additional forms of compensation such as healthcare, retirement contributions, bonuses, and allowances. Local tax obligations include taxes imposed by the host country on both employers and employees, such as income tax, Social Security contributions, and any other mandatory payroll taxes. These components constitute the core elements of labor costs associated with staffing an offshore location and are critical for accurate financial planning and budgeting. Options A and C vary depending on the nature of contracts in place and the company staffing strategies, and Option D is included in the correct answer.

47. D. In some countries, there are regulations or laws that require employers to contribute to government-sponsored training programs through payroll taxes or other means. These programs aim to enhance workforce skills, promote lifelong learning, and address the training needs of employees. Such laws are designed to ensure that employers invest in the continuous development of their workforce. Option A is incorrect as it does not represent an international labor law in the area of learning and development, but rather an organizational strategic approach. Option B is incorrect as it is not a legal requirement or an international labor law but can be a policy or practice. Option C is incorrect as requiring employees to translate compliance-related training into the local language may be a corporate policy or practice in some organizations; however, it is not a standard international labor practice.

48. A. When multinational enterprises (MNEs) use third-country nationals to staff open positions in a foreign location, language barriers and communication difficulties can be a significant culture-related problem. Third-country nationals may not be fluent in the language of the host country, making it challenging to effectively communicate with local employees, clients, or customers. Misunderstandings and miscommunication can arise, potentially leading to conflicts, inefficiencies, and a lack of cultural integration within the workplace. Option B is incorrect as it is not necessarily a culture-related problem. Option C is incorrect because while resistance from the home country's workforce may be a concern in certain situations (particularly if third-country nationals are perceived as taking jobs that could have gone to local employees), this is more of an employment and labor relations issue rather than a culture-related problem. Similarly, Option D is incorrect as it speaks more to an individual personal and social adjustment of individuals rather than organizational culture.

49. D. A works council is a formalized representative body of employees within an organization that is responsible for addressing various workplace issues, including matters related to employment conditions, workplace safety, and employee welfare. They act as a channel of communication between employees and management, often facilitating discussions, negotiations, and the resolution of workplace concerns. Option A describes a labor union or trade union rather than a works council. Option B is incorrect as a works council consists of employees, not senior executives. Option C is incorrect because this option describes a safety committee or safety representatives, not a works council.

50. A. The "hands off by headquarters" approach to managing the union/multinational enterprise relationship is characterized by granting overall decision-making control to local management. In this approach, the headquarters of the multinational corporation allows local management in each country or subsidiary to handle labor relations, union negotiations, and related issues independently. Headquarters does not intervene directly and trusts local management to make decisions in alignment with local labor laws, customs, and market conditions. This approach reflects a decentralized and localized approach to labor relations. Options B, C, and D reflect a more involved approach by home-country headquarters.

51. A. Unions often fear that MNEs can exploit the global competition among workers by threatening job loss or outsourcing to regions with lower labor costs. This can put pressure on workers in one country to make concessions in terms of wages, benefits, or working conditions to remain competitive. Option B is incorrect as safety standards and protocols can vary across industries and countries, and many of these rules are now regulated by the government. Option C is incorrect as the cost of administering collective bargaining agreements may vary but is not the central concern. Labor practices, competition, and the potential exploitation of workers' vulnerabilities are more significant factors contributing to union mistrust of MNEs. Option D is incorrect as union strikes that extend across borders are less common compared to strikes that are confined to a single country or workplace, making Option A the better answer.

52. C. When faced with a situation where an employment practice that is illegal in the home country is acceptable in the host country, the first approach senior HR leaders should take is to research and understand why the practice is acceptable in the host country. This option acknowledges the importance of cultural and legal differences between countries. Understanding the reasons behind the acceptance of such practices is essential to make informed decisions on how to proceed. Option A is incorrect because following the home country practice without understanding the host country's context can lead to cultural insensitivity and noncompliance with local laws and customs. Option B is incorrect as automatically adopting the host country's practice without understanding its implications may result in noncompliance with international standards or even violate human rights. Option D is incorrect as while considering whether the practice is a violation of human rights is an important step, it should not be the first approach. The initial step should be to research and understand the practice's acceptability in the host country. This research may involve evaluating human rights concerns, but it should be preceded by a broader examination of the cultural, legal, and societal factors that influence the practice's acceptance.

53. B. Chinese employees, like many others, value work-life balance and flexibility. Offering flexible work arrangements, such as remote-work options or flexible hours, and implementing work-life balance initiatives can significantly contribute to motivating employees beyond financial rewards. It aligns with the importance of harmonious work environments and employee well-being in Chinese culture. Options C and D are partially correct in that recognition for hard work in the forms of title and praise can indeed be motivating for workers. However, in cultures that place particular emphasis on collectivism, humility, and modesty, grand titles and public praise would not be the most appropriate way to motivate employees.

54. C. In a rapidly growing international economy, organizations often face the challenge of sourcing qualified candidates from around the world. This is because in many developing countries qualified regional talent is not available, so organizations may need to tap into talent pools across different countries and regions to meet their workforce demands. This involves understanding and navigating various cultural, legal, and logistical considerations when recruiting and hiring international talent. Option A is incorrect as the demand for skilled labor often outpaces the supply, making it difficult for organizations to find and retain the right talent. Option B is incorrect as ensuring consistency in hiring practices can be addressed through standardized processes, which is important but not the central challenge. Option D is incorrect as in rapidly developing economies turnover rates may vary depending on factors such as market competition, talent mobility, and workforce demographics.

55. C. In egalitarian countries, such as Scandinavian nations like Sweden and Norway, the culture context often emphasizes equality, cooperation, and a strong sense of social responsibility. In such societies, employees are seen as stakeholders in the organization. This means that their opinions and well-being are valued, and they are considered integral to the success of the company. Option A is incorrect in the context of egalitarian countries. In such countries, there is a low power distance between management and employees. Option B is not necessarily true in all egalitarian countries. While unions may exist and play a role in labor relations, it is not a universal requirement mandated by governments in such countries. Option D is incorrect as work councils, which are representative bodies of employees, tend to have a significant degree of influence in egalitarian cultures.

56. B. Ethical absolutism is a perspective that asserts that ethical principles and moral values are universal and apply consistently across all cultures and situations. In cultures characterized by ethical absolutism, there is a belief in objective moral standards that should not change based on cultural or situational factors. These principles are viewed as timeless and unchanging, providing a consistent ethical framework that transcends cultural differences. Options A and C describe ethical relativism, not ethical absolutism. Ethical relativism is the belief that ethical principles are culturally determined and vary from one culture or group to another. Option D is contradictory and inaccurate as ethical absolutism and ethical relativism represent opposing viewpoints.

57. A. Cultural awareness in business involves understanding and recognizing the cultural norms, values, customs, and behaviors of other countries to effectively navigate and engage in intercultural business interactions. In Chinese business culture, it is customary to leave some food on your plate at the end of a meal to indicate that you are satisfied. Finishing all the food on your plate may imply that the host did not provide enough, while leaving some food shows appreciation for the meal and hospitality.

58. A, B, D. Handshakes are a common greeting in many Western cultures, but they may not be universally accepted or appropriate in all cultures. In some cultures, alternative greetings such as bowing or the exchange of verbal greetings may be preferred or expected. In Japanese culture, exchanging business cards is a formal ritual that carries significant cultural etiquette. Presenting and receiving business cards with both hands, along with a slight bow, is considered respectful and proper etiquette in Japan. This practice may not be observed in the same way in other cultures. While email is a widely used form of business communication in many parts of the world, its usage and appropriateness may vary depending on cultural preferences and norms. In some cultures, face-to-face or phone communication may be preferred for certain business matters, while in others, email communication may be perceived as impersonal or less effective. Option C is incorrect because punctuality is often considered important in various cultures around the world, although the degree of strict adherence to punctuality may vary.

59. D. While international trade with any region can present challenges, the qualifications of the labor force in Africa are not a universal barrier to trade. Africa has a diverse workforce with varying levels of qualifications and skills, and there are skilled professionals and workers in various sectors across the continent. Options A, B, and C are all factors that are barriers to the development of MNEs in Africa. The lack of predictability in the labor market can indeed be a challenge in some African countries, affecting factors such as workforce availability, labor regulations, and market conditions. Political instability may lead to disruptions, regulatory changes, and security concerns that affect trade operations and investment decisions. An unfriendly business climate, characterized by regulatory hurdles, corruption, and unfavorable business conditions, can be a significant barrier to international trade in some African countries.

60. C. Free market policies in countries (such as those in the Asia-Pacific) refer to economic principles and policies that prioritize minimal government intervention, open competition, private ownership, and the free exchange of goods and services within the region, often aimed at promoting economic growth and efficiency. In many free-market economies, there is a transition from government-sponsored or heavily regulated retirement plans to a greater reliance on individual retirement savings and private pension schemes. This shift places more responsibility on individuals to plan and save for their retirement, impacting HR practices related to employee benefits and retirement planning. Option A is incorrect as this option does not directly relate to HR trends. Option B is incorrect as wage suppression, or the limitation of wage growth, can be influenced by economic policies, but it may not be a direct result of free-market policies; the normalization of wage suppression varies heavily by region and industry. Option D is incorrect as the decline in union organizing is a trend that can be influenced by various factors, including labor laws, social attitudes, economic conditions, and population density.

61. A. In a country that prioritizes free trade to boost economic prosperity, the government and policymakers are likely to adopt a pro-business and market-oriented approach. As a result, labor markets in such countries are often characterized by significant flexibility in hiring and firing practices, and labor laws may be less stringent in terms of job protection and regulation. Low security means that workers in such countries may have relatively lower job security and fewer social safety nets compared to countries with more protective labor laws. Employment contracts may offer fewer long-term guarantees, and there may be limited access to unemployment benefits or comprehensive healthcare coverage.

62. D. European countries often have a comprehensive system of labor laws and regulations that cover various aspects of employment, including working hours, paid leave, employee rights, and collective bargaining. These laws are often more detailed and prescriptive compared to the less extensive labor laws in the United States. Options A, B, and C are not necessarily true when it comes to the key distinctions of European labor laws.

63. A. Global HR systems are designed to align with the organization's overall strategy and goals. They provide a standardized framework for HR processes and data management across different countries or regions. On the other hand, HR policies and practices can vary by country or region to comply with local labor laws, cultural norms, and specific needs. The

key distinction is that HR systems aim for standardization, while policies and practices allow for flexibility to adapt to local contexts. Options B, C, and D do not accurately reflect the key distinctions between systems and practices.

64. B. The correct first step when designing expatriate crisis management plans is to conduct risk assessments of host countries. This involves evaluating the potential risks and threats that expatriates might encounter in the host country, such as natural disasters, political instability, security issues, health emergencies, and other crisis scenarios. By conducting thorough risk assessments, HR can identify and understand the specific challenges and vulnerabilities associated with each host country, which forms the foundation for developing effective crisis management plans. Options A, C, and D are all necessary components of an expatriate crisis management plan that should come after the initial risks have been assessed.

65. B. One of the key benefits of developing an international human resources website is the administrative support tailored to the unique requirements of managing a global workforce. This includes accommodating differences in character lengths for names, addressing global address protocols, handling currency conversions for payroll, differences in leave requirements and more. Options A and C are incorrect because maintaining separate systems can decrease cohesiveness. Option D is incorrect because it is not a specific benefit of an international HRIS.

66. A. Management techniques that work well in one country may not be as effective or applicable in another due to variations in cultural norms, business practices, legal frameworks, and societal expectations. Adapting management techniques to fit different cultural contexts is a significant challenge for global managers. Option B is incorrect as it is not accurate to generalize that employees of some countries universally have stronger work ethics than others. Option C is incorrect because the goal of global HR practices is not always consistency but rather alignment with business strategy social norms, and laws of the host country. Option D is incorrect because while true, this is a strategic management challenge more so than a talent management challenge.

67. C. Employee relations encompass the interactions between employers and employees, including aspects such as communication, conflict resolution, collective bargaining, and labor rights. In many countries, labor unions negotiate on behalf of workers to secure better wages, working conditions, benefits, and rights. The presence or absence of labor unions can greatly influence HR practices, policies, and strategies in multinational corporations operating across different countries. Options A, B, and D are all related to navigating the relationship with labor unions within the domain of employee relations.

68. A. In planned economies, such as those seen in communist or socialist systems, the government plays a central role in planning and controlling economic activities, including production, distribution, and resource allocation. In market economies, such as capitalist systems, the allocation of resources, production decisions, and distribution of goods and services are primarily guided by market forces such as supply and demand, competition, and consumer preferences. Options B, C, and D do not accurately define the differences between planned and market economies.

Chapter 12: Diversity, Equity, and Inclusion

1. D. Diversity as the act of valuing human differences, whereas equity is the adjustment of employment treatment based on an individual's unique circumstances, aiming to achieve fairness and equality in outcomes despite differences in starting points. When combined with inclusion, these principles support a workplace culture where all individuals feel respected, valued, and empowered to contribute their unique perspectives and talents.

2. B. By ensuring that all employees, regardless of their background or identity, have access to the same opportunities for career advancement, skill development, and recognition, HR professionals contribute to creating a more inclusive workplace through their performance management systems. Option A is incorrect because surveys are not part of the performance management process but rather the larger organizational DEI efforts. Option C is incorrect because it is focused on pay equity, which is an essential aspect of fairness in the workplace within the function of Total Rewards. Option D is incorrect because inclusivity should be integrated into performance management to ensure that evaluations are fair, unbiased, and consider factors that contribute to a diverse and equitable workplace.

3. B. A microaggression is a subtle, often unintentional, verbal or nonverbal behavior or comment that communicates derogatory or negative assumptions about a person's race, gender, religion, or other aspects of their identity, contributing to a hostile or belittling environment. By privately discussing her feelings with Howie, Kathy can help him understand the impact of his comment and potentially prevent similar incidents in the future. Options A, C, and D are not as appropriate in this context because they either ignore the issue or escalate it too quickly without attempting to resolve it through communication.

4. A. Employee resource groups (ERGs) are voluntary, employee-led groups that promote diversity, inclusion, and employee engagement within organizations. In this context, creating an ERG specifically for employees with disabilities can provide a dedicated platform for them to collaborate, share their experiences, advocate for change, and work toward increasing representation in leadership roles. Option B is incorrect as focus groups lack the structured and ongoing nature that an ERG provides. Option C is incorrect as a whistleblower hotline does not directly address the issue of underrepresentation and engagement among employees with disabilities. Option D is incorrect as while policies and training are essential components of a broader diversity and inclusion strategy, they should be informed by the recommendations of the ERG.

5. A. Executive sponsorship refers to the active support and commitment of senior leaders and executives within an organization to drive and champion DEI efforts throughout the organization. Leaders play a crucial role in setting the tone, allocating resources, and making key decisions that impact equity initiatives. Option B is incorrect because diversity among employees is an asset and can contribute positively to the success of equity initiatives by providing a variety of viewpoints and experiences. Option C is incorrect because transparent and inclusive communication is a facilitator rather than a barrier to the implementation of successful equity initiatives. Option D is incorrect because having adequate funding and resources is generally a necessary factor for the successful implementation of equity initiatives, not a barrier.

6. D. When companies prioritize DEI, they create a more inclusive and welcoming work environment. This inclusivity helps employees feel valued and accepted, which in turn reduces the likelihood of them leaving the organization. Lower attrition rates can save the company money on recruitment, training, and productivity losses associated with turnover. A psychologically safe workplace, sense of personal belonging and equitable compensation programs (Options A, B, and C) are better examples of the benefits of DEI efforts for employees rather than the organization.

7. A. One of the major disadvantages of the COVID-19 pandemic on an organization's DEI efforts was the disproportionate impact on women. Many women, especially mothers, were forced to leave the workforce or reduce their work hours due to increased caregiving responsibilities brought on by school closures and the lack of affordable childcare during the pandemic. This not only hindered gender diversity efforts within organizations but also highlighted systemic challenges and disparities in the workforce. Option B, C, and D are incorrect as the options do not directly relate to DEI initiatives in the workplace.

8. C. DEI initiatives should involve continuous conversations that allow employees to express their concerns, share experiences, and provide valuable feedback. Organizations need to collect data, analyze it, and make data-driven decisions to enhance their DEI efforts. Inclusivity efforts go beyond diversity numbers; they focus on creating a welcoming environment for all employees. This includes addressing unconscious bias, providing training and resources, and implementing policies that promote equitable opportunities. Option A is incorrect because quotas, while well-intentioned, can sometimes lead to tokenism, where individuals from underrepresented groups are hired to meet the quota, without considering their qualifications or experiences. Affirmative action quotas are unlawful. Option B is incorrect as one-time DEI training is insufficient on its own. Option D is incorrect because assimilation policies are often problematic as they can promote a "one-size-fits-all" approach that expects individuals to conform to a dominant culture.

9. B. A pay audit involves a thorough review of the company's compensation practices identifying any patterns of discrimination or unfair pay disparities. Addressing pay disparities is essential for maintaining employee morale, equity, and legal compliance. Option A is incorrect as under the National Labor Relations Act in the United States employees have the right to discuss their pay and working conditions with each other. Disciplining employees for sharing pay information would be a violation of their legal rights. Option C is incorrect because HR should first investigate and rectify any potential discriminatory practices. If pay disparities are the result of factors such as experience or education, that should be explained when sharing the findings of the audit. Option D is incorrect because conducting a pay audit or addressing the issue internally first to determine if there are discriminatory practices is a more proactive and cost-effective approach. A labor attorney's involvement may come later in the process if legal concerns arise.

10. B. Connecting DEI efforts to organizational results in a meaningful way requires a transparent and explicit understanding of how DEI initiatives positively impact performance, productivity, innovation, and other key organizational outcomes. When organizations clarify this relationship, it not only emphasizes the importance of DEI but also provides a compelling reason for stakeholders to actively support and engage in these efforts. Option A is incorrect because while transparency about the outcomes of DEI initiatives is important, it may not on its own effectively connect DEI efforts to organizational results. Option C is incorrect because the

quarterly timing may be insufficient to establish a meaningful connection between DEI efforts and organizational results. Option D is incorrect as this option highlights recognition but does not address the need for understanding the relationship between DEI and performance.

11. D. Training in unconscious bias and other behaviors that result in inequity helps raise awareness among managers about their implicit biases and how these biases can influence decision-making processes such as hiring, performance evaluations, promotions, and resource allocation. By providing managers with the knowledge and tools to recognize and mitigate biases, HR can foster a more equitable workplace culture and ensure fair treatment of all employees. Options A and B are incorrect as employees have complained and HR has already investigated and found disparities. The next step would be to take action. In Option D, hiring practice equity is important; however, it should be part of a broader strategy to improve DEI outcomes in all HR programs, not just in a single area.

12. D. A diverse applicant pool indicates that the organization is attracting candidates from various backgrounds and demographics. By tracking this metric, organizations can assess whether their recruitment efforts are effectively reaching a diverse range of potential employees. Option A is incorrect because focusing on the first 90 days of employment may not provide a comprehensive view of the impact of hiring practices on DEI goals, and turnover can be influenced by various factors, including onboarding, job fit, and workplace culture. Option B is incorrect because the rate of promotion based on demographic data primarily reflects the effectiveness of internal promotion and advancement practices rather than the initial hiring practices. Option C is incorrect because unless the organization is attracting and hiring diverse candidates, measuring equity in salaries is a moot point.

13. A. To assess whether DEI initiatives are positively impacting employee retention, measuring employee engagement survey scores is a relevant metric. Higher scores often correlate with better retention rates in inclusive workplaces. Options B, C, and D are metrics relevant to other organizational results such as recruitment, revenue, and attendance.

14. C. Explicitly prohibiting targeted or discriminatory treatment of LGBTQ+ team members is a fundamental and effective strategy that ensures that LGBTQ+ employees are protected from discrimination and harassment, creating a safer and more inclusive work environment. Clear policies and guidelines send a strong message that discrimination will not be tolerated, fostering trust and inclusivity among employees. Options A and B are incorrect because while they aim to raise awareness of the specific issues these workers face, they do not address or protect discrimination or harassment. Option D is incorrect because this approach can perpetuate invisibility and hinder progress toward inclusivity by not acknowledging and addressing the unique challenges that LGBTQ+ employees may face.

15. A. Treating DEI as seriously as other initiatives through planning, resourcing, implementation, and evaluation efforts reflects a commitment to creating a culture of fairness and inclusivity. It ensures that DEI is not seen as a side project but as a core component of the organization's overall strategy. Option B is incorrect as the effectiveness of the DEI officer depends on how seriously the organization takes DEI as a whole. Option C is incorrect as building a DEI initiative should involve internal leadership and ownership, with consultants as a supplementary resource. Option D is incorrect as relying on government regulations alone may not lead to a culture of genuine diversity, equity, and inclusion within the organization.

16. B. The CROWN Act is a legislative initiative that prohibits discrimination against individuals in the United States based on their natural hair texture and protective hairstyles, such as braids, twists, and locs, aiming to promote diversity and combat hair-related bias in workplaces and schools. Changes in societal attitudes and expectations regarding DEI directly impact an organization's approach to diversity and inclusion. Legal trends encompass changes in laws, regulations, and government policies that can have a significant impact on organizations.

17. C. Employers can use their DEI initiatives to create a positive brand image by emphasizing their commitment to diversity and inclusion. Customers who perceive a company as socially responsible and inclusive are more likely to remain loyal, even in the presence of substitutes. Option A is incorrect because it focuses on cost-cutting more than brand loyalty. Option B is incorrect because it offers more options but does not inherently address the threat of substitutes or build brand loyalty based on DEI initiatives. Option D is incorrect because it may not align with the goal of building brand loyalty through DEI initiatives and could create conflicting interests in the market, which does not support business results.

18. A. HR can partner with business leaders to improve equity in outcomes by collaborating on DEI initiatives such as workforce development, cultural celebrations, and internships. This approach fosters a culture of equity and helps bridge societal gaps. Options B and C are incorrect because focusing on community engagement or employee volunteer programs without clear internal equity initiatives may not align efforts with organizational results. Option D is incorrect because corporate social responsibility (CSR) initiatives do not reflect the concepts of DEI.

19. B. Offering flexible work hours and remote options promotes equity for a multigenerational workforce by accommodating different generational preferences and needs. Option A is incorrect because age-based promotions would likely lead to discrimination and inequality. Options C and D are unrelated to generational diversity and equity.

20. B. Blind recruitment practices, such as removing personally identifiable information (like names and addresses) from résumés, can help reduce unconscious bias in the hiring process. It ensures that candidates are evaluated based on their qualifications and skills rather than their gender, race, or other characteristics. While involving peers in the interviewing process (Option A) brings diverse perspectives into the hiring process, it is essential to have a structured and unbiased recruitment process that addresses potential bias prior to the interviews being scheduled. Option C is incorrect because an employer's focus should be on creating a more balanced and inclusive workforce rather than excluding over-represented ones. Option D is incorrect because it can perpetuate biases and overlook candidates with valuable skills and potential who may not fit traditional molds.

21. D. One of the main challenges to the use of mentorship programs for developing a diverse and inclusive workplace is the presence of institutional and systemic bias in the workplace. Such bias can create barriers for individuals from underrepresented groups to access mentorship opportunities, hindering their career development and advancement. Option A is incorrect as individual experiences and perspectives are what make diverse mentors valuable as they can relate to the challenges of their mentees. Option B is incorrect because lack of diversity at the institutional level contributes to the reinforcement of stereotypes. In Option C, the lack of diverse mentors in senior roles is the result of institutional and systemic bias.

22. B. The most suitable accommodation to support lactation needs is to provide a private and comfortable lactation room. This ensures a private and hygienic space for mothers to express breast milk. Options A, C, and D are incorrect because they are either not private, not suitable, or not in compliance with regulations governing accommodating nursing mothers in the workplace.

23. B. Imposter syndrome is a personal barrier to DEI efforts. It is a psychological phenomenon where individuals, despite their accomplishments and qualifications, feel like frauds and doubt their abilities. This mindset can hinder their career advancement and full participation in DEI initiatives as they may not feel they deserve recognition or opportunities. HR systems can support employees with imposter syndrome by providing access to professional development resources, mentorship programs, and psychological support services, helping individuals build confidence and recognize their true value within the organization. Option A is incorrect because confirmation bias is a cognitive bias where individuals tend to favor information that confirms their preexisting beliefs or values. Option C is incorrect because stereotype threat refers to a situation where individuals, especially those from underrepresented groups, feel anxiety or pressure because they fear conforming to stereotypes about their group. Option D is incorrect because anchoring bias is a cognitive bias where individuals rely too heavily on the first piece of information they encounter when making decisions.

24. C. The manager displayed stereotype bias by assuming that a candidate's age and assumption about childbearing would determine their commitment to work overtime. Stereotype bias involves making generalizations or assumptions about individuals based on characteristics such as age, gender, or other protected factors. Option A is incorrect because microaggressions are subtle, often unintentional, discriminatory behaviors or comments directed at individuals based on their race, gender, age, or other protected characteristics. Option B is incorrect because age discrimination occurs with individuals older than 40, and the candidate's age is not specifically mentioned in the question. Option D is incorrect because same-sex bias refers to bias or discrimination based on an individual's sexual orientation or the assumption that individuals of the same sex share certain characteristics or preferences.

25. B. An empathy index survey is a tool that can assess the experiences and perspectives of employees from diverse backgrounds. Such a survey can gauge how employees feel they are treated, whether they perceive empathy and understanding from their colleagues and supervisors, and whether they believe their unique perspectives and needs are considered in decision-making processes. Option A is incorrect as an annual diversity report does not directly assess the experiences and perspectives of employees and are more focused on statistics related to diversity representation. Option C is incorrect because an organizational hierarchy analysis focuses more on structural aspects of equity, such as the distribution of power and resources. Option D is incorrect as it is an operational sampling audit that involves randomly selecting a subset of data or records for examination to assess compliance or specific aspects of an organization's operations.

26. C. Tangible diversity targets are specific, measurable goals and objectives that organizations set to increase diversity and inclusion within their workforce and workplace culture, often related to numerical representation, pay equity, or procurement from underrepresented groups. Collecting and analyzing inclusivity efforts over the next 12 months represents an ongoing process of data collection and analysis, but it lacks a specific, quantifiable goal or target. Options A, B, and D are tangible diversity targets because they involve specific, measurable goals.

27. C. An effective mentoring program for supporting DEI initiatives involves providing diverse mentor-mentee pairings, where individuals from different backgrounds, genders, races, and experiences are matched. This approach promotes cross-cultural learning, empathy, and the development of a more inclusive workplace culture. Option A is incorrect because exclusively pairing mentees with mentors from the same background can reinforce homogeneity and limit the potential for diverse perspectives and cross-cultural learning. Option B is incorrect because DEI-focused mentoring programs are often more successful when they are tailored to the specific needs and experiences of different groups. Option D is incorrect because limiting mentoring programs to high-potential employees may exclude many individuals who could benefit from mentorship, especially those who may face barriers to advancement due to systemic bias or lack of access to opportunities.

28. B. HR professionals acting as diversity advocates should have a global mindset to understand and respect diverse cultures, backgrounds, and perspectives. Effective communication skills are vital for conveying the importance of diversity and inclusion, engaging employees, and fostering a more inclusive workplace. Options A, C, and D are incorrect because the question speaks specifically about competencies that allow HR professionals to act as advocates for diversity initiatives in the workplace. While each of these competencies in their own way can help support diversity in the workplace, the global mindset and communication competencies are more directly related to diversity advocacy.

29. A. To assess the effectiveness of DEI initiatives, measuring employee satisfaction through surveys is the most relevant metric for understanding retention and inclusivity. High satisfaction rates can indicate a positive and inclusive work environment, which often leads to higher retention. Option B is incorrect because the number of employees in leadership positions focuses on representation, not retention. Option C is unrelated to assessing DEI initiatives, and Option D focuses on training but doesn't directly measure retention or inclusivity.

30. A. Organizations can effectively measure and increase equity in their workplace culture by conducting regular audits of diversity levels at various organizational levels. These audits provide data to identify disparities and implement strategies for improvement. Option B is incorrect because relying exclusively on the empathy index may not provide a comprehensive understanding of equity. Option C is incorrect because avoiding the use of reports and assessments hinders transparency and accountability. Option D is incorrect because focusing exclusively on organizational hierarchy overlooks other aspects of equity.

31. B. Transparent pay structures ensure that compensation decisions are based on clear and consistent criteria, making it less likely for pay disparities to occur due to bias or discrimination. Transparency also allows employees to understand how their pay is determined and can identify and rectify any existing inequities. Option A is incorrect as pay equity initiatives require specific actions to review and adjust compensation practices to ensure fairness. Option C is incorrect because increasing the salary of diverse employees without addressing the underlying causes of pay inequity can exacerbate the problem and create further disparities. Option D is incorrect because ignoring issues can lead to employee dissatisfaction, legal issues, and a negative workplace culture.

32. C. Cross-functional structures encourage employees to work across departments and gain diverse skills and experiences. This can lead to a more equitable distribution of career advancement opportunities and help break down silos that may contribute to inequity. Option A is incorrect because hierarchical structures often have a centralized decision-making process that may contribute to inequity if decisions about promotions and career advancement are based on seniority. Option B is incorrect because a matrix structure, which involves employees reporting to multiple managers, does not inherently address issues of equity in career advancement unless specific equity-focused policies and practices are also implemented. Option D is incorrect as self-directed work teams can improve employee autonomy and decision-making but do not support the broader structural needs that drive diversity outcomes.

33. C. The most empathetic and inclusive action for the leader is to privately check in with the team member to understand their needs. This action demonstrates the competency of empathy and inclusivity because it shows genuine concern for the well-being and feelings of the team member. Option A is incorrect because while respecting an individual's privacy is important, making assumptions without checking in can lead to missed opportunities to provide support or address any underlying issues. Option B is incorrect because using humor to address someone's disengagement may not be appropriate or effective. Option D is incorrect because while reminding team members of their value and contribution is important, it should be done in a way that promotes open communication and understanding rather than creating potential guilt or negative perceptions.

34. C. When an underrepresented employee with excellent performance is consistently passed over for promotions, it may indicate systemic biases or barriers within the promotion process. Conducting a thorough review can help identify and address any such issues, ensuring a more equitable and inclusive promotion process for all employees. Option A is incorrect because promoting candidates based only on seniority may perpetuate inequities and not address potential biases or barriers that may exist in the promotion process. Option B is incorrect because promoting one individual without understanding the reasons behind the lack of promotions may not solve the broader problem. Option D is incorrect as this option does not directly address the need to investigate potential biases and barriers, and it's important to ensure that promotion decisions are based on fairness and equity for all employees, not just individual preferences.

35. A. By seeking input and understanding the unique challenges, preferences, and perspectives of team members, a leader can tailor their approach to create a more inclusive work environment. This action demonstrates a commitment to listening, acknowledging differences, and addressing them effectively. Option B is incorrect as segregating similar groups into pods may inadvertently reinforce silos and hinder diversity and inclusivity efforts. Option C is incorrect because discouraging conversations about diversity can lead to a lack of awareness and understanding among team members; avoiding these discussions may perpetuate biases and misunderstandings. Option D is incorrect because promoting a culture of competition may lead to individuals prioritizing their personal success over collaborative teamwork and can create a less inclusive environment. Inclusivity often thrives in an atmosphere of cooperation and mutual support rather than intense competition.

36. C. Conducting open conversations with under-performing employees to understand the root cause of any performance issues allows managers to identify whether performance challenges are related to individual job performance or potentially influenced by DEI-related factors, such as bias, discrimination, or lack of inclusivity, or protected conditions such as medical issues. By engaging in open dialogue, managers can gain insights into the specific challenges an employee may be facing and determine the appropriate actions to address those challenges. Options A and B are incorrect because they do not specifically address the distinction between performance issues and DEI differences, and relying just on the job requirements may inadvertently result in discrimination. Option D is incorrect as avoiding discussions related to protected information can hinder the ability to address potential DEI-related challenges effectively.

37. B. Affinity diagrams are a structured facilitation exercise that allows participants to write their responses to a query on sticky notes or index cards. The cards are then collected and grouped into like categories, and a discussion ensues in small or whole groups. Facilitation techniques such as this foster unbiased, open discussion and consensus building and promote equal participation. Option A is incorrect as it is by nature exclusionary by being focused on the more vocal meeting attendees. Option C is incorrect because rewarding only those who speak up can inadvertently discourage quieter or introverted team members from participating. Option D is incorrect because it can be challenging for introverted individuals to be active participants in a meeting without specific structures or techniques in place to support their contributions.

38. A. Interpersonal risk-taking as an HR professional competency involves taking bold steps to advocate for positive changes, even when there is potential resistance or pushback. Options B and C do not demonstrate the courage necessary, making them incorrect. Option D is incorrect because it is more a reflection of a collaborative approach to conflict resolution, as opposed to taking more proactive actions that are likely to be unpopular or questioned.

39. B. Allyship in the workplace refers to actively supporting and advocating for colleagues from underrepresented groups. It involves actions that go beyond passive support and includes speaking up against discrimination, bias, and inequality to create a more inclusive environment, and taking concrete actions to promote equity and diversity. Option A is incorrect as it extends beyond aligning with people and involves actively supporting and advocating for colleagues from underrepresented groups. Options C and D are incorrect because they do not adequately capture the concept of allyship at work.

40. B. Reverse mentoring involves younger employees mentoring older ones, facilitating knowledge sharing and mutual learning, and fostering a culture of respect and collaboration. This approach promotes psychological safety by encouraging open communication and the exchange of skills and perspectives between generations. Option A is incorrect because it is not a direct contributor to psychological safety. Option C is incorrect because psychological safety is more about fostering collaboration, not competition. Option D is incorrect because disciplining team members who discriminate based on age is an important action to address age-related bias, but it is a response to a problem rather than a direct contributor to psychological safety.

41. D. Diversity training needs to occur at three levels: organizational, individual, and department. Organizations often implement diversity training to address gender disparities and promote women's representation in leadership roles. Option A is incorrect as it is an example of individual diversity training needs. Options B and C are incorrect as they are better examples of departmental training needs, and the supply chain issue reflects a CSR challenge more so than a diversity challenge.

42. B. Developing a comprehensive succession planning program is the most suitable approach for an organization facing staffing challenges due to an aging workforce. This option involves identifying and grooming potential successors from within the organization to take over key roles as older employees retire. It ensures a smooth transition of knowledge and skills and minimizes disruptions in operations. Options A and C are incorrect as they can lead to legal and ethical issues related to age discrimination and can lead to a lack of experience and institutional knowledge within the organization. Option D is incorrect because it is important to have a comprehensive strategy beyond incentives to ensure long-term workforce sustainability.

43. A. Executive sponsorship involves top-level leaders taking responsibility and being held accountable for the success and progress of DEI efforts within an organization. This includes setting goals, allocating resources, and ensuring that DEI initiatives are effectively implemented throughout the company. Options B and C are incorrect as they exemplify external DEI efforts rather than leadership commitment and accountability. Option D is incorrect because an employee resource group (ERG) is a specific action that may be part of a broader DEI strategy, but it does not encompass the entire concept of executive sponsorship.

44. C. Mabel's assertive and quick-speaking behavior, as well as her tendency to take the lead during discussions, reflects her personality traits. In contrast, Oliver's preference for listening, taking time to process information, and being quieter also reflects his personality traits. This scenario highlights the diversity in how individuals' personalities shape their communication styles and behaviors within the team. Option A is incorrect because the internal layer of diversity represents aspects that individuals are born with, such as age, gender, and race. Option B is incorrect as external dimensions of diversity include factors influenced by life experiences and choices, such as educational background and marital status. Option D is incorrect because the term *preferences* is broader and can encompass various aspects, but in this context, personality traits drive these preferences.

45. C. The key tenet of Gardenswartz and Rowe's Four Layers of Diversity model at the organizational level is to value the uniqueness of each individual by considering all layers of diversity. This model emphasizes that individuals are shaped by multiple dimensions of diversity, including personality, internal dimensions, external dimensions, and organizational dimensions. Organizations should recognize and appreciate the richness of diversity across all these layers, promoting inclusivity and equity. Options A, B, and D are not accurate representations of the model.

46. A. The primary difference between an employee resource group (ERG) and a diversity council lies in the level of leadership involvement and decision-making authority. ERGs are employee-led and provide a platform for employees with shared characteristics or interests to come together, support each other, and advocate for change within the organization. While ERGs may have some interaction with leadership, they do not have a significant role in decision-making at the organizational level. Option B is incorrect as ERGs often focus on providing support and representation for specific employee groups, while diversity councils are more involved in shaping overall diversity and inclusion strategies within the organization. Options C and D can both vary depending on factors other than the purpose of the groups.

47. B. When forming an employee resource group (ERG), it is most important that the members self-select. This means individuals who share a common characteristic, interest, or background should voluntarily choose to join the ERG because they identify with the group's

mission and objectives. Self-selection ensures that ERG members are genuinely interested and committed to the group's goals, creating a more engaged and effective group. Option A is incorrect because even in organizations that have strong diversity representation, ERGs provide support, promote diversity, and advance specific interests to both respond to and prevent under-representation in the workplace. Options C and D are incorrect as lack of influence or not perceiving themselves as advocates may be the result of systemic lack of diversity, and it is important to hear from multiple individuals for a well-rounded and inclusive group.

48. C. Allyship requires individuals to have the courage to speak up, challenge biases and stereotypes, and take action to support underrepresented groups. It involves confronting uncomfortable situations, advocating for change, and actively participating in efforts to create a more inclusive and equitable workplace. Without courage, other qualities like compassion (Option A) and advocacy (Option B) may not be effectively put into action (Option D).

49. D. Unconscious bias refers to the automatic and unintentional biases or prejudices that individuals hold, often based on societal stereotypes and preconceived notions. In this case, the employee conducting the interview is unconsciously favoring male candidates over the female candidate by consistently. Option A is incorrect because the question does not note that this employee is generally a rude person, so the underlying issue causing the rudeness is more likely to be unconscious bias. Option B is incorrect as a stress interview is a type of job interview where the interviewer intentionally creates a stressful or challenging environment to assess how a candidate responds to pressure, which is not indicated in the scenario. Option C is incorrect because same-sex harassment refers to harassment based on an individual's gender or sex by a person of the same gender or sex; this scenario does not rise to the level of ongoing or pervasive harassment but rather unconscious bias that affects the interview process.

50. A. Using preferred gender pronouns of employees is important because it creates a climate of inclusiveness. By respecting and using an individual's preferred pronouns, an organization signals that it values and acknowledges the diverse identities of its employees. This fosters a more inclusive and welcoming workplace environment where individuals feel seen, respected, and safe to be themselves. Option B is incorrect as the primary reason for using gender pronouns goes beyond politeness. Option C is incorrect as in some jurisdictions, there may be legal requirements related to gender identity and pronoun usage. However, the primary importance of using preferred pronouns is rooted in fostering inclusivity, and it may still be important even in the absence of legal mandates. Option D is not necessarily true, in fact, some customers may be bothered by it, and customer demands should not be the driver for using (or not using) preferred gender pronouns within the organization.

51. A. Mentoring in DEI involves an experienced individual (the mentor) providing guidance, support, and advocacy to someone from an underrepresented or marginalized group. Allyship similarly entails individuals (allies) advocating for and supporting marginalized or underrepresented groups. Allies actively work to understand the experiences and challenges faced by these groups and use their privilege and influence to help create a more equitable and inclusive environment. Option B is incorrect as coaching focuses on skill development, performance improvement, and goal achievement. Options C and D are incorrect because, similar to coaching, they involve imparting knowledge and helping in the skill development of others, while mentoring in DEI involves a more holistic approach, including emotional support, advocacy, and guidance tailored to an individual's unique experiences and challenges.

52. C. Psychological safety is the correct choice because it encompasses the characteristics of empowerment, humility, accountability, and courage. Psychological safety is a key principle within the context of DEI. It refers to creating an environment in which individuals feel safe and comfortable to express themselves, take risks, and contribute their perspectives without fear of negative consequences. In such an environment, individuals are empowered to speak up, leaders exhibit humility by actively listening and learning from others, there's a sense of accountability for promoting inclusion, and it takes courage to address biases and challenge the status quo.

53. A. Neurodiverse employees are individuals with a wide range of neurological conditions, including autism, ADHD, and others, who bring unique perspectives and talents to the workplace. Adjustments such as sensory-friendly workspaces with adjustable lighting can help reduce sensory overload and create a workspace where neurodiverse employees can focus and perform at their best. Option B is incorrect as neurodiversity encompasses a wide range of conditions, and some individuals may thrive with routine, while others may prefer more flexibility. Option C is incorrect as asking neurodiverse employees to assimilate is not the most inclusive approach. Option D is incorrect because minimizing communication channels and options can be isolating, especially for neurodiverse individuals who may benefit from alternative communication methods.

54. B. Affinity bias occurs when individuals show favoritism or preference toward others who share a similar background, characteristics, or experiences with them. Option A is incorrect as social comparison refers to the tendency of individuals to evaluate themselves in comparison to others. Option C is incorrect because the halo effect is a form of bias when an individual attributes greater weight to positive characteristics and overlooks negative ones. Option D is incorrect as the term *unconscious bias* refers to biases that individuals hold without awareness or deliberate intention.

55. D. Leader-Member Exchange Theory (LMX) suggests that leaders form different exchange relationships with their followers, divided into two groups: the in-group and the outgroup. Leaders tend to develop a closer, more positive relationship with members of the in-group, characterized by higher trust, support, and influence. This theory inherently leads to the creation of ingroup and outgroup distinctions, resulting in potential perceptions of bias and inequity. Option A is incorrect because Theory X and Theory Y (McGregor) focus on contrasting assumptions about employee motivation and behavior, not comparing groups. Option B is incorrect as Acquired Needs Theory (McClelland) explains how individuals have different needs for achievement, affiliation, and power in the workplace. While this theory helps leaders understand the motivations of their team members, it also does not inherently lead to ingroup/outgroup bias. Option C is incorrect because the Two Factor Theory (Herzberg) distinguishes between hygiene factors and motivators and doesn't directly involve ingroup/outgroup bias.

56. A. Cultural taxation refers to the phenomenon where individuals from underrepresented or marginalized groups are often expected or burdened with additional responsibilities related to DEI efforts within an organization. This can include activities such as serving on diversity committees, leading diversity training, and being advocates for DEI initiatives.

57. B. Grooming policies can often lead to behaviors where protected-class employees feel compelled to "cover up" or downplay certain aspects of their identity to conform to the policy's

standards. For example, they may alter their hairstyle or clothing choices to conform to the policy, even if it conflicts with their cultural or personal preferences. Option A is incorrect as it is more applicable to neurodiverse individuals who conceal or suppress one's neurodivergent traits, behaviors, or characteristics (such as stimming) to fit in or conform to societal or social expectations, often leading to mental and emotional exhaustion. Options C and D are incorrect as quiet quitting and defensiveness are generally in response to larger issues of systemic exclusion.

58. A. Unlawful discrimination refers to actions or behaviors that are intentional, deliberate, and illegal under anti-discrimination laws. These actions involve treating individuals unfairly or adversely based on their protected characteristics, such as race, gender, or age. Microaggressions are subtle, often unintentional, and may not be illegal in themselves. Microaggressions are comments, behaviors, or actions that convey bias or stereotypes toward individuals based on their identity, but they are not necessarily deliberate or malicious.

59. D. Quiet or prayer rooms in the workplace are designed to provide a peaceful and accommodating environment where individuals from diverse backgrounds, including those who may have religious or sensory needs, can engage in practices such as meditation, prayer, or sensory self-regulation. These spaces promote inclusivity and well-being by recognizing and addressing the unique needs of various individuals. Options A, B, and C are partially correct but do not capture the primary purpose of quiet or prayer rooms in the workplace.

60. D. Pay equity reports are specifically designed to measure and analyze the degree to which positions with similar responsibilities are comparably compensated within an organization. These reports involve a detailed examination of salary data, job roles, and other relevant factors to identify and address any pay disparities, particularly related to gender, race, or other protected characteristics. Pay equity reports help HR professionals ensure that employees are being fairly compensated for their work, regardless of their backgrounds. Option A is incorrect as HR audits involve a comprehensive review of HR policies, procedures, and practices within an organization and are not specifically focused on measuring compensation comparability. Option B is incorrect because diversity audits are conducted to assess an organization's diversity and inclusion efforts, policies, and practices, not comparable worth. Option C is incorrect as adverse impact formulas are used to analyze whether employment practices, such as hiring or promotion decisions, have a disproportionate negative impact on protected groups, not equitable pay practices.

61. B. Implicit biases are unconscious attitudes or stereotypes that individuals hold without being consciously aware of them. These biases can affect decision-making, hiring, promotions, and day-to-day interactions in the workplace. They often result from societal and cultural conditioning and can lead to unintended discrimination or unequal treatment.

62. D. Stereotypes are preconceived and consciously held beliefs or generalizations about a particular group based on characteristics such as race, gender, age, or religion. In the workplace, explicit biases in the form of stereotypes can lead to biased decisions, discriminatory behaviors, and unequal treatment of individuals from different groups. Option A is incorrect as unlawful discriminatory behaviors are the outcomes or consequences of biases, not the biases themselves. Options B and C are incorrect because unconscious bias and microaggressions represent implicit biases as they are not consciously intended.

63. B. The diversity dividend refers to the tangible benefits that organizations can gain by actively promoting diversity and fostering an inclusive workplace culture. When an organization creates an inclusive environment where individuals from diverse backgrounds feel valued and can contribute their unique perspectives, it can lead to increased innovation, improved problem-solving, enhanced creativity, and, ultimately, greater profitability.

64. A. Equity refers to fairness or justice in the way people are treated, and especially freedom from bias or favoritism. Equality refers to the quality or state of having the same rights and opportunities, such as equal pay for women.

65. B. This type of diversity encompasses the traditional dimensions we're familiar with, such as gender, race, age, and ethnicity. It acknowledges the unique perspectives and experiences that individuals from different backgrounds bring to the table. These characteristics can be considered part of an individual's legacy because they are passed down through generations. Option A is incorrect as the term *protected* in the context of diversity often refers to characteristics that are protected under anti-discrimination laws, such as race, gender, disability, or age and may or may not be physical characteristics. Option C is incorrect because experiential diversity relates to individuals' unique life experiences, backgrounds, and perspectives. Option D is an answer distractor as it is not a typical dimension of diversity.

Chapter 13: Workforce Analytics and Technology

1. B. The primary goal of workforce analytics is to optimize workforce productivity by using data analysis to identify patterns, trends, and factors affecting productivity. This involves analyzing various workforce-related metrics to make informed decisions and improvements. Options A is incorrect as reducing employee turnover is a benefit of using workforce analytics, but not its primary goal. Option C is incorrect as customer satisfaction is accomplished through more customer-centric activities, not internal workforce analytics. Option D is partially correct as optimizing workforce productivity can lead to cost savings; however, the primary focus is on improving productivity and efficiency within the workforce.

2. C. An HR benchmark is a standardized metric or performance indicator used to measure, compare, and assess various aspects of human resources management, such as workforce productivity, employee turnover, or compensation levels, against industry standards or organizational goals to inform decision-making and improve HR practices. HR departments often work closely with production and operations teams to optimize workforce performance and productivity. Tracking the number of units produced per hour is a common HR benchmark used to assess the efficiency and output of manufacturing employees. Options A, B and D are incorrect because they are examples of quality, energy efficiency and supply chain benchmarks, not HR benchmarks.

3. D. A cost-benefit analysis quantifies the expected return on investment (ROI) over time by comparing the anticipated benefits of the software (such as increased efficiency, cost savings,

or revenue generation) against the costs associated with its acquisition, implementation, and maintenance. It helps stakeholders understand whether the investment is financially justified and what they can expect in terms of ROI. Option A is only partially correct as while a cost-benefit analysis does involve detailing the costs associated with a plan, its primary role is to assess whether the benefits of the plan outweigh the costs, not just to list the costs. Option B is incorrect because a cost-benefit analysis does not focus on how a plan will be funded. Option C is incorrect because it is not the primary role of a cost-benefit analysis.

4. A. Lack of quality data is a common challenge in workforce analytics implementation. To perform effective analytics, you need reliable, accurate, and complete data. When data is of poor quality, it can lead to incorrect analyses and unreliable insights, undermining the effectiveness of workforce analytics initiatives. Option B is incorrect because this challenge pertains more to change management efforts and organizational culture than to data analysis. Option C is incorrect because having a wealth of data can be advantageous if it is well-organized and analyzed effectively. Workforce analytics often focuses on selecting relevant data points rather than analyzing every piece of data. Option D is incorrect because workforce analytics seeks to provide insights into employee behavior, performance, and trends, not. Have employees offer insights into organizational initiatives. That is more the role of surveys, focus groups and other feedback mechanisms.

5. B. Predictive analytics can help you forecast which employees are at risk of leaving in the future, giving you an opportunity to intervene proactively. Prescriptive analytics goes a step further by providing actionable recommendations on how to prevent turnover based on the predictions. Predictive and prescriptive analytics not only identifies the problem but also suggests solutions to address it, making it a powerful combination for reducing turnover. Options A and C are only partially correct because descriptive analytics focuses on summarizing historical data and providing insights into what has happened in the past but does not provide actionable insights for preventing future turnover. Option D is incorrect as diagnostic analytics involves analyzing data to understand why certain events occurred in the past rather than preventing them from occurring in the future, making B the better answer.

6. A. When HR is drafting a request for proposal (RFP) for a new applicant tracking system, it's important to specify the desired features and functionality required to meet the organization's hiring needs. This information helps potential vendors understand the HR department's specific requirements and capabilities they should offer in their system. It ensures that the chosen system aligns with HR's goals and objectives for recruitment and applicant management. Option B is incorrect as it's not a component that HR should include in the RFP itself. Instead, HR should use the RFP to request pricing details from vendors based on the specified features and functionality. Option C is incorrect because Proprietary information belongs to the organization or the vendor and should not be disclosed in the RFP document, as it could compromise confidentiality, security, or intellectual property rights. Option D is incorrect as marketing and advertising strategies are unrelated to the selection of an applicant tracking system.

7. C. One of the primary advantages of using external collaboration software in the workplace is to facilitate and streamline collaboration with external partners, clients, vendors, or other stakeholders. This software allows organizations to securely share information, documents, and collaborate on projects with external parties, improving communication and efficiency

in external-facing processes. Option A is incorrect as the use of external software can expose an organization to threats, not necessarily enhance security. Option B is incorrect because external collaboration software is primarily focused on facilitating communication and collaboration with external parties, not on improving internal communication within an organization. Improving internal communication is usually the role of internal collaboration tools. Option D is incorrect because while external collaboration software can increase efficiency, its primary purpose is to enable better collaboration with external partners, not automate or reduce internal workloads.

8. D. Blockchain technology offers a decentralized and secure way to verify credentials. It ensures data integrity and authenticity by creating a tamper-proof record of qualifications. This method can streamline the verification process, improve efficiency, and reduce the risk of hiring unqualified candidates. Option A is incorrect because manual verification is prone to errors, time-consuming, and inefficient for handling large volumes of international credentials. Option B is incorrect as outsourcing verification can be expensive, introduce delays, and may not provide the level of control needed for efficient credential verification. Option C is incorrect because artificial intelligence may struggle with diverse international credential formats and standards, potentially compromising the accuracy and reliability of the verification process.

9. C. Natural Language Processing (NLP) in the workforce refers to the use of artificial intelligence and computational linguistics to enable computers to understand, interpret, and generate human language. NLP algorithms can process and analyze large volumes of text-based data, such as employee feedback, emails, and chat interactions. It can identify trends, sentiments, and key insights within this unstructured data, helping HR teams gain a deeper understanding of employee opinions, concerns, and satisfaction levels. Option A is incorrect because NLP does not generate feedback. Option B is incorrect because NLP's primary function is not necessarily to translate all communications into a single language. Option D is incorrect as NLP cannot replace the role of HR personnel in conducting surveys and interviews, which involve human interaction, empathy, and contextual understanding that NLP cannot replicate.

10. B. When historical data used to train AI systems contain bias or reflects past discriminatory practices, the algorithm can perpetuate those biases, leading to biased outcomes in promotion recommendations. Addressing this type of bias often requires data cleansing, bias mitigation techniques, and a careful examination of the training data to ensure fairness and equity in AI-driven decisions. Option A is incorrect because while technical errors can cause issues in AI systems, the scenario described indicates a consistent pattern of favoring one gender over another, which is more indicative of bias rooted in the data used to train the algorithm. Option C is incorrect because while diversity in the HR team is important for addressing biases, this was not apparent in the question. Option D is incorrect because the complexity of the algorithm may affect HR's ability to manage it effectively, but it's not the root cause of the bias.

11. C. Blockchain is a technology that securely records transactions on multiple computers, ensuring data is transparent, secure, and cannot be altered. Processing payroll in real-time often involves complex financial transactions and compliance requirements that may not align with blockchain's current capabilities. Payroll systems require integration with financial institutions and real-time regulatory reporting, which can be challenging to achieve through blockchain technology. In option A, blockchain excels at providing tamper-proof records,

making it suitable for maintaining employee records, credentials, and other HR-related data securely. In Option B, blockchain can enhance privacy and confidentiality by allowing individuals to have greater control over their personal data while securely sharing it as needed. In option D, decentralized identity verification is a way for people to prove who they are online without depending on a central authority, making online identity checks more private and secure. Blockchain can facilitate decentralized identity verification, reducing the need for centralized identity verification services (such as government agencies) and enhancing security and trust in HR processes.

12. A. In this scenario, blockchain-enabled capabilities are digital identity management platforms that provide individuals with a secure way to manage and control their personal identity online. It offers a unique and decentralized identity solution that can be used for various authentication and verification purposes, but it is not based on options B, C and D-traditional passwords, fingerprints, or CAPTCHA-style security features. Once an employee uploads proper documents that have been authenticated, they receive a digital key that is used to access various HR services, such as updating personal information, viewing pay stubs, and enrolling in employee benefits. The digital id also provides for a legally binding digital signature for use on confidentiality agreements or performance related documents.

13. B. Phishing is a type of cyberattack where the attacker impersonates a trustworthy entity or individual to deceive the target into revealing sensitive information, such as login credentials or personal information. Phishing attacks often rely on social engineering tactics to manipulate victims into taking actions that compromise their security. Option A is incorrect because hacking refers to the unauthorized access or intrusion into computer systems or networks to gain control, steal data, or disrupt operations. Option C is incorrect because Ransomware is a distinct type of cyberattack where malicious software encrypts a victim's files or systems and demands a ransom to provide the decryption key. Option D is incorrect because social engineering is a broader concept that encompasses various techniques used to manipulate individuals into divulging confidential information or performing certain actions. While phishing is a form of social engineering, the scenario provided specifically focuses on the deceptive email and the attempt to trick employees into revealing their account information.

14. A. The key difference is that social engineering targets human behavior, while hacking targets technical weaknesses. Social engineering involves exploiting individuals through psychological manipulation or deception to gain access to confidential information or systems. Hacking, on the other hand, primarily focuses on exploiting technical vulnerabilities in computer systems or networks to gain unauthorized access.

15. D. An offsite network access policy outlines the specific security measures and protocols that employees must follow when accessing the company's network remotely. It includes requirements such as multi-factor authentication and encrypted connections to maintain the confidentiality and integrity of corporate data when employees are working offsite. Option A is incorrect as personal use policies focus on guidelines and rules related to employees using their personal devices for work purposes, rather than the specific security protocols required for remote network access. Option B is incorrect because social media policies are unrelated to the security measures needed for remote network access. Option C is incorrect as internet messaging policies primarily address the use of messaging applications and platforms for communication, which is distinct from remote network access security protocols.

16. A. A BYOD policy aims to define clear guidelines and rules for employees who opt to use their personal devices (such as smartphones or laptops) for work-related tasks. This includes rules related to security, data protection, acceptable use, and other considerations to ensure a secure and compliant environment when personal devices are used for work. Options B, C and D are not true.

17. B. Human resources is responsible for supporting the creation and implementation of data backup and recovery policies and procedures. This includes determining what data needs to be backed up, setting retention policies, and ensuring compliance with data protection laws, especially when it comes to personnel records and sensitive HR data. Option A is untrue, and options C and D are handled by other departments such as IT or outsourced to specialized technicians.

18. B. Scale in microlearning pertains to the capacity to efficiently disseminate and manage microlearning content to a wide range of learners or employees. It refers to the ability of the program to "scale up or down", depending on audience size. Options A, C and D are incorrect because scale is more about the delivery and distribution of content to a broad audience than it is about the size, duration or depth of training modules.

19. C. Micro-learning by definition is designed for targeted learning outcomes, and thus, appealing to large groups of employees is not an important element of the design of these programs. Option B involves adding game-like elements to the content to enhance engagement and motivation. Gamification can make learning more interactive and enjoyable, which can lead to improved retention and participation. Option D, personalization, can make microlearning more effective by providing content that is relevant to each employee's specific learning goals and performance gaps.

20. D. The most critical element in designing a DEI (Diversity, Equity, and Inclusion) survey for informing strategic initiatives over the next 5 years is to clearly define the objectives. This is important because without well-defined objectives, the survey may lack focus and fail to gather the necessary data to inform the company's strategic decisions. By clearly defining the objectives, you ensure that the survey questions are aligned with the specific goals and outcomes the company wants to achieve through its DEI initiatives. This clarity will drive success of the other options such as who should be included in the survey and obtaining their consent (option A) how to conduct the survey (option B) and once designed, the proper validation procedures (option D).

21. A. The primary purpose of validating a workplace assessment tool or survey is to ensure that it accurately measures what it intends to measure. Validation involves a rigorous process of testing the survey's questions and methodology to determine if they effectively capture the intended concepts, variables, or characteristics. It assesses the survey's reliability and validity, ensuring that the collected data can be trusted to represent the targeted aspects of the workplace accurately. Option B is incorrect because response rate is a separate consideration related to survey administration. Option C is incorrect because the Uniform Guidelines on Employee Selection Procedures (UGESP) are a set of federal guidelines in the United States that provide standards for evaluating and ensuring fairness in the use of selection procedures in employment, with the aim of preventing unlawful discrimination. Validating the results will align with the requirements of the UGESP's, making A the better option. Option D is incorrect because comparing survey results to industry benchmarks is a post-survey analysis and benchmarking exercise.

22. C. The HR department in this scenario is engaged in data mining. Data mining involves the process of analyzing large volumes of data to discover patterns, trends, and insights that may not be readily apparent through traditional analysis. In this case, HR is examining historical employee data to uncover key traits and practices associated with high-performing and long-tenured employees, which is a classic example of data mining. Option A is incorrect because statistical analysis involves applying statistical techniques to analyze workforce data, such as identifying the relationship between employee performance and training hours or uncovering patterns in employee turnover rates over different departments, which is not described in this scenario. Option B is incorrect because while the HR department may generate reports based on their data mining findings, the primary activity described in the scenario is the analysis typical of mining, not reporting. Option D is incorrect because trend analysis is a specific type of analysis that involves identifying and analyzing patterns or trends within data over time, also not the focus of the example.

23. D. Managing the process of data cleansing as a strategic initiative involves dedicating resources, time, and effort to systematically identify, correct, and prevent data errors and inconsistencies. It is a proactive approach that can significantly improve the issues and lead to enhanced patient satisfaction and operational efficiency. Option A is incorrect as the core issue here is not just about managing large quantities of data but rather about the quality and accuracy of the data. Option B is incorrect because it does not directly address the underlying problem of data errors and inconsistencies in patient records. Option C is incorrect because training employees makes more sense once the issue has been resolved and understood and new procedures are set in place to prevent the issues from getting out of hand.

24. B. Data visualization skills are necessary to transform complex data into visually appealing and easily understandable formats such as charts, graphs, and dashboards. This competency enables HR professionals to present insights in a more accessible and compelling manner, which is critical when communicating with senior management about talent acquisition, employee engagement, and retention strategies. Option A is incorrect as project management skills are more relevant when planning and executing the process of improving HR data analysis and presentation, but they do not directly address the need to visualize and communicate the data effectively. Options C and D are incorrect because simply having strong communication or presentation skills may not be sufficient to transform overwhelming data into easily understandable insights. Data visualization skills play a more direct role in creating visual representations of data that facilitate comprehension, which is the primary challenge described in the scenario.

25. B. Integrating HR systems allows for the centralization of HR data from various sources and systems into a single, unified platform. Real-time analytics capabilities help HR teams make data-driven decisions regarding talent management and workforce planning. They can analyze trends, identify skill gaps, and plan for talent needs more effectively when armed with this centralized, real-time data. Option A is incorrect as they safeguard employee information but do not directly facilitate better talent management and workforce planning. Option C is incorrect because Employee Self-Service (ESS) capabilities primarily empower employees to access and manage their own HR-related information, activities more narrowly focused than talent management or workforce planning. Option D is incorrect as HR professionals play a crucial role in strategizing, planning, and implementing effective talent management and workforce planning initiatives, so eliminating their roles is not the goal of automation and other uses of technology.

26. A. Payroll processing is one of the HR tasks that are best suited to automation. It involves complex calculations, tax deductions, and compliance requirements, which can be efficiently handled by HR software, reducing errors and saving time. Option B is incorrect as while some aspects of employee onboarding can be automated, such as electronic document signing or training module assignments, the personal and human-centric aspects of onboarding, like team introductions and culture assimilation, are best handled by humans. Option C is incorrect as performance evaluations involve subjective assessments of employees' performance, including feedback and goal-setting often requiring human judgment and interaction. Option D is incorrect because workplace conflict resolution is a highly sensitive and interpersonal HR task that involves understanding complex human emotions and dynamics. It is not well-suited for automation, as it requires empathy, communication skills, and nuanced judgment to resolve effectively.

27. D. Continuous improvement involves the ongoing process of assessing and refining data-driven initiatives and strategies. By continuously improving their data-related practices, HR can adapt to changing circumstances, address emerging challenges, and enhance their ability to leverage data for talent management, employee engagement, and overall organizational performance. Option A is incorrect because it focuses solely on the technological aspect of data advocacy. Continuous improvement encompasses a broader scope, including refining strategies, processes, and approaches, rather than just tool updates. Option B is incorrect because it is not its primary purpose in the context of HR's role as data advocates. Option C is incorrect because continuous improvement is not limited to tracking data trends but rather involves actively improving data-related efforts.

28. A, B. While HR Generalists may be involved in using HR metrics to understand organizational performance, promoting the use of HR metrics across the entire organization is a responsibility that falls more squarely on senior HR leaders. Senior HR leaders often play a strategic role in advocating for the use of metrics, setting the direction for data-driven decision-making, and ensuring that HR metrics align with the organization's overall goals and objectives. This responsibility is more closely associated with senior leadership roles within HR. In option B, senior HR leaders must demonstrate an understanding of the use of data to inform business decisions, evidenced by the business credits recertification requirement of the SPHR, but not the PHR. It is a fundamental competency for HR professionals at all levels, not exclusive to senior leaders. Option C is incorrect because maintaining a working knowledge of data collection methods is a responsibility that should be shared by HR professionals at different levels, including HR Generalists and senior HR leaders. Option D is incorrect because maintaining objectivity when interpreting data is a fundamental principle for all HR professionals, regardless of their specific role or level within the HR department.

29. B. Cloud-based HR software offers increased accessibility, allowing HR professionals to access data and applications from anywhere with an internet connection. This enhances flexibility and collaboration. Option A is incorrect because scalability refers to the system's ability to handle increased workload or users without compromising performance or requiring significant changes to the infrastructure and does not directly relate to HR technology management and its advantages. Option C is incorrect as cloud-based software often allows for significant customization, enabling organizations to tailor the system to their specific needs and requirements. Option D is incorrect as data security is not necessarily an advantage, rather, it is a fundamental requirement that must be adequately addressed.

30. B. Evidence-based decision making is characterized by using research and best practices as the foundation for building strategies to achieve organizational results. It involves relying on empirical evidence, data, and research findings to inform and support decision-making processes. In this approach, decisions are based on what has been proven to work effectively in similar situations or contexts, leading to more informed and successful organizational strategies. Option A is incorrect because data analysis involves examining and interpreting data to derive insights, whereas evidence-based decision making encompasses a broader process that includes using research, best practices, and empirical evidence in addition to data analysis to inform decisions. Options C and D are incorrect as they do not represent the broader concept of using research and best practices to build organizational strategies, as specified in the question.

31. B. Evidence-based decision making in the workplace involves gathering and considering data and input from a diverse group of employees or stakeholders. Seeking input from a diverse group ensures that decisions are based on a broader range of evidence, leading to more informed and effective solutions. Option A is incorrect as it alone may not encompass the full scope of evidence-based decision making. Option C is incorrect as evidence-based approaches prioritize the use of credible data, research, and diverse input to inform decision-making, rather than relying on the opinions or guidance of a select group of leaders. Option D is incorrect because this option does not directly the need for a focus on the broader use of empirical evidence, research, and diverse input to inform decisions, not just legal considerations.

32. A. When presenting the annual financial performance to the board of directors, using a narrative that incorporates storytelling and visualizations is the most effective communication approach. It helps engage the audience, makes complex financial data more accessible, and allows for the highlighting of key insights. Storytelling can provide context, while visualizations, such as charts and graphs, can make the data more understandable and memorable, leading to a more compelling and impactful presentation. Option B is incorrect as it may not be as effective as option A because it lacks the narrative and storytelling elements, subjecting the recipient to interpret the data in a vacuum. Options C and D are incorrect as written reports and raw data can be dense, and board members may not absorb all the key insights without context and interpretation.

33. C. Benchmarking is not an internal source of information. Benchmarking involves comparing an organization's practices and performance with those of external entities, such as competitors or industry peers. It is an external source of information that helps organizations assess their relative performance but is not generated from within the organization itself. In option A, employee wellness programs are an internal source of information that HR teams can use to gather data on employee health, participation rates, program effectiveness, and feedback. This information can inform the development of initiatives related to employee health and wellbeing. In option B, performance reviews provide internal data that HR teams use to assess individual and team performance, identify areas for improvement, and make decisions related to promotions, training, and development. In option D, focus groups are organized discussions involving employees to gather qualitative insights on various HR-related topics, initiatives, or challenges and are an internal source of information that helps HR teams gain diverse perspectives and feedback from employees, which can be valuable in shaping HR initiatives.

34. B. When conducting an external scan to understand data utility needs in the workplace, one of the key considerations is obtaining data from reputable and legitimate sources. This is important to ensure the credibility and accuracy of the data being used for decision-making. Data from unreliable or questionable sources can lead to poor decision-making and inaccurate insights. Option A is incorrect because while it is important to act in an ethical fashion, relying on credible external resources is likely to allow for this, making B the better answer. Option C is incorrect because the question is more broadly about understanding data needs in the workplace, which can extend beyond just competitors. Option D is incorrect because budget considerations are relevant, but not at the expense of relevance or accuracy.

35. C. One of the primary challenges organizations may face when implementing AI in human resource applications is the inability to integrate AI systems with existing HR software. This challenge arises because many organizations already have established HR software and systems in place, and integrating AI seamlessly can be technically complex. Compatibility issues, data synchronization, and ensuring that the AI system complements the existing HR infrastructure can be challenging. Option A is incorrect as finding qualified talent is not unique to AI but rather dependent on many other variables. Option B is incorrect as organizations often aim for a balance between scalability and security when implementing AI in HR. Option D is incorrect because AI's limited capacity to handle routine HR tasks is a limitation of AI technology but is not one of the primary challenges faced by organizations when implementing AI. The challenge lies more in the successful integration and adoption of AI within HR processes.

36. D. When there is a significant gap in human relations experience within the AI implementation team, one of the key challenges that may arise is difficulties in understanding and addressing the nuanced needs of employees. Human resource applications often deal with complex and sensitive aspects of employee relations, and lacking the necessary human relations experience can hinder the team's ability to effectively address these nuanced issues. Option A is incorrect as this option does not address the specific challenge related to understanding and addressing employee needs. Option B is incorrect as difficulty in finding AI talent for HR applications is a separate challenge related to staffing the implementation team. Option C is incorrect because the inability to align AI initiatives with organizational goals is a broader challenge that may arise in AI implementation but does not specifically address the issue of a gap in human relations experience within the team. It focuses more on strategic alignment rather than the understanding of employee needs.

37. C. Employee self-service (ESS) technologies are most suited to support updates to sensitive personnel data. These systems allow employees to independently and securely update their personal information, such as contact details, emergency contacts, or changes in marital status. This reduces the administrative burden on HR staff, ensures data accuracy, and empowers employees to maintain their records efficiently. Option A is incorrect because legal compliance often involves complex issues and may require legal expertise and oversight from HR professionals. Option B is incorrect because employee coaching involves interactions between employees and coaches or mentors. Option D is incorrect because HR professionals monitor and facilitate such events in coordination with employees.

38. A. HR is most likely to demonstrate the competency of negotiation when implementing a new process or technology change. This is because these types of implementations often involve negotiations with software vendors, service providers, and internal stakeholders.

Options B and C are incorrect because interpreting workforce data and predicting trends are more about using competencies related to data analysis and understanding trends within the data. Option D is incorrect because dealing with a data security breach primarily involves incident response, security protocols, and compliance with data protection regulations and is more likely to require the competencies of communication and consultation.

39. B. After identifying HR needs and requirements, the next step is to assess the scalability and integration capabilities of HRIS systems. This ensures that the selected system can grow with the organization and seamlessly integrate with existing HR processes and software. Options A, C, and D are incorrect because they do not represent the appropriate next step in the HRIS selection process and may lead to inadequate evaluation or premature implementation.

40. D. Addressing how the HRIS system aligns with the organization's international expansion strategy, compliance goals, and long-term growth is a crucial consideration for making a strong business case. It emphasizes the strategic benefits of the HRIS implementation and shows that the investment is not just about efficiency but also about achieving the company's broader objectives. Option A is incorrect because it may not be the most compelling argument for a global company with strategic international expansion goals. Option B is incorrect because it is essential to emphasize the long-term return on investment (ROI) and strategic benefits of the HRIS system rather than focus on short-term budgetary challenges. Option C is incorrect as the focus should not be on staying competitive in the industry but rather how the initiative affects both short and long term strategic targets.

41. A. Software as a Service (SaaS) is a cloud computing model that delivers software applications over the internet on a subscription basis, allowing users to access and use the software without the need for local installations or maintenance. SaaS in HR technology is often used to efficiently manage payroll processing and employee benefits administration, offering cloud-based solutions for these tasks. Option B is incorrect because SaaS is ready-made HR software and thus, is not used to develop other solutions. Option C is incorrect as SaaS is known for its cloud-based delivery model, which eliminates the need for maintaining on-premises databases. Option D is incorrect because SaaS is more commonly used for online and remote HR functions rather than in-person training sessions.

42. B. Applicant Tracking Systems (ATS) are primarily designed to manage and streamline the recruitment process. They help HR departments post job listings, track and organize applicants, screen resumes, schedule interviews, and ultimately improve the efficiency of the hiring process. ATS plays a crucial role in sourcing, evaluating, and selecting the right candidates to fill job vacancies. Options A and D are partially correct in that an ATS should feature functions that help an employer comply with non-discriminatory and other regulatory hiring factors. However, the purpose of ATS technology is primarily focused on acting as a database for the recruiting and hiring process. Option C is incorrect as an ATS does not track software applications, but rather, employment applications.

43. B. A learning portal is specifically designed to provide access to educational content, resources, and tools for the purpose of training, skill development, and knowledge sharing. It is a digital platform tailored for learning and development. Option A is incorrect because while a learning portal is a type of website, not all websites are dedicated to education, training, or knowledge sharing, which is the primary focus of a learning portal. Option C is incorrect because an intranet is a private network used within an organization to share information and resources among its employees. Option D is incorrect as a "Learning machine" is not a commonly recognized term in the context of digital platforms for education and training. It does not accurately describe the concept of a platform providing access to educational content and resources.

44. B. The scenario described is an application of wearable technology in the workplace to enhance employee productivity and safety. Smartwatches are used to monitor employees' movements and provide real-time feedback on posture, helping prevent workplace injuries and improve work efficiency.

45. C. One of the potential risks associated with using wearable technology, such as smart clothing, in the workplace, is the heightened risk of privacy and data security concerns. When employees wear devices that collect and transmit data, it raises questions about how that data is stored, accessed, and protected. Privacy and security breaches can occur if this data is not properly safeguarded, leading to potential legal and ethical issues. Options A, B and D are not directly related with the wearable technology itself.

46. B. The greatest risk associated with the use of VPNs (Virtual Private Networks) in the workplace is an increased vulnerability to social engineering attacks. VPNs are designed to secure data transmission over the internet, but they do not protect against social engineering techniques where attackers manipulate individuals into revealing sensitive information or access credentials. Employees connecting to the workplace via VPNs might assume a false sense of security, making them more susceptible to social engineering attempts. Option A is incorrect because while VPNs can increase internet bandwidth consumption slightly due to encryption overhead, it is not considered the greatest risk associated with their use. Option C is incorrect as system crashes are related to hardware or software issues unrelated to VPN usage. Option D is incorrect because VPNs do not lead to decreased storage capacity.

47. A. Policies alone may not provide the same level of security as the other techniques, as they rely on employees following guidelines and may not prevent unauthorized access or data breaches on their own. Option B, passwords, are a commonly used and effective technique for protecting employee information. Tiers presented in Option C, are an effective technique used by employers to restrict access to employee information and help ensure that only authorized personnel can access certain types of data. Option D, data keys, or cryptographic keys, are a highly effective technique for protecting employee information. They are used in encryption and decryption processes, adding an extra layer of security to sensitive data. When data keys are implemented correctly, they can provide strong protection against unauthorized access.

48. C. When analyzing Requests for Proposals (RFPs) for the acquisition of new technology, the criteria should be considered by weighing them in order of feature importance. This means that you prioritize the features and capabilities that are most critical to your organization's needs and objectives. Option A is incorrect as it's a project management consideration rather than a criterion for evaluating the technology itself within an RFP. Option B is incorrect as ordering criteria from price, highest to lowest, may not necessarily reflect the most important factors for selecting the right technology solution. Price is just one aspect to consider among many others like features, scalability, support, and fit with organizational needs. Option D is incorrect as it should come after assessing the core features and fit of the technology with your organization's requirements.

49. B. When selecting HR technology, prioritizing how the technology supports organizational strategy is crucial. Ensuring that the technology aligns with organizational strategy helps in achieving a more strategic and value-driven approach to HR. Option A is incorrect because compliance is important, but it should not be prioritized over aligning with organizational strategy, which can drive broader business success (and include compliance). Option C is incorrect as ownership can be determined once the technology choice aligns with organizational strategy and HR needs. Option D is incorrect because it is a technical consideration that should come after ensuring that the technology supports organizational strategy and meets HR requirements.

50. B. IT can be a strong business partner for HR when selecting an HRIS (Human Resources Information System) by providing the necessary integration support with enterprise-wide systems. IT departments have expertise in system integration, which is crucial for ensuring that the HRIS can seamlessly work with other organizational systems, such as finance, payroll, and email, to create a unified and efficient technology ecosystem. Option A is incorrect as the final decision on selecting HR software should ideally involve HR stakeholders, as they are the ones who will primarily use the system to manage HR processes. Option C is incorrect because the purchasing decision should involve collaboration between both departments to align technical requirements with HR's functional needs. Option D is incorrect as the expertise on how to best secure confidential employee data should be a shared responsibility between IT and HR, as HR holds valuable insights into data privacy and compliance specific to HR-related information.

51. A, D. AI-powered tools can analyze large volumes of resumes and job applications quickly and accurately, saving time for recruiters and HR professionals. These tools use algorithms to match candidate skills and qualifications with job requirements, thus streamlining the initial screening process. Time-to-hire is a metric used to evaluate how long a position remains open until filled, and a streamlined applicant system can greatly improve this metric. Option B is incorrect as AI systems can inherit biases present in the data they are trained on, and algorithmic decision-making can sometimes introduce new biases. Option C is incorrect as this option presents a potential disadvantage rather than an advantage of using AI in the hiring process.

52. A, B, C, D. Digital monitoring has both positive and negative consequences. Digital monitoring of employees can provide valuable data on productivity and efficiency by tracking their performance metrics. This data can be used to identify areas for improvement and optimize workflows, leading to increased productivity. It also allows employers to ensure that employees adhere to company policies and regulatory requirements. By tracking employees' actions and behaviors, employers can identify and address any compliance issues more effectively, thus improving overall compliance within the organization. Conversely, employees report lower levels of job satisfaction and increased stress due to digital monitoring, and in some cases, respond with an increase into counterproductive work behaviors such as wasted time.

53. B. Anthropomorphized robot leaders refer to robots or artificial intelligence systems that are designed or portrayed with human-like qualities such as emotions, decision-making abilities and communication skills, and even physical appearances of humans. Research suggests that when anthropomorphized robots deliver negative feedback, they may be perceived as possessing agency, leading to perceptions of abuse and higher levels of retaliation from employees. This can result in feelings of mistrust and resentment among employees, ultimately impacting morale and productivity. Options A, C and D are not true.

54. B. Descriptive statistics involve summarizing and presenting data in a meaningful way to provide insights into the current state of affairs. This includes measures such as mean, median, mode, range, and standard deviation, which help in understanding the central tendency and variability of the data. Option A is incorrect because it describes the role of predictive analytics which uses historical data to forecast future trends and outcomes by applying statistical algorithms and machine learning techniques. Options C and D are incorrect because they refer to the role of inferential statistics which are used to make inferences or conclusions about a population based on a sample of data.

55. C. Mode is the value that appears most frequently in a dataset, so 4 is the correct answer.

56. C. Mean, also known as the average, is calculated by taking the sum of all the values in the dataset and dividing it by the total number of values:

    `4+3+5+2+5+4+5= 28/7=4`

57. B. Concurrent validity involves comparing the scores obtained from a new assessment tool with scores from an established criterion (such as supervisor ratings) to determine whether the new tool accurately measures the same constructs or competencies. Option A is incorrect as it refers to predictive validity rather than concurrent validity, which assesses the extent to which assessment scores predict future job performance over time. Option C is incorrect because it describes the assessment of reliability which is the consistency or stability of measurement over repeated administrations. Option D is incorrect as it refers to construct validity, which assesses whether an assessment tool measures the intended construct or trait, including whether it captures unique aspects not measured by other tools.

58. A, B, C. Automating unemployment claims processing can significantly reduce processing time and streamline efficiency by eliminating manual tasks, reducing errors, and accelerating the overall processing workflow. Automation can also help organizations comply with documentation requirements including storage and retention imposed by laws that can vary from state to state. It also enhances data security and confidentiality to help protect sensitive information related to unemployment claims, including personal and financial data, from unauthorized access or breaches. Option D is incorrect because the likelihood of winning an appeal depends on various factors, including the strength of the evidence presented and compliance with relevant laws and regulations.

59. A. After a reduction in force, revoking security clearances and other access to company assets becomes a priority to ensure that only authorized individuals have access to sensitive information. This helps mitigate the risk of data breaches and ensures the security of company assets. Options B and C do not directly relate to technology needs after a reduction in force. Option D is incorrect because it may not necessarily be the top priority immediately after a reduction in force. Other technology needs, such as security measures and optimizing operations, may take precedence in such situations.

60. C. Evidenced-based decision making involves gathering and analyzing empirical evidence and data to make informed decisions in the workplace. Option A is incorrect as intuition and gut feelings are not legally defensible nor are they part of the scientific approach that underscores evidenced based decision making. Option B is incorrect as while precedent and case law may be relevant in legal contexts, evidenced-based decision making in the

workplace involves utilizing empirical evidence and data analysis from various sources, not just legal ones. Option D is incorrect because evidenced-based decision making goes beyond following tradition and involves staying current with new academic and other industry related findings.

61. C. Many global organizations indeed face challenges in accessing certain websites and utilizing specific software due to regional restrictions and censorship policies. This can impact their ability to conduct business efficiently in certain regions and requires them to adapt their strategies accordingly.

62. A. Global organizations have teams spread across different regions, and thus scalability is crucial for collaboration software to effectively support communication and collaboration among diverse teams. The software should be able to handle a large number of users, diverse communication needs, and varying technological infrastructures across different locations. Option B is incorrect as it may not be feasible to decrease complexity, particularly for organizations in multiple countries. Option C is incorrect as compatibility with a single language may not adequately address the needs of a global organization. Option D is incorrect because exclusivity to a specific region would limit the software's usability and effectiveness.

63. A, B. E-Verify is a government-sponsored system that allows employers to complete and submit form I9 online. The website provides an automated link to Government records to help employers confirm the employment eligibility of new hires. For employers with multiple hiring sites, they have two ways to participate. The first is that each site can enroll separately, sign its own MOU, and create cases for its newly hired employees. This approach allows for decentralized enrollment and case creation, ensuring that each site manages its own employment verifications. The second is that one site can create cases for all of their sites. When enrolling, the employer can select "multiple site registration" and specify the number of sites per state that will use E-Verify. This option provides flexibility for employers who prefer to centralize case creation while still allowing each site to participate in E-Verify.

64. C. Automating HR audits through technology allows for efficient and systematic verification of compliance with labor laws, employment regulations, and other legal requirements. Automated audits can help identify potential risks and gaps in compliance, enabling HR professionals to address issues proactively. Option A is incorrect because it primarily addresses document management rather than directly enhancing the due diligence process. Option B is incorrect because in the early stages of an M & A, this would not take precedence over risk analyze of labor law compliance. Option D is incorrect as the focus of the due diligence process is on data analysis, compliance verification, risk assessment, and strategic planning, not necessarily keeping the project on track using technology.

65. A. Geofencing technology allows organizations to define virtual boundaries around specific geographical locations, such as the workplace premises. By implementing geofencing in the mobile time card app, employees would only be able to clock in when their mobile devices are within the designated on-site locations, ensuring greater accuracy and integrity in time tracking. Option B is incorrect as biometric authentication verifies the identity of the individual but does not confirm their physical presence at the workplace. Option C is incorrect because GPS tracking may raise privacy concerns among employees, and it may not be feasible to continuously monitor employees' locations in real-time, especially during non-working hours. Option D is incorrect because it may not directly address the issue of employees clocking in from off-site locations unless the access control system is expanded to cover all entry points and accurately track employees' movements both inside and outside the workplace premises.

66. C. Biometric authentication methods such as fingerprint scans, iris scans, or facial recognition provide a high level of security because they are based on unique physical characteristics of individuals. Unlike traditional authentication methods like passwords or ID cards, biometric data is difficult to forge or replicate, enhancing overall security in the workplace. Option A is incorrect as biometric data, such as fingerprints or facial features, is highly personal and sensitive. Therefore, the collection and storage of biometric data must be carefully managed to ensure privacy compliance and prevent unauthorized access or misuse of this information. Option B is incorrect as some individuals may experience challenges or discomfort with biometric scanners, leading to potential delays or inconveniences during the authentication process. Option D is incorrect because implementing biometric systems may require additional administrative tasks, such as data management and compliance with privacy regulations.

67. B. Asset management in Human Resource Management Systems encompasses tracking and managing both physical assets (such as laptops and mobile devices) and intangible assets (such as software licenses and intellectual property) throughout their lifecycle. It involves processes such as assignment, monitoring, maintenance, and disposal of assets within the HR management platform.

68. D. Encrypting personal data collected and stored by the company is essential for compliance with the General Data Protection Requirements (GDPR). It ensures that even if unauthorized access occurs, the data remains unreadable and unusable to potential attackers. This measure helps prevent identity theft by safeguarding sensitive information from unauthorized access or breaches. Options A, B, and C are important security measures but may not directly address the need for compliance with GDPR and prevention of identity theft as effectively as data encryption.

69. A, B, C, D. A data controller, under the General Data Protection Requirements (GDPR), is an entity or organization that determines the purposes, conditions, and means of processing personal data, thereby holding primary responsibility for ensuring compliance with GDPR regulations regarding data protection and privacy. A data controller could be a private company or any other legal entity including an incorporated association, incorporated partnership, or public authority. A data controller could also be an individual person such as a partner in an unincorporated partnership, a sole trader, or any self-employed professional.

70. D. As long as HR is able to provide an accurate reporting of the meeting (such as notes or minutes), and the employee was given the opportunity to exercise their Weingarten rights to have another person present during the session, it is reasonable to deny the employees request to record the disciplinary session. HR could record the meeting as part of the accuracy, provided they also offer a copy of the recording to the employee.

Chapter 14: Human Resource Competencies

1. C. HR leaders need business acumen to align HR strategies with the organization's broader business goals. This alignment helps drive organizational success by ensuring that HR initiatives support the company's strategic objectives. Options A, B, and D are incorrect because they either focus narrowly on HR functions or do not address the strategic aspect of business acumen.

2. A, C. Designing recognition and rewards programs that acknowledge employees who exemplify the organization's values and contribute to its goals is a clear demonstration of HR's ability to support the company's vision through HR systems. It aligns HR practices with the broader organizational objectives, values, and mission, making it an essential competency for HR professionals. Option B is incorrect because it refers to the ability to understand and work within the organization's structure, culture, and dynamics. Option D is incorrect because this competency is more focused on interpersonal skills and fostering positive relationships within the organization.

3. C. HR professionals are responsible for identifying and attracting candidates who possess the skills and qualifications required for the specific job roles within the marketing department's new advertising campaign. This involves conducting interviews, assessing candidates, and ultimately selecting the right creative professionals to join the team, and demonstrates the competencies of talent acquisition and knowledge of best people practices. Option A is incorrect because the primary role described in the scenario is related to hiring creative professionals, which is more aligned with the recruitment and talent acquisition competency rather than distributing workflow. Option B is incorrect as identifying potential advertising channels is a task associated with the marketing department itself, not HR. HR's role in this scenario is more focused on staffing the marketing department with the necessary creative professionals. Option D is incorrect because HR's primary role in this situation is not related to brand communication (unless it specified the employer brand) but rather the recruitment of creative professionals needed for the advertising campaign.

4. A. HR can support the R&D department's need for confidentiality by implementing strict nondisclosure agreements (NDAs) with candidates during the hiring process. This demonstrates HR's competency in legal and compliance matters as well as business acumen. NDAs are legally binding agreements that protect sensitive information and ensure that candidates understand the importance of maintaining confidentiality when joining the project. Option B is incorrect as it does not directly address the issue of maintaining confidentiality during the hiring process as background checks don't safeguard against disclosure. Option C is incorrect because relying on candidates' discretion without consequence may result in leaks of protected information. Option D is incorrect as using threatening language during the hiring process may send the wrong message and discourage candidates from accepting a job offer should one be offered.

5. D. Human resources primarily focuses on supporting organizational results through people management strategies. This includes activities such as workforce planning, talent acquisition,

performance management, employee relations, and organizational development. By aligning HR practices with business objectives, HR professionals contribute to the overall success and effectiveness of the organization. Options A, B, and C all fall under the umbrella of HR responsibilities that support organizational outcomes.

6. C. HR can assist the finance department by supplying payroll and benefits data, which is essential for cost allocation and financial planning. Options A, B, and D are incorrect because they involve financial responsibilities that are not within HR's scope.

7. C. The primary goal of active listening is to understand and empathize with employees. This demonstrates HR's competency in communication and interpersonal skills. Active listening involves giving full attention to employees, seeking to understand their perspectives, and showing empathy toward their concerns. By doing so, HR professionals can build trust, enhance employee relations, and address workplace issues effectively. Option A is incorrect because it is not the primary goal of active listening. Active listening is more focused on the initial step of understanding employee concerns and needs before taking action or using influence. Option B is incorrect as providing timely solutions is an important aspect of HR's role, but it comes after the process of active listening. Option D is incorrect because active listening is about building relationships and understanding employee experiences, which can be used as a foundation for addressing workplace culture issues. However, the primary goal is understanding and empathy.

8. B. Neutrality ensures that HR professionals do not take sides and do treat all parties involved in the conflict impartially. Fairness means that HR professionals adhere to established procedures and principles of justice when addressing the conflict. This demonstrates HR's competency in conflict resolution and mediation. Option A is incorrect as positive relationships may result from successful conflict resolution, but they should not come at the expense of fairness or impartiality. Option C is incorrect as policies provide a framework for addressing conflicts, but the HR professional's primary role is to ensure that the resolution process is fair and impartial, even if it means deviating from strict policy adherence in some cases. Option D is incorrect because offering a solution without first ensuring neutrality and fairness can lead to perceived bias.

9. B. HR can support the production department by providing additional training for production employees. This demonstrates HR's competency in talent management and training. By offering training programs to enhance employees' skills and addressing their needs, HR can help reduce turnover and increase efficiency on the factory floor. Option A is incorrect because HR's role is more focused on managing human capital and addressing issues related to employee turnover and performance. Option C is incorrect because it does not directly address the issue of high turnover and its impact on production disruptions. Option D is incorrect as setting production quotas is the responsibility of the production department itself, not HR.

10. D. Closed-ended questions in HR interviews have answers that are limited to "yes" or "no" or involve providing specific factual information. Open-ended questions such as those described in Options A, B, and C encourage the candidate to provide a detailed narrative about their work experience. Open-ended questions require HR to use the competencies of communication and listening.

11. A. In this situation, HR should prioritize empathy and emotional support. Doing so shows HR's competency in interpersonal skills and emotional intelligence. The right empathetic approach acknowledges the employee's emotions, expresses understanding and support, and

allows the employee to feel heard and valued. This compassionate approach helps create a safe and supportive environment for the employee to express their feelings and eventually continue the discussion. Option B is partially correct in that giving the employee a moment to compose themselves is important, but HR should proactively offer emotional support by showing empathy as well through body language, actions, and choice of words. Options C and D are incorrect as neither of them properly express empathy and may lead to additional discomfort or escalation of the situation.

12. C. HR should initially have a one-on-one discussion with the employee to understand the reasons behind their declining performance. This demonstrates HR's competency in communication and problem-solving. Understanding the underlying causes allows HR to address the issue effectively and determine if there are any legitimate reasons for the issues, such as personal challenges or supervision. Option A is incorrect as jumping directly to disciplinary action without understanding the reasons behind the behavior may not be the most effective approach. Option B is partially correct in that involving the employee's manager is an important step in making a decision about what should be done; however, HR should first gather information directly from the employee to gain a clear understanding of the situation (which may or may not involve the supervisor's action themselves). Option D is incorrect because it does not address the root cause of the problem.

13. B. Cultural sensitivity helps HR professionals create an inclusive and respectful training environment where participants feel valued and understood, regardless of their cultural differences. This competency involves being aware of and respectful toward the diverse cultural backgrounds, beliefs, and values of the employees they are training. Option A is incorrect as conflict resolution may come into play if conflicts arise during training, but cultural sensitivity is more fundamental to fostering a welcoming and inclusive learning environment. Option C is incorrect because the focus during training should be on creating awareness, understanding, and inclusivity rather than attempting to influence participants in a particular direction. Option D is incorrect as a global mindset is valuable in HR, especially in organizations with a global presence, but it may not be directly relevant to diversity and inclusion training within a specific local or organizational context, making Option B the better answer.

14. A. Sharing personal stories can help team members get to know each other on a deeper level, foster empathy, and create a sense of connection. This demonstrates HR's competency in team development and relationship building. Option B is incorrect as it is a fine line between personalized performance management and gathering information that may create bias or judgment unrelated to the employees' primary responsibilities. Option C is incorrect because the storytelling is influenced by many factors other than sharing a personal anecdote, which can make someone more uncomfortable and thus not an accurate gauge of their storytelling abilities. Option D is incorrect because team-building workshops are more focused on strengthening team dynamics, communication, and relationships rather than identifying individual weaknesses for development.

15. A. In negotiating employee benefits packages, assertiveness is a valuable interpersonal skill for HR professionals. This competency demonstrates HR's ability to confidently and effectively advocate for employees' needs and interests while also considering the organization's policies and budget. Assertiveness helps HR professionals ensure that employees receive competitive and fair benefits packages. Options B, C, and D are incorrect because assertiveness in these situations should be balanced with fairness and professionalism in this context, particularly with written communication that can be easily misinterpreted.

16. B. Concise communication promotes professionalism by ensuring that messages are to the point and easy to understand, which is crucial in a business context. This demonstrates HR's competency in communication skills. Option A is incorrect because although using technical jargon may be necessary in certain contexts, it can lead to confusion and miscommunication, especially if not all recipients are familiar with the terminology. Option C can add a human touch to communication and engage the reader, but they should be used judiciously and only when relevant to the message. Option D is incorrect because the level of formality should be adjusted based on the specific audience and purpose of the message, not so much to impact clarity.

17. D. Navigating the organization involves understanding and respecting the dynamics, relationships, and hierarchies within the workplace. It also includes recognizing the influence of key stakeholders, even if they do not hold formal positions within the company. In this scenario, the HR manager should have recognized the importance of the CEO's family members as stakeholders and considered their input, regardless of their level of experience. Option A is incorrect as situational awareness involves understanding the context and dynamics of a situation, but it is not the primary competency lacking in this scenario. The HR manager's failure to navigate the organization and consider the CEO's family members as stakeholders is a more significant issue. Option B is incorrect as the scenario centers on the HR manager's ability to navigate the organization and recognize the significance of key stakeholders. Option C is incorrect as professional integrity relates to ethical conduct and honesty in one's work. In this scenario, the HR manager's actions do not necessarily implicate a lack of professional integrity but rather a failure to navigate the organization effectively.

18. B. In navigating workplace conflict, consensus involves reaching an agreement where all parties align their opinions or preferences to some degree. It may not necessarily require complete agreement but aims for a middle ground or compromise that satisfies everyone involved. On the other hand, commitment goes beyond mere agreement and focuses on ensuring that all parties are dedicated to achieving a common goal or outcome. It emphasizes a shared sense of purpose and determination, even if individual opinions may still differ. Competent HR professionals should understand these distinctions and choose the conflict-resolution approach that best suits the situation and the desired outcomes. Options A, C, and D do not accurately describe the main differences.

19. D. Compromise involves finding a middle ground where both parties make concessions to reach an agreement that is mutually acceptable. It is most effective when both parties value the resolution and are willing to work together to find common ground. When HR professionals are able to facilitate the compromise process to ensure fairness and collaboration, it demonstrates their competency in conflict resolution. Option A is incorrect as compromise is not necessarily tied to the speed of resolution. Option B is incorrect because compromise involves both parties making concessions, so it should not be employed when one party is willing to give in entirely. Option C is incorrect because compromise is not contingent on the absence of urgency but rather on the mutual investment in the outcome.

20. C. A key advantage of using alternative dispute resolution (ADR) techniques such as mediation or arbitration in the workplace is that they promote open and effective communication. This demonstrates HR's competency in conflict resolution and communication skills. ADR

methods encourage parties in conflict to engage in constructive dialogue, express their concerns, and work together to find mutually agreeable solutions. By fostering communication and understanding, ADR techniques can help resolve conflicts more amicably and potentially preserve working relationships. Options A, B, and D are not completely accurate representations of ADR techniques.

21. C. Perspective taking is a negotiation technique that involves understanding and acknowledging the other party's perspective before presenting your offer. Demonstrating the perspective-taking competency shows empathy and the ability to understand the employee's point of view, which can lead to a more collaborative and mutually beneficial negotiation. Option A is incorrect because principled bargaining, also known as interest-based or integrative bargaining, involves focusing on interests and needs rather than positions. Option B is incorrect as positional bargaining is a negotiation approach where each party takes a fixed position and seeks to compromise or reach an agreement. Option D is incorrect as win-lose negotiation, also known as distributive bargaining, is a competitive approach where one party seeks to gain advantages at the expense of the other. Options A, B, and D do not emphasize understanding or acknowledging the other party's perspective but rather aims for maximizing one's own gains.

22. D. The training manager's lack of awareness of the effect her behaviors are having on the impact of her sessions points to a deficiency in self-awareness, a key component of emotional intelligence (EQ). Self-awareness involves recognizing and understanding one's own emotions and actions and their impact on others. The training manager's inability to perceive how her interruptions, lengthy explanations, and personal anecdotes affect the participants indicates a lack of self-awareness regarding her own behavior. Option A is incorrect because cultural sensitivity is the ability to recognize, respect, and consider the cultural differences and perspectives of individuals and groups in a way that promotes understanding, inclusivity, and effective communication. Option B is incorrect because self-awareness focuses on understanding one's own emotions and their impact, while relationship management involves effectively interacting with and managing relationships with others. Option C is incorrect because self-management is the ability to control and regulate one's own emotions and behavior, and the core issue here is her lack of self-awareness regarding the impact of her actions on others.

23. C. By discussing their professional background and interests, you can establish common ground, identify potential areas of collaboration, and build a meaningful connection based on shared professional interests. This demonstrates HR's competency in networking and relationship building. It shows genuine interest in the other person's professional life, which is likely the primary focus of the conference. Option A is incorrect as doing so quickly without engaging in a meaningful conversation may come across as insincere or transactional. Option B is incorrect as while some personal conversation can help build rapport, it should be balanced with discussions of professional backgrounds and interests. Option D is incorrect because complaining about the conference's organization and logistics is generally not a productive way to initiate a connection. It can create a negative impression and may not lead to a meaningful professional network.

24. C. Cross-functional projects require employees from different departments to work together on common goals, fostering interactions, collaboration, and relationship-building. It promotes teamwork, breaks down silos, and allows team members to gain a deeper understanding of each other's roles and contributions. This demonstrates HR's competency in relationship management and collaboration. Option A is incorrect because forced interactions may not lead to authentic connections, and the effectiveness of such meetings can vary. Option B is trickier but still incorrect because leading volunteers is a positive initiative but may not necessarily lead to building relationships with other department leaders in a work context where credibility, trust, and relationships matter. Option D is incorrect because the infrequency of company events may not lead to sustained collaboration.

25. D. Building a network of mentors and advisors in your industry is most likely to be achieved by attending industry-specific events and actively engaging with participants. This allows you to establish connections, exchange ideas, and seek mentorship opportunities from experienced professionals and demonstrates your competencies in networking and relationship management. Option A is incorrect because it casts too broad of a net and may not be as effective as in-person interactions and engagement at industry-specific events. Option B is incorrect because it may not help you build a network of mentors and advisors in your industry, focusing on a single perspective. Option C is incorrect as coaches have a specific role in skill development and may not provide the same type of mentoring relationship that industry-specific contacts can offer.

26. B. By educating the managers on their responsibilities and the importance of meeting deadlines, you can potentially prevent future delays in time card approvals. This demonstrates HR's competency in communication, training, and problem-solving. Option A is incorrect as jumping to hiring additional staff does not resolve the root cause of the issue, which is managers failing to follow procedure or a procedure that is a barrier to efficiency. Option C is a temporary workaround leading to ongoing issues and does not promote a solution-focused approach. Option D is incorrect as HR professionals should actively seek ways to improve processes and address issues that hinder efficiency and effectiveness in their roles. Ignoring the problem could lead to continued payroll delays and frustration among employees (including the HR team!).

27. B. A flat team structure promotes a collaborative approach to teamwork, where employees have a say in the decision-making process and there is less hierarchy and bureaucracy. HR competencies necessary to support a flat team structure include business acumen, leadership, and conflict management. Option A is incorrect because hierarchical team structures involve a clear chain of command, where decisions are made by higher-ranking individuals or managers. Option C is incorrect because functional team structures are organized based on specific functions or departments within an organization and so decision-making authority may vary based on the department or function. Option D is incorrect as an autocratic team structure is characterized by a single decision-maker or a small group of leaders who make most decisions without significant input from team members.

28. D. Cross-functional teams are formed by bringing together members from various functional areas or departments within an organization to work on specific projects or tasks. One potential challenge of such teams is the difficulty in coordinating and integrating the diverse functional areas. HR competencies necessary to address this challenge include communication, conflict resolution, and team building. Option A is incorrect because effective communication and collaboration are generally considered goals of cross-functional teams. Option B is incorrect as limited diversity of skills and perspectives is not a common challenge but

rather a potential strength. Option C is incorrect because there are several factors related to organizational culture (such as competitiveness of individualism) that lead to unhealthy alliances but not necessarily the structure of the team itself.

29. C. Virtual teams are made up of members who work together remotely, often in different locations. Maintaining strong team cohesion, where team members feel connected and work well together, is crucial for the success of virtual teams. HR competencies necessary to foster strong team cohesion in virtual teams include communication, relationship building, team building, and conflict-management skills. Option A is incorrect because it is not a practical solution when managing remote teams. Option B is incorrect as frequent face-to-face meetings are not likely to be practical in the daily management of virtual teams. The degree of trust and how well the team communicates is a higher priority than the mode in which they connect. Option D is incorrect because virtual teams often require a balance between autonomy and collaboration.

30. D. A "parking lot" is a facilitation technique where the facilitator temporarily sets aside unrelated or off-topic issues and notes them for discussion later. This allows the facilitator to refocus the group on the main topic and the agenda at hand while still capturing (potentially) important topics for future consideration. HR competencies necessary to effectively use this technique include facilitation skills, time management, and influence. Option A is incorrect as allowing the group to continue discussing unrelated topics without addressing them can lead to inefficiency and loss of focus. Option B is incorrect because it's generally more effective to address unrelated issues separately, rather than introducing more distractions. Option C is incorrect because while gently guiding the discussion back to the main topic is a valid facilitation technique, using a parking lot can be more effective.

31. A. This response demonstrates strong problem-solving competency because it takes a proactive and strategic approach to address the issue of excessive and ineffective meetings. HR professionals, by championing such an initiative, show leadership and consultative and analytical skills. Option B is incorrect as conducting a survey is a valuable step in collecting input from managers, and it demonstrates active listening and engagement with stakeholders. However, it alone may not fully demonstrate problem-solving competency unless followed by concrete action. Option C is incorrect because it does not necessarily address the root causes or improve the effectiveness of the remaining meetings. The policy itself could then become part of a workflow bottleneck. Option D is incorrect because it essentially deflects the issue and places the responsibility back on the managers and does not support HR's role as advisors. HR should be proactive in addressing workplace challenges and facilitating solutions rather than leaving it to the affected parties.

32. C. Pathos is a persuasive communication technique that involves using emotional appeals to connect with your audience. HR professionals often need to use emotional appeals when communicating with employees, stakeholders, or leaders to influence their opinions or decisions. This technique involves tapping into the audience's emotions, values, and beliefs to create a persuasive message. HR competencies necessary for effectively using pathos include emotional intelligence, active listening, and empathy. Option A is incorrect because logos is a persuasive technique that relies on logical reasoning, facts, and evidence to persuade an audience. It appeals to the audience's rational thinking rather than their emotions. Options B and D are incorrect because both are forms of nonverbal communication, not a persuasive technique.

33. C. Coaching involves providing guidance and support to individuals to help them improve their skills and problem-solving abilities. In this case, coaching the managers on breaking down the procedure into simple steps aligns with HR competencies related to communication, training, and collaboration. Option A is incorrect because it does not offer a comprehensive solution to the managers' struggle with conveying the procedure effectively or developing the skills in the manager, thereby developing the knowledge of the entire team. Option B is incorrect because it does not empower the managers to improve their own communication skills. Option D is incorrect because the managers need more immediate support in effectively communicating the procedure to their team members and does not demonstrate team or advisory skills necessary for HR to be a credible and trusted business partner.

34. C. When addressing C-suite executives about a sensitive HR issue, it's essential to communicate in a way that aligns with their level of responsibility and interest in the organization's strategic goals. This option demonstrates competencies such as communication, strategic thinking, risk management, and confidentiality/employee privacy. Option A is incorrect because this option lacks the interpersonal communication and strategic thinking required for this type of conversation, and HR can document the relevant information in other, more effective ways. Option B is incorrect as sharing all the details of the issue, including confidential information, is not advisable when addressing C-suite executives. It can compromise confidentiality, and it may overwhelm them with unnecessary information. Option D is incorrect because, especially with sensitive issues, HR should maintain professionalism and address the issue seriously, focusing on facts, risks, and solutions.

35. A. Sending an email is an effective way to communicate when providing documents or forms. This scenario aligns with HR competencies related to delivering messages and exchanging organizational information. Option B is incorrect because, where possible, HR should opt for more personal and engaging methods, such as in-person gatherings, video messages, or social recognition platforms, to convey warmth and appreciation during these moments. Option C is incorrect because interpersonal and nonserious situations may benefit from more immediate and informal communication methods, such as instant messaging or in-person discussions. Conversely, perception matters, and while an issue may seem to be a minor inconvenience to one person, it may be a big deal for others (such as the temperature in the office or cleanliness of the lunchroom). These issues may require a more formal approach. The scenario does not provide enough information to determine if Option D is correct; depending on the situation, HR professionals may choose to communicate through email when time is limited, but they may also explore alternative methods based on other variables.

36. B. Competitive awareness involves the ability to understand and respond to external factors that can impact an organization's ability to attract, retain, and engage talent effectively. This includes monitoring industry trends, labor market conditions, and the practices of competitors to ensure the organization remains competitive in talent acquisition and retention. Because competitive awareness involves understanding the external factors that affect an organization's placement in its relevant market, Options A, C, and D are incorrect as they reflect internal activities.

37. D. Human resource professionals must stay informed and competent as strategic partners by relying on credible and trustworthy sources of information. Websites that end in .org (organization) or .edu (educational institution) or .gov (government) are often considered reliable because they are associated with nonprofit organizations, educational institutions, and the

U.S. government. These sources generally provide well-researched and unbiased information on various HR topics, including labor laws, best practices, and industry trends. Option A is incorrect as social media headlines may not always provide the depth, credibility, or reliability required for strategic decision-making and competence development. Option B is incorrect as labor law newsletters have a narrower focus on legal matters and may not cover the broader spectrum of strategic HR topics that HR professionals need to be competent in. Option C is incorrect as HR networking groups often rely on a variety of sources, including websites, research, and publications that may not have been vetted against peer-reviewed or other credible standards.

38. C. The Delphi facilitation technique primarily involves participants anonymously ranking and voting on various options or ideas. In contrast, the nominal group technique centers around open discussions and consensus-building among participants to arrive at a collective decision. HR competencies that support both of these techniques include training, decision-making, listening and exchanging organizational information. Options A, B, and D do not accurately reflect the primary differences between the facilitation techniques.

39. B. The HR department in this scenario is likely applying the statistical principle of analysis of variance (ANOVA). ANOVA is a statistical technique used to analyze the variation in a dataset and determine whether there are statistically significant differences between groups or categories. HR competencies necessary for this include analyzing data, evaluating business challenges, and making decisions based on evidence. Option A is incorrect because regression analysis is used to predict or explain the behavior of a variable based on other variables. Option C is incorrect because simple random sampling is a method of selecting a subset of individuals from a population in a way that each individual has an equal chance of being chosen. Option D is incorrect as descriptive statistics involve summarizing and describing data using measures such as means, medians, and standard deviations, which is not noted in the scenario.

40. A. A correlation coefficient measures the strength and direction of a linear relationship between two variables. A positive correlation coefficient indicates that as one variable (training hours) increases, the other variable (performance scores) tends to increase as well. The value of 0.75 is close to 1, which suggests a strong positive linear relationship. This means that, in the startup company's data, employees who have completed more training hours tend to have higher performance scores. HR professionals should be competent in understanding and interpreting correlation coefficients to make data-informed decisions related to employee performance and training.

41. B. Strategic planning is essential for effectively connecting DEI initiatives with organizational performance. HR professionals need to develop and implement strategic plans that integrate DEI goals with broader organizational objectives. This involves analyzing data, identifying key areas for improvement, setting measurable targets, and aligning DEI initiatives with the company's long-term vision and values. Option A is incorrect as the employee relations competency primarily focuses on managing relationships between employees and the organization, addressing concerns, and fostering a positive work environment. Option C is incorrect because it is not specifically a competency required for connecting DEI initiatives with organizational performance. Option D is incorrect because while conflicts related to diversity and inclusion may arise, strategic planning is necessary to proactively address systemic issues, set priorities, and allocate resources effectively to achieve desired outcomes in terms of organizational performance.

42. C. By starting meetings with an activity that encourages interaction and sharing in a non-threatening manner, facilitators can help participants feel more at ease, build trust, and establish a sense of psychological safety within the group. This, in turn, fosters greater participation, collaboration, and openness to sharing ideas and perspectives during the meeting. Option A is not correct because while ice-breakers or warm-up activities can sometimes incorporate energizing elements or begin to introduce content, that is not really their primary purpose. In fact, some ice breakers should move at a slower pace, particularly if the topic is sensitive. Option B is incorrect because there are several variables that affect whether people "like" each other or not that often go deeper than an ice-breaker. Option D is partially correct as it is true that engaging in these activities may indirectly stimulate participants' cognitive abilities; however, the goal is to create a psychological safe and inviting room to set the tone for effective collaboration rather than sharpening critical thinking skills directly.

43. A. In labor negotiations, HR often supports the negotiation process between labor unions and management. This requires competencies such as negotiation, relationship building, and facilitation skills. In the case of UPS negotiating with the drivers' union for increased total rewards, HR likely played a significant role in coordinating and facilitating these discussions to ensure a mutually beneficial outcome for both the company and the union members. Option B is incorrect as while HR may consider cultural factors in their overall strategy, it's less directly related to the negotiation process itself. Options C and D are HR responsibilities but not within the scope of contract negotiations.

44. C. HR and leadership professionals, particularly those involved in internal communications or employer branding, play a crucial role in ensuring clear and effective messaging. They are responsible for conveying information about company initiatives to both internal and external stakeholders, including customers, employees, and the media. If HR fails to deliver messages accurately and transparently, it can lead to confusion, backlash, and reputational damage. Option A is incorrect as the primary issue lies in the delivery of the message about the dynamic pricing strategy, rather than conflicts arising from unclear communication within the organization or between stakeholders. Option B is incorrect as conflict-management skills come into play after a conflict has arisen, and the lack of communication occurred prior to any pushback against the initiative. Option D is partially correct as HR may or may not have been invited to the table in conversations about new strategic roll outs. However, HR's involvement may have been indirect, such as providing guidance on effective messaging strategies or assisting in crisis management efforts following the backlash. Therefore, while HR's involvement may not be direct, they can still contribute to addressing challenges related to messaging and reputation management.

45. B, C, D. HR professionals need to possess a strong understanding of business operations, financial principles, and market dynamics to contribute effectively to strategic initiatives such as designing and implementing in-house certificate programs. Understanding Walmart's goals, market trends, and the impact of training programs on the company's bottom line requires a keen sense of business acumen. They must also have a clear vision of the organization's future direction and be able to anticipate the company's needs to align HR strategies with broader organizational goals. Visionary thinking enables HR teams to proactively address talent gaps and support long-term growth objectives. Influencing skills are crucial for navigating complex organizational dynamics and securing resources necessary for program success. Option A is incorrect because negotiation skills are not as central to the core competencies required for acting as a strategic business partner in this context.

46. A, C. Transitioning from remote work to a hybrid model involves significant changes in work arrangements and employee expectations. HR leaders need strong change management skills to effectively communicate the reasons for the transition, address employee concerns, manage resistance, and facilitate a smooth adjustment to the new working environment. HR is also being tasked with leading conversations around how to redesign office space for a new hybrid work model. Option A is incorrect as proficiency in graphic design software is not the most crucial competency for HR leaders in this context and communicating the rationale for the transition and addressing employee concerns can be achieved through strong verbal and written communication skills. Option B is incorrect because while logistics are important, the primary focus during the transition process should be on addressing employee concerns, managing resistance, and facilitating the adoption of new work practices to ensure a smooth return to the office. Option D is incorrect because this is a separate issue from a return to office in that teams are coming back into a brick-and-mortar environment that should be more secure than having open portals from remote work locations.

47. A, B, D. In hybrid work structures, employees may experience uncertainty about their roles and responsibilities, particularly when transitioning between remote and in-office work. This ambiguity can lead to confusion, inefficiency, and decreased productivity if not addressed effectively by HR leaders and managers. Hybrid work arrangements may exacerbate proximity or "face-time" bias, where employees who are physically present in the office are perceived as more committed or productive than those working remotely. These structures can also inadvertently perpetuate gender discrimination, as many workers who benefit the most from remote work are women and women of color. This is because these groups often bear a larger share of caregiving responsibilities, making remote work arrangements more appealing or necessary for them, potentially leading to their absence from the office being misconstrued as lack of dedication or productivity. Option C is incorrect as it is not a challenge inherent to the structure of a hybrid work model but rather a variable based on the type of work being performed.

48. A. The No Surprises Act is a 2021 legislative measure aimed at protecting patients from unexpected medical bills by establishing guidelines for resolving billing disputes between healthcare providers and insurers, particularly in cases of out-of-network care. This legislation mandates that employer-based health plans submit annual prescription drug data reports to the Centers for Medicare and Medicaid Services (CMS). HR leaders are responsible for ensuring that their organizations comply with these reporting requirements to help control prescription drug costs and improve transparency in healthcare coverage.

49. B, C, D. Option B is correct because HR leaders can fulfill their fiduciary responsibilities by seeking transparency regarding the pricing mechanisms of prescription drugs within the health plan. Understanding the spread between the actual drug cost and what is charged to the employer plan helps ensure that the plan is not being overcharged, thus protecting the interests of the employees and the plan itself. Option C is correct because clear and understandable pricing helps employees make informed decisions about their healthcare options, promoting transparency and accountability within the plan administration. Option D is correct because it is important to request detailed information on costs, coverage, and any potential conflicts of interest, ensuring that the plan operates in the best interests of the employees. Option A is incorrect because while negotiating lower costs for prescription drug coverage is a valid strategy for controlling healthcare expenses, it does not directly address the fiduciary responsibility of HR leaders in health plan administration. Fiduciary responsibilities focus more on transparency, accountability, and acting in the best interests of the employees rather than only on cost negotiation.

50. D. Fiduciary responsibility in HR refers to the legal obligation of employers to act in the best interests of their employees when managing employee benefits and retirement plans. The lawsuit alleges that the company's actions, such as overpaying for prescription drugs and incentivizing the use of a specific mail-in pharmacy with higher costs, resulted in significant financial losses for the ERISA plans and their participants, amounting to millions of dollars in alleged overpayments. Options A and B are incorrect because while auditing and oversight of drug costs could potentially help identify overpayments, the primary breach is the company's agreement to terms that were not in the best interest of the plan members. Option C is incorrect because the allegations center around the company's actions related to prescription drug coverage and costs, not the cost of premiums.

51. C. Center of Excellence (CoE) are dedicated teams within HR departments that focus on specific areas of expertise, such as talent acquisition, learning and development, or performance management. This specialization allows CoEs to design tailored HR solutions that are aligned with organizational objectives and deliver high-quality services to employees. Options A and D are incorrect because CoEs go beyond administrative and routine tasks, offering deep levels of knowledge to advise on HR solutions. Option B is incorrect as they do not fully capture the scope of CoEs' responsibilities.

52. B. Option B correctly identifies the commonality among decentralization, Human Resources Information Systems (HRISs), and Human Resources to Full-Time Equivalent (HR:FTE) ratio as elements of an HR department structure. Each of these factors directly relates to how an HR department is organized and services are delivered and managed within an organization. Options A, C, and D are all incorrect because they are dependent on a number of structural factors, making B the better answer. For example, if the HR:FTE ratio is small, digitization may be a cost-effective option. If the workforce is geographically spread out, decentralization or the creation of centers of excellence may be effective HR structural strategies.

53. A, B. Option A demonstrates HR navigating the organization by working closely with department heads and middle managers to address resistance to a new performance evaluation system. HR must navigate conflicting interests and build consensus among stakeholders to ensure successful implementation. Option B also exemplifies HR navigating the organization by strategically networking with influential stakeholders to gather support for a diversity and inclusion initiative. By leveraging relationships across departments, HR ensures the initiative's successful integration into the organizational culture. Option C is incorrect because this option primarily focuses on ensuring compliance with regulations and benchmarking against market standards rather than navigating organizational dynamics and relationships. Option D is incorrect because it primarily involves collaboration between HR and another department to champion HR initiatives as opposed to the broader aims of organization-wide needs.

54. B. In many organizations, complex dynamics and politics can impact the successful implementation of HR initiatives. HR professionals must possess the ability to navigate these complexities, build relationships across different departments and levels of the organization,

and understand the informal power structures that influence decision-making. Option A is incorrect because while understanding the structure facilitates collaboration, it does not necessarily address the challenges posed by organizational politics. Option C is incorrect because it does not explicitly address the competency of navigating the organization. While navigating the organization may involve aligning HR strategies, the focus of this competency is more on managing interpersonal relationships and political dynamics within the organization. Option D is incorrect because it does not fully encompass the competency of navigating the organization. Navigating the organization may involve gaining support for initiatives, but it also includes understanding and maneuvering through complex political dynamics and relationships.

55. C. HR often relies on research findings and data to inform decision-making processes regarding various HR initiatives, policies, and strategies. Critical evaluation ensures that HR professionals assess the credibility, accuracy, and relevance of the research and data sources they utilize. By critically evaluating the information, HR can make informed decisions that are based on sound evidence, ultimately contributing to effective HR management and organizational success. Option A is incorrect as critical evaluation involves more than just assessing outcomes; it also entails scrutinizing the quality and validity of the information used to inform decision-making. Option B is incorrect because while critical evaluation may be involved in the process of identifying areas for improvement, this option focuses more on problem-solving and strategic thinking rather than evaluating the quality of information. Option D is incorrect as critical evaluation extends beyond performance metrics to encompass the evaluation of various types of HR-related research, data, and information sources.

56. A, B. Option A is correct as the need for connectedness and mentoring are important competencies for supervisors to have in order to build relationships and effectively build their teams. For this reason, HR can support leadership development by implementing training programs in coaching and mentoring. Option B acknowledges the reality that younger workers are turning to alternative sources, such as ChatGPT, for advice and guidance. By introducing ChatGPT as a supplementary resource, HR recognizes the importance of leveraging technology to meet the evolving needs of employees, integrating ChatGPT as a digital tool to enhance managerial support and guidance. Option C is incorrect as it lacks a specific strategy for leveraging technology to supplement managerial support. Option D is incorrect as it focuses on gathering information rather than implementing a solution to address the identified gap and integrate the prevailing needs and interests of a younger workforce.

57. A, B, C, D. Younger workers, especially millennials and Generation Z, often prioritize a healthy work-life balance, personal well-being, financial stability, and career advancement opportunities. These benefits address their diverse needs and priorities, fostering greater job satisfaction, engagement, and loyalty among younger employees.

58. A. Option A demonstrates HR's competency by analyzing employees' health benefit usage data to identify cost-saving opportunities, aligning with organizational goals and enabling evidence-based decision-making for designing HR solutions. Options B and C are incorrect because they rely on external expertise rather than utilizing internal HR capabilities for data analysis and solution design. Option D is incorrect as it is a simplistic approach that does not involve comprehensive data analysis or strategic planning.

59. C. This option addresses the root cause of the retention issue by recognizing the need for career advancement opportunities within the company and requires that HR demonstrate the competencies of communication and managing HR initiatives. Option A is incorrect because increasing salaries and benefits may provide short-term relief, but it may be impractical and does not address the underlying issue of limited career advancement opportunities. This option demonstrates a lack of strategic thinking and fails to leverage other retention strategies beyond monetary incentives. Option B is incorrect as it does not directly address the issue of career advancement opportunities. Option D is incorrect because it is not a sustainable solution and does not address the root cause of the retention issue.

60. C. Building an employee pipeline in the tech sector involves fostering interest and developing skills in science, technology, engineering, and mathematics (STEM) from a young age. By mentoring middle school students on STEM skills, companies can help cultivate a future talent pool while also promoting diversity and inclusion in the tech industry. This initiative supports long-term workforce development and ensures a sustainable pipeline of skilled workers for the organization and requires the HR competencies of communication, strategic talent acquisition, and evaluation of business challenges. Options A, B, and D are all partially correct in that they can develop a pipeline of employees prior to the need for them. However, these options fall short because they miss the opportunity to connect with individuals at various stages of their educational journey (including those at a younger age) to cultivate interest and skills in relevant fields like STEM.

61. D. By collaborating with the manager to create a replacement plan, the HR manager acknowledges the difficulty of the situation while still taking proactive steps to maintain adherence to company policies and ensure the smooth functioning of the production line. Option A is incorrect because issuing verbal warnings and write-ups without considering the broader context could exacerbate tensions and undermine the HR manager's relationship with the manager. Option B is incorrect as it does not engage the competency of advising on HR solutions to help the manager with the issue. Option C is incorrect as it doesn't directly address the current problem of absenteeism and lateness on the production line, nor does it effectively address the manager's concerns about finding qualified replacements.

62. D. An affinity-based employee resource group's (ERG's) key feature is the similarity of the participants that come together to provides support, resources, and advocacy for DEI initiatives in the workplace. "Affinity" diagrams are also used as a facilitation technique where similar ideas are grouped together to identify larger patterns of data.

63. C. Political savvy and navigating the organization best reflect the competencies needed for the HR leader to advocate for DEI initiatives in a challenging environment where there are external pressures such as potential legislation limiting the reach of DEI initiatives and reports of consumer backlash. Political savvy involves understanding the organizational dynamics, including the influence of external factors such as legislation and public perception, and navigating these complexities to advance the organization's goals. Navigating through such challenges while advocating for DEI initiatives requires a deep understanding of the political landscape, strategic communication skills, and the ability to build alliances and influence stakeholders effectively. Option A is incorrect as the situation described involves broader challenges related to external factors and potential shifts in strategic priorities. Option B is incorrect because they may not be sufficient in addressing the specific challenges related to DEI initiatives in the described scenario. Option D is incorrect because the lack of

DEI awareness and skill sets is not the specific challenge but, rather, the inhospitable/changing climate in which these skills must be applied.

64. B. By requiring team members to attend training events at a University of California campus and take courses taught by university professors, they are implementing creative methods to align employees' passion for learning with the company's purpose. This demonstrates a proactive approach to human resources management that emphasizes innovation and creativity in achieving organizational goals. Options A and C are incorrect because they do not fully encapsulate the essence of what the HR team is doing. The focus is not just on training and developing employees or engaging with the company's purpose but rather on finding innovative ways to engage employees with a higher purpose. Option D is incorrect because while relationship building might be a competency of the HR team, it's not the central focus described in the scenario.

65. D. By emphasizing outcomes rather than physical presence, HR can ensure fair and equitable evaluations for both remote and in-office employees, thereby addressing proximity bias effectively. Option A is incorrect because proximity bias is rooted in favoring employees who are physically present in the office, and implementing progress reports may inadvertently reinforce this bias without addressing its underlying causes. Option B is incorrect as training managers may not alone be sufficient to address proximity bias in the performance review process. Option C is incorrect because quotas may create additional challenges and tensions within the organization and may not effectively address proximity bias in the performance review process.

Chapter 15: Leadership

1. B. Effective leaders set a vision for the organization, communicate it to their team members, and work with them to define and pursue common goals. Leadership involves creating a sense of purpose and motivating individuals to work together cohesively to achieve these objectives. While inspiration and guidance are key components, leaders also consider the well-being and development of their team members. Options A, C, and D are also important features of leadership; however, it is not their primary purpose, nor do they encompass the entire role of leadership as well as option B.

2. C. This approach demonstrates active listening and involves the employee in finding a solution to their workload frustration. It empowers the team member by allowing them to voice their concerns and suggest potential solutions. This collaborative approach fosters a sense of ownership and can lead to more effective problem-solving while also showing that the leader values the team member's input. Option A is incorrect because it is not always feasible to take on additional workload, and it doesn't directly address the team member's frustration or help them develop problem-solving skills. It might temporarily alleviate their workload, but it doesn't promote a sustainable solution. It also does not build the leader's delegation or problem-solving skills. Option B is incorrect as it may come across as dismissive of their concerns or automatically assume it is something the team member is doing incorrectly. Option D is incorrect because this option, while empathetic, may not always be realistic, as workloads can fluctuate due to organizational needs. It also doesn't actively involve the team member in finding a solution and may not address the underlying issue causing their frustration.

3. B. Open and transparent communication, especially in difficult situations, demonstrates honesty and integrity. Actively seeking input and feedback from team members fosters a sense of inclusion and trust, as it shows that you value their perspectives and are willing to listen and consider their ideas. Option A is incorrect because trust is built through collaboration and support, and failing to follow up can lead to mistrust if team members feel neglected or unsupported. Option C is incorrect because blurring the lines between personal and professional boundaries can sometimes lead to challenges and conflicts. Option D is incorrect because maintaining excessive professional distance can hinder the development of strong interpersonal relationships and trust. While professionalism is important, building trust often involves some degree of personal connection and understanding, as long as it is done in an appropriate and respectful manner.

4. B. By providing employees with a way to voice concerns anonymously, you create an environment that encourages open communication, transparency, and accountability. This approach can help identify and address issues that may be contrary to the organization's values, allowing for continuous improvement and reinforcement of the desired organizational culture. Option A is incorrect because it promotes a siloed approach where individual targets take precedence over broader organizational values and sustainability goals. Option C is incorrect because prioritizing cost-cutting measures without considering their impact on the organization's mission, values, and sustainability goals may lead to decisions that contradict the desired culture. Option D is incorrect because while it promotes ethical considerations, a rigid and inflexible approach may stifle innovation and adaptability. Effective workplace practices should encourage ethical behavior while allowing for some flexibility to adapt to changing circumstances and challenges.

5. A. A leader who can foster strong relationships among team members and maintain open and transparent communication channels is more likely to create a positive and cohesive team environment. Good relationships and effective communication can help resolve conflicts, build trust, and promote a sense of unity within the team. Option B is incorrect in the context of improving team morale and cohesion. Business acumen primarily involves understanding the financial and strategic aspects of an organization, which may not directly address interpersonal dynamics within a team. Option C is incorrect because these skills are more relevant in resolving disputes and reaching agreements in situations of conflict, which may arise in any team. However, they do not necessarily foster a positive team atmosphere on their own. Option D is incorrect as empathy in teams refers to the ability of team members to understand and share the feelings and perspectives of their colleagues, fostering a more compassionate and supportive work environment, while diversity in teams signifies the presence of individuals with various backgrounds, experiences, and characteristics, contributing to a broader range of perspectives and ideas within the team.

6. C. Team leadership, with each member responsible for their assigned role, is a characteristic of leadership on a self-directed work team. In self-directed teams, leadership is often distributed among team members, and each member takes ownership of their specific responsibilities. Option A is incorrect as in such teams, leadership is more collaborative and shared. Option B is incorrect because these teams typically have a more decentralized leadership structure with members taking responsibility for their tasks. Option D is incorrect because minimal leadership is not a defining characteristic of self-directed work teams.

7. B. Balancing the demands and priorities of both functional managers and project managers is a characteristic of leadership within a matrix organizational structure. Leaders in this context must navigate the competing interests and ensure alignment with organizational goals. Option A is incorrect as centralized decision-making is more characteristic of a traditional hierarchical structure. Option C is incorrect as leadership in a matrix structure involves shared responsibilities and coordination between these two roles. Option D is incorrect because a complete separation of roles and responsibilities between functional and project leaders is not a characteristic of a matrix organizational structure.

8. B. Institutions such as banks and universities often operate within a strict hierarchy. Given the university's long history, well-funded status, and the importance placed on tenured professorships, it is likely to have a top-down hierarchical leadership structure with a strong emphasis on administrative control. Such universities often have a president or chancellor who holds significant authority. Option A is incorrect as the emphasis on a tenured professorship may suggest a more hierarchical structure with administrative control. Option C is incorrect because a cooperative and egalitarian structure with shared leadership among faculty and administration is less likely in a university environment where tenure and administrative control are highly valued. Option D is incorrect because a leadership structure based on student input and decision-making is uncommon in traditional universities. While student input may be considered, the primary leadership roles are typically held by faculty and administrators.

9. A. A divisional organizational structure allows each business unit to operate semi-autonomously, with its own functional departments, including individual leaders in the support functions of HR, accounting, and finance. Leadership structures typically follow the organizational structure, a divisional approach to leading the business units makes most sense and aligns well with the distinct and separate nature of the business units. Option B is incorrect because a hierarchical structure typically involves a single, top-down chain of command that would not be appropriate for the distinct needs of each business unit. Option C is incorrect because a functional organizational structure is characterized by grouping employees by their specific functions or roles (e.g., HR, accounting, finance), so there would be one business unit manager for the entire operation. Option D is incorrect because a flat organizational structure typically has few or no levels of middle management between staff and leadership, which is not described in the scenario.

10. B. Emotional regulation is a highly valuable characteristic for leaders in managing difficult conversations. It allows leaders to stay composed, empathetic, and focused during challenging discussions. It helps prevent emotional outbursts or overreactions, promoting a more constructive dialogue. Option A is incorrect as effective leadership in these situations involves openness and transparency, not hiding one's emotions. Authenticity and emotional honesty can help build trust and facilitate productive discussions. Option C is incorrect because recognizing one's own emotions are important; that alone may not be sufficient for effectively handling difficult conversations. Option D is incorrect because it can be very difficult and inappropriate to try to manage another person's emotions, especially in difficult situations. In challenging discussions, leaders should primarily focus on managing their own emotions and facilitating productive communication.

11. B. Constructive discipline, characterized by providing timely and specific feedback, coaching, and guidance, is suitable for isolated incidents or one-time mistakes. Leadership competencies like effective communication, conflict resolution, and performance coaching are essential here to take a growth oriented as opposed to punitive approach. Option A is incorrect because a more formal feedback approach is necessary, especially if the consistent lateness affects team morale or productivity. Option C is incorrect as while constructive discipline might still be applicable in some cases, it should not be used to overlook policy violations simply because others are doing the same; either the policy needs to be reviewed or team members consistently corrected for policy violations. Option D is incorrect because while it may seem that the disrespectful behavior has not directly affected the other person, such conduct still needs to be addressed as it can create a toxic work environment over time. Constructive discipline alone may not be sufficient to maintain a respectful and inclusive workplace culture.

12. A. Self-discipline is characterized by the ability to set clear goals and stick to them, often requiring perseverance to overcome challenges and distractions. Self-motivation, on the other hand, involves the internal drive to pursue goals without relying on external rewards. Leaders need to be both self-disciplined and self-motivated to set a strong example for their teams, maintain focus on long-term goals, and inspire others to achieve excellence through their own commitment and determination.

13. D. The leader is making a bold decision to invest significant company resources despite the inherent uncertainties and potential for both rewards and failure. This demonstrates their willingness to take calculated risks for the potential benefit of the organization. There are components of courage, business acumen, and strategic thinking (Options A, B, and C) in the scenario; however, the core competency being outlined in the scenario is a business strategy with the potential for success or failure, making risk-taking the more appropriate answer.

14. C. The trait theory of leadership suggests that effective leaders possess specific, inherent traits or characteristics that distinguish them from nonleaders. It suggests that leaders are born with certain qualities, such as intelligence, charisma, and assertiveness, which make them effective in leadership roles. Option A is incorrect as situational leadership theory focuses on the idea that effective leadership is determined by adapting one's leadership style to match the specific situation or context. Option B is incorrect because transformational leadership theory emphasizes how leaders can inspire and motivate their followers to achieve exceptional performance through shared vision, values, and charisma. Option D is incorrect as contingency theory emphasizes that effective leadership depends on various situational factors and how well a leader's style matches the specific situation. These incorrect options do not focus on unique leader traits as the primary determinant of effective leadership.

15. B. Path-goal leadership theory suggests that a leader's role is to help followers achieve their goals by providing guidance and support. Sophie's adaptability based on the needs of the team aligns with this theory. Option A is incorrect as charismatic leadership theory emphasizes a leader's ability to inspire and motivate followers through their personal charisma and vision versus adaptability. Option C is incorrect because authentic leadership focuses on leaders being true to themselves, displaying transparency, and building trust with their followers. Option D is incorrect as laissez-faire leadership is characterized by a hands-off approach, where leaders provide minimal guidance or direction. While Sophie's approach with Luc involves some degree of autonomy, it is not entirely hands-off. Her adaptability in addressing James's inconsistency also suggests a more involved leadership style than laissez-faire.

16. C. The Situational Leadership Matrix is used as a framework for leaders to adapt their leadership style based on the readiness and competence levels of their followers in various situations. The categories include the following:

M1: Low competence, high commitment—Enthusiastic but lacking skills.

M2: Some competence, low commitment—Possesses some skills but lacks motivation.

M3: High competence, variable commitment—Skilled but commitment varies.

M4: High competence, high commitment—Highly skilled and motivated.

Carl is described as having strong technical skills, with a potential variable commitment to growing within the organization. Therefore, he falls into the category of high competence, variable commitment (M3) on the situational leadership matrix.

17. D. Participating involves collaborating with team members to make decisions collectively. With an employee who has high commitment but variable competence, involving them in decision-making processes and seeking their input can help bridge competence gaps and ensure that they are engaged and motivated to address their areas of weakness while allowing them the opportunity to contribute in ways aligned with their skills and commitment. Option A is incorrect as telling involves providing specific instructions and expecting compliance, which may not be suitable for an employee with variable competence. While they have high commitment, their varying competence levels require a more adaptable leadership approach. Option B is incorrect as selling involves explaining decisions and persuading team members to buy into a course of action. Option C is incorrect as delegating involves entrusting tasks and responsibilities to team members who have both high competence and commitment.

18. B. The contingency theory of leadership suggests that the most effective leadership style depends on the specific situation, including factors like the nature of the task, the maturity and readiness of the followers, and the external environment. It emphasizes that different situations may require different leadership approaches. Options A and C are more in line with trait-based theories of leadership, and Option D is more aligned with leader-member-exchange theory of leadership.

19. A. The leader-member exchange (LMX) theory focuses on the quality of the relationship between the leader and individual followers. It emphasizes that leaders often have different levels of relationships with their followers, and the quality of these exchanges can impact various outcomes, including job satisfaction, performance, and commitment. Option B is incorrect because path-goal theory is more concerned with how leaders can help followers achieve their goals by providing guidance and support. Option C is incorrect as situational leadership theory centers on adapting leadership styles based on the readiness and maturity of followers and the specific situation, rather than primarily focusing on the leader-follower relationship. Option D is incorrect as servant leadership theory emphasizes leaders serving the needs of their followers and the community, prioritizing others' well-being.

20. B. John demonstrates servant leadership by actively engaging with his team to discuss their challenges, stressors, and jointly exploring solutions. Servant leadership principles emphasize empathy, support, and collaboration. Option A is incorrect because while team-building activities can be valuable, especially for team cohesion, it may not directly address the team's current workload-related stressors and, in fact, add more stress as some team members don't enjoy these events, or it can backfire and cause the team to fall further behind. Option C is incorrect because servant leadership typically involves more direct involvement, support, and collaborative action. Option D is incorrect as providing additional PTO does not directly address the team's current workload challenges or provide the support and engagement associated with servant leadership.

21. A, D. Laissez-faire variably translates into English as "let go" and "allow to do," and this leadership style is designed to be more empowering and hands-off when applied appropriately. It trusts team members to take ownership of their tasks and decisions, empowering them to use their expertise and judgment to achieve goals, and involves minimal interference from the leader, giving team members more autonomy. Because it is a more passive leadership style, it can be ineffective if applied to a team that lacks self-discipline or requires more guidance and, thus, is often misunderstood. Option C describes a leadership style that is disengaged without the intention and empowerment of a laissez style. Option B is not true.

22. B. In the context of leader-member exchange (LMX) theory, when team members feel excluded, leaders should acknowledge their concerns, provide explanations if possible (such as clarifying why certain team members have higher-quality exchanges), and actively work to build better relationships with all team members. This approach promotes fairness, inclusivity, and improved team dynamics. Option A is incorrect as maintaining the status quo without addressing the concerns of excluded team members can lead to morale issues, reduced trust, and potentially higher turnover. Option C is incorrect as dismissing the concerns of excluded team members is not a constructive response and LMX theory does not advocate for ignoring or dismissing concerns related to perceived exclusivity. Option D is incorrect because LMX theory is not rooted in favoritism, rather in the level of trust and investment present in the relationship dynamic between the leader and employee, and LMX theory is not intended to be used as a front for discriminatory behavior against the out group members.

23. C. The contingency theory of leadership is based on the idea that the most effective leadership style depends on specific situational contingencies, including factors such as the readiness and maturity of followers and the external environment. Option A is incorrect as the trait theory of leadership focuses on identifying specific traits or qualities that are inherent in effective leaders, such as charisma, intelligence, and confidence. It does not emphasize adapting leadership styles based on situational contingencies, as Mark believes. Option B is incorrect as the path-goal theory is not primarily concerned with adapting to broader situational contingencies that Mark is experiencing, such as changes in the company's financial stability or market conditions. Option D is incorrect because transformational leadership focuses on leaders inspiring and motivating their followers to achieve exceptional outcomes. While it recognizes the importance of leadership flexibility, it does not emphasize adapting leadership styles based on the broader contingencies that Mark is dealing with.

24. A. A high-performance culture is characterized by a strong emphasis on achieving exceptional results and outcomes, often setting ambitious goals and encouraging continuous improvement to maintain top performance. Option B is incorrect because it is a characteristic of an authoritarian culture, where authority and control are concentrated at the highest levels of the organization, and employees have limited input into decisions. Option C is incorrect as it is a characteristic of a mechanistic culture with well-defined roles, responsibilities, and

processes. This culture often values stability, consistency, and adherence to established procedures. Option D is incorrect because it is a characteristic of a leader in a participative culture, which encourages collaboration, open communication, and empowerment.

25. C. One potential advantage of the autocratic leadership style is that it can lead to quick decision-making and enhanced efficiency. In this approach, the leader has sole authority and can make decisions rapidly without the need for extensive consensus-building or consultation. Option A is incorrect because autocratic leadership is typically associated with low employee morale and job satisfaction because it involves a top-down approach with limited input from team members, potentially leading to feelings of disempowerment and dissatisfaction. Option B is incorrect as autocratic leadership tends to stifle creativity and innovation since it often does not encourage open communication and idea-sharing among team members. Option D is incorrect as autocratic leadership does not involve an equal distribution of decision-making power among team members, which is more characteristic of democratic or participative leadership styles.

26. A. While these two styles have distinct approaches, they both recognize the importance of employee empowerment, albeit in different ways. Transformational leaders empower their employees by inspiring and motivating them to reach their full potential, fostering personal growth and development. Autocratic leaders, on the other hand, may not prioritize empowerment to the same extent, but they still involve employees in certain decision-making processes, providing a sense of involvement and ownership in their tasks. Options B and D are not true. Option C is incorrect because in practice, follower perceptions can vary widely, and the reception of these leadership styles depends on various factors; transformational leadership is generally more positively received than autocratic leadership due to its emphasis on employee development and empowerment.

27. A. Transactional leaders operate on the basis of exchange and rewards, where they offer incentives and rewards to employees in exchange for their compliance and adherence to rules and tasks. This "quid pro quo" (this for that) approach involves a clear system of rewards and consequences based on performance and compliance with established standards. Option B is incorrect as transactional leaders are often quite active in setting expectations and are not passive in their leadership approach. Option C is incorrect because the defining feature of transactional leadership is the exchange-based approach rather than being primarily assertive. Option D is incorrect because charismatic leadership is characterized by the leader's ability to inspire and motivate through their personal charisma, while transactional leadership relies more on structured systems of rewards and punishments rather than charismatic qualities.

28. A. Transactional leaders excel in situations where they can set clear expectations, provide immediate feedback, and use rewards and punishments to ensure compliance and performance. In the context of manufacturing, it is useful to employ a transactional leadership style where expectations are clear and objective criteria is available to measure success or failure. Option B is incorrect because nursing management often involves a complex and dynamic healthcare environment where patient care and employee engagement are critical. In healthcare, a more transformational or supportive leadership style that emphasizes collaboration, motivation, and empathy may be more effective than a strictly transactional approach. Option C is incorrect because project management typically requires a blend of leadership styles depending on the project's nature, team dynamics, and project phases. Option D is incorrect as HR managers must call upon a more transformational leadership style to balance the needs of multiple stakeholders.

29. B. Mentorship programs provide ongoing support, guidance, and a personalized learning experience for employees. Senior leaders can share their knowledge, experiences, and insights with junior employees, helping them develop leadership skills over an extended period. This type of program encourages continuous learning, promotes long-term relationships, and aligns with the goal of nurturing a culture of growth and development within the organization. Option A is incorrect as a one-time, intensive leadership training workshop provides a single, concentrated burst of training but may not sustain ongoing development or support a long-term culture of learning. Option C is incorrect because coaching tends to be more individualized and may not reach a broad range of employees. Option D is incorrect as an annual leadership conference is a periodic event and may not provide the sustained, ongoing learning and growth opportunities needed to create a culture of continuous development within the organization.

30. B. For a distributed workforce, an online leadership training platform with self-paced modules is the most suitable choice as it allows employees in different time zones to access the material at their convenience. In-person workshops may be challenging for remote employees due to geographical constraints. Weekly virtual meetings are valuable but may not provide comprehensive leadership development. An annual retreat is logistically challenging for a distributed workforce and may not provide ongoing development opportunities.

31. C. Experiential learning allows participants to apply leadership skills in real-world situations, leading to better skill retention and practical knowledge. Option A is incorrect because experiential learning may require additional resources, potentially increasing program costs. Option B refers to theoretical knowledge, which is not the primary focus of experiential learning. Option D is not necessarily a benefit, as program duration should align with learning objectives.

32. B. Self-assessment in a leadership development program helps individuals reflect on their strengths and areas for improvement, which is essential for personal growth and leadership development. Options A, C, and D may play roles in leadership development but do not specifically focus on self-awareness and self-assessment.

33. B. The 360-degree feedback process in leadership development programs involves collecting feedback from various sources, including peers, subordinates, and supervisors, to provide a comprehensive assessment of an individual's leadership skills and behaviors. Options A, C, and D do not accurately describe the 360-degree feedback process.

34. C. Succession planning involves identifying and nurturing individuals within the organization who have the potential to fill key leadership roles in the future. Talent reviews are regular assessments of employees' skills, potential, and performance to identify those who have the ability and readiness to take on leadership positions. These processes help organizations proactively develop a pool of qualified internal candidates for leadership roles, aligning with their long-term strategic goals. Option A is incorrect because promoting employees based on seniority does not necessarily identify high-potential leaders. Option B is incorrect because

relying on external hiring for leadership positions does not focus on identifying and developing internal high-potential employees. Option D is incorrect because career development modeling refers to models that establish a pattern of professional development for all employees, not just for high performers.

35. A. Providing leadership development opportunities can lead to decreased employee turnover because it helps employees feel valued and invested in their career growth within the organization. When employees see a clear path for advancement and development, they are more likely to stay with the organization, reducing turnover rates. Option B is incorrect because leadership development complements performance evaluations but doesn't replace them. Option C is incorrect as operational efficiency depends on various factors beyond leadership development, such as processes, technology, and resource management. Option D is incorrect because leadership development aims to develop capable leaders who can handle more complex roles and responsibilities within the organization, and organizational structure is determined by the organization's size, goals, and complexity.

36. C. Job enrichment is a common approach to building a leadership pipeline that involves rotating high-potential employees through various roles and departments. It aims to provide employees with a broader set of experiences and responsibilities, which can help them develop leadership skills and gain a more comprehensive understanding of the organization. Options A, C, and D do not involve moving high-potential team members through different roles for skill development.

37. A. Overemphasis on bottom-up communication is not typically considered a common barrier to leadership effectiveness in a diverse workplace. In fact, encouraging open communication from all levels, including bottom-up, is often seen as a positive practice that promotes inclusivity and diverse perspectives. Challenges such as lack of transparency in Option B exist because when decisions are made without clear communication or understanding, it can lead to misunderstandings, distrust, and disengagement among employees from different backgrounds. In Option C, misalignment of organizational resources such as budget allocation and resource distribution, is a common barrier to leadership effectiveness in a diverse workplace and results in unequal opportunities and resource disparities among different groups. The absence of diverse mentors (Option D) is also a common barrier to leadership effectiveness in a diverse workplace. Having diverse mentors can provide guidance and support to individuals from underrepresented backgrounds and help them advance in their careers.

38. A. David's strong communication and collaboration skills are essential competencies for effective remote leadership. Remote teams heavily rely on clear communication, and strong collaboration ensures that team members can work together seamlessly, even when physically distant. The other options all have merit, however, technical and problem-solving abilities, adaptability and project management, and strategic thinking with conflict management skills are all secondary to the need for remote leaders to be strong communicators and collaborators.

39. C. As counterintuitive as this may seem, scheduling more frequent daily check-ins has been found to be effective in helping team members manage burnout or stress. However, it should be done in conjunction with other supportive actions. Simply scheduling more meetings without addressing the underlying causes of stress may not be sufficient. Option A is incorrect because it is unfair and unlikely to address the root cause of the issues. Option B could have been correct if the question had suggested that senior leaders' expectations are indeed unreasonable and contributing to the team member's stress. Option D is incorrect because stress and overwhelm can lead to burnout and reduced productivity if left unaddressed, and ignoring the approach does not demonstrate the leadership competency of managerial courage.

40. A. The primary difference between succession and replacement planning is that succession planning emphasizes identifying and developing internal candidates within an organization to fill key positions when they become vacant. Replacement planning, on the other hand, involves seeking external candidates to quickly fill a vacant role. Succession planning is about nurturing talent from within, while replacement planning looks externally for immediate solutions. Options B, C, and D are not accurate.

41. B. Leadership succession planning involves identifying and nurturing internal talent to prepare them for leadership positions. By offering employees the chance to advance and assume leadership roles, it provides a clear path for career growth and development, which can significantly enhance their commitment and engagement. Option A is incorrect because leadership succession planning should focus on identifying and developing employees with the necessary skills and potential to fill future leadership positions rather than promoting based on seniority, which can be counterproductive and does not guarantee employee engagement. Option C is incorrect as this option does not accurately describe the core purpose of succession planning, which is to prepare and promote employees from within the organization. Option D is incorrect because it is not true.

42. D. A cost leadership business strategy involves becoming the lowest-cost producer or provider within an industry. Engaging in workflow analysis helps identify areas of redundancy, inefficiency, and opportunities for streamlining operations. By conducting such analyses, HR can contribute to cost reduction efforts and operational improvements. Option A is incorrect because layoffs should be approached with care and as a last resort. HR's focus should be on finding ways to optimize the workforce, reduce labor costs through attrition, and improve workforce deployment. Option B is incorrect because as business partners, HR can take more strategic action than that of an event planner. HR's primary focus should be on initiatives related to cost reduction, process efficiency, and workforce optimization, rather than organizing morale-boosting events. Option C is inaccurate as pricing decisions are typically made by marketing.

43. A. In their consultative role, human resource leaders should collaborate with other organizational leaders to gain insights into their specific HR challenges and needs. By understanding these challenges, HR leaders can provide tailored advice, solutions, and strategies to address them effectively. Options A, C, and D are all important competencies for HR professionals; however, they are not in alignment with the consultative role of HR, which involves collaboration and problem-solving related to HR challenges faced by leaders, rather than the direct execution of engagement initiatives.

44. C. Relationship-building with other organizational leaders involves effective communication and collaboration. Responding promptly to work assignments and requests from colleagues demonstrates reliability, responsiveness, and a willingness to work cooperatively, all of which are essential for building positive relationships with leaders in different departments or areas of the organization. Option A is incorrect as facilitating difficult interactions with employees focuses more on employee relations and conflict resolution, rather than building relationships with fellow leaders within the organization. Option B is incorrect because it primarily relates to an individual's ethical conduct and professionalism. Option D is incorrect as this initiative focuses more on HR's role in fostering an inclusive workplace, whereas relationship-building involves interpersonal interactions and collaboration with leaders from various parts of the organization.

45. B. In their consultative role, HR leaders can support organizational leaders in talent acquisition by providing valuable market analysis, including insights into industry trends, competitive salary information, and candidate recommendations. They help leaders make informed decisions about recruiting and hiring strategies. Option A is incorrect as HR leaders may be involved in the interview process, but their consultative role involves providing expertise, guidance, and support to organizational leaders rather than directly making hiring decisions. Option C is incorrect because HR leaders may provide training and guidance, but their consultative role involves broader strategic advice and support related to talent acquisition. Option D is incorrect as it focuses more on compensation and benefits than on the consultative role in talent acquisition.

46. B. Senior leader service excellence competencies involve the ability to identify and address larger system-level needs and issues within the organization. Senior leaders with this competency are skilled at recognizing systemic challenges, improving processes, and creating strategies to enhance overall service quality. Service excellence in senior leaders goes beyond addressing individual stakeholder requests, identifying early stage needs, or maintaining service quality (Options A, C, and D). These are responsibilities at all levels of HR service excellence.

47. D. Effectively managing the initiative involves engaging with the resistant department heads, understanding their concerns, and actively seeking their input and feedback. Incorporating their suggestions where feasible demonstrates a willingness to address their concerns and collaborate on a solution that works for everyone. Option A is incorrect because implementing a performance management system without the involvement and buy-in of department heads who are resistant can lead to conflicts, resistance from their teams, and potential implementation challenges. Option B is incorrect because relying on other leaders to advocate for the changes might not address the underlying resistance (and potential legitimate concerns) from the department heads directly affected by the new system. Option C is incorrect as abandoning the initiative due to resistance from department heads is not a productive solution.

48. B. 360-degree feedback assessments involve gathering feedback from multiple sources, including peers, subordinates, superiors, and self-assessments. This method provides a well-rounded and comprehensive view of a leader's performance, including their strengths and areas for improvement, making it a common and effective approach. Option A is incorrect as this option is not as effective because self-assessments can be biased, and leaders may not always provide an objective evaluation of their own performance. Option C is incorrect because employee feedback is essential, but it should be complemented by input from other sources to ensure a well-rounded assessment. Option D is incorrect because evaluating leaders based on their tenure (the length of time they've been in a position) does not consider the quality or impact of their leadership during that time.

49. C. Social media popularity and the number of followers are not direct indicators of a CEO or senior leader's effectiveness in driving organizational success. More important considerations are Option A, which reflects the organization's success and the leader's ability to make sound financial decisions. Option B is also critical in that engaged and satisfied employees are more likely to be productive and contribute positively to the organization. Option D is a useful leadership metric because market share and competitive positioning indicates their ability to position the company in a competitive market and gain a larger share.

50. B. A potential drawback of relying solely on quantitative metrics for evaluating leader performance is that they may not capture all aspects of leadership effectiveness, such as soft skills and interpersonal relationships. Option A is incorrect because quantitative metrics provide an objective rather than subjective assessment. Option C is incorrect as the breadth and scope of metrics may vary based on leadership roles. Option D is incorrect; quantitative metrics may not necessarily be the most time-consuming method.

51. C. When leading projects that involve diverse teams and multitasking, effective communication is paramount. Managers must ensure that team members understand their roles, responsibilities, and expectations clearly. Option A is incorrect because many managers are promoted to leadership roles because they are good at their technical jobs without necessarily having the interpersonal skills necessary to lead others. Options B and D are incorrect as time and budget management address the multitasking portion of the question, but not necessarily the managing diverse component of where leaders can struggle.

52. B. A crucial element in building diverse leadership development programs is tailoring the programs to meet the specific needs and backgrounds of participants (personalization). Option A, a one-size-fits-all approach, may not address diverse needs. Option C, excluding underrepresented groups, goes against the goal of diversity. Option D, focusing on technical skills, neglects the importance of inclusive leadership development.

53. B. High-potential employees often value work-life balance, a positive workplace culture, and opportunities for growth and development. A flexible work environment that accommodates their needs and promotes inclusivity can contribute to job satisfaction and employee retention. Such an environment also encourages innovation, collaboration, and engagement, which are important for retaining top talent. Option A is incorrect as it only fits a limited population of the high-potential employees. Some may prefer to advance in their careers while staying in their current location. Option C is incorrect because competitive compensation is important, high-potential employees often seek other benefits such as career development, a positive work culture, and work-life balance. Option D is these individuals are often looking for a holistic package that includes opportunities for growth, a supportive work environment, and work-life balance, not just financial incentives as retainers.

54. D. Coaching involves providing guidance, feedback, and support to team members to help them improve their skills, improve their performance, and achieve their goals. This is the most appropriate people management technique in the given situation because it allows the manager to adapt their approach to the individual needs of each team member, whether they are new or experienced. Coaching encourages skill development, fosters growth, and supports all team members in achieving their goals effectively. Option A is incorrect as delegating might work well with more experienced team members, but it may not provide the necessary

guidance and support to newer or less experienced members. Option B is incorrect because mentoring typically involves a senior or experienced team member providing guidance, advice, and support to a less experienced colleague. Some team members may already have significant experience, making a mentoring approach less relevant to them. Option C is incorrect because directing may limit the autonomy and growth opportunities for more experienced team members and could lead to disengagement among the newer ones.

55. D. In this scenario, the senior manager is demonstrating the leading by example influence technique by personally adopting eco-friendly practices to encourage employees to do the same. In Option A, forming coalitions involves the process of building alliances or partnerships with individuals or groups to work collectively toward a common goal or objective. Option B is inaccurate because rational persuasion is an influence technique that relies on presenting logical arguments, data, and evidence to convince others to adopt a particular viewpoint or take a specific action. Option C is incorrect as personal appeal is an influence technique that relies on building personal relationships, trust, and emotional connections with others to gain their support or cooperation.

56. C. The key distinction between personal appeal and rational persuasion is that personal appeal focuses on building trust and personal relationships to influence others, while rational persuasion relies on logical arguments, data, and evidence to persuade through reasoning and facts. Options A, B, and D are not accurate distinctions.

57. A. Leading by example involves setting a positive and credible model of behavior for others to follow. When leaders demonstrate the values, work ethic, and behavior they expect from their team, it can build trust and credibility more effectively than forming coalitions. Trust and credibility are vital for influencing others and gaining their commitment. Option B is incorrect because the effect of leading by example can require reinforcement and trust building, which can be time-consuming. Option C is incorrect as leading by example primarily focuses on an individual's behavior and actions, rather than collective decision-making. Option D is incorrect because leading by example often requires self-awareness and self-discipline, which are important features of high emotional intelligence.

58. B. In Fiedler's contingency theory of leadership, the goal is for leaders to change conditions to be more favorable. The theory notes that effective leadership depends on the match between a leader's preferred leadership style, either task-oriented or relationship-oriented, and the favorability of the situational context in which they operate.

59. D. The impact of high power distance—where there's a significant level of unequal distribution of power and authority—on the leader-team relationship depends on various contextual factors, including the cultural norms, leadership style, and specific circumstances. In some cases, a high power distance may lead to more hierarchical and less collaborative relationships, while in others, it may be mitigated by factors such as the leader's approach or the team's dynamics. Options A, B, and C are not accurate.

60. A. Both contingency theory and the job characteristics model (JCM) acknowledge that the characteristics of the job or situation can have a significant impact on employee satisfaction and performance. Contingency theory suggests that task structure can improve situational favorableness, while the JCM focuses on how specific job characteristics, such as skill variety, task identity, task significance, autonomy, and feedback, can influence job satisfaction and motivation. The other options are inaccurate statements.

61. A. Elon Musk's leadership style is best characterized as transformational because he combines visionary thinking with active involvement in pushing the boundaries of innovation, motivating his teams to achieve ambitious goals, and fostering a culture of creativity and problem-solving within his companies. Option B is incorrect because while Musk is known for being highly involved in decision-making and having a strong vision for his companies, his leadership style is not characterized by authoritarian control or dictatorial tendencies, which are typically associated with autocratic leadership and present in more institutional or formalized work structures. Option C is incorrect because Musk's leadership style extends beyond mere charm or persuasion. He actively engages in problem-solving and implementation, which goes beyond the scope of charismatic leadership. Option D is incorrect as a laissez-faire leadership style involves minimal interference and allows employees a high degree of autonomy, which is not reflective of Musk's hands-on approach and direct involvement in the operations of his companies.

62. D. Steve Jobs demonstrated a clear vision for Apple and its products, driving the company forward with his innovative ideas and inspiring his teams to achieve ambitious goals. Additionally, his charismatic leadership style allowed him to influence and motivate others effectively. Option A is incorrect because while Jobs was indeed transformational in his approach, inspiring innovation and motivating his teams to achieve greatness, the question does not suggest that he practiced transactional leadership, which involves rewarding or punishing based on performance. Option B is incorrect because although Jobs fostered a culture of creativity and innovation at Apple, his leadership style extended beyond merely being creative and innovative himself. Option C is incorrect as while Jobs could be demanding and had high standards for his teams, his leadership style was not solely characterized by authoritarian or autocratic tendencies. He valued collaboration and input from his team members, albeit with a strong guiding vision.

63. A, B, C, D. The third-party logistics (3PL) industry involves the outsourcing of logistics services, such as transportation, warehousing, and distribution, to specialized companies to efficiently manage and streamline supply chain operations. In a 3PL, leaders need to have a strong grasp of strategic planning to ensure efficient operations and effective utilization of resources. Additionally, expertise in supply chain management is crucial for optimizing processes and meeting customer demands. Effective communication is essential for building relationships with clients, suppliers, and team members in the logistics industry, and negotiation skills are also vital for securing favorable contracts, resolving conflicts, and navigating complex business arrangements. Because the logistics industry is constantly evolving, with advancements in technology and shifts in market dynamics, leaders must possess the agility to adapt their strategies and operations to stay competitive and capitalize on emerging opportunities. Leading teams in a third-party logistics organization requires strong leadership skills to motivate employees, foster collaboration, and drive performance. Additionally, the ability to resolve conflicts efficiently is crucial for maintaining productivity and harmony within the workplace.

64. A. Self-awareness is foundational to effective leadership. Leaders who are self-aware can recognize their own limitations and areas for growth, allowing them to make informed decisions and seek support or development where necessary. Option B is incorrect because while self-awareness does contribute to improved communication and relationships, it's not the only

factor. Effective communication also requires active listening, empathy, and understanding of others' perspectives, which may not be solely dependent on self-awareness. Option C is incorrect because while self-awareness does contribute to adaptability, it's also not the sole determinant. Adaptability involves factors such as flexibility, openness to change, and willingness to learn, which may not be entirely dependent on self-awareness. Option D is incorrect because while self-awareness does contribute to authenticity and integrity, these qualities also rely on other factors such as ethical principles, consistency, and transparency in leadership, which may not be only determined by self-awareness.

65. A. Upskilling employees can provide them with the necessary tools and knowledge to increase their productivity and value to the organization, thereby justifying pay increases based on performance. Providing a clear path to advancement can help employees see a direct connection between their contributions and compensation, fostering greater motivation and engagement. Option B is incorrect as it does not directly address the issue of struggling to absorb pay increases and may not be practical in terms of adding more overhead without other strategic considerations. Option C is incorrect because freezing pay increases may lead to decreased morale and employee motivation, especially if employees already feel their contributions are not being recognized or rewarded. Additionally, it does not address the underlying issue of employees struggling to connect their contributions to their compensation. Option D is incorrect, because it can have negative implications for employee morale, organizational culture, and long-term productivity. Additionally, it does not address the root cause of the issue, which is the disconnect between pay increases and productivity gains.

Chapter 16: Organizational Development and Design

1. A. While often used interchangeably, organizational development and design are two separate activities. Organizational design primarily focuses on the arrangement of structures, roles, processes, and systems within an organization to ensure efficiency, effectiveness, and alignment with strategic objectives. It involves decisions about the division of labor, hierarchy, communication channels, and workflow optimization. Organizational development centers around enhancing the organization's human capital, including improving employee skills, knowledge, attitudes, and behaviors. This often involves interventions such as training programs, leadership development initiatives, team-building exercises, and cultural change efforts.

2. A, C. Job restructuring is a common activity during organizational redesign. This involves reshaping job roles, responsibilities, and reporting relationships within the organization to improve efficiency, effectiveness, or adaptability to changing circumstances. Span of control refers to the number of subordinates or employees that a manager or supervisor directly oversees. During organizational redesign, adjustments to the span of control may occur to streamline reporting relationships, improve communication channels, or enhance managerial effectiveness. Options B and D are incorrect as both activities are functions of organizational development, not organizational design.

3. A. Span of control refers to the number of subordinates or employees that a manager directly supervises. By adjusting the reporting relationships, it is also likely that the manager's responsibilities will be redistributed to ensure that the manager's tasks and personnel are appropriate for effective supervision and management. Option B is incorrect as demotion is a disciplinary action and it does not inherently focus on adjusting the number of subordinates under the manager's supervision. Option C is incorrect because changing the manager's direct supervisor may impact the chain of command or managerial oversight but does not specifically address the optimal number of subordinates that a manager should supervise. Option D is partially correct because restructuring to a cross-functional team may influence the distribution of responsibilities and reporting relationships within the department. However, cross-functional teams are more about enhancing collaboration and leveraging diverse skill sets across different functions or disciplines rather than specifically focusing on managerial span of control.

4. B, D. Job restructuring involves reorganizing or redefining job roles within an organization to improve efficiency, effectiveness, or adaptability. As part of this process, existing job descriptions may be refined or updated to reflect changes in responsibilities, required skills, or reporting relationships. During job restructuring, changes in job roles or responsibilities may necessitate updates to existing workflows and reporting channels to ensure that procedures are aligned with new processes, reporting relationships, or organizational priorities. Option A is incorrect because layoffs are not necessarily directly associated with job restructuring, although they can sometimes occur as a result (as can hiring). Option C is not correct as job restructuring primarily involves reorganizing or redefining existing job roles within the organization rather than adding new positions.

5. B. In organizational restructuring, task specialization often occurs to improve efficiency and effectiveness. By breaking down complex tasks into smaller, specialized components, organizations can allocate resources more effectively, increase productivity, and enhance quality control. This approach allows employees to focus on specific aspects of their work, leveraging their expertise and skills to achieve better outcomes. Additionally, task specialization can facilitate clearer role definitions and responsibilities, leading to smoother workflow and coordination within the organization.

6. B. With employees working both remotely and in the office, it becomes essential to create a workspace layout that fosters effective collaboration and communication regardless of location. Redesigning the workspace to support seamless interaction between remote and in-office employees can enhance teamwork, boost productivity, and maintain a sense of cohesion within the organization. Option A is incorrect because it does not directly address the need for collaboration between remote and in-office employees in a hybrid work model. Option C is incorrect because hot-desking (unassigned work stations) primarily focuses on optimizing space utilization and flexibility in office arrangements, but it may not directly contribute to enhancing communication and teamwork across different work settings. Option D is incorrect because such a rigid seating arrangement may not foster the flexibility and adaptability required for effective collaboration across different work settings.

7. B. The primary purpose of implementing an organization chart is to provide a clear overview of the company's structure, including reporting relationships, hierarchies, and departmental divisions. By visually depicting how different roles and departments are interconnected within the organization, the organization chart helps employees understand their position in the company's structure and to whom they report. This clarity fosters better communication, coordination, and alignment of efforts across the organization, particularly during periods of growth and restructuring.

8. B. Automation can be particularly beneficial when organizations seek to streamline operations, improve efficiency, and reduce costs by automating repetitive and labor-intensive tasks. By replacing manual processes with automated systems or technologies, organizations can increase productivity, minimize errors, and allocate human resources to more strategic and value-added activities. Option A is incorrect because automation may not necessarily enhance employee autonomy, as it can lead to a shift in job roles or require employees to adapt to new technologies. In some cases, automation may even limit employee decision-making capabilities if it restricts the flexibility or customization of processes. Option C is incorrect because in some cases, automation may replace certain collaborative tasks previously performed manually, potentially reducing opportunities for teamwork. Option D is incorrect because prioritizing traditional manual processes over automation may result in inefficiencies, higher operational costs, and missed opportunities for improvement.

9. D. A sole proprietorship is a business structure where the owner has full personal liability for the business's debts and legal obligations. This means the owner's personal assets can be used to satisfy business debts. Options A, B, and C are incorrect because sole proprietorships do not provide limited liability protection, create a separate legal entity, or involve multiple owners.

10. C. In a partnership, the income is passed through to the individual partners, who report their share of the income on their personal tax returns and pay taxes at their individual tax rates. Options A, B, and D are incorrect because partnership income is subject to taxation, but it is not taxed at corporate tax rates or a fixed government rate.

11. B. Multinational organizations commonly adopt a corporate structure due to its ability to raise capital through the sale of stock, its legal distinctiveness from its owners, and its capacity to operate globally with subsidiaries in multiple countries. Option A is incorrect as limited liability corporations (LLCs) are used for smaller businesses or startups due to their flexibility in management and taxation. Option C is incorrect because sole proprietorships are businesses owned and operated by a single individual, and they lack the scalability and international reach required by multinational organizations. Option D is incorrect because "Global" is not a specific business structure but rather an adjective describing the reach or scope of operations. While MNEs may indeed have a global presence, they adopt a specific legal structure such as a corporation to manage their operations efficiently across borders.

12. B. A cross-functional organizational structure is a framework where employees from different functional areas or departments collaborate on projects or tasks, breaking down traditional silos to promote interdisciplinary teamwork and innovation. By facilitating effective communication channels and fostering collaboration initiatives, HR helps ensure that teams can work together seamlessly to achieve common goals. Option A is incorrect as in a cross-functional organizational structure, HR's role is to move away from traditional hierarchical management. Option C is incorrect because broad banding is a compensation strategy driven by factors other than the organizational structure, such as increasing flexible reward options or simplifying pay administration. Option D is incorrect as these activities are secondary to HR's primary goal of facilitating interdepartmental communication and collaboration and may or may not be directly related to the organizational structure.

13. A, B, C. In a matrix structure, employees often report to both functional managers and project managers simultaneously, leading to potential conflicts of interest, priorities, or

directives and lack of clear lines of authority. HR professionals must navigate these conflicts diplomatically to maintain employee morale and productivity. Option D is not correct as standardized performance evaluation metrics are not always necessary nor significant in a matrix structure.

14. A. The primary objective of corporate governance is to ensure that the interests of shareholders are protected and that the company's management acts in their best interests. Maximizing shareholder wealth involves making decisions that enhance the long-term value of the company, such as increasing profitability, growth, and share price. Options B and C are incorrect because even though employee satisfaction and addressing the impact of business on the environment are important considerations for any organization, they are achieved in ways other than through corporate governance such as strategic initiatives and corporate social responsibility. Option D is incorrect because executives' compensation should be aligned with the company's performance and long-term shareholder value creation.

15. A. The primary difference between shareholders and stakeholders is that shareholders are individuals or entities that own shares or equity in the company, making them partial owners and giving them a financial interest in the company's performance and profitability. In contrast, stakeholders include a broader group of individuals or entities (such as employees, customers, suppliers, and the community) who are affected by or can affect the company's actions but do not have a financial ownership stake in the company.

16. B. In this scenario, local residents and community members are the primary stakeholders who are likely to be most concerned about the project. The construction of the new factory will directly impact their lives, environment, and local economy. Option A is incorrect because shareholders, while interested in the company's expansion, may not be as directly affected as the local community. Option C is incorrect because competing manufacturing companies may view this as a competitive challenge but are not considered stakeholders in this context. Option D is incorrect because the company's board of directors is generally focused on governance and strategic decisions but may not be directly impacted by the local community's concerns.

17. B. Corporate governance boards are responsible for overseeing the strategic decisions of the company to ensure they align with the company's mission, values, and legal obligations. Outsourcing customer support services could raise concerns related to maintaining service quality, data privacy, compliance with regulations, and potential impacts on the company's reputation. Options A, C, and D are not likely to be concerned with this type of strategic initiative.

18. B. Tying CEO compensation to long-term performance, such as through performance-based stock options or bonuses, is a best practice in corporate governance as it aligns the CEO's interests with the long-term success of the company and encourages responsible leadership. Option A is incorrect because providing generous stock options can lead to short-term focus and potential misuse. Option C is incorrect because offering a fixed salary without variable components may not sufficiently incentivize performance. Option D is incorrect because keeping CEO compensation details confidential goes against the principle of transparency in corporate governance.

19. D. One of the primary roles of HR professionals in corporate governance is to establish and enforce policies and practices that promote ethical behavior and integrity throughout the

organization. This includes developing codes of conduct, providing ethics training, investigating misconduct allegations, and fostering a corporate culture that values transparency and accountability. Options A and B are incorrect because they are parts of other functional areas of human resources that are separate from corporate governance. Option C is incorrect because hiring the board of directors is the responsibility of the shareholders or a nominating committee of the board, not HR professionals. While HR may provide support in the recruitment process, such as facilitating candidate interviews, their primary role in corporate governance relates more to ensuring ethical conduct and fostering a culture of integrity.

20. C. In the absence of a board clerk or other administrative support, HR is often tasked with compliance with the Brown Act. The Brown Act requires that meetings of public bodies, including those involving boards of directors, be open and transparent to the public. HR plays a crucial role in ensuring that board meetings are conducted in accordance with the act, including providing access to meeting agendas, allowing public attendance, and facilitating transparency in decision-making processes. HR is also responsible for ensuring that proper notice of board meetings is given to the public and interested stakeholders in compliance with the act's requirements such as publishing meeting agendas, dates, times, and locations in advance to allow for public participation and observation. HR is responsible for creating an official record of the proceedings.

21. B. The balance sheet provides a snapshot of a company's financial position at a specific point in time, at the end of a reporting period, such as a quarter or a year. It presents the company's assets, liabilities, and shareholders' equity, showing what the company owns (assets), owes (liabilities), and its net worth (shareholders' equity) at that moment. Option A is incorrect because the income statement, also known as the profit and loss statement, provides a summary of a company's revenues, expenses, and net income or loss over a specific period, such as a quarter or a year. Option C is incorrect because the cash flow statement reports the cash inflows and outflows from operating, investing, and financing activities over a specific period, such as a quarter or a year. Option D is incorrect as the statement of retained earnings shows changes in a company's retained earnings balance over a specific period, a quarter, or a year.

22. C. An increase in overtime expenses can be a result of a shortage of skilled workers, which requires existing employees to work longer hours to meet demand. Option A is incorrect because more vacation days would likely reduce overtime expenses. Option B is incorrect because flexible work hours are designed to provide employees with work-life balance and are not necessarily related to increased overtime. Option D is incorrect because using sick leave would not consistently result in an increase in overtime expenses.

23. C. The scenario suggests that the company lacks adequate internal controls to prevent and detect fraudulent activities like Ricky's embezzlement. Internal controls include the proper separation of tasks and other check and balance mechanisms designed to safeguard company assets, prevent fraud, and ensure accurate financial reporting. The absence of such controls allowed Ricky to manipulate vacation days and cash out time undetected. Option A is incorrect as the primary issue lies in the lack of proper internal controls rather than only managerial oversight. Option B is incorrect because a background check may not reveal behaviors like embezzlement unless the applicant had been caught and convicted in the past. Option D is partially correct in that policies, procedures, and rules are suggested internal control mechanisms, but without other controls such as task separation and audits, they would be insufficient by themselves to have prevented the fraud.

24. B. Organizational structures primarily focus on defining roles, hierarchy, and reporting relationships within a business. They establish the framework for how tasks and responsibilities are distributed and how employees interact within the organization. Options A, C, and D are incorrect because they represent different aspects of business operations that are not the primary focus of organizational structures.

25. C. Organizational systems include frameworks, procedures, and mechanisms designed to streamline workflows, enhance efficiency, and achieve operational excellence. By implementing effective organizational systems, businesses can improve productivity, reduce costs, and maintain a competitive edge in the market. Option A is incorrect because organizational systems encompass broader functions beyond just defining reporting structures, such as optimizing processes and facilitating efficient operations. Option B is incorrect as organizational systems may include elements related to job roles and responsibilities, but their primary focus is on managing and optimizing operational processes to achieve the organization's objectives. Option D is incorrect because employee engagement initiatives are part of broader human resources strategies rather than organizational systems specifically focused on operational processes and efficiency.

26. B. Organizational structures establish a clear hierarchy of authority and responsibility within the business. This hierarchy helps define who has the authority to make decisions, who is accountable for their outcomes, and how information flows through the organization. Clear lines of authority facilitate efficient decision-making processes and ensure accountability for outcomes. Option A is incorrect as organizational structures primarily focus on establishing frameworks for how authority, responsibility, and communication flow within the organization, rather than directly dictating data analysis methods. Option C is incorrect because supply chain management involves a broader set of processes and strategies beyond just organizational structures, including procurement, logistics, inventory management, and supplier relationships. Option D is incorrect as collaborative and creative decision-making often relies on organizational culture, leadership style, and team dynamics in addition to structural factors.

27. C. A functional organizational structure groups employees by common functions or departments, such as marketing, finance, and operations, each with its own area of expertise and decision-making authority. This allows for specialization and efficiency within each department while still providing a clear overall direction set by the executive leadership team. Option A is incorrect because a centralized organizational structure involves decision-making authority concentrated at the top of the hierarchy, with little autonomy given to lower-level employees or departments. Option B is incorrect as a flat organizational structure has few levels of hierarchy and encourages decentralized decision-making by empowering employees at various levels of the organization. Option D is incorrect because a matrix organizational structure combines elements of both functional and project-based structures, where employees report to both functional managers and project managers.

28. D. A matrix organizational structure combines elements of both functional and project-based structures, where employees report to both functional managers and project managers simultaneously. In the scenario described, employees report to multiple team leaders (project managers) while also collaborating across teams, indicating a matrix structure where employees have dual reporting relationships and work on cross-functional projects. Option A

is incorrect because a centralized organizational structure involves decision-making authority concentrated at the top of the hierarchy, with little autonomy given to lower-level employees or teams. Option B is incorrect as a flat organizational structure has few levels of hierarchy and encourages decentralized decision-making by empowering employees at various levels of the organization. Option C is incorrect as a functional organizational structure groups employees by common functions or departments, such as marketing, finance, and operations, each with its own area of expertise and decision-making authority. In the scenario described, teams are organized around specific projects rather than functions, suggesting a project-based structure rather than a functional one.

29. D. An integrated systems approach refers to the use of systems and technologies, such as enterprise resource planning (ERP) systems, to integrate data and processes across different departments or functions within an organization. The use of an ERP system enables seamless information flow and decision-making by integrating data and processes across all departments. Option A is incorrect as a centralized organizational structure involves decision-making authority concentrated at the top of the hierarchy, with little autonomy given to lower-level employees or departments. Option B is incorrect because a flat organizational structure has few levels of hierarchy and encourages decentralized decision-making by empowering employees at various levels of the organization. Option C is incorrect because in a functional organizational structure, employees are grouped by common functions or departments, such as production, finance, and sales, each with its own area of expertise and decision-making authority.

30. B. Change management involves strategies and processes aimed at preparing, equipping, and supporting individuals and teams to adopt organizational changes successfully. By implementing change management initiatives, such as communication plans, stakeholder engagement, training programs, and addressing concerns, HR can help employees navigate through the uncertainties and challenges associated with organizational redesign. Option A is incorrect as it may not directly address the challenges of employee resistance and uncertainty during organizational redesign. Option C is incorrect as it does not address the root cause of the resistance, which is the organizational redesign. Option D is incorrect as it also does not directly address the underlying issues.

31. C. In Lewin's theory of change management, the first stage is "unfreezing," which involves creating a sense of urgency and motivation among employees to recognize the need for change. By emphasizing the importance of change and the reasons behind it, management can overcome resistance and prepare employees for the upcoming transitions. This step sets the stage for the subsequent stages of change, making it crucial for successful implementation. Option A is incorrect because it does not directly align with Lewin's theory's initial stage of "unfreezing." This step occurs later in the change process as part of the "changing/moving" stage, where organizations evaluate current practices and identify areas for improvement. Option B is incorrect as KPIs are established after the change has been initiated, during the "moving" stage, to track progress and outcomes. Option D is incorrect because stabilizing the organizational chart is part of the "refreeze" stage of Lewin's model.

32. A, B. Establishing feedback systems allows organizations to continuously gather input from employees regarding the implemented changes. This feedback can provide valuable insights into the effectiveness of the changes, identify areas for improvement, and address any concerns or challenges encountered during the change process. Implementing reward systems can incentivize and motivate employees to embrace and support organizational changes. Rewards can take various forms, such as bonuses, recognition programs, promotions, or other tangible incentives, depending on the organization's culture and objectives. Options C and D are incorrect because identifying barriers to change and breaking down the status quo primarily pertains to the initial stages of change implementation, such as the "unfreezing" stage in Lewin's model. Anchoring change involves sustaining and embedding change initiatives within the organization over the long term, which may involve establishing mechanisms such as feedback and reward systems to reinforce desired behaviors and outcomes.

33. B. In Kotter's model, building a guiding coalition involves assembling a group of influential individuals within the organization who can champion the change effort and drive it forward. This coalition includes key stakeholders, leaders, and influential employees who can advocate for change and garner support from others. By prioritizing this step, the company can address employees' concerns by ensuring that their voices are represented within the guiding coalition. Option A is incorrect as creating a sense of urgency does not necessarily ensure that employees feel heard or involved in the change process. Option C is incorrect because focusing on short-term wins may not directly address the underlying issue of employees feeling excluded from decision-making and unheard regarding their perspectives. Option D is partially correct in that removing barriers to communication may be necessary to help employees embrace the change; however, it does not inherently involve employees in decision-making or address their need for involvement and feedback.

34. D. One potential challenge associated with John Kotter's change management model is its reliance on a small group of leaders or individuals to drive the change process forward. This challenge may hinder the effectiveness of the change effort by limiting input from a diverse range of stakeholders, overlooking critical insights, and creating bottlenecks in decision-making processes. Option A is incorrect because Kotter's model is generally well-defined and structured, consisting of eight distinct steps. Option B is incorrect as Kotter's model advocates for active employee participation to facilitate change acceptance and adoption. Option C is incorrect as Kotter's change management model places significant emphasis on establishing a clear vision and goals for change, as well as celebrating short-term wins to maintain momentum and motivation.

35. C. The ADKAR model for change is a structured approach that focuses on individuals' Awareness, Desire, Knowledge, Ability, and Reinforcement to facilitate successful organizational change. The primary focus is to support employees throughout the change process. Option A is incorrect because while the model may provide guidance on how to support employees through the change process, it does not focus on providing detailed instructions for implementing change initiatives. Option B is incorrect because the ADKAR model is not focused on ensuring a smooth transition for leaders but rather on addressing the needs and concerns of all employees during the change process. Option D is incorrect as organizational goals are not the primary focus of the model.

36. D. The Kubler-Ross change curve depicts the emotional stages individuals experience when confronted with significant change, including denial, resistance, exploration, acceptance, and integration, similar to the stages of grief. Effective communication, coupled with empathy, helps address employees' concerns, alleviate fears, and build trust, ultimately fostering a sense of inclusion and involvement in the transformation. Without empathy and communication, employees are more likely to feel left out and disconnected from the change effort, impeding its successful embedding within the organization.

37. A. Nudge theory emphasizes making small, subtle changes in the environment to influence people's behavior in predictable ways. In this scenario, the manager is subtly nudging the employee toward accepting the proposed change by finding common ground and connections. Option B is incorrect as Kotter's change model focuses on eight steps for leading organizational change. It includes establishing a sense of urgency, creating a guiding coalition, developing a vision and strategy, communicating the change vision, empowering broad-based action, generating short-term wins, consolidating gains and producing more change, and anchoring new approaches in the culture. Option C is incorrect as the bridges transition model emphasizes managing the human side of change. It involves three stages: ending, neutral zone, and new beginning. While finding connections and common ground might facilitate the transition from the ending stage to the new beginning stage by building rapport and trust, it doesn't necessarily reflect the unconscious personal approach described in the scenario. Option D is incorrect as the ADKAR model focuses on five elements: awareness, desire, knowledge, ability, and reinforcement. While building connections and rapport might contribute to creating awareness or fostering desire for the change, it doesn't directly align with the unconscious personal approach described in the scenario.

38. B. The Twitter example highlights the challenge of balancing the speed of change with resource limitations and organizational needs. Elon Musk's swift action in firing more than half of the employees upon taking over Twitter demonstrates the desire for rapid change. However, the subsequent rehiring of some employees and consideration of limited resources and organizational needs suggest the importance of carefully balancing the speed of change with these factors. This emphasizes the necessity of aligning the pace of change with the organization's resources and requirements to ensure effective implementation and sustainable outcomes.

39. C. The primary focus of Frederick Taylor's theory of scientific management is to increase productivity and efficiency in the workplace. Taylor believed that by scientifically analyzing tasks, optimizing work processes, and providing appropriate training and incentives, organizations could achieve higher levels of productivity and efficiency. Options A, B, and D do not accurately reflect Taylor's scientific theory.

40. C. The chaos theory of management recognizes that organizational systems are inherently complex and nonlinear, influenced by numerous factors that can lead to unpredictable outcomes. It emphasizes the importance of embracing uncertainty, adapting to change, and leveraging complexity as a source of innovation and competitive advantage. Options A, B, and D are not characteristics of the chaos theory of management.

41. B. Scalar chain is a principle of Henri Fayol's administrative theory that emphasizes the importance of establishing a clear and unbroken line of authority and communication within an organization, where instructions flow from top management down through various levels of hierarchy. In the scenario, the CEO's emphasis on establishing clear lines of authority and communication channels reflects the concept of scalar chain. Option A is incorrect as unity of command is a principle within Fayol's administrative theory that emphasizes that employees should receive orders from only one superior to avoid confusion and conflicting instructions. Option C is incorrect because span of control refers to the number of subordinates a manager can effectively supervise. Option D is incorrect as the division of labor is a principle that involves breaking down tasks into specialized roles to improve efficiency and productivity.

42. C. In an ethnocentric approach, headquarters maintains tight control over subsidiaries, and there is a tendency to standardize practices and policies across different regions to reflect the dominant culture and practices of the home country. This approach can significantly impact global organizational design principles by prioritizing centralized decision-making and uniformity across geographically dispersed units.

43. D. In the context of global organizational design, emphasizing uniformity and centralization may hinder the organization's ability to adapt to diverse market conditions and cultural differences across different regions. By maintaining tight control and standardizing practices from headquarters, the organization may overlook the unique needs and preferences of local markets, potentially leading to missed opportunities or inefficiencies. This approach limits the responsiveness of the organization to local market dynamics, which can be critical for success in international markets.

44. D. In response to challenges related to role ambiguity and overlap among employees due to rapid growth and expansion, the tech startup introduces a new organizational structure. By clarifying the structural framework, the company aims to improve efficiency, coordination, and accountability within the organization, addressing the specific challenges arising from its growth and expansion. Option A is incorrect as employee wellness program focuses on promoting the physical, mental, and emotional well-being of employees, which do not directly address the challenges related to role ambiguity and overlap within the organization. Option B is incorrect because overhauling the performance appraisal system involves revising the methods and processes used to evaluate employee performance, which also does not directly address the challenges of role ambiguity and overlap among employees. Option C is incorrect because while leadership changes can influence organizational dynamics, they may not necessarily provide the structural clarity needed to address the specific challenges outlined in the scenario.

45. A, B. An organizational culture with a strict hierarchy and centralized decision-making can create an environment where employees feel they lack influence and representation, leading to an increased likelihood of considering unionization to address their concerns collectively. A culture that promotes open communication and employee empowerment often reduces the need for unionization by addressing employee concerns within the organization. Option C is incorrect because organizational culture can significantly influence employees' perceptions and collective actions, including unionization. Option D is incorrect as the impact of a culture promoting innovation and adaptability on unionization can vary.

46. C. Edgar Schein's layers of culture theory suggests that organizational culture consists of three levels: artifacts and symbols, espoused values and beliefs, and basic assumptions and unconscious values, with each level representing progressively deeper and less visible aspects of culture. Artifacts are the most visible and tangible aspects of culture, including behaviors, practices, and physical manifestations. In this case, the dress code policy is an observable artifact that dictates how employees should dress in the workplace. Option A, symbols, are often more abstract representations of culture, such as the company logo or mission statement. Option B, beliefs, are part of the "Espoused Values and Beliefs" level, which encompasses the stated values and beliefs of the organization. Option D, unconscious values, are part of the deepest level of culture, "Basic Assumptions and Unconscious Values." These are deeply ingrained and often unspoken beliefs and assumptions that guide behavior.

47. B. Geert Hofstede's cultural dimension of masculinity versus femininity focuses on the extent to which a society values assertiveness, achievement, and material success in the workplace. In cultures characterized by masculinity, there is an emphasis on competition, assertiveness, and the acquisition of wealth and material possessions. Conversely, in cultures characterized by femininity, there is a greater emphasis on cooperation, quality of life, and caring for others. Option A is incorrect as individualism versus collectivism focuses on the extent to which individuals prioritize their own interests and the interests of their immediate family or social group. Option C is incorrect as power distance is a cultural dimension that reflects the extent to which less powerful members of a society accept and expect unequal distribution of power. Option D is incorrect because the cultural dimension of long-term versus short-term orientation focuses on the extent to which a society values long-term planning, perseverance, and tradition versus short-term results, quick gratification, and adaptation to changing circumstances.

48. C. In leveraging Hofstede's theory of power distance, HR can design organizational interventions by encouraging open communication channels and transparency. This promotes collaboration, enhances teamwork, and creates a more inclusive workplace culture where all employees feel valued and empowered. Additionally, transparency in decision-making processes helps employees understand the rationale behind organizational actions, reducing ambiguity and increasing trust. Option A is incorrect as hierarchical structures can inhibit communication, limit upward feedback, and create barriers to innovation and creativity. Option B is incorrect because addressing power distance requires more than just awareness; it necessitates structural and behavioral changes to reduce power differentials and promote equality. Option D is incorrect as it may not address broader cultural dynamics or structural barriers that contribute to power imbalances within the organization.

49. A. The most prominent characteristic of individualism in organizational culture is decentralized decision-making. Individualism emphasizes autonomy and independence, allowing individuals to make decisions and take ownership of their tasks and outcomes. This approach empowers individuals to exercise autonomy in their roles, make decisions aligned with their personal goals and priorities, and take ownership of their work, reflecting the characteristic of individualism in organizational culture. Options B, C, and D reflect a more collectivist approach to work structures.

50. C. Restructuring the company's top management team is an example of an organizational-level strategic intervention. This intervention involves significant changes to the leadership structure and hierarchy within the organization, which can have widespread impacts on decision-making processes, organizational culture, and overall strategic direction. By restructuring the top management team, the organization can realign its leadership capabilities with its strategic objectives, address performance issues, and drive organizational change more effectively at a systemic level. Options A, B, and D are all examples of tactical interventions, characterized by their specificity and focus on implementation.

51. B. Total quality management (TQM) is a strategic intervention approach that emphasizes employee involvement, problem-solving, and continuous improvement to drive organizational change. TQM focuses on enhancing product and service quality by involving employees at all levels of the organization in problem identification, solution development, and implementation of process improvements. Option A is incorrect because a top-down leadership approach involves decision-making and direction coming primarily from senior management or leadership without much input or involvement from lower-level employees. Option C is incorrect because an outsourcing strategy involves contracting out certain business functions or processes to external vendors or partners to reduce costs, increase efficiency, or access specialized expertise. Option D is incorrect because a market expansion strategy involves entering new markets or expanding operations to increase market share and revenue.

52. C. Company VII can foster a culture of innovation by implementing an innovation lab where employees have the freedom to collaborate, brainstorm, and work on new ideas. This approach encourages creativity and aligns with the objective of enhancing innovation. Options A, B, and D do not directly contribute to fostering a culture of innovation and may even hinder it.

53. C. During a major organizational restructuring, HR professionals need to prioritize building relationships with key stakeholders, such as executives, managers, and employees, to understand their interests, perspectives, and concerns. By fostering open communication and collaboration, HR can gain valuable insights into the impact of the restructuring on different stakeholders and work toward addressing their needs effectively. Option A is incorrect because avoiding any involvement in office politics entirely may hinder their ability to effectively navigate the complexities of organizational restructuring. Option B is incorrect because ignoring employee concerns during a restructuring can lead to low morale, increased resistance to change, and decreased productivity. Option D is incorrect because implementing strict policies to eliminate all political discussions may stifle open communication, hinder collaboration, and be an unfair labor practice.

54. C. Cross-training involves providing employees with training and development opportunities to acquire skills and knowledge beyond their current job responsibilities. By upskilling employees to adapt to changes in the production process, the organization aims to increase flexibility, reduce bottlenecks, and improve overall efficiency. Option A is incorrect as techno-structural interventions focus on aligning technology with organizational structures and processes to improve efficiency and effectiveness. While the scenario mentions the adoption of new technology contributing to inefficiencies in the production process, the proposed intervention focuses on upskilling employees rather than restructuring technology or organizational processes. Option B is incorrect as job enrichment involves redesigning jobs to provide employees with increased autonomy, responsibility, and opportunities for personal growth and development. Option D is incorrect because the proposed intervention in the scenario specifically targets addressing current inefficiencies in the production process caused by the adoption of new technology, not planning for labor surpluses or shortages.

55. D. In the scenario described, the most appropriate organizational intervention strategy for addressing the identified challenge of low morale, high turnover rates, and dissatisfaction with communication and decision-making is a leadership development program. By providing training and development opportunities to improve leadership capabilities, the organization can empower managers to communicate effectively, make better decisions, and foster a positive work environment. Option A is incorrect as techno-structural interventions focus on upgrading technology infrastructure rather than addressing communication and decision-making issues within the organization. Option B is incorrect as job enrichment focuses on enhancing individual job roles rather than addressing broader organizational leadership challenges. Option C is incorrect because the issue is not described as lack of teamwork or collaboration, issues that are best solved by cross-functional training.

56. D. By bringing together representatives from different departments and stakeholders, HR can foster collaboration, address concerns, and ensure that proposed changes are well-understood and supported across the organization. Facilitating these meetings helps promote transparency, communication, and, ultimately, successful implementation of organizational design initiatives. Options A, B, and C are incorrect because while all are important and will add value, as a temporary fill-in for a specific role on the team, HR's immediate focus should be on activities that directly contribute to advancing ongoing organizational design efforts.

57. B. Option B effectively simplifies the original statement by conveying the essence of the talent acquisition strategy without using technical jargon. It maintains the focus on efficiency improvement through AI and data analysis, which are the key components mentioned in the original statement. This simplified version ensures clarity and accessibility for a broader audience without altering the context or meaning of the original statement. While Option A simplifies the statement, it does not fully capture the role of data analytics in predictive hiring models, which was highlighted in the original statement. This option also lacks specificity compared to Option B. Option C accurately simplifies the statement but does not explicitly mention the role of data analytics in predictive hiring models. Option D mentions technology and data without highlighting the specific role of AI-driven ATS platforms and predictive hiring models, which are crucial aspects of the original statement.

58. B. Translating the program's impact into financial value is the correct answer because Lucy effectively demonstrated the value of the talent development program by quantifying its potential impact on key financial metrics, such as revenue growth and ROI. This approach helps senior leadership understand the tangible business value of investing in talent development and increases the likelihood of gaining their buy-in and support for the program. By fluently speaking the language of business and connecting the human process intervention to financial outcomes, Lucy successfully made a compelling business case for the talent development program.

59. A. Active listening is essential for HR professionals to effectively communicate organizational change to a geographically dispersed team. By actively listening to the concerns, questions, and feedback of team members across different locations, HR professionals can better understand their perspectives, address their needs, and ensure that the communication of organizational change is tailored to meet the diverse needs of the dispersed workforce. This competency allows HR professionals to foster trust, engagement, and alignment among remote team members, ultimately facilitating successful change implementation. Option B is incorrect because technical expertise alone does not guarantee effective communication, especially when it comes to understanding and addressing the unique challenges and concerns of remote employees across different locations. Option C is incorrect as the primary focus of communication in this context is on fostering understanding, engagement, and alignment among remote team members rather than resolving conflicts. Option D is incorrect because while having business acumen can help HR professionals articulate the strategic rationale behind the change, active listening is more critical for ensuring effective communication and engagement with remote team members during the change process.

60. D. The competency of listening involves understanding information provided by others and seeking feedback. This includes the need for HR professionals to clarify ambiguous situations. This competency involves actively seeking clarity and understanding in situations where there is uncertainty or complexity, which is crucial for making informed decisions and leading successful change initiatives. Options A, B, and C are all behaviors associated with listening; however, the scenario did not explicitly describe competing points of view, asking for feedback or interpreting context.

61. B. Developing a comprehensive briefing tailored to the board's perspective and concerns is the best step for an HR professional when creating board-level communication on organizational change. By tailoring the briefing to the board's perspective, the HR professional ensures alignment and informed decision-making at the highest level of the organization. Option A is incorrect as boards rely on HR professionals to provide them with well-thought-out recommendations rather than presenting various options for consideration. Option C is incorrect because HR should maintain ownership of the communication strategy and ensure that it aligns with the organization's goals and the board's expectations. Option D is incorrect as it could be time-consuming and may not be practical, especially if there are many board members. Additionally, this approach may result in inconsistent messaging and lack of alignment among board members, as each member may have different perspectives and priorities. It's more efficient and effective to present the change collectively to the board in a comprehensive briefing.

62. A. The HR manager encounters resistance from employees who are anxious about the changes but handles the conflict constructively. By listening attentively to employees' concerns, facilitating open dialogue, and collaboratively working toward solutions that address both employee needs and organizational objectives, the HR manager effectively manages conflict. Option B is incorrect as it does not directly involve managing conflict. While observations may inform the redesign process, this option does not address the conflict that may arise among employees or stakeholders during the restructuring initiative. Option C is incorrect because the HR manager's proposed solution of advocating for leadership development training does not directly address conflict management within the context of job redesign. Option D is incorrect as holding a focus group after imposing changes may be reactive rather than proactive in addressing conflicts, potentially exacerbating tension and resistance among employees.

63. A, B, C, D. Clear and transparent organizational policies and procedures provide employees with guidelines for ethical behavior, helping to clarify expectations and minimize ambiguity in decision-making situations. Fostering a culture of accountability and integrity from top leadership down to all levels of the organization emphasizes the critical role of organizational culture in influencing ethical decision-making. Providing channels for employees to report ethical concerns confidentially and without fear of retaliation creates a supportive environment for ethical decision-making. Regular ethics training and workshops help to raise awareness about ethical principles and dilemmas, equipping employees with the knowledge and skills needed to navigate ethical challenges effectively.

64. C. Culture encompasses the values, norms, and behaviors shared within an organization, including attitudes toward diversity and inclusion. Cultural interventions may involve initiatives such as diversity training, promoting inclusive leadership practices, and establishing

policies and practices that support diversity and equity. Option A is incorrect as human process interventions focus on interpersonal dynamics and group processes rather than diversity-related issues. Option B is partially correct as change management interventions are designed to facilitate organizational change initiatives and transitions. While addressing lack of diversity within teams may require organizational change, change management alone may not specifically target diversity-related issues within teams if the culture does not change first. Option D is also partially correct as training and development interventions can play a role in promoting diversity and inclusion within teams by providing education on topics such as unconscious bias, cultural competence, and inclusive leadership. However, these programs may not adequately address the underlying cultural and structural barriers contributing to lack of diversity within teams.

65. C. Conducting regular employee satisfaction surveys and taking action to address issues is an effective organizational intervention strategy for overcoming a poor employer brand. By regularly seeking feedback from employees, HR can gain insights into areas where the organization may be falling short in terms of employee experience and employer reputation. Option A is incorrect because while advocacy programs can amplify positive aspects of the organization, they may not effectively address or resolve existing negative perceptions among employees and external stakeholders. Option B is incorrect because this strategy focuses primarily on attracting new talent rather than addressing the existing perception of the organization among current employees and external stakeholders. Option D is incorrect as they do not specifically target the issues contributing to a poor employer brand.

66. A. Employee satisfaction surveys are commonly used to measure organizational health because they provide insights into employees' perceptions, attitudes, and engagement levels within the organization. By gathering feedback on various aspects such as workplace culture, leadership effectiveness, job satisfaction, and opportunities for growth, employee satisfaction surveys help assess the overall health and well-being of the organization's workforce. Positive survey results indicate a healthy organizational culture, strong employee morale, and effective leadership, while negative feedback may highlight areas for improvement and intervention to enhance organizational health. Options B, C, and D are all examples of organizational performance and strategic results, reflecting more of the success at the decision-sciences than true organizational health nor do they provide a holistic view of organizational health, as they do not consider internal factors such as employee morale, teamwork, or leadership effectiveness.

67. C. Continuous monitoring is the best method for total quality management (TQM) interventions because it aligns with the principles of TQM, which emphasize continuous improvement and ongoing measurement of processes and outcomes. Continuous monitoring involves regularly collecting and analyzing data to assess performance, identify areas for improvement, and implement corrective actions. Option A is incorrect because it is not specifically tailored to total quality management interventions. Option B is not correct as although KPIs may include quality-related metrics, such as defect rates or customer satisfaction scores, they are not specifically designed for total quality management interventions. KPIs provide a snapshot of performance at a specific point in time. Option D is incorrect because balanced scorecards provide a broad overview of organizational performance across various dimensions.

68. B, C, D. One of the best evaluation methods to measure the impact of leadership development initiatives is through a combination of qualitative and quantitative approaches. Implementing 360-degree feedback assessments to gather feedback from multiple sources, including supervisors, peers, subordinates, and other stakeholders, provides insights into the effectiveness of the leadership development initiatives. Conducting pre- and post-training assessments measures changes in leadership competencies, knowledge, skills, and behaviors among participants. Pre-training assessments establish baseline data, while post-training assessments measure the impact of the leadership development initiatives on participants' performance and growth. By capturing employees' perspectives and experiences, organizations can assess the impact of these initiatives, identify areas for improvement, and make data-driven decisions to optimize future leadership development efforts. Option A is incorrect because ROI often overlooks the intangible and long-term benefits of improved leadership capabilities, such as enhanced employee engagement, culture change, and innovation, which are challenging to quantify in financial terms.

69. A. Aligning total rewards with organizational goals and values to reinforce desired behaviors and outcomes is the best way for HR to optimize the use of total rewards systems to support organizational development initiatives. This approach fosters a culture of performance, accountability, and engagement, ultimately supporting the achievement of organizational development goals. Option B is not correct as optimizing total rewards involves more than just incentives and recognition; it requires a holistic approach that considers various elements of rewards. Option C is incorrect because the focus of OD goes beyond compliance and competitiveness. Option D is only partially correct as transparency and communication about total rewards offerings are essential; however, this alone may not fully optimize the use of total rewards systems to support OD initiatives.

70. A. Conducting thorough risk assessments to identify potential challenges and cultural differences in different regions is a crucial risk management best practice when designing global OD initiatives. By conducting comprehensive risk assessments, HR can proactively identify potential barriers, cultural nuances, legal considerations, and other challenges that may impact the success of OD initiatives in diverse global contexts. Option B is incorrect because it is not specifically focused on risk management. Option C is incorrect as compliance measures do not fully address other potential risks such as cultural differences, operational challenges, or geopolitical factors. Option D is incorrect because it primarily focuses on building capabilities rather than risk management.

Appendix B

Answers to Terminology Knowledge Test

Chapter 2: U.S. Labor Law

The following are the answers for Chapter 2's terminology knowledge test:

1. Arbitration
2. Overtime
3. Qualifying event
4. Major life activity
5. Advance notice
6. Affirmative defense
7. Unlawful discrimination
8. BFOQ
9. Qualifying event
10. Unionization
11. Modified duty
12. Pay equity
13. Compensable time
14. Validity
15. Reliability
16. Hostile workplace
17. Unconscious bias
18. Prevailing wage
19. Confidentiality
20. Amendments

Chapter 3: Business Management and Strategy

The following are the answers for Chapter 3's terminology knowledge test:

1. Strategic planning
2. Business plan
3. Kaizen

4. Action plan
5. Cost leadership
6. Strategic alignment
7. Differentiation
8. Environmental analysis
9. SWOT analysis
10. Competitive analysis
11. Joint ventures
12. Focus strategy
13. Process improvement
14. Process flowchart
15. Evidenced-based decision-making
16. Return on investment (ROI)
17. Management
18. BCG matrix
19. SMART goals
20. Total Quality Management (TQM)

Chapter 4: Talent Planning and Acquisition

The following are the answers for Chapter 4's terminology knowledge test:

1. Recruitment
2. Job description
3. Internal job posting
4. Candidate evaluation
5. Candidate selection
6. Talent strategy
7. Job offer
8. Applicant tracking system (ATS)
9. Succession planning
10. Qualifications

11. Candidate relationship management (CRM)
12. Passive candidate sourcing
13. Employee development
14. Résumé screening
15. Temporary staffing
16. External hiring
17. Performance management system
18. Skills gap analysis
19. Diversity recruitment
20. Rehiring
21. Talent analytics
22. Recruitment technology
23. Global talent acquisition
24. Competitive compensation
25. Employment contract
26. Employee separation
27. Background screening
28. Employee referral program
29. Workforce planning
30. Career development

Chapter 5: Learning and Development

The following are the answers for Chapter 5's terminology knowledge test:

1. Learning
2. Soft skills training
3. Needs assessment
4. Development
5. Active learning
6. Development plan
7. Peer learning
8. E-learning
9. Evaluation

10. Lifelong learning
11. Skills assessment
12. Simulation
13. Coaching
14. Onboarding
15. Self-paced learning
16. Goal setting
17. Instructor-led training
18. High-potential development
19. Competency assessment
20. Career development
21. Scenario-based training
22. Succession planning
23. Experiential learning
24. Learning culture
25. Job rotation
26. Leadership development
27. Progress monitoring
28. Compliance training
29. Self-study
30. Recognition

Chapter 6: Total Rewards

The following are the answers for Chapter 6's terminology knowledge test:

1. Total rewards
2. Performance bonus
3. Base salary
4. Additional leave
5. Stock purchase plan
6. Noncash compensation
7. Education assistance
8. Flextime

9. Job evaluation
10. Disability income
11. Healthcare reimbursement account
12. Compensation philosophy
13. Salary range
14. Incentive compensation
15. Merit increase
16. Job classification
17. Employee assistance program
18. Longevity bonus
19. Wellness program
20. Perks

Chapter 7: Risk Management

The following are the answers for Chapter 7's terminology knowledge test:

1. Risk identification
2. Risk tolerance
3. Risk transfer
4. Risk mitigation
5. Risk impact
6. Risk acceptance
7. Risk assessment
8. Risk monitoring and control
9. Enterprise risk management (ERM)
10. Supply chain risk management
11. Financial risk management
12. Risk avoidance
13. After action review
14. Risk scoring
15. Insider threat
16. Natural disaster

Chapter 8: Employee Engagement and Retention

The following are the answers for Chapter 8's terminology knowledge test:

1. Employee feedback
2. Realistic job preview
3. Goal alignment
4. Employee involvement
5. Flexible work arrangements
6. Job satisfaction
7. Engagement dashboard
8. Employee wellness
9. Expectancy theory
10. Exit interviews
11. Self-determination theory
12. Culture building
13. Equity
14. High-potential development
15. Maslow's hierarchy
16. Employee engagement
17. Job characteristics
18. Performance appraisal
19. Employee development
20. Employee connection

Chapter 9: Employee and Labor Relations

The following are the answers for Chapter 9's terminology knowledge test:

1. Arbitration
2. Code of conduct
3. Collective bargaining agreement

4. Due process
5. Employee complaint process
6. Employee participation
7. Employee relations
8. Employee rights
9. Good faith bargaining
10. Grievance procedures
11. Labor dispute resolution
12. Labor-management cooperation
13. Mediation
14. Positive employee relations
15. Retaliation
16. Standard operating procedures
17. Strikes
18. Trade union
19. Union election
20. Workplace policies

Chapter 10: Ethical Practice and Corporate Social Responsibility

The following are the answers for Chapter 10's terminology knowledge test:

1. Privacy
2. Self-dealing
3. Ethics
4. CSR reporting
5. CSR policy
6. Good faith and fair dealing
7. Morals
8. Transparency
9. ESG rating agencies
10. Conflict of interest
11. Environmental stewardship

12. Utilitarian ethics
13. Social responsibility
14. Compliance
15. Integrity
16. Unconscious bias
17. Employee welfare
18. Political pressure
19. Authenticity
20. Deontological ethics
21. Honesty
22. Ethical controls
23. Triple bottom line
24. Consistency
25. Moral imperative

Chapter 11: Managing a Global Workforce

The following are the answers for Chapter 11's terminology knowledge test:

1. International human resource management (IHRM)
2. Work visa
3. Immigration specialist
4. Host country
5. Cultural intelligence
6. Global mindset
7. International trade
8. Repatriation
9. Expatriate
10. Foreign law defense
11. Global mobility
12. Cultural etiquette
13. Global competencies
14. Social mores

15. Tax equalization
16. Multinational enterprise (MNE)
17. Reverse mentorship
18. Ad hoc
19. Travel advisory
20. Works council

Chapter 12: Diversity, Equity, and Inclusion

The following are the answers for Chapter 12's terminology knowledge test:

1. Equity policies
2. Inclusion policies
3. Diversity audits
4. Equity audit
5. Inclusion dialogue
6. Reporting channels
7. Physical accessibility
8. Advocacy
9. Employee feedback
10. Equality
11. Bias training
12. Neurodiversity
13. Accommodation
14. Diversity training
15. Discrimination
16. Equity
17. Diversity goals
18. Cultural awareness
19. Diversity
20. Inclusion

Chapter 13: Workforce Analytics and Technology

The following are the answers for Chapter 13's terminology knowledge test:

1. Applicant Tracking System (ATS)
2. Employee collaboration platform
3. HR process automation
4. HRIS
5. Onboarding technology
6. People analytics
7. Remote work technology
8. Retention analytics
9. Internet of Things (IoT)
10. Employee self-service
11. Survey tool
12. Talent analytics
13. Time and attendance system
14. Workforce utilization
15. Employee engagement score

Chapter 14: Human Resource Competencies

The following are the answers for Chapter 14's terminology knowledge test:

1. Leadership
2. Vision
3. Influence
4. Personal integrity
5. Professional integrity
6. Relationship management
7. Networking
8. Negotiation

9. Teamwork
10. Conflict management
11. Listening
12. Growth mindset
13. Advocacy
14. Business acumen
15. Competitive awareness
16. Strategic alignment
17. Evaluating business results
18. Change management
19. Service excellence
20. Data advocacy

Chapter 15: Leadership

The following are the answers for Chapter 15's terminology knowledge test:

1. Autocratic
2. Democratic
3. Laissez-faire
4. Servant
5. Transactional
6. Development
7. Trait
8. Contingency
9. Leader-member exchange (LMX)
10. Situational
11. Behavioral
12. Visionary
13. Transformational
14. Authentic
15. Path-goal

Chapter 16: Organizational Development and Design

The following are the answers for Chapter 16's terminology knowledge test:

1. Organizational design
2. Structure
3. Centralized
4. Matrix
5. Project-based
6. Organization chart
7. Functional
8. Flat organization
9. Task specialization
10. Team building
11. Restructuring
12. Phased implementation
13. Organic
14. Automation
15. Change management
16. Training and development
17. Workspace redesign
18. Span of control
19. Organizational development
20. Total quality management

Appendix C

Answers to Research Challenge Questions

Chapter 2: U.S. Labor Laws

The following are the answers to the research challenge questions from Chapter 2:

Research Concepts Question 1:

The Portal-to-Portal Act of 1947 was a significant amendment to the Fair Labor Standards Act in the United States. Its primary purpose was to clarify and narrow the definition of compensable working time for employees. The activities are classified as principal activities, such as time spent working on a construction site or answering phones, preliminary work such as time putting on a uniform, and postliminary activities such as time spent showing and changing clothes after working with hazardous materials.

Research Concepts Question 2:

The risk to employers in this area include employee health and safety, discrimination, and retaliation, just to name a few. There is confusion in the HR industry about how to address medical marijuana use as there are conflicting federal and state laws. HR can best serve their employers by engaging in the following activities:

- **Familiarize yourself with state laws:** Medical marijuana laws vary from state to state, and some states have specific employment protections for individuals who use medical marijuana. HR professionals should be aware of the laws in their particular state and any local regulations that may apply.
- **Engage in interactive discussions:** If an employee discloses their use of medical marijuana due to a disability or medical condition, engage in an interactive discussion with them. Explore possible accommodations that can be made while ensuring workplace safety and productivity.
- **Maintain a safe workplace:** Regardless of state laws, employers have a duty to maintain a safe working environment. If an employee's use of medical marijuana could pose a safety risk or impair their job performance, consider reasonable accommodations or work modifications to address these concerns.
- **Review drug testing policies:** Review your company's drug testing policies and procedures. Determine whether you need to make any adjustments to align with state laws and ensure fairness in how drug tests are administered and evaluated.
- **Implement education and training:** Train managers and supervisors on the company's policies regarding medical marijuana and how to handle related issues sensitively and consistently.
- **Stay informed:** The legal landscape surrounding medical marijuana is evolving, so it's essential to stay informed about any changes in state laws, court decisions, and best practices in the industry.

- **Consult legal counsel:** Consider consulting with legal counsel who specializes in employment law to ensure that your company's policies and practices are compliant with both state and federal regulations.

Research Concepts Question 3:

The Lilly Ledbetter Fair Pay Act, enacted in 2009, aims to combat pay discrimination based on factors such as gender, race, age, religion, and national origin. Its key provisions reset the statute of limitations for filing pay discrimination claims with each affected paycheck. This was achieved by eliminating the "paycheck rule," which previously required employees to file claims within 180 days of the initial discriminatory decision, even if they were unaware of it at the time. The act established that the statute to file a claim is reset every time a paycheck is issued and broadened the definition of compensation discrimination, allowing claims based on any discriminatory compensation decision or related practices.

Chapter 3: Business Management and Strategy

The following are the answers to the research challenge question from Chapter 3:

1. What are at least three ways that organizations can adapt their business practices to adopt a more environmentally oriented mission, vision or values?

   "The Good Life" sustainable business goals typically encompass a range of objectives aimed at achieving environmental, social, and economic sustainability. While specific goals may vary depending on the organization and its context, here are some common examples:

   1. Environmental stewardship:
      - Reduce greenhouse gas emissions and minimize carbon footprint.
      - Conserve natural resources such as water, energy, and raw materials.
      - Implement sustainable sourcing practices to minimize environmental impact.
      - Adopt renewable energy sources and increase energy efficiency.
      - Implement waste reduction and recycling programs to minimize waste generation.
   2. Social responsibility:
      - Ensure fair labor practices throughout the supply chain, including living wages and safe working conditions.
      - Support diversity, equity, and inclusion initiatives within the workforce and the community.

- Engage in philanthropic efforts to support local communities and social causes.
- Promote employee well-being and work-life balance.
- Respect human rights and adhere to ethical business practices.

3. Economic prosperity:
    - Foster economic growth that benefits all stakeholders, including employees, customers, and communities.
    - Ensure transparency and accountability in financial reporting and business operations.
    - Invest in innovation and research to develop sustainable products and technologies.
    - Support small and local businesses through partnerships and supply chain initiatives.
    - Generate long-term value for shareholders while considering broader societal impacts.

These goals align with the principles of sustainability, aiming to create a "good life" not only for current generations but also for future generations by balancing economic prosperity, social well-being, and environmental protection.

Chapter 4: Talent Planning and Acquisition

The following are the answers to the research challenge questions from Chapter 4:

Research Concepts Question 1:

The demographic shifts outlined in the Indeed and Glassdoor 2023 report call for innovative technology strategies to address labor market shortages effectively. HR can recommend a range of technologies, including AI-powered tools such as chatbots and virtual assistants to help streamline the recruitment process, online learning and training platforms to upskill and reskill teams, and data analytics for workforce planning and retention predictions, and remote work solutions to ensure that companies remain competitive in acquiring and retaining top talent. These technologies can empower HR teams to adapt to changing labor market dynamics and secure the best candidates for their organizations.

Research Concepts Question 2:

Human resource professionals should adapt to the evolving psychological contract between employers and employees by creating a strong employee value proposition (EVP). Key strategies include staying informed about workforce dynamics, customizing EVPs for different employee segments, and ensuring clear communication to align employee expectations. The EVP should reflect the organization's culture, offer opportunities for development and work-life balance, and provide competitive compensation and benefits. HR should establish feedback channels to assess EVP effectiveness, remain adaptable to changing workforce needs, and measure its impact through metrics like retention and engagement. Competitive analysis of industry EVPs helps HR stay relevant. Lastly, HR should ensure the EVP adheres to legal and ethical standards, including diversity and inclusion.

Research Concepts Question 3:

Questions that require critical thinking will include realistic scenarios asking you to bring together multiple concepts including:

- **Business acumen in action:** HR professionals delve into market research to understand the unique demands and competitive landscape of the new region. They collaborate with the company's leadership to define the precise skills, qualifications, and cultural traits required in candidates to drive success in the startup's expansion.
- **Analytical approach:** HR leverages analytical tools to collect data on the local tech talent pool, identifying potential candidates and assessing their qualifications. Data-driven insights guide decisions on candidate sourcing, selection criteria, and compensation packages tailored to the regional market.
- **Team collaboration:** HR collaborates closely with hiring managers and department heads who provide critical insights into the specific job requirements and nuances of the local market. Together, they create a comprehensive talent acquisition strategy that aligns with the company's broader expansion objectives.

Chapter 5: Learning and Development

The following are the answers to the research challenge questions from Chapter 5:

Research Concepts Question 1:

The ADDIE (Analysis, Design, Development, Implementation, Evaluation), SAM (Successive Approximation Model), and Action Mapping models are three distinct approaches to instructional design, each with its own set of principles and methodologies. Understanding their key differences can help instructional designers choose the most appropriate model for a specific project and achieve better outcomes in training development:

- **ADDIE Model:** ADDIE consists of five sequential phases—Analysis, Design, Development, Implementation, and Evaluation. It follows a linear and systematic approach, with each phase building upon the previous one. The model can be seen as rigid and time-consuming because it requires completing one phase before moving on to the next. ADDIE places a strong emphasis on evaluation and feedback throughout the entire process to ensure the training's effectiveness.
- **SAM:** SAM is characterized by an iterative, cyclic approach, where design and development activities are carried out in multiple, smaller cycles. It offers greater flexibility and allows for course corrections based on frequent client and user feedback. SAM encourages collaboration between instructional designers, stakeholders, and end users at every stage and places a strong emphasis on understanding and meeting the client's needs and expectations.
- **Action Mapping Model:** Action Mapping is centered around achieving specific performance goals and focuses on identifying and addressing performance gaps. It emphasizes a thorough needs analysis to determine the root causes of performance issues before designing training solutions. Action Mapping advocates for creating training content that is minimal and directly relevant to achieving performance goals, avoiding unnecessary information. The model prioritizes the desired behavioral changes in learners and aligns training with those behaviors.

Research Concepts Question 2:

Organizational learning techniques encompass various strategies and practices that promote continuous learning and knowledge-sharing within an organization. These techniques are crucial for enhancing a company's ability to adapt, innovate, and grow in today's dynamic business environment, and they emphasize the importance of creating a culture where employees freely share knowledge, insights, and best practices.

Learning organizations encourage employees to reflect on their experiences, extract lessons, and apply them to future endeavors. Organizational learning techniques enable companies to adapt to changing circumstances and market dynamics. This adaptability is achieved through a willingness to experiment, take calculated risks, and adjust strategies based on feedback. The process also relies upon continuous improvement efforts to actively find ways to support competitiveness through efficiencies, under-scored by a highly developed stakeholder feedback loop. A hallmark of organizational learning is a robust learning and development system championed by HR teams. These systems must be capable of deep knowledges sharing often using technology and have the appropriate degree of leadership support to me sustained over time.

Chapter 6: Total Rewards

The following are the answers to the research challenge questions from Chapter 6:

Research Concepts Question 1:

Certain small employers—generally those with fewer than 50 employees that don't offer a group health plan—can contribute to their employees' healthcare costs through a Qualified Small Employer Health Reimbursement Arrangement (QSEHRA).

A QSEHRA allows small employers to provide nontaxed reimbursement of certain healthcare expenses, such as health insurance premiums and coinsurance, to employees who maintain minimum essential coverage, including an individual marketplace plan. In many states, QSEHRAs allow small employers to provide their employees with additional plan choices without managing group health plan coverage.

Research Concepts Question 2:

The U.S. Department of Health and Human Services, in collaboration with the Department of Labor, has concluded that chronic disease is a public health issue. As such, regulatory agencies took steps to provide incentives for employers to promote employee wellness as part of the Patient Protection Affordable Care Act (also known as the ACA and ObamaCare). These are the main principles of eligible employer programs:

- **Participatory:** A program that reimburses employees for all or part of the cost of membership in a fitness center; a diagnostic testing program that provides a reward for participation and does not base any part of the reward on outcomes; and a program that provides a reward to employees for attending a monthly, no-cost health education seminar.
- **Health-contingent:** A program that requires an individual to satisfy a health-factor standard to obtain a reward, such as performing or completing an activity relating to a health-factor, or it may be attaining or maintaining a specific health outcome. Health-contingent programs have two subcategories:
  - **Activity-only:** Under an activity-only wellness program, an individual is required to perform or complete an activity related to a health factor to obtain a reward. Activity-only wellness programs do not require an individual to attain or maintain a specific health outcome. Examples of activity-only wellness programs include walking, diet, or exercise programs.
  - **Outcome-based:** Under an outcome-based wellness program, an individual must attain or maintain a specific health outcome (such as not smoking or attaining certain results on biometric screenings) to obtain a reward. Generally, these programs have two tiers: a measurement, test, or screening as part of an initial standard; and a larger program that then targets individuals who do not meet

the initial standard with wellness activities. For individuals who do not attain or maintain the specific health outcome, compliance with an educational program or an activity may be offered as an alternative to achieve the same reward. Examples of outcome-based wellness programs include a program that tests individuals for specified medical conditions or risk factors (such as high cholesterol, high blood pressure, abnormal BMI, or high glucose level) and provides a reward to employees identified as within a normal or healthy range (or at low risk for certain medical conditions), while requiring employees who are identified as outside the normal or healthy range (or at risk) to take additional steps (such as meeting with a health coach, taking a health or fitness course, adhering to a health improvement action plan, or complying with a healthcare provider's plan of care) to obtain the same reward.

The final regulations increase the maximum permissible reward under a health-contingent wellness program offered in connection with a group health plan (and any related health insurance coverage) to 30 percent of the cost of coverage. The final regulations further increase the maximum permissible reward to 50 percent for wellness programs designed to prevent or reduce tobacco use.

Chapter 7: Risk Management

The following are the answers to the research challenge questions from Chapter 7:

Research Concepts Question 1:

Creating a safe, cost-effective, and healthy workplace is a goal that many employers aim to achieve, and drug-free workplace programs can play a pivotal role in achieving this objective. These programs typically consist of the following four essential components critical for success:

- **Written policy:** A "drug-free in the workplace" policy should encompass various aspects, including the rationale behind it, such as alignment with organizational goals and adherence to legal requirements. It should specify expectations for compliance and outline the available assistance options to support employees in adhering to it and the consequences for policy violations.
- **Employee education:** Comprehensive education and training are essential to provide everyone in the organization with insights into the challenges associated with substance misuse. These efforts should reinforce healthy attitudes and behaviors while increasing awareness of how substance misuse can impact employee health and employment.
- **Supervisor training:** Supervisors play a vital role in upholding the effectiveness of the drug-free workplace policy and program. It is imperative that they are well-versed in both the policy and the program. This includes having a clear

understanding of legally sensitive areas and knowing how to document potential problems fairly and systematically. They should also be trained in maintaining confidentiality and referring employees to appropriate services. Supervisors may require training on helping employees reintegrate into the workplace after receiving necessary services.

- **Drug testing:** Implementing drug testing measures is a proactive step to protect the workplace from the adverse effects of substance misuse. This practice can help organizations ensure compliance with federal regulations and insurance carrier requirements. It serves to enhance workplace safety and mitigate costs associated with alcohol and drug misuse on the job. A well-structured drug-testing program can act as a deterrent, discouraging employees from reporting to work while unfit for their duties.

Research Concepts Question 2:

Best practices for business continuity planning (BCP) involve comprehensive strategies to ensure organizations can continue their critical operations during and after disruptive events. Here are a few best practices:

- Complete a risk assessment:
  - Conduct a thorough risk assessment to identify potential threats and vulnerabilities that could disrupt your business operations. This includes natural disasters, cyberattacks, supply chain disruptions, and more.
  - Analyze the potential impact of these threats on your organization, considering factors such as financial losses, reputation damage, and regulatory compliance.
  - Perform a BIA to prioritize critical business functions and processes. Determine recovery time objectives (RTOs) and recovery point objectives (RPOs) for each function. Identify dependencies between different functions and processes to understand how disruptions in one area may affect others.
- Develop a comprehensive business continuity plan (BCP).
  - Create a well-documented BCP that outlines the strategies, procedures, and resources required to maintain essential operations during a disruption.
  - Establish clear roles and responsibilities for key personnel involved in BCP execution.
  - Ensure that the BCP addresses communication plans, data backup and recovery, alternate site locations, and resource allocation.
- Conduct regular testing and drills.
  - Conduct regular testing and exercises to validate the effectiveness of your BCP. This includes tabletop exercises, simulations, and full-scale tests.
  - Identify weaknesses or gaps in your plan during testing and use these findings to make improvements.

- Educate through training and awareness.
  - Ensure that employees at all levels are trained in BCP procedures and are aware of their roles in case of a disruption.
  - Foster a culture of preparedness and resilience within the organization, emphasizing the importance of BCP and individual responsibility.

Chapter 8: Employee Engagement and Retention

The following are the answers to the research challenge questions from Chapter 8:

1. What are the different ways human resource teams can support employee engagement?

   Gallup defines employee engagement as the involvement and enthusiasm of employees in their work and workplace. It involves measuring and managing employees' perspectives on crucial elements of workplace culture and aims to improve the connection between employees and their work and company. Engagement is important because employees produce better business outcomes than others, regardless of industry, company size, or economic conditions. Engaged employees positively impact absenteeism, patient safety, turnover, shrinkage, safety incidents, quality, customer loyalty, productivity, and profitability.

   There are four levels in Gallup's employee engagement model, based on employees' performance development needs. These levels include Basic Needs (What do I get?), Individual Contribution (What do I give?), Teamwork (Do I belong?), and Growth (How do I grow?). Meeting needs in these levels creates an environment of trust and support, enabling personal growth.

2. Give an example of retention efforts at each stage of the employee life cycle.

   Based on recommendations from `Indeed.com` and other best practices, there are several opportunities to increase employee retention throughout the employee life cycle. The employee life cycle aligns well with the functional areas of HR covered on HR exams. They include the following:

   - **Recruiting and selection:** Welcome new employees with a positive first impression. Offer straightforward training materials, support, and guidance.
   - **Talent management:** Invest in employees' growth by providing coaching, mentoring, training, education, and opportunities for advancement within the company.
   - **Total rewards:** Reward employees with competitive compensation, bonuses, retirement plans, health benefits, fitness classes, and stress management resources to enhance job satisfaction. Offer perks such as flexible schedules, paid parental

leave, remote work options, and smaller-scale benefits like casual Fridays or occasional treats.

- **Employee relations:** Recognize and appreciate employees' hard work, whether through direct acknowledgment or company-wide announcements. Support a healthy work-life balance by offering flexible schedules, remote work options, and other accommodations. Prioritize employees' well-being to demonstrate care and improve retention.

Finally, be sure to promote an open-door policy, enabling employees to share ideas, questions, and concerns. Listening and engaging with employees fosters a sense of belonging and helps with retention.

Chapter 9: Employee and Labor Relations

The following are the answers to the research challenge questions from Chapter 9:

Research Question 1:

After a period of significant decline due to the evolution of labor laws protecting all employee rights (as opposed to just union members), there is a renewed push by unions to organize industries such as the medical and retail communities. According to the AFL-CIO, 71% of Americans support unions, the highest level in nearly 60 years. There are many reasons that employees choose to join unions.

- **Improved wages and benefits:** One of the primary motivations for unionization is the pursuit of better wages, salaries, and benefits. Unions negotiate on behalf of their members to secure higher pay rates, better healthcare coverage, retirement benefits, and other perks.
- **Better working conditions:** Unions often advocate for improved working conditions, such as safer workplaces, reduced working hours, and adherence to health and safety regulations. They may also seek to address concerns related to excessive workload and stress.
- **Job security:** Unionized workers may feel that union membership offers them greater job security. Through collective bargaining agreements, unions can negotiate for job protection provisions, including rules regarding layoffs, seniority-based retention, and procedures for addressing job terminations.
- **Employee rights and protections:** Labor unions can help protect employees' rights by providing legal representation and assistance in cases of workplace disputes or unfair treatment. Union members often have access to grievance procedures to address workplace issues.

- **Voice and representation:** Many employees join unions to have a collective voice in decision-making processes within the workplace. Unions give workers a platform to influence company policies, participate in negotiations, and advocate for their interests collectively rather than individually.

Research Question 2:

There are several ways employers can remain union-free, and they exist on both a large scale, such as lobbying for governmental changes, and a small scale, such as written policies prohibiting solicitation. As a general rule, the following strategies can help employers create and maintain a positive workplace culture so that employees do not seek out union representation:

- **Education and training:** Employers often provide education and training programs to inform employees about the potential disadvantages of unionization, the company's perspective, and the benefits of maintaining the current work environment. This may involve conducting mandatory meetings, distributing informational materials, and using workplace communication channels to convey the employer's viewpoint.
- **Employee engagement:** Employers may focus on actively engaging with employees, fostering open communication, and addressing their concerns. By creating a positive workplace culture, employers aim to reduce the appeal of union representation. This can involve soliciting employee feedback, addressing grievances promptly, and involving employees in decision-making processes.
- **Effective communication:** Employers develop communication plans that allow them to convey their stance on unionization and address any misconceptions or concerns. They may use various communication channels, such as emails, newsletters, company meetings, and one-on-one discussions with supervisors, to maintain a clear and consistent message.
- **Response to union activities:** Employers monitor and respond to any signs of union-organizing efforts. This may involve hiring consultants or law firms specializing in avoiding unions, conducting counter-campaigns to address union activities, and legally countering any perceived violations of labor laws by unions.

Chapter 10: Ethical Practice and Corporate Social Responsibility

The following are the answers to the research challenge questions from Chapter 10:

Research Concepts Question 1:

As a general rule, companies should strive to put public health and safety at the top of their decision-making list. In many circumstances, this internal decision-making mechanism can help avoid the situation as described in the Ford Pinto case study. Beyond complying with government safety standards, other internal controls that could have been considered include the following:

- **Ethical oversight:** Ford could have established an ethical oversight committee responsible for reviewing critical decisions with ethical implications. This committee should have included safety and ethics experts who could assess the risks and benefits of design choices and advocate for consumer safety.
- **Whistleblower mechanisms:** Creating mechanisms for employees to report safety concerns and ethical issues without fear of retaliation is crucial. This would encourage employees to raise alarms about potential hazards, ensuring that critical information reaches decision-makers.
- **Cost-benefit analysis with ethical considerations:** When conducting cost-benefit analyses, Ford should have integrated ethical considerations and human safety into the equation. While cost savings are important, they should never take precedence over human lives and safety.

Research Concepts Question 2:

Your answer will likely be based on your specific place of work or industry; however, the following example uses Google's mission, which is "Committed to significantly improving the lives of as many people as possible." Google further explores a commitment to "Protecting Users, Building Belonging, Expanding Opportunity, Responding to Crisis and Advancing Sustainability" (`https://about.google/intl/ALL_us/commitments/#responding_to_crises`).

Google's CSR initiatives could include the following:

- Protecting users
  - **Online safety tools:** Google can develop and improve tools to enhance online safety, such as anti-phishing measures, content filtering, and privacy controls.
  - **User education:** Launching educational campaigns and resources to raise awareness about online safety and digital literacy.
- Building belonging
  - **Diversity and inclusion programs:** Implementing programs to foster a diverse and inclusive workplace, including mentorship, diversity hiring initiatives, and employee resource groups.
  - **Community engagement:** Supporting local communities through partnerships, grants, and volunteer opportunities.
- Expanding opportunity
  - **Digital skills training:** Providing training and resources to help underserved communities acquire digital skills and access online opportunities.

- **Small business support:** Offering tools and resources for small businesses to expand and thrive online.
- Responding to crisis
  - **Disaster Relief Efforts:** Mobilizing resources and technology to respond to natural disasters and emergencies, such as crisis mapping and communication tools.
  - **Crisis Information:** Providing accurate and timely information during crises through platforms like Google Search and Maps.
- Advancing sustainability
  - **Renewable energy investment:** Investing in renewable energy projects to reduce the company's carbon footprint.
  - **Green data centers:** Designing and operating energy-efficient data centers to minimize environmental impact.

Chapter 11: Global Human Resource Management

The following are the answers to the research challenge questions from Chapter 11:

Research Concepts Question 1:

While the individual answers will vary based on the country you chose, this example uses the Czech Republic:

a. Who is required to obtain a visa?
You do not need a Schengen visa to visit the Czech Republic if you are an EU/EEA/Schengen citizen. You can work, live, and visit the Czech Republic without any restrictions. Everyone else must apply for a visa before entering the Czech Republic.

b. How long is a visa valid for work?
For a long-term work visa, you can stay for more than 90 days, provided you have a sponsor.

c. What limitations, if any, are there for visa while in the host country?
You must enter the country prior to the expiration date listed on the visa and obtain a temporary residence permit if staying for longer than 90 days.

Chapter 12: Diversity, Equity, and Inclusion

The following are the answers to the research challenge questions from Chapter 12:

Research Concepts Question 1:

Based on the Body of Applied Skills and Knowledge, which is the framework for the SHRM CP and SHRM SCP exams, the basic competencies necessary for an HR professional to drive diversity, equity, and inclusion results in the workplace include the following:

- **Creating a diverse and inclusive culture:** HR professionals should be capable of fostering an environment where diversity is valued and inclusion is encouraged. This involves implementing strategies like executive sponsorship, leadership buy-in, and employee resource groups.
- **Ensuring equity effectiveness:** HR professionals need to ensure that policies and practices within the organization are equitable, addressing disparities related to gender, race, age, abilities, and other factors. This may involve conducting pay audits, promoting pay transparency, and monitoring diversity at all organizational levels.
- **Connecting DEI to organizational performance:** HR professionals should understand how DEI initiatives can positively impact organizational performance. They should be able to measure and analyze DEI metrics, such as gender and race diversity, retention rates for diverse employees, and external stakeholder diversity.

In addition to these competencies, HR professionals should have a deep understanding of the various barriers to DEI success, including conscious and unconscious bias, stereotypes, and microaggressions. They should also be familiar with techniques to measure and increase equity, such as using the SHRM Empathy Index and conducting diversity surveys.

HR professionals should also be aware of the benefits and programs that support DEI, including caregiver options, workplace flexibility policies, and global festivities and events calendars.

HR professionals need a combination of knowledge, skills, and the ability to apply these competencies effectively to drive meaningful diversity, equity, and inclusion results in the workplace.

Research Concepts Question 2:

HR leaders can significantly enhance the results of their organization's diversity, equity, and inclusion efforts by focusing on three key areas, as highlighted in the SHRM report.

- **Communication:** HR leaders should continue to engage in open and transparent dialogue with their workforce. Hosting town hall meetings and releasing statements about racial injustice and protests demonstrate a commitment to addressing these issues internally. However, HR should also look beyond the organization's walls and consider external communication. Expressing public support for the Black community and addressing racial issues with customers and external stakeholders are becoming increasingly important.
- **Education:** Prioritize training programs that educate employees about racial inequality, implicit bias, and racial inclusion, which continue to be important for multiple reasons. These programs should be tailored to the organization's unique culture and workforce needs. HR's expertise is invaluable in designing training that encourages candid conversations and promotes a more inclusive workplace.
- **Investment:** True commitment to DEI goes beyond words—it requires financial investment. HR leaders can advocate for allocating resources to support diversity programs effectively. Some organizations are taking it a step further by donating to nonprofit advocacy groups dedicated to diversity, equity, and inclusion. These financial contributions can help drive systemic change and promote a more inclusive society beyond the organization's boundaries.

Chapter 13: Workforce Analytics and Technology

The following are the answers to the research challenge questions from Chapter 13:

Research Concepts Question 1:

Company culture in the workplace has impact on employees' emotions, beliefs, behaviors, and overall well-being. In the context of AI at work, culture plays a crucial role beginning with the need for AI initiatives to be aligned with the company purpose. When AI initiatives align with the organization's cultural values and mission, they can contribute to a shared sense of purpose, making employees feel that technology is used to achieve meaningful goals. Additionally, effective communication and trust are vital components of a positive culture.

When employees trust that AI technologies are used transparently and for their benefit, it fosters a culture of openness and collaboration. Employees are more likely to embrace AI when they understand its role and impact on their work. Helping employees understand how the use of AI can improve the culture itself is another way communicating the benefits can increase buy-in.

Finally, a positive culture nurtures employee well-being, both physical and emotional. AI can contribute to well-being by automating repetitive tasks, allowing employees to focus on more meaningful work. When employees feel valued and supported by AI-enhanced processes, it positively influences their well-being. When AI technologies are aligned with the organization's culture, values, and purpose, they can contribute to a positive workplace environment, improved employee engagement, and a lasting legacy of purpose and innovation. A strong and supportive culture provides the foundation upon which AI can amplify its benefits and drive positive change within the organization.

Research Concepts Question 2:

While the automation of HR continues to grow at a rapid pace, there are both benefits and challenges. The benefits include increased efficiencies. Automation speeds up HR tasks that are repetitive, time-consuming, and prone to human error. By automating processes such as onboarding, payroll processing, time and attendance tracking, and performance management, HR professionals can save time and resources. Automation reduces the need for manual data entry and administrative work, allowing HR teams to focus on more strategic initiatives and employee-centric activities.

Another benefit to automaton is an improved employee experience. By automating processes related to onboarding, performance management, employee feedback, and recognition, HR can create a smoother and more engaging experience for employees. This improvement in employee experience can lead to higher job satisfaction, better retention rates, and increased productivity.

Automation also comes with specific challenges. Many HR professionals and candidates alike complain about the lack of personal touch in processes such as recruiting. HR tasks often involve sensitive or emotional aspects, so striking the right balance between automation and personalization is a challenge. Implementing HR automation requires training not only for HR professionals but also for the entire workforce. Employees need to understand how to use and interact with automated HR systems effectively. And HR automation systems often handle sensitive employee data, so security and compliance training are essential to protect data integrity and privacy.

Chapter 14: Human Resource Competencies

The following are the answers to the research challenge questions from Chapter 14:

Research Concepts Question 1:

Many recertification activities can fulfill requirements for the HRCI or the SHRM exams. These activities may be preapproved, or you can upload a description of the activity to your recertification application.

Here are the main recertification requirements for each exam:

a. SHRM CP and SCP

There are three categories from which you may earn PDCs for recertification: advance your education, organization, or profession. Sample activities include instructor-led or self-paced courses, strategic work projects, volunteering for HR-related associations, or teaching classes on HR or business topics.

There are two primary options for recertification. Whichever option you choose should be completed by your recertification end date, which is the last day of your birth month, three years after you first earn SHRM certification, and every three years thereafter. Your new three-year cycle will begin the day after you recertify.

1. **Option 1:** Earn 60 professional development credits (PDCs) within your three-year recertification cycle.
2. **Option 2:** Retake the certification exam within the last year of your recertification cycle.

b. PHR, PHRi, SPHR, SPHRi

Similar to the SHRM exams, recertification must be completed on a three-year cycle. Sixty credits are necessary to recertify, and this can be done through personal professional development activities such as online courses or conferences, or professional achievement, such as publishing or implementing a new program at work. For SPHR/i candidates, at least 15 of the 60 credits must add to your knowledge of your organization and how it operates. This is generally done by engaging in activities related to the "Leadership and Strategy" functional area of the SPHR/i exam content outline. All recertification candidates for HRCI must earn at least one ethics credit within the recertification cycle.

Chapter 15: Leadership

The following are the answers to the research challenge questions from Chapter 15:

Research Concepts Question 1:

Emotional intelligence enables HR and other leaders to better understand and respond to the emotions and needs of their employees, fostering trust, engagement, and loyalty within the organization. By effectively managing emotions, building rapport, and resolving conflicts, leaders with high emotional intelligence create a positive work culture, enhance team performance, and drive organizational success. Characteristics of emotionally intelligent leaders may include:

- **Self-awareness:** Involves recognizing and understanding one's own emotions, strengths, weaknesses, values, and motivations, leading to greater self-understanding and adaptability in various situations.

- **Self-management:** Encompasses the ability to regulate and control one's emotions, impulses, and behaviors, fostering resilience, integrity, and effective decision-making in personal and professional contexts.
- **Social awareness:** Entails perceiving and understanding the emotions, needs, and perspectives of others, cultivating empathy, compassion, and interpersonal sensitivity for building positive relationships and rapport.
- **Relationship management:** Involves effectively navigating and influencing social interactions and dynamics, utilizing communication, conflict resolution, and collaboration skills to foster trust, teamwork, and mutual respect within personal and professional relationships.

Research Concepts Question 2:

Leadership development initiatives play a crucial role in nurturing talent, empowering individuals, and driving organizational success. By investing in leadership development, companies can cultivate a pool of capable leaders who inspire, motivate, and guide teams to achieve strategic objectives. These initiatives not only enhance employee engagement and retention but also foster a culture of innovation, adaptability, and continuous improvement, ensuring long-term competitiveness and growth in today's dynamic business environment.

HR leaders can effectively support leadership development programs by focusing on whole-person growth, providing opportunities for self-reflection and meaning-making, offering targeted programs to address stress, acknowledging and addressing psychological barriers to growth, and ensuring that short-term growth leads to sustained, long-term impact.

Chapter 16: Organizational Development and Design

The following are the answers to the research challenge questions from Chapter 16:

Research Concepts Question 1:

In this research question, you were asked to think about your current organization or a company that you have worked for in the past and then select one of the challenges you experienced there from a list. While each individual will have a different answer, here are examples of strategies that can help with the specific challenges:

- **Lack of teamwork:** Implementing cross-functional team-building workshops and collaborative projects to address lack of teamwork.
- **Task redundancies:** Conducting a thorough review of processes and restructuring tasks to eliminate redundancies.

- **Poor leadership:** Providing leadership development training programs and mentoring initiatives to improve poor leadership.
- **Outdated technologies:** Upgrading software systems and investing in training sessions to address outdated technology.
- **Lack of communication:** Establishing regular communication channels, such as weekly team meetings and digital platforms, to tackle lack of communication.
- **Unsafe working conditions:** Conducting safety audits and implementing necessary measures to improve unsafe working conditions.
- **Wasted time:** Introducing time management training sessions and implementing productivity tools to minimize wasted time.
- **Lack of diversity:** Implementing diversity training programs and actively recruiting from diverse backgrounds to address lack of diversity.
- **Low morale:** Organizing team-building events and recognition programs to boost low morale.
- **Poor company reputation:** Launching a public relations campaign focusing on company values and positive contributions to improve poor company reputation.

Research Concepts Question 2:

HR as a strategic partner encompasses many of the valuable outcomes that derive from the organizational development and design processes. HR can strategically influence organizational development success in several ways:

- **Understanding organizational objectives:** HR professionals need to align themselves with the broader strategic goals of the organization. By understanding the business objectives and challenges, HR can tailor organizational design initiatives to support these goals effectively.
- **Data-driven decision-making:** Utilizing data analytics and metrics, HR can assess current organizational structures and performance to identify areas for improvement. By gathering insights on employee engagement, productivity, turnover rates, and other relevant metrics, HR can make informed decisions about organizational design changes.
- **Collaboration with leadership:** HR should collaborate closely with top leadership to gain buy-in and support for organizational design initiatives. By engaging executives and key stakeholders in discussions about the rationale behind proposed changes and the expected outcomes, HR can ensure alignment with the overall strategic direction of the organization.
- **Talent management integration:** Integrating talent management practices with organizational design can enhance the effectiveness of both processes. HR can ensure that the organizational structure supports talent acquisition, development, and retention strategies, thereby fostering a high-performance culture.

- **Change management expertise:** HR plays a crucial role in managing change effectively within the organization. By leveraging change management principles and techniques, HR can minimize resistance to organizational design changes and facilitate smooth employees transitions.
- **Continuous improvement:** Organizational design is an ongoing process that should adapt to evolving business needs and market dynamics. HR can champion a culture of continuous improvement by regularly evaluating the effectiveness of organizational structures and processes and adjusting as needed.
- **Employee involvement and communication:** Involving employees in the organizational design process can increase acceptance and engagement with proposed changes. HR can facilitate communication channels for employees to provide feedback, voice concerns, and contribute ideas, fostering a sense of ownership and empowerment.

By employing these strategies, HR can position itself as a strategic partner in driving organizational design and development approaches that support the achievement of business objectives and enhance overall organizational performance. These are all competencies and subcompetencies that are evaluated on the HR exams.

Index

C

D

E

F

G

H

K

L

M

N

O

P

Q

R

S

T

U

V

W

Y

Online Test Bank

To help you study for your PHR, PHRi, SPHR, SPHRi and SHRM CP/SCP certification exams, register to gain one year of FREE access after activation to the online interactive test bank—included with your purchase of this book! All of the chapter review questions and the practice tests in this book are included in the online test bank so you can practice in a timed and graded setting.

Register and Access the Online Test Bank

To register your book and get access to the online test bank, follow these steps:

1. Go to `www.wiley.com/go/sybextestprep`. You'll see the **"How to Register Your Book for Online Access"** instructions.
2. Click "here to register" and then select your book from the list.
3. Complete the required registration information, including answering the security verification to prove book ownership. You will be emailed a pin code.
4. Follow the directions in the email or go to `www.wiley.com/go/sybextestprep`.
5. Find your book on that page and click the "Register or Login" link with it. Then enter the pin code you received and click the "Activate PIN" button.
6. On the Create an Account or Login page, enter your username and password, and click Login or, if you don't have an account already, create a new account.
7. At this point, you should be in the test bank site with your new test bank listed at the top of the page. If you do not see it there, please refresh the page or log out and log back in.